GUIDE TO THE STUDY OF RELIGION

GUIDE TO THE STUDY OF RELIGION

Edited by

WILLI BRAUN AND RUSSELL T. McCUTCHEON

CASSELL
London and New York

Cassell

Wellington House, 125 Strand, London WC2R 0BB

370 Lexington Avenue, New York, NY 10017-6550

http://www.cassell.co.uk

First published 2000

British Library Cataloguing-in-Publication Data

A catalogue record for this book is available from the British Library.

ISBN 0-304-70175-0 (hardback)

0-304-70176-9 (paperback)

Library of Congress Cataloging-in-Publication Data

Guide to the study of religion / edited by Willi Braun and Russell T. McCutcheon.

   p. cm.

Includes bibliographical references and index.

ISBN 0–304–70175–0. – ISBN 0–304–70176–9 (pbk.)

   1. Religion. I. Braun, Willi, 1954– . II. McCutcheon, Russell T., 1961– .

BL48.G83 2000

200′.71–dc21

99-30537

CIP

Typeset by BookEns Ltd, Royston, Herts

Printed and bound in Great Britain by Redwood Books, Trowbridge, Wiltshire

CONTENTS

Contents

CONTRIBUTORS

Gregory D. Alles is Chairperson and Associate Professor, Department of Philosophy and Religious Studies, Western Maryland College, Westminster, Maryland.

Veikko Anttonen is Professor of Comparative Religion, Department of Cultural Studies, University of Turku, Finland.

William E. Arnal is Assistant Professor of Religious Studies, Department of Classics, New York University.

Gustavo Benavides is Associate Professor of Religious Studies, Villanova University, Pennsylvania.

Willi Braun is Associate Professor of Religion and Director of the proposed Centre for the Study of Christianity, University of Alberta, Edmonton, Canada.

David Chidester is Professor of Comparative Religion and Director of the Institute for Comparative Religion in Southern Africa, University of Cape Town, South Africa.

Timothy Fitzgerald is Associate Professor, Aichi-Gakuin University, Japan.

Sam D. Gill is Professor in the Department of Religious Studies, University of Colorado, Boulder, Colorado.

Ronald L. Grimes is Professor of Religion and Culture, Wilfrid Laurier University, Waterloo, Ontario, Canada.

Stewart Elliott Guthrie is Professor of Anthropology, Fordham University, New York.

Jeppe Sinding Jensen is Senior Lecturer in Religion and Chair of the Department of the Study of Religion, Aarhus University, Denmark.

Contributors

E. Thomas Lawson is Professor and Chair of Comparative Religion, Western Michigan University, Kalamazoo, Michigan.

Gary Lease is Professor in and the Chair of the History of Consciousness Program, University of Santa Cruz, California.

Bruce Lincoln is Professor of History of Religions, an Associate Member of the Departments of Anthropology and Classics, the Center for Middle Eastern Studies and the Committee on the Ancient Mediterranean World, University of Chicago.

Burton L. Mack is Emeritus Professor of New Testament, Claremont School of Theology, Claremont, California.

D. Bruce MacKay is Assistant Professor, Department of Geography, University of Lethbridge, Alberta, Canada.

Luther H. Martin is Professor of Religion, Department of Religion, University of Vermont, Burlington, Vermont.

Tomoko Masuzawa is Associate Professor, Department of Religious Studies, University of North Carolina, Chapel Hill.

Arthur McCalla is Research Reader and Instructor, Department for the Study of Religion, University of Toronto, Toronto, Canada.

Russell T. McCutcheon is Associate Professor of Modern Religious Thought, Department of Religious Studies, Southwest Missouri State University, Springfield, Missouri.

Tim Murphy is a Mellon Postdoctoral Fellow, Department of Religion, Case Western Reserve University, Cleveland, Ohio.

William E. Paden is Professor in and Chair of the Department of Religion, University of Vermont, Burlington, Vermont.

Daniel Pals is Associate Dean in the College of Arts and Sciences and Professor in the Department of Religious Studies, University of Miami in Coral Gables, Florida.

Hans H. Penner is Preston Kelsey Professor of Religion, Department of Religion, Dartmouth College, Hanover, New Hampshire.

Thomas Ryba is the Notre Dame Theologian in Residence, St. Thomas Aquinas Center and Adjunct Professor of Philosophy and Jewish Studies, Purdue University, West Lafayette, Indiana.

Jonathan Z. Smith is the Robert O. Anderson Distinguished Service Professor of the Humanities, University of Chicago.

Contributors

Rodney Stark is Professor of Sociology and Comparative Religion, University of Washington, Seattle, Washington.

Randi R. Warne is Associate Professor and Chair of Religious Studies, Mount St. Vincent University, Halifax, Nova Scotia, Canada.

Harvey W. White is Associate Professor, Department of Religion, Bishop's University, Lennoxville, Québec, Canada.

Donald Wiebe is Professor of the Philosophy of Religion and Dean of the Faculty of Divinity, Trinity College, University of Toronto, Toronto, Canada.

Johannes C. Wolfart is Assistant Professor, Department of Religion, University of Manitoba, Winnipeg, Canada.

For
Bruce, Don, Neil, Peter
Vive la différence!

ACKNOWLEDGMENTS

One weekend, early in the autumn of 1996, we met in Springfield, Missouri, and—in keeping with the culinary metaphor used in the Prologue—we began to imagine a stew something like this volume turned out to be. The basic ingredients were its rationale, its organization and its topics. Its seasoning and spice would be provided by a dream team of contributors. Despite the fact that there are already far too many dictionaries and encyclopedias of religion available to interested readers, we thought that our concoction would be interesting fare with a distinctive flavor, not only because it would try to dish up a thoroughly anthropological study of religion, but also because it would include the discipline of studying religion within its critical mix.

We jotted down the recipe and sent it off to a few people whose tastes we valued. Their encouraging replies confirmed our hunch that what we had begun calling simply the *Guide* would make a needed contribution to the field. We approached our wish list of authors and discovered, to our delight, that almost all of them were eager to join the project. Many put other simmering projects on their backburners to make time for stirring their contributions into our broth.

What we needed was a publisher. One November evening, during the annual conference of the American Academy of Religion and the Society of Biblical Literature (held in New Orleans that year) we found ourselves at dinner in a memorable restaurant in the French Quarter with Janet Joyce, the Editorial Director at Cassell Academic Press. One of us had brought along a copy of the recipe in a jacket pocket, just in case. Over good food, splendid wine, a great jazz ensemble—the sound of the band's CD, *Two Clarinets on a Porch*, is turned up in one of our offices even as we write this—punctuated by the occasional break with Ben at the bar for goodies not found at the table, it became clear to us that Janet began to savor the dish promised in the recipe. By the end of the evening, the recipe was on its way to the kitchen.

As with any project such as this, the debts are too great and too many to list here fully. Suffice it to say that we are grateful for Janet's judgment in her

Acknowledgments

choice of publishing projects and for the incredible energy and enthusiasm she has spent on the *Guide*. Many of the contributors are colleagues and good friends, without whom we likely would not have developed our particular tastes in the study of religion.

Since both of us learned to cook "religion" in the Centre for the Study of Religion at the University of Toronto in the late 1980s, we dedicate this volume to four people who defined for us a stimulating but all too brief moment in the history of that institution.

Willi Braun
Russell T. McCutcheon

PROLOGUE

❧ ❧

Lacking a clear articulation of purpose, one may derive arresting anecdotal juxtapositions or self-serving differentiations, but the disciplined constructive work of the academy will not have been advanced, nor will the study of religion have come of age.

Jonathan Z. Smith (1990: 53)

1

RELIGION

Willi Braun

❧❧

Aristotle, legendary for his relentless insistence on classifying the terms, categories and objects of knowledge, once remarked that the beginning of wisdom is the definition of terms. And why not? Some initial, even if imprecise demarcation of something we want to know or explain, or of something we set out to discover, is in the order of common sense. If, for example, I want to study the craft of pottery making—about which I know nothing—I should know that the object of my interest is not the evolution of reptiles. Or, although I know next to nothing about linear algebra, I would know that I was not in a linear algebra tutorial if the tutor's talk was about plot variations in detective fiction. These examples may be uninteresting, but they do serve to indicate that researching the world we live in, including comparatively across time (worlds of past societies) and space (worlds other than our own), is always a complex exercise of selecting, inventing, and fiddling with categories in order to render—to force—the natural world and the range of human doings as intelligible, differentiated, ours to respond to, to make and remake.

"Religion" as Specter

What, then, about "religion"? As is the case with many other common words in the large domain of cultural studies—think of "culture" itself, or of "society," "ideology," "experience," "history," "tradition" (and many more in Raymond Williams, *Keywords*)—the term "religion" is as familiar as it is difficult to contain within a cogent, agreed-upon, manageable frame of reference. Like the apparition of ghosts which often are a feature of religious talk and behaviour, "religion" is a phantom-like category, a specter (on the idea of "specter" see Derrida 1994; Žižek 1994), a free floating Something. As a specter, "religion" presents us with the dual problem of being flamboyantly real, meeting us in all forms of speech and in material representations, on the one hand, and frustratingly apt to turn coy or disintegrate altogether when put under inquisition, on the other.

As a linguistic denomination "religion" is very real, evidently one of those "experience-near" categories (Geertz 1983: 56–59) used by millions of Western people as routinely as they use the words "politics" or "sex," and with an apparently effortless sense of its self-evident meaning. If a class of fifty undergraduate students in an introductory course on the study of religion may stand as a sample of popular knowledge, it demonstrates that people, whether they describe themselves as religious or not, do not need to have studied religion in order to think they know what it is. A general, if fuzzy, knowledge of "religion" seems to be a precipitate of formally untaught learning (Atran and Sperber 1991), whereby people simply absorb elements of their cultural marinade—*à la* the lines from rocker John Mellencamp's song: "I was educated in a small town / taught to fear Jesus in a small town." As a culturally induced mental representation (on which see Shore 1996; Sperber 1996) "religion" is articulatable either as something-in-itself or, by a process of ostention, usable as a descriptor of differentiated sets of phenomena: religious ideas, religious experiences, religious rituals, religious art, religious traditions, religious fanatics and the like.

In my tabulary of student definitions, "religious" seems to have no domain limits and therefore no discriminatory utility when it is the adjective of choice to describe the state one feels when writing poetry or the rush that comes from riding a motorcycle or spending quality time with one's pet. Just as pop-singer Paul Simon knows "fifty ways to leave your lover," so students in my classroom have no trouble counting at least "fifty ways to meet your religion," confirming Jonathan Z. Smith's response to some professional thinkers' lament over the impossibility of defining religion. From James Leuba's (1912) list of fifty definitions, Smith draws the moral not that religion *cannot* be defined, "but that it can be defined, with greater or lesser success, more than fifty ways" (1998: 281). The problem of "religion" in popular speech thus is the problem of excess and spectrality: there are too many meanings and the meanings are too indeterminate (or, perhaps, too over-determined) to be of value for sustained and thoughtful public discourse—to which we might add that the indeterminacy of meanings tends to be prized and protected with appeals to the immediacy and inscrutability of "private" experience and opinion, effectively setting up taboo-like barriers to a bit of rough critical handling of the ubiquitous popular "religion" talk, lest, one suspects, "the mystery that appears to surround ['religion'] is entirely superficial and fades upon closer scrutiny" (Durkheim 1995 [1912]: 431). (I have been at more than one dinner party where "religion" has been ceremoniously declared off-limits as a subject of discussion!)

If we add to the popular understandings of "religion" the definitional offerings of scholars, the inordinate strength of "religion" as an uncontrollable, wind-driven reference is underscored. As surveys of the career of the category "religion" indicate (Despland 1979; Bossy 1982; J. Z. Smith 1998), the word is a "floating signifier" capable of attaching itself to a dizzying range of objects— many of them remarkably obscure—to countless blurry ideas and a host of often imprecise definitional propositions. Little wonder that in the history of theorizing "religion" the term has tended to fidget nervously in its own opaqueness and that it therefore has not infrequently transvested itself to play peek-a-boo behind substitute terms such as "the holy" (the spectral legacy of Otto 1969 [1917]) or "the sacred" (the conjuring influence of Eliade 1959b). However, both of these substitute terms are equally mysterious, making their use conducive to explaining *obscurium per obscurius*, to account for one mystery by means of other mysteries. Readers may wish to consider the counsel of Marvin Harris (1979: 315–41), whose exposition of obscurantism in the social sciences applies aptly to a dominant discourse in the academic study of religion. Little wonder, too, that the history of the category "religion" is at the same time in part a history of the category's vanishing act in the folds of confessional (theological, apologetic) discourses of religious communities or, more generally, in what Jacques Derrida calls discourses of "hauntology" (Derrida 1994: 51): discourses such as theology, even "global theology of world religions" (Whaling 1999), and ontology (talk about the Being of being) that are spent on discussing the realities and presences of absences (ghosts are and are not!). Without denying their noble aims, necessity and appropriateness for confessional locales, these hauntologies are obscurantist in that they subvert a research strategy whose aim is to enlist the study of religion as a contributing partner in the pursuit of a science of human social life, an exercise that could be credible within the family of human and social sciences in the modern university. In the effort to counter obscurantist strategies in the study of religion, other approaches have divested "religion" of utility altogether, claiming that it has no independent, proper-to-itself substance. Such approaches prefer to collapse "religion" into other classes of social life and to talk about it in terms of the vocabularies drawn from the social sciences or comparative "cultural studies" (Fitzgerald 1999).

The spectrality of the category "religion" and the fact that divergent, conflictual, even contradictory incantations of "religion" are not only possible but vigorously alive side-by-side in hundreds of university religion departments whose knowledge is relayed for scholarly and popular consumption by an astonishing volume of publications, is almost enough reason for a *Guide to the Study of Religion*. The field of religious studies is a bewildering jungle. If one wants to slash one's way into it and come out the other end with an increase of critical judgment and theorizing potential about what "religion" is or does, especially what it is not, and what ought usefully to be entailed (or not entailed) in calling some aspect of human doing "religious," then a direction-whispering companion is something to take along. This *Guide* has pretensions of being just such a companion. Intended for students from undergraduate to professional levels, the collection of substantial essays presented here are a concert of critical expositions of the ways that "religion" and "religious" are used by scholars intent on defining, describing, classifying and explaining sets of human performances as well as social and cultural processes. Just to be sure that readers are not misled, a cartographical metaphor may help to sharpen the identity of this volume: think of the *Guide* as an "atlas" of "maps" to the "field" of the study of religion. It is therefore not another encyclopedia that catalogs descriptions of religious artifacts, practices, heroes and saints, authoritative texts, myths and rituals—in short, it is not a compendium of the phenomena central to a religious tradition or commonly shared by religious traditions. Nor is it a dictionary that gives thumbnail descriptions of predominantly native (i.e., a community's own) religious terms and facts compiled on the model of language dictionaries. These kinds of deposits of knowledge are abundant in every academic library and there is no need to add to this crowd.

Rather, the *Guide* takes as its focus of interest precisely those intellectual processes and choices in the study of religion that few encyclopedias and dictionaries of religion put up for inspection—namely scholars' conceptual key terms and their theory-loaded methods of explanation, their translations of religious insider terms into the language of scientific social and cultural studies, their practices of comparison and their attempts to set boundaries between what counts as religious and what does not. Most simply put, this *Guide* is a multi-faceted asking of and replying to two basic questions that students of religion must sooner or later take up with some degree of seriousness as a matter of remaining transparent and cogent about what they are up to when they study religion: what is religion? how is it successfully investigated within the shared aims of the family of human and social sciences in the modern university? If readers need an analogy, the relationship of the *Guide* to actual "fieldwork" in religion—whether that fieldwork consists of students' research in the archives and encyclopedias of religions, of specialists' expositions of the properties of religious communities, or of ethnographers' documentaries of the religious life of group X or Y—is like a guide to historiography (the theory of history) is to the fieldwork of historians, or like a handbook on theories of lexicography stands as a second-order reflection in relation to the work of compiling actual dictionaries. In the turbulent intellectual storms of late modernity, likely to buffet us well into the next millennium, the *Guide* presents an attempt at second-order reflection so as to retain, perhaps regain or gain for the first time, some purchase on the core concepts in the study of religion.

"Religion" in Concept

This volume does not make an argument for a single "grand theory" of religion, nor does it offer an exhaustive set of unified methods for studying religion. But the essays here do participate, more or less, in a common stance on matters of theory and method. It will quickly become evident to readers that the *Guide* is not neutral on what makes for "greater or lesser success" (J. Z. Smith 1998: 281) in positioning the study of religion as a viable and sustainable academic pursuit within the terms of knowledge production that distinguishes the modern academy. The *Guide* thus comes with a bit of "attitude" and the articulation and rationalization, quite explicitly in some essays and more tacitly in others, of this attitude is a second major reason for the labors contained here. The elements of this attitude need to be explicated for the benefit of general readers.

1. *Gifts from the past*. The critical study of religion—a creation of European cultures—historically developed simultaneously as a negative process of disaffiliation from Christian theology and as a positive process of affiliation with the values of scientific rationality associated with the European Enlightenment (see Preus 1987, 1998; Capps 1995). Out of this struggle of estrangement and affinity emerged the possibility of a research stance outside the indigenous perspectives and knowledge frameworks of religious structures, one that was driven by uncensored curiosity rather than by the confessional and apologetic requirements of religious bodies. It became possible to become an observer of religion without being a participant in religion; it was now conceivable to distinguish the *study* of religion from the *practice* of religion; it was now reasonable to separate caring, either positively or negatively, for religion from analyzing, comparing and explaining religion; it was now justifiable to use nonreligious theories of knowing (epistemologies) to generate knowledge about religious phenomena. What is astonishing is not that these possibilities emerged, but that the research activity (*Wissenschaft*) which formed itself around these possibilities was specifically called religion-science (*Religionswissenschaft*), in polemical opposition to the study of the (Christian) "faith in faith for faith" (*Glaubenslehre*). "Religion" thus had its modern (re)birth as a signifier of difference from theological inquiry where the difference was, in the first place, "a sort of absence" (Preus 1998: 3), a way of saying "not this." This emptiness of "religion" would not last, of course, and "not this" (i.e., theology) had to be changed to "not this, but that." I will return to "that" below. In the meantime, it is interesting to note that this binary logic of A / not-A may in effect continue its force in marking religion off from non-religion. That is, the not-A modern origin of "religion" is the legacy we have inherited today with our more than fifty ways to define religion. If religion is not-A, then definitionally it includes about everything and anything.

    It is worth noting in the past of "religion" a second moment when the word was employed as a category of comparison to signify some difference between "us" and "them." As David Chidester demonstrates in his essay in this volume on "religion" in the management of "the natives" on colonial frontiers,

European explorers, travelers, missionaries, settlers and colonial administrators recorded their findings on indigenous religions all over the world. With remarkable consistency over a period of five hundred years, these European observers reported that they had found people in the Americas, Africa and the Pacific Islands who *lacked any trace of religion.* (my emphasis; see also Chidester 1996)

"Religion," filled with some generic (but nevertheless Christian-informed) essence distilled by the emerging science of comparative religion (Sharpe 1986), could be used as a mark on the colonial periphery, one that differentiated the civilized, properly religious European *homo urbanus* from the uncivilized "savage" who was thought to have no religion or, at best, whose religion did not measure up and whose practices therefore had to be called something else. "Superstition" was, and for some still is, the age-old handy term for flawed, futile or false religion—as judged from the powerful defining centers of normative religion.

The lesson to be drawn from this brief look at the recent past of "religion" is that the term has had a more consistently successful career as a marker of difference and separation than as a container and carrier of an irreducible, stable and inspectable knowledge. Or, more precisely, the substance supposedly contained in "religion" seems to be utterly variable and the variation is dependent on the term's classifying function as determined by the interests of the classifiers. The editorial attitude in this volume—readers will have to judge to what extent it is shared by the essayists—is to seize with appreciation one gift of our field's past and regard "religion" as essentially empty, of use only as a marking device. It should go without saying that in accepting this gift from our past we do not also have to take over the classifying interests and social values of the past, those that constructed such oppositions as *their* conjuration versus *our* knowledge, *their* superstition versus *our* religion. These polarities are not useful in the study of religion and ought to be regarded as conceptual relics in the museum of our discipline's past.

2. *From substance to concept.* If "religion" is substantively empty—or infinitely fillable with aeolian qualities, as we have noted—let us abandon the eschatological hope, so tenaciously persistent in our field, that by some brilliant hermeneutical can-do we will spook the true genie out of the bottle of "religion." If "religion" is substantively empty, then there is no genie in the bottle! In more genteel terms, the problem with using "religion" as a nominal for a substance with its own inherent characteristics is that it conjures definitions that are *"ad hoc* and / or taken-for-granted (and ultimately incoherent)." Moreover, such incoherence is generally unnoticed by scholars who, instead, "tend to take the *significance* of [any] definition for granted" (Arnal, Chapter 2), as if it was sheltered from critique. To be

sure, it is possible for faith-generated premises to secure for those who believe in them credibility supports *a fortiori* by means of intellectual crafts. But the attitude embraced in the *Guide* is to forsake the ethereal and exalted "It" of religion and, instead, to use "religion" to retrieve something on the ground, something on the hard surface of social life in time and space, something that counts as data according to the generally shared, scientific evidentiary principles of the modern academy. That is, the editorial attitude in this volume *reverses* the well known interdict offered by one of the grandfathers of religious studies, Rudolf Otto (1869–1937), in the opening pages of his *The Idea of the Holy*; contrary to Otto, the *Guide* advises that whoever has an "intimate personal knowledge" of the *ontos* (Greek, "being") of religion "is requested to read no further" (1969: 8). In other words, the contributors to the *Guide* make no claim to privileged, intuitive knowledge about what "religion" really is or is not. Instead, they set out to develop taxonomies and theories to assist them in answering questions about the nature, origin and functions of that part of the social world which they call "religion."

This means that we must regard religion as a concept, in the technical sense, and not as a substance that floats "out there," a something that might invade and enlighten us if we should only be so fortunate as to have the right kind of receiving apparatus. Concepts are ideas used to allocate the stuff of the real world into a class of objects so as to position these objects for thought that is aimed toward explanation of their causes, functions, attractiveness to individuals and societies, relationships to other concepts, and so on. Norwood R. Hanson's conceptual distinction between two kinds of terms might help us to think about this. He differentiates, albeit on a line of continuum, "sense-datum" words or "data-words" from more or less "theory-loaded" words, using as his illustration of their difference the data-word "hole," a spatial concavity, and the concept "crater": "To speak of a concavity as a crater is to commit oneself as to its origin, to say that its creation was quick, violent, explosive" (Hanson 1958: 56–60). Simply, for our purpose, concepts are products of scholars' cognitive operations to be put to work in the service of scholars' theoretical interest in the objects of their research. Concepts are not given off by the objects of our interest. They neither descend from the sky nor sprout out of the ground for our plucking. Claiming that "religion" is a concept is to say something like what Hanson suggests and to subscribe to what Olin Wright states with reference to the concept of "class":

Concepts are produced. The categories that are used in social theories, whether they be the relatively simple descriptive categories employed in making observations, or the very complex and abstract concepts used in the construction of "grand theory," are all produced by human beings ... They are never simply given by the real world as such but are always produced through some sort of intellectual process of concept formation. (Wright 1985: 20)

3. *Owning our concepts*. Concept formation, which is never a once-for-all-time process, in the service of a successful research strategy, is not just the prerogative of the scholar, but it is indeed her or his primary obligation as a scholar. In the study of religion no one has recognized this obligation for self-conscious concept formation more clearly and stated it more sharply than Jonathan Z. Smith. Though often cited, it is worth intoning once again his words from the introductory paragraphs of his influential book, *Imagining Religion*:

> *there is no data for religion*. Religion is solely the creation of the scholar's study. It is created for the scholar's analytic purposes by his imaginative acts of comparison and generalization. Religion has no independent existence apart from the academy. For this reason, the student of religion, and most particularly the historian of religion, must be relentlessly self-conscious. Indeed, this self-consciousness constitutes his primary expertise, his foremost object of study. (J. Z. Smith 1982: xi, emphasis in original).

Let us then regard "religion" as a concept, as a semantic marker in a specific sense of the Greek word *sēma*: a boundary indicator around particular and conspicuous things in the observable, real world, analogous to the markers that designate places for playing football or burying the dead. Or, better, let us understand "religion" as analogous to the manner in which the Library of Congress or the British Library divides published material quite artificially among "classes of conceptual and topical relations in the service of data retrieval" (J. Z. Smith in this volume).

4. *Defining the "religion" concept*. But what kind of marker is "religion"? What conspicuous things does it pick out and bring into relations for our inspection? Here is a proposal that expresses the orientation of this volume. Tinkering just a bit with Bruce Lincoln's definitional thesis (Lincoln 1996b: 225), let us think of "religion" (a) as ordinary and mundane (i.e., in this world) discourses or *arts de faire* ("practices of everyday life" [Certeau 1984]) that are characterized (b) by an orientation to speak of matters transcendent (i.e., beyond the limited spaces of this world) and eternal (i.e., beyond the limits of time) and (c) by a desire to speak of these matters "with an authority equally transcendent and eternal" (Lincoln 1996b: 225). Or, very plainly, "religion" is a kind of human talk that can be differentiated from other human talk by its topical content and its rhetorical propensity (see Spiro 1966: 98).

"Religion" in Theory

Readers will no doubt detect that defining "religion" in this way is to push it well into the domain of Hanson's theory-loaded terms (on theory see Achinstein 1968; Anon. in J. Z. Smith 1995: 909–910). Perhaps "theory-redolent" is preferable, indicating that the concept gives off some theoretical odors, in that it is dependent on some moves of theoretical proposition-making in the formulation of the concept itself. But it is also theory-suggestive, indicating that the term "religion" is subject to further intellectual maneuvers in the direction of generating more fecund explanations of those things contained and entailed in the definitional concept.

As to indications of the first kind, notice first that the concept implicitly locates the origin (not to be thought of in primordial absolute terms but in terms of ongoing beginnings) and explicitly the "life" of religion within the complex fabric of active interests of people in the real world. The "transcendent" beyond-human beings, such as gods, spirits, ancestors, or whatever else one would name to this class, have their lives not in some ontic selfhood, but as discursive entities (see Murphy in this volume). To phrase it another way, Lincoln's definition implies that, insofar as the gods or ancestors "live," it is contemporary people who give them life by talking about, to and with them. This, in turn, suggests that the object of the scholar's study is not the gods but the complex social operations by which, and the conditions under which, people discursively bring the gods to life. This orientation opens new lines of inquiry: what human interests are served in keeping the gods alive? What are the variety of ramifications for self, society and culture in the cultivation and preservation of the gods?

Second, the proposed religion concept is redolent of an act of general classification for the purpose of delimiting the objects of our inquiry. It retrieves not invisible things, but conspicuous *arts de faire* or what we can simply term discourses—a term used most capaciously to include "not only verbal, but also the symbolic discourses of spectacle, gesture, costume, edifice, icon, musical performance, and the like" (Lincoln 1989: 4). From these proliferations of socially cultivated discourses, our concept "religion" selects not all, not just any, but specifically some, those marked by an orientation to certain topics (the transcendent) that are then handled within a rhetorical framework of self-authorizing credibility structures. That is, there is enough discriminating power in our concept to distinguish specifically religious discourses from other ideological discourses with which they may share enough similarities in rhetorical orientation so as to allow us to regard religious discourses as but one type of ideological discourse, but without holding the converse, that is, that all ideological discourses are also religious (see Chapter 30).

It is important to observe that the formula, though theory-loaded, does not *explain* religious discourses. To do this, more is needed. Lincoln's concept gives no indication, for example, that it contains even an implied explanation of the *arts de faire* that his definition selects and retrieves for us. By what networks of operations and dynamics, we might ask for example, do religious discourses maintain (or lose) their credibility in the lives of people and societies who live in them? What are their intended goals and their unintended consequences? Supposing, for the moment, that religion is among the hundreds of human universals (D. E. Brown 1991)—meaning that religious discourses are cultivated in all societies across time and place (Burkert 1996)—how do we account for them as both ubiquitous and resiliently persistent? How do we explain the peculiar nature of the authority of, and the authority-orientation in, religious discourses (see Lincoln 1994)? And so on.

That Lincoln's formula does not contain answers to these and many other questions is not, however, a mark of its weakness. Concepts, after all, are not full-fledged theories, but somewhat elastic, provisional set-ups for theories; they axiomatically delimit the focus and types of theorizing that are possible. Concepts thus select theories appropriate to the concept, which also means, obviously, that they exclude some types of theorizing as *not* apropos. For example, a concept that defines religion as a human discourse is not hospitable to explaining religion in terms of propositions that postulate it as a *sui generis*, one of a kind of substance set apart and existing apart from human discourses, an explanatory option that Weston La Barre characterizes as explaining religion "in the terms provided by religion" (1970: xi). Concepts simply are jealously discriminating romancers and lovers of explanatory stratagems that are commensurate with (faithful to) the core sensibilities of the concept. The mark of a strong religion concept for our research purposes is its ability to initiate, direct and sustain a rich historical, world-oriented, social "science" (*Wissenschaft*) of religious *arts de faire*. At the very least, this means that a religion concept ought to make possible a critical inquiry whose theories, methods and results are not esoteric, private and intelligible only within the terms of a special-to-religion epistemology and credibility structure.

Third, the specific expertise that is the aim of religion scholars is made apparent when we notice that the classificatory act expressed in the definitional concept relativizes "religion" taxonomically. "Religion" is not a *summum genus* (J. Z. Smith 1998: 281), but a sub-class of human *arts de faire* or discourses. Hence, the specificness of the scholar's expertise in various religious discourses is similarly subordinated to an overarching, more general critical purpose of which the core problem, always to be theorized itself, concerns the complex and multiple interrelated processes of cultural production, structuration and representation (e.g., Giddens 1984; J. Goodman 1997). The religion scholar is thus a social theorist whose distinction from other social theorists is marked by the data-focus of her or his labors, that is, that part of the observable world named religion.

This, I should point out, is not really all that novel or outrageous a plea for the rectification of religious studies as a species of social studies. It is, rather, a reminder of, and an attempt to recover, a generative orientation in the modern study of religion's past. Recall that the study of religion (*Religionswissenschaft*) emerged in post-Enlightenment, scientific-oriented Europe. Out of the processes of shaping the emergent sense of what religion is, and how to investigate it scientifically, arose a general commitment to explain religion as a natural phenomenon, as opposed to a divine phenomenon—to regard the religious practices of societies as discursive devices generated by human beings to make sense of their world. Let's regard Ludwig Feuerbach's famous translation of theology into anthropology as an example of the general orientation of this period toward secular theories of religion: "Theology is anthropology, that is, in the object of religion which we call *Theos* in Greek and *Gott* in German, nothing but the essence of man is expressed" (Feuerbach 1967: 10). Of interest to us here is not Feuerbach's *particular* psycho-philosophy of human consciousness and cognition (on this, see the essays by Guthrie and White in this volume), but the fact that he, along with many others of his time, sought to explain religion and its postulated superhuman objects as the precipitates of entirely human doings. To understand religion thus inescapably entailed as the investigative starting and ending point the very anthropological and social questions of the what, how and why of human "religious" being and doing in historical, material and social situatedness.

It is hardly coincidental that this turn to natural, anthropological explanations of religion roughly coincided with the modern beginnings of the disciplines known as anthropology, psychology and sociology (Anon. in J. Z. Smith 1995: 909). Most of the so-called founders of these social-scientific disciplines formed the fundamentals of these sciences more or less in their effort to explain religion. This can be said of W. Robertson Smith, Edward B. Tylor, James G. Frazer and David Hume (anthropology); Ludwig Feuerbach, Sigmund Freud and Carl G. Jung (psychology); and Auguste Comte, Émile Durkheim, Karl Marx and Max Weber (sociology); to call the roll of merely the most famous. I sometimes tease my colleagues in the social sciences that if it had not been for the problem of religion, they might not have quite the job they now have! What all these scholars had in common was their effort to answer the what, how and why of "religion" without appealing to a divine being, a god, or any other nonhuman transcendent "other" reality. All of them basically agreed that it is not the gods that make people revere and fear them, but, on the contrary, that people make their gods whom they then revere and fear. To readers who have a popularly mediated knowledge of religion along lines described above, this may sound horrifyingly counter-intuitive, but this is nonetheless the core premise of studying religion in an anthropological key.

Now, this brief rehearsal of the anthropological foundations of modern religious studies' beginnings is not meant as an exhortation that religion scholars ought restrictively to become Durkheimians, Freudians or Marxists.

The point is more general and it concerns the religion scholar's theoretical orientation: when it comes to theorizing religion and explaining religious *arts de faire*, let us not abandon, but rather continue to explore and refine the naturalistic, anthropological and sociological turn that marked *Religionswissenschaft* from its beginning.

"Religion" and Disciplinarity

What about the disciplinarity of religious studies? Readers may well take what has been said so far as an implicit subversion of the specialized technologies and disciplines that have been developed around "religious studies" and that have garnered for the study of religion an officially sanctioned place in the university. There is, however, neither subversive intent nor any suggestion that religion scholars should rename themselves and reappear as generic social theorists or ethnographers. On the contrary—and here I have in mind the recent trend in some North American universities to see religion departments as unrationalizable in these economically stringent times (Lease 1995)—a wide collaborative expertise-coalition of scholars (see Capps 1995: 336–337), intentionally gathered around religious *arts de faire* makes a great deal of sense. Thick knowledge, unlike revelations, about highly complex social practices comes neither by *ad hoc* pursuit nor without costly investment in disciplinary props. We will need a set of cooperating methods and foci of study for the purpose of compiling an "archive" of these *arts*. We will require a "critical mass" of intelligence, a grouping of disciplined specialists, to manage that archive with self-consciously critical practices of concept formation, theory construction, classificatory and interpretive operations. We will need thoughtful curricula for the distribution of our knowledge, and so on. The larger purpose of generating and disseminating an academically credible public knowledge about religion is therefore undoubtedly best pursued in an institutionally designated and licensed place.

It is also to be acknowledged that the data-domain "religion" is extensive and almost limitlessly varied across time and locale, from one culture to another, on the large scale, and within bounded cultural domains, on a more restricted scale. Even descriptive mastery of mere subsets of the facts of "religion" will require a range of technical knowledges such as archeology, art history, demography, linguistics, philology, and so on, none learnt or taught overnight. In the real world of academic practice the mastery, use and teaching of these technologies will undoubtedly take up the bulk of the religion scholar's day and days.

But at the end of the day there remain the conceptual and theoretical problems posed by "religion" which the specialized, empirical technologies of "field work" in religion will not solve. In the final analysis, then, the *sine qua non* of the religion scholar's contribution to a general science of culture and society lies less in disciplined employment of this or that *technē*, though this is not unimportant by any means, than in the theoretical imagination that can translate the merely curious or puzzling data of "religion" or the self-evidently significant but spectral objects of religious discourses into categories that can help us as scholars of religion—and the various publics who value (or merely tolerate) our labors—to understand the human interests and social arrangements in which religious discourses play their various generative and representational roles. Thought of in this way, the study of religion is more like an organized, specific-purpose field-trip into the general region of social and cultural processes than it is a fenced-in disciplinary or departmental acre with its own, non-shared, special-to-religion methods.

Reading the *Guide*

The *Guide* consists of thirty essays, written specifically for this volume by some of the world's leading theorists of religion. Essays are grouped under three general organizational headings that reflect the editorial attitude outlined above.

1. *Description*. Essays in the first section deal with specific theoretical and methodological issues around the question, what is religion? These essays further articulate the assumption that "religion" comprises a range of ordinary human practices and that the category "religion," when used as a scholarly term, is a label, a taxonomic tool by which certain human practices are isolated for scholarly attention. But how will the marks of identification be determined? Definition is not an innocuous matter of merely pointing out what is self-evident. Take the example of a meal, an almost universal site of social formation and thus a practice that is often wrapped up in religious significations. Is a meal simply a biological activity of replenishing the body's nutritional needs? Is it an aesthetic activity insofar as mere food is generally the raw material for a cuisine? Is it also a social and political activity that is constrained and directed by cultural norms of power, rank, proper table company and dining etiquette? Is it a ritual activity that suspends the messy ambiguities of real life if only for a momentary representation of what life ideally ought to be? When does a meal become a religious practice and what distinguishes the religious aspect of a meal from its other dimensions? And precisely how, if at all, is a religious meal distinct from a nonreligious one both in type and function? These questions press the need for definition as a basic theoretical beginning and a constant accompanying value in any study of religious *arts de faire*, of which meals are a type. It will become evident in reading the first four

essays, that in order to describe religion one must first define it, an act that is inextricably linked to the acts of classification, comparison and the interpretive choices and categories that are involved in all definitional thought. Readers thus should not regard definition, classification, comparison and interpretation as cleanly independent topics. While each essay does stand on its own, the potential to stimulate thought on describing "religion" lies in large part in reading these essays as a quartet.

2. *Explanation*. In the second set of essays the focus of attention turns from questions on defining and describing religion to issues related to explaining religious practices. Each essayist in this section was invited to describe and evaluate a *theoretical system* (for example, structuralism, exchange theory, social structuration, world-building) or an *analytic category* (for example, gender, ethnicity, myth, ritual, sacred) by which those artifacts and practices defined as religious have been or might be explained. Each essay follows, more or less sharply, a similar pattern: it outlines the key features of a particular theoretical system or analytic category; locates it historically and with reference to its representative theorists; classifies subsets within the system; evaluates the approach for the contributions it has made to the scientific study of religion; and assesses its future usefulness. Because one aim in this section is to present both traditional approaches and to identify emergent approaches, the entries in this section far outnumber the usual "approaches to the study of religion" that are found in most introductory textbooks.

A second aim is to redescribe some traditional categories, because in our view there is nothing particularly self-evident about the theoretical value of some keywords—"sacred," for example—that have long had pride of place in the academic study of religion. Similarly, we could not convince ourselves of the value of lumping, say, all anthropologists into a category called "anthropological approaches," for some anthropologists operate with an implicit theory of religion as an autonomous, non-reducible (non-anthropological) entity, just as some religion scholars rigorously and consistently base their theories on a foundation of "religion" as an "anthropological category" (J. Z. Smith 1998: 269). The study of religion is a disciplinary boundary-crossing pursuit in any case, and in the interest of highlighting theoretical concerns and preferences, grouping scholars of religion into several homogenized "approaches"—a common discipline-mapping genre (Waardenburg 1973; Whaling 1995; Connolly 1999)—seemed to be a restrictive classificatory option.

3. *Location*. In the third set of essays, authors explore aspects of the making of the scientific study of religion as a Western intellectual enterprise. J. Samuel Preus (1998: 3) has nicely articulated a central question that is implied and variably addressed in these essays:

Something in our culture that nobody has quite figured out is this: why is the modern study of religion an invention of the West; why is it not done anywhere else quite like the way it is done here? Why does it not even seem to make sense in other [non-Western] cultures? For some reason, in the West people had motive, learning and opportunity to make a distinction between doing religion and studying it, or between doing theology and analyzing it.

Preus' use of the term "invention" is appropriate. "Disciplines" or "fields" of study, though they appear to us as natural and concrete in their institutional "department" forms and in their officially practiced regimens—formal courses of study leading to general examinations and other performance tests that certify whether students have mastered the discipline—are actually quite novel historical forms of producing and purveying knowledge (Messer-Davidow et al. 1993). "Religion" as an academic field in the university is no different. Indeed, religion departments are very recent tenants in the halls and towers of the academy—the study of religion was reborn in North American universities only an academic generation ago. Although the essays in the "Location" section do not give a detailed history of "the making of a discipline" (see Capps 1995; McCutcheon 1997b; Sharpe 1986; D. Wiebe 1999), they do attempt to put up for critical thought some of the conditions, the general intellectual and cultural environments of Western modernity, that help us to understand both the rise and the particular orientation(s) of the academic study of religion. Turning the spotlight from the study of "religion" to the *scholars* who have done and are doing the studying, these essays demonstrate that the pursuit of "religion" neither was nor is a pure and isolated affair; instead, it is deeply embedded in wider conditions of motive and possibility: conceptual, social, institutional, political, even geopolitical forces, constraints and interests.

The *Guide*'s final word consists of Sam Gill's meditation on some of the ambiguities and conundrums that face the scholar of religion who works with entirely nonreligious concepts of religion in order to understand people and their religious *arts de faire*.

If readers notice that over the course of its sections, the *Guide*'s lens has gradually been pulled back, further and further, until scholars of religion themselves, as intellectual, social and political actors, are brought into view as the object of critical reflection, then they will have spotted an editorial intention. The volume begins with issues and problems of concept formation and ends with the reflexive impulse to stand watch over the utter historicity of concept-making, concept-makers and the effects of concept-making. What Michel Foucault once said about people in general is an apt word not only on the *Guide*, but on scholars of religion: "People know what they do; they frequently know why they do what they do; but what they don't know is what what they do does" (quoted in J. Goodman 1997: 783). The *Guide* is an attempt to lay out what religion scholars do, provide some insight into why they are doing it, and, in the final section of essays, give some thought to the question of what effects religion scholars' doings have.

Suggested Readings

Bossy, John
    1982   "Some Elementary Forms of Durkheim." *Past and Present* 95: 3–18.
Capps, Walter H.
    1995   *Religious Studies: The Making of a Discipline*. Minneapolis: Fortress.
Harris, Marvin
    1979   *Cultural Materialism: The Struggle for a Science of Culture*. New York: Random House.
Lincoln, Bruce
    1996b   "Theses on Method." *Method and Theory in the Study of Religion* 8: 225–277; reprinted in Russell T. McCutcheon (ed.), *The Insider/ Outsider Problem in the Study of Religion: A Reader*. Controversies in the Study of Religion, London: Cassell, 1999.
Smith, Jonathan Z.
    1998   "Religion, Religions, Religious," pp. 269–284 in Mark C. Taylor (ed.), *Critical Terms for Religious Studies*. Chicago: University of Chicago Press.
Spiro, Melford E.
    1966   "Religion: Problems of Definition and Explanation," pp. 85–126 in Michael Banton (ed.), *Anthropological Approaches to the Study of Religion*. A.S.A. Monographs, vol. 3. London: Tavistock.
Williams, Raymond
    1976   *Keywords: A Vocabulary of Culture and Society*. London: Fontana.

I

DESCRIPTION

When the most basic concepts—the concepts from which we begin—are suddenly seen to be not concepts but problems, not analytic problems either but historical movements that are still unresolved, there is no sense in listening to their sonorous summons or their resounding clashes.

Raymond Williams (1977: 11)

2

DEFINITION

William E. Arnal

Defining "Definition"

Surprisingly enough, the *definition* of religion has not been a consistent major concern either for students of specific religious traditions or for theorists of religion. We would expect, at least under ideal circumstances, that any academic inquiry would begin with a careful circumscription of its subject matter, not to mention an at least passing attention to the question why that subject matter is worth studying in the first place. In other areas of study these sorts of issues tend only to be neglected when the discipline is so firmly entrenched, institutionally and ideologically, that it does not even occur to anyone to ask the question of definition in the first place, as may be the case with Classics or English or History, for example. The study of religion, by contrast, is both a relatively new addition to the academic repertoire, and by no means has a secure position within the secular university curriculum (Juschka 1997: 8–10).

Part of the difficulty lies in the fact that, while the academic *study* of religion may be a recent enterprise, the popular use of the term "religion" is not. Even when we (wisely) refuse to claim that we *understand* religion, at the level of common sense we are fairly certain that at least we know what it *is*. Perhaps this assumption is true at the level of common sense and popular discussion, but it is certainly unable to withstand scrutiny at the level of academic analysis. Some of the most important theorists of religion—Karl Marx (1818–1883) and Sigmund Freud (1856–1939) spring immediately to mind—not only fail to define what religion is, but actually describe it in conflicting and inconsistent terms; in terms, that is, that suggest multiple definitions of religion. Marx, for instance, in a single paragraph, calls religion "[alienated] man's self-consciousness and self-awareness," an "inverted world-consciousness," "the general theory of [the] world," a "general basis of consolation and justification," a "fantastic realization of the human being," and the "spiritual aroma" of the world (Marx 1844: 11–13). These comments are really theoretical or explanatory assertions, but they also have significant definitional force: Marx assumes that religion *is* some sort of affect-laden intellection, and proceeds to circumscribe the subject matter of that intellection in several different—perhaps mutually exclusive—ways. Freud does no better: religion is sometimes a set of (false) *beliefs* (Freud 1989 [1927]), delimited in terms of their supernaturalism; and at other times, it is constituted by a set of (ritualistic and obsessional) *practices* (Freud 1907).

These examples of inconsistency regarding the question of what religion *is*—and the examples could be multiplied—raise a further concern, directly relevant for what follows. This is the question of defining definition. In the case of religious studies, the issue of definition overlaps so extensively with the issue of general theories that, in some instances, the two appear to be almost entirely coextensive. How are we to separate the two concerns? *Can* they be separated?

The short answer is "no, not entirely." For the concept of religion is a sufficiently artificial or *synthetic* construct that its very creation is itself an implicit theorization of cultural realities. As Russell McCutcheon (1998a: 52) puts it,

> it is the act of scholarship itself that (in Jonathan Z. Smith's well-known words) "invents" such categories as religion, myth, ritual, sacrifice, pilgrimage, etc., uses them to construct theoretical "models" of how minds or institutions work, and then "maps" these models onto what might otherwise simply be termed observable human behaviors.

What this means, of course, is that no statement about what religion *is* can avoid at least partially *explaining* what religion *does*, where it comes from, and how it works. Nonetheless, in what follows attention will be directed primarily to explicit efforts within the study of religion to define the concept—that is, to determine its fixed limits, to offer a precise descriptive characterization of it— rather than to those various theoretical assays which may have implicit definitional import. Still, it should be kept in mind throughout that each and every definition of religion implies at least *some* theoretical conclusions, while any effort to theorize religion is, concomitantly, utterly dependent on, and even derivative from, the way in which the concept is defined in the first place.

Some Major Scholarly Contributions

The effort to define religion is as old as the academic study of religion itself. F. Max Müller (1823–1900), who is sometimes credited with the "invention" of modern religious studies (see especially Masuzawa 1993: 58–60; Sharpe 1986: 27–28, 30–31, 31 n. 7; cf. Pals 1996: 7–8, 19), strictly delineates "religion" proper from the "myths" with which he is more concerned (and for whose study he is more renowned). Religion, for Müller, is quite broadly the primitive intuition and adoration of God, the "perception of the infinite," the natural and transcultural awareness that some Other is responsible for one's own existence and that of the world (Masuzawa 1993: 67, 192–193 n. 42; Morris 1987: 93).

The anthropological pioneers of religious studies—E. B. Tylor (1832–1917) and J. G. Frazer (1854–1941)—who criticized Müller's philological focus did not dramatically depart from his understanding of what religion *is*. Tylor's uniquely straightforward definition of religion was, simply, the "belief in spiritual beings" (Pals 1996: 24), arising out of a primitive conception of ghosts. It is on this basis—that is, defining religion exclusively or primarily in terms of conscious mental activity: "I am religious because I *believe that gods exist*"— that he could easily divide and categorize three distinct ways of thinking about nature: magical, religious and scientific. Frazer, likewise, not only invoked this same threefold typology, but believed that it represented successive stages in human intellectual evolution. Religion, he claimed, is to be defined in terms of "propitiation and conciliation of powers believed to be superior to man" (Morris 1987: 104). Although some effort is made here to clarify what is meant by "spiritual" (i.e., superior to human beings) and although a dimension of behavioral or emotional connection (a desire to propitiate a personal agency of some sort) is introduced into the definition, Frazer's conception is no less focused on the intellectual content of belief than is Tylor's. Religion is just a *particular way of understanding the world*, characterized, in contrast both to "magic" and to "science," by its personalized and non-mechanistic dimension, and destined to be overtaken by more progressive modes of thought by virtue of religion's essential falsity.

This *intellectualist* approach to religion can be traced back to David Hume (1757–1838) and beyond, and is linked to the interests and projects of the Enlightenment. All three definitions focus on the belief in gods (or "spiritual beings"), and in so doing make the (mental) positing of some non-temporal realm the defining hallmark of religion. Tylor's and Frazer's definitions, however, are even more revealing than Müller's, for they provide us with a *contrast* between religion and science. Hence it should be clear in this case that (at least part of) the guiding impulse for intellectualist definitions of religion is the archetypal Enlightenment contrast between "dogma," on the one hand, and "rational and scientific" knowledge, on the other. This contrast, of course, is itself part of a larger *political* program in which ecclesiastical institutions and the late absolutisms which derived some measure of legitimacy from them were subjected to "rational" critique. That the earliest academic efforts to define religion bear traces of this program should alert us to the possibility that "religion" itself may be an intellectual *invention* of modernity, and especially of Enlightenment; its cogency may depend on the socio-political circumstances and agenda of the Modern world.[1] This is not to say that Tylor and Frazer—much less Müller—were themselves advancing the political interests of Enlightenment but, rather, that the success of the Enlightenment project had *created* an entity, "religion," which these later thinkers attempted to account for. That they, and those who followed them in this approach, did so in terms of Enlightenment presuppositions, therefore, should hardly surprise us.

Another body of efforts to define religion has attempted to do so in terms of the precise character of its connection to, or *function* within, other aspects of human reality. That is, a given phenomenon is identified as a religious phenomenon less because of its intellectual or propositional *content* and more in terms of *the task the phenomenon serves* with respect to psychological, social or political operations:

> Functionalists prefer to define "religion" not in terms of *what* is believed by the religious but in terms of *how* they believe it (that is in terms of the role belief plays in people's lives). Certain individual or social needs are specified and religion is identified as any system whose beliefs, practices or symbols serve to meet those needs. (Clarke and Byrne 1993: 7)

The superiority of this approach lies not least in its recognition of the extra-intellectual aspects of religion, in its appreciation that the spectrum of phenomena embraced by the term "religion" includes powerful emotional states, particular types of action and, of course, serious consequences for behavior, rather than consisting exclusively of a set of (mistaken) mental conclusions. Moreover, by stressing the *work* religion performs, whether at the individual or the social level, functional definitions allow for a more complex understanding of the various different forms taken, historically or individually, by diverse religious phenomena, and thus they make it possible to avoid the peculiar problem for the intellectualist approach that religious belief has not ceased with the advent of the Age of Science.

The classic functionalist definition of religion is that of Émile Durkheim (1858–1917), a French sociologist whose 1912 work, *The Elementary Forms of Religious Life* (Durkheim 1995), marked a watershed in genuinely sociological investigation of religious phenomena. Durkheim sought to explain not so much the original genesis of religion in the mists of the past as the grounds for its persistence and diversity in the present. His investigation of *totemism*, which he thought to be the "original form" of religious belief and practice, was designed to reveal the social functions of religion in their most primitive—and hence obvious—form, rather than to posit a specific event that "got the ball rolling." Noting that earlier definitions of religion, which focused on the "supernatural" or on "divinities," had misconstrued the nature of religious belief (warping it too far in the direction of modern manifestations of religious belief), Durkheim proposed instead a definition of religion based on the distinction between sacred and profane: "a religion is a unified system of beliefs and practices relative to *sacred things*, that is to say, things set apart and forbidden" (Durkheim 1995: 44). What is meant by this distinction may seem strange at first, for as far as Durkheim is concerned, it has nothing to do with holiness, goodness or supernatural characteristics; in fact, the content of each of the categories is essentially arbitrary. Anything can be sacred in a given society, provided only that it is not profane; and vice versa. If there is no fixed content to the distinction between "sacred" and "profane," if the distinction is purely formal and arbitrary, what is its point? According to Durkheim, the point of this distinction is to offer a representation for society as a whole, or, by the same token, for the feeling of "effervescence" that accompanies occasions of communal solidarity. Religion is thus the symbolization of the whole of the social body; that is, religion is defined by its social function rather than by any distinctively religious content. By such a definition, the flag, for instance—at least in the United States—is an object of genuinely religious veneration. Conversely, for Durkheim, magic, which bears many of the supernatural characteristics (i.e., content) of what is ordinarily designated as religion, is excluded from this category by virtue of its private character: as a private act, it cannot fulfill precisely the *social* functions by which Durkheim can identify a phenomenon as a religious one.

One could apply the functionalist mode of defining religion in ways other than those adopted by Durkheim, of course. From a Freudian perspective, for instance, religion could be functionally defined in terms of its collective obsessional character (Freud 1907); thus religion is identified in terms of its task of providing a neurotic outlet for the social necessity of the repression of anti-social drives (see also Freud 1930). Marx's understanding of religion as ideology might similarly fit the bill: religion, from a Marxist perspective, *might* be defined in terms of its function to occlude the truth and provide mystic consolation for the afflictions of this world.[2]

There are, in addition, those definitions that understand religion in terms of some basic and irrepressible human instinct, an impulse toward the ultimate or infinite which cannot be *reduced* to (translated into) any other type of human needs, such as material consolation or psychological gratifications. The human being is thus understood as a *Homo religiosis*—a being fundamentally hard-wired with an orientation toward a greater and awesome Other. Such is the definition of religion, implicit or explicit, in the work of thinkers such as Rudolf Otto (1869–1937), or, somewhat more recently, Mircea Eliade (1907–1986). Otto described religion in terms of the individual's unique experience of the *mysterium tremendum et fascinans*, the personal encounter with the numinous whose overpowering and fundamentally ineffable character renders mere human existence contingent and small (Otto 1969 [1917]). Eliade, somewhat similarly, took religion to be the apprehension of or orientation to the Sacred: religion consists of those beliefs, practices, rituals and feelings that are directed toward the Center, the primal time, the "zone of absolute reality"

(Eliade 1954: 17–18). Such definitions of religion as these are of course non- and even anti-reductionistic. Otto, Eliade and others who adopt such an understanding of religion ensure by their very act of defining it this way that—*unlike* functional definitions—an "explaining away" of religion in extra-religious terms is impossible.

Finally, one of the most concerted and explicit efforts to define religion may be found in Clifford Geertz's essay, "Religion as a Cultural System" (Geertz 1966). Geertz attempted to be as thorough and precise as possible, while providing a definition that would allow anthropologists, including those working with non-Western traditions, to approach religion in a productive way. His dense and multi-part definition is:

> Religion is (1) a system of symbols which acts to (2) establish powerful, pervasive, and long-lasting moods and motivations in men by (3) formulating conceptions of a general order of existence and (4) clothing these conceptions with such an aura of factuality that (5) the moods and motivations seem uniquely realistic. (Geertz 1966: 4)

This extended and detailed definition has been extraordinarily influential, and it is not easily categorized as either functional *or* substantivist, reductionistic *or* non-reductionistic. Geertz paid careful attention both to the intellectual and to the emotive aspects of religion, as well as to its symbolic function within a given culture. Of all of the important academic definitions of religion, that of Geertz appears to be the most careful and thorough—and probably the least open to charges of special pleading.

Critical Evaluation

The various definitions of religion that have been suggested in the last hundred years or so—a rather bewildering array, in fact—might be more easily apprehended and understood in terms of a simple twofold typology. The first category may be designated "substantivist" definitions of religion. Such definitions, regardless of the actual and specific content imputed to religion, locate the definition of religion with its key internal attributes. That is, religion *is*, and can be identified by, particular features that inhere in its particular expressions. These features may be the necessary and sufficient qualities for designating a given phenomenon as "religious," or they may constitute the elements of a system of "family resemblances" whereby no *single* feature is absolutely required for a phenomenon to be—more or less—religious (Clarke and Byrne 1993: 11–15; Saler 1993).

The second category defines religion in terms of what a phenomenon accomplishes for the social or individual *context* in which it occurs, or in terms of the use to which it is put; that is, these definitions are essentially functionalist. As already noted in connection with Durkheim, one result of functionalist definitions of religion is that they make the content of "religion" wholly arbitrary. One person's "sacred," as it turns out, is someone else's "profane." I have chosen to call such definitions "culturalist" because they tend to identify religion in terms of some fixed *cultural* role, whether in a reductionist fashion or not.

Each type of definition—in spite of the variety internal to each type—tends to have a number of different shared characteristics.

Characteristic	Substantivist Definitions	Culturalist Definitions
Basis of definition	Ontological	Functionalist
Point of religious language	Refers to religious objects	Symbolic, communicative
Content	Cross-culturally stable	Arbitrary, historically specific
Referent	Extra-mundane	Mundane
Value of religion	Good or bad	Often neutral

Not all theorists or definitions are equally susceptible to easy categorization, but the foregoing typology may suggest some of the salient features—and perhaps even some of the strengths and weaknesses—of each *type* of approach to defining religion.

The attributes most commonly associated with the several substantivist definitions of religion have to do, of course, with things "supernatural" or "spiritual." There are two major problems here. The first is that the definition of religion in terms of spiritual or supernatural content, while seemingly straightforward, actually only defers the question: we are left wondering how to define "spiritual" or "supernatural," neither of which, it turns out, is much easier to define clearly than is religion itself. We may wish to clarify what is meant by "spiritual" in a variety of ways, but the problem does not go away. For instance, we cannot say, " 'spiritual' refers to entities which are not real"; not only does this beg the question of the referential truthfulness of religion as well as the question what is meant by "real," but it additionally would imply that novelistic fictions, such as, say, Heathcliffe in Emily Brontë's *Wuthering Heights*, fall into the category of religion, while real human beings, such as Jesus or Mohammad, do not. Nor can we say, " 'spiritual' refers to strictly non-material entities," because such a definition could include *all* ideas and concepts. Nor is it clear that animistic religions, for example, posit any alternative or non-material order at all.

The second problem with substantivist definitions is that they assume, without giving any particularly good reasons *why*, that whatever characteristics they identify as constitutive of religion are *important* characteristics. Why, if at all, is it important for me to distinguish between a political activity and a religious activity? Even if the two *could* be separated, why bother? Or again, on what basis should we draw a line between ourselves as human beings and the gods? Why invoke such a subtle distinction when there are other, much more consequential ones to be made? To put it differently: I could, if I wanted, come up with a definition for "blue" that allowed me to categorize almost anything in the world as "blue" or "not-blue." But simply being able to do so would not mean that the distinction was useful for anything, or that academics should start constructing testable general theories of blueness or that universities should start opening Departments for the Study of Blue. So, in addition to working with what appears to be an essentially *ad hoc* and / or taken-for-granted (and ultimately incoherent) definition of religion, substantivist definitions also tend to take the *significance* of that definition for granted.

Culturalist or functionalist definitions, by contrast, at least avoid this latter problem. By describing religion in terms of a particular cultural, social or psychological function, culturalist definitions from the start impute a distinctive practical significance (and hence, by extension, an obvious intellectual significance) to the phenomena they identify. But their definitional success remains open to question. The biggest problem with such "culturalist" definitions is that while they provide good criteria for including those phenomena we normally and unself-consciously designate "religious" within the category of "religion," they usually do not offer any substantial grounds for *excluding* certain phenomena that we normally do *not* consider religious. This seems to me to be part of the reason that neither Marx nor Freud employed functionalist *definitions* of religion in spite of developing functionalist *theories* of religion: religion may serve a mystifying, consoling or neurotic function without by any means being the only social entity that does so. Literature, philosophy or even, in our day, television, might fulfill such functions, all without being religious in any discernible way. Perhaps this only means that we need to reconsider the parameters of religion; but if we do so in any substantial way, what we are dealing with is really no longer "religion" at all. Thus, ironically, it is the *absence* of the very feature whose (indefinable and question-begging) *presence* is ruinous for substantivist definitions that turns out to be the central weakness of culturalist or functionalist definitions. If, say, Marxism, television, the United States flag, and driving on the right-hand side (or left-hand side) of the road can all be called religious, the term is so broad as to be meaningless, and needs to be replaced.

Geertz, while offering essentially what I have called a "culturalist" definition of religion, attempts to avoid this problem by specifying within his definition the *kinds of topics* with which religion deals, while leaving the actual content of those topics open, historically contingent and, hence, potentially arbitrary. Geertz suggests that while religion may be recognized essentially in its function to provide a culturally-shared system of symbols, evoking moods and motivations that seem uniquely realistic (Geertz 1966: 4), that function circumscribes somewhat the content of the symbols that are used in this fashion. Driving on the right-hand side of the road, for instance, while it may indeed depend on an emotionally-charged symbol system, is recognized to be strictly conventional, and hence has no "uniquely realistic" component. Even the cultural symbolism used to represent such things as awe at the wonders of nature is at least theoretically ruled out of Geertz's definition of religion:

> That the symbols or symbol systems which induce and define dispositions we set off as religious and those which place those dispositions in a cosmic framework are the same symbols ought to occasion no surprise. For what else do we mean by saying that *a particular mood of awe is religious and not secular except that it springs from entertaining a conception of all-pervading vitality like mana and not from a visit to the Grand Canyon*? (Geertz 1966: 12, emphasis added).

But it is precisely at this point that the definition starts to become circular. Geertz here *assumes* a distinction between mana and the Grand Canyon, rather than providing any grounds for it. His notion that one pertains to "a conception of all-pervading vitality" while the other does not is simply a restatement, without elaboration or argument, that one is religious and one is not. The characteristic referents of religious symbols—"a general order of existence," "all-pervading vitality," and so on—are sufficiently vague that they can be (and are) simply attributed to those phenomena Geertz believes to be religious (on the basis, it seems, of *a priori* judgments that actually are *not* functions of the definition itself) without providing any compelling reason to avoid associating these referents with *other* (i.e., "non-religious") phenomena.

Geertz's effort to specify the function of religion more precisely in terms of the generally-human desire to assert in the face of life's torments and unintelligibility its ultimate comprehensibility and sense does not, despite appearances, much clarify things. On the one hand, not all of the phenomena identified by Geertz as religious serve to make sense of the cosmos. Religious *practices*, for instance, seem more concerned with building or reinforcing communal solidarity than asserting the meaningfulness of creation: even when some (and certainly not all!) of those practices are *rationalized* through recourse to symbol-systems that *do* assert cosmic order, the practices themselves are normally understood to be intrinsically religious, quite without recourse to their developed theological rationalizations (cf. Asad 1993: 36). On the other hand, there are phenomena that *do* attempt this, including secular political ideologies (whether Marxism's evolutionary notions or capitalism's rationalizations about the invisible hand of the market—and surely these latter would fall into the category of religion by almost *any* of the definitions so far discussed) and including scientific research,[3] that are, according to both Geertz and common sense, *not* religious at all. In other words, it appears that this characteristic—asserting the sensibility of the cosmos—is neither necessary *nor* sufficient for a phenomenon to be designated as "religious," and hence has no definitional import at all.

In addition, it must be conceded that any effort to define religion as such, that is, as a human entity, culturally and functionally determined or otherwise, that is meaningfully distinct from other types of human cultural production, entails an implication or assumption that religion is, in fact, *sui generis*. It appears impossible to avoid this unfortunate conclusion, even within functionalist approaches to religion. "The insistence that religion has an autonomous essence—not to be confused with the essence of science, or of politics, or of common sense—invites us to define religion (like any essence) as a transhistorical and transcultural phenomenon" (Asad 1993: 28). The reverse is also true, of course: if we define religion in transhistorical or transcultural terms, we are necessarily imputing to it a fixed essence. Since no one has yet isolated that essential kernel without invoking specific and specifically *theological* assumptions, perhaps it is time—at least for secular students of religion—to abandon the effort altogether.

Future Prospects

What, then, is to be done? What shall we do with this intractable word and concept that, on the one hand, we seem unable to do without and that, on the other, we are incapable of defining in any coherent way? One possibility is to acknowledge the artificiality of the concept, but not to abandon it on that account. This suggestion recognizes the synthetic or arbitrary nature of most mental categories (see especially Lakoff 1987), and so concludes that there is no especial difficulty in using "religion" taxonomically—even if it fails to correspond perfectly to some real object in the world—so long as our intellectual creativity in so doing is kept firmly in mind (see J. Z. Smith 1990: 51, regarding comparative projects; Arnal 1994: 191–192, McCutcheon 1998a: 52 and D. Wiebe 1992, regarding the concept of religion itself). The difficulty with such a view is that the utility of religion as a taxonomy is only a function of its persistence in our common-sense views of the human universe. To assert that this makes its use inevitable or even valuable is akin to suggesting that the idea of the soul should be pursued—albeit with a recognition of its strictly taxonomic character!—by psychology. This will not do.

Instead, I think, the academic future of religion as a concept will need to focus on deconstructing the category and analyzing its function within popular discourse, rather than assuming that the category *has* content and seeking to specify what that content is. This task has already begun to be undertaken, most successfully by Talal Asad (Asad 1993). Asad argues not only that the concept of religion as a universal entity is incoherent but, further, that past (or non-Western) forms of what we would identify as "religion" operated in terms of mechanisms and self-understandings that we no longer associate with religion as such. Instead, he argues, the concept of religion as we understand it (and hence, tend to define it) is a by-product of the special historical and political circumstances of Western modernity (Asad 1993: 28, 39–43, 47–48). As Asad (39) puts it:

> Several times before the Reformation, the boundary between the religious and the secular was redrawn, but always the formal authority of the Church remained preeminent. In later centuries, with the triumphant rise of modern science, modern production, and the modern state, the churches would also be clear about the need to distinguish the religious from the secular, shifting, as they did so, the weight of religion more and more onto the moods and motivations of the individual believer. Discipline (intellectual and social) would, in this period, gradually abandon religious space, letting "belief," "conscience," and "sensibility" take its place.

In other words, our definitions of religion, especially insofar as they assume a privatized and cognitive character behind religion (as in religious *belief*), simply reflect (and assume as normative) the West's distinctive historical feature of the secularized state. Religion, precisely, is *not* social, *not* coercive, *is* individual, *is* belief-oriented and so on, because in our day and age there are certain apparently free-standing cultural institutions, such as the Church, which are excluded from the political state. Thus, Asad notes, it is no coincidence that it is the period after the "Wars of Religion" in the seventeenth century that saw the first universalist definitions of religion; and those definitions of "Natural Religion," of course, stressed the propositional—as opposed to political or institutional—character of religion as a function of their historical context (Asad 1993: 40–41).

Since these views, as noted above, do indeed bolster the *normative* character of the separation of state from cultural institutions,[4] the concept of religion serves modern political ends and reflects modern political circumstances. Again, quoting Asad (1993: 28):

> It may be a happy accident that this effort of defining religion converges with the liberal demand in our time that it be kept quite separate from politics, law, and science—spaces in which varieties of power and reason articulate our distinctively modern life. This definition is at once part of a strategy (for secular liberals) of the confinement, and (for liberal Christians) of the defence of religion.

I would go even farther than this: the very concept of religion as such—as an entity with any distinction whatsoever from other human phenomena—is a function of these same processes and historical moments that generate an individualistic concept of it (in fairness, Asad 1993: 29 hints at this). The concept of religion is a way of demarcating a certain socio-political reality that is only problematized with the advent of modernity in which the state at least claims to eschew culture *per se*. Further, one of the current political *effects* of this separation—one of the political ends served currently by it—is the evisceration of substance, that is, collective aims, from the state. That is to say, the simple positing of religion is a covert justification for the modern tendency of the state to frame itself in increasingly negative terms: the secular state is the institutional apparatus by which the social body *prevents* the incursion by others into the personal and various other goals of individuals, rather than being the means of achievement for common projects and the collective good. This very definition of the modern democratic state in fact creates religion as its alter-ego: religion, as such, is the space in which and by which any substantive collective goals (salvation, righteousness, etc.) are individualized and made into a question of personal commitment or morality. This phenomenon is a feature of modernity, and as such it will be found in the political theories of centuries past. But it clearly affects our present understanding of politics as well. This effect is described succinctly as an *ideological* effect in our own day by Slavoj Žižek (1994: 15):

> the form of consciousness that fits late-capitalist "post-ideological" society—the cynical, "sober" attitude that advocates liberal "openness" in the matter of "opinions" (everybody is free to believe whatever she or he wants; this concerns only his or her privacy), disregards pathetic ideological phrases and follows only utilitarian and / or hedonistic motivations—*stricto sensu* remains an ideological attitude: it involves a series of ideological presuppositions (on the relationship between "values" and "real life," on personal freedom, etc.) that are necessary for the reproduction of existing social relations.

That the effort to define religion should serve as the opening contribution to this volume is, paradoxically, simultaneously ironic and appropriate. It is ironic because such an endeavor must result in negative conclusions—that there is no such thing as "religion," that cross-cultural or non-specific characterizations of so-called religious phenomena are distorting, that the phenomenology of religion is in fact a phenomenology of the Modern state, and so on—and so this *Guide* now opens with a declaration of its own impossibility. This is appropriate, however, precisely because the recognition of this impossibility is probably the anthropological *precondition* for any (at least putatively) non-hegemonic analysis of those types of practices that we moderns tend to designate as religious. "Religion," in other words, may be an *obstacle* to cross-cultural (including cross-temporal) under-standing; hence it must be theorized, as a concept, for that very reason. Talal Asad's description (1993: 54; cf. 37) of this project may thus stand as our conclusion:

it does not follow that the meanings of religious practices and utterances are to be sought in social phenomena, but only that their possibility and their authoritative status are to be explained as products of historically distinctive disciplines and forces. The anthropological student of particular religions should therefore begin from this point, in a sense unpacking the comprehensive concept which he or she translates as "religion" into heterogeneous elements according to its historical character.

Notes

1. By "modernity" I do not mean simply "recent times," but rather something quite specific (hence Modern with a capital M): the historical transition in Western Europe (and to a much more limited extent in Eastern Europe) from medieval and feudal institutions to those which have characterized the post-medieval and increasingly-capitalist West up to the twentieth century. Thus private property, for instance, or the idea of the essential equality of persons, or the definition and understanding of the "person" as a willful and self-interested subject, are all "modern" even if the roots of such concepts—and other ideas and social constellations typical of the Enlightenment—can in fact be traced to the Renaissance and Reformation periods, if not to several centuries earlier.
2. While such a functionalist reading of Marx is not *too* far removed from his own comments about religion, Marx himself would never have offered these characteristics as a sufficient *definition* of religion: for him, religion seems to be a self-evidently *particular* type within the broader functional framework of generalized "ideology." In fact, philosophical idealism is functionally identical to religion according to Marx's theories. Hence an acceptance of his theory of religion might generate a functional definition of religion, but Marx himself does not employ one.
3. Geertz attempts to avoid this problem by carefully distinguishing between scientific and religious "perspectives" (Geertz 1966: 26–28). But there is nothing intrinsic to scientific investigation that ensures its utilitarian character or its methodological skepticism. Pure research, even when it fails, implicitly imputes intelligibility to aspects of the cosmos we do not understand, and science has not always or consistently defined itself in terms of an institutionalized skepticism. Note also how similar this religion versus science typology is to the intellectualist definitions of Tylor and Frazer.
4. Or, at least, this *particular* cultural institution. In fact, however, apart from the recent phenomenon of public primary and secondary education, Western democracies seem to have at least some aversion to the state's control over culture. This aversion can be seen, for instance, in the pejoratively-intended description of the media in non-democratic countries as "state-controlled."

William E. Arnal

Suggested Readings

Asad, Talal
  1993 "The Construction of Religion as an Anthropological Category," pp. 27–54 in *Genealogies of Religion: Discipline and Reasons of Power in Christianity and Islam*. Baltimore: Johns Hopkins University Press.

Freud, Sigmund
  1907 "Obsessive Actions and Religious Practices," pp. 116–127 in *The Standard Edition of the Complete Psychological Works of Sigmund Freud*, vol. 9. James Strachy (ed. and trans.), in collaboration with Anna Freud. London: Hogarth.

Geertz, Clifford
  1966 "Religion as a Cultural System," pp. 1–46 in Michael Banton (ed.), *Anthropological Approaches to the Study of Religion*. A.S.A. Monographs, vol. 3. London: Tavistock.

Guthrie, Stewart Elliott
  1996 "Religion: What is It?" *Journal for the Scientific Study of Religion* 35: 412–419.

Idinopulos, Thomas A. and Brian C. Wilson, editors
  1998 *What is Religion? Origins, Definitions, and Explanations*. Leiden: E. J. Brill.

Marx, Karl
  1844 "A Contribution to the Critique of Hegel's *Philosophy of Right*: Introduction," In Robert C. Tucker (ed.), *The Marx-Engels Reader*. New York: Norton, 1972.

McCutcheon, Russell T.
  1997b "The Category of Religion in Recent Scholarship," Ch. 5 in *Manufacturing Religion: The Discourse on Sui Generis Religion and the Politics of Nostalgia*. New York: Oxford University Press.

Smith, Jonathan Z.
  1982a *Imagining Religion: From Babylon to Jonestown*. Chicago: University of Chicago Press.

Žižek, Slavoj
  1994 "Introduction: The Spectre Of Ideology," In Slavoj Žižek (ed.), *Mapping Ideology*. London: Verso.

3

CLASSIFICATION

Jonathan Z. Smith

❧ ❧

Methodological and Theoretical Elements in Classification

Two beginnings, which, between them, display three modes of comprehending the classificatory enterprise: In the one, Thomas Hobbes reflects on the paradigmatic moment in Genesis 3:20 when Adam imposes names on the animals YHWH parades before him (Hobbes 1968: 100–101). These names, in one of Hobbes's understandings, were only names of the "first intention," the "names of things." What Adam lacked were names of the second intention, "names of names and speeches, as universal, particular, genus, species, syllogism, and the like." The first set of names is that of the realm of commonplace, utilitarian knowledge; the second is that of "such things as pertain to science, that is . . . our second intention was to give names to names" (Hobbes 1839: 20–21). In the other, Claude Lévi-Strauss has recalled, on a number of occasions, a Proust-like reverie triggered by contemplating a dandelion one Sunday in May, 1940, near the Maginot line (Pingaud 1965: 3; Tréguier 1970: 173; Akoun et al. 1972: 78; Lévi-Strauss 1978: xi–xii). In order to "see" the dandelion, Lévi-Strauss discovered, one must, at the same time, "see" the other plants which differ from it. The dandelion cannot be "intelligible" by itself, but only as "much more," as constituted by the totality of those relations of similarities and differences that allow one to "isolate" it (Pingaud 1965: 3). In both accounts, denomination is placed in relation to classification, as it must be. But in Hobbes's view, classification is a second order activity, posterior to (as well as superior to) naming. His view of Adamic language is much like that fabled report of the Bakairi of Brazil, often cited by advocates of "primitive prelogical thinking"; while the Bakairi have names for each sort of parrot or palm, they have no word for the genus parrot or palm. "They attach themselves so much to the numerous particular notions that they take no interest in the common characteristics" (Steinen 1894: 81). Lévi-Strauss, by contrast, insists that classification, comparison and naming be seen as a single, indissoluble process. For Hobbes, named objects are independent monads with relations secondarily predicated to them. For Lévi-Strauss, objects are "given" as "bundles of relations" as part of the process of intellection itself. Either view supports both interest in taxonomy and the necessity of classificatory projects as characteristic of either science or cognition.

Many students of religion, with their exaggerated ethos of localism and suspicion of generalization, tend to treat their subjects in an Adamic fashion as if they were naming entities, often exacerbated by their insistence on employing native terminology which emphasizes the absolute particularity of the data in question rather than deploying a translation language which already suggests that the data are part of a larger, encompassing category. As such, their projects fall well within the sort of philosophical difficulties with respect to proper names, raised since Frege (1960: 56–78), as to the relations of denotation and connotation, as to whether naming is prior or posterior to describing (Searle 1967: 487–491; Chomsky 1993). Such approaches give every appearance of rejecting explicit taxonomic enterprises, although the use of geographical or linguistic nomenclatures, the deployment of categories such as "living religions," "monotheism" or "mysticism" suggest the presence of implicit taxonomies.

By contrast, a number of fields have long focused attention on issues of taxonomy, with classic works, journals devoted to the topic, and lively theoretical debates. One thinks of areas as diverse as linguistics (Ruhlen 1991), archeology (Clarke 1968; Dunnell 1971; Conklin 1972: 197–213) and library science (Shera 1965, 1966; Barbosa 1969). The first two are primarily concerned with "natural" classes in the service of establishing historical filiation; the last is concerned with "artificial" classes of conceptual and topical relations in the service of data retrieval. But it has been in the biological sciences, with its concern for systematics—whether understood as phenetic relations of similarity based on shared characteristics or as phylogenetic groupings of species by common ancestry—that the most sustained attention has been given to theories, methods and controversies with respect to classification (Mayr 1988: 268–288), from older essentialist systems (Gotthelf and Lennox 1987; Daudin 1926a, 1926b) to evolutionary classifications (Simpson 1961; Mayr 1969, 1982) and the newer, still controversial (Hull 1988), approaches of numerical phenetics which quantitatively measures similarity by aggregating and clustering characteristics (Ainsworth and Sneath 1962; Sokal and Sneath 1963, 1973; Johnson 1970; Abbott, Bisby and Rogers 1985; achieving its most influential results in the works of Young and Watson 1970; Watson and Dallwitz 1985; Watson, Dallwitz and Johnson 1986) and phylogenetic cladistics which classifies species by the recency of their common ancestry (Hennig 1950, 1966; Ridley 1986; Hoenigswald and Wiener 1987; now best represented by Kenrick and Crane 1997). Moreover, the emergent anthropological field of ethno-classification (Conklin 1972; Berlin, Breedlove and Raven 1973; C. H. Brown 1977, 1979, 1984, Berlin 1992), focussing on native classificatory procedures, and the ensuing controversies as to the relationship of "folk" taxonomies to "scientific" taxonomies (Atran 1990, 1994, 1996a, 1996b; Sperber 1996b [1975]; S. Carey 1996), among other matters, echo debates between emic and etic perspectives that have long preoccupied students of religion (Saler 1993). Most classical biological classifications employ the hierarchical model of logical division and are *monothetic* in that a single property held in common is definitive of a class, the *sine qua non* without which an "x" would not be an instance of "x," but of "something else." Numerical phenetics, by contrast, is self-consciously *polythetic* in that each member of a class possesses a large, but unspecified number of properties, with each property possessed by a large number of individuals in a class, but no single property needs be possessed by every member of the class (Beckner 1959: 22–25). Some scholars (Needham 1972: 110–121, 1975, 1980: 6–9, 41–62; Lakoff 1987: 11–18) have suggested a similarity between biological polythetic classification and the notion of "family resemblances" advanced by Wittgenstein (1953: 66–71) and extended by Austin (1961). It is this philosophical rather than the biological model which has been appealed to by some students of religion, either explicitly (Alston 1967; Edwards 1972: 14–39; Southwald 1978), or implicitly (Smart 1969, 1973a).

While most biological classifications are, as in Hobbes, conceived of as second-order procedures for establishing similarity classes of selected characteristics, various cognitive studies of the mental procedures by which concepts, categories and classes are formed come closer to Lévi-Strauss's understanding of classification as part of a single process of perception/ intellection (see, however, Boyer 1990: 24–45). Moreover, unlike biological taxonomies which have held little interest for students of religion (J. Z. Smith 1982a: 1–18, 1990: 47–48, n.15), cognitive studies of classification have begun to be influential in some recent theoretical works on religion (Lawson and McCauley 1990: 148–157; Saler 1993: 158–226; Boyer 1993, 1994: 62–67, 171– 184; McCutcheon 1997b: 131–132; Paden 1998a) as well as a few studies of specific religious traditions (e.g., Ferro-Luzzi 1986).

The origin of many of these empirically based cognitive studies can be traced to the work of Berlin and Kay (1969) on basic color terms. Although modified in a series of subsequent investigations (D'Andrade 1995: 106–115; Lakoff 1987: 26–30), their work appeared to establish that there are innate structures of color classification which have both extreme economy and predictable levels of complexity. Perhaps the most influential development out of Berlin and Kay has been the notion of "prototypes" as first developed by Eleanor Rosch and her colleagues (Rosch and Mervis 1975; Rosch et al. 1976; Rosch and Lloyd 1978; Rosch 1978, 1981; Mervis and Rosch 1981; as well as the important summary of the different stages of Rosch's theories in Lakoff 1987: 39–57) and extended by others (e.g., E. E. Smith and Medin 1981; Barsalou 1987; E. E. Smith 1988). Prototype theories describe classification and category formation in terms of an ideal exemplar of the type with decisions as to whether another object is a member of the same category being based on matching it against the features of the prototype. The match, in a polythetic fashion, does not have to be exact; it requires a judgment that the object (or concept, or word) is sufficiently similar, a judgment not made primarily on the basis of visual appearance. While researches in category formation have moved well beyond Rosch's proposals (Rips 1995), they made urgent a renewed interest in the psychological processes of forming judgments and relations of similarity (Tversky 1977; Tversky and Gati 1978; Gati and Tversky 1984; Nosofsky 1988; Medin, Goldstone and Getner 1993; Jones and Heit 1993; E. E. Smith and Sloman 1994; Hahn and Chater 1997)—processes that stand at the very heart of classificatory as well as comparative enterprises. The issue remains that was formulated by Émile Durkheim nearly a century ago: "a feeling of similarity is one thing, the notion of genus is another" (1912: 208).

Classification in Religions

Religions are not only the objects of classification, they are themselves powerful engines for the production and maintenance of classificatory systems. Unfortunately, most scholarship on religions, while treating some classificatory topics in isolation, rarely displays the full range of a given religious tradition's taxonomic enterprise—Brian K. Smith (1994) is a recent, stunning exception. However, a number of these more topical studies have proved provocative of theory. Perhaps the best known set clusters around taxonomic distinctions with respect to pure and impure (Leach 1964; Douglas 1989 [1966]; Beck 1969; Tambiah 1969; Neusner 1973, 1974–1977; Dumont 1980).

The most fundamental classificatory distinction deployed by religions, as represented by modern scholarship since Durkheim, is that between the "sacred" and the "profane." In the case of Durkheim's privileged example of the Australian aborigines, subsequent scholarship (e.g., Yengoyan 1989) has tended to bear out both the general and the specific critique of W. E. H. Stanner (1967: 229–34) who notes that "historians of ideas will no doubt wish to say much about Durkheim's inclination to dichotomism and dualism," and goes on to argue for the presence of "intermediate forms" or degrees of sacredness and profaneness. There is little doubt that students of religions have shown a marked preference for sharply dualistic or oppositional classes, not simply because they are commonplace (Needham 1973; Maybury-Lewis and Almagor 1989), but also because they often allow scholars to assert some form of affirmation of transcendence. In fact, much of the intellectual work of religions is devoted to the making of fine distinctions (even within apparently dual categories) and to the organization of these in classificatory schema. Religious expertise, in part, consists of the ability to think with and to manipulate these structures.

Classification of Religions

"Religion" is itself a classificatory term that is usually treated in the scholarly literature as preeminently a matter of definition. However, as legal procedures from Roman codes to the United States Supreme Court make plain, the decision in those societies where the term is appropriate to classify a given activity or group as religious or not (let alone judgments on matters such as magic/sorcery/witchcraft, licit or illicit religion) carry substantial consequences. From a taxonomic viewpoint, an urgent question is whether religion be understood as the unique beginner, by no means the suppressed premise of those who would characterize religion as *sui generis* (McCutcheon 1997b), or whether religion is to be classified as a genus within a larger, encompassing family as is more characteristic in the human sciences where, quite typically, culture is the *summum genus*—social institution is the genus and religion a species (Spiro 1966: 98).

Given the importance of these matters, it is noteworthy that studies devoted wholly to the classification of religions as a general topic are rare, chiefly affairs of dissertations (Ward 1909; Parrish 1941), encyclopedia articles (Adams 1974; Partin 1987), or chapters in older handbooks (Saussaye 1891: 50-66; Jastrow 1902: 58–128), with the latter being replaced in more recent works by a chapter on the definition of religion.

Perhaps the most fundamental classification of religions is "ours" and "theirs," often correlated with the distinction between "true" and "false," "correct" and "incorrect." At times, a comparative dimension will be added: "theirs is like ours" in some stipulated respect. Such comparisons are most frequently accompanied by a genealogical narrative which accounts for the perceived similarities in terms of filiation. All of these elements, except the term "religion" and the correlation with true and false, are already to be found in Herodotus's descriptions of the religious customs and practices of others (J. Z. Smith 1992).

Within early Christian apologetics, as well as in the later development of Christian anthropological theory, this paradigm was to have decisive influence in the development of a totalistic system of comparison that prevented surprise whenever similarities or differences were observed in the peoples mapped upon it. The genealogies that underlay the system, as well as the biblical anthropogonic narration, guaranteed the essential unity of humankind; all were children of Adam and Eve, even though their lineages must be traced through Noah's three sons. Differences were, therefore, accidental. Somatic and economic differences were the results of climate and ecology. Cultural, and most especially religious, variegations were caused by a particular group's forgetfulness of primordial truth as well as by mixtures brought about by processes of contact, conquest, migration and diffusion (J. Z. Smith 1999a, 1999b). Remembering produces unconscious "traces" of truth and unity, recoverable by the Christian scholar, amidst palpable diversity. Most frequently, the results of forgetting are described by the lump-term "idolatry." This theory paralleled the Christian understanding of heresy. Truth, by definition, is singular and eternal. Therefore only error (i.e., heresy) can have a history of plurality and difference. "The true church is always true... Only deviants introduce new ideas ... or create division... [The apostolic faith] had shown itself to be the original and oldest religion given by the gods" (Wilken 1972: 74–76). Both models—singularity and heresy—were especially prevalent in the early history of Christian encounters with Islam. The first model may be seen in its simplest form in medieval Latin and vernacular usage where *mahomet* or *mahommet* mean "idol" and *mahummetterie* means "idolatry," even when applied to non-Islamic religions, a usage found also in the early English words, *mamet*, *maumet*, *mawmet* (Du Cange 1733–1736 vol. 4: 178; Tobler and Lommatzsch 1962: 278; Shipley 1963: 418). The second model treats Islam as an apostasy from Christianity, including the fantastic fourteenth-century legend that Muhammad was a Catholic cardinal in Rome who invented his own religion after being denied the papacy (Doutte 1898–1899).

Both models are strikingly deployed in the journal of Columbus's first voyage. Here, the most common religious term, referring always to Roman Catholicism is that of "the Faith" (21 occurrences). The term, "religion" (3 occurrences) is, likewise, reserved for Catholicism. The language of deviation is first used of Europe where "so many peoples were lost, believing in idolatries and receiving among themselves sects of perdition." In contrast, the Spanish rulers were sworn "enemies of the sect of Mahomet and of all idolatries and heresies" (Dunn and Kelly 1989: 16, 18). This same language is routinely applied to the natives. While Columbus's reports are often translated as saying that the *Indios* had no religion, a categorization he limits to Catholicism, in fact, Columbus insists six times that the natives "have no sect" (*secta*)—the latter a pluralist term which does not carry the full modern meaning—thus Christianity can be described positively, since Tertullian, as a sect. Columbus twice couples this claim with the observation, "nor are they idolaters," thus easing their conversion to "our customs and faith" (Dunn and Kelly 1989: 68, 88, 126, 142, 184, 234).

Given these models, it is not surprising that the earliest works devoted to the history of religions (plural) are works describing Protestantisms in which geographical dispersion as well as genealogical history are central, and in which, as is characteristic of *secta* in its double sense (positively as "school," negatively as a schismatic group), attention is paid to "founders" (e.g., Ursin

1563; Pagitt 1635). Nor is it surprising that the three "monotheistic" religions, a term that became important only in the sixteenth-century European unitarian disputes—Judaism, Christianity and Islam—will be joined together in one taxonomic unit as reflecting various degrees of recollecting primordial truth, while all other religious traditions can be classified in the single taxon, "idolatry," "polytheism" (in contrast to "monotheism," an ancient term), or "pagan." This dual classification continued at least through the late nineteenth century (J. Z. Smith 1998), as, for example, in Vincent Milner's 1872 reference work in which all of the crucial terms figure already in the title: *Religious Denominations of the World, Comprising a General View of the Origin, History and Condition of the Various Sects of Christians, the Jews, and Mahometans, as Well as the Pagan Forms of Religion Existing in the Different Countries of the Earth*. Even today such models persist when religions are named for their founders (W. C. Smith 1964), and in introductory textbooks, where religions are classified by geographical and historical criteria (Partin 1987). In all of these developments, Christianity, either Catholic or Protestant—depending on the author—is taken taxonomically to be the "prototype" of religion.

In the seventeenth and eighteenth centuries, the model was revised, following the repression of the biblical framework and the rejection of the myth of primordial knowledge. The presupposition of essential unity, giving priority to similarities, was recast through the postulation of some Kant-like universality of cognitive or innate capacities—what will become, in the nineteenth century, the notion of the "psychic unity of humankind"—still linked to historicistic, genealogical explanations of difference. The best known form of this revision is that of "natural religion" with its postulation of innate "common notions" of religion (Pailin 1984; Harrison 1990; J. Z. Smith 1996a). But the same taxonomic classes—Christianity, Judaism, Islam, and Idolatry—remained largely in place.

It is in the nineteenth century, with the advent of the science of religion (*Religionswissenschaft*) developed within a university context, that classificatory questions concerning religions take on new urgency, resulting in the formulation of a set of categories, with "world religions" or "universal religions" at the apex of the hierarchy (J. Z. Smith 1996a, 1998). While not without predecessors (Saussaye 1891: 54), this classification received its most sophisticated formulation in the writings of C. P. Tiele (1877, 1884)—a figure who deserves, in many respects, to be considered the founder of the science of religion.

Tiele begins his work by accepting a clearly apologetic distinction between "nature religions" and "ethical religions," working out a complex classification of nine types and subtypes of nature religions, but only two divisions of ethical religions: "national/nomistic religions" and "universalistic religions" (the latter, a term with an Hegelian pedigree) or "world religions." As the characterization, "nomistic," makes clear, the contrast, at this level, is essentially that between Judaism and Christianity, although the list of national / nomistic religions is expanded to include Taoism, Confucianism, Brahmanism, Jainism, "Primitive Buddhism," Mazdaism (or Zarathustrianism), Mosaism (by which Tiele means the religion of the Hebrew Bible) and Judaism (by which he means "rabbinism"). Universalistic religion is a class with only three members: Christianity, Buddhism and Islam. This list is, in fact, generous. When Abraham Kuenen delivered his 1882 Hibbert Lectures, *National Religions and Universal Religions*, he demoted Islam to a national religion in conscious opposition to Tiele. The universalistic religions are book religions, they are devoted not to the special interests of a nation or people but to humankind in general, and, therefore, they are proselytizing traditions. Subsequent understandings of this classification, most recently in Mensching (1959, 1976), continue Tiele's divisions, adding only brief essentialist characterizations of each religion (J. Z. Smith 1996a: 395–396). Note that this classification replicates the older division of Christianity, Judaism, Islam, and Idolatry by demoting Judaism, promoting Buddhism (which formerly functioned as the very type of idolatry in the older Christian literature, at least since the thirteenth century), and renaming Idolatry as nature, ethnic, or national religions.

In subsequent formulations, popular since the 1930s, the original list of three world religions has been expanded to seven by means of a sort of pluralistic etiquette. If Christianity and Islam are world religions, it would be rude to exclude Judaism (the original model for the opposing type of ethnic or national religions). Likewise, if Buddhism, then Hinduism. And again, if Buddhism, then Chinese and Japanese religions. Unlike Tiele's system, these religions are all "living," consequently the taxonomic nomenclature is often altered to "religions of the world" or "the world's religions"—terminology likely influenced by the 1893 Chicago World's Parliament of Religions (Kitagawa 1983).

In fact, "a world religion is a religion like ours; but it is, above all, a tradition which has achieved sufficient power and numbers to enter our history, either to form it, interact with it or thwart it" (J. Z. Smith 1978a: 295). This understanding is explicit in the title, "The Conference of Great Religions," an 1896 gathering held in Lahore, India. Today, "we recognize both the unity within and the diversity between the 'great' World Religions because they correspond to important geo-political entities with which we must deal. All 'primitives' by way of contrast may be simply lumped together as may the so-called 'minor religions' because they do not confront our history in any direct fashion. They are invisible" (J. Z. Smith 1978a: 295). This may be seen in the prevalent category in religious population statistics, "others or none." Ernst Troeltsch affirms similar values in a slightly revised classification. The "limitless, subterranean field of primitive ethnic religions" exhibits considerable uniformity; "polytheistic religions of a cultured peoples ... have highly differentiated forms," while "the great world religions are found to be extraordinarily involved in similarities and in differences." Continuing the use of Christianity as a prototype, Troeltsch concludes with the following political implications: "oriental religions, with their numerous analogies to Christianity and their own peculiar religious and ethical values, are even more in view; they demand that we come to terms with them practically" (1913: 94).

Scholars have been more successful in framing a set of middle-range categories, at times explicitly related to theoretical concerns, such as the typologies of church, sect, and cult (e.g., Stark and Bainbridge 1996 [1987]). Students of ritual have proposed suggestive distinctions between spectacle, festival, ceremonial, drama, ritual, and game (MacAloon 1984); others have worked out various genera of rituals, usually aggregated under the two families of periodic and non-periodic rites (Grimes 1985). In the case of van Gennep (1960), a taxonomic investigation has yielded an important and influential theory. Likewise, while there is a considerable list of types of myth, the usual practice has been to take one of these as a prototype in order both to characterize and explain myth, such as Eliade's (1959b, 1963a) and Long's (1963) focus on cosmogony. A more promising example has been the development, in folklore studies, of a comprehensive and shared classification of both tale-types (Aarne and Thompson 1961) and motifs (S. Thompson 1955–1958) tied to the methodological principle that the former can be properly used to establish diffusion and filiation, but that the latter cannot (S. Thompson 1946).

There have been surprisingly few recent meditations on classification by scholars of religion. Bruce Lincoln (1989) remains an important exception. There are certainly none that have taken fully into account the discussions of methods and theories of classification in other areas of research as reviewed above. For many in the study of religion, when not asserting some ethos of uniqueness and locality (J. Z. Smith 1990; Moran 1992), classification is seen as an instrument of power (Foucault 1970), a point clearly illustrated in that rich series of studies of the Indian Census (Appadurai 1996) that build on the pioneering researches of B. S. Cohn (1987). But this is to present the study of religion with an occasion for rectification, not resignation or renunciation. For the rejection of classificatory interest is, at the same time, a rejection of thought.

Suggested Readings

Adams, Charles J.
>   1974   "Religions, Classification of." *Encyclopaedia Britannica*. 15th edn, Vol. 15, 628–634.

Lincoln, Bruce
>   1989   *Discourse and the Construction of Society: Comparative Studies of Myth, Ritual, and Classification*. New York: Oxford University Press.

Parrish, Fred L.
>   1941   *The Classification of Religions: Its Relation to the History of Religions*. Scottdale, PA: Herald Press.

Smith, Jonathan Z.
>   1974   "Animals and Plants in Myth and Legend." *Encyclopaedia Britannica*. 15th edn, Vol. 1, 911–918.
>   1982a   "Fences and Neighbors: Some Contours of Early Judaism," pp. 1–18 in J. Z. Smith, *Imagining Religion: From Babylon to Jonestown*. Chicago: University of Chicago Press.
>   1996a   "A Matter of Class: Taxonomies of Religion." *Harvard Theological Review* 89: 387–403.

Ward, Duren J. H.
>   1909   *The Classification of Religions: Different Methods, Their Advantages and Disadvantages*. Chicago: Open Court.

4

COMPARISON

Luther H. Martin

∽∝∽

It has long been recognized that "[c]omparisouns doon offte gret greuaunce" (Lydgate 1967 [c. 1430]: iii, 1.2188). And yet, comparison is so common in the modern study of religion that "comparative religion" is often used to designate the field itself. The modern field of comparative religion was born, like that of anthropology, largely of the encounters with other cultures consequent upon seventeenth- and eighteenth-century Western exploration and colonialism. Whereas anthropologists, however, have consistently if inconclusively reflected upon the numerous theoretical and methodological issues incumbent upon comparing data cross-culturally (Lawson and McCauley 1993; see Poole 1986 for a recent consideration of issues focussing on the comparison of religion from an anthropological perspective), virtually no such sustained attention has been given comparison by scholars of religion (the exception being the work of J. Z. Smith 1978a; 1982a; 1987b; 1990). When the issue of comparison is attended to, it is usually as a question of method. Since method is dependent, however, on "the theory that shapes one's problematic" (McCutcheon 1997a: 9), the following will emphasize the theoretical issues concerning comparison, discuss how these issues have been dealt with in the study of religion, then conclude with a brief view of prospects.[1]

Comparison

Human beings, it is argued, observe and enumerate, often in great detail, various aspects of their environment. They then compare these data and group or classify them (Latin: *gener*, *genus* = class) according to generalizations they make about the similarities, and consequently the differences, among them (Latin: *comparare*) (Lévi-Strauss 1966: 10). These acts of comparison and generalization represent fundamental ways in which human minds order the

45

world (Schacter 1996: 52, 55). Considerations of data in terms of such constructed categories, for example, enable previous "knowledge about similar objects" to be applied to all newly perceived entities (Pinker 1997: 12). The question, then, is not whether to compare but how best to understand and effectively to go about this task (Lawson 1996: 32).

Comparative generalizations represent attempts to account for the greatest amount of data in terms of the least number of principles. Generally, only a single principle is assumed in their construction (Brody 1967: 60). Such a principle might predict, for example, that generalizations about similarities admit more shared data and fewer non-shared data than those about dissimilarities (Pinker 1997: 13). But what constitutes "similarity"? This judgment raises further questions of whether the principle whereby data is admitted to a common class is, for example, that of homology or of analogy. Homologies are understood by biologists as similarities produced by descent from common ancestors whereas analogies are similarities produced in some other way (Saler 1993: 174–177). Animals, for example, may be grouped into taxa that presume natural relationships by genealogy but also into "guilds," into herbivores, carnivores or omnivores, according to analogous ways of obtaining food. Depending upon the explanatory principle employed, "chimpanzees and gorillas are similar category-mates or as different as people and cows" (Pinker 1997: 128). The principle or principles of generalization, in other words, must be explained if they are to be accorded any intellectual integrity.

Different social groups pay attention in varying degrees of intensity to different environmental details. Consequently, every society produces principles of generalizations which are common only to that group (Lévi-Strauss 1966: 2, 10). Such "common sense" may be defined, with Giambattista Vico, as "judgment without reflection, shared" by a particular social group (Vico 1948 [1744]: 142). The common-sensical aggregate of generalizations included in any group's "circle of knowledge" constitutes its "encyclopedia," indeed, its "encyclopedia of comparative knowledge" (Berger 1969: 21). When observers encounter the data of others, data that often appear novel in that they do not fit the conceptual or interpretative categories of the observer, they tend to make generalizations about this data based upon their own common-sensical encyclopedia. As the fifth-century B.C.E. historian Herodotus already recognized:

> if it were proposed to all peoples to choose which seemed best of all customs, each, after examination made, would place their own first; so well is each persuaded that their own are by far the best. (Herodotus 3.38)

Generalizations about one's past are, as in the case of individual memory (Schacter 1996: 26), especially accorded familiarity. However, recent historiographical theory, influenced by ethnography, has emphasized that the character of the past is also "other" with respect to the historian/observer (Pocock 1962; Silk 1987). In other words, neither the customs of contemporary China, for example, nor those of the Western Middle Ages accord with a modern Western observer's common-sense data and rules for classifying these data. Consequently, simplistic attempts at a description of others often represent, as do naïve historiographies, a reduction of the data of others to the generalizations / categories of the observer, creating, thereby a perception of similarities where none exist.

In addition to common-sense generalizations, which are based on a sort of "soaking up of [cultural] correlations among properties" (Pinker 1997: 127), generalizations may be based on the ideological commitments of special interest groups. Such propagated views, be they political, religious or moral, need not necessarily be false and may, indeed, represent an evaluative response to an uncritical social consensus (Merton 1968: 160, 563). Nevertheless, the self-interested basis of such views ensures a perspective on others, whether positive or negative, that finally is as unreflective as the common-sense generalizations of which it is initially so critical. In fact, if successful, such propaganda may itself achieve over time the status of common sense.

In contrast to common sense, which may well be characterized by stereotypes, or to propaganda, which is often associated with ideological fictions, effective generalization requires the formal and critical considerations that may be afforded by theoretical reflection. As M. I. Finley concluded of historical generalizations, one of the most common types of generalization in the human sciences alongside comparison, unexamined assumptions "may impose an unexplained or unjustified organization of the subject matter to be presented and may bring in their wake other unexamined assumptions or generalizations" (Gottschalk 1963: 197).

Theoretical generalizations define "categories in terms of rules that apply to them, and that treat all the members of the category equally" (Pinker 1997: 127)—in our context, the rules of posited similarity (Pinker 1997: 309). Louis Gottschalk's prescription for the place of theory in historiography suffices for comparison as well. Theory, he writes, is the "attempt to find in ... [the] subject matter a *basis* for comparison, classification, interpretation, or generalization" (Gottschalk 1963: v; emphasis added). Theory, in other words, allows us "to rise above mere similarity and reach conclusions based on explanations" that are extrinsic to and different from the subject matter (Pinker 1997: 127; Poole 1986: 413; Gopnik and Wellman 1994: 260). Although historiographical generalizations are contingent upon a specific context or tradition, whereas comparative generalizations are not so constrained, the explanatory requirement is the same for both: to possess intellectual efficacy, generalizations must be formulated as "systematically related sets of empirically testable deductive hypotheses" (McCutcheon 1997a: 9).

Clearly the human sciences cannot evaluate their theories in ways appropriate to those of the natural sciences. Unlike the invariable laws of nature sought by the natural sciences, however, the human sciences *can* attempt to differentiate between *valid* and *invalid* generalizations. The conclusions of historical study together with those of anthropological research provide sufficient measure against which such generalizations, formulated as hypotheses, may be tested. Eric Hobsbawm offers the example of "Hindu zealots" who

> destroyed a mosque in Aodhya, ostensibly on the [propagandistic] grounds that the mosque had been imposed by the Muslim Moghul conqueror Barbur on the Hindus in a particularly sacred location which marked the birthplace of the god Rama.

However, Indian historians have demonstrated:

> (a) that nobody until the nineteenth century had suggested that Aodhya was the birthplace of Rama and (b) that the mosque was almost certainly not built in the time of Barbur. (Hobsbawm 1997: 6)

Thus, as Gottschalk concludes, generalizations must conform "at least ... to all the known facts" as well as "to certain general standards and tests—of human behavior, of logical antecedents and consequences, of statistical or mass trends" (Gottschalk 1963: vi; see Hobsbawm 1997: 6). If deemed valid, hypotheses can be held to be explanatory or causal and are differentiated, thereby, from both common sense and propaganda (Poole 1986: 413; McCutcheon 1997a: 9). As such, at the Xth Congress (Marburg, 1960) of the International Association for the History of Religions (IAHR) a number of leading members endorsed as part of their statement on the "basic minimum presuppositions" for the study of religion the proposition that "Comparative Religion" can make *scientifically legitimate* generalisations concerning the nature and function of religion" (Schimmel 1960: 236).

Comparing Religions

"Religion", in an oft-cited observation by Jonathan Z. Smith, is a creation of the scholar's "imaginative acts of comparison and generalization" (J. Z. Smith 1982a: xi). Some students of religion have appropriated from this statement support for idiosyncratic projects of "imagining religion" (indeed, the title of Smith's volume from which this prefatory line is taken); the poet has said, "I will not Reason and Compare: my business is to Create" (Blake, 1997: f. 10, l.21). Any study of religion in the absence of comparison and reasoned generalization is, however, but a common-sensical or propagandistic reiteration of itself, however creatively it may be formulated and however this creation may be ornamented with the conventions of scholarship. As Poole (1986: 413) concludes, the encapsulation of any analysis within a single religious system—and thus within the semantic networks of the religion's own terms, categories, and understandings—entangles the analysis with the very discourse it seeks to interpret and explain.

Too few scholars have heeded Smith's admonition that "imaginative acts of comparison and generalization" are not for poetic fabrications but for "analytic purposes" and are subject, thereby, to scientific (i.e., *wissenschaftliche*, "academic" or "theoretical") constraints (J. Z. Smith 1982a: xi). Or, as Smith has put it elsewhere, "the enterprise of comparison ... brings differences together solely within the space of the scholar's mind. It is the individual scholar, for his or her own good theoretical reasons, who imagines their cohabitation, without even requiring that they be consenting adults" (1990: 115).

Students of religion first attempted to apply scientific principles to the comparison of religions in the latter part of the nineteenth century. These early proponents of comparative studies based their generalizations on the "raw material" of "empirical data" provided them by the historical and philological studies of particular religious traditions (Müller 1871: 5; Jastrow 1981 [1901]: 21; Jordan 1905: 9–10), a view that still has currency (Sharpe 1987: 578). Theoretical reservations about nineteenth-century positivistic claims to the veracity of factual objectivity aside, the question remains about what exactly constitutes the evidentiary data of religion that historians and philologists might amass. Given that differing cultures have produced differing "religious" data, what, in other words, are the units of comparison to be? Should they be selected *aspects* of what the observer considers to be religious data (Poole 1986: 414)? Comparisons have been made, for example, of religious ideas, their teachings or beliefs; they have been made of religious symbols or of religious experiences (on "intellectualist," "symbolist" and "emotivist" theories of religion which identify these differing classes of data, see already Marett 1932: 1). Is there some *essential* aspect of these data that identifies them as religious and differentiates them, thereby, from those of analogous forms of human behavior? In other words, are such data to be construed as independent variables which may exert causal influences upon other cultural formations or as variables dependent upon other social and cultural factors (Krymkowski and L. H. Martin 1998)? Or, perhaps, should the data of religion be situated in and comparison made of entire religious systems? But, again, what constitutes a "religious" system and in what sense are entire systems comparable when by definition they are "different"? Stipulations of which data, or which sets of data, to compare and upon which generalizations might subsequently be made are not, in other words, self-evident, even as a consequence of meticulous historical and philological research, but already presume some operative theory of religion.

Further, an understanding of comparison and generalization as an operation following upon the gathering of the evidentiary data of particular religions by historical specialists raises its own theoretical problems. For historical data is the raw material of common-sensical and propagandistic *as well as* of comparative generalizations (Hobsbawm 1997: 5, 275). Is the observer to notice the similarities or the differences among these data? If similarities, how is their presence to be explained? Are there theories of comparison based upon differences?

Many scholars who have emphasized the *differences* among religious data have been impressed by their particularity, that is, by their socio-cultural contingency and specificity. Accordingly, they have questioned the significance if not the validity of any cross-cultural generalization. Some "postmodernists," for example, understand any attempt at generalization, including theoretical and even scientific generalizations, to be linguistically standardized cultural constructs (Pinker 1997: 308; Hobsbawm 1997: 6). Such well-meant attempts to preserve the integrity of "others" (Hewitt 1996), however, often result simply in a reiteration by paraphrase of what others say of themselves, preserving, thereby, their difference from the generalizations/categories of the observer (Poole 1986: 413; Gopnik and Wellman 1994: 260). Since the categories of such observers are, by this view, not subject to generalization, they remain, consequently, propagandistic. The results tend, therefore, to be similar to those produced by pre- or non-scientific comparativists, namely an evaluation of the "beliefs and practices [of the observer] in relation to those of other peoples and races" (E. O. James 1961: 15). So understood, the comparative project remains a reflexive exercise within the religious context of the observer—a limitation such views share with earlier comparative practices informed by religious apologetics.

While differences among particular data may well be important to specialists, they may have but minor significance for the generalizations of comparativists. One of the more interesting examples of a theoretical model of comparison based on difference rather than resemblance is Lévi-Strauss' attempt to establish the meaning of myths in terms of a differential, oppositional logic (Penner 1989: 179). Lévi-Strauss nevertheless argues that "[i]t is through the properties common to all thought that we can most easily begin to understand forms of thought which seem very strange to us" (Lévi-Strauss 1966: 10). Whereas comparison requires, in other words, "the postulation of difference as the grounds of its being interesting," it is the similarities that make it possible (J. Z. Smith 1982a: 35; Poole 1986: 417); and it is the perception—or conception—of similarities that has dominated the comparative agenda (J. Z. Smith 1982a: 21). But how might the presence of "properties common to" religion be explained?

An early view of similarity among religions was based on the assumption that the religious data of others are simply variations upon those of the observer and, consequently, these data may simply be identified. This view can be traced from the *interpretatio Graeca* or *Romana* of Western antiquity (the term is Tacitus', *Germania* 43.4). Herodotus, for example, identified Egyptian deities with his own Greek deities (Herodotus 2.42, 144) and averred that the Thracians "worship no gods but [the Greek] Ares, Dionysus and Artemis" (Herodotus 5.7). His synthesis was guided, of course, by his own Greek theological categories, i.e., the mythological encyclopedia of Homer and Hesiod (Herodotus 2.53).

Modern comparativists, more influenced by models of scientific generalization than of religious synthesis, seek theoretical explanations for perceived similarities among the diversity of religious data. Such theoretically formulated explanations have most often attempted to establish a homologous basis for these similarities, either by scholarly accounts of historical processes of diffusion or contact or, similar to folk psychology, by assuming some "underlying constitution" (Pinker 1997: 324).

Historical diffusion is the view that families of religion share a common genealogy. Max Müller, for example, modeled his proposal for a "scientific study of religion" on that of comparative philology which, at the time, was intent upon tracing the historical diffusion and development of Indo-Aryan languages (Müller 1871). Analogously, many scholars sought to explain the homologies they perceived among religious data as traces of primitive religious origins that had survived among the "more developed religious" traditions. This view of religious "survivals" gained theoretical support from evolutionary theories borrowed from biology and was illegitimately adapted to social development (J. Z. Smith 1982a: 24). On the other hand, attempts have been made to explain religious similarities by historical contact. According to this "syncretistic" view, some aspects of an originally autonomous religious tradition were influenced by or became blended with (or were corrupted by) those of one or more others as the consequence of cultural contact, whether through conquest, through commerce or through the centrifugal tendencies of political development.

Theories of diffusion and contact both assume some view of an original religiosity from which the various historical religions either diverged or converged. Such genealogical views based upon origination are unhelpful, however, since such origins are finally unavailable to historical or anthropological research and, consequently, tend simply to be retrojections of contemporary imaginings, indefensibly based, for example, on stereotypical assumptions about primordial survivals identified from among contemporary "primitive" peoples.

The dominant rationale to explain apparent similarities among the various religions when historical diffusion or contact cannot be demonstrated or assumed has been the positing of some kind of "primordial tradition" or of some sort of "psychic unity of mankind" from which religious themes or motifs derive (Faivre 1998: 120; J. Z. Smith 1982a: 26). Such homologous patterns as "sky gods," "solar worship," "lunar deities," "water symbolism," "sacred stones," "earth and women," "vegetation rites," and so on (see the table of contents to Eliade 1963b; van der Leeuw 1938) purportedly "reveal themselves" through a comparison of the multiplicity of historical religious expressions and practices (Eliade 1964: xiv–xix). The problem with such archetypal or morphological catalogs of religious themes, apart from the questionable assumption about their source, is, of course, their discounting of any historical and cultural significance. Rather, the amassing of such acontextual data has been most often in service to the culturally shaped, that is, common-sensical or propagandistic, agenda of the comparativist. Thus, the "recurrent" themes have tended to be derived from religious traditions of the Western scholar, the autonomous character attributed "the sacred," for example.

Comparativists who explain similarities among the diversity of religious data in terms of homologies tend to presume some essential "religiosity" common to these data. This presumption has led some among them to propose, consequently, an eventual synthesis of the world's "great" religions based on a recovery of the commonalities they "discover" among them. Irenic pursuits of comparative religion have resulted in such generic religious quests as the founding of "theosophy" in the nineteenth century (e.g., Blavatsky 1889) and the construction of "world theologies" in the twentieth (e.g., W. C. Smith 1981; Reat and Perry 1991; Grünschloss 1994). Even Max Müller (1884: 80–81), one of the first to argue a scientific character for the comparative study of religion, anticipated a

> new religion . . . for the whole world . . . firmly founded on a belief on the One God, the same in the Vedas, the same in the Old, the same in the New Testament, the same in the Korân, the same also in the hearts of those who have no longer any Vedas or Upanishads or any Sacred Books whatever between themselves and their God.

This goal of seeing in the gods of differing religions "nothing but names of what [is] beyond all names" is, Müller concluded, "[o]ne of the many lessons" which a comparative study of the historical religions may teach us (Müller 1997 [1878]: 363–364).

At best, the perception of similarities among religious data remains an unexplained recognition of intuitive familiarities observers tend to find in traditions different from their own (Pinker 1997: 324; Malley 1997: 389). "Even the barbarians have gods," Aristophanes assured his fifth-century B.C.E. Greek audience (*Aves* 1525). Rather than portending a reduction to some essential "religiosity," however, such recognitions might better be understood as *analogies* among the complexities of historical and cultural data. Jonathan Z. Smith, for example, has argued that religious similarities may be understood as the consequence of "analogical processes, responding to parallel kinds of religious situations" in a shared, historically constituted cultural field (J. Z. Smith 1990: 112–113). The question remains, however, how to explain perceived *cross-cultural* analogies, should the validity of such generalizations be admitted.

An approach alternative to the comparison of religions based upon generalizations about the data of particular religious traditions would be a theoretical development at the outset of general categories and / or formal frameworks of religion (D. Wiebe 1996). Apart from the recognition that what counts as religious data is itself a theoretical question, the quandary remains that an accumulation of even more data will not satisfy questions associated with comparison. Since "religion," like "literature," "philosophy" and "history," is but a discursive formation with its own history and historically constituted set of rules (Foucault 1972: 22, 38), rules for such generalizations might well be formulated according to scientific principles which are not contingent upon any one culture.

An example of theoretically constructed generalizations that might provide categories adequate for comparison is the "ideal types" first proposed by Max Weber (Weber 1946: 323–324). Although these "logically precise conceptions," as employed by Weber, tended to be modeled on Western religions, for example, "gods," "priests," "prophets," "salvation religions," "ethics" (Weber 1963: Contents), such theoretically formulated categories need not *in principle* conform to any specific cultural classification system (Gerth and Mills 1946: 59–60). A second example of theoretically constructed generalizations is modeled upon contemporary linguistics which has recognized, since the work of Saussure at the beginning of the twentieth century, a "constant data" that make up the multiplicity of human languages and that constitute a basis for comparison while still respecting the differences among the various languages (Saussure 1983 [1916]).

Formal, theoretically constructed generalizations about religion can finally be filled in or amplified with the data of particular religious traditions, data that establish each and every religious system as a unique system of meaning for its particular participants and practitioners. Such theoretically formulated generalizations about religion would, of course, also define the data of religion, insuring thereby the evidentiary confirmation of that theory. Nevertheless, such an approach would seem to offer the optimum possibility for diminishing culturally specific orientations in comparative research.

Prospects

Although the scientific comparison of religions has made remarkable progress since its nineteenth-century origins, metaphysical (i.e., theological) concerns, with which comparisons of religions have been implicated in Western culture since antiquity (Aristotle, *Metaphysics* 1026a19; see 1064b3), continue to infect generalizations about religion (L. H. Martin 1999). The term "metaphysics" was first employed by Hellenistic commentators on Aristotle with reference to the untitled group of texts the philosopher wrote "after those he wrote on nature" (*meta ta physika*). Medieval philosophers, however, imputed to "meta" a "philosophical" rather than its simple prepositional meaning, transforming its temporal into a transcendental sense (Hancock 1967: 289). Since the Enlightenment, however, epistemology in the human sciences has been reverting from the metaphysical to the physical sciences. Consequently, "naturalistic theories" have been defined for the study of religion simply as those whose "commitments" are no "different from the assumptions one might use to understand and explain other realms of culture" (Preus 1987: x). The best prospect for "scientifically legitimate generalizations" about religions would seem to rest, consequently, in the abandonment of theological presumptions about and concerns with ahistorical origins and essences and an acceptance of naturalistic theories, a direction that provides the basis for what has been loosely designated the "new comparativism" (L. H. Martin 1996).

Like scientific generalizations generally, naturalistic theories of religion are based upon theoretical reductions (Poole 1986: 417) and, consequently, understand religion primarily as a dependent variable. Some of these theories of religion suggest a developmental homology between biological patterns of behavior and culturally "refined" religious practices and suggest these biological substructures as the formal basis for comparison (Burkert 1996). These theories must remain vigilant, however, against a return to earlier views of a social evolution from the "primitive" to the "civilized" (Harris 1979: 139).

A second significant development for developing a naturalistic theory for comparing religions is the implications of cognitive psychology. The ultimate, while still distant, goal of cognitive psychology is a global explanation and mapping of the physical structure of the human mind and how it operates. In contrast to biologically based theories of phylogenetic adaption, the mental structures being identified by cognitive psychologists act as trans-historical as well as cross-cultural constraints upon the production of human cultures, including their religions (Lawson and McCauley 1990; Boyer 1994; Sperber 1996a). The identification of these common mental constraints promises to provide, therefore, a non-ethnocentric framework for analogical religious constructs.

Biologically based theories of cultural production have led to consideration of the social dynamic of "world construction" without yet offering a clear theoretical explanation for these social structures. What we regard as "religion" is fundamentally a social reality in which socially defined "sacred orders" maintain an "inhabited program of highlighted or bounded categories" for various social units. Whether the social construction of religion is understood as cultural adaptations of biology (Boyer 1990; Burkert 1996) or as the consequence of a domain-specific competence of the human mind (Hirschfeld 1994), such "religious worlds" can offer "a matrix" for "comparative inquiry" that "shows common, analogical factors in human behavior," on the one hand, and establishes "a standard against which cultural differences may be highlighted," on the other (Paden 1996a, 1998b; Luckmann 1967). Consequently, a comparative study of religion requires also cross-culturally valid theories of social formation and maintenance.

Scholars in the traditions of Durkheim, Marx and Weber have all produced significant social theories of religion. Although only Weber concerned himself specifically with issues of comparison, theories produced by the Durkheimian and Marxist traditions also have clear cross-cultural implications. Since the work of W. Robertson Smith, for example, a major influence on Durkheim's thought, anthropologists have identified but two types of social systems: "kinship" and "kingship" (W. R. Smith 1972 [1889]: chap. 2). "Kinship societies" may be defined as those in which "[e]very human being, without choice on his own part, but simply in virtue of his birth and upbringing, becomes a member" (W. R. Smith 1972: 29). Membership in these "natural societies," a notion that may be traced from Aristotle (*Politics* I.1.4–6), may be augmented by kin recruitment, for example, adoption, and kin alliances, for example, marriage (L. H. Martin 1997a, 1997b). By contrast, "kingship" may be defined as a transformation of kinship groups into "an aristocracy of the more powerful kins" with a consequent consolidation of power (W. R. Smith 1972: 73). Historical societies and their correlative religious forms represent, of course, sundry incremental variations between these two "ideal" types of social formation. Yet, such universal patterns of social formation and organization suggest the possibilities inherent in such theories for comparative study.

Naturalistic theories raise once again the Enlightenment proposal of human universals but without the metaphysical / theological assumptions (D. E. Brown 1991). As a basis for a comparative study of religion, such theories are promising. And yet, they remain provisional; none have yet been developed into a complete theory for a competent comparing of religions that has been fully "tested" against the cross-cultural and historical data. By paying attention, however, to the role that human biology, minds and social organization play in the production and constraint of cultural forms and expression, such empirical "mappings" of the architecture of human behavior and thought promise to contribute not only to our knowledge of the ubiquity of religion in human culture and its persistence in human history but to suggest also a formal framework of mental and behavioral constraints upon which might be constructed a theoretical explanation for the comparative enterprise that is so central to the way in which human beings organize their world and to academic generalizations alike.

Note

1. Portions of the following have been taken from arguments and observations first suggested in Luther H. Martin 1993, 1994, 1996, 1997a, 1997b, 1999 and forthcoming.

Suggested Readings

Brown, Donald E.
    1991   *Human Universals*. Philadelphia: Temple University Press.
Martin, Luther H. (Ed.)
    1996   "The New Comparativism in the Study of Religion: A Symposium." *Method and Theory in the Study of Religion* 8: 1–3.
Paden, William E.
    1994   *Religious Worlds: The Comparative Study of Religion*. 2d edn. Boston: Beacon.
Poole, Fitz John Porter
    1986   "Metaphors and Maps: Towards Comparison in the Anthropology of Religion." *Journal of the American Academy of Religion* 54: 411–457.
Sharpe, Eric J.
    1986   *Comparative Religion: A History*. 2d edn. La Salle, IL: Open Court; original edn, London: Duckworth, 1975.
Smith, Jonathan Z.
    1982   *Imagining Religion: From Babylon to Jonestown*. Chicago: University of Chicago Press.
    1990   *Drudgery Divine: On the Comparison of Early Christianities and the Religions of Late Antiquity*. Chicago: University of Chicago Press; London: School of Oriental and African Studies.

5

INTERPRETATION

Hans H. Penner

To experience is to interpret. To misunderstand is to misinterpret. Most disagreements are probably caused by misinterpretations. To interpret is to translate. All of these assertions sound like common sense. What is a valid interpretation? How do we know, if at all, a good translation from a bad one? Is it true that every generation makes its own translations. Do all texts need context for interpretation? If so, what is context? What is text? Are there universal rules of interpretation? What is a symbol? These questions and many more make this topic crucial for the study of religion.

Hermeneutics

From Hermes to Ricoeur

For many centuries the term "interpretation" was understood to be synonymous with "hermeneutics." In fact, most entries in dictionaries and encyclopedias of religion refer us to "hermeneutics" when we look up the entry "interpretation" (e.g., V. A. Harvey 1987). Hermeneutics, we discover, was at first used as a technical term in philology, biblical studies, law and theology. It is only since the nineteenth century, however, that the term has become important for theories in cultural studies, religion and literary criticism.

Most stories about "interpretation" begin with the Greeks and the Greek word *hermaios* which refers to the Delphic oracle. Some scholars think—but it is quite doubtful—that the term was derived from Hermes, son of Zeus and Maia. Hermes is the wing-footed messenger of the gods and friend of humans, an interpreter or translator. The significance of hermeneutics as a theory of interpretation, message or proclamation, a translation or transmission of knowledge from one domain (the gods) to another (humans), is that this theory clearly entails a relation between language and understanding. Thus, language and understanding become essential elements in theories of interpretation. In fact, we might say that any theory of interpretation involves the triad:

interpretation→language→understanding.

The Art of Understanding

Friedrich Schleiermacher (1756–1834), the father of modern theology, was also called "the Kant of Hermeneutics." Given his Kantian roots, Schleiermacher wanted to write a fourth critique, "The Critique of Understanding." This is clear from his lectures on hermeneutics (1819) in which he claimed that at the present time a general theory of understanding simply did not exist (Schleiermacher 1977). Rejecting the speculations and abstractions of metaphysics and ethics as adequate foundations for the study of religion, Schleiermacher sought for a theory of understanding that would unify the various methods for interpreting texts, grammars and rhetoric.

Although Schleiermacher clearly did see the relevance of language in his quest for a unified theory of understanding, he focused on the re-experiencing of the mental processes of the author of a text. He concluded that the tension between the subjective mental processes of authors and the objective context in which they exist can never be resolved. It is this tension between the particular and the universal, the specific and the general, the part and the whole, the individual and history, that became known as "the hermeneutical circle." The act of understanding entails knowledge of the particular, but knowledge of the particular entails knowledge of the universal. In order to understand a text we must understand the concrete, individual mental processes of the author. But, to know the author's mental processes we must also know the historical context of the author. To know one presupposes that we must know the other. This vicious circle is a major problem for many contemporary studies of interpretation.

Schleiermacher is important to the topic of interpretation for three reasons. First, he established the beginnings of a new "science," the "science of understanding." Second, this science is obviously different from the search in the natural sciences for explanations by causal laws. Third, his emphasis on religion as the feeling of absolute dependence (Schleiermacher 1928 [1821–1822]), an experience to be differentiated from physical or moral feelings, marks the beginning of a general study of religion that is not reducible to ethics, aesthetics or natural law.

Lived Experience, Interpretive Understanding and World-View

Wilhelm Dilthey (1833–1911) brings our subject into the modern world (see selected writings in Dilthey 1976). In fact, the terms *Erlebnis*, *Verstehen* and *Weltanschauung* (lived experience, understanding and world-view) are synonymous with Dilthey. Unfortunately, as Ermarth has pointed out, "It must be said that his notion of understanding is, ironically, one of the most misunderstood concepts in the theory of knowledge and science" (1978: 242). Although it is true that Dilthey drew a sharp line between the cultural sciences (*Geisteswissenschaften*) and the natural sciences, Ermarth shows beyond doubt that for Dilthey the theoretical and methodological procedures in both were as rational as can be. Nevertheless, it is ironic that the intellectual history of interpretation should rest on the proper translation and understanding of Dilthey's famous assertion, "*Die Natur erklären wir, das Seelenleben verstehen wir*" (We explain nature, we understand the mind). We will not be able to set the record straight in this essay, but do recommend Ermarth's excellent evaluation of Dilthey's theory of interpretation and historical reason to anyone interested in the *Verstehen* debate.

Dilthey raised the concept of interpretation to a level of general validity. He called the critical theory "hermeneutics," a fundamental science encompassing all modes of interpretation. His theory of interpretation begins with "lived experience." This is the familiar, unreflective, everyday world which involves a tacit knowledge and orientation. We often call this level of interpretation pre-theoretical. Ermarth makes the crucial observation that for Dilthey this level of interpretation is anything but "private" or "esoteric," since it is constituted by language, history and community (1978: 248).

The aim of all human sciences is to relive and represent this lived experience on a more conceptual and abstract level. Although he gave many examples of this task—the application of general rules of truth, comparative procedures, the importance of linguistic, logical and symbolic structures in this elementary level of human interpretation—it is clear that throughout his life Dilthey found the notion of "lived experience" very difficult to articulate.

Regardless of the difficulties with Dilthey's view of lived experience and interpretation, it is of profound importance for our critical analysis of interpretation in the history of the study of religion. Dilthey rejected such notions as "pure consciousness," "subjectivity" or a "transcendental ego" as the foundation for a theory of interpretation. As Ermarth (1978: 228) puts it:

> To be experiencing is already a kind of proto-interpretation, for we do not exist *de novo* out of our own immediate subjectivity but rather "live through" life in a vast network of accumulated meanings and life-values. In what might seem paradoxical or logically circular move, Dilthey suggests that such a general experience of life is not only the pre-condition

of human understanding, but also its result. Experience of life and understanding are mutually implicated and work together reciprocally to promote ever-higher levels of consciousness.

Once again we find the hermeneutical circle at work here. Dilthey resolves this paradox by grasping both horns of the dilemma. The question of the logical priority of either the historical context or the logical form must be suspended. This basic relation is a reciprocal one: experience and understanding, the temporal and the logical exist in a double relationship. Dilthey seems to resolve the dilemma, says Ermarth, "in terms of the relation of identity-in-difference which permeated German thought ever since Nicholas of Cusa: it is a *Grenzbegriff* [limiting concept] which we must assume but cannot demonstrate conclusively" (1978: 285–286).

The consequences of this theoretical shift remained ambiguous in Dilthey's life. Although he would certainly reject the Nietzschean notion that "language is a lie," the first cause of our alienation from lived experience, Dilthey remained caught betwixt and between the extreme forms of romantic subjectivism and philosophies of radical historicism. Although his theory did produce insights into the importance of language and community, Dilthey remained wary of language throughout his life.

The influence of the romantic presupposition that language betrays experience not only infected Dilthey's thinking but remains a powerful idea in the history of the study of religion into our own time. When all is said and done it is clear that Dilthey thought there was an unbridgeable gap between lived experience and expression. Although it may be impossible to resolve interpretive problems by a transcendental reduction into a pre-linguistic life of pure experience, Dilthey posited "a gap between inner and outer modes of existence and stressed that there were dimensions of inner life which cannot find expression in language ... While expression may be natural, it is partial and wanting in comparison to the ineffable fullness of lived experience" (Ermath 1978: 281). As Dilthey put it, "in a certain sense all knowledge, like poetry, is only symbolic" (quoted in Ermarth 1978: 251).

Lived Experience, Interpretation and World-View

Dilthey was well aware of one important consequence of his Kantian theory of interpretation: we can no longer speak of knowing things as they are in themselves. The levels of interpretation from lived experience to abstract, formal, logical thought were no longer secured by the existence of a rational, universal subject. Knowledge of a world *an sich* (in itself) became knowledge *Ansicht* (in perspective). The outcome, Dilthey knew, was "the subjectivity of the modern way of looking at things" (Ermarth 1978: 323). Looking at things from a vantage point, a perspective, is a necessary condition for lived experience. Perspectives are "world-views."

"World-view" is a central concept for most approaches to the study of religion. It is a notion that is seldom defined or described in explicit terms. Here is one of the best descriptions of world-view that I have discovered. According to Ermarth (1978: 326–327), Dilthey thought of world-view as

> at one remove from reality—it is not reality itself, but an interpretation of reality. This interpretation is not merely an aggregate of separate experiences but tends toward an integrated whole. The world-view is not given to us like a discrete fact or object in the world; it is a total outlook compounded of experience, reflection, and interpretation. It is not purely theoretical, scientific, or "philosophical" in character; it is not constructed like an argument or hypothesis—though it is not therefore irrational. It contains unconscious attitudes and deep presuppositions, but these are not wholly inaccessible, since lived experience is permeated by incipient elements of silent thought and reflection. The world-view unites different levels of meaning and integrates different aspects of experience.

> The world-view is not knowledge, science, or "theory" in the strict sense: it might be called a belief-system. It is not simply the construction of purely rational thought, for, as Dilthey stresses, man does not think, let alone believe, by sole means of theoretical reason. The world-view is not a logical system of judgments but a configuration which integrates cognition, volition, and affection; it is a synthesis of facts, values, and ends. Compounded of both subjective and objective conditions, the world-view arises from the perspective of factual states of affairs but also from the deepest attitudes of personality, which Dilthey sometimes called "moods of life."

> World-views are products of history, not just inner life for they reflect the influence of cultural tradition, nationality and epoch ... There always remains an elusive and unfathomable personal factor in the formation of any world-view, but no world-view is wholly individual, for it is constituted in relation with other persons and other world-views ... World-views are "creative, formative, and reformative." [Finally], transparent to those who hold them, world-views require great effort "underground" in order to be brought into view. This is the task of the hermeneutic science of world-view—a science extending beyond the conventional bounds of epistemology and even philosophy itself.

Faced with the doctrine of a multiplicity of world-views Dilthey clearly recognized two perplexing problems.

The first problem is known as conceptual or cultural relativism. Briefly, if the theory of world-views is true then truth and the content of truth is relative to a particular world-view. Pressed to its logical conclusion, relativism asserts that world-views are incommensurable, that is to say, not translatable, since there is no universal truth, or grammar that provides a bridge between them. As Peter Winch (1970) once put it, "what is real and what is unreal shows itself in the sense that a language has." Thus we cannot conclude that the belief system of one religion rather than another is "in accord with reality" or that it is mistaken, because what is or is not in accord with reality is dependent on the sense that the language of that religion has. It is not just opinions, interests, lifestyles or skills that are relative to a culture but fundamental concepts; it is the very propositional attitudes that constitute cognition and culture that are culturally specific. Benjamin Lee Whorf seems to think that people actually live in different worlds (see Carroll 1956: 213). Truth is relative to a world-view. The first problem then is one of translation. It is not religions that are ineffable, inscrutable, incapable of interpretation or translation but languages and cultures themselves. Notice, the logic of relativism does not claim that we have good or bad translations; rather, it claims that translations are impossible because cultures or languages are incommensurable.

The second problem is as devastating as the first. What do we make of relativist propositions as such? What sense does it make to say that "all world-views are relative to some context," or that "what is real and what is unreal is given in the sense that a language has?" Are these statements also relative to some context or language? If not, are such statements applicable to all world-views? Are they universal? An affirmative answer to this question seems to entail a contradiction. There seems to be one statement, the statement that relativism is true, that escapes the claims of relativism. We can put this argument in slightly different terms. How could we go about validating the hypothesis that meaning, beliefs, truth, are culturally determined? Is it not the case that the question itself arises out of a specific cultural context, a particular language? In order to answer these questions does not the relativist somehow have to rise above all contexts, including the language in which the hypothesis is stated, to judge whether it is true? Relativism entails its own destruction.

Most scholars, including Dilthey, do not follow the logic of relativism to its absurd end. The slippery slope of relativism is checked by an appeal to "the given." For some scholars this is usually described under the rubric of "phenomenology" where the given of religion is posited as transcendence, the sacred or ultimate reality. What recent introductory or specialized text on religion would disagree with the following interpretive principles?

1. Religious symbols reveal a modality of the real that is not evidenced in immediate, empirical reality.
2. Religious symbols point to something *real*, the sacred, a presystematic ontology.
3. Religious symbols entail a multiplicity of meanings.
4. Religious symbols signify a unity, destiny and integrating function for

human beings. Religious symbols express the contradictory aspects, the *coincidentia oppositorum* of ultimate reality.

5. Religious symbols have the capacity for expressing paradoxical situations or structures of ultimate reality that are otherwise quite inexpressible.
6. Religious symbols bring meaning into human existence. (Eliade 1959a)

Dilthey, of course, would have little to do with Mircea Eliade's romanticism. Nevertheless, fully aware of the profound consequences of the antagonism between the relativism of historical consciousness and the claims of universal world-views Dilthey did yearn for the universal truth that is disclosed in the dialectic relations that hold between the conditioned relations of history (see Ermarth 1978: 337). History and interpretation, for Dilthey, yield a paradoxical double relation of meaning and truth.

Dilthey's problem can be described as follows: How do we explain the claims of universal truth if lived experience, subjectivity or consciousness is constituted by history, language and culture? Moreover, how do we explain the persistent ignorance of human beings with regard to the relative truth value of their religious symbols and world-views?

There is, of course, another, an alternative solution. We can simply deny that religious language or beliefs contain any cognitive or propositional values whatsoever. Interpret religion as expressive of emotions, as similar to poetry or music, or as dramatic, and the problem is solved. As one scholar put it, "if they think deeply about it they will see that their religious beliefs are purely symbolic" (Beattie 1966: 69–70).

Unfortunately, this solution is illusory since we may ask the same question all over again: why do human beings believe that their religious beliefs and symbols are cognitive, that they assert truth values about the world? Marx, Freud, Durkheim and Weber give us various answers based on the premises of functionalism. Although people do believe, albeit falsely, that their world-views are true, the persistence of such beliefs functions to fulfill certain needs that must be satisfied both for the maintenance of the person and society. Religion, according to the functionalists, is what it does. The truth value of religion is in its use. A proper interpretation of religion is thus reduced to the satisfaction of certain needs—semantics is reduced to causality. This solution seems to avoid the pitfalls of interpretive relativism. Unfortunately, it does not escape the devastating critique of functionalism that demonstrates the invalidity of the theory on both logical and semantic grounds (Penner 1989).

Interpretation and Present Meaning

Hans-Georg Gadamer's *Truth and Method* (1989 [1960]) remains the definitive work on interpretation in the post-Dilthey tradition. Thoroughly at home in this tradition, Gadamer locates his theory in the radical historicism of Martin Heidegger (1889–1976). Gadamer takes Dilthey's contextual hermeneutics to its logical conclusion. If the author and intentionality are irrelevant to the interpretation of a text, then the text itself has an autonomous meaning. But, given the historicity of interpretation, the autonomous meaning of a text is always a "meaning for us." As Hirsch puts it, "reduced to its intelligible significance, the doctrine of the autonomy of a written text is the doctrine of the indeterminacy of textual meaning." "No method can transcend the interpreter's own historicity, and no truth can transcend this central truth" (Hirsch 1967: 249, 245). Interpretation becomes a never ending process or production and the notion of a "true" or final interpretation is simply a misunderstanding of the interpretive process. In brief, there is no fact of the matter.

Gadamer is well aware of the consequences of a theory of interpretation that denies that there are any criteria for deciding whether one interpretation is more valid than another. Hirsch quotes Gadamer: "There is no criterion of validity. Nor does the poet himself possess one ... rather, each encounter with the work ranks as a new creation. This seems to me an untenable hermeneutic nihilism" (Hirsch 1967: 251). Interpretation is always participation in a present meaning (Gadamer 1989: 370; Hirsch 1967: 252). This is indeed relativism with a vengeance. And, as Hirsch demonstrates, no appeal to relations between past and present will overcome the contradictions inherent in such hypotheses.

Interpretation, Double Meaning and Symbol

Paul Ricoeur begins his long monograph on Freud with the following premise: "language itself is from the outset and for the most part distorted: it means something other than what it says, it has a double meaning, it is equivocal" (Ricoeur 1970: 7). From this basic premise Ricoeur goes on to define interpretation: "to interpret is to understand a double meaning." Hermeneutics is defined as "the theory of the rules that preside over an exegesis—that is, over the interpretation of a particular text, or of a group of signs that may be viewed as a text" (1970: 8). Thus, "double meaning" is the "hermeneutic field," the object of interpretation, and this field is called "symbol" (1970: 7). Moreover, symbols are a group of expressions "that share the peculiarity of designating an indirect meaning in and through a direct meaning and thus call for something like a deciphering, i.e., interpretation, in the precise sense of the word. To mean something other than what is said – this is the symbolic function" (1970: 12).

After a very confusing, if not mistaken, interpretation of Ferdinand de Saussure's concept of sign and signification, Ricoeur states that the difference between a sign and a symbol is that "in a symbol the duality is added to and superimposed upon the duality of sensory sign and signification as a relation of meaning to meaning, it presupposes signs that already have a primary, literal, manifest meaning. Hence, I deliberately restrict the notion of symbol to double- or multiple-meaning expressions whose semantic texture is correlative to the work of interpretation that explicates their second or multiple meanings" (1970: 12–13). "In hermeneutics symbols have their own semantics, they stimulate an intellectual activity of deciphering, of finding a hidden meaning" (1970: 19).

The problem is this: we simply do not have an agreed upon set of rules that could be called a general theory of hermeneutics. On the contrary, what we find is a situation in which modes of interpretation are in conflict.

Several years later Ricoeur thought that it might be best to take linguistics into account and to trace the history of hermeneutics back through Gadamer, Dilthey and Schleiermacher (Ricoeur 1976, 1981). There is indeed much erudition and insight in these essays along with a great deal of complexity, dialectics, opacity and confusion. Yet, the one thing that remains steadfast and clear is that symbolic interpretation manifests a double meaning: faith versus suspicion, proclamation versus iconoclasm, alienation versus belonging, reader versus interpreter, text versus author, text versus reader, language versus speaking, understanding versus explanation, sign versus icon, theories of logic versus theories of iconicity, hermeneutics versus phenomenology.

For Ricoeur, symbols not only entail a double meaning, but a surplus of meaning. Symbol, like metaphor, "tells us something new about reality." "Symbolic signification, therefore, is so constituted that we can only attain the secondary signification by way of the primary signification, where this primary signification is the sole means of access to the surplus of meaning. The primary signification gives the secondary signification, in effect, as the meaning of meaning" (1976: 52, 55). Symbolic meaning is opaque to linguistic interpretation. Symbolic meaning "resists any linguistic, semantic, or logical transcription" (1976: 57).

Ricoeur's theory of interpretation, especially as it relates to symbolic meaning, ends where Schleiermacher began. "As I said," concludes Ricoeur, "a general hermeneutics does not yet lie within our scope" (1970: 494). We might add, and it never will if, as with Dilthey, Gadamer and Ricoeur, we begin with the ineffable fullness of lived experience, if the symbolic remains opaque to interpretation.

Summary

There are three fundamental assumptions in the history of hermeneutics that remain central to the study of religion.

1. Experience as lived experience (*Erlebnis*) is a unified primary interpretation of life. It is this lived experience that must be grasped by the scholar. For purposes of study we may focus on different modalities of lived experience, such as "poetic" or "estranged" or an experience of "the sacred." Scholars of religion have usually described the experience of the sacred as "a total," "cosmic," "ultimate" or "transcendental" experience. However, the validity of the concept of lived experience as the given and the scholar's interpretation of that experience are left either unresolved or never raised.

2. Lived experience, together with consciousness and interpretation, is thoroughly and radically historical. This thesis leads us into the inescapable problems of relativism. The question of truth is either placed in "brackets" or dissolved into incommensurable truths of different world-views. Eliade, as you may recall, dealt with this problem by calling it a "fall into history," "a second fall" which he thought to be the mark of modernity (Eliade 1954).

3. For better or for worse, interpretive theory since Dilthey views the history of science with suspicion. The debate about whether the study of religion is or is not a "science of religion" is the best evidence for this suspicion. The contemporary emphasis on pluralism, dialogue and discourse, rather than on analysis, comparison, universal rules and unity are some of the products of the suspicion.

There is one question that remains fundamental: how would one go about confirming that the basic premise of what we could call the history of hermeneutics is true? Sellars called this basic premise "the myth of the given" (Sellars 1997).

Interpretation, Language and Belief: Outline for a New Theory

Interpretation: A Radical Proposal

As usual, some of the problems that hermeneutics struggles with are real, and many of the insights are important. However, there may be a way out of the paradoxes and contradictions we encountered.

First of all, let us simply drop the quest for "the given." In other words, let us resist the notion of "lived experience" as the starting point for our theory of interpretation. This is a radical proposal. It entails the conscious removal of all theological and metaphysical traditions that continue to haunt the study of religion; all notions of "the given," the numinous, transcendence, ultimacy, the flux of experience, sensations, the really real and the like need to be set aside.

Let us begin, instead, with the simple assumption that we are all interpreters who have the uncanny ability of making sense out of what others say every day of our lives. As Davidson says, "without interpretation there would be no such thing as speech, no such thing as communication" (1980: I.1). He points out that our ability to interpret goes far beyond the important point made by linguists about our "knowing a language." As interpreters we are able to identify many of the beliefs, intentions, desires, fears and hopes of those we interpret. The point here is "that there is no way of understanding the words unless we are correct in much of what we think the speaker thinks and knows." The ability to interpret, therefore, entails a massive agreement between speakers about the world. To disagree, to detect false beliefs, presupposes that agreement. As Davidson points out, "without a fund of agreement, there would be no comprehending the differences—we would not know what we were differing about . . . But of course it would be a mistake to think that because we can be wrong about *anything*, we can be wrong about *everything*" (1980: II.3).

Second, let us make and consistently hold to a distinction between language and speech, meaning and use, competence and performance, semantics and pragmatics as we build a theory of interpretation. There is nothing more confusing in the hermeneutic tradition, and in the study of religion, than the use of these terms in writing about interpretation, semantics and meaning. As Davidson points out, "there is no single relation between what our words mean and what we want to, or do, accomplish by uttering them." As Saussure said, "I speak a language" (1983 [1916]). Thus interpretation entails the principle of the autonomy of meaning.

Here is a simple example. We might think that the sentence, "Alan Turing invented the computer" is meaningful when it is used to inform us that Alan Turing invented the computer. But what if the sentence is used to tell a lie, amuse us, irritate us or to create interest in graduate work? Davidson put it this way: "what we say does not depend on what we want or intend to achieve beyond words, in the saying" (1980: III.8). In fact, we may not know whether a person is joking, quoting a source or asserting something, yet have no doubt at all about what the sentence as uttered means.

Communication thus depends upon interpretation, not on shared speech or *use* of language. Thus Dilthey and his followers are quite correct in asserting that no amount of knowledge about an author's intentions allows us to interpret what the sentences mean. But, the popular saying, "tell me its use and I will tell you its meaning" is, as with most popular sayings, wrong.

Third, our theory of interpretation must be holistic; the parts cannot stand alone. Examples: no language, no belief; no language, no speech; no belief without many other beliefs. To put it in other terms, no theory of interpretation will be successful if we begin block by block or attempt to posit a "given" as the foundation for interpretation (Penner 1994, 1995).

Fourth, to interpret entails that we share a world with others. This is not something we might discover as an empirical fact. Community, social relations, a shared world with others is coeval with interpretation. To interpret is to assign meanings to the sentences of a speaker; to assign meanings to sentences is to assign truth conditions to what the speaker says. We understand what a speaker says because "means" translates as "believes true." If this were not the case, lying would be impossible. Thus to interpret makes the speaker our "co-believer."

Interpretation Entails Truth Conditions

Whatever the outcome regarding the acquisition of language, we may be certain that,

> Before the utterer of sounds can be said to have *said* something [asked a question, asserted something, made a promise] he must intend to achieve his purpose by dint of having caused an interpreter to understand his words. To have this intention, to be a speaker, the utterer must have a complex picture of the thoughts and abilities of his audience, and this he cannot have unless he is himself an interpreter. (Davidson 1980: III.8)

Davidson makes it clear why this must be the case:

> An interpreter has the concept of objective truth—the way things really are, in contrast perhaps to how they are believed to be—because in order to interpret, he must know under what conditions a sentence of a speaker is true, and because he must, in arriving at this knowledge, make use of facts about when the speaker holds a sentence true. The interpreter cannot fail, therefore, to recognize that a speaker holds some sentences true that are not, which is to say he attributes a false belief to the speaker. Truth is thus from the start conceived as objective and intersubjective. (1980: III.8–9)

To put this in other terms, there are two principles at work when I interpret what you say (utter). The first says that we both have an indefinite number of beliefs that we agree upon as true. This principle holds for all speakers and hearers, that is, for all contexts of interpretation, whether it be from English to English, Hindi to English or Japanese to Russian. The second principle tells us that the first principle must hold if I interpret what you say to be false. That is to say, we must first of all be in a linguistic context of massive agreement before we can disagree. Thus to assert that people live in different worlds, or that they hold incommensurable world views, or that something can be true in one culture but false in another, is incomprehensible. This conclusion should not be taken to imply that therefore all cultures or religions are the same. It should be clear that "translatability" or "interpretation" entails different languages, cultures, religions (see Penner 1995).

Interpretation Entails Translatability

This theory of interpretation entails a crucial principle for the study of religion: interpretation is a community project. "My image of myself, like my picture of others and the world, is a joint creation" (Davidson 1980: I.1). Once again, this is in agreement with Dilthey and those who have worked on the concept of "lived experience." The difference, of course, is that the dualism of "subject–object" and the "ineffable" given of experience have been dropped. Moreover, we avoid the pitfalls of relativism because to interpret means to translate. The notion then that someone speaks an uninterpretable language is incomprehensible—language *entails* translatability. Thus, it makes no sense to say, "people live in different worlds" or that language is a world-view, schema, paradigm, episteme, symbolic model or framework for the "given" of experience. In brief, language is not a representation of anything. As Davidson points out, "Nothing, however, no *thing*, makes sentences true: not experience, not surface irritations, not the world, can make a sentence true" (Davidson 1984: 194; Penner 1995).

Interpretation Entails Literal Meaning

Finally, if what we may call a "truth-conditional theory of interpretation" is anywhere near right, then the notions of "hidden meaning," "double meaning," "second meaning," all of which require deciphering language as a code, also become incomprehensible. This strikes at the heart of a long tradition in the study of religion, myth, ritual and belief as symbolic, or, as Ricoeur thinks, as containing a "double meaning." What we must learn to do is ask the following question as we read books and articles on religion: why do scholars of religion assert that religious language contains a hidden or symbolic meaning, or, that the task of interpretation is to equip ourselves with the right translation code?

It is precisely at this crucial pause in our reading that the importance of theory will disclose itself to us. When we raise the question, "what is the right, fitting, adequate translation code?" we are raising the question of theory. As we have noted, some scholars think that the most adequate interpretive code tells us that religion is void of propositional content, that is, religion does not contain truth values; religious language, religious symbolism is neither true or false, containing nothing of cognitive significance. Religion, as they say, is like music (as if music is not cognitive). Or, we often read that religion is symbolic, bearing a special or double meaning that can be deciphered only on its "own plane"; a valid interpretation can be given only by those who are themselves religious or have experienced "the other," "the sacred" or "the numinous." The important point to remember is that such assertions entail an interpretive theory that is founded on "the myth of the given."

The fact that after more than one hundred years we have not reached agreement on just what the code or double meaning is should have alerted us to the possibility that it may well be wrong to approach religion as a schema or framework that symbolizes, represents or transforms some content, *Erlebnis* (lived experience) or "the given."

A truth-conditional theory of semantics leads us to the inevitable conclusion that there is no such thing as symbolic, secondary or double meaning. The quest for such meanings is illusory. We must give up the idea that the semantics of religious language has a content or a meaning other than literal meaning because there simply is none (see Davidson 1984: 245–264, 183–198). There are no exits from the scheme / content theory of interpretation.

What we must grasp, and grasp firmly, is the premise that there is no such thing as "religious language" in need of a special grammar, semantics or code book. We must also hold firm to a second premise, the distinction between the meaning of a sentence and its indefinite uses in a variety of contexts. Saussure was right to argue that we must make a theoretical distinction between language and speech for a development of an adequate theory of interpretation (Saussure 1983 [1916]; Penner 1989). This proposal is a wager: a valid general theory of interpretation may yield an adequate theory of religion—I speak (use) a language; I practice a religion.

I am aware that any proposal that stresses theory goes against the stream in the academic study of religion. Nevertheless, it seems clear that to interpret religion or the practice of religion, we need a theory about what religion and ritual are. Given the above proposal, I am suggesting that we follow the success in linguistics and explain ritual, for example, as the "practice," "pragmatics" or "context" of religion, just as we explain how someone is able to "speak" (use) a "language," or how certain "ideolects" (religions) entail the same linguistic system (religion). This theory would make a distinction between the semantics and structure of religion as a cognitive system and the use, context or practice of the system in various societies and cultures. In other words, we would divide the theoretical task into an explanation of the semantics / syntax of religion and an explanation of the pragmatics of religion.

"I practice religion," then, discloses two theoretical tasks that we could call the "semantic task" and the "pragmatic" or "use task." The theory explains religion as constituted by the relation between these two elements. Two things need to be said about this theoretical approach to the interpretation of religion. First, and most obvious, although the two parts of religion can be divided among scholars of religion, they are inseparably linked in the history of religions, just as the division between "language" and "speech" or "competence" and "performance," though separable in theory, are inseparable in the history of languages. Second, and not so obvious, we cannot derive the first element from observing or studying the second. We cannot derive semantics, language, competence from a study of pragmatics, speech, performance or use; we must first of all know the world before it can become useful to us. The popular notion of "family resemblance" will not do simply because it presupposes what we are in need of: a theory of resemblance that allows us to pick out the families.

My appeal to linguistics is simply founded on the fact that religion is thoroughly based in language, both in beliefs and in practices. If the "myth of the given" is true—and I think it is—then we have no choice but to face and resolve the theoretical task before us. Interpretation demands theory. If the linguistic model is inadequate, then my question is, "with what do we replace it?"

Suggested Readings

Davidson, Donald
    1984   "On the Very Idea of a Conceptual Scheme" and "What Metaphors Mean," pp. 183–198 and 245–264 in *Inquiries into Truth and Interpretation*. Oxford: Clarendon.
    1989   "The Myth of the Subjective," pp. 159–172 in Michael Krausz (ed.), *Relativism: Interpretation and Confrontation*. Notre Dame: University of Notre Dame Press.

Dilthey, Wilhelm
    1976   *Selected Writings*, Hans Peter Rickman (ed. and trans.). Cambridge: Cambridge University Press.

Ermarth, Michael
    1978   *Wilhelm Dilthey: The Critique of Historical Reason*. Chicago: University of Chicago Press.

Gadamer, Hans-Georg
    1989   *Truth and Method*, Garret Barden and John Cumming (trans.). New York: Crossroad; original German edn, 1960.

Gumperz, John J. and Stephen C . Levinson, editors
    1996   *Rethinking Linguistic Relativity*. Studies in the Social and Cultural Foundations of Language, vol. 17. Cambridge: Cambridge University Press.

Harvey, Van Austin
    1987   "Hermeneutics," pp. 279–287 in Mircea Eliade (ed.), *The Encyclopedia of Religion*, vol. 6. New York: Macmillan.

Hirsch, E. D.
    1967   *Validity in Interpretation*. New Haven: Yale University Press.

Penner, Hans. H.
    1995   "Why Does Semantics Matter to the Study of Religion?" *Method and Theory in the Study of Religion* 7: 221–249.

Sellars, Wilfrid
    1997   *Empiricism and the Philosophy of Mind*, With an Introduction by Richard Rorty and a Study Guide by Robert Brandom. Cambridge, MA: Harvard University Press.

II

EXPLANATION

Religion has never been explainable in the terms provided by religion.

Weston La Barre (1970: xi)

6

COGNITION

E. Thomas Lawson

❦❦

Cognition is the set of processes by which we come to know the world. Cognitive science is the set of disciplines which investigate these processes and propose explanatory theories about them. Such theories display considerable variation depending upon whether they assume *classical* or *connectionist* forms, but both types of theorizing assume some form of *computational* account of cognition.

Computational accounts of the mind / brain employ the analogy of the computer to describe cognitive processes and products (Thagard 1996, 1998). They assume that we can model our cognitive processes and specify the products that these processes generate much like we specify mathematical operations. *Classical* computational theories employ rules to describe the conceptual operations of the mind without regard to their mode of implementation in the brain. Many classical theories argue that human beings possess innate mechanisms acquired via evolution and which require only environmental cues to trigger their operation. For example the dominant theory in linguistics argues that human beings come equipped with a universal grammar which constrains the construction of particular grammars. According to this approach, children acquire a language easily, efficiently and quickly because they are biologically equipped to do so. Classical theorists describe the process of acquiring a language by employing formal principles that account for why some forms of culture are readily assimilated whereas other forms are very difficult to acquire. *Connectionist* theories attempt to take into consideration, and, in fact, to model the mind / brain's processes by devising networks that in very limited ways simulate these processes in order to show how the mind/brain can rapidly acquire knowledge by exposure to aspects of the environment. Connectionist theories emphasize the plasticity of the mind/ brain, and while not denying that human beings are born with certain predispositions, for example, the ability to acquire a language, nevertheless argue that the evidence from developmental psychology shows that experience plays a fundamental role in the acquisition of the various forms of knowledge. Connectionists also employ computational principles to describe how such networks work (Bechtel 1991; Elman et al. 1996). Both approaches focus upon the acquisition of knowledge, but whereas classical theorists emphasize the *speed* of acquisition connectionists point to the processes of cognitive *development*.

Such approaches give rise to questions about the primary focus of the inquiry. One of the key issues in cognitive science involves the kind of knowledge, if any, that newborn infants possess or with which they come equipped. The facts of the situation seem reasonably clear. From the moment of birth, every infant is faced with the problem of appropriating the information provided by the world by engaging in the processes of interpretation and explanation. In the case of human beings, parents or their surrogates are typically available to nurture and instruct the child, but the world into which all of us are born is a very complicated place and consists of more than parents. From the child's point of view, the behavior of the parents, and all the other things in the environment requires as much interpretation and explanation as all of the other things and events that the child encounters. Who can deny that from the moment of birth infants are surrounded by massive amounts of information; sounds, colors, shapes, movements, people, physical and artificial objects, and events come and go with reckless abandon? This is the world that William James (1902) described as a booming, buzzing confusion.

Presented with such a world, infants have to be capable of acquiring a great deal of information rapidly and systematically. There are faces to recognize, languages to learn, foods to like or dislike, sounds to interpret, values to acquire and so on. Although some animals are ready to hit the ground running, it takes humans a little longer to get going. Nevertheless, as we examine the complex properties of the information that young children need to acquire in order to survive, we begin to realize that they acquire these various forms of knowledge with astonishing speed. At an early age, all things being equal, all children have already developed a significant command of their native language.

Because of the rapidity with which such knowledge is acquired, psychologists and other social and behavioral scientists have focused upon the issue of what is given by nature and what is acquired through nurture. Except for the behaviorists, most psychologists, and some social scientists now agree that the minds of infants are not Lockean blank slates; they appear, rather, to be predisposed to acquire certain kinds of information with ease and others with great difficulty. For example, as we have already seen, language comes easily and calculus is acquired only after strenuous effort. Learning how to talk one's native language requires very little instruction. By the age of five a mature grammar is in place. This fact has led some cognitive scientists to develop theories about the constraints on the acquisition of various forms of knowledge. Whereas the empiricist tradition has placed a great deal of emphasis upon instruction, socialization and experience as the primary means of acquiring knowledge, cognitive science has placed much more emphasis on the non-cultural foundations of knowledge: a complex interaction between the environment and innate predispositions. In fact this has led to considerable investigations into the plasticity of the human mind / brain in order to attempt to separate the cognitive equipment that is in place from that which requires development.

The tendency in cognitive science, in order to deal with this problem of the initial conditions necessary for the acquisition of knowledge, has been to conceive of the mind / brain in modular terms. This means that the mind / brain is not conceived of as a general all-purpose mechanism for the acquisition of knowledge, but consists of a set of autonomous mechanisms each designed to acquire specific kinds of information. One of the reasons for adopting a modular approach is precisely that while some forms of knowledge come easily others do not. Those who postulate one mechanism for the acquisition of all forms of knowledge would have a difficult time accounting for differential learning. Jerry Fodor (1983), working in the classical tradition, has been a key figure in arguing for the mind/brain's modular organization. Fodor argues that modules are domain specific (that is to say, they respond only to information from a specific domain, for example, face recognition). One of the issues which divide connectionists and classical theorists is whether the mind / brain is modular to begin with, requiring only triggering events in the environment in order for specific competencies to develop, such as the acquisition of a language, or whether the modules are the *consequence* of cognitive development leading to domain specific forms of knowledge. The facts at present support both interpretations.

No one denies, of course, that the cross-cultural research engaged in by linguists, anthropologists and scholars of comparative religion has as its consequence the recognition of the considerable variation in the contents of knowledge that exists from individual to individual and from culture to culture. Languages, religions, political, economic and moral systems differ in significant ways geographically and historically. In fact this variation has led to the dogma of cultural and even conceptual relativism among students of culture. But while, for example, the linguistic forms and modes of expression differ profoundly from culture to culture, the science of linguistics has been remarkably successful in demonstrating that the grammars of particular languages are constrained by universal grammar. Their obvious diversity has been shown to possess an underlying unity.

Classical cognitivists have focused upon the rule-governed nature of the acquisition of at least some forms of knowledge and developed theories emphasizing the principles that aid in such acquisition and parameters that are necessary to specify the particular forms acquired. Connectionists, on the other hand, have called our attention to the ability of neural networks to recognize patterns, to be trained by presenting them with a large number of examples, and then to recognize novel instances on the basis of such training. In this view knowledge of the world *becomes* modular rather than commencing as modular, at least in the case of language. But in both cases computational methods are employed to demonstrate that there are constraints on the acquisition of forms of knowledge.

As we have said at the beginning of this essay, computational approaches to describing the mind/brain employ the analogy of the computer. Just as a computer processes information according to a set of principles, so the human mind engages in the act of computation when it processes input provided by the senses. What distinguishes such a computational approach from behaviorism is the willingness of cognitive scientists to propose that an understanding of the mind/brain requires the postulation of theoretical (unobservable) entities. Such postulation, characteristic of the natural sciences, permits cognitive scientists to theorize about the internal processes involved in such processing from a number of perspectives (Thagard 1996).

The underlying unity that characterizes human mental processes is apparent not only in the universal principles that linguists have identified, but also in the categories that human beings employ in their on-line reasoning about the world. Cognitive scientists have thus also focused upon *category formation*. This is particularly the case when we study the *intuitive ontologies* that people employ (Boyer 1994). An intuitive ontology is an implicit theory of the kinds of things that there are in the world. (I say "implicit" because one can employ such a categoreal scheme without being aware that one is using it.) According to many cognitive scientists everyone employs an intuitive ontology of some sort in their conceptual traffic with the world. Some cognitive anthropologists (see, for example, Boyer) argue that people the world over employ the same sets of categories in their everyday traffic with the world. For example, all human beings distinguish between inanimate and animate things, and, more specifically between persons, animals, plants, artificial objects and physical objects. And they have the same basic expectations about the world based upon such an intuitive ontology. A case in point: no one thinks that a solid object can pass through another solid object except under very special conditions. People do not try to walk through walls. People also, unless they are engaged in metaphorical thought, avoid predicate spanning. Predicate spanning means applying predicates appropriate to one categoreal domain to another. Even very young children when told that an object of a certain kind sleeps know automatically that such an object cannot be made of metal. Or that an object made of metal cannot sleep. Our basic expectations or assumptions that we employ when thinking about physical objects made of metal would not be regarded as applicable to human beings or animals. In fact to say that the teakettle is sleeping is automatically regarded as a non-standard mode of discourse. People know the difference between the literal and the metaphorical.

Some students of religion have paid attention to the findings of cognitive science and have begun to theorize about how religious ideas are structured, acquired, retained and transmitted and how such ideas are related to our common-sense notions. Rather than assuming that religious ideas require special mental operations radically distinct from all other cognitive processes, students of religion operating from within a cognitive perspective have suggested that our ordinary, garden-variety cognitive equipment provides sufficient representational resources to account for their structure, acquisition, retention and transmission. In other words, *whatever it takes to explain how minds work generally will be sufficient to explain how religious minds work* (Lawson and McCauley 1990). Not surprisingly perhaps, this has proven to be a controversial idea because some scholars of comparative religion have claimed that the study of religion constitutes an autonomous level of analysis which is neither related to, nor reducible to any other level. According to these "autonomists," religion is *sui generis* and requires special and unique methods for its explication not available in the other disciplines. Some go so far as to argue that scientific theorizing in general makes little if any contribution to our understanding of what they consider to be specifically religious ideas and practices. Obviously such an approach makes science irrelevant for developing an explanatory understanding of religious thought and practices.

The study of religion from a cognitive perspective is actually a relatively recent affair and a new form of the "science of religion." One reason for this is that the study of religion has been largely an activity in the context of the humanities which values interpretive rather than explanatory approaches to the subject matter of religion. According to this hermeneutic approach, proposing a reading of a text (and by extension the "reading of a culture") requires only the expertise acquired from literary analysis plus the historical and philological knowledge that accompanies it. (Although some would insist upon having a religious experience as a necessary condition for understanding religion.) But even when scientific theorizing is taken into consideration the focus of such research, that is, the theoretical object of study, has either been on unusual and extraordinary experiences or on processes of socialization. Much of the work on religion in psychology, for example, has focused upon unique religious experiences, such as trances, ecstatic states or mystical episodes rather upon widespread religious ideas and the practices they inform. To the extent that the mind is even an issue, the major search in this tradition of scholarship has been for neurological correlates for religious experience. Such work stands squarely in the tradition of William James who, in his *Varieties of Religious Experience* (1902), treated such extraordinary experiences as paradigmatic of religion.

In the social sciences the work on religion has either been of the hermeneutic variety, thus echoing the concerns of the humanities, or has focused upon the processes of socialization (i.e., instruction and indoctrination) or has focused not upon the *structure* of religion and upon the constraints upon the acquisition and transmission of religious ideas, but upon the social *functions* of religion. Of particular interest has been the question of how religion fulfills psychological and social needs such as personal and social integration. Such approaches, unfortunately, have presupposed very simplistic theories of the mind as the conduit for the transmission of information and the functions such information serves, without paying much attention to the mind's architecture.

The first cognitive scientist to pay attention to religion was Dan Sperber (1975) who analyzed religious symbolism in the context of a general theory of the acquisition of knowledge. Sperber not only provided a critique of semiotic approaches to religious symbolism, but also argued for the importance of studying the inferential processes tacitly employed in religious modes of thought. Semiotics is the science of signs. In his critique of semiotics Sperber showed that the interpretation of symbolism was an extension rather than an explication of the symbolic process. His challenge was to rethink symbolism in such a way that it could lead to the development of an explanatory understanding of the epidemiology of religious representations. In such an epidemiological approach the issue involves the principles and processes by which some religious ideas are selected for transmission and others simply wither away. Sperber showed how some ideas achieve a remarkable stability and nearly everyone in a particular cultural context acquires them, whereas other ideas are entertained by only a few and, if transmitted at all, remain the purview of only a few—unless, by happenstance, they are recorded in literature. Otherwise they vanish from the scene. But even in literate cultures some ideas are transmitted even if they are never written down. Jokes and rumors spread with amazing rapidity. What is especially interesting about religious ideas is that they are so easily acquired no matter what the cultural context. This has led to research about what it is about human minds that makes them susceptible to religious ideas.

Pascal Boyer (1994) has primarily focused upon the relationship between religious ideas and the intuitive ontologies that people employ in their everyday affairs. Continuing the epidemiological theme proposed by Sperber, Boyer argues that an idea cannot be transmitted unless it combines two aspects. First, it must be sufficiently familiar so that it is not automatically rejected as nonsense. It must conform in most respects to our intuitive ontology. Second it must be sufficiently interesting or attention-grabbing so that it becomes memorable enough to be transmitted. What makes an idea interesting is when it goes against our expectations of what the world is like. Interesting ideas are counter-intuitive. They surprise us. Boyer calls this delicate balance between the intuitive and the counter-intuitive the state of *cognitive equilibrium*. Ideas that balance our standard intuitive ontological assumptions with notions that are quite uncommon have more chance of being transmitted than ideas that do not. And religious ideas are particularly good at perpetuating themselves, hence their widespread occurrence.

What makes religious ideas attention-demanding, according to Boyer, is that they either violate one of the default assumptions normally associated with the categories in our intuitive ontologies, or transfer some of these default assumptions from one category to another. For example, given the category "person," the default assumptions of which are intentional, biological and physical, one only needs to violate one of these default assumptions, the physical, to produce the notion of a living, intentional being without a body. Or, to take another example, given the category "artificial object," the default assumptions of which are physical, to transfer the property of either life or mind to such an object permits religious people to entertain the idea that a particular statue might, for example, weep and even consider answering their prayers. Here an artificial object has transferred to it biological (weeping) and mental (considering) properties. Boyer's claims about the role that intuitive ontologies play in our on-line reasoning about the world are not merely speculative. He has engaged in cross-cultural research which seems to demonstrate that ideas that balance the intuitive and the counterintuitive are more memorable and, therefore, more transmittable.

Lawson and McCauley (1990) have also argued for some time that our garden-variety cognitive equipment is largely sufficient for the generation of religious representations, especially representations of religious ritual actions. They have couched their argument in the context of theorizing about religious ritual action. They have shown how our ordinary cognitive representations of action (agent acting upon patient by means of some instrument or other) are capable of being organized by a small set of principles to provide structural descriptions of religious ritual acts. The only significant way in which the structural descriptions of religious ritual actions differ from the descriptions of everyday actions is that the former presuppose the presence of agents with special qualities in these descriptions. For example "man washes baby with water" and "priest baptizes baby with water" have the same actional description. In each case someone is doing something to someone by means of something. No special representational equipment is required to describe the priest baptizing the baby with water. One only has to specify the quality of the agent involved. The priest is a real agent in the real world. One only needs to know that in order to engage in the act of baptism the priest needs to have been ordained. The significance of these claims lies in their ability to show that religious ideas and the practices they inform do not require special cognitive resources for their implementation. The minds that we have inherited from our evolutionary ancestors are sufficient to acquire, structure, store and transmit religious ideas from one person to another and from one generation to another. People are equipped to create and employ religious ideas because they are equipped to create and employ ideas.

Focusing upon religious ritual representations permits Lawson and McCauley to theorize about this religious ritual competence, this ability not only to conceive of a world of actors and their actions but also to show how such a world can be transformed into a religious one simply by focusing upon the quality of the agent, the action or the patient.

Of course there are also matters of performance. How do religious systems ensure that the ideas they contain are transmitted? What does it take in actual ethnographic situations for such transmission to occur? One technique that religious systems have evolved over time involves the frequency effect. Granted that people are already susceptible to acquiring religious ideas with ease (because, as Boyer has shown, they are attention-demanding enough to capture human interest and, as Lawson and McCauley have shown, they have available an action representation system), the frequency with which these ideas are emphasized and employed in religious contexts clearly makes them transmittable. People are born into a world replete with religious ideas. The more frequent the ideas are discussed, insisted upon, taught, the more likely it is that those ideas will be attended to, and the more that they are attended to the more likely it is that they will survive through time and be transmitted to succeeding generations. For example, ideas such as agents with special qualities, experiences with unusual power, moral systems with sufficient bite, all of which serve to structure a way of life, are particularly compelling if they are frequently emphasized in a large variety of contexts. Religious systems seem capable of consistently providing the conditions for their own transmission, and instruction plays an important role. But a number of other resources besides the frequency effect are also available to religious systems. Perhaps the most powerful of these is the manipulation of the emotions. Those ideas are held in memory most easily, and therefore transmittable most readily, that are acquired in powerful emotional contexts. Thus elaborate ceremonies, massive celebrations, as well as situations requiring pain, punishment, fasting and so forth act to ensure the memorability of the ideas—even if the ideas themselves are bizarre or out of the ordinary. One only has to consider the rites of passage in various societies in order to recognize the difference between those rites which require a great deal of planning and resources because they only happen once in the life of an individual and those rites which are performed frequently.

Agents with special qualities of various sorts play a fundamental role in religion and can be found in all religious traditions even those traditions which are thought to be "atheistic." Of particular importance are their role in bringing about changes in states of affairs. For example, in a particular tradition before a person becomes an adult she or he would have to undergo a rite of passage. Such a rite might very involve a ritual official who engages in a set of actions which enables the person to successfully pass from one religiously defined state to another. The ritual official involved in performing the necessary acts would be required to be qualified to perform these acts.

This would mean that the observed act of transition from one state to another presupposes a prior act in which the ritual official was the patient of a ritual act legitimating her or him to perform the act in question. This would apply to the entire series of acts in which a succession of ritual officials ritually acquired their legitimacy. Such a succession is not infinite and the hypothesis is that in a tradition such as this there would be an initial act by an agent with special qualities who instituted the successive series of acts culminating in the actions performed by the ritual official in the specific rite of passage under consideration. In many religious traditions this initial act is conceived of as being instituted by a superhuman agent, that is, an agent with special qualities. Unlike ordinary causal processes which can always be pushed back one step further, such religious series of acts presuppose a starting point. The buck stops with the gods. Of interest to the cognitive scientist is why such a concept of agency plays such an important role in religion. The answer is interesting. Agency is important in religion because it is important in ordinary life.

Considerable work in developmental psychology has demonstrated the important role that agency plays in human cognitive traffic with the world. Human beings consistently adopt the intentional stance in their dealings with each other. That is to say, they attribute both to themselves and to others a theory of mind. Agents have minds. They are capable of desiring, believing, wanting, knowing, intending, hoping and so on. It is precisely because human beings treat each other as agents (i.e., as having minds) that they are so efficient at predicting the behavior of others. Sometimes it only takes the recognition of a glance to expect another person to behave in a certain way. Even infants are experts, long before they are efficient users of language, at communicating by glance and expecting parents and others to respond to their glances.

Now, if the attribution of agency to others is so efficient, even when the other agent is not present, it becomes relatively easy to recognize that people can conceive of agents that are very much like us (i.e., they can know our thoughts, respond to our wishes, consent to our actions) even if they are not observable. The superhuman agents that populate religious systems are frequently represented in this manner. Many of their properties conform to our ordinary assumptions about what agents are like. But agents which are *just* like us would not possess the efficacy which we require to presuppose their role in bringing about the states of affairs which religious people regard as necessary. The fact that they are agents at all is a necessary condition for their efficacy. The fact that they are regarded as having special qualities makes it possible for them to ground the kinds of actions in religious ritual contexts which have the effects that they possess. Without such special qualities they would be nothing but fictional characters. Fiction might entertain us, but religious rituals make ordinary actions, and the ideas that inform them, serious business indeed.

Suggested Readings

Barsalou, Lawrence W.
　　1992　*Cognitive Psychology: An Overview for Cognitive Scientists*. Hillsdale, NJ: Lawrence Erlbaum.

Boyer, Pascal
　　1994　*The Naturalness of Religious Ideas: A Cognitive Theory of Religion*. Berkeley: University of California Press.

Lawson, E. Thomas and Robert N. McCauley
　　1993　"Crisis of Conscience, Riddle of Identity: Making Space for a Cognitive Approach to Religious Phenomena." *Journal of the American Academy of Religion* 61: 201–223.

Sperber, Dan
　　1975　*Rethinking Symbolism*, Alice L. Morton (trans.). Cambridge Studies in Social Anthropology. Cambridge: Cambridge University Press.

Thagard, Paul
　　1998　*Mind Readings: Introductory Selections in Cognitive Science*. Cambridge, MA: MIT Press.

7

DEPRIVATION

Harvey W. White

❧ ❧

> How, then, do I seek You, Lord? For in seeking You, my God, I seek a happy life. I will seek You that my soul may live ... Is not the happy life the thing that all desire, so that there is no one who does not wish it at all? (Augustine, *Confessions* X.20)

In this famous statement, Augustine expresses a desire for complete fulfillment (*beatus*). Like Aristotle's notion of happiness (*eudaimonia*), it has the status of an intrinsic, basic and universal need for something not yet possessed or accomplished.

This view, which was part of the fundamental outlook of the classical and medieval periods, took happiness to be fulfillment of that which is properly needed and desired by persons. However, a distinction was made between what is properly needed and what is not. In Augustine's terms the distinction is between *beatus* and *gaudium*, the latter being—roughly—pleasure, while the former is fulfillment or, ultimately, beatitude—perfect happiness or, simply, specific perfection. Thus while *gaudium* seems to many people to be that which they need, in truth they need *beatus*, and this can only be acquired through faith. One might say that a person without faith is deprived of *beatus*. Thus Aristotle defines "privation" (*sterēsis*) as a lack of something that would be naturally possessed. (Aristotle, *Categories* 12.a.26ff.).

Similarly, in many modern theories, religion is deemed to be something that fulfills a need. However, such theories claim that that which can properly grant what is needed is not religiosity *per se* (or that which only religiosity can properly grant), but something else for which religion serves as a substitute, compensation or surrogate. Religion may be a reaction to a lack of something of great importance, but it is not religion that is the basic privation. A short analysis of the ways we use the terms "need" and "deprivation" will help clarify matters.

First, we note that needs and deprivations can range from significant (including urgent) to trivial: for example, "I need an antibiotic" versus "I need a second helping of cake." Our interest will be in significant needs. Needs can also range from realistic to outlandish. It not only makes no serious sense to say that persons are deprived of faster-than-light travel (since that is not possible), but it would be absurd, in most contexts, to speak of being deprived of a lack of transportation at half the speed of light (even though it is theoretically possible). In many cases, the context will indicate the significance and realism of the need.

Second, the presence of a need does not imply a deprivation. A well-fed person will still need food, albeit not immediately. We need air to breathe, even though we are not (yet!) deprived of it. Thus we speak of deprivation *when one lacks that which is required for meeting an immediate and significant need*. This disentangling of deprivation from need will be useful in discussing some of the theories below.

Third, one can distinguish between "perceived" needs and "real" needs, where the former is what one believes is needed and the latter what is in fact needed. We may understand perceived needs as including those with an affective component (feeling hungry or unloved) as well as needs that one believes one has even though there may be no present significant affective component (though I am not now hungry, I know I need food). Our term "perceived" will include both kinds. Clearly, the perceived need and the real need may or may not be the same ("deprivation" takes on a corresponding ambiguity). Augustine, for example, describes his own life to show that one may not be aware of the difference between the real need and the perceived need. While he knew that he needed to be loved, he came to realize that the love of other persons was not what would satisfy that need; for even when loved by persons, he really needed the love of God. Freud, in contrast, reverses this: a person who perceives a need for the love of God may really need the love of certain persons.

A difference between a perceived and a real need, if there is one, can only be known when the real need is identified as such. Indeed, the fundamental difference between classical and modern accounts of religion lies not in the distinction between real and perceived needs, but in what is identified as being the real need. This is a difference that is far reaching, for in specifying a real and significant need, one is simultaneously saying something theoretical about the nature of persons who have the need; that is, to claim that X really needs Y is to say that X is the sort of being who would be harmed in being deprived of Y.

Finally, though we use the same word, "need" to refer to what is immediately needed and what can supply that need, a distinction between them will prove convenient. Immediate needs, real and perceived, pertain to personal requirements, and thus involve the nature of the person, but that which is needed to satisfy the need may be material, psychological, social or metaphysical. An unemployed person may need a job, but what is more immediately needed is the money that the job supplies, and the money is needed to acquire the most immediate needs for food, shelter, and so on. Augustine may need God, but the immediate need is the love which only God can properly grant.

Ludwig Feuerbach, Karl Marx and Sigmund Freud represent basic approaches of the modern theoretical understanding of religion. Each sees religion in terms of real needs and deprivations that must be different from the need that is perceived by the believer. Feuerbach (1804–1872) is at once one of the most influential and neglected intellectuals in the post-Hegelian era. Feuerbach's analysis (1972: 241) represents a radical departure from previous theological explanations for religion: "The new philosophy is the *complete* and *absolute dissolution of theology into anthropology*."

Writing in response to Hegel, in *The Essence of Christianity* (1957 [1841]), Feuerbach focused on the quintessential human ability and immediate need for self-understanding, deeming self-consciousness to be the human characteristic *par excellence*. While Hegel had understood human thought and reflection—especially consciousness of one's own self—to be a sign of self-transcendence and thus a manifestation of transcendently conscious Spirit, Feuerbach sees no need to refer it to something that is beyond human being itself. In other words, a person's "species, his essential mode of being—not only his individuality—is an object of thought to him." Moreover, this is "no abstract, merely ideated or imaginary being, but rather the most *real* of all beings, the true *Ens realissimum—man*" (Feuerbach 1972: 254).

Insisting that this idea does not arise out of an awareness of an actually existing supernatural being, Feuerbach understands it in sociological and psychological terms: "Its principle is the most positive and real, and it generates thought from the opposite of thought; namely, *matter*, *being*, and the *senses*" (Feuerbach 1972: 254).

Feuerbach also takes it that persons require an object to which they can refer the idea of essential human being. This objectification of essential human attributes is simply what the mind does, how it thinks. Since this ideal humanity is only imperfectly realized in one's individual self—or any individual person—it is imaginatively objectified in thought as a particular idealization of such qualities: a supra-human being who is the perfect embodiment of ideal humanity which, in religious terms, is named God. This needed act of reason and imagination involves an affective sense, which Feuerbach calls "feeling": "Longing is the necessity of feeling, and feeling longs for a personal God ... Longing says, 'There must be a personal God,' i.e., it cannot be that there is not; satisfied feeling says, 'He is.'" (Feuerbach 1957 [1841]: 146).

Feuerbach's analysis makes a distinction between what we have termed the perceived (belief and longing) need—God—and the actual need—awareness of self. The immediate, natural and real need of consciousness to understand and to objectify what is otherwise abstract becomes transformed into a different perceived need. He understands this transformation as projection, that is, the act of creatively objectifying, in a god, those human species-attributes of which one becomes conscious.

But when cast in religious terms, this is an alienated self-consciousness; for while it is really consciousness of human nature, it is deemed by believers to be awareness of some non- or super-human being, in comparison with which actual individual human beings are correspondingly denigrated. The irony, Feuerbach points out, is that the very human and immediate need for *affirmative* self-understanding becomes inverted into a negative self-understanding: "To enrich God, man must become poor; that God may be all, man must be nothing ... Everything he takes from himself is not lost, but preserved in God" (Feuerbach 1957 [1841]: 26).

In short, one creatively imagines a perfected self, having all that the person lacks as well as having the power and will to judge, punish or forgive, and, indeed, eventually to endow (in some future life) the person with these desirable qualities. But this perfect divine being is, in actuality, nothing more than the consciousness of the ideal human being (the species) thought as particularized (God). Thus Feuerbach's revolution in understanding religion is not only in terms of the difference between the perceived need and the real need, but, in addition, in terms of the question what constitutes the real deprivation.

It would misconstrue the sense of "deprivation" to think of the need for self-understanding as a response to a deprivation. While it is a real need, self-understanding is always at hand to fill that need. However, in pursuing fulfillment of the real need under terms of the perceived need, a real deprivation is *created*: one is really deprived of self—thus, one is in a state of alienation. The irony is that in seeking to fill a need by religious faith, one *becomes* deprived—and worse, for faith actually prevents people from perceiving their real need.

The earlier outlook, exemplified by Augustine, was that the object of religious faith, God, provided just what one in fact desired and needed. Even Hegel conceived religion as the penultimate human attainment of the fundamental metaphysical ground of being—Absolute Spirit. With Feuerbach, however, religious belief—indeed, the Hegelian ideal itself—is an instance of *false* consciousness. It is based in reality itself, but becomes a way of failing to accept and come to terms with the real. Thus the specifically human need for concrete self-understanding turns into an alienated expression of the same.

This inversion—that religious belief is not the way to attain true fulfillment and happiness, but is rather a way of failing to do so—becomes one of the common critical propositions in subsequent analyses of religion. While explanations of religion take it that true fulfillment involves acceptance of and commitment to reality (including human nature), what is at stake here is what it is that constitutes reality. For Feuerbach, the real consists of this world that is experienced sensually, the world within which we live our lives. It does not include a transcendent reality; or, more cautiously, even if it does, the latter is not available to us as sensual beings:

> The all-inclusive and all-encompassing reality is nature (taken in the most universal sense of the word). The deepest secrets are to be found in the simplest natural things, but, pining away for the beyond, the speculative fantast treads them under his feet. The only source of salvation lies in a return to nature. (Feuerbach 1972: 94)

While Feuerbach posits humans as essentially material sensuous beings, his early analytic emphasis was on the intrinsic nature of human thought and self-consciousness (alienated or otherwise) rather than upon sensuous and material conditions and deprivations which give rise to the psychological process of alienation. In his later work he moved his emphasis in this latter direction.

According to Karl Marx and Friedrich Engels, Feuerbach failed on two counts: he did not adequately emphasize that self-consciousness and under-standing is a *response* to material and social conditions rather than an intrinsic movement within consciousness; and merely *understanding* religious false consciousness, as Feuerbach had done, was not enough: one must also get rid of the causes or conditions under which religion arises. Thus Marx's famous statement: "Philosophers have only interpreted the world in various ways; the point is to change it" (Marx and Engels 1970: 123).

One might think of alienation as being deprived of one's self. In more economic terms, an alienated person is one that no longer "owns" one's self. Feuerbach emphasized the essential nature of persons, what he called the "species-being." Marx, however, came to reject such a view. Instead, he increasingly saw persons as engaged in self-creation—a human activity (praxis)—as they engage themselves in the social-material world. Persons are self-expressive: as material social beings, we self-express ourselves in the world. However, as we are part of the world, we appropriate the world to ourselves, thus (dialectically) being formed by the very conditions we create.

> As individuals express their life, so they are. What they are, therefore, coincides with what they produce, with *what* they produce and *how* they produce. The nature of individuals thus depends upon the material conditions which determine their production. (Marx and Engels 1970: 42)

> [People], developing their material production and their material intercourse, alter, along with this their real existence, their thinking and the products of their thinking. Life is not determined by consciousness, but consciousness by life. (Marx and Engels 1970: 47)

The problem—alienation—is one of *ownership* of the self-expressions we create. In more material terms of production, a worker with his or her own labor produces an object for an employer who then owns that product. Or, more extremely, consider the cases in which an employer not only owns the fruits of the worker's labor, but also the worker himself or herself, and generally treats the latter as a mere commodity or machine of production. Such conditions, together with the explicit material inequities of life that accompany a capitalist system, serve as the "material" bases for our selves, including our religiosity. Note that those who materially benefit from the system may be just as self-alienated as the workers, for although they own the product, they have not created and produced it.

For Marx, religion is an ideological *expression* of material conditions, conditions which generate alienation and deprivation in particular. It expresses what is—and ought—be the case; but rather than doing so in realistic terms of undeserved material deprivation and the real need for economic justice, it does so in unrealistic terms of sin, human imperfection and the righteous will of God. It expresses material deprivation in terms of spiritual hope and thereby not only deflects attention from the real needs, but even justifies them: religious ideologies place a transcendent imprimatur upon the economic system itself. So long as deprivation of material satisfaction is reinforced by religion with its promise of fulfillment and reward as eventual compensation for that deprivation, religion suppresses the possibility of acquiring those immediate needs. Marx's solution, of course, calls for the creation of a society in which the real alienating factors, the material deprivations, are eliminated.

Religion for Marx is an expression of a deprivation that is created by an economic system. We might term it a pathological expression of a legitimate need where the expression is itself induced by pathological life conditions.

Sigmund Freud, on the other hand, represents a somewhat different development of Feuerbach's position. Freud sought to provide a complete scientific psychological model for the phenomenon of projecting one's unfulfilled desires onto a divine being. Unlike Feuerbach, who was concerned with human rational consciousness and feeling, and different from Marx, whose emphasis was on material economic conditions, Freud focused on fundamental non-rational instinctual drives or needs (which constitute the id), and which strongly seek satisfaction (which, when attained, is experienced as pleasure). The converse is the need to avoid frustration and pain.

This fundamental libidinal need—Freud often focused upon the sexual drive—is directed toward something that appears capable of providing satisfaction. Thus a child, needing affection and security, will seek and normally receive maternal and paternal satisfaction. The child is, however, confronted by a contradiction: there is a fundamental libidinal bond between the two parents, resulting in the child's experiencing a basic sense of jealous competitiveness. The male child, although loving and needing the father, also fears him—indeed, at an unconscious level, may hate him—as the competition for his mother's affection. This love–fear–hate tension requires sorting out, for such tensions are not easily bearable. Here, then, a basic need generates a conflict and a fear of deprivation, a fear that is made explicit in Freud's notion of the male's castration complex and his notion of the female's penis envy.

But the effective source of deprivation is the super-ego, constituted by psychologically internalized anti-libidinal instincts, including a very strong internal prohibition of incestuous desires. The super-ego inflicts psychological pain (guilt) even at the thought of such desires, and thus such thoughts are repressed. Freud considered both these opposed forces, the id and the super-ego, to be non-rational and non-realistic. Each of these, the libidinal need for satisfaction of which one may be deprived, and the super-ego which seeks to enforce deprivation, are psychological functions. That is, both need and deprivation have internal sources.

The ego has the dual job of managing the conflicts between id and super-ego, and of providing the individual with an effective and rational awareness of reality. However, in the absence of resources and strength to realize the latter, the ego does what it can in regard to the former. Ironically, with this work of the ego religion arises, Freud thought. For even though religion is an illusion with no foundation in sensible reality, it arises from the ego's attempt to mitigate the basic internal conflict by projecting a "super-parent," one who fulfills all the positive functions of one's real (or ideal) parent: loving, forgiving, providing security, and so forth, psychologically playing out one's deep desires or needs in relative safety by disguising them. Dreams have the same function. In this way the ego seeks to satisfy libidinal needs, circumventing the super-ego's attempts to deprive and punish by providing a surrogate fulfillment: for example, religion. The problem that arises, of course, is that insofar as the satisfaction is pursued in terms of the perceived religious need, the person is self-deprived of that which can adequately meet the real need.

This deprivation is not solely a matter of the unavailability of sources of satisfaction. For Freud it is an instinctively and unconsciously self-imposed deprivation that occurs as a natural, albeit neurotic, process of the psyche. In fact, insofar as the real need is incestuous, fulfillment would have negative consequences. Thus the prohibitions, though irrational, are not misplaced. Freud deems the optimal real need to be "education into reality" in which a person's behavior is under conscious ego-based control rather than ruled by unconscious defensive strategies.

An instructive contrast is afforded by Erik Erikson's psychoanalysis of religion, in which he places more emphasis upon the positive role religion may play in dealing with real psychological deprivation. In his famous psycho-biography, *Young Man Luther* (1962), Erikson makes the developmental point that significant deprivation at a natural stage of development may result in psychological problems in later stages. In Luther's case it was a matter of somehow recouping an underdeveloped sense of trust—in his own trustworthiness as well as his being able to trust his world—and this he accomplished through his re-conceiving God as one who justifies and loves irrespective of what that person had done or was: the doctrine of justification by faith alone. Here a real deprivation occurring at a natural early developmental stage is dealt with later by acquiring something else that helps meet that need. Generally, religion, though a matter of psychological projection, can appropriately assist in the meeting of immediate real psychological needs.

Similarly, Carl Jung deemed religion to be an appropriate way of fulfilling basic psychological needs. Jung's basic drive mechanism was the libido which he, like Freud, characterized as the source of psychic energy. Both understood psychological and behavioral activity in terms of releasing excessive energy into some object, or process ("cathexis"; Freud 1935: 368). It is the failure to release such energy in appropriate ways that leads to neurosis. Jung's emphasis in this regard was on the role played by the collective unconscious, consisting of a number of basic universal human instinctual needs (archetypes) for typical behavioral expressions, attitudes and manifest personality traits. Since these are psychologically effective and appropriate forms for releasing psychic energy, anything that elicits such expressions contributes to psychological well-being. Religion can be an optimally healthy way of accomplishing this, insofar as it includes within itself basic archetypical manifestations (iconic, dogmatic, conceptual and liturgical) which thereby directly encourage cathexis, and with particularly emotive force. In contrast to Freud, Jung claims that there is little or no difference between the real and the perceived need; that is, the archetypically formed need for religious belief and behavior is the same as the perceived need. Religion, therefore, fulfills basic natural needs, and it can do so in the very terms of the content of what it is that is believed. Religious belief and behavior, then, are not in response to a deprivation. Indeed, pathology may result from a *failure* to acknowledge one's legitimate religious needs or from otherwise being deprived of being able to express them adequately.

It should be noted, however, that a theory, such as Augustine's, that enjoins religious belief in a transcendent God makes significantly different ontological claims from a theory, such as Jung's, that refers simply to psychological archetypes. Thus, despite Jung's positive valuation of religion, in order to cast him as a theologian one must overlook significant and fundamental theoretical differences.

These psychological approaches, despite their differences, characterize religion in terms of real immediate needs, though they differ in regard to the role of deprivations. A more fundamental distinction in modern psychological theories is provided by what is often referred to as the "humanist" tradition in which religion is not understood in terms of the satisfaction of needs or drives, but as something intrinsically valued for its own sake. Here we encounter a distinction between "need" and "want." The latter is characteristic of the mature and well developed personality for whom religion is not a response to a need but, rather, a conscious and intentional recognition and appropriation of goals. Gordon Allport (1950: 149), for example, represents this position:

> Faith is basically man's belief in the validity and attainability of some goal (value). The goal is set by desires. Desires, however, are not merely pushes from behind (drive ridden). They include such complex, future oriented states as longing for a better world, for one's own perfection, for a completely satisfying relation to the universe.

On this view, it is immature and neurotic religiosity that is a response to a need that, in itself, is not religious. Mature and healthy religion, by contrast, is one's pursuit of some higher goal, not in response to a need, deprivation or stimulus, but as a *desire* for "more." Thus, given the humanist perspective with its distinction between needs and intentions, "religion meets a need" turns out to not be a trivial claim.

Nonetheless, as a non-trivial *explanation* for religion, "it meets a need" must identify the real needs and what sources provide what is needed. Only thus can they indicate whether religion meets the need. As we have seen, some of the modern need-based theories have it that the real need is different—or it is met differently—from that which is substantively claimed in the beliefs. The strength of these theories lies in their ability to convincingly distinguish between the immediate real need and the perceived need and, if they are the same, between the perceived source of satisfaction and the real source. Augustine claims that the immediate need for happiness and love is met by God. While Freud might agree with such general claims, his position is that these needs are falsely (albeit symbolically) met by religious belief. In so doing, and in specifying what really will meet those needs, he also must differently construe the specific nature of the real immediate needs. Thus neither the real needs nor the optimal means of meeting them are specified by what it is that is believed. Jung, on the other hand, is closer to Augustine in this regard.

Despite the similarities and the closeness in time, there are important differences between these theoretical approaches. Feuerbach and Marx, for example, viewed human beings as essentially conscious, moral and active, and saw religion as the result of human consciousness and activity gone awry. But whereas Marx saw religion in terms of a real deprivation of basic material needs, Feuerbach's analysis focused on intrinsic psychological needs which generate perceived but non-real deprivations. Freud viewed human beings as fundamentally instinct-driven and amoral, and religion as a pathological result of repressed primitive instinctual drives / needs which deprive people of the real sources of fulfillment Thus, insofar as a real need is non-religious, and as that which is required for meeting it is non-religious, it follows that a religious response to a need will create (in the theories of Freud and Feuerbach) or reinforce (in the theory of Marx) a real deprivation—that is, it will prevent a person from effectively seeking that which is really needed.

Moreover, in order to take account of the utmost seriousness with which believers hold their beliefs, it is also necessary that there be a mechanism of "delusion" involved, in which the real need or the source of fulfillment is transformed into a different perceived need or source. At the same time, the perceived need must maintain those attributes of the real need to the extent that the fulfillment of the perceived need remains functionally related to the real need. The common route is to maintain that what is perceived as needed is generically the same as what is really needed: for example, love (Freud), material and social needs (Marx), conceptual needs (Feuerbach), but to make the distinction at the level of *how* those needs are to be optimally met. In doing the latter, however, the apparent generic sameness of real and perceived needs is transformed into specific differences. If, as Freud has it, the need is sexual, presumably Augustine's God cannot fulfill *that* need. If security or personal fulfillment is the need, then Augustine, while agreeing that those are real human needs, will claim that God can truly meet those needs; but, Freud or Marx would claim that a strong ego or a socialist society are required.

Thus there are at stake basic assumptions concerning the nature of persons: if religion is a response to a real need, then the nature of the real need will imply something of the nature of the being who has that need. Moreover, while it is common for explanations of religion to avoid any sorts of theological or metaphysical judgments, such judgments are at least implicit in the positions concerning how the real needs are effectively to be met and what the source of real fulfillment might be. Let us seek a general characterization: the difference between the classical religious view and the modern theoretical one is that, while they can agree that needs are based in human nature and existence, the religious view sees need and fulfillment in theological terms and the modern theories see them in psychological / social / historical / economic terms. How one is to decide between the two is a matter of hermeneutical and metaphysical presuppositions.

Suggested Readings

Allport, Gordon W.
   1950   *The Individual and His Religion: A Psychological Interpretation*. New York: Macmillan.
Erikson, Erik H.
   1950   *Childhood and Society*. New York: Norton.
Feuerbach, Ludwig
   1957   *The Essence of Christianity*, George Eliot (trans). New York: Harper & Row; English translation 1854, original German edn, 1841.
   1967   *Lectures on the Essence of Religion*, Ralph Mannheim (trans). New York: Harper & Row.
   1972   *The Fiery Brook: Selected Writings of Ludwig Feuerbach*, Zawar Hanfi (trans. and Introduction). Garden City, NY: Anchor.

Freud, Sigmund
    1935   *A General Introduction to Psychoanalysis*, Joan Riviere (trans.). New York: Washington Square Press.
    1989   *The Future of an Illusion*, With a biographical Introduction by Peter Gay, James Strachey (ed. and trans.). New York: Norton; original German edn, 1927.

Harvey, Van Austin
    1995   *Feuerbach and the Interpretation of Religion*. Cambridge Studies in Religion and Critical Thought, vol. 1. Cambridge: Cambridge University Press.

Jung, Carl Gustav
    1938   *Psychology and Religion*. New Haven: Yale University Press.

Marx, Karl
    1844   "A Contribution to the Critique of Hegel's *Philosophy of Right:* Introduction." In Robert C. Tucker (ed.), *The Marx-Engels Reader*. New York: Norton, 1972.
    1964   "Theses on Feuerbach," pp. 69–72 in Reinhold Niebuhr (ed. and Introduction), *On Religion: Karl Marx and Friedrich Engels*. New York: Schocken.
    1987   *Economic and Philosophic Manuscripts of 1844*, Martin Milligan (trans.). Buffalo, NY: Prometheus.

Marx, Karl and Friedrich Engels
    1970   *The German Ideology, Part One*, C. J. Arthur (ed. and Introduction). New York: International Publishers.

8

ETHNICITY

D. Bruce MacKay

Ethnicity and religion are words that often overlap in discourse about the identity of groups of people. Indeed, in many ways religion and ethnicity seem inextricably tied together. This is not surprising, perhaps, when one considers that adherence to a particular religious tradition inevitably puts a believer in league with others who follow the same path, who practice the same rituals, who observe the same divisions of time, or who speak the same language. Allegiance to a particular religion generally involves membership in a group of like-minded people and much religious activity involves interaction, some of which may be ritualized, with others of the same group. Membership also often involves formal interactions with other people explicitly outside of the group as, for example, when engaged in an effort to win new members through conversion or to engage in battle over issues defined, at least in part, by religious ideology. Such activity and interaction, both within groups and between groups, underline that religious group identity and ethnic group identity clearly have much in common.

The apparent congruence between ethnicity and religion observed in discourses about the identities of particular groups of people has often supported an assumption that one category simply explains the other. Such a starting point underlies the facile argument that the ethnicity of a given group can be explained simply as the result of their religious beliefs and practices. An example is a description of Jewish ethnicity as the result of the practice of Judaism. The key point from this perspective is that religion is seen as the primary element of Jewish identity. But the opposite point of view may also be held: religion may be explained as the result of ethnicity. From this perspective, for example, the argument may be made that a particular group's Muslim beliefs and practices are the result of their Arab ethnicity. In this case, the group's identity is the primary unifying element and religion is secondary, the result and not the cause of the group's identity.

However, the construction of group identity is not as simple, unidirectional, or monolithic as either of these points of view would suggest. For one thing, a religious group and an ethnic group are not always congruent. A particular religion may be the religion of choice for a number of different ethnic groups. Furthermore, when religion and ethnicity do appear to coincide, explanations for the apparent congruence or for how religious groups construct and maintain their group identity are often based on theoretical perspectives that obscure underlying assumptions about the construction and maintenance of ethnicity. A closer look at theories and models of ethnicity will enable us to better analyze the evident congruence of religious identity and ethnicity.

The point of congruence between religious identity and group identity is a location where the anthropological study of ethnicity can inform the study of religion. In very broad terms, ethnic theory suggests that an individual's identity is constructed and operates at a number of intertwined levels which may include, for example, individual psychology, relationships, family, community, nation and people. Ethnic identity is a group identity. It is an identity which is constructed, defined, maintained and changed by and for a group, a people whose members perceive and are perceived by others as having a sense of commonality and unity which may allow them to claim, but which does not necessarily require, a common history, language, homeland, ancestry and religion. In addition, ethnic identity may run through other levels of identity and may cut across other boundaries and divisions such as the state, nation, class or community.

The focus of this essay is the study of ethnicity and how it has informed and can inform the study of religion. It will examine theories about ethnic identity and consider how more clearly understanding the study of ethnic identities may help us to better study religious identity. We will consider first the nineteenth-century view of the divisions of humanity. We will then examine developments in the twentieth century which set the stage for our present understanding of ethnicity. The initial phase of our modern understanding followed on the heels of the nineteenth-century view in assuming that ethnic groups were relatively static and stable. However, in the late 1960s and early 1970s this view was supplanted by one suggesting that ethnicity was completely defined by particular circumstances and through the intentionality of groups members. After summarizing each of these perspectives, we will examine what has been proposed as a more balanced approach, one where the instrumentalist view has been tempered by an understanding of the deep, almost coercive, force that allegiance to a group often imposes on its members. This balanced, or constructivist, approach perhaps offers most for understanding the relationship between ethnicity and religion.

Race, Place and Religion in the Nineteenth Century

Scholarship of the nineteenth century tended to explain the congruence of religion with group identity in terms of race. Enlightenment thinkers held a Eurocentric view which stood directly on the shoulders of earlier classical Greek views of "other" people. The Greek writers had used *ethnos* to describe large amorphous groups of animals or humans. For instance, Sophocles labeled groups of wild animals as *ethnos* (*Philoctetes* 1147; *Antigone* 344) and Aeschylus used it for the Furies (*Eumenides* 366) and for the Persians (*Persai* 43, 56). Aristotle used the term when he described foreign and barbarous peoples in contrast to civilized "Hellenes" like himself (*Politics* 1324.b.10; all quoted in Chapman, McDonald and Tonkin 1989: 12). Thus, the Greek word *ethnos* signified on a general level a distinct group of creatures, animals or people, who lived together and who could be separated from other groups (Liddell, Scott and Jones 1968).

In a more narrow sense, Aristotle used *ethnos* to label those who dwelt primarily in northwestern Greece and whose social organization he considered to be "primitive" (*Politics* 1324.b.10). He saw these people as different and separate from the inhabitants of the Greek city state, or *polis* (Just 1989). He understood the members of such rural groups to be "outsiders," provincial foreigners, and uncivilized, uncultured, irreligious barbarians who spoke unintelligible languages in contrast to the civilized folk of the cities. Echoes of these ideas are contained in the modern words "ethnicity" and "ethnic."

Adoption of this ancient Greek view during the Enlightenment meant that all inhabitants of the non-European, nonwhite, "uncivilized" world were assumed to be inferior and barbaric (Eze 1997b: 4). The growth of a scientific approach and world-view codified these assumptions; all living things, including humans, were classified and grouped in terms of a "natural" hierarchy. At the pinnacle, of course, were Europeans and all others were arrayed below according to their supposed mental, physical, and spiritual abilities (Eze 1997b: 5). Thus, the Enlightenment view was that the people inhabiting the earth could be classified as different, separate and distinct from each other, and that they were created this way, if not by God, then by evolution. Hegel, for instance, argued that differences in climate were at least partially responsible for causing the differences between groups of people (Eze 1997b: 110–112). The result was, among other things, that groups of people were assumed to have different conceptions of religion, as natural and as basic as their group identity. For the Enlightenment thinkers, this group identity was essentially defined in terms of race. So, for example, Hegel argued that African religion was without morality and without awareness of a supreme being (Eze 1997b: 129). He suggested, therefore, that the religions of African peoples reflected the fact that they were "incapable of any development or culture, and their present existence is the same as it has always been," for, he said, the land was still "enmeshed in the natural spirit" which defined Africa as an "unhistorical" land (Eze 1997b: 142).

In general, the Enlightenment scientists and thinkers classified the world they observed and the human groups which populated it in a way that tied together race, place and religion into concrete and essential categories. These elemental classifications resulted in a static view of human groups, denied any creative independence to the people being classified, and placed European cultures above all others. In part it was the apparent congruence between race and religion which they observed that supported the categories they constructed. The assumed connection between the two became part and parcel of thinking about group identity at the end of the nineteenth century and in the first half of the twentieth century.

Max Weber and Émile Durkheim are perhaps the most influential and significant of the theorists in this period who wrote about the relationship between religion and group identity. They had quite different views about religion, however, and about the links between religion and how a group defines itself and is defined by others.

Durkheim saw religion as a reflection of society itself and as a coercive force that molded and shaped society (Durkheim 1995 [1912]; Nisbet 1974). Indeed, one of the functions of religion in his view was to create a sense of membership in the society of which people were a part (Nisbet 1974: 165). The role of the rituals performed by members of the society, therefore, was to inculcate the values of the society, to renew the sense of belonging to that society, and to maintain and uphold the community. Religion and group identity were therefore inextricably tied together in Durkheim's view. The social group was at the root of religion and the social group depended on religion for its continuing solidarity. The identity of groups of people, what we would describe as their ethnicity, was defined, therefore, at least in part by religion.

Weber saw religion as providing values which, in his view, did not originate with some transcendent other but rather with human decisions and actions taken in the realm of history (Aron 1970). Humans, beginning especially with prophetic figures but then increasingly guided by processes of rationalization and bureaucracy, were instrumental in developing and defining their own religious expressions. However, the underlying ethic expressed by religions, especially the ethic of brotherly love, was derived from the primary, or primordial, relationships of one's community or neighborhood (Weber 1963 [1922]: 211–212). This relationship with the members of one's closest community circle was the basis for the economic aspects of religious behavior as well. Judaism best exemplified this point for Weber; it illustrated the double economic standard which he argued was derived from the primordial relationship of the basic community: certain behaviors are permitted between members of the primordial community while the same behaviors are prohibited with people who are not members of the community (Weber 1963: 250–251).

The key point for us is that the community demarcated by specific permitted and prohibited transactions was, in Weber's view, originally a primordial community; that is, it was an elemental unit, a group defined not by choice but by birth. The identity of the primordial group, its ethnicity, was, therefore, at least part of what defined a particular religion. Despite differences in their individual theories of religion, both Durkheim and Weber viewed the identity of the core, elemental group as a factor in religion. Moreover, their shared view of the group as a static entity continued throughout the first two-thirds of the twentieth century.

Primordialism and Universalism

The structural-functionalist paradigm of anthropology tended to underlie most models of ethnicity until the late 1960s. Like its nineteenth-century predecessors, its focus was on how cultural systems functioned in coherent and static social units (Buchignani 1982: 1). Most research aimed to explore how assumedly homogeneous social groups maintained stability, how parts of the stable social system related to each other and to the whole (the pluralist model), and how the complete social unit responded to changing physical and socio-cultural systems impacting it from outside its own borders (R. Cohen 1978: 381). Overall, the structural-functional approach tended to assume that the homogeneous ethnic group was a concrete and immutable social fact. Ethnicity, therefore, was an *a priori* category, a primordial feature which identified and defined the social group under examination. Furthermore, the religious beliefs and practices of members of the group were one set of cultural elements which identified and characterized a particular ethnic group and which helped to maintain the group's stability and order. Analysis focused on the function of religion within the group.

As noted above, the structural-functionalist analysis of large-scale societies often characterized them as pluralistic. The argument was that the identity of the whole was defined by rigid boundaries, supported institutionally, which enclosed smaller mutually discrete groups (Nagata 1979: 185). The smaller groups, however, retained their distinct identity in spite of being enclosed within a larger society. This approach assumed a "mosaic" picture of society; different religions, as part and parcel of different ethnic groups, continued to exist within the bounds of the larger society.

During the 1950s and 1960s this model gained some prominence. However, despite the apparent pluralism or dynamism of such a view, it nonetheless supported a long held presumption about the static nature of the basic group. Because the existence of distinct and concrete ethnic groups was still assumed, research focused on the processes by which supposedly mosaic social groups simply disappeared into the dominant "ethnic-less" community (Nagata 1979: 186–187). This process was studied in terms of *assimilation* and *acculturation*. Different localized religions, brought to the melting pot by different ethnic groups, were thus analyzed in terms of how such primordial identities slowly and inevitably give way to the supposedly unified universalism (i.e., melting pots) of the modern world.

When ethnic identity is presented as a primordial identity, it is viewed as a powerful coercive force which determines an individual's group affiliation and identity. It is understood to be a primary bond rooted in blood and kinship that ties a group's members together, determines their behaviors and customs, gives them their language, and defines their ethnicity. Edward Shils was among the first to analyze the attachments between members of a primary group in these terms, arguing that what held the group together was not personal qualities or interactions between group members, but irreducible relational qualities formed by birth into the group (Shils 1957: 122). Clifford Geertz (1973: 259) also emphasized the primordiality of the ties that bind the members of an ethnic group together when he argued that the determining factors in one's ethnic identity are ties stemming from the particular social features of language, location, religion, kinship, and custom—all of which he suggested were acquired at birth (1973: 263). Ethnicity is thus something very deep within people and it establishes their ethnic affiliation and identity no matter what the external realities may be (see also Grosby 1994).

Ethnicity therefore has an ahistorical quality in primordialist discourse (Scott 1990: 149). Language, location, kinship, custom and religion are all described as persistent and immutable elements of social identity. Features such as these are explained as the sources for an ethnic group's solidarity and longevity. Furthermore, primordialists suggest ethnicity has an ascriptive quality and that it determines behavior. Ethnic group members feel loyalty, solidarity and trust toward other group members and act in accordance with these feelings, not because of the quality of interpersonal relationships between individuals, but because fellow group members are perceived as kin (G. M. Scott 1990: 151; Dubetsky 1976: 435). Members of other ethnic groups are treated with mistrust and suspicion because they are perceived as unrelated. Thus, in the primordialist view, both the cultural attributes of an ethnic group and the actions of members of an ethnic group are determined by primordial ties and forces. Among the cultural attributes of an ethnic group is its religion; primordialist discourse therefore understands religion also to be an *a priori* given. It is presented as a feature of society which, through its coercive power, determines ethnic association (see Geertz 1973: 109–110). It is characterized as a stable, conservative and traditional social force which keeps ethnic group members true to the ordained order of being. From this viewpoint, myths about the role of the ultimate sacred reality in the origins of the group are taken to be essentially true and determinative for the social order and cohesion of the society.

Circumstantialism and Particularism

By the mid-1960s it was clear that the modernist agenda which had foreseen the development of a more and more efficient social machine which would erase, dominate, unify and make obsolete local, ethnic differences so as to bring about a productive, peaceful and undifferentiated mass of humanity was, in fact, not happening. In particular, the civil rights movement in the United States showed that differences were not being erased, boundaries between groups were not melting away but were becoming stronger, and the imposition of the idea of a single humanity unified by mass communication and common economic markets was not bringing about unity but, instead, was destroying the sense of identity, independence and autonomy which was vitally important for many people. Anthropological examination of these phenomena led to the articulation of what we can term a circumstantial view of ethnicity.

Circumstantialist discourse understands ethnicity as a variable that depends upon particular circumstances and interactions. Whereas primordialists tend to depict ethnicity as an *a priori* category and reduce all ethnic sentiments and action to static structures of difference defined by birth, circumstantialists tend to present ethnicity as the result of particular interests and specific strategies (Nagata 1979: 188). They argue that people define ethnic identities themselves in response to unique interests, goals and agendas, and that these tactical identities are expressed primarily in political and economic spheres of human activity. Furthermore, as conditions change so too do goals and interests, and thus ethnic identity may also change. In the circumstantial view, particular ethnic configurations are dependent upon the circumstances and the situation; in the primordialist perspective, particular ethnicities are completely independent of accompanying conditions.

Fredrik Barth (1969) is recognized as one of the first to have articulated the circumstantialist position. He argued that ethnic groups were forms of social organization that were not *a priori* categories but, instead, were dependent upon interaction for their configuration (1969: 13). The primary characteristic of an ethnic group, in his view, is that the members of the group use their ethnicity in a transactional way to describe themselves and others through their interactions. Therefore, in Barth's view, ethnic groups are defined only to the extent that group members use an ethnic identity as a category (1969: 13–14). Furthermore, it is the relative success of an ethnic identity in meeting group goals and satisfying group interests during interactions with others that is fundamental to the creation and continuance of ethnicity.

Barth suggested, therefore, that "ethnic categories provide an organization vessel that may be given varying amounts and forms of content in different sociocultural systems" (1969: 14). Ethnic groups are not fixed and immutable things; they are forms, without fixed shape or content. The focus of study should therefore be the boundary that demarcates and defines the group, not the "cultural stuff that it encloses" (1969: 15), because the borders of ethnic groups are fluid and are determined by changing needs and interests. Thus, language, location, kinship, customs and religion are defined and used as elements of a group's identity in the course of social action and interaction by the people involved. Ethnicity, in the circumstantialist view, is a dynamic process, not a stable given.

Because the circumstantialist position focuses on the boundaries between ethnic groups, it is presumed that, in order for differences to be identified and for dichotomies to become salient, ethnic identities are mobilized and boundaries are constructed in particular contexts and in light of specific issues (R. Cohen 1978: 397). A problem with this focus, however, is that these otherwise fluid boundaries may be reified and treated as static entities to the same extent that the ethnic group itself is reified in the primordialist position (R. Cohen 1978: 387). Furthermore, Barth's emphasis on individuals and interaction tends to ignore the large-scale social and institutional power of ethnic groups which can influence and constrain the actions of individuals (Buchignani 1982: 6). As well, the emphasis on interests and circumstances can lead to the question of how ethnic groups differ from any other interest group such as, for example, unions or political organizations.

Religion, in the circumstantial view, is not a cause of ethnicity or an *a priori* marker of ethnic identity. Religion is an aspect of the social system like any other aspect of a group's social system: economic, political, kinship or custom. As is the case with these elements of a social system, any part may or may not be mobilized to define the borders of a group's ethnic identity. In fact, an expression of religious difference need not overlap necessarily with other aspects of ethnic identity. Canfield's study (1978) of sectarian myths in Afghanistan, for example, indicates that, although stories told about religious heroes support and reinforce differences between Sunni and Shi'ite Muslims, these sectarian differences may not correspond with ethnic differences expressed through tribal and kin alliances.

Abner Cohen's research on the Muslim Hausa of West Africa (1969) demonstrates the same point. The Hausa held an economic advantage in long distance trade from the interior to the coast until Nigeria gained independence in the 1950s. This economic activity, together with differences of language, residence and place of origin, enabled the Hausa to construct an ethnic boundary between themselves and other groups, especially the Yoruba. However, once Nigeria became independent, the Hausa's economic advantage was threatened as broader systemic supports changed. One of the results of independence and changing trade conditions was that the Yoruba began to gain some advantage, especially in economic and political spheres. The Hausa responded to the new circumstance by adopting a Sufi sect, the Tijaniyya Order, which provided a means for them to re-articulate and reassert a distinct identity in the face of the homogenizing forces of nationalism. The group's religion, a sect of Islam in this case, was not defined primordially, but was adopted in this particular context as a means to maintain distinctiveness.

The circumstantialist view, to summarize, does not suggest that there is a necessary one-to-one correspondence between religion and ethnicity. Rather, a group may or may not use religion as a means to articulate its ethnic identity, it all depends upon the situation. If, in the course of its interactions with others, the members of the group use religion as a marker of their ethnicity and if that marker is used to demarcate a boundary between them and others, then religion may indeed be a part of their ethnic identity. If, on the other hand, a group defines a distinct ethnicity for itself without claiming allegiance to or defining a particular set of religious beliefs and practices, then religion need not be a part of the group's ethnic identity. The overriding factor which determines this is the particular circumstances which confront the group.

Constructivism

The potential for extreme rigidity in the primordialist interpretation of ethnicity, on the one hand, and for extreme relativism in the circumstantialist position, on the other, have led some to articulate a middle ground, what they term the constructivist view. In essence, the constructivist position combines the primordialist position with the circumstantialist in an attempt to include the most valuable and analytically useful insights of both (Vincent 1974; McKay 1982; G. M. Scott 1990; Tambiah 1989; Cornell 1996; Tilley 1997).

From the primordial perspective, the constructivist approach recognizes that ethnicity has an ascriptive and determinative aspect. One's ethnic identity is formed, at least in part, not because of choice, but because of birth and socialization into a particular group. Location, language and kinship are all parts of an identity which may be perceived and presented by members of groups as long-standing or even eternal elements of who they are. Often, these persistent features of a group's identity are defined by the group as having originated far in the group's mythic past. Narratives containing elements of this mythic past are created and retold by a group over many generations. New experiences and events considered significant are incorporated into these narratives, which are used by group members to understand and describe to themselves and each other who they are (Spicer 1971: 796; G. M. Scott 1990: 159).

The constructivist position recognizes the key point that these ascriptive aspects of identity, although acquired by group members simply by birth into a group, are continually reconstructed by members of the group for the group. Although the processes of construction may be so slow and constrained by tradition as to appear timeless to group members, even apparent timeless truths about group identity can be shown to have been created and formed within particular historical contexts. This leads to the second facet of the constructivist position, the circumstantial aspect of ethnicity. This perspective recognizes that ethnicity is an identity formed through interaction and in dialogue with members of a group and with other people outside of the group as they all work to achieve goals and realize interests. Ethnic identity is flexible and changes as the circumstances in which it is articulated change. Ethnicity is *responsive* rather than *timeless*.

A key step in the analysis of ethnicity, therefore, is discussion of the circumstances in which an ethnic identity is expressed. Particular economic, political, social or religious situations can influence the shape and strength of the ethnic boundaries groups may define through internal debate or through interaction with others (A. Cohen 1969). The boundaries are critical for seeing these processes of ethnic interaction, as Barth pointed out, for it is at the boundary where ethnic identities are most clearly articulated and defined in response to changing circumstances. If there is conflict over access to political, economic or social resources or if the group has particular political and economic interests which it is trying to realize, then these may provide the situations in which a particular ethnic identity can coalesce and where distinctions between ethnic groups are drawn and expressed most clearly. The circumstantial aspect of ethnicity focuses on the issues around which ethnic identities become salient and change.

G. M. Scott (1990), following Spicer (1971), highlights this point in terms of opposition. The opposition between or among groups may crystallize around and be motivated by any number of issues (e.g., political, economic, social or religious), depending upon the circumstances (Olzak and Nagel 1986). In Scott's view it is the opposition experienced subjectively by members of the group which mobilizes them to assert a collective identity in primordial terms and to define their distinctiveness over against another group (1990: 162–166).

Thus, in the constructivist approach there are two facets to expressions of ethnicity. One facet is the primordial. A particular ethnic identity is expressed in terms of cultural features which are said to be ancient and perceived to be *a priori* characteristics by which its members define the group in distinction to other groups. On the other facet, ethnicity is circumstantial. An ethnic identity is expressed in varying intensity through the interactions of the group and its members with neighboring groups as individuals are mobilized in response to issues which focus groups in opposition.

The Construction of Ethnicity and Religion

There are myriads of possible ways that the categories religion and ethnicity can be analyzed in light of the constructivist position outlined above, for, as we suggested at the beginning, they are often closely intertwined in the creation and maintenance of group identity. I wish, however, to touch on three issues:

religion as a constraining primordial force, the role of religion in changing circumstance, and religion as a focus for conflict.

Religions often provide a myth of origins for their followers. Such presentations of the past are, in many ways, the epitome of a primordial expression of identity. A myth of origins need have no basis in historical reality and yet it can articulate for the members of the group who they are, how they came to be who they are, and how they differ from other groups. It carries an air of timeless truth and communicates an *a priori* identity for those who accept it. As well, myths of origin may outline primordial differences between groups and explain how and why neighboring groups are mortal enemies. Contemporary conflicts can then be explained away and justified as having roots that are beyond examination or question since they are so ancient as to have "always" been a part of relations between the involved groups.

Furthermore, the coercive and conservative authority of primordial expressions of identity can be furthered by legal traditions within a religion which serve to define and limit behavior. The rules governing action and interaction, practices that are allowed and disallowed, and treatment of both outsiders and insiders to the group may all help to define and maintain borders around the group. As well, rituals may be proscribed which socialize individuals into the culture of the ethnic group.

Religion, however, is not a completely static or stable social structure. All religions change and develop as both internal and external pressures and forces lead to new formulations and reformulations of prior configurations. There are two aspects of this that are significant for exploring the relationship between religion and ethnicity. First, it is possible that if the leadership, practices, or main tenets of a religion change, this can alter the definition of the group's identity or even motivate the construction of a new ethnicity. When radical change in these areas leads to a split within a previously unified group, the possibility of a new ethnic group being formed is greater. And, when a religious split is supported further by changes in other aspects of ethnic group identity such as location (as with migration to a new place and especially if such a move results in linguistic isolation), political situation (during escape from or fight against marginalization or powerlessness), economic status (when class struggle differentiates groups of people), or outright conflict (as during religious persecution), then the possibility for the creation of a new ethnic identity is increased even more. But since ethnicity includes a primordial aspect, time is essential for myths of origin, memories of collective experience and structures of social organization to become so much a part of the group's identity that they are given an air of timelessness.

Second, ethnic change can influence religion. As ethnic identities change due to changing circumstance, such as in the social, political, economic, geographic or linguistic spheres of human action and interaction, developments in the definition of group identity can influence the formulation of religious ideas and practices. Primordial myths can be articulated in new ways to support a new identity. Primordial beliefs can be altered and reformulated to make sense in a new situation. Old practices can be reformed and replaced by newer behaviors that, in time, can also be accepted as tradition. Indeed, religion and ethnicity are alike in the way both are responsive to changing circumstances and both are molded and shaped by the humans who create and maintain the categories as ways of defining who they are.

Finally, the intersection between religion and ethnicity is significant for the way in which religion can serve to focus conflict. Since religion and the value system it engenders can have an obvious effect on behavior, foodways, dress, cultural practices and relations with others, it can serve as a visible marker where conflicts coalesce. The primordial facet of ethnicity, often expressed in discourse that is, at least in part, religious, can influence the basic and emotional level of identity that in times of conflict can inspire struggle against others who express a different identity through other primordial traditions. And, as we have pointed out, circumstances also play a part in motivating conflict. The setting may include competition over economic, political, or social factors and the particular situation will serve to initiate or exacerbate what is expressed as a primordial difference. The responsive and flexible side of religion can take a part on this side of conflict as it is changed and adapted in changing situations, for example, to help hold a group firm to its primordial identity, to mobilize a group to armed defense of its identity, or to motivate a group to dominate or conquer another group. As such, ethnic identity can be a part of religious conflict, either in a defensive mode as in times of persecution, or in an offensive mode as in times of forced conversion.

Conclusion

I will conclude this brief discussion of religion and ethnicity by suggesting how the constructivist position could be used to examine the construction of Jewish ethnicity in the state of Israel. The primordial facet of Jewish ethnic identity is carried by the Tanak (Hebrew Bible), the Talmudic and Midrashic legal traditions which are central to the religion, and a body of culture which defines practices and values in communities. The tales of the past recorded in the Tanak represent a record of primordial events which describe the birth, growth and creation of a people. The Talmud and Midrash then communicate and extend the authority of primordial traditions in defining what constitutes appropriate action in the present. In addition, there are the memories, traditions and experiences of local communities—such as Ethiopian or Hasidic Jews—which, although pledging a common allegiance to Judaism in the abstract, have sufficiently different locations, traditions and values as to lead to considerable differences of opinion over how to respond to the specific circumstances of the modern state of Israel.

Study of Jewish ethnicity in Israel must look further than primordial statements of identity, however, and must also treat the ways ethnic identity continues to develop and to respond as the members of the ethnic group face new challenges. In this case, a key area for examining the continuing definition of Jewish ethnicity is the response of the community to conflict with neighboring countries and to pressures of Western secularization. Conflict, as we have suggested, is a circumstance that can mobilize a group and unify people in response to an outside threat. Israel's conflicts with neighboring nations in the late twentieth century have been significant unifying circumstances. In addition, these conflicts have contributed to the definition of clear geographic and cultural borders that mark differences between Jew and non-Jew in the Middle East.

Finally, studies of ethnicity and religion must also examine the various debates within an ethnic group concerning how its members feel they should respond to changing circumstances and how best to transform and define their identity in new situations. In Israel the broad parameter of one such debate is between more orthodox communities opposed to secular Western values and practices and other more secular groups who participate to varying degrees in the socio-economic behaviors typical of late twentieth-century capitalist nations. Such debates affect the definition of ethnic boundaries. For example, the amounts and kinds of activities allowed on the Sabbath are highly contentious issues. Many orthodox communities vehemently oppose, for example, driving vehicles, shopping or attending movies on the Sabbath. Some secular Israeli Jews, on the other hand, do engage in these activities on the Sabbath. Some orthodox communities are actively seeking, through debate, political alliance and action, demonstrations and education, to ensure that Sabbath behavior is maintained according to primordial traditions as they interpret them. More secular Israeli Jews seem to suggest, however, their distinctive identity can be maintained and supported without strict attention or appeal to such primordial traditions. In terms of the analytic approach suggested here, secular Israeli Jews are not maintaining as stringent an ethnic boundary as are more orthodox Israeli Jews.

How or if this internal debate will be resolved in the future remains to be seen. It is clear, however, that more research is needed to examine the interplay between primordial expressions of identity, such as those championed by orthodox Israeli Jews, and the debates and conflicts of the present, such as over Sabbath practices, in order to understand more about the interplay between these two facets of ethnic identity in various expressions of Jewish ethnicity. The constructivist approach suggested here can be one fruitful line of inquiry to use in examining this and other cases where ethnicity and religion are a part of the discourse about group identity.

Suggested Readings

Amit-Talai, Vered and Caroline Knowles
  1996   *Re-Situating Identities: The Politics of Race, Ethnicity, and Culture.*
          Peterborough, ON: Broadview.
Ben-Rafael, Eliezer
  1982   *The Emergence of Ethnicity: Cultural Groups and Social Conflict in Israel.*
          Contributions in Ethnic Studies, vol. 7. Westport, CT: Greenwood.
Cartledge, Paul
  1997   "Historiography and Ancient Greek Self-Definition," pp. 23–42 in Michael
          Bentley (ed.), *Companion to Historiography*. London: Routledge.
Jacobson, Jessica, Atsuko Ichijo and Anthony D. Smith, (Eds.)
  1997   "Ethnicity and Religion." Special Issue: *Ethnic and Racial Studies* 20, 2.
Olzak, Susan and Joane Nagel, editors
  1986   *Competitive Ethnic Relations.* Orlando, FL: Academic Press.
Tilley, Virginia
  1997   "The Terms of the Debate: Untangling Language about Ethnicity and
          Ethnic Movements." *Ethnic and Racial Studies* 20: 497–522.

9

EXCHANGE

Gregory D. Alles

> Exchange is a universal activity ... it is the chief means by which useful things move from one person to another; ... it is an important way in which people create and maintain social hierarchy; ... it is a richly symbolic activity. (J. Davis 1992: 1)

As I was reading the newspaper one day, my eyes were drawn to an advertisement that took up roughly a fourth of a page. At the top of the ad large, bold letters proclaimed: "Christ is Coming 'Very, Very Soon'." Somewhat smaller, less prominent letters promised "8 Compelling Reasons Why." At first I kept reading because I was curious. What compelling reasons would the ad give to demonstrate that "History's Greatest Event" was about to occur? The reasons ranged from what I had expected, such as famines, wars and earthquakes, to what I had not: the current "explosion of travel and education." What eventually struck me, however, was the way the ad underscored exchange as an important topic in the study of religions. After enumerating the eight reasons why Jesus would return soon, the ad recounted some basic Christian notions about sin, God's judgment and the way to escape that judgment. Then it reached its climax: "In any gift exchange, there has to be giver and receiver. God has already given us the gift, His Son; now we must receive Him."

The Scope of Exchange

Anyone who watches, hears or reads the news encounters exchange. Think of stock market reports, analyses of economic activity (how much did people buy during the Christmas shopping season?), U.S. Federal Reserve decisions on interest rates, the latest figures on inflation, tax policies and arguments over free trade versus protectionism. Although some forms of economic exchange may be uppermost in the minds of middle-aged professionals, including professors, who are investing for retirement, exchange is hardly limited to economic activity. It characterizes relations between parents and children, spouses, friends and neighbors. It creates and maintains groups from the level of a simple two-person unit (dyad) to the United Nations. It is an important tool in national and international politics. It provides the intersubjective component that is crucial in the development of knowledge. It is central not only to conversation but to all communication. In addition, exchange defines means of assessing human activity; think of the spectrum defined by altruism, reciprocity and theft. Even more broadly, exchange extends beyond human activity. Primatologists have studied exchange and distribution among animals such as chimpanzees (e.g., Waal 1982: 200–207; but compare Lee 1979: 489–494). On much different scales exchange appears within fundamental topics of biology, chemistry and physics; consider thermodynamics.

To state the obvious: the study of religions is concerned with exchange as a human activity. A number of fields have developed theories that pertain to these kinds of exchange. Economics is a good example, but not the only one. The economic study of exchange ranges from a micro-economic analysis of individuals and their activities to a macro-economic consideration of broader processes and collectives, but it generally concerns the trading of commodities in markets and involves money as a standard of value and a medium of exchange (Mair and Miller 1991). Sociologists have used social exchange theories for a variety of purposes, such as explaining the creation of social solidarity, analyzing power and dependence, and attempting to generate the foundations of macro-sociological structures from micro-sociological events (Homans 1974; Blau 1964; Emerson 1962, 1964, 1972a, 1972b; R. Collins 1981). Anthropologists have been particularly interested in the exchange of gifts and relationships of reciprocity, in the exchange of spouses, especially of women by men, and in economic activity (Malinowski 1922; Mauss 1990 [1925]; Komter 1996; Lévi-Strauss 1969; Sahlins 1972; Appadurai 1986; Parry and Bloch 1989; Narotzky 1997). In the realm of ethics, appropriate forms of exchange constitute a central topic in theories that emphasize justice and fairness, whether justice is seen as rooted in proper procedures or in the equitable distribution of goods, services and costs. A good example of such a theory is the work of the well-known liberal ethicist, John Rawls (1971).

The theme of exchange cuts across virtually all of the social sciences. In the study of religions, however, the theoretical consideration of exchange is relatively underdeveloped. Exchange did provide one of the oldest theoretical models for understanding the widespread ritual of sacrifice: the notion that sacrifices are gifts given to gods or ancestors in the hope of receiving a gift in return. This perspective is often summed up in three Latin words: *do ut des*, "I give [to you], so that you will give [to me]." In addition, most scholars of religions are familiar with several classical accounts of exchange by anthropologists: Franz Boas' (1966) accounts of the potlatch in the American Northwest, events in which people competed in the destruction of property; Bronislaw Malinowski's (1922) study of the *kula* in Melanesia, analyzed as a ring of exchanges in which necklaces circulated clockwise and armshells circulated counterclockwise; Marcel Mauss' (1990) [1923] analysis of the gift in its primitive form as a "total prestation" as opposed to the limited exchange of commodities in money-based markets; and Claude Lévi-Strauss' (1969) analysis of kinship systems as the exchange of women by men, especially through cross-cousin marriages. Until recently, however, the closest that most scholars of religions came to a consideration of exchange was an occasional reference to reciprocity.

One set of events illustrates well the place of exchange as a topic in the study of religions: the different reception given to two quite different definitions of religion advanced in 1966. In a volume entitled *Anthropological Approaches to the Study of Religion* Melford Spiro proposed a definition that employed crucial elements of an exchange model. Religion, he said, was "an institution consisting of culturally patterned interaction with culturally postulated superhuman beings" (Spiro 1966: 96). In the same volume Clifford Geertz proposed to define religion as a system of symbols that integrates a people's world-view and ethos, that is, the way they think about and live in the world (Geertz 1966: 3–4). Spiro's definition was largely rejected. Geertz's became the definition of choice for an entire generation.

One problem with Spiro's definition was that it encompassed too narrow a range of data. Not all religions involve interactions with culturally postulated superhuman beings. But the preference for Geertz's definition also reflected a preference for his general approach to religion, which he stated programmatically in the opening of the essay (Geertz 1966: 1–3). Geertz equated the study of religions with the understanding and elucidation of religious symbols and meanings. Today that approach is less popular, and many anthropologists have recently questioned Geertz's orientation and assumptions. Some of these scholars have studied meanings, both religious and anthropological meanings, in terms of ideological practice. Drawing metaphors from architecture and economics, they have talked about the construction and production of meanings (Asad 1993). Indeed, references to production and consumption have become fairly common in cultural studies, including religious studies. In their wake, metaphors drawn from other aspects of economic life, including exchange, have also begun to appear (e.g., Olivelle 1993; Nattier 1995; Patton 1996). In a somewhat different tradition, the historian of ancient Greek religions, Walter Burkert (1996), has discussed religious reciprocity in the context of human evolution, with heavy emphasis on evidence from ancient Greece and the ancient Near East.

Although scholars of religions have generally shown little interest in exchange, the theme actually pervades religious speaking and acting. Consider the following lengthy list of examples. In "Western" Christianity, that is, in Roman Catholicism and Protestantism, the central theological vocabulary derives from the economic marketplace; redemption, grace and forgiveness are all at root economic terms. A part of the Lord's Prayer reads, "Forgive us our debts, as we forgive our debtors."[1] The covenant obligations in the Hebrew Bible begin by invoking the act which indebted the chosen people to their God: "I am your God YHWH, who brought you out of the land of Egypt, the house of bondage: You shall have no other gods besides Me" (Exodus 20:2–3; also Deuteronomy 5:6–7). The Qur'an continually emphasizes one form of exchange, charity to widows and orphans and others who are less well off. So important is this obligation that *zakat* (almsgiving) became one of the five pillars of Islam. More broadly, monotheistic religions like Judaism, Christianity and Islam speak of worship as something human beings owe their creator. Worship at a Hindu temple prominently involves acts of exchange: *dāna*, in which worshippers present offerings to the enshrined deity, and *prasāda*, in which they receive tokens of grace from the deity, such as coconut bits, nuts, sugar crystals or water. Those religions that derive from the ancient *śramana* movements in India, Buddhism and Jainism, divide their practitioners into monastics and laypersons, as did the religion of Manichaeism, which is no longer practiced. A significant component of Buddhist and Jain religious life is the practice of exchange between monastics and lay supporters. Similar exchanges once took place between the Manichaean elect and their supporters and still do take place between devout Hindus and male and female ascetics known as *sādhus* and *sādhvīs*. Buddhism has often used a mercantile image and spoken of "stores of merit" upon which devotees can draw, relying upon the boundless compassion of various Buddhas and bodhisattvas. Chinese tradition has been more real-political; it has thought of offerings to the deities and spirits as bribes. Among the ancient Maya bloodletting rituals attempted to maintain the universe by perpetuating a relation of reciprocity between human beings and the gods. On the ethical plane, balanced exchange or reciprocity underlies the so-called *lex talionis*: "the penalty shall be life for life, eye for eye, tooth for tooth, hand for hand, foot for foot, burn for burn, wound for wound, bruise for bruise" (Exodus 21:23–25). It also appears to underlie the Golden Rule: roughly, treat others as you wish to be treated. This rule appears to have been a common piece of Asian moral wisdom, for it appears in sayings attributed to Confucius in east Asia, the Buddha in south Asia, and Jesus in west Asia.

Limits and Advantages

Exchange is universal; all human beings exchange. Indeed, the anthropologist Richard Lee once suggested that the development of distinctive methods of exchange was a crucial step that made the evolution of human beings possible

(Lee 1979: 489–494; compare Burkert 1996: 132, 134, 140, 150). Even if that is the case, exchange does not provide a complete account of human life. It also does not provide a complete account of human religious life.

Exchange is not the "essence" of religion. It is, at most, a theme that pervades the world's religions. In part this statement reflects a more general position: it seems doubtful that religion has an essence, that is, a common defining character that is everywhere the same. But in any case it would be misguided to think that a single process of exchange stands at the heart of all religions, as Spiro's definition, quoted above, seems to imply. Similarly, it would be misguided to attribute to processes of exchange in religions a single, universal function, as Geertz mistakenly does in a different sphere when he defines religious symbols in terms of their role in integrating a world-view and an ethos. The term "exchange" denotes the generic set of all transactions found in the world's religions. Specific transactions vary considerably.

The consideration of exchange provides a particular perspective on human religious life, an interactionist perspective (Fig. 9.1). It directs attention to transactions that take place between elements in a broader set. One obvious instance comprises exchanges of objects (O) between individual persons (P_1 P_2, ... P_n) within a single social group (S).

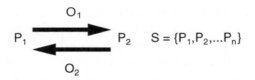

Figure 9.1   Reciprocal exchange

In attempting to understand religions, we reach one limit of exchange analysis when we encounter events for which we can give a satisfactory account solely by examining isolated elements within the broader set, such as individual human beings (P_1, P_2). An example might be the activities and expectations of a person sitting in *zazen* (Zen meditation). In the social sciences this limit appears prominently in psychology: theories of exchange have been primarily useful to social psychologists.

We reach another limit of exchange analysis when we encounter events for which we can give a satisfactory account solely by examining the broader set, such as the social group (S). In that case we can afford to disregard the constituent elements of the set and the interactions between them. An example might be a study of the composition of a large-scale religious community. In the social sciences this limit appears prominently in sociology. Theories of exchange have been most useful to micro-sociologists. Attempts to derive macro-sociology from micro-sociological processes have generally been deemed unsuccessful, at least to date (Blau 1986).

Yet a third limit of exchange analysis appears when we encounter events for which we can give a satisfactory account solely by examining the content of the objects exchanged—the commodities, if you will (O_1, O_2)—quite apart from their involvement in exchange. An example might be a desire to understand the generally accepted meaning of a group of symbols, provided these symbols do not themselves point to activities and relationships of exchange. (Because a private language is impossible [Wittgenstein 1953: §243–308], all symbols are in some way or other commodities in communicative exchange.) In the social sciences this limit appears prominently in linguistics: theories of exchange are primarily useful to linguists interested in pragmatics.

Thus, exchange analysis has very real limits. But it has very real advantages, too. These advantages stem in part from the relation of exchange analysis to the recent history of the study of religions.

During roughly the last hundred years the most influential approaches to the study of religions have been sociological, psychological and anthropological. Most educated North Americans are familiar with the ground-breaking work of Karl Marx, Max Weber and Émile Durkheim in sociology, Sigmund Freud and C. G. Jung in psychology and, perhaps less familiar, with James G. Frazer, Bronislaw Malinowski, Claude Lévi-Strauss and Clifford Geertz in anthropology. The influence of these viewpoints extends well beyond their own disciplinary boundaries. For example, their influence appears in one area of the study of religions that has adopted the label "history of religions." An early exemplar of this approach, Joachim Wach, was heavily influenced by sociology, especially the interpretive sociology of Max Weber, as was Wach's student and successor Joseph Kitagawa. Like Wach and Kitagawa, Charles H. Long devoted much attention to the art of interpretation, although with interests that were as much anthropological as sociological. The thought of Mircea Eliade, probably the best-known representative of this approach, has affinities with Jungian psychology and the anthropological study of symbols. Like Eliade, Wendy Doniger has studied myths and symbols, but she has been more influenced by Freudian psychology. The insights and problematics of anthropology significantly inform the writings of Jonathan Z. Smith and Bruce Lincoln—for Smith anthropology as the investigation of local systems of meaning, for Lincoln anthropology as cultural critique.

One contribution that the analysis of exchange can make to the study of religions is that it can help introduce models from two important but neglected social sciences: economics and political science. For example, Geertz's definition of religion as a system of symbols suggests an overly intellectualized view of human religious activity. It implies that religion is a way people contemplate the world. Thus, Geertz juxtaposes the religious "perspective" with several others, the common-sensical, the scientific and the aesthetic. As a result, approaches such as Geertz's generally neglect important questions about the implication of religion in the creation and negotiation of wealth and poverty, power and subordination. More recent scholars have begun to note that religions are extensively linked with wealth and power (e.g., Asad 1993; Lincoln 1989, 1994). An analysis of exchange can help provide detailed and nuanced accounts of how.

In addition, the study of religions has generally stressed functioning structures and systems. In doing so, it has adopted a view of human reality that is too homogeneous and static. It has treated symbols as if their meanings were universally shared within a culture and religion. Indeed, in Eliade's hands it treated symbols as if their meanings were shared by all people, regardless of whether those people were aware of the meanings. Such views have made it impossible to conceive of history as anything more than deviations from stable systems of meaning.

An analysis of exchange is not automatically free from a systemic bias. Malinowski's (1922) account of the *kula* is a good example of how it is not. His account is entirely systemic, because his strategy is entirely ethnographic. That is, he takes specific events that he observed and generalizes them. He does so by shifting verbs from what they should be, verbs in the past tense with adverbs specifying time and place, to verbs in an unqualified present that describe what "always" happens—at least, what would always happen if history in the form of European influence had not intervened. Malinowski does occasionally add geographical and temporal specificity, but he does so primarily to give his account dramatic interest. What results is an image of a tight, closed system of exchange, but one of which, Malinowski notes, the "natives" are themselves unaware (compare Leach and Leach 1983).

All of us engage in behavior whose full implications we do not understand. But the point here is that exchange analysis can do much better than repeat Malinowski's fabrication of a closed, tight system. It can help the study of religions move away from thinking in terms of integrated and closed systems and structures by encouraging scholars of religions to think instead in terms of complex processes that occasionally reach states of equilibrium. An example of such a shift is Lawrence Rosen's (1984) densely written account of "bargaining for reality" in Morocco.

Models of Exchange

Social scientists have often worked with models of exchange that are much too restricted. They have imagined that parties to exchange are totally rational agents, that is, agents whose aim is to maximize their own self-interest. They have imagined that these agents operate within a closed system of elementary forms. In addition, they have assessed the results of exchange solely in terms of the accumulation of objects exchanged. These presuppositions do result in tight, economical models that can be analyzed as games. They bear little resemblance, however, to the richness that characterizes exchange in actual practice (see J. Davis 1992).

In its current form, the notion of the rational agent derives from Francis Y. Edgeworth (1961: 16). In 1881 he wrote, "The first principle of Economics is that every agent is actuated only by self-interest." To be sure, some thinkers, such as Jon Elster (1989a, 1989b) and Howard Margolis (1982), have vigorously defended this view. But it seems open to several objections. One crucial challenge is posed by apparent acts of altruism—in terms of exchange, by giving that is motivated without any expectation of a reciprocal gift. An example would be the behavior of those who risked their lives to save Jews from the Holocaust, at what would seem to be great personal risk with little promise of personal gain. Some religious thinkers suggest that such a willingness to forego self-interest is a mark of the saint (Wyschogrod 1990). Nancy Hartsock (1983) points to similar behavior in a relationship that is much more common than sainthood, the relation between mothers and children. In her view, the notion that human beings are rational economic agents fails to consider the experiences of the large numbers of women who are mothers. Under the title "Rational Fools," Amartya Sen (1979) has explored various ways in which all people act apart from the dictates of self-interest. In addition, some experimental evidence indicates that in processes of exchange people do not always act to maximize their own personal benefit to the detriment of others (J. Turner 1986: 234–235; Molm 1986: 125). So in the study of exchange, including religious exchange, it seems better not to presume that all parties to exchange are always seeking to maximize their own personal gains. Instead, one needs to explore the actual motivations of people and the extent to which self-interest is involved.

In addition to talking of rational agents, social scientists have often reduced exchange to elementary forms. One example is a particularly helpful distinction drawn by the anthropologist Marshall Sahlins (1972: 188–189). Sahlins identifies two very different types of exchange, reciprocity (Fig. 9.1) and redistribution (Fig. 9.2). Reciprocity, Sahlins suggests, "is a *between* relation, the action and reaction of two parties," whereas redistribution "is socially a *within* relation, the collective action of a group." In reciprocity, two persons exchange goods with one another, but in redistribution goods are funneled through a central point in order to be shared by members of the entire group. This distinction is not without significance in the study of religions. For example, some scholars have asserted that the effective redistribution of agricultural products was a central function of ancient temples.

It can certainly be helpful to identify elementary forms of exchange, but it is also important to note that acts of exchange are rarely if ever primal, elementary forms. They are complex acts that occur within human society and culture. Pierre Bourdieu (1990: 98–111) has made this point nicely in talking about the kinds of exchange and counter-exchange that occur as members of certain Mediterranean societies jockey for honor and social status. He uses the

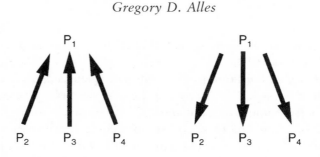

Figure 9.2   Redistributive exchange

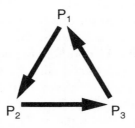

Figure 9.3   Generalized exchange

analogy of sports. In learning a sport it is often necessary to concentrate on basic moves or maneuvers, but playing a sport is more than performing the basic moves or maneuvers. It is the artful, innovative use, at just the right time and in a situation of actual competition, of the moves or maneuvers that one has practiced. So, too, the actual practice of exchange is not identical with the elementary forms to which analysts sometimes reduce it. It is rather the artful exploration of the immense possibilities of application present in those forms.

Again, social scientists often analyze exchange as if its ultimate focus were to maximize or at least to redistribute most effectively the objects exchanged. That notion is implicit, for example, in Bourdieu's notion of the virtuoso who attempts to maximize status and honor. But people actually enter into exchanges with other goals in mind, too. For example, Claude Lévi-Strauss (1969: 58–60) once noted how patrons at certain restaurants in southern France used to, and perhaps still do, exchange bottles of wine. Neither party to the exchange gained or lost in regard to either the quantity or the quality of the wine that he (or she?) enjoyed. Each had an identical, small bottle of wine set at his place. But each patron poured his bottle of wine into the glass of another. In doing so, the patrons created temporary social bonds between strangers who happened to be sitting at the same small table.

Scholars have linked exchange to a variety of purposes and functions. Consider a common form of exchange, the giving of gifts. Aafke Komter (1996: 3), a Dutch social psychologist, sees gift-exchange as the cement that holds society together. Others see gift-giving as a means to create or to contest social identity and status. An example is the potlatch, in which the goal is to attain supreme status by outdoing one's opponents in gift-giving. Some argue that because gifts are redundant, that is, given from surplus holdings, they are a way of creating voluntary social relationships (Cheal 1988). But in some cases that analysis may be too innocent. To non-Christians the excessive emphasis in North America on the giving of Christmas gifts may seem to be a not so subtle instrument by which Christians dominate the cultural and religious consciousness of others (e.g., Schwartz 1967).

Religious Exchanges

Regardless of what models of exchange one prefers, applying such models to religious exchange often presents special challenges. That is because religious exchanges themselves often present special challenges to description. They often involve either objects, such as merit, or parties, such as gods, that are non-empirical (see also Burkert 1996: 145–149).

To be sure, exchange always involves a non-empirical element: it is not simply the giving and receiving of objects but the giving and receiving of objects of value, and value is non-empirical. But consider the case of gifts given to a spirit to assuage its anger so that it will stop afflicting one with illness. Should this action really be described and analyzed as exchange, or is something else taking place, say, the intentional destruction of property, to which the human being simply applies the language of exchange as a metaphor? A related difficulty appears when, from the empirical point of view, exchange occurs, but from the religious point of view something else actually takes place. Consider a festival that, from the empirical point of view, redistributes goods brought to a temple as offerings, but that participants describe as dissolving the universe into its elements so that the god can reconstitute it at the opportune moment. Should one simply suggest that the views of participants provide a smoke screen that allows them to undertake exchanges that they would not otherwise perform? Those who follow interpretive approaches, such as symbolic anthropologists and some historians of religions, might counter that to dismiss the views of the participants would be to miss the most important point, the religious meaning. Politically astute critics might see an account that discounts local views as an intellectual parallel to the economic imperialism that post-colonial powerhouses are visiting upon the rest of the world. These and similar difficulties of description often plague the study of religious exchanges, whether those exchanges are found in ritual activity, in daily relations between human beings or in the formulation of religious thought.

Some ritual exchanges seem very easy to describe. Consider, for example, acts of reciprocity between parties to a marriage, whether between the bride and groom, as in an exchange of rings, or between extended families, as in dowry or bride wealth. At the very least, these exchanges are "starting" exchanges in the sense that they initiate new social roles. But the description of other rituals may not be so easy. One difficulty, as we have seen, is whether to consider the exchange to be real or imaginary. That difficulty does not just concern offerings and sacrifices presented to non-empirical beings. It also concerns gifts allegedly received from non-empirical beings in the course of rituals. Consider the *prasāda* received at Hindu temples or the body and blood of Jesus which Catholic, Orthodox and some Protestant Christians believe they receive with the bread and wine of communion. The description of these exchanges will vary considerably depending upon how seriously one takes the religious claims.

Another classic difficulty concerns the issue of self-interest. Some parties to rituals of exchange readily admit that they are acting out of self-interest. Consider the large, redistributive feasts that took place at public festivals in ancient Greece. According to a traditional Greek story, the gods were duped into taking the most undesirable portions of the sacrificial victim. Consider, too, traditional Chinese, who give gifts to a god solely in order to receive divine favor. If that favor is not forthcoming, they select a different god to be the recipient of their gifts. But participants and observers may part company with regard to sacrificial ideologies that emphasize renunciation, as the traditional commentaries on Vedic sacrifices do. Where some see renunciation, others will insist on veiled self-interest. That may be true not simply of Vedic sacrifices but of practices patterned after them, as when the *Yogasūtras* or the *Bhagavadgītā* urge aspirants to renounce the fruits of their actions by giving them to God.

Difficulties of describing religious exchange also occur when the exchanges to be described are exchanges between human beings in daily life. In societies with sufficient social differentiation, exchange may characterize the relations between religious functionaries and others. The *saṅghas* found in Jainism and many forms of Buddhism are ideal examples. Those who take monastic vows live off the material generosity of those who do not. So important is this religious duty that Melford Spiro (1982: 456–459) once estimated that in upper Burma people spent between 25 percent and 40 percent of their annual income on gifts to monks and nuns. The lack of balance in these material transactions—monks and nuns receive a lot more material than they give—is a sign of the inequality of power between the two groups. As a general rule, the powerful benefit from material exchange more than the less powerful. But the lack of balance also points to a descriptive difficulty. Economists see no benefit from gifts to monks and nuns, but Buddhist laity clearly do. Gifts to monks and nuns are an especially important source of the merit that will improve one's status in the round of rebirths (Spiro 1982 [1970]: 460–463). It remains an open question what role this merit should play in exchange analysis. Is it parallel to other non-tangible but significant social returns from exchange, such as honor, repute and status? Or is it equivalent to promises of tangible returns that, for reasons of duplicity, are not fulfilled? To be more blunt, are monastics con artists in disguise?[2]

Exchange also figures prominently in some religious ideas, but to what extent are these exchanges real, and to what extent are they metaphorical? According to James Fowler, thinking in terms of exchange typifies the second stage of the development of faith, represented by the religious ideas of, say, a ten-year-old. Around that age people adopt a view of the "world based on reciprocal justice and [they assess events in terms of] an immanent justice based on reciprocity" (Fowler 1981: 149). One presumes that many people grow out of this view. Religious people may use ideas of exchange to provide religious explanations for what might otherwise be seen simply as natural processes. Thus, one Christian hymn uses economic language to convey a perspective on both the world of nature and the world of human commerce: "We give thee but thine own, whate'er the gift may be; all that we have is thine alone, a trust, O Lord, from thee." Notions of reciprocity and exchange are often involved in the important intellectual problems of theodicy. Examples include both the operation of karma, according to which every act is paid back in kind, and promises of an ultimate, final recompense in the world to come, as in Qur'anic injunctions against stinginess and in some beatitudes attributed to Jesus: "Blessed are you who are poor, for yours is the kingdom of God. Blessed are you who are hungry now, for you will be filled" (Luke 6:20–21). The illustration at the beginning of this essay showed how people may use the language of exchange to formulate the central message of Christianity. One attempt to do so with scholastic sophistication was Anselm's widely influential account of the substitutionary atonement.

Opportunities

The ultimate goal of using exchange as a model in the study of religions is not to provide an ever more thorough, refined or fashionable description of processes of exchange, whether material or imagined, as these appear in the world's religions. It is to develop accounts that help explain specific religious events. Few if any such accounts have wide currency in the study of religions today. Here, then, I will suggest four rough, untried opportunities for applying exchange analysis. Two of them relate to transactions in equilibrium (structures); two relate to transactions in change (history).

Social solidarity—what makes disparate persons into a social unit—has been a common topic of sociology at least since the days of Durkheim. A common metaphor for this force is social glue or cement, and scholars have applied that metaphor to both religion and exchange. Now, some scholars have suggested that certain forms of exchange, namely, generalized forms, are more helpful in producing social solidarity than other forms, namely, specialized forms. In generalized exchange, everyone gives and receives, although each person receives from one person and gives to another (Fig. 9.3). In specialized exchange, two persons enter into reciprocal relations with one another, so that the person to whom one gives is at the same time the person from whom one receives (Fig. 9.1). Some experimental evidence does indeed indicate that generalized exchange produces social solidarity whereas specialized exchange does not (Gillmore 1986). If this hypothesis holds, it invites a consideration of the specific processes by which religious exchanges contribute to social solidarity.

Power and domination are also common topics in the study of societies, religion and exchange (e.g., Emerson 1962, 1964; Cook 1986). Indeed, relations of power and domination in religions are often characterized by practices of unequal exchange, such as the giving of offerings and sacrifices. This is especially true of the interactions of religious people with non-empirical beings, such as gods, spirits and ancestors. At least to outsiders, this behavior is a puzzle. Why should religious people devote so many resources to exchange with beings who actually seem not to exist? Detailed analysis of such interactions in terms of exchange could attempt to answer this question. That is, it could try to identify the forces and dynamics at work in such relationships that create long-term equilibrium, and it could try to locate what factors make this equilibrium preferable to situations that do not involve unequal exchange with non-empirical beings under conditions of power and domination.

Perhaps more interesting than the possibility of using exchange models to explain religious structures is the possibility of using them to explain processes of religious history. That is because scholars of religions have generally been content simply to observe and describe these processes rather than to offer any explanations for them. I will give two examples.[3]

In the broadest terms, one may say that the development from Theravada Buddhism to Mahayana Buddhism involves a shift in processes of exchange. In Theravada exchange occurs primarily between two stratified groups of human beings, monastics and laypersons. In Mahayana, the patterns of gift exchange shift. The difference in power is heightened, so that exchange takes place with a smaller number of beings who are now non-empirical: celestial Buddhas and bodhisattvas. The focus has shifted from a redistribution of material goods (food) to a redistribution of spiritual goods (blessings), with possible consequences in the world of tangible objects. In addition, the Buddhist layperson has been transformed from being primarily a giver into being primarily a receiver. Any account of this shift needs to take note of the variety of factors that are at work in it, including such standard topics as the development of arguments within Buddhist philosophy. Nevertheless, exchange analysis faces a twofold challenge. First, it must elucidate the instabilities within the organization of exchange in Theravada Buddhism that have led to disequilibrium. Second, it must identify the factors under which equilibrium is disrupted, so that a shift in processes of exchange occurs in some settings but not in others.

The second example concerns not a shift in the kind of exchange, but a change in the quantity of objects exchanged. Although such shifts may appear mundane, they have at times had world-historical significance. For example, there are periods when the quantity of economically significant goods presented to non-empirical beings grows tremendously. A representative instance would be the presumed growth over time in the number of victims offered in Vedic *śrauta* sacrifices until it ultimately became staggering. At other periods the quantity of economically significant goods presented to non-empirical beings diminishes, so that, in economic terminology, religious benefits are sold at a discount, sometimes a tremendous discount. A representative instance might be the history of indulgences in the Middle Ages. This history culminates in Luther's proclamation of what one might call the ultimate discount: forgiveness of sins and the bliss of eternal life in heaven are absolutely free for the taking and require no human effort. Economists know some of the factors that result in changing prices, such as the well-known "law" of supply and demand. But what factors govern shifts in the amount of tangible goods and services that religious people offer to their gods?

I can give no good answers to any of these four problems. To the best of my knowledge, no good answers are available. That state reflects the neglect from which the analysis of exchange has suffered in religious studies. But the possibility of finding answers to these and other problems raises the prospect that the study of exchange may yet make useful contributions to the study of religions.

Notes

1. Other translations read "trespasses" or "sins." The original, Matthew 6:12, uses the Greek word *opheilēma*, an economic term whose primary meaning is "debt." I have heard, although I cannot confirm, that the alternate translations developed in relatively high-class churches whose members tended to be creditors and found the notion of debt forgiveness economically distasteful if not threatening.
2. This question may sound harsh, but the view that it suggests often has proponents in countries where monastics live.
3. In oral discussion David Hein, Department of Religion and Philosophy, Hood College, suggested that a greater emphasis on the dynamics of exchange—what the Christian owes to and receives from God—might provide one explanation for the disproportionate growth of conservative churches in the United States during the last third of the twentieth century.

Suggested Readings

Burkert, Walter
    1996   *Creation of the Sacred: Tracks of Biology in Early Religions.* Cambridge, MA: Harvard University Press.

Komter, Aafke E. (Ed.)
    1996   *The Gift: An Interdisciplinary Perspective.* Amsterdam: Amsterdam University Press.

Mauss, Marcel
    1990   *The Gift: The Form and Reason for Exchange in Archaic Societies.* W. D. Halls (trans.), Foreword by Mary Douglas. New York: Routledge.

    1954   *The Gift: Forms and Functions of Exchange in Archaic Societies,* Ian Cunnison (trans.), Introduction by E. E. Evans-Pritchard. Glencoe, IL: Free Press; original French edn, 1925.

Olivelle, Patrick
    1993   *The Asrama System: The History and Hermeneutics of a Religious Institution.* New York: Oxford University Press.

Spiro, Melford E.
    1982   *Buddhism and Society: A Great Tradition and Its Burmese Vicissitudes.* 2d expanded edn. Berkeley: University of California Press; original edn, New York: Harper & Row, 1970.

10

EXPERIENCE

Timothy Fitzgerald

"Religious experience" is widely used by theologians, philosophers, anthropologists, comparative religionists and psychologists, and to inform the reader about all the different applications of the expression in the voluminous literature across the humanities is impossible in one short essay. Indeed, I will suggest that the term is so wide that it has little analytical value. The term itself is radically open-ended, sliding in scholarly usage from relatively specific situations within the Judeo-Christian traditions to all-encompassing cross-historical and cross-cultural claims.

Different Constructions of "Religious Experience"

There are a number of different ways the notion of religious experience has been, or might be, construed:

1. "Religious experience" often refers to a personal encounter with the God of the Judeo-Christian tradition. This tradition conceives itself to have arisen from major experiences or revelations of this god granted to (or through) special individuals. But the term is taken even more widely by theological ecumenicists and comparative religionists to be a cross-cultural category referring to some specific kind of experience of a god which is in principle available to individuals everywhere, regardless whether the dominant collective representations of their culture are biblical or monotheistic or Judeo-Christian or not. This modern emphasis on personal encounter with a god derives to a large extent from Protestantism and has entered fully into the writings of comparative religion scholars such as F. Max Müller (1878), Rudolf Otto (1969 [1917], 1932) and Joachim Wach (1944, 1951). Psychologists such as William James (1902) and Charles Tart (1964) have

extended this individualistic focus to include, as a personal experiential mode, "peak" or ecstatic experiences generally.

2. A second possibility, still within the Western monotheistic context, is that religious experience might be extended to include the totality of an individual's experience of the world as it is interpreted within the terms of Christian institutions, symbols and meanings. In this case the term "religious experience" does not only include the extraordinary revelations, epiphanies and visions which are usually once-off, unique and *discontinuous*, but also the ordinary events of day-by-day life which acquire an on-going *continuous* significance in so much as they are interpreted in theistic terms. Thus, for example, a conversion experience need not be of the dramatic kind reported by the early Christian missionary Paul. Instead, it might be understood to consist of a conviction which gradually develops in the course of one's ordinary life—that life does, after all, make sense if interpreted as being governed by God. "Religious experience" in this sense permeates the whole of one's life through "faith," through day-by-day commitment, through ritual participation. This much wider concept allows so-called mystical, peak or ecstatic experiences to be treated as sub-categories of religious experience in general (Ellwood 1980; A. E. Taylor 1964).

3. This wider category of religious experience, however, has been extended by scholars to non-theistic systems such as Theravada Buddhism, Confucianism, humanism, nationalism, liberal democratic capitalism and Marxist socialism. Many of these are atheistic and impersonal, focused not on deities but on principles, concepts of order or ideas of human relationships. There are also the many societies in which witchcraft, sorcery, ancestor cults, forms of "divine" kingship and other kinds of ritual institutions provide a framework for experiences of an "ultimate" kind. (I do not imply Paul Tillich's theological assumption about what constitutes "ultimacy"; see a more detailed discussion below.) This wider, cross-cultural use generally includes those experiences which, within the specific configuration of values and institutions (cultures) which frame the experiences and make them intelligible, are attributed widely by the people involved with special significance. These are often connected to the protection and maintenance of sacred boundaries and concepts of social and cosmic order. A wide range of experiences of deeply-felt "special significance" therefore include characteristics such as "sacredness," "ultimacy," solemnity, transcendence (though not necessarily the ontological transcendence of personal divine beings), qualities and characteristics which are given a special symbolic and ritual expression presumed to be close to a people's identity and which they will honor and protect. In this sense, an ultimate commitment is better understood as a collective and not necessarily conscious value or ideal, but which at certain times becomes explicit and pressing for an individual or group. It might, for example, be an experience of some deeply idealized

form of human relationship that connects the particular experience to a wider system of referents and values, such as those pertaining to "the nation," "the race," "the land" or to those principles which are felt by the collectivity to be self-evident, beyond question, that is, sacred.

Mystical or Numinous Experiences of the God of the Bible

One legacy of Protestantism is that many people in modern Western societies think of spirituality as essentially private and subjective, while public institutions and practices are understood to be merely secondary phenomena. The Christian Bible contains accounts of powerful and unrepeatable "religious experiences" understood as the revelation of God's will to outstanding human individuals such as Moses, Abraham, the Prophets, Jesus and Paul. These major experiences have been characterized by Rudolf Otto as "numinous," typified by the participant's sense of a *mysterium tremendum et fascinans*—a feeling of awe and fear in the presence of God, the wholly Other (Otto 1932, 1969 [1917]). Such experiences are *discontinuous* in the sense that the numinous Transcendent breaks into the mundane consciousness powerfully and unexpectedly, the Infinite rupturing the finite and dramatically effecting (and affecting) the consciousness of the chosen individual who experiences fear, awe and new understanding about the nature and purpose of life and death. Such visions are often understood as once-off revelations and they are represented by both the Catholic and Protestant traditions as sources of authority and validation. For example, the medieval Catholic philosopher Thomas Aquinas, who believed that human reason could provide some legitimate knowledge of God and the world, accepted that the full story of Christ's redemptive power depends on such revelation. For Christians, the revelation of God through Jesus Christ's life, death and resurrection was a unique, unrepeatable historical event, as was Paul's vision on the road to Damascus (see Acts 9:1–22).

Within such traditions, the overwhelming sense of the numinous which breaks into the consciousness of the unsuspecting (though culturally and ritually prepared) individual presupposes a fundamental distinction between the independent Creator and the dependent creature. Yet classically, "mysticism" has been understood as an inner contemplative quest for union with God, a quest which implies an inner identity with or an absorption into God. There has thus been a tension within Christianity between these two emphases. This quest for mystical union with God is often associated with the special training entailed in living a life of monasticism, celibacy and asceticism. The aim is to reduce the human ego to nothing in order to make it fit for the beatific vision. (Among the vast amount of literature on mysticism, see the classic account of Evelyn Underhill [1911].) Mysticism is seen by participants as a process of stripping the self. But despite the long training, the devotee cannot force the experience; it is a divine gift and the devotee within the Christian tradition is conscious of a radical sense of dependence on God (or the saints, angels, Holy Mother, etc.), of his or her own worthlessness and sinfulness, of being joyfully saved by an external power, of being transformed as a person.

In Roman Catholic culture, ritual has been especially important for mystical groups (as it has been in other cultures; see Zuesse 1987: 406). Since ritual is centered on the body, the body must be considered in the analysis of mysticism. The tendency to abstract the personal encounter from the public, bodily ritual context derives mainly from the theological assumptions of Protestantism. This emphasis on the interior and private creates problems not only in cross-cultural analysis, but also in the analysis of the wider sociological context of Protestantism itself, for it prompts scholars to ignore the fact that all societies (even those that deny the centrality of ritual) generate ritual, and that *all significant personal experience is significant precisely because it is generated within and interpreted by means of an institutional, social context.*

Problems of Interpretation

The inseparable, though often complex, link between ethnographic context, personal biography and the contents of the experience is a methodological issue. It implies that even the most personal and private experience, if it is to be interpreted, needs to be placed within the context of collective, institutional realities. Whether stated explicitly or not by the participant, the biography of the mystic is by definition part of a ritual and political nexus. This insight has implications for scholarship on religion, for a frequent assumption made by comparative religionists is that so-called religious experience is an intensely personal matter that provides the basis and primary datum which, through a secondary process, becomes institutionalized in collective forms of organization, such as churches or priesthoods (see, for example, W. James 1902: 31; Otto 1932: xvi; Tart 1964: 4; Wach 1944: 28). To claim, as William James does (1902: 31), that churches grow out of the primary experiential data as a secondary process of institutionalization is therefore misleading. Even in a book titled *The Sociology of Religion* (1944), Joachim Wach makes the theologically posited relationship between the individual and God primary, and all human social relations secondary (Wach 1944: 28). However, I agree with Ellwood when he says: "All that is observable about mysticism interfaces with the ideologies, practices and sociologies of its total religious environment. To isolate the mysticism of a religion from this matrix is to make its ecology as unnatural as that of zoo animals taken away from the field" (Ellwood 1980: x; however, precisely because we are trying to theorize on religion, I would substitute "cultural environment," i.e., ritual, political, institutional milieu, for

Ellwood's "religious environment," for otherwise we get caught in a circularity). The point here is that *the semantic context for having and interpreting an experience is necessarily also a social, institutional context*. For instance, the context in which someone describes having an experience of, say, Jesus Christ, is not one which is informed by the abstract assumptions of a comparative religionist who collects the experience of Christ into the same basket as a reported experience of Krishna (the ecumenical view being that they are both encounters of the individual soul with "the sacred," despite being filtered through the secondary forms of different cultures). Rather, the experience is meaningful (i.e., the experience counts as significant to the devotee) in light of the actual ritual and political context in which the participant is located.

"Religious" Mysticism and "Secular" Mysticism

As noted earlier, the focus on personal encounters in religious experiences has been stretched, for example by psychologists, to cover a whole range of "peak" or transcendental experiences in Western societies. This has led to attempts to identify distinctions between religious and non-religious peak experiences. For instance, Zaehner (1957) distinguishes between sacred and profane mysticism. Ellwood similarly distinguishes between "mystical ecstasy" and "secular ecstasy." Although, according to Ellwood, these two forms of mysticism are more or less the same in physiological and behavioral terms, the difference is in the interpretation: "true" mystical experiences are those which are interpreted according to a system of religious symbolism. Specifically religious systems are characterized by offering a means to a goal of "ultimate transformation of self, or world or both" through concepts such as worship, conversion, salvation and "other means of integrating oneself absolutely into the true nature of the universe" (Ellwood 1980: 34).

Although Ellwood's characterization is useful for conveying what some participants report to be the subjectively experienced ultimacy of "peak" experiences, it is not clear that such concepts would help us distinguish between religious and non-religious experiences—nor does it help us to explain the causes of these so-called peak experiences. One can imagine examining, as I do in a subsequent section, the non-theistic representations of Humanism which offer an interpretation of the whole of reality and the meaning of life, and demand total loyalty and commitment. In such a case it is not immediately clear what is to be gained by distinguishing this social value system from a "religious" value system. Moreover, the need for ethnographic data and contextual interpretation in specific cultural situations tends to reduce the usefulness of the common but troublesome distinction between "religious" and "non-religious," a distinction which is itself culturally determined (Fitzgerald 1997, 1999).

Mysticism and Intelligibility

From the point of view of some theologies, an "experience" of a transcendental god in the form of a mystical union between the creature and his or her Creator might be considered logically and / or ontologically impossible for a finite consciousness. One response to the logical gulf which might be held to exist between an infinite eternal god and a finite and temporal individual might be to claim that assertions about the gods are not factual and that religious experiences are really projections of ideal human qualities (Feuerbach 1957 [1841]) or of this-worldly ethical commitments (Braithwaite 1964 [1955]). These interpretations imply "religious humanism" discussed below.

The position of some Christians who do assert an ontologically transcendent God would be to hold that such a state of consciousness goes beyond "experience" in any normal sense of that word and that, consequently, a different form of language becomes necessary to indicate that which paradoxically cannot be indicated. This paradoxical language is used, for example, by such mystics as Meister Eckhart, St. John of the Cross and by the anonymous author of *The Cloud of Unknowing*. In such cases the concept of "religious experience" would itself be subsumed under a mystical theological position that God is radically unknowable and cannot be experienced simply because human experience implies the limitations of the subject–object distinction, a distinction which is wholly transcended by God. Religious knowledge and experience therefore becomes a kind of "unknowing" and non-experiencing of Reality or Truth, a notion which has been radically explored by J. Krishnamurti (1969; Fitzgerald 1991).

In this case, the limits of insider terminology for the scholar of religion is all too apparent. Although one might expect paradoxical language to be used by people who participate in those social systems (such as mysticism) which are the subject of scholarly study, one can hardly expect to derive from participants' reports and language a lucid, cross-cultural, analytical vocabulary—such that "religious experience" is understood by some scholars to comprise a *non-social* type of *non-experience*, an understanding that presents some obvious difficulties for historically and socially based scholarship on religion.

Despite these dangers, some writers, including theosophists, ecumenical theologians and even some comparative religionists, have attempted to extend this kind of paradoxical language into a cross-cultural context, connecting the "unknowing" of some Christian mystics with the *nirguna* Brahman of the Upanishads, the *nibbana* of Theravada Buddhism, the emptiness (*sunyata*) of Nagarjuna and the *satori* of Zen. Even assuming that these states of mind do contain the same ineffable core, all that is actually available for public analysis are the interpretations given by the relevant individuals in their language and their institutional context. Thus, for example, the aims and techniques of Zen meditation, when considered in the immediate context of the master–pupil relation as it is conceived in Japan, and also in the wider cultural context, will have importantly different semantic implications when compared to the strivings of a Sinhalese *bikkhu* in a Sri Lankan forest *vihara*. The assumption that they are both experiencing the same transcendental reality behind the different forms of life is itself properly understood as a *theological* assumption. Although it provides a speculative metaphysical starting point, such an assumption must not be confused with an empirically-based conclusion (as an example of the former, see Hick 1987). Indeed, familiarity with specific, historically based, institutional contexts may lead the observer to conclude that these various states of mind have fundamentally different aims and values—in short, that the experiential content is quite different.

Religious Experiences and Legitimation

On the one hand, claims by mystics and saints to revelatory experiences of gods can raise a problem of legitimation within their respective communities because they frequently have doctrinal and political implications. Such reported experiences of the divine do not always legitimate the existing social order, but may be seen to challenge it, just as the history of the ancient Hebrew prophets suggests. Inspired preachers who claim to have received some special calling from a god have frequently been a challenge to the status quo and the source of new sects, churches or traditions. Not infrequently such prophets, mystics and preachers have been understood and condemned as heretics.

On the other hand, the institutionalization of such revelatory experiences in the on-going framework of a ritual community and its values may also provide a continuous source of legitimation for the status quo and the framework of dominant values and ideology. Though revelatory experiences appear to the experiencer as self-validating, the criteria for distinguishing between valid and invalid experience lies with the dominant tradition within which the experience is had and interpreted. This may be ultimately a matter of power, exercised, for example, by the elders or some kind of élite.

Experience and Ritual Process

The potential ambivalence in the relation between individual mystical states and the ideological context within which they occur suggests that mystical experiences originate within marginalized social contexts and can function to confer power. Such power is dangerous, however, and needs to be made to conform to the on-going norms of institutionalized life, to be bolted down like a loose cannon. Rudolf Otto's characterization of the numinous not only as "beautiful and pure and glorious" but also as "demonic" (1932: 12–13) suggests the ambiguity of the numinous from a theological angle. Otto, and Wach who followed him in his characterization of religion (Wach 1944: 13), are mainly concerned with the individual and his or her relation to God or some similar concept. Where they may be held to have failed is in not taking adequate account of the relationship between the numinous as an individual experience and the social contexts in which such experiences are made possible and understood as meaningful, contexts that include ritual orthopraxy, political authority and ideological conformity.

They also tend to ignore the extent to which, cross-culturally, the focus of ritual is actually atheistic and centered on values such as *duty*. For example, even in an apparently theistic system such as Hinduism, the ritual performance of the sacrifice in some forms is explicitly atheistic (e.g., *purva mimamsa* or *karma mimamsa*); and there is a significant link between the principles of sacrifice as the reproduction of cosmic order and those principles underlying the performance of caste duty (*dharma*). Ritual here has a structural rather than personal focus because its aim is the regeneration of cosmic, ritual and social order. Even in the oft-cited experience of the character Arjuna in the *Bhagavad Gita*, the revelation of Krishna's mystical nature has as much to do with the duty (*dharma*) of Arjuna as a warrior prince (*kshatriya*), and indeed of the *avatars* themselves in the whole project of regenerating the ritual order of the world, as it does about other-worldly salvation (*mukti*). The two are inextricably inter-linked. As another example of religious experience as "duty," James Martin has pointed out that "[i]n the Confucian tradition, the religious significance of acting according to *li* (an informed sense of propriety) in a carefully structured system of human relations is widely stressed" (1987: 325).

In fact, the framing of experience by means of ritual is demonstrated by Victor Turner in his concepts of structure and anti-structure, both of which are inseparable social processes (V. Turner 1968, 1969). For Turner, the ideological or normative and the sensory aspects of meaning come together in ritual and produce powerful emotional effects and real transformations of character and social relations. In his concept of *communitas*, Turner (1969) uses basically the same scheme as Arnold van Gennep in his *Rites of Passage* ([1909] 1960) but from the point of view of the group. In the stage of *communitas* all structures of hierarchy and status distinction that separate people within the society are suspended and often reversed (anti-structure), and a state of temporary equality prevails. Such a stage in the ritual process might occur in the context of rites of passage such as initiations, pilgrimages, festivals and in theater, and might involve possession states, shamanism, renunciation and asceticism. Turner notes that the cathartic effects of ritual reversal restore and legitimate the established structures. This anti-structure by definition poses a challenge to the status quo by abolishing it, and can thus only be a temporary phase or stage in a total ritual process. As such, it can paradoxically strengthen what it appears to destroy.

More recently, Maurice Bloch (1992) has suggested that most of what is conventionally referred to as religious experience is fundamentally a ritual process or a family of processes by which people in different societies create and recreate the transcendental as a permanent reality in order to deny the vicissitudes and contingency of life, death and biological indeterminacy. A crucial aspect of the ritual process is the construction of some kind of transcendental representation through a process involving violence turned initially against oneself. This act of self-destructive violence, as for example in the symbolic killing of initiates in initiation rites or the methodical self-denial and even self-mutilation of monks, shamans and renouncers, constitutes a symbolic denial of the natural process of birth, growth and decay, and at the same time it serves as an acknowledgment of a transcendental life constructed out of the negation of that natural process (see also Parry 1982).

As should be clear, the specific content of the transcendental will be intelligible only in the ethnographic context. It might be conceived as an ancestral lineage, a place on an empty mountain, a place under the earth, a permanent descent group, a heaven and so on. To frame the transcendental in this way marks the concept off as entirely different from the theological–phenomenological approach which starts from a Judeo-Christian ethnocentric idea of the transcendent God of the Bible and then looks for "religions" defined in terms of it (see Bloch 1992: 3, explicitly repudiating Mircea Eliade). This simultaneous emphasis on the ritual procedures adopted and the conception of the transcendental which is reported indicates the inseparable (though not always direct) link between the specific experience and its interpretative sociological context.

Continuous Religious Experience as an On-Going Feature of Day-to-Day Life

We can acknowledge that special mystical, numinous and peak experiences are dramatic and transforming without at the same time denying that these are a sub-category of religious experience in a more general and pervasive sense. This latter concept would be (in the biblical theistic context) equivalent to Hick's "experiencing-as" (Hick 1964): experiencing the world as created by God for a divine purpose. Hick makes a working distinction between special powerful experiences of God epitomized by the beatific vision of God, and a more diffuse sense of religious experience which makes it virtually the same as the day-to-day on-going religious faith of the individual believer, "the ordinary believer's awareness of God in our present earthly life" (Hick in Schedler 1974: 280; A. E. Taylor 1964). It means that the same natural and historical world can be experienced "on the one hand as purely natural events and on the other hand as mediating the presence and activity of God" (Hick in Schedler 1974: 281). Members of a faith community experience the same natural world as non-believers, but interpret it differently within the framework of Christian theistic beliefs and values. (One should note, however, that Hick's distinction between the world as experienced theistically and the world as experienced naturalistically is not satisfactory because ideas of nature are themselves results of interpretations derived from specific ideological and cultural situations.) Thus they experience it as a world created by God and as being imbued with the guiding presence of God. It is this latter, more diffuse sense of religious experience which Hick wishes to formulate epistemologically as "experiencing-as." Religious experience here means the experience of life "as a continual interaction with the transcendent God," an experience which may sometimes erupt into special epiphanies and revelations but which is also a continuous interpretation of the world in theistic terms.

What must be stressed is that few members of Christian communities get a beatific vision of God, Jesus, angels, saints or the Virgin Mary. It is regular involvement in the network of ritual institutions rather than a claimed direct experience of God which counts to make an experience a religious experience. For example, attending a Latin mass, a holy communion, a snake-handling convention, a Friends' meeting, hearing an evangelical preacher on TV, praying to a saint or the Mother of God, making a confession, or reading the Bible or the prayer book might seem unarguably legitimate circumstances in which to have a religious experience even in the absence of special visions and revelations, and regardless as to whether one does or does not think it is logically conceivable to have an experience of God himself. While these day-to-day activities might be occasions for direct revelations of God to chosen individuals, it is more usual for believers and active members of a church to have an on-going, continuous, comprehensive experience of the world through the framework of their particular tradition.

The experience of committed participation in such authoritative offices, institutions, rituals, values and the world-view which provides participants with an overall structure of meaning, seems as legitimately described as "religious experience" as the more dramatic sense of the numinous or the mystical union with a god. In other words, if one is consciously participating in a Christian or some other religious framework of ideas and ideals which have been defined as "religious," then one's experiences will be religious, even though one might want to say that they are continuous, less intense, providing the on-going structure of one's life. Within this habitual framework and day-by-day form of life there may occur to anyone specially intense moments of conviction and commitment, or situations where the truth of one's commitments seem especially compelling.

Western Religions of Humanity

Compelling commitments and even conversion experiences do not, however, require commitment to an Infinite God. It is not only biblical theism and Christian communities which can provide a symbolic framework for "experiencing-as"; so can beliefs and values, current since the Enlightenment, expressed in what can be termed the religion of humanity, the religion of reason, civil religion, nationalism, Marxism and Freudianism (see Smart 1969: 647–670; Wach 1951: 219; Fromm 1950; B. K. Smith 1987). Many nineteenth-century intellectuals shared Comte's belief in a "religion of humanity," though some rejected his authoritarian concept of the church of science. Today many humanists refer to themselves as "religious humanists." For example, Herbert W. Schneider in his essay "Religious Humanism" sees humanist religion as "an effort to free religious faith and devotion from the dogmas of theistic theologies and supernaturalist psychologies" (quoted by J. E. Smith 1994: 33).

Deism, with its idea of a core universal content in "religion," was one link between the old hierarchical theistic doctrines and institutions of unique salvation through Christ, on the one hand, and the emergence of non-theistic, non-biblical concepts of religion, on the other. Romanticism provided another stage, for romanticism "provided the basis for the 19th century's abiding concentration on the self. The romantic conception of religion marked no going back to a pre-Enlightenment view of religion as providing an ordered framework for humanity, but the reinvention of religion as a communion of the self with nature" (Purdue 1998). Liberal democratic capitalism, nationalism, socialism or fascism, in their different institutionalized forms, are arguably all capable of providing a framework for conversion experiences, a deep conviction of truth and reality, and an on-going context for a total life commitment which would be the equivalent of "experiencing-as."

Robert Bellah (1970) has argued that the Declaration of Independence and the Constitution are foundational texts for the American civil religion which includes the American revolution itself, patriotism, rights to property and freedom of speech and worship. In the USA, the flag, the presidency, democratic values and procedures all demand an allegiance and sense of ultimacy in human life. Arguably, the dominant religious humanism in the world today is the destiny of the American nation to defend and promote the ideology of democratic, free-enterprise capitalism. The most important sacred texts include the American Declaration of Independence and the Constitution, or the Enlightenment declaration of the Rights of Man. When the modern believer in democratic values reads the Declaration of Independence, he or she may well get shivers up the spine, feel inspired, wiser, conscious of reading, in language which strikes one's sensibility as noble and profound, one of the earliest and clearest proclamations of the fundamental values of Western democracy, values which underpin most public discourses in art, politics and economics, and which generations of Americans and other Westerners have fought and died to achieve and defend. Such an experience might be accompanied by the conviction that, among the collectivity of equal nations, America has a special historical mission and destiny to ensure the realization of these universal democratic values in all societies around the world. Furthermore, the belief in American destiny (a doctrine termed Manifest Destiny) is closely linked to a belief in one's duty and destiny as an individual, that the meaning of one's own life is located within the context of national identity and transcendental values, including radical freedom and moral autonomy.

Some might argue that this sense of transcendental values, of epochal significance, of historical mission and destiny, which is conveyed to the committed reader of the Declaration of Independence, is a truly religious experience. But it is no longer "religious" as defined by biblical theism, because the semantic context, including the elaborate and carefully defined doctrine of God which is fundamental to the legitimate concept of religious experience within Christianity has been replaced by an institutional context which is entirely different. There are references to God in U.S. nationalist documents, but of a Deistic kind and taken out of the context of a specific church confession. Not only does a view of the document as having a transcendental significance which provides a sense of sacredness or an experience of ultimacy not require membership in a specific traditional church, but its appeal can be felt by atheists too. But it does require committed membership (i.e., citizenship) in the Western liberal democratic community.

Many comparative religionists would want to argue, along Tillichian theological lines, that only an experience of God is a truly "ultimate experience" and, therefore, that any object such as nature, the self, the nation, the race, the principles of democracy or socialism are not the basis of "true" religious experiences. Instead, they would argue, these should be understood as pseudo-religious or quasi-religious experiences (see, for example, J. E. Smith 1994); Wach labels them "semi-religious experiences" which he also describes as "idolatrous" (Wach 1951: 33). But this clearly is a theological judgment, and it is difficult to know what objective criteria could decide that the experience of an uncanny power from an invisible, supernatural world is more of a genuine religious experience than the sense of awe and wonder of the naturalist in the face of the sheer size and majesty of the universe; or what objective criteria could judge that giving one's life for America and the cause of human freedom is less of a religious experience for a committed democrat and patriot than giving one's life for "the Infinite" or for one's caste *dharma*.

Religious Experience as a Cross-Cultural Category

As has become evident, the range of possible applications for the category "religious experiences" gets progressively wider and therefore more diluted. We have seen how anthropologists such as Victor Turner and Maurice Bloch have linked, theoretically and ethnographically, religious experience to ritual context. I. M. Lewis (1971, 1976, 1986) has shown in ethnographic detail how the experience of misfortune in different societies is attributed to witchcraft, sorcery, spirit possession or the ancestors. Can we say that spirit possession or witchcraft is a form of religious experience? One could have an experience of a demon or an angry ghost which requires ritual healing or exorcism, and which might be diagnosed as the result of the breaking of a taboo or as a form of punishment. It seems likely that purity and danger, the protection of boundaries and structures from pollution or disruption from a vast range of imagined enemies, involves the deepest concerns for all societies and social groups.

Possibly when writing about American civil religion, Bellah had in mind a structural parallel with an entirely different culture, Japan. Bellah has written extensively on Japan, where the state cult of the Emperor has often been referred to as a form of "religion," and where fundamental values concerning Japanese identity, the state and the hierarchical ordering of social relations have an aura of sacredness and demand a high degree of commitment. Such commitment often seems to have little to do with personal, other-worldly, soteriological meanings. There may be other, sectarian contexts (for example, the dubiously named "new religions") or, alternatively, shamanism as found in Shugendo, for example, which provide a more individualistic context for personal soteriological aspirations. Yet, such sects have to define themselves in the context of a society in which the dominating code is one of the nation or the race or some lesser collectivity, such as the corporation or the *ie* (household). Only ethnographic research can help us understand to what degree, if at all, any sectarian group in Japan can avoid simply reproducing the dominant ethos of hierarchy and provide a genuinely individualistic form of renunciation or even of world affirmation. The experience of Buddhism for most ordinary Japanese is mainly an honored relationship with a specific neighborhood temple where the ancestral tablets are maintained, a commitment to family and national values of social conformity, and a commitment to Japaneseness and all that such a concept implies. The ancestors are more guardians of the social order and guarantors of the purity of the race than enlightened Bodhisattvas. The personal religious experience may have a sectarian context, but the sect will also have a wider social context. All three levels of analysis are interdependent.

Conclusion

The actual and the possible usages of the term "religious experience" have been shown to be rather wide. Anything which is connected to matters of "ultimate concern" for a specific collectivity can involve "religious experience," though clearly Tillich's stance that "ultimate" must mean God is a theological judgment which many would reject. An interesting counter-example to Tillich is Krishnamurti, who is frequently described by others as a religious teacher and who, for the best part of his life, taught the possibility of what he called "unconditioned insight." One result of insight, he once said to the physicist David Bohm, is that "if I had a belief in God it would drop instantly" (Krishnamurti 1985: 27). On another occasion he said: "We have invented God ... out of our misery" (quoted in Lutyens 1988: 60). Whether we like or reject what Krishnamurti taught, acquaintance with the facts of his life would make it difficult to deny that he was a person of ultimate concern (see Fitzgerald 1991).

It seems important to bear in mind that the term "religious," if it is to be used at all, cannot be consistently applied only to pleasant or uplifting experiences. Experiencing the world as meaningful within the context of a dominant set of ultimate symbolic meanings, both theistic and non-theistic, cannot logically only include the erotic-like joy of St. Theresa (M. Warner 1976: 299–300), or the contentless ecstasy of Nagarjuna or the ongoing sense of peace and contentment which results from a deep conformity with the values of one's tradition. It may also include the slaying of demons, the throwing into outer darkness where there is wailing and gnashing of teeth, stonings, the Jihad of Islam and the bombing of Iraq. To be cured of possession, or of an evil dictatorship, might involve considerable traumas. Would being educated by the Jesuits or the Puritans or the Japanese Ministry of Education count as a continuous religious experience? And being punished by them? This would seem to be legitimate, for within the rationale which (for example) the Jesuits would presumably give themselves, an awareness of the saving power of the Lord Jesus Christ can, for example, be inculcated into Boarding School boys through rigorous and punitive schooling. Being made to do penance, being exposed to the terrors of the ancestors in initiation, being martyred, cured and purified, may all be part of the experience of the world as conforming to a particular concept of sacred order, whether this is in a British public school, in communist China or among the Orikaiva (Bloch 1992).

John Carey, in his review of a recent biography of St. Thomas More, mentions that More used to chastize himself with a whip and his daughters with peacock feathers. Carey (1998) writes about the saint:

> As the government's chief heretic hunter, he had organised a thought-police of spies and informers, interrogating and intimidating suspects at his grand house in Chelsea, and, it was said, attending the torture

chamber at the tower to see them racked. When they were burnt alive at Smithfield, he rejoiced at their sufferings with ghastly relish, jubilantly predicting that they would roast in hell for all eternity. His victims were not criminals but devout men, guilty of nothing more heinous than doctrinal difference from Rome and the desire to read the Bible in the English language.

This is conceivably true, and the hunting, torturing and burning make sense within the theistic context: defending the church, as the continuous repository of God's revealed truths, from its enemies and from false knowledge. And More's enjoyment of his victims' suffering would make sense in the context of his Christian assumption that he was succeeding in that defense and that his punishment of heretics was righteous in the eyes of his Lord. This is an example of religious experience as "experiencing-as." Various examples can be found from many other cultures where suffering is an integral part of one's experience of the world as having a sacred order and in which each member of the society has a sacred duty to defend it (the McCarthy witch-hunts of American Communists come to mind). Such considerations suggest that the term "religious experience" has become extended to the point where its analytic power has all but disappeared, and where the uncritical assumptions of a past generation of comparative religionists must be abandoned in favor of a range of more critical categories and methods of ethnography.

Suggested Readings

Proudfoot, Wayne
    1985   *Religious Experience*. Berkeley: University of California Press.
Scott, Joan Wallach
    1991   "The Evidence of Experience." *Critical Inquiry* 17: 773–797.
Sharf, Robert H.
    1998   "Experience," pp. 94–116 in Mark C. Taylor (ed.), *Critical Terms for Religious Studies*. Chicago: University of Chicago Press.

11

GENDER

Randi R. Warne

Key Features of the Category

Gender distinguishes humans into "women" and "men." It is based on the notion of difference, arranged dyadically. This male / female dyad is often understood in terms of opposition (e.g., "the opposite sex"); the qualities or properties of the two parts of the dyad are assumed to be not only different in kind (as is an apple from an orange, or a tree from a motorbike) but different through mutual definition (e.g., concave vs. convex, a "male" plug vs. a "female" socket). Gender is also often understood hierarchically, with one part of the dyad seen as preeminent over the other. Complicating and skewing the practice of mutual definition is the ascription of greater cultural authority to one part of the dyad in naming the nature of that definition (McClung [1915] 1972: 70; de Beauvoir 1949; Ellmann 1968). While some scholars have posited the existence of a primitive matriarchy (Gage 1985 [1893]), in general "women" have not been consistently valued *over* those designated "men." The reverse, however, has been the case. Gender is thus about power, or rather, issues of power inhere in the deployment of gender. The tension implicit in opposition is given concrete form in gender relations, the interactions between "women" and "men."

The making of humans into women and men through gender operates both at the conceptual level and at the level of social practice. One's gender ascription is a shaping factor in one's life possibilities, assumed capabilities, symbolic representation, social power, cultural authority, expectations, dress, positioning in relation to physical violence and of what kind, permissibility of emotional expression and of what kind, how one's sexual desires and practices are understood and named, one's social value and one's religious status. The extent and particulars of gender ascription vary from culture to culture. Some limit gender sharply to specifics like external genitalia or pregnancy (Lepowsky

1993; Sered 1998b). Others expand the meaning of gender to include the structure of the entire universe, such as in the yin-yang polarity of Asian cultures.

Though gender is ubiquitous, it has often been invisible as an analytic category, even as it was being employed. Minnich (1990: 136–146) describes it as a "mystified concept" which is both symptom of and remedy for the hierarchical arrangement of the gender dyad and its consequences. That is, gender is the product of the hierarchical distinction of humans into women and men, but it is also a concept which alerts us to the fact of that construction, and hence its possible transformation. This apparent contradiction may be better understood after considering some of the strategies or operations to which gender is subject. In no particular order these are:

> *ontologizing*—ascribing to the level of Being;
> *essentializing*—positing as an essential (eternal) defining characteristic;
> *cosmologizing*—ascribing to a cosmic order;
> *naturalizing*—making something "natural," that is, free from (humanly constructed) conventions;
> *reifying*—converting something mental to a thing, that is, materializing;
> *authorizing*—sanctioning, giving authority;
> *valorizing*—imputing value;
> *idealizing*—exalting to perfection or excellence;
> *normalizing*—establishing as a rule, setting up a standard by which to judge deviation;
> *pathologizing*—naming as a disorder;
> *problematizing*—making into a problem requiring or implying a solution.

These strategies combine in different ways to deploy gender in specific cultural circumstances. The great variety of combination of these strategies has contributed to much of the debate and, indeed, confusion about gender as a social practice.

A further complication is presented by "sex," that is, specificities in anatomical form and function related to bisexual reproduction. Anthropologist Nicole-Claude Mathieu (1996) offers three main models of the relationship between sex and gender. In the first, sex and gender are *homologous*. Human identity is "sexual." That is, "sex is experienced as an individual anatomical destiny which one follows through the gender that conforms to it. Here gender translates 'sex' " (Adkins and Leonard 1996: 17). This has been a long-standing view of sex and gender in Western culture. Sociobiology, discussions of "brain sex," research into possible physiological bases for homosexuality, and many popular studies of differences in male and female communication styles all reflect the assumption undergirding this model, that is, the assumption of a naturalized and essentialized difference between women and men reified at the physiological level. Here, one's gender is an inevitable result of the body with which one was born. The exaggeration of difference through clothing styles, range of allowable physical activity, desirability of particular body shapes (e.g., broad shoulders in men, curvaceousness in women) is read as a biological programme which human culture shapes only slightly. On this account, gender is as "natural" as sex.

In the second model, gender and sex are *analogous*. Human identity is "sexed." That is, "gender consciousness is seen as based on lived experience in a group (i.e., from 'socialisation; and living as a woman within the group of women'). Here gender symbolises sex (and sex symbolises gender)" (Adkins and Leonard 1996: 17). Put another way, gender is the social meaning given to sex. Sex is natural while gender is cultural, subject to human variation and construction (King 1995: 4–6). This viewpoint is common in the social sciences and is congenial to a range of disparate analyses. For example, both socialist and cultural feminist positions find this model acceptable, the former because it allows for the politicization of existing gender relations (social meanings can be contested) and the latter because it affirms cultural difference between women and men, and allows for the valorization of "women's experience and perspectives." This sex/gender model retains the notion of normative heterosexuality grounded in biological nature, although it allows for particular cultural constructions which transgress a strict linkage of sex and gender. The *berdaches* of some North American Plains and Western Indian tribes are one example: after adolescence some males become social women and some females social men, having sexual relations with persons of the same sex and opposite gender. Similarly, Albanian "vowed virgins" take on the role of *paterfamilias* and live as men, with all the rights and privileges pertaining thereto, so long as they follow the unwritten rule never to marry or have children. The view that sex and gender are analogous, and that gender expresses diverse cultural understandings of biological sex, has also had many adherents.

The third model sees sex and gender as *heterogeneous*. Human identity comes from one's "sex-class." Neither sex nor gender are natural. Rather, "a social/political logic is seen to exist between sex and gender, and identity is based on sex-class consciousness: on recognizing male domination. Here, gender is seen to construct sex (and heterosexuality is viewed as a social institution)" (Adkins and Leonard 1996: 17; also Rubin 1975). The notion that "gender precedes sex" appears counter-intuitive in a culture dominated by the notion that gender is *caused* by sex. However, there is a kind of circular reasoning which both posits and assumes one form of anatomical difference (that related to bisexual reproduction) to be foundational and definitional of all human life. Further, sexual dimorphism is not absolute: "nature" produces humans with a range of combinations of hormones, chromosomes and sexual apparatuses (Stoltenberg 1989: 25–39). The selection of the extremes of a "male / female" continuum is a human choice and conceptual construct. For this reason, some (Guillaumin 1982, 1985; Mathieu 1980; Wittig 1992) oppose use of the term "gender" entirely, as it implies there is an actual "natural" biological basis for "sex" upon which gender is then grafted. Others argue that since the very term "sex" denotes and connotes something natural (that is, "naturalness" is part of its definition), another term (first "sex roles" and then "gender") was a necessary step in showing that "sex" is "applied to divisions and distinctions which are social" (Delphy 1996: 36). The term "gender" therefore retains some usefulness as a marker of the constructed character of the categories "male" and "female."

Postmodernist discourses shift the language from gender to the body and its practices, particularly its sexualities (Foucault 1978). Specific attention is paid to psychoanalytic categories and the symbolic order, within which there is a "masculine" (a linear, goal-driven, order imposing modality) and a "feminine" (a chaotic, infinitely open, multi-faceted, transgressive modality). The notion of gender as a male/female dyad (in which the female is defined by the male as "not-male" or Other) is seen as a product of the masculine modality, to be resisted. Gender neutrality is not an option, however. Trying to be neutral is both futile (everyone is positioned somewhere) and morally misguided, in that it obscures the positioned speaker (Irigaray 1985; Tong 1998). The extent to which postmodernist discourses participate in essentializing gender is a complex and unresolved issue. Theresa de Lauretis concludes that gender "exists," but it "is neither an unproblematic procession from biologically determined sex nor an imaginary construct that is purely arbitrary. Rather, gender is the product and process of a number of social technologies that create a matrix of differences and cross any number of languages" (de Lauretis 1987, in Tong 1998: 209).

Historical Development

The division of humans into males and females is an ancient practice, as is theorizing about the nature and meaning of that difference (Gleason 1990, 1995; Tuana 1993). As Thomas Laqueur has shown, a shift took place in late eighteenth-/early nineteenth-century Euro-North American culture regarding the dominant understanding of human nature. Prior to that time, the prevailing gender ideology presumed a "one sex / flesh" model of humanity in which "women were essentially men in whom a lack of vital heat—of perfection—had resulted in the retention, inside of the structures that in the male are visible without ... [thus] women are but men turned outside in" (Laqueur 1990: 4). This is not to suggest that egalitarian social relations were enjoyed between men and women: maleness was still valorized, such that those designated women were understood to be lesser or damaged forms of the full human norm and ideal. However, at least one consequence of the "one sex/flesh" model was the assumption that men and women naturally experienced sexual desire, as might be expected of the same flesh, whether obverted or inverted.

Since the late eighteenth century in Western culture much of the social practice and reflection upon gender has been done from a "two sex / flesh" model (Laqueur 1990: 8) in which sex and gender are presumed to be homologous. That is, male / female oppositional difference is assumed, named and naturalized; it is often cosmologized and ontologized as well. However, the vast amount of prescriptive literature on how females and males ought to behave suggests that, while normative, these distinctions are transgressed with sufficient frequency that further guidelines are required to reinforce what nature (ostensibly) intends. Hence even when gender is theorized as weak (physical male / female difference reflects and embodies the structure of the universe; human shaping of that difference is minimal or non-existent), in practice human ability to act differently is acknowledged, though not necessarily approved of. Those who deviate from the normative gender script are pathologized, and / or special categories are set up to allow for the maintenance of the dominant system while ensuring that "anomalies" do not disrupt its fundamental logic.

It is important to remember that not every member of *homo sapiens* is necessarily granted the cultural status of humanity (and hence the opportunity to be male or female). For example, when Plato is considering whether women can be Philosopher Kings, or when Aristotle is noting that man's virtue is in commanding and woman's in obeying, neither are including slaves in their analyses (Spelman 1988). Two contradictory operations are going on simultaneously in this literature. On the one hand, a norm is being established: How is the category "human" to be boundaried? What distinguishes human from non-human? At the same time an ideal is being set up, not just what humans are (an aggregate of all the qualities of those designated "human") but what humans ought to be (amongst those qualities, which are the best?). In the case of both Plato and Aristotle, slaves are not human in the same way women and men are. Humanity is thus a cultural distinction. By extension, even when writers naturalize gender, their normative understandings of humanity (often, in the West, "Man") suggest a deeper construction of the categories of male and female even, perhaps especially, when it is not acknowledged.

Just as gender difference has been maintained in theory and cultural practice, so too has it been resisted. Celibacy, for example, as a requirement of religious orders, has been one way of "transcending" the disabilities imposed by one's gender ascription. Other forms of resistance have been more overt, manifesting themselves in specific written objections to the cultural gender script, and in direct transgressions of that script in lived experience. Feminist scholarship has paid particular attention to women's resistance to gender asymmetry and androcentric misogyny, in both historical studies and contemporary feminist theory. Recent scholarship in lesbian / gay / queer studies have foundationally challenged the practices of gender ascription as well (Duberman et al. 1989; Feinberg 1996; Comstock and Henking 1997).

The history of the term "gender" *per se* is complicated by its slippage in usage with the term "sex roles," the social possibilities and expectations accorded those designated female and male. To see what women and men do as "roles" it is first necessary to disrupt the notion of biological inevitability in female and male behavior. Margaret Mead is credited with this move, arguing on the basis of her anthropological research in Samoa that most societies establish a dualistic division of human characteristics, arbitrarily assigning some to women and some to men (Mead 1935). Yet as Delphy notes (1996: 31), Mead was less concerned with "sex roles" than with masculine and feminine psychological dispositions or "temperaments." The real development of the idea of "sex roles" took place from the 1940s to the 1960s, in the work of Komarovsky (1950), Myrdal and Klein (1956) and Michel (1959, 1960). Influenced by the work of Talcott Parsons, they all "saw a *role* as the active aspect of a *status*," the position one is given in a social hierarchy (Delphy 1996: 31). Where Mead saw a fundamental division of labor between men and women as natural, these authors stressed that the position of women was both socially determined and changeable. Moreover, they challenged Parsons' assumption of harmony between the sexes, and his belief that women's "traditional" subordinated, domestic role was good for both women and society.

The specific term "gender" first began appearing in the 1970s, in works such as Ann Oakley's *Sex, Gender and Society* (1972). Oakley upheld the distinction between biological "sex" and cultural "gender," but rejected all forms of biological determinism, on the grounds that cultural variability in gender demonstrated that it was social in nature. Despite its presence in the earlier work on sex roles, Oakley's definition did not address gender asymmetry or gender hierarchy (Delphy 1996: 32).

Since the 1970s there has been an explosion of scholarship on gender (Kramarae and Spender 1992). The category was widely adopted both in the social sciences and in the humanities, and was particularly visible in work proceeding from feminist perspectives. Some attempts were also made to rethink maleness and masculinity (Petras 1975). Prior normative gender positions were reinscribed in response to these initiatives (Gilder 1973). Others advocated "androgyny," understood either as the integration of "masculine" and "feminine" qualities in a kind of Jungian hybrid or else as obliterating these distinctions altogether (Heilbrun 1973). The first formulation was soon rejected by radical feminists such as Mary Daly (1978: xi) as reinforcing the very gender stereotypes it was intended to overcome. Neither did obliterating gender distinctions in androgyny gain widespread currency.

This theorizing was not done in a gender neutral environment. Historically the vast preponderance of authoritative reflection on female / male difference had been done by those with male gender ascription. The result was an androcentric asymmetrical account which valorized maleness. Attempting to redress this imbalance, some gender essentialists identified a problem of omission, with the inclusion of "women's perspective" as its remedy. For social constructivists, the real issue lay in the way the whole gender *system* had been named, constructed and programmed to maintain male interests. A wide range of analyses were produced (Tong 1989, 1998; Tuana and Tong 1995) contesting the naturalness of received gender arrangements. These were usually identified as feminist in that they explicitly contested the appropriateness of the depiction and social constraints of women, and the social mechanisms which produced and reinforced them.

The attempt to redress the imbalance of androcentric accounts by focusing on women meant that maleness was not always fully theorized, although it was problematized, and sometimes naturalized and pathologized as well (Dworkin 1981, 1987). On this account, women were seen as (inappropriately) constructed and constrained by patriarchal culture. Men, the beneficiaries of that culture, were seen to intend or sustain women's oppression due to inherent flaws in their nature which made them act unjustly and/or violently, such as the "necrophilia" attributed to them by Mary Daly (1978: 59–64), a model which reversed the formerly conventional construction of "natural" woman and more "cultural" man (Eliade 1959b, 1969; Ortner 1974). Investigations proceeded in any number of directions and from a range of assumptions. A new gender essentialism emerged, with femaleness now occupying the valorized position and, by implication, an authorized position in a new social order (Griffin 1978). Radical constructivists maintained a critique of prior social arrangements of gender, acknowledged their contemporary phenomenological reality and looked for resources to transform those arrangements to ones of greater equality.

In the 1980s the singular focus on gender to the exclusion of other cultural variables was now rejected in favor of a more complex analysis which included race and class, sexualities, age, (dis)ability and ethnic and colonial positionings. An emphasis on "difference," fueled in large measure by the increasing influence of postmodernist and poststructuralist theories on academic discourse, fractured formerly (assumed to be) coherent concepts like gender, locating them within a matrix of multiple and changing "techniques" in which power and authority were deployed. Postcolonial critiques further moved to decenter Euro-North American hegemony, offering new accounts of gender and its implication in imperialism (Mohanty 1991a, 1991b). A significant tension has developed between those who see a continued need to redress the imbalance of traditional gender accounts by a specific focus on women (with continued attention to the material conditions of those so designated) and those whose theoretical commitments make "woman" an "empty category" (Downs 1993, Scott 1993). Some contemporary scholars question the very existence of gender, arguing that the multiplicity of other variables shaping human life, such as race, social class, ethnicity, age, physical size, shape and health, make the concept at best an artificial one, and at worst a homogenizing and totalizing obliteration of the reality of difference amongst women (and by extension, amongst men) (Butler 1990). Others argue that while at the level of theory "gender skepticism" has a certain salience, at the level of social practice gender persists to inscribe both normative heterosexuality and male dominance.

Scholarship which reflected on maleness and masculinity developed a higher profile in the 1980s and 1990s. Here, too, numerous positions were articulated. Some sought to reinscribe an essentialized masculinity through male bonding and self-discovery (Bly 1990; Keen 1991). Others took seriously the critiques of gender ideology being generated by feminist scholars and writers to consider the deployment of masculinity historically (Tosh 1991) and in contemporary culture (Kaufman 1987; Brittan 1989; Brod 1987). Masculinities were denaturalized and pluralized, with a variable degree of attention to power inequities in past and current gender systems. Still others argued the incompatibility of humanity and manhood (Stoltenberg 1993), holding with French materialist feminism the position that gender creates hierarchy and hence must be abandoned. Against these constructivist approaches in scholarship, sociobiological accounts of sex / gender and sexualities have gained popular visibility.

Contemporary scholarship thus displays a bewildering array of positions on gender, from the most sociobiological and deterministic (in which "gender" hardly exists at all) to the most constructivist (where gender's component categories of "men" and "women" are seen as so unstable and fragmentary that they are meaningless). Between these extremes inquiry into the making of "women" and "men" continues, as does the social practice of distinguishing humans into those categories.

Major Subsets within the Category "Gender"

The categories below provide four major frameworks within which the techniques and strategies of gendering (e.g., ontologizing, pathologizing, idealizing, normalizing and so forth) have been undertaken. They may be summarized as follows:

1. No (or minimal) gender. Biological sex is strong, cultural gender is weak to non-existent. Male superordination and female subordination is inevitable, a fact of nature, cosmically determined, divinely ordained. Heterosexuality is normative. A subset holds that female subordination is a distortion of the natural order which has emerged out of an imbalance caused by cultural practices such as technology. On this account, balance needs to be restored by revalorizing "woman's nature." Male / female difference, signaled by biological difference around reproductive heterosexual sex is taken as (properly) foundationally determinative of human life.

2. Sex is natural, gender is cultural. There is immense variation within this category, depending on how strongly or weakly either sex or gender is construed. A politicized understanding of gender is inherent in its logic. Because gender is variable, it is changeable. If changeable, in what direction and for whose benefit? Equally, who is benefiting now?

3. Neither sex nor gender are natural. There is no logical reason for some biological markers to determine human culture and selfhood. It would be equally reasonable to categorize people on the basis of their nostril shape (people breathe twenty-four hours a day; presumably they do not employ their sex organs so frequently). Gender is a misleading category because it suggests that there is something natural about "sex"; however, it has been a useful conceptual tool to decenter "sex" as the necessary and sufficient condition for determining human identity. Division and hierarchy have been inherent to gendering hitherto; overcoming sex/gender hierarchy would end sex/gender distinctions. Material conditions which result from sex/gender division and hierarchy need to be challenged and transformed. Sexual practices are multiple; some practices (rape, for example) are unacceptable.

4. Whatever sex is, gender is discursively constructed. Nothing is natural, inevitable, given. There is no inherent logic which impels transformation of material conditions of human life. Gender is performative, sexual practices are multiple and non-normative, and continued focus on one component of the gender dyad (i.e., "women") may actually maintain gender hierarchy by reifying its component parts.

Critical Evaluation of Past Uses and Contributions to the Scientific Study of Religion

Academic fields emerge out of particular social and historical contexts. These contexts set the terms of debate for their practitioners, foregrounding specific concerns and problematics, and obscuring or ignoring others. Increasing attention has been paid to the role of imperial and other political interests in setting the intellectual and investigative agendas of the scientific study of religion, illustrating its implication in a variety of colonial practices and strategies (Chidester 1996; McCutcheon 1997b). What has been insufficiently considered within the scientific study of religion, however, is how the techniques of empire—and hence the theoretical paradigms generated within those contexts—are gendered (Mills 1994; Blunt and Rose 1994).

As we have seen, there is no neutral, self-evident rendering of gender. Each gender ideology is at some level a decision about how the world is to be configured and understood, establishing normative social, political and cultural practices which set the parameters and possibilities for how human life might be lived. The context out of which the scientific study of religion emerged was marked by a specific, highly contested prescriptive gender ideology which, in the circular, mystified process outlined by Minnich (1990) became so ubiquitous as to be virtually invisible to the subsequent majority culture knowledge makers in religion.

That gender ideology emerged during the expansion of Euro-North American empire, a time marked by a series of social debates occasioned in part by changing social and economic conditions of developing industrial capitalism. Industrialization and urbanization had a number of significant social effects, amongst which was the development of a bourgeoisie, or middle class. In contrast to élites (who had no workplace as such) and the peasantry (whose work and home were coterminous), the middle class enacted a distinction between the "private" sphere of the home and the "public" sphere of the workplace. This private / public distinction was also gendered; "women's sphere" was the (ostensibly private) home while "men's sphere" was anything outside of it. At the same time waged labor and the widespread availability of manufactured goods shifted the household from a producing to a consuming economic unit. This made a distinction between the world of home and the world of work somewhat more plausible, while having the practical effect of rendering women's ongoing domestic labor invisible (since women in the home "don't work"). Moreover, the prescriptive and constructed distinction between public and private obscured and elided the widespread involvement of working women in waged labor in the (presumably male) "public" sphere.

These cultural renegotiations occasioned by industrial capitalism in the nineteenth century were aided by intellectual perspectives such as Darwin's theory of evolution, which explained this rapid social change in terms of "the differentiation and specialization of function," as the sign of evolutionary advance. This gave further weight to a dual nature view of humanity grounded in (ostensibly non-cultural) biologically determined sex in which reproductivity (a version of survival) was its central driving force.

Religionswissenschaft, the comparative, non-confessional scientific study of religion called for by Max Müller, embodied and valorized a number of intellectual stances which characterized these developments. Following the nineteenth-century penchant for oppositional dualisms, a sharp line was drawn between science and religion (which later shows up in distinctions between, and arguments about, religious studies and theology). Reason and emotion too were polarized, so that within the realm of science disembodied reason was seen to function independently, "objectively," from a position of epistemic acontextuality known as the "god's-eye view" or "view from nowhere." Religious commitment was and is seen, in this account, to interfere with the analytical, comparative project undertaken in the scientific study of religion. In keeping with the location of religion and morality in "women's sphere," such faith was construed as a "feminine," an interior stance rightly subject to the external, scientific, analytical male gaze. Unacknowledged in this version of scientific objectivity is the male gender-embeddedness of the vast majority of its practitioners, and their thoroughgoing implication in the prescriptive gender ideology of androcentrism in its specific nineteenth- and twentieth-century cultural form of "separate spheres." This requires some unpacking.

The construction of any new ideology does not proceed without opposition. Central amongst the social debates which marked the nineteenth century was the contestation over "Woman's True Place," and what has been called "the Cult of True Womanhood" (Welter 1966; Smith-Rosenberg 1985). The new prescriptive gender ideology of "separate spheres" embodied Laqueur's "two sex/flesh" model: a sharp oppositional distinction was made between women and men as social and biological bodies, and those distinctions were naturalized in terms of both evolutionary theory and culturally reinforced social arrangements (for example, legal prohibitions against women undertaking lucrative and prestigious professions such as medicine or the law, enforced economic dependency by denying married women the right to own their own property, and sanctioned sexual slavery by the legal obligation of a wife to provide sexual services to her husband at his command). This configuration was vigorously resisted. Women insisted upon the right to vote, to own property, to the sanctity of their own bodies, to education, to access to professions, to marry or not, and to exercise their reproductive capacities as they chose. These vocal, public, insistent struggles made the so-called "Woman Question" one of the most lively debates of the nineteenth and early twentieth centuries (Engels 1972 [1884]; Mill 1988 [1869] ; Martineau 1840, 1985; Gilman 1966 [1898], 1911; McClung 1972 [1915]; Rossi 1988; Schreiner 1914; Spender 1983; Stanton 1974 [1895]; Wright 1913).

Yet despite this sustained, visible, and vocal problematizing of gender as an analytical and social category, the prescriptive gender ideology of separate spheres, marked by an aggressive, rational, public, culturally authoritative male and a passive, receptive, emotional, private and nurturant female was naturalized, ontologized, and authorized in the scientific study of religion from its origins. The scientific study of religion thus is implicated in a particular construction of gender, one which is enmeshed in notions of male cultural dominance and female passivity. A culturally normative "Mankind" is posed against "the Sex," as women were identified and delimited in male cultural discourses, a construction which by the twentieth century came to include both single-nature (women as deficient) and dual-nature (women as oppositionally different) versions of male / female gender difference.

The continued male domination of the field of the scientific study of religion is both symptomatic of this gender ideology and a mask of its male gender-embeddedness, facts which served and still serve to distort and render unreliable the knowledges being generated about religion. Circularity of reasoning is a key problem. The asymmetry of androcentrism assumes that what men do is of preeminent human importance. The "self-evidence" of that importance is then naturalized and its gender-embeddedness obscured. When men then do what now is considered "objectively" important (often because it is "public," itself a construct and consequence of a particular gender ideology), men and their actions become not only a "serious" subject for intellectual investigation and analysis, but also *representative* of humanity overall (Warne forthcoming b). In similar circular fashion, what women do is less important by definition, because women do it; alternately, what women do is important only in the terms set down for them within the androcentric frame (Lerner, 1979).

Just as imperialist agendas have been made visible when Euro-North American normativity is queried, so too the extent of androcentric distortion becomes evident once women are placed at the center of the study. The issue of secularization pointedly illustrates both these concerns. As the nineteenth century progressed, religion was increasingly theorized in evolutionary terms. Renunciation of religion was seen to be a natural process as "mankind" moved from its "childhood" into "adulthood." This process was both personal (in that rational adults—epitomized by males—would relinquish their childish dependency on religion), and global and pan-historical (in that scientific Euro-North American culture represented the highest evolutionary state of "mankind" while the "primitives" of the "Dark Continent" of Africa and elsewhere represented "Man's infancy"). Secularization theory builds on these presumptions, positing an originally sacralized cosmos which (in its dystopic form) falls victim to, or (in its utopic form) is released from superstition by, an enlightenment of reason, particularly that marked by technological, scientific advance. And indeed, public social power in Euro-North America did shift from the ranks of the (male) clergy to a "new priesthood" of (male) scientists and government officials. But did the ongoing religious life of humanity actually demonstrate the process of renouncing religion which secularization theory asserts?

The secularization narrative presumes at least three things: first, that the so-called public sphere is preeminent (Ammerman 1994: 291). Religious leadership and received institutional forms are taken as the proper barometers for assessing the vitality of religions. Second, by implication in an androcentric frame, male religious behavior (as culturally authoritative speakers in religion's public forms) is assumed to be the significant marker of human cultural development. Thirdly, it conflates "religion" with Euro-North American Christianity, a highly problematic and underinvestigated formulation. All these assumptions are plausible within an ideological framework which assumes Euro-North American superiority and masculine dominance. Yet as Ann Braude has shown regarding the American context, there has been no falling away from religion if women are taken into account. Instead, "per capita church membership in the United States increased steadily throughout the nineteenth century, beginning at less than 10 percent and reaching stunningly high rates (67–76 percent) that have persisted throughout the twentieth century" (Braude 1997: 95). Indeed, the narrative construction of Christianity's "declension, feminization, and secularization" in North America only makes sense if men's religious lives are assumed to be more important than women's: percentage-wise, women have always been in the majority (Braude 1997: 93–94). Moreover, women are increasingly taking public and institutional positions within Christianity, effecting considerable liturgical and theological change (Braude 1997: 101–103). As Braude lays out in detail, once the presumption of male preeminence is dislodged—and with it, the ideological construct of gendered public / private spheres in which women are "contained" in the private, non-normative, and culturally less evolved—"secularization," in North America at least, is either reconfigured or disappears altogether (Warne forthcoming a). The decentering of colonialist assumptions of European cultural normativity yields similar results.

As the example of secularization suggests, it is high time that the scientific study of religion scrutinized the cultural assumptions of its own theory base. Yet (to take the category explored here), rather than seeing gendering as a central element in world-building—one of religion's main projects—the scientific study of religion has proceeded within an obscured and unacknowledged gender ideology marked by androcentrism. The human cultural project of gendering (Ortner 1996), and the asymmetries of power and authority which are established via that process, have not received the kind of critical scrutiny that could reasonably be expected from an intellectually rigorous scientific study of cultural forms and processes. Instead, engagement with the question of gender in religion has been marginalized, placed in "women's sphere" of connection, commitment and "advocacy." The strong version of objectivity that has characterized the scientific study of religion from its inception, with its notion of human understanding unenmeshed in human selves, has stood as a barrier and functioned as the ideological justification for marginalizing or ignoring gender and leaving androcentrism intact.

Nevertheless, despite these obstacles, gender-critical work on religion has been widely undertaken. It first emerged in Christian theological contexts, as women (and some few men) challenged traditional renditions of women's deficiency and/or unfitness for religious leadership (Saiving 1960; Tavard 1973). Feminist theology (Warne forthcoming a) has continued the project of gender critique with great vigor, and is now being undertaken in traditions other than Christianity and Judaism, such as Rita Gross' (1993) feminist reconstructions of Buddhist traditions. Gender-critical scientific studies of religion have proceeded since the early 1970s (Plaskow and Romero 1974; Gross 1977, 1996), although the specter of "advocacy" has served to inhibit their acceptance and application in the malestream, with a few welcome exceptions (MacQueen 1988). "Women in" and "women and" studies examined the characterization and theorization of women within religious tradition and moved beyond those boundaries to suggest other religious possibilities for them (Clark and Richardson [1977] 1996; Cooey et al. 1992; Holm and Bowker 1994). Goddess worship, both historical and contemporary, also became a growing focus of scholarship (Olson 1987; Christ 1987; Eisler 1987). As Carol Christ (1992) and others (Warne 1998) have shown, although gender-critical studies of religion have been increasingly available (Bendroth 1993; Hawley 1994; King 1987, 1990, 1995; Joy and Neumaier-Dargyay 1995; A. Sharma 1987, 1994a, 1994b; S. Young 1993), they retain the status of a kind of "expertise of the margins," produced and read by those who do not fit the received cultural gender script of male pre-eminence and normativity. A partial exception is the interesting new work being produced on masculinities by Jewish scholars such as Daniel Boyarin (1993, 1997) and Lawrence Hoffman (1996), which complements feminist analyses of the construction of gender in Judaism (Sered 1999). Gendered studies of Islam are also available (Haddad and Esposito 1998), although there is still a tendency, with religion as in other areas, to treat gender as something which has to do more with women than with men. However, these explorations of located knowing and cultural gender construction have yet to transform dominant discourses in method and theory in the scientific study of religion.

Prospects for Future Usefulness

As long as we distinguish humans as "women" and "men," and as long as these distinctions carry symbolic meaning and cultural authority which shape human life possibilities, the concept of gender will be essential to any adequate analysis of religion. Gender as an analytical category, and gendering as a social practice, are central to religion, and the naturalization of these phenomena and their subsequent under-investigation have had a deleterious effect on the adequacy of the scholarship that the scientific study of religion has produced. Until the scientific study of religion becomes intentionally gender-critical in all of its operations, it will unwittingly reproduce, reify and valorize the nineteenth-century gender ideology which marks its origins, rendering suspect any claims to the scientific generation of reliable knowledge it seeks to make.

Randi R. Warne

Suggested Readings

Blunt, Alison and Gillian Rose (Eds.)
   1994   *Writing Women and Space: Colonial and Postcolonial Geographies*. New York: Guilford.
Comstock, Gary David and Susan E. Henking (Eds.)
   1997   *Que(e)rying Religion: A Critical Anthology*. New York: Continuum.
Gleason, Maud W.
   1995   *Making Men: Sophists and Self-Presentation in Ancient Rome*. Princeton: Princeton University Press.
King, Ursula
   1995   "Introduction: Gender and the Study of Religion," pp. 1–38 in Ursula King (ed.), *Religion and Gender*. Oxford: Blackwell.
Kramarae, Cheris and Dale Spender (Eds.)
   1992   *The Knowledge Explosion: Generations of Feminist Scholarship*. New York: Teachers College Press.
Laqueur, Thomas
   1990   *Making Sex: Body and Gender from the Greeks to Freud*. Cambridge, MA: Harvard University Press.
MacQueen, Graeme
   1988   "Whose Sacred History? Reflections on Myth and Dominance." *Studies in Religion/Sciences religieuses* 17:142–158.
Minnich, Elizabeth Kamarck
   1990   *Transforming Knowledge*. Philadelphia: Temple University Press.
Tuana, Nancy
   1993   *The Less Noble Sex: Scientific, Religious, and Philosophical Conceptions of Woman's Nature*. Bloomington: Indiana University Press.
Warne, Randi R.
   1998   "(En)Gendering Religious Studies." *Studies in Religion/Sciences religieuses* 27: 427–436.
   Forth-   "Making the Gender-Critical Turn." In Tim Jensen and Mikael Rothstein
   coming   (eds.), *Secular Theories on Religions: A Selection of Recent Academic Perspectives*. Copenhagen: Museum Tusculanum.

12

INTELLECT

Daniel L. Pals

❦ ❦

Intellectualism stands for a perspective in the comparative study of religion traceable to the theories of the Victorian English ethnologist Edward Burnett Tylor (1832–1917) and his disciple James George Frazer (1854–1941), author of the widely read *Golden Bough* (1924 [3 editions: 1890, 1900, 1915]). Predicated on the common-sense notion that religious behavior is activity governed by religious beliefs, intellectualist theory holds that ideas about the gods have arisen mainly from human efforts to explain events that occur in the natural world. It contends that in non-literate cultures especially, people attribute the causes of certain events, both routine and exceptional, to the agency of supernatural beings, with the result that in such communities religion plays a role quite similar to that of science in the secular societies of the modern West. The purpose of religious belief and practice is therefore to provide an understanding of nature, to communicate with the spiritual beings that govern its course, and thereby to predict and control its processes. At first widely accepted, especially in Anglo-American discussion at the close of the Victorian era, intellectualism came in the early and middle decades of the twentieth century to be just as widely rejected, due largely to: the influence of reductionist thinkers such as Sigmund Freud, Karl Marx and Émile Durkheim on the study of religion; the work of myth-and-ritual theorists, who argued that religious practice is logically and historically prior to belief; and the findings of a new generation of professional field-working anthropologists, who were severely critical of the methods employed by Tylor and Frazer. In the later decades of the twentieth century, intellectualism has undergone a limited but vigorous revival, chiefly in the work of Robin Horton, the British anthropologist of Africa.

E. B. Tylor

A self-taught student of folklore and myth who as a young man traveled to Mexico to record the customs and ideas of native Americans, E. B. Tylor in 1871 published a seminal two-volume study entitled *Primitive Culture: Researches into the Development of Mythology, Philosophy, Religion, Language, Art, and Custom.* In this widely influential book, which earned him acclaim in some circles as the "father of anthropology," he contended that the origin of religion lay in the intellectual strivings of individuals in early non-literate societies to explain certain important, puzzling or mysterious events encountered in everyday life. Thus when the early "savage philosopher" reflected on encounters with the motionless bodies of the sleeping or the dead and associated them with the animate figures experienced in dreams, he drew the inference that every human being consists of a physical body activated by a spiritual principle or "soul" within (1903 [1871]: vol. 1: 429). From this fundamental premise—that the soul is the cause of life and activity in the human body—he then reasoned by analogy and extension to the more general theory that spiritual agency was the source as well of other instances of motion or life in the natural world. Accordingly, "animism" (from the Latin *anima*, meaning "spirit" or "soul") became the key and comprehensive explanatory principle adduced in early human thinking to account for activity of almost any kind in the natural world. The presence of souls explained not only the enterprises of human agents, but also the growth of plants and trees, the movements of rivers and winds, the activities of animals and even the motions of planets and stars. Further, since souls were fully separable from bodies, early peoples drew the inference that there could also be spiritual beings of a sort that did not possess, and did not need, attachment to a body at all. These were the demons, angels and the gods.

In the course of describing this wide-ranging system of early ideas and beliefs, Tylor, a sturdy Victorian rationalist, offered two rather divergent appraisals of its merits. Looked at from one perspective, animism was a colossal fabric of delusion—one of the great errors of the human race. Tylor believed it obvious to any intelligent observer that there are no such things as spiritual beings and that human beings do not have souls. Still less do trees, animals, planets or any of the other living, moving entities we meet in daily experience. To cling to such notions, as early peoples did, was in his opinion to reason in a way that must be described as naïve, simplistic and childlike.

On viewing it from another perspective, however, Tylor recognized that animism was not entirely irrational or absurd. It was, after all, the product of undeniably human reasoning diligently employed in an effort to account for phenomena that would otherwise have remained disconnected and devoid of explanation. Whatever may be thought of it in modern times, early belief in souls and spirits was the work of minds that were at least attempting to be rational in their effort to make sense of the experiences of everyday life. In fact, animism, for all its limitations, needs to be recognized as the first "general philosophy of man and nature" ever devised by the human intellect (1903 [1871]: vol. 2: 356). It was so comprehensive and adaptable that it spread easily into almost every aspect of the life and thought of non-literate cultures. Moreover, animism, like modern science, lent itself to extended application and progressive intellectual development. Over the course of the centuries, the simple animism of the earliest societies (Tylor's word for these was "savage") came gradually to be replaced by the more elaborate polytheism of the later "barbaric" ages, when agriculture, literacy and communal life formed the first great civilizations of the ancient world. Polytheism in its turn was capable of being developed into the still higher form of thought on display in the Judaism and Christianity of the modern Western world—that is, monotheism, the belief that all of nature is created and guided by one and only one divine being. With the appearance of monotheism, Tylor argued, the system of animist thought achieved the most sophisticated and appealing of its several forms, though it was of course nonetheless mistaken for that (1903 [1871]: vol. 2: 335–336).

J. G. Frazer

It was left for Tylor's famous successor, J. G. Frazer, to adopt the general thesis of *Primitive Culture*, weave it into the three editions of his monumental study, *The Golden Bough*, and in the process incorporate the story of animism into his own, more comprehensive theory of human intellectual development through three successive stages of magic, religion and science. According to Frazer the earliest human efforts to understand the world took the form not of religion, but of magic, which offers the prospect of changing the course of nature through impersonal and invisible "sympathies" that work by way of either contact or imitation. Imitative magic proceeds by noticing instances of resemblance between objects and processes in nature and manipulating them to change its course, as when a tribal magician tries to bring rain by making a sound similar to that of thunder. Contagious magic operates on the basis of physical connection, as when hair or fingernails of a targeted enemy are attached to a voodoo doll with the expectation that any curse placed upon the image will transfer to its victim (Frazer 1924: 11–48).

In appealing to these universal, impersonal principles of likeness and contact in nature, Frazer notes that magic operates in a way not unlike that of modern science, but of course it is not at all the same thing. For the explanatory principles of magic are mistaken, whereas those of modern science are not. Magic is in fact false science—a fact which over the course of time becomes all too apparent in its numerous failures.

It is the inevitable decline of magic that over the centuries leads to the rise of religion, which Frazer proceeds to describe in terms very similar to those adopted by Tylor. Religion attempts to understand the world by appealing not to regular, impersonal and universal "sympathies" within nature, but to the spontaneous and often inscrutable ways of powerful, personal beings who stand outside of it. These supernatural agents—the gods—determine the course of events in accord with purposes which are their own and in a manner that goes beyond any human power effectively to alter or amend. In the stage of religion, pleadings and prayers to the gods replace the spells and rituals of magic, and all efforts to change the course of nature take on a much more uncertain aspect. The laws of magic are coercive; the spell rightly spoken must yield the result it promises. The prayers of religion, no matter how sincerely uttered, offer no such guarantee; for the designs and rivalries of the gods determine events, not the fears or wishes of humanity. At the same time, it is precisely because prayers do rise to the gods unanswered, and the wishes of the devout often do go unfulfilled, that the affirmation of religion can be seen, in intellectual terms, to mark an improvement on magic. When people embrace a vision of life in which outcomes are not guaranteed, and accept the world as a theater of events controlled by interests apparently indifferent to their own, they have in hand a general philosophy that fits closely the pattern of natural events as actually encountered in everyday life. The principles of magic may be fixed and regular, promising control of nature; but the world as we actually meet it for the most part eludes both prediction and control (R. A. Jones 1984: 39).

Though magic and religion are distinct, Frazer concludes that in the end there is little to choose between them since both have been replaced in the modern age by science. Over the last several centuries, he notes, the methods of both the magician and the priest have been pushed aside by the steady advance of this new, disciplined and more cautious form of explanation that emphasizes observation and experiment. With the arrival of science and its new way of explaining the world, the old ways of both magic and religion can be seen rightly to have come to an end (Frazer 1924: 712).

Though *The Golden Bough* exercised influence well beyond the borders of anthropology and the study of religion, careful observers noticed early on that its sequence of broad stages in the growth of the human intellect was problematic. Much of the information which Frazer had gathered on tribal societies through correspondence with traders, travelers, missionaries and colonial officials was difficult to corroborate and almost impossible to locate in any specific historical period, so it could hardly be used to prove, or even disprove, the claim of a broad evolutionary sequence (Fraser 1990: 75–85). In addition, insofar as a clear delineation could even be made between the stages of magic and religion, most of the evidence seemed to show that they were not sequenced but simultaneous. The reports of most observers suggested that magical and religious customs were almost invariably intertwined, with little evidence to indicate which form of thought might have come before the other.

Further, in gathering his materials Frazer, like Tylor, relied almost exclusively on what later anthropology described with disdain as "the comparative method" (Hodgart 1955; Leach 1961a, 1965; Harris 1968: 204–205, 562). Like a tourist circling the globe, he traveled from source to source and place to place, assembling reports on supposedly similar customs from peoples of differing times and locales, but proceeding with little regard for the specific social and historical contexts which were crucial to any clear grasp of their meaning. For example, Frazer saw no difficulty in associating fire festivals from Scandinavia which occurred at one time of year with Celtic rites in Scotland which occurred at another, while at the same time using both to make an even more dubious connection with the Roman festival of Diana, which was itself reconstructed from second-hand accounts of events reported to have occurred in central Italy nearly 2,000 years earlier (Pals 1996: 41–42, 46). These casual associations, made by theorists who almost never left the armchair, earned both Frazer and Tylor a strong measure of contempt from their successors in anthropology who in the early years of the twentieth century turned their attention to a new and radically different kind of inquiry. Following the lead of the Polish emigré Bronislaw Malinowski, who introduced professional fieldwork as a standard, they insisted that serious explanation of either a society or its religion could not even begin until the theorist, departing sharply from the older comparative method, had exchanged superficial and second-order acquaintance with sources drawn from many cultures for thorough, extended, first-hand observation of just one or a few.

To all of this must be added, finally, the fact that the thinking of both Tylor and Frazer was colored lifelong by a decidedly anti-religious prejudice. Rationalists to the bone, they could see little in religion of any kind that did not deserve to be dismissed as ignorance, opportunism or naïve superstition (Pals 1996: 17, 30). The prospect of entering "sympathetically" into the conceptual framework of people who genuinely believed in miracles, demons and deities was to them an intellectual impossibility. More pointedly still, the subtext of the evolutionary model that both thinkers endorsed made it clear that in the end there was relatively little to distinguish the more recent forms of religion from the more ancient. What else was the everyday theology of England's Christian populace, they intimated, if not a residue of the childish animism devised by savages in the intellectual half-light of a primitive age?

Intellectualism in Eclipse

For the reasons noted above, the intellectualism of Tylor and Frazer entered a phase of almost unanimous repudiation in the decades after World War I. Leaving aside the matter of their instinctive distaste for religion (perhaps the one article in their creed which certain of their successors shared), most anthropologists, social theorists and historians of religion labored hard through the middle years of the twentieth century to put as much distance as possible between themselves and the "armchair" anthropology of their Victorian predecessors (Sharpe 1986: 87–96; Morris 1987: 103–106). But while it was possible to reject the methods of Tylor and Frazer, there was no escape from their influence. On the contrary, the work of these early intellectualists set the agenda for a great deal of subsequent discussion of the origin and nature of religion. They framed problems and initiated debates that, beginning still in their lifetimes, would continue for three generations into the latter half of the century. How did this come about?

The key point to notice is that the general effect of intellectualist theory of religion was to frame for later theorists the troublesome cross-cultural problem of understanding alien systems of belief. Specifically, if the claims of religion are, as Tylor and Frazer contended, manifestly false and mistaken, why is it that so many people have for so long persisted in holding them—and with such deep and tenacious conviction? If (to phrase the question in Victorian evolutionary terms) religious claims are so obviously a feature of the childhood of the race, why does so much of humanity, now in a more mature phase of its development, still insistently cling to them as truths virtually beyond refutation?

Reductionist Theories

In addressing these questions, Tylor proposed what he thought was an answer in the form of his celebrated "doctrine of survivals," which held that the broad rule of evolutionary intellectual progress naturally has its exceptions (Hogden 1936). Not all cultures, he noted, and not all things in any one culture, evolve at the same pace. In Europe the practice of bloodletting persisted on the strength of cultural inertia long after the medieval physiology on which it was based had disappeared from the scene. So too with other customs; often they linger in obsolescence, as flotsam on the tides of history (Tylor 1903 [1871]: vol. 1: 97–102, 108–111). Unfortunately, as later social anthropologists were quick to notice, the difficulty with this doctrine is that it purports to be an answer when in fact it is only a restatement of the question. It merely gives a name—"survival"—to a phenomenon when what we really want to know is why it is that the "survival" has survived. It is not enough to explain the presence of religious beliefs in the modern secular age as a survival from the animist past. We want to know what it is about both the belief and the culture in which it persists that has enabled it to survive when other such ideas may have long since disappeared (Burrow 1966: 240).

If intellectualism was unable to account for the persistence of religious ideas, the same could not be said of its social-scientific successors. Already in the first decade of the new century, while *The Golden Bough* was at the height of its fame, Freud, Durkheim, the disciples of Marx and assorted others working in the fields of psychology, sociology and anthropology were beginning to supply explanations that Tylor and Frazer could not. Freud found the answer in the individual personality, arguing that religion persists despite its transparent falsehood because it is rooted in psychic needs that lie deeper than the rational human intellect. Anchored in the unconscious fears and anxieties of the personality; it is "the universal obsessional neurosis of the human race" (Freud 1989 [1927]). At almost the very same moment Émile Durkheim in France was making analogous arguments, though he appealed to conditions that were social rather than psychological. For Durkheim religion persists because it offers symbolic expression of the loyalty felt by all individuals to the social group that enfolds and sustains their lives. "The god of the clan," he wrote in *The Elementary Forms of Religious Life*, "can be none other than the clan itself, but the clan transfigured and imagined in the physical form of [the] totem" (1995 [1912]: 208). As is well known, Marxist theory drew on economics to reach a similar conclusion. Though for him religion is manifest illusion, Marx was convinced that it survives because it is a perniciously useful falsehood in an unjust social order. Religious institutions sanction the mechanisms of oppression that protect the rich, while its otherworldly ideas conveniently channel into passivity the revolutionary energies of the poor (Niebuhr 1964: 41).

In all three of these classic reductionist theories, the main agenda is the penetration of surface appearances. Each contends that religious traditions are things quite different from what intellectualists presume them to be. Though on the surface they appear to be systems of doctrine and practice that relate to the realm of the supernatural, they are in fact exercises in symbolism—Durkheim's term is "representations"—that express in indirect form realities that are entirely historical and natural. On the reductionist view, intellectualism explains religion by naïvely accepting the otherworldly claims that lie on its surface; in so doing it entirely misses social, psychological or economic circumstances that are its real and underlying substance.

Symbolic Anthropology

The anti-intellectualist contention that religion is essentially a mechanism for translating this-worldly human concerns into other-worldly images and symbols was certainly not limited to the theories of Freud, Marx and Durkheim alone. Due in part to Durkheim's influence, a perspective on religion not too distant from his reductionist sociology has guided much of the work done by the leading figures in Anglo-American social science during the early and middle years of the twentieth century. This can be seen most clearly in what has been called the "expressivism" of interpreters such as

A. R. Radcliffe-Brown (1952), Edmund Leach (1954; 1961b), Raymond Firth (1973), John Beattie (1964) and others in the tradition of contemporary symbolic anthropology. The position taken by these "symbolist" interpreters, nearly all of whom have adduced the results of anthropological field work to support their views, can perhaps best be understood as an endorsement of the Tylorian stance in one respect and a clear rejection of it in another. Symbolist interpreters readily agree with the intellectualist judgment that the claims of religion, especially the traditional religions of non-literate peoples, cannot be seriously believed. At the same time, they emphatically reject the notion that the people who hold these invalid beliefs are in any way inferior—that is, childish, savage or superstitious—in comparison to ourselves. They proceed to justify this "untrue but not unworthy" verdict on the religions of non-literate cultures by appealing to a critical divide in the nature of human thought.

In all cultures, symbolists insist, human beings make use of two quite different forms of thinking. The one, which we find in everyday conversation, as well as in science and technological discourse, is instrumental and literal. It identifies objects or processes in the external world and makes logical connections between them. It discovers causes and effects, grasps relationships, distinguishes differences, proves and disproves assertions. Its aim is to explain, predict and control events in the world. The other form of thinking, which we find especially in the realm of the arts, is best described as symbolic and expressive. In such thought, and the language that conveys it, the purpose is not to apply words literally, with their obvious referents and meanings, but to use them figuratively to refer in an indirect way to emotions, conditions or realities that do not lend themselves easily to literal description. In light of this distinction, the symbolists go on to argue, it is not hard to see where intellectualists like Tylor and Frazer made their great mistake. Invariably, they took the language of religion to be instrumental, logical and literal when in fact (and especially in non-literate cultures) it is meant to be expressive, emotional and symbolic. Intellectualism thus does a double disservice to the people of non-literate societies; first, it misunderstands the language and gestures of traditional religions; then, on the basis of this misunderstanding, it demeans as ignorant and childish those people who practice them (Leach 1966: 41).

In sharp contrast to all of this, symbolic anthropology claims to understand the subtlety entailed in recourse to religious images and rituals. When in non-literate cultures people offer prayers for the planting, they may *seem* to be literally expecting the gods to give rain, but the symbolic theorist knows at once that they are simply (and correctly) expressing in figurative language their deep sense of dependence on the natural world. And if in such a culture a father were to plead with the god of healing, he should not be thought to be literally (and mistakenly) expecting health to be returned to his son, but only (and correctly) expressing in symbols his parental love for his child. Thus, in dealing with religion the main explanatory mission of symbolic anthropology is one of translation, of finding avenues of meaning that take the interpreter through the literal sense of words to their real and symbolic purpose. The aim of symbolist theory is to penetrate the intellectualist surface of language and action directed toward the supernatural world of the gods and to seek, beneath the literal sense, the real, this-worldly conditions, circumstances and emotions they express (Beattie 1964: 71–72, 212–215).

The Return of Intellectualism

By and large, the aggressive reductionism of thinkers like Marx and Freud and the rise of symbolic interpretation among professional anthropologists succeeded in placing intellectualism on the periphery of theoretical discussion through the middle decades of the twentieth century. Since that time, however, there have been signs in certain quarters of a return to intellectualism in a form that recognizes, and seeks to overcome, the problems that attended the work of its founders. A first clue indicating that intellectualist theory might have been too easily dismissed was the publication in 1937 of one of the pivotal works in modern anthropology, E. E. Evans-Pritchard's classic study, *Witchcraft, Oracles, and Magic among the Azande*. In this impressive analysis, the product of meticulous field work in East Africa, Evans-Pritchard undertook a detailed, critical examination of the very beliefs and practices which, in symbolist theory, could not be taken at face value unless one were to concede—as no responsible Western observer now would—that the Azande were fundamentally ignorant and irrational people. Departing from symbolist methods, Evans-Pritchard chose to take the entire system of Zande magic and assess it as believed by the Azande themselves. This method clearly did not lead him to the conclusion that the Azande were ignorant or irrational. On the contrary, the more intimately Evans-Pritchard came to know this magical system in all its nuances and multiple functions, the more convinced he became that it was not a jumble of absurd and childish superstitions, but rather an orderly, rational and coherent network of ideas (Pals 1996: 204–209). Evans-Pritchard concluded that given the assumptions on which it rested (and which he himself did not accept), Zande doctrines of witchcraft and magic could be seen not only to form an integrated conceptual system, but to provide a framework that guided individuals into pathways of socially constructive behavior. If the system were removed, the society would almost certainly have been thrown into serious disarray.

One clear implication of this landmark study was to place a note of caution before any theorist too readily disposed to treat the religious and magical ideas of non-literate peoples as expressive rather than instrumental. Among the Azande, magical ideas seemed to be socially constructive precisely because they made literal and instrumental reference to the realm of the supernatural.

The full impact of Evans-Pritchard's work was not felt until after World War II, when its exploration of rationality within cultural frameworks attracted the interest of analytical philosophers as well as professional anthropologists. Since that time, others have traveled similar paths, raising new questions about both the case for reductionism and the merits of the symbolist style. Though their lines of argument differ, strong misgivings about the symbolist consensus have been registered by Jack Goody (1961), M. E. Spiro (1968), J. D. Y. Peel (1969) and by Ian C. Jarvie in a provocative monograph entitled *The Revolution in Anthropology* (1964).

Perhaps the most notable of these dissenting voices, however, is the British anthropologist of Africa, Robin Horton. In a number of journal articles and essays published from the 1950s through the early 1980s, Horton has drawn on his training in English analytic philosophy and extensive anthropological work among the Kalabari and other African peoples to frame a cogent critique of symbolist interpretation, while at the same time pressing the case for Tylorian intellectualism in a revised and updated form. Since Horton's writings offer the most comprehensive and compelling version of the intellectualist program to appear in recent years, this essay will conclude by exploring several major themes in his work and assessing their significance for present and future theoretical discussion.

Earlier Intellectualism

In Horton's view it is important to notice that certain major failings of the Victorian intellectualists were in some respects quite separable from their intellectualism. Though not always noticed by their critics, the intellectualist claims of Tylor and Frazer were not dependent on the uncritical evolutionary assumptions, the casual handling of evidence and dubious comparative method they employed to support them. Unburdened by these liabilities, which have been well and widely exposed, the intellectualist stance can be seen to show promise that its critics have been slow to notice (Horton 1993: 53–62).

The Limits of Symbolic Interpretation

In framing its critique of the older intellectualism, symbolic anthropology has relied heavily on the distinction between the expressive and instrumental modes of thought, insisting that the language (and actions) of both religion and magic belong to the former rather than the latter. Religious thought, like artistic endeavor, is expressive and satisfying in itself; it is not used instrumentally either to explain events, to enter relationships with gods or to effect a change in this-worldly circumstances. Unfortunately for this thesis, says Horton (1993: 114), our actual encounters with traditional religion and magic suggest precisely the opposite:

Surely all the evidence from fieldwork in religious cultures is that, when men talk about the gods, they are talking about beings that are as real to them as men and women, sticks and stones, rivers and mountains. Surely all the evidence is that when people say their crops have been destroyed by the anger of the gods or prospered by their approval, they are talking literally.

In traditional cultures, moreover, people do not just speak as if they believe quite literally in the gods and the supernatural; they act upon such beliefs, often at great personal sacrifice and in ways that make sense only if those beliefs are in fact being taken as genuine.

Again, it should be noted that many people in traditional cultures make the same distinction between literal and symbolic language that modern symbolic theorists do, yet when they consider their own religious claims, they invariably categorize them not as symbolic, but as literal. Not surprisingly, then, when such people are confronted with Western symbolic reinterpretations of their own beliefs, their usual reaction is bewilderment. It is inconceivable to them that their beliefs should be read in any other way than as referring to precisely those spiritual beings or supernatural realities that they are meant to designate. Nor will it do to claim, along Freudian lines, that while traditional peoples themselves think they are making claims about the gods, their discourse is unconsciously symbolic. By symbolic theorists' own admission, the subjects that are said to be symbolized in religious discourse bear none of the anxiety-inducing characteristics that would merit them a place in the Freudian unconscious.

Given these and other obstacles to symbolist interpretation, Horton suggests that it is only reasonable to return to the original premise of intellectualism and assume that when people in traditional cultures employ religious discourse or resort to ritual action, they should be understood to mean just what they say and do just what they intend. Just as importantly, the distinction between expressive and instrumental modes of thought seems itself to be of questionable value. In aiming to correlate literal thought and language exclusively with the instrumental end of gaining practical control of the world, and symbolic thought and language just as exclusively with aesthetic, expressive purposes that are satisfying in themselves and devoid of practical intent, symbolist theory distorts by oversimplification a set of relationships which is actually quite complex and overlapping. Just as some scientific thinking, which is supposedly literal and instrumental, makes extensive use of symbols, so some religious thinking, which is supposedly symbolic and purely expressive, turns out to be quite undeniably literal and instrumental (Horton 1993: 122–124).

Ethnocentrism and Explanation

Of the various criticisms leveled against intellectualist interpretation, none is more serious than the claim that it has been an ethnocentric exercise in Western self-congratulation. Symbolist interpreters, well aware of the frequent and demeaning references to "savage superstitions" and "childish ignorance" that appear in the pages of both *Primitive Culture* and *The Golden Bough*, have been wary of any attempt to take at their face value the claims of tribal magic or traditional religion—and for good reason. Since in their view there is no way to avoid the conclusion that compared to Western thought, these systems are irrational and inferior, the better course is to assign all such traditional thinking to the realm of aesthetic or expressive thinking (Leach 1966: 39–49). In Horton's view, however, this strategy, though widely practiced in professional anthropology, is a needless and ideologically driven evasion of responsibility. If "rationality" is defined not just as what appears familiar to the modern interpreter, but as that which, in the light of knowledge available to the subject at the time and criteria of verification shared by *both* the interpreter and the subject, leads to plausible conclusions or actions, then traditional peoples fare no worse in such appraisals of rationality than moderns do (Horton 1993: 127–129). Further, to the degree that we measure traditional and contemporary cultures alike against impartial criteria, we shall find that both kinds of society are built on mixtures of rationality at the core and varying degrees of irrationality on the periphery. To concede, as intellectualists must, that traditional cultures do display some elements of the irrational is hardly an act of arrogance when the very same thing is admitted as equally true of the modern West. Conversely, it *is* a mark of Western arrogance when symbolist interpreters insist that the only mode of thought appropriate to the description of traditional religion is the symbolic and expressive rather than the literal and instrumental. They too easily forget that our notions of symbolism and aesthetic expression are, no less than other categories, also a product of uniquely Western intellectual history—specifically, the reaction of Romanticism against the cold, impersonal reasoning that has fueled the rise of the sciences. To put the matter simply, the taboo on ethnocentrism can be seen to cut both ways in modern interpretation (Horton 1993: 132–133). Intellectualist theory is no more naturally disposed to transgress it than any other.

Though these themes are central, they are by no means the only ones that Horton explores in essays that range widely in subject and demonstrate the rich resources of the intellectualist perspective, whether it is brought to bear on classic interpretations of religion, key problems in cross-cultural understanding or comparative inquiry into the forms of thought that govern both traditional societies and the culture of the modern West. Analyses and discussions such as these suggest not only that the intellectualist tradition is very much alive in the last decades of the twentieth century, but that it offers considerable promise both as a general theoretical perspective and as a guide to fieldwork, archival research and other first-order inquiry in the century to come.

Suggested Readings

Ackerman, Robert
  1987   *J. G. Frazer: His Life and Work.* Cambridge: Cambridge University Press.
Dorson, Richard M.
  1968   *The British Folklorists: A History.* Chicago: University of Chicago Press.
Frazer, James George
  1924   *The Golden Bough: A Study in Magic and Religion.* Abridged edn. New York: Macmillan.
Horton, Robin
  1993   *Patterns of Thought in Africa and the West: Essays on Magic, Religion and Science.* Cambridge: Cambridge University Press.
Jarvie, Ian C.
  1964   *The Revolution in Anthropology.* New York. Humanities Press.
Marett, R. R.
  1936   *Tylor.* London: Chapman and Hall.
Pals, Daniel L.
  1996   *Seven Theories of Religion.* New York: Oxford University Press.
Preus, J. Samuel
  1987   *Explaining Religion: Criticism and Theory from Bodin to Freud.* New Haven: Yale University Press.
Ross, Gillian
  1971   "Neo-Tylorianism: A Reassessment." *Man* N. S. 6: 105–116.
Tylor, Edward Burnett
  1903   *Primitive Culture: Researches into the Development of Mythology, Philosophy, Religion, Language, Art, and Custom.* 2 vols. 4th revised edn. London: John Murray; original edn, 1871.

13

MANIFESTATION

Thomas Ryba

❧ ❧

Manifestation as a Problematic Category

The history of the category of manifestation in the Western study of religion is a checkered one, one colored by a unique set of Western theological and philosophical assumptions. These assumptions are part of the thicket of Western intellectual history and cannot be easily disentangled from the historical development of religious studies, the phenomenology of religion, ideas of representation and allied epistemological notions. Related to these assumptions are two distinct sets of difficulties. One of these has to do with the meaning of manifestation; the other has to do with the significance of this meaning.

Like the proverbial moonless night in which all cows are black, the categorical meaning of manifestation inherited by today's religious studies is one so ambiguous as to be useless. The works of Rudolf Otto, Gerardus van der Leeuw and Mircea Eliade have led to its indiscriminate application to any religious phenomenon. In the broadest sense, religious manifestation has come to mean anything whereby religious power or agents are in any way sensed, perceived, felt, thought or communicated.

Views about the *significance* of manifestations are also problematic. Historically, two different perspectives have emerged about the salience of religious manifestations. For religious adherents, their importance lies within general schema of demonstration, manifestations (among other things) counting as evidence for the existence of religious objects. For academics studying religions, the attestation to manifestations within a particular tradition is usually the occasion to reflect on how these manifestations may be explained, instead of seeing them as functioning as evidence. For the believer, a manifestation is religious evidence; for the academic, a manifestation is precisely that which is to be explained.

Semantic Field of Manifestation

The verb "manifest" entered the English universe of discourse before its corresponding noun form. Its first entry (*manyfest*) occurred around 1380 in Chaucer's translation of Boethius' *Consolation of Philosophy*, Chaucer probably borrowing form and meaning from both the Old French *manifeste* and the Late Latin *manifesto* (Barnhart 1988: 630a). The intended meaning behind this borrowing is complicated by a dual etymology for *manifesto*, one which derives it from *manus* + *festus*, meaning "to be able to be seized by hand, palpable," and one which derives it from *manus* + *fendo*, meaning "to strike with one's hand, to slap, and particularly to slap to awareness or to attention" (Barnhart 1988: 630a; Onions 1966: 552a). Thus, the relevant meaning of the Latin *manifesto* is "to make clear, public or manifest but to establish this clarity is in a way that cannot be ignored"; it means "to make something palpably or forcefully clear." The noun *manyfestacioun* entered English around 1425 as a word borrowed through the Middle French *manifestation* and the Late Latin *manifestatio* (Barnhart 1988: 630a).

The Latin *manifesto* is the synonym of the Greek *phainō* which means: "to bring or come to light or sight, to make to appear or come to appearance, to make known or reveal by baring, to exhibit, to make clear to the ear, to sound true, to show or display as one's own, to be evident, plain or certain" (Liddell et al. 1968: 1912a–1913a). The Greek stem *phan-* means either "to illumine / make visible" or "to speak / make audible." In contrast, the Latin sense is not focused on the metonymic relation between sense modalities and the meaning of manifestation but on the forcefulness of the manifestation's presentation. This Latinate emphasis on force has had great consequences for the way in which the category is developed in the academic study of religion. Although the main Greco-Roman notions of manifestation have the sense of "something brought palpably or forcibly to attention," there is another connotation that links this idea to socio-political power. The adjective, *phaneros*, also has the sense of "what is distinctive, famous, renowned" or indicating the palpable evidence of aristocracy, wealth or importance based on the ownership of land (Liddell et al. 1968: 1915a).

The most common German word for manifestation—as understood in the English sense—is *Offenbarung*, from the German verb *offenbaren* which, like the Greek *phainō*, has the sense of "to bare, reveal, make public, obvious or evident." Less common are the verb *manifestieren* and the noun *Manifestation* which also have the same sense as the English "manifestation" but also that of "demonstration." The two German words for appearance are *Schein* (verb: *scheinen*) and *Erscheinung* (verb: *erscheinen*). *Schein* means "a shining, glow or appearance, semblance, illusion (to appear, resemble or seem)"; *Erscheinung* means "appearance" or "phenomenon" but with the sense of veridicality and no suggestion of illusion. *Täuschung* (deception, illusion) and *Erscheinung* are both associated as varieties of *Schein*. It is *Erscheinung* that is most often used as a synonym of *Offenbarung*, particularly in the theological sense when the veridical appearance is that of a god or gods or of a revelation. Thus, *Offenbarung*, perhaps, finds its closest English synonym in the Greek-borrowed "theophany" (Inwood 1995: 38–40).

In contemporary English, to manifest something is "to make evident to the eye or to the understanding; to show plainly, disclose, reveal." It is "to give evidence of, prove or attest" to the presence or reality of the thing or for something "to reveal itself as existing or operative." In the lingo of Spiritualism, to manifest a spirit means to give a perceptible appearance of it or reveal its presence. In the most general sense, to manifest anything means to display (a quality, condition, feeling, etc.) by one's action or behavior; to give evidence of possessing, reveal the presence of, evince a mental state or quality through one's action or behavior. As a noun, manifestation refers either to the process of manifesting something, an instance of something being manifested or (instrumentally) the means by which something is manifested. In each of these meanings, the manifestation is not intended as identical to the object it mediates. This establishes the first important characteristic of how a manifestation was understood in its historical development.

Contemporary English makes manifestation a process, thing or sign through which the presence or qualities of an otherwise invisible thing are made known. As such, a manifestation is always mediatory; it is something through which something else is known. It would be an obvious mis-locution to speak about a manifestation in exactly the same sense as one might about a phenomenon. Although a bare phenomenon is conceivable as a mere appearance without signifying some underlying reality (a mirage being an example), a moment's reflection on the idea of a bare or empty manifestation makes it clear that there can be no such thing. If a manifestation were either thought or proven to be empty, then—by the very meaning of the word—it could no longer be properly designated as a manifestation.

Theological and Philosophical Development

To understand how the notion of manifestation came to be employed as a category of religious experience within Western religious studies requires us to explore briefly some of its theological and philosophical roots. From the religious and theological origins of manifestation, Western religious studies has collected the data for investigations, taxonomies and explanations, while from its philosophical origins have come epistemologies and criteriologies for determining the cognitive status and warrant of manifestations.

Israelite, Greco-Roman, and Early Christian Origins of Manifestation

In its earliest history, the notion of manifestation was a native idea common in the religious texts and experiences of some Western religions.

In the Tanak, or Hebrew Bible, theophanies were characterized by a set of features and powers of humans or nature, many of which had negative emotional associations with terror and fear. Lightning, thunderheads, whirlwinds, hail, volcanic eruptions, subterranean fire, and so forth, were the elemental powers through which the God of the Israelites was manifested. The development of the Israelitic religion meant a progressive spiritualization of God's presence away from the face-to-face appearances portrayed in the earlier Genesis narratives to more indirect representations. The angel of YHWH was an example of how the speech and glory of YHWH were transferred to a mediating manifestation. This was presumably the solution to the problem of squaring the posited transcendence of God with his perceived, immanent energy. As such it offered a solution to the reconciliation of opposites (immanence and transcendence) which is not unlike that at the heart of the modern notion of presentational signs, the class of signs whose sensible qualities are instrumental in expressing the reality of that which they signify.

In addition to the angel of the Lord, another of YHWH's theophanies was his glory (Hebrew, *kavod*), a theophany whose subjective effect was like the gravity, weight or heaviness experienced in the presence of the wealthy, the honorable, the powerful and the successful. Objectively, the *kavod* was described as accompanied by perceptual effects such as lightening, fire, radiance and blinding lights. Here, again, is the common occurrence in religious history that what begins in the subjective experience of social power is transferred to a religious object (Eichrodt 1961, vol. 2: 29–35).

A third theophany in the Tanak (Psalm 54:3, 89:25, 44:6, 118:10–12) was the *pânîm* (or face) of God, originally intended quite literally in the folk tales of the Israelites but later becoming a metaphorical expression, probably borrowed from the Babylonian, indicating one had been granted an audience (had seen the countenance) of the Potentate. "To have seen God's face" thus expressed a complicated panoply of affections associated with the absolute power of the Theocrat to whom one had come to plead one's case, ask for assistance and find favor. Although the *pânîm* and *kavod* have no apparent connection, Carthaginian votive tablets refer to the goddess Tanit as "the face [or manifestation] of Ba'al," which parallels the Egyptian *Ennead* and the Hindu god Shiva and his shakti, or female consort (Eichrodt 1961, vol. 2: 35–39; Morenz 1973: 142–146; Muller-Ortega, 1989: 86–88).

Finally, the name of YHWH itself became a theophany following from the ancient Israelite notion that knowing a name was equivalent to knowing the nature of that which was being named. The Israelites progressively exaggerated this tendency so that the hypostatized name became YHWH's manifestation at work in the world. Because calling upon the name of the Lord immediately put one in his presence, the places of invocation became known as the places where the Lord's name dwelt (Deuteronomy 12:5, 11, 21, 14:23–24; 1 Kings 11:36, 14:21; 2 Chronicles 6:20).

Religious manifestations in Greco-Roman religion were almost always theophanies (showings of gods). In fact, there was rarely a manifestation without attachment to a supernatural person, even though these manifestations were polymorphous (Schilling 1987). Thus, the eagle, lightning and the world order were different epiphanies of Zeus, while other gods, such as Athena, manifested themselves anthropomorphically and directly (though sometimes privately) to their favorites (Burkert 1985: 125–131, 139–143). The inspiration, close presence and assurance of the gods was also "perceived" emotionally by their favorites. Sometimes the gods went so far as to possess their favorites and drive their enemies mad.

Even in the case of the much-discussed notion of *numen*—the divine power, will, sanction, majesty, or manifestation which is the origin of the later word for the *uncanny Other*, the *numinous*—it made its appearance almost always in connection with a specific god or supernatural beings. The Roman scholar Varro (116–27 B.C.E.) provided an etymology that reflected its personalistic associations when he derived it from *nutus* or the nodding assent of Jupiter possessing the greatest *imperium* or power (*De Lingua Latina* 1.7.85). Like the socio-political connotations of *phaneros*, *numen* was probably transferred from the might, power and authority of important humans to the gods and then back again to rulers such as Caesar; it was through this *numen* that a ruler's importance was manifested.

In the New Testament, *phainō* was used only to describe the shining of celestial bodies. *Phainomai* (passive form), or *phaneroō* were used with greater frequency (and more in keeping with the English word "manifestation") in the sense of "to make visible, manifest, to show oneself, to make an impression, to strike one, to look like" or, even, "to occur." These senses of *phainomai* were applied to dreams, to miracles and to appearances of the risen Christ—the distinction between a manifestation perceptually experienced and a manifestation psychologically experienced was blurred and not always easy to disentangle (Kittel and Friedrich 1964–76: 9.2).

In contrast, the verb *phaneroō* was used very frequently to mean to make visible what is invisible, or in the sense of a revelation. In the Pauline literature it is used synonymously with *apokaluptein*, evoking common New Testament themes having to do with the mystery of concealment and revelation. In the Johannine literature, the mediate nature of the revelation of God showed itself in Jesus and his works, in God's prophets and especially in the post-resurrection appearances of Jesus (Kittel and Friedrich, 1964–76: 9.4–5). *Epiphaneia*, from which we get the English word epiphany, is used of God's interventions or Jesus' future eschatological works. It does not seem to be used as a synonym of manifestation.

Accordingly, from the ancient Greco-Roman and Judeo-Christian religious complexes came two senses of the term manifestation: one concentrated on manifestations as objective media that presented transcendental beings whereas the other thematized manifestations as subjective (or intersubjective) experiences of transcendental beings.

Manifestation in the Theology of Augustine of Hippo

As early as the late fourth and early fifth centuries C.E., Augustine of Hippo made an analysis of the subjective locus of visions and manifestations that was far from theologically credulous. Augustine's thought is important because he also provided some rudiments for manifestation's epistemological analysis. His was an early recognition of the importance of ideology for the interpretation and for the certification of religious experience, no matter how vivid.

In interpreting the vision of Paul of Tarsus' ascent to the third heaven (2 Corinthians 12:2–4), Augustine provided a reading which established some characteristics of subjective manifestations. He compared the veridicality of such manifestations to the confusion one experiences in a awakening, semiconscious state, where one half-believes the images before one are realities and when one is half-aware that they are dreams. Confusion occurs because the state is experienced as more real than, different from and not quite as vivid as waking consciousness but more real, different from and more vivid than sleep (*The Literal Meaning of Genesis* 2.2.2.3–5).

For Augustine, the object of the manifestation (or vision) also brings with it the criteria for its typification. Because Paul claimed to have seen the third heaven (whether in or out of body he knew not), problems arose as to the vision's medium. According to the imputed cosmology, the third heaven is the place of God's presence, a place where corporeal vision would be impossible. The word that Augustine used for vision (*ostensio*) signals a primitive epistemology at work; *ostensio* is the kind of vision caused by an image presented to the imagination that need not have an objective correlate (*The Literal Meaning of Genesis* 2.12.3.8).

Basing his argument on accounts of Paul of Tarsus' celestial voyage, Augustine distinguished three varieties of visions: corporeal, spiritual and intuitive. The first is the vision of sight activated by corporeally present objects. The second is that of imagination activating stored images in the absence of their objective correlates. The third is that of intellection, or the intellectual grasp of the nature of things without imaginal representations. Realizing that imaginative visions do not always come replete with interpretation, Augustine concludes that imaginal manifestation will have intelligibility only if it is given along with its code. Thus any unequivocal imaginative manifestation requires an imaginal component and an intellectual component that decrypts its meaning (*The Literal Meaning of Genesis* 2.12.8–9.19–20).

The causal order of vision—under normal circumstances—requires the following sequence: sight to imagination to intellection, but Augustine maintained that the regulatory order is the reverse, so that if either nervous exhaustion, disease or supernatural agency interferes in this sequence, it disrupts the intellect's imaginational control. Intellectual *ecstasis* leaves the person catatonic, while interference in the intellect's regulation means experience of apparitions, hallucinations and delusions. What makes a subjective manifestation (or vision) truthful is the compatibility of its intelligible code to the ideology of the Christian Church.

Anticipating later developments in European philosophy, Augustine argued that one may be deceived about the referentiality of a manifestation but one cannot be wrong about *thinking* that one has experienced a manifestation (Ryba 1994b: 311–314). Although certainty about what-appears-to-have-been-experienced is absolute, safeguards against deception about referents are primarily intersubjective and thus external to the visionary's experience. For Augustine, Christian orthodoxy always sets the frame within which manifestations are evaluated.

Philosophical Conceptions of Phenomena and Manifestations

René Descartes and Manifestation

The Archimedian point for both modern and postmodern analyses of religious manifestations is the Cartesian epistemology. Descartes' philosophy may be taken as an extended meditation on manifestation, if manifestation is understood as the way that reality is presented to consciousness through its representations. In considering grounds for certainty, Descartes not only takes up the Augustinian and Skeptical discoveries, he also deepens the application of methodological (or hyperbolic) doubt by imagining the consequences that would follow from subjecting human experience to it. The instrumentality of this hyperbolic doubt means that it *is not* tantamount to genuine skepticism. Thus, when he problematizes human consciousness by positing it as an illusion wrought by a malicious demon, his goal is to discover what in human experience would be indubitable and thus incapable of false presentation to consciousness. Indubitable are those *cognitions* which are clear and distinct, clarity meaning having *efficient force* sufficient to make it present and apparent to the attentive mind, distinctiveness meaning having a precise difference so great that whatever the thought contains is clear and unconfused. For Descartes a perception, cognition or manifestation may be clear without being distinct but not the reverse.

Although he is not interested in the certification of religious manifestations *per se*, the problems that arise in his attempt to discover indubitable foundations for knowledge arise in any attempt to certify religious manifestations. Cartesian analysis of knowing thus amounts to the following, "How can I know that anything exists or is the way it presents itself to me, if I do not know it immediately?" "How can I move from the immanent data of consciousness to the transcendental objects of consciousness?"

If religious manifestations (and indeed every variety of veridical representation) present the experienced object as mediated but certain, then the problematic of the Cartesian analysis of consciousness hinges on how one understands that mediation. If everything including the *cogito* and *cogitationes* are mediated, the question is whether (and how) this mediation distorts the causal presence of the object? Alone, clarity based upon presentational efficacy, and distinctness reliant upon clarity and difference, do not suffice to establish the truth of representation.

For ancient realists, the mediation of intentionality meant that two (somewhat) different things were brought into an ontological relationship of identity or participation; the knower, in a way, became the known. However, if the religious object is "wholly Other," as some like Rudolf Otto have maintained, then it is difficult to see—according to the Cartesian analysis— how the cognition of a manifestation can be considered an icon, index or other kind of veridical representation of its religious object. A critique of the Cartesian understanding of representation can be fundamentally devastating to the Western epistemological project and leads ultimately to the critique of representation mounted by postmodernists.

Appearance and Manifestation in the Thought of Immanuel Kant

Fundamental to an understanding of the Kantian take on religious manifestations is his doctrine of appearances and the distinction he makes between *Erscheinung* (appearance) and *Schein* (illusion). A phenomenon is perceived in accordance with our forms of sensibility and understanding in contrast to the *noumenon* as the super-sensible reality or object in-itself. All appearances are therefore forms of our "external sensible intuitions" and can never be noumenal things-in-themselves but only "subjective modes of representation of objects in themselves unknown to us" (Kant 1985: 53–54). Kant maintained that appearances are not empty illusion (*Schein*) but entail something that appears. Although we may have no knowledge of noumenal objects, we may, at least, know them as transcendental objects.

According to the Kantian understanding, all religious manifestations (as mediations of "information" about a noumenal reality) are either miracles or illusion. If miraculous, they are either super-sensible or revelatory. As either, they cannot be known through pure reason, but they may be postulated by practical reason as transcendental events whose laws and causes are necessarily inaccessible to us (Kant 1960a: 81). Moreover, their veridicality can never be practically proven, only disproven. Kant takes the Genesis tale of Abraham's sacrifice of his son Isaac as an example of how this negative proof is applied. God's manifestation *to* and command *that* Abraham sacrifice his son "cannot, despite all appearances, be of God" because it "flatly contradicts all morality" (Kant 1960a: 82). Even manifestations that correspond to moral precepts, or at least do not violate them, are not susceptible to verification because—at least within the Christian tradition—demons can appear as angels of light.

Although the possibility of religious manifestations cannot be denied, as miracles they would be *rationally* inexplicable and *practically* worthless. The Kantian world-view's Newtonian causal horizon necessarily entails that religious manifestations be susceptible to explanation only as *Schein* or illusion, because such illusions and hallucinations are explicable according to the determinative categories of human experience: space, time and causation. As *Schein*, manifestations are delusions. Following such intellectual predecessors as John Locke and David Hume, Kant maintains that there are two varieties of delusions: the fanatical and the visionary, both of which are types of mental illness.

Appearance and Manifestation in the Thought of G. W. F. Hegel

Hegel's reinterpretation of appearance accompanies his discussions of Logic, a science that considers the laws of thought as equivalent to metaphysics. The categorical structure of Hegel's absolute idealism dictates the rejection of the Kantian distinctions between *Schein* (illusion) and *Erscheinung* (appearance) as well as the distinction between noumenon and phenomenon. Though Hegel distinguishes *Erscheinung* from *Schein*, the latter is no longer illusion, nor is the former an indeterminate content of a sensuous intuition, nor is there any longer any need to posit a noumenon or unknowable thing-in-itself. Everything is ultimately intelligible, and to know anything is to know it as mediated. In the Hegelian system, then, both *Schein* and *Erscheinung* are different modes of the appearance of Essence—Essence being sublated and negated Being.

Schein (semblance) is the mediate mode that both presents Essence (*Wesen*) and partially occludes it. Hegel associates *Schein* and *scheinen*, with the meaning of "a glowing" or "to glow (shine)" as well as with the meaning of "reflection." The "shining" of Being is twofold: internal and external. An Essence actualizes itself as such by "shining" outwardly and then inwardly. Without having shown itself, an essence is a mere potential essence, an in-itself as a mode of Being. An essence shining outwardly constitutes itself as a particular showing of itself for another, a showing that is partial and incomplete. Finally, Essence shining inwardly—its *scheinen* reflecting off an *other*—constitutes itself as Essence in-and-for-itself, as an essence fully realized (Inwood 1995: 184). Semblance can only express Essence fractionally, perspectivally and serially but never as a whole and never exhaustively. Essence is the plenum, the unbroken completeness that achieves only piecemeal expression in semblance (Inwood 1995: 39).

Erscheinung (appearance) and *erscheinen* (shining-from-within) are differentiated from semblance and shining as a higher and more important mode of Essence. Appearance does not veil or mask Essence. Rather, appearance is the existence of Essence. As the truthful expression of Essence, appearance forms a connected totality of the ways the Essence shows itself from within, a totality whose horizon is the world as the collection of all possible relationships between the Essence and other things. Essence always stands to appearance as what is mediated by it; the form this mediation takes is the showing forth of Essence in the sensible and the perceptual. Even so, appearance is a mode of mediation expressing the inexhaustibly diverse sets of perceptions and sensations that express an Essence. As such it is contradictory, fleeting and contingent; it is not stable and rational.

For Hegel, the notion of *Erscheinung* comes close to the notion of manifestation, especially with respect to the mediacy of each. However, for Hegel, appearance properly characterizes an evolutionary category of Being; it does not refer to a miraculous revelation. What Hegel says about miracles indicates the inapplicability of appearance to these events.

Manifestation as a Category for the Study of Religion

It is within religious studies that manifestation came into its own as a descriptive and (implicitly) explanatory category. What characterized its construction, there, aside from the search for a universe of regular features under which different phenomena could be collected, was the narrower search for a set of common powers which explains the *doxastic* efficacy of manifestations—that is, the perceptual power of manifestations whose strength causes belief (Alston 1993: 78–81). In describing this power, religionists treated this efficacy not only descriptively but sometimes uncritically as evidence for the realities behind the phenomena.

The Holy as Manifestation and A Priori *Category in the Thought of Rudolf Otto*

In his attempt to argue that the holy was an *a priori* category, Otto produced a religious epistemology of sophistication and wide-ranging influence. Those influenced by Rudolf Otto's exposition of the holy read like a twentieth-century

Who's Who. The later works of Nelson, Heiler, Wach, van der Leeuw, Nygren and Eliade all show a marked debt to this exposition, particularly as each attempted to work out the notion of religion as a *sui generis* (autonomous or self-caused) category (Ryba 1994a: 24).

For Otto, the meaning of the holy is best understood through the objective and subjective correlates of the emotion (or feeling) which mediates the sacred object for an experiencing subject. The word Otto employs for this emotion is *Ahndung*, meaning "presentiment, foreboding apprehension" (Otto 1959: ch. 28). Its corresponding faculty is the capacity for "divination." He believes that there is a variability in the activation threshold of this faculty across humans. In religious specialists it is activated by peculiar external circumstances with the ease that some people's artistic acuity is activated in the presence of beauty (Ryba 1991: 28). But even if an analogy holds between the aesthetic faculty and the faculty of divination, it is not possible to reduce the latter to the former. It is not reducible to the subjective response of its possessor nor is it the result of an *a priori* judgment. Its validation is bound up with its content, a content which is given with an intensity that makes it indubitable. Here it is clear that the warrant for the truthfulness of the experience is based in part on the power of the experience as well as the presence of the holy object conveyed by the experience's indexical qualities.

The content of *Ahndung* can be explicated according to the terms *tremendum*, *mysteriosum* and *fascinans*. Otto couples these three terms as *mysterium tremendum* and *mysterium fascinans* to suggest the object-taking intentionality of each. *Mysterium tremendum* describes the intentionality of an experience of marrow-penetrating dread, majesty and urgency in the presence of the uncanny and disquieting Other (Otto 1959: 12–24). At the same time, *Ahndung* may be explicated according to the intentionality of an experience of attraction based upon the wonderful love, mercy, pity and comfort that is attached to the beatitude of the thrilling Other (Otto 1959: 31–40). The *mysterium*, or object-pole, of this experience can be grasped ideogrammatically on analogy with a mystery that is "alien, uncomprehended and unexplained" (Otto 1959: 26). In its religious sense, it is best understood as *mysteriosum*, as the wholly Other that is in its very nature beyond the pale of the "usual, the intelligible, the familiar" and "the canny" (Otto 1959: 26). In its presence we are filled with "blank staring wonder" (Otto 1959: 26, n. 1). As *mysteriosum* it cannot be confused with those analogous mysterious beings of the natural and supernatural worlds because it transcends them all. It alone is inexhaustible in its depth, emptiness and hyper-essential being (Otto 1959: 30).

Otto believes that both the capacity of the religious subject and the development of the religious culture to which the subject is attached determine the experience of a religious manifestation. This implies significant complexity in the analysis of any manifestation because of the variability of both the receptivity of the subject and the nature of the object. The same sacred object may be experienced in a deeper or shallower fashion by different subjects depending upon their spiritual virtue and their religio-cultural development. Moreover, a religious object is not even required for a religious manifestation to take place. In this case the holy is presenced according to the subject's religious development, spiritual technology and so on. Otto also allows that the holy "acts" to reveal itself beyond the conditions which a subject can control.

Essence and Manifestation in the Thought of Gerardus van der Leeuw

Gerardus van der Leeuw's characterization of religious phenomena contained in his *Phänomenologie der Religion* (1933) represents the second major influence on the development of the category of manifestation in the twentieth century. Because his discussion of methodology contained in the epiglomena relies on some Husserlian terminology, his phenomenology of religion has sometimes been touted as a Husserlian model of religious phenomenology. This is almost certainly misguided. Both the placement of his discussion of method at the end of the book and the way he structures the content of the preceding chapters suggest that the inclusion of the Husserlian method was largely an afterthought. Indeed, his conception of religious phenomena is most decidedly non-Husserlian. Most likely it was influenced by both the Hegelian philosophy (indirectly through Chantepie de la Saussaye) and Heideggerian philosophy (directly and indirectly through the New Testament scholar, Rudolf Bultmann) (Murphy 1994: 125–135; Waardenburg 1978).

For van der Leeuw, a phenomenon (or appearance) "refers equally to what appears and to the person to whom it appears"; it is neither pure object nor subject, nor does it refer to the reality "whose essential Being is merely concealed by the 'appearing' of the appearances." Although a phenomenon is a relation between subject and object, this does not imply either that the subject modifies the subject or the subject modifies the object. "Its entire essence is given in its 'appearance' and its appearance [is given] to someone" (van der Leeuw 1938 [1933]: 107).

The phenomenon subsists in consciousness "as an image" possessing perspectives, backgrounds, planes, similarities, differences, position and numerous other relationships which are "perceptible" and structurally connected with other phenomena; these structural connections explain nothing about their factual or causal connections. The "image" of van der Leeuw bears and obvious resemblance to the ideograms of Otto and Eliade and to the Hegelian notion of representation inasmuch as it is an attempt to describe the naive imaginative representation of the sacred prior to philosophical critique. It is the uncritical precursor to the notion of an ideal type. The nexus of structural relationships disclosed by phenomena and as applying to persons, historical situations or religions are called "ideal types" (van der Leeuw 1938 [1933]: 107). These types are timeless, irreal and need not be historical (van der Leeuw 1938 [1933]: 107).

The presentation of a phenomenon to a subject follows three levels of disclosure. A phenomenon is experienced, first, as mediating a relatively concealed essence, then as acquaintance grows, a gradual revelation of the essence occurs, ultimately culminating in the final transparent mediation of the essence. The evolution of the presentation of phenomena corresponds to three levels of life: experience, understanding and testimony. Experience is the unity of the "actually subsisting life," incomprehensible in its particularity but reconstructed according to abiding, discernible structures which cohere in understanding as wholes (van der Leeuw 1938 [1933]: 107). Meaning is a third realm existing above mere objectivity and subjectivity not fully separable into subjective and objective contributions to understanding (van der Leeuw 1938 [1933]: 107). These levels of disclosure mirror both the structure of the book—which begins in objectivity, moves to subjectivity, and then unites the two—which also follows the Hegelian sequence of the development of religion.

The meaning of religious phenomena "dawns" on the religionist much in the way the Hegelian essence reveals itself as semblance, partially, momentarily, but instantaneously. The Husserlian notion of essence is implicitly evoked when van der Leeuw discusses the fullness of a phenomenon's meaning, a meaning that is never fully disclosed in a perspectival experience. It must also be related to the full series of similar experiences which "in and through understanding . . ., manifests itself as community of essential nature" (van der Leeuw 1938 [1933]: 107). But this essence requires a larger "objective connection" suggesting that the essence-manifesting phenomenon only has meaning against a wider horizon of meanings.

Of importance to note is that, for van der Leeuw, the phenomenological experience of the religionist is not identical to the phenomenal experience of the religious individual. For the religious subject, religious experience is concerned immediately with a *somewhat*, a somewhat which, like Rudolf Otto's sense of the *wholly Other*, forces itself upon the subject and opposes her/him as "*highly exceptional* and *extremely impressive 'Other'*" (van der Leeuw 1938 [1933]: 1). Here, van der Leeuw takes up a notion of affective efficacy that is evident in the writing of numerous early anthropologists of religion such as Tylor, Codrington, Hewitt, Marett, Lévy-Bruhl and Lehmann, while eschewing accompanying intellectualist projections. This efficacy takes the subjective form of emotions such as amazement, fear, awe that causes it to be regarded as extraordinary and uncanny. However, in a curious reversal of naturalistic and sociological explanations of power, van der Leeuw argues that religious power is "authenticated in things and persons" and, on the basis of this authentication, "these are influential and effective" (van der Leeuw 1938 [1933]: 1). This, however, raises the problem of the chicken or the egg: is the power abstracted from a powerful person / thing or is it a preapprehesion so that the person / thing is recognized as a locus of power? Van der Leeuw finds that the unifying feature of "primitive" religious experience is that it is a naively empirical experience of an *Other*, "a departure from all that is usual and familiar" as a "consequence of the *Power* it generates" (van der Leeuw 1938 [1933]: 1). It is an experience of the power of the religious Other that is given pre-scientifically and pre-theoretically.

From the above, one can see that van der Leeuw uses the term "manifestation" in two related senses, one which suggests that religious experience is characterized by manifest perceptual immediacy of an uncanny Other, one which suggests that phenomenological understanding is equivalent to the mediate disclosure of religious essences through a broad horizon of religious phenomena. For the religious subject, the mark of the primordial religious manifestation is disturbing power. For the phenomenologist of religion, the mark of essential manifestation is the disclosure of the invariant structural features of religious persons and things through an understanding of the phenomena.

The most interesting question about van der Leeuw's dual use of manifestation is whether he considers the experiences of the religious "primitive" and of the phenomenologist as parts of the same developmental continuum, especially since his characterization of both varieties of experience bears a similarity to the Hegelian spectrum beginning with natural religions and ending with the absolute religion devoid of sensuous representations. If van der Leeuw's descriptions of manifestation imports a Hegelian analogy between primordial and phenomenological religious knowledge so that the knowledge of the phenomenologist represents a positive advancement in the development of religious consciousness, then the claim about van der Leeuw's implicit theological agendum finds further support (for such a critique see Waardenburg 1978).

Theophany and Manifestation in the Thought of Mircea Eliade

According to Eliade, anything that, in some way, manifests some modality of the sacred, at some moment of its history, to someone, is a hierophany (*hieros* + *phainein* = "a *showing* of the holy"). Eliade takes this term in the broadest sense of a sacred epiphany; it applies to anything which in any way may signify the sacred. He recognizes that this broadest category may be subdivided into two constituent categories according to whether a hierophany is primarily a kratophany, or a showing of a sacred power (from *krasis* + *phainein* = "a showing of power"), or whether a hierophany is a theophany, or a showing of a god (from *theos* + *phainein* = "a showing of god"). Other subdivisions of the category of hierophany would also seem to be possible according to the nature of the sacred being. Moreover, not all kratophanies are hierophanies because there may be impressive showings of natural power which are not integrated into a religious system.

The value of this definition is in pointing attention toward two aspects of a hierophany: that it is a manifestation of the sacred's modality and it reveals the historical subject's attitude toward the sacred (Eliade 1963b: 2). In order to understand how a hierophany is a modality of the sacred, however, one must understand what Eliade intends by sacred, manifestation and by modality.

Eliade provides no handy definition of the sacred, preferring to *illustrate* it through an extensive series of historical examples. The closest he does come to venturing a definition is through negation; he chiefly tells us what the sacred *is not* by describing it in dialectical contrast to the profane. In a Saussurean vein, Eliade describes the sacred as defined by the field of its oppositions to the profane (Saussure 1983). He further mystifies this relationship by arguing that ultimately, the sacred medium exists in opposition to itself because it consists of profane and sacred aspects. It still remains what it profanely was, even with the sacred added to it, but both aspects are united in tension (Eliade 1963b: 13). This evocation of the Hegelian and Marxist notion of contradictions as the "motors" of the historical dialectic is reflected in Eliade's notion of a sacred dialectic whose purposes curiously resemble themes in Jewish and Christian iconoclasm (Stace 1955: 94–96, 101, 102; Lenin 1976: 357–363). Ultimately, he does provide a positive, minimalist definition of the sacred, describing it as designating an order of being which is qualitatively different from the profane but is richer, transcendental, eternal and more real (Eliade 1963b: 32, 460). He also discloses the ways that the sacred is known, that it (purportedly) can manifest itself through any profane thing (Eliade 1963b: 30). Hierophanies are ubiquitous; they are recognizable "absolutely everywhere, in every area of the psychological, economic, social and spiritual life." Eliade goes so far as to state that more than likely that anything that has been "handled, felt, come into contact with or loved" by anyone has been or can be a hierophany (Eliade 1963b: 11).

Therefore, to call something a *manifestation* means for Eliade that it "embodies and reveals" something other than itself and that in the process of this revelation the manifesting object, itself, becomes sacralized. To become the manifesting medium of a sacred *Other* thus means to become differentiated from other profane things, even though its physical attributes remain apparently unchanged (Eliade 1963b: 13). Thus at the heart of every hierophany there is a paradox because "every hierophany whatever ... shows, makes manifest, the co-existence of contradictory essences: sacred and profane, spirit and matter, eternal and non-eternal, and so on" (Eliade 1963b: 29).

Eliade admits that even though the word "hierophany" appropriately designates a wide field of religious phenomena—they are all phenomena which in some way "show" the sacred—manifestation *may not* be exactly interchangeable with it. This is because hierophanies form a series ranging from the cryptic to the holistic. At one extreme, they may reveal the sacred according to a secret code or those, at the other extreme—those "more truly *manifestations*"—may display the sacred clearly in a wealth of its modalities (Eliade 1963b: 10). A holistic manifestation is one whose connection with a "network of myths, symbols and customs" is so evident that its original meaning may be easily uncovered. A cryptic manifestation—though presupposing "a system of coherent statement"—is not so easily decoded (Eliade 1963b: 10). Eliade places little value on living-informant reports for uncovering the meaning of a manifestation, denying that either "explicit beliefs or logical actions" will serve as adequate keys for unlocking their meaning. He prefers to rely on scholarly reconstruction based on extensive researches into sacred and profane history (Eliade 1963b: 10).

Hierophanies may also be differentiated according to whether they are simple or complex and dialectical or non-dialectical (idolatrous). Simple hierophanies are those in which sacredness is mediated by simple objects or symbols; complex hierophanies are those in which the sacredness is mediated by complex rituals, artifacts or sacred beings. The former are always elements in a larger network of meaning and often acquire their sacred power by being implicated in a wider network of meaning, whereas the latter usually establish that network.

Dialectical hierophanies are the product of the paradox at the heart of sacred things and a tradition's ongoing reevaluation of the sacred. Iconoclasm—in the broad sense of the term—designates a tendency on the part of some traditions to supplant older manifestations with newer more adequate ones. This involves the supersession of older hierophanies in favor of later ones and marks one of the evolutionary characteristics of some religions. According to Eliade—who shows his cards in favoring this fusion of Hegelian evolutionary and Christian dispensationalist ideas—this process is derivative from an incisive grasp of the nature of a hierophany to be partial, incomplete and indirect (Eliade 1963b: 25). In contrast are those traditions that place hierophanies on equal footing only to call them aspects of the same sacred whole. With these, Eliade associates the pejorative adjectives "non-dialectical" and (more astoundingly) "idolatrous." Eliade resurrects the latter word but puts a Hegelian spin on it by intimating that non-dialectical religions naively accept all sensuous representations of the sacred as being equally truthful.

The modality of the sacred is the aspect that allows Eliade to link the subjectivity of the religious adherent to the various relations a hierophany possesses to the complete network of religious ideas and practices. Eliade's reifying manner might seem to suggest that hierophanies are so objective as to be susceptible to scientific verification. But this would be a misunderstanding. At points, he clearly denies the public objectivity of a hierophany; it is merely a "manifestation in the mental world of those who believe it" (Eliade 1963b: 10). The historicity of a hierophany does not diminish its universality, though some hierophanies have strictly local significance. Because hierophanies appear at specific times, they are indexed to the historical circumstances of their emergence and to the historical limitations of the subjects who experience them (Eliade 1963b: 2–3). Indeed, the localization of a hierophany may mean that its universal aspects are not significant for the individual members of a religious tradition. Nevertheless, this inherent historicity is no barrier to either the phenomenologist or historian of religions. The former seeks to establish the universal meaning of the hierophany while the latter studies its complete history in order to understand it in all of its modalities (Eliade 1963b: 5).

Toward the Rehabilitation of the Category of Manifestation

One might criticize the Western category of manifestation along many lines. An obvious criticism is that the term means so many things that it is hard to recommend its serviceability for any course of research. Some scholars came to this conclusion long ago and have simply taken it for granted that far from being *sui generis*, religious manifestations are explicable according to natural processes. Some have attempted to explain manifestations reductively, according to different physical, neurophysiological and psychological models (Freud 1913, 1963; Burkert 1996: 156–176; P. Wiebe 1997: 172–211; Persinger 1987). Accordingly, manifestations become instances of psychopathology or neuropathology, and manifestation as a religious category is dissolved. But despite their exaggerated claims, these models are still in their infancy and their explanatory power is quite limited. The jury is still out on the ultimate explicability of manifestations according to a naturalistic ontology.

Instead of marshaling arguments based upon immature empirical models, I should like, instead, to make a few modest suggestions as to how the category of manifestation might be rehabilitated for provisional use in a program of empirical research. My suggestions follow from four observations about the weakness of the category of manifestation as it has been construed in religious studies.

First, attempts to generalize about manifestations are defective because they collapse all *purported* indications (phenomena) of the sacred under the category of manifestation. Instead, manifestation should be narrowed and reserved as a subset of the larger class of purported religious *indices* that Eliade called "kratophanies" (showings of power).

In the etymological discussion at the beginning of this essay, I suggested that "manifestation" (by its Latin roots and some of its English connotations) signified an appearance of something which was veridical, something whose sensorial or perceptual force was so striking that it could not be ignored. Otto, van der Leeuw and Eliade all neglected this connotation in an obvious way. Recognizing that religious objects were the source of profound feelings, they descriptively leveled emotional reactions by ignoring the variability of experiential intensities beyond a minimum threshold. Anything on the other side of this threshold, they simply equated with the feeling of the holy. The impression left is that all appearances of the sacred are manifestations because all appearances possess the same emotional and perceptual efficacy. There is also the unintended effect that all experiential modalities are equated in significance.

I think this is wrongheaded, a symptom of imprecision and creeping apologetics. Instead, it seems to me, we ought to take a cue from the philosophers and attempt to distinguish between a religious semblance (or specious appearance), a *purported* appearance (or *phenomenon* in the sense of "a showing") and a *purported* manifestation (or *epiphany*). A religious semblance designates any experience of a religious thing (and / or process) in which the object of the experience seems charged with force but the subject of the experience is mistaken about the *reason* that she or he experiences that force. In contrast, a purported appearance designates any experience through which forces or beings are *apparently* indicated. Finally, a purported manifestation is a subset of purported appearances reserved for those experiences in which the perceptual, emotional and / or cognitive force is so great that the experience is taken as veridical—that is, as forcefully demonstrating the existence of the object of the experience.

A religious semblance roughly corresponds to either of the Freudian notions of error or delusion. It is an error, if (after rational persuasion) the subject will admit that the power attached to the thing (or process) has causes other than those she or he attributed to it. It is a delusion, if upon being shown the causes of the semblance, the subject rejects the explanation. In contrast, a purported religious appearance is an experience that is construed as mediating a hidden or partially-hidden object, an experience for which no naturalistic explanation has (or, perhaps, can) be given. This variety of religious experience corresponds to the Freudian notion of illusion, but the way I am employing it suggests that to describe it as such is useful only retrospectively. Thus, it retrospectively applies to any experience (characterized as showings of a religious being or force) before a naturalistic explanation is provided. If the subject still adheres to a religious explanation, beyond the moment an adequate explanation is provided, then her or his experience becomes an example of religious semblance or delusion. Finally, religious manifestation represents a new sub-category of appearance whose veridicality suggests that—if it is delusion—it is better described as hallucinatory. As inexplicable, it may legitimately be taken by the subject as *warrantably* real, especially if no other explanation is either *a priori* possible or *a posteriori* forthcoming (Yandell 1993: 256–275).

When the notion of what the *sui generis* nature of manifestation is considered, it is best made clear by contrasting it with semblance, on one hand, and appearance, on the other. What seems implicit in the notion of a manifestation is the force of its veridicality, and this distinguishes it from both appearance and representation. An appearance is validated as what it is by its context and the various causal relations that can be established between it and what it discloses. If these prove to be non-existent or illusory then, as appearance, it is illusory—it is a mere semblance. If, on the other hand, an undeniable veridicality is part of the experience of the appearance, then it is a manifestation. What differentiates both appearances in the broad sense and manifestations from representations, therefore, is what John Locke understood as the distinguishing feature of ideas and perceptions: perceptual vividness or efficacy. We might also add that position and presence within the sensorial field and the simultaneous awareness of the activation of the senses (eyes, ears, nose, tongue and skin)—whether veridical or not—is also another characteristic of appearances and manifestations different from ideas. Finally, there is the fact that the appearances and manifestations seem to have a causal spontaneity and causal texture quite different from ideas, which seem more generally under willful control. Those ideas which border on spontaneity and independence—and which are often linked to human compulsions—may more closely resemble appearances and manifestations in this respect. It is also not uncommon for psychopathologic experiences to have a more vivid quasi-sensorial signature and presence than ideas typically have.

In attempting to associate these varieties of religious experience with Freudian notions, I am not foreclosing the possibility that powers and beings beyond naturalistic explanation exist. As a principle of methodological agnosticism, I am simply advocating that, before our credulity is given free rein, naturalistic explanations should be sought. In recommending a distinction between manifest phenomena and other appearances, it is my contention that the force connected with some religious object can, indeed, be scaled. Take a simple case: in comparing the experiences of two religious objects—x and y—one might be able to elicit from one's informant whether x was experienced as more uncanny than y. Thus it should be possible to scale qualitatively different experiences of the same (or different) objects on analogy of the scaling of sensory force much in the same way we do when we ask someone whether they are more bothered by a child's crying or a faucet dripping.

Following from the first point, my second recommendation goes to the nature of the Eliadean taxonomy of religious appearances. I would like to recommend that the Eliadean taxonomic arrangement which makes theophanies and kratophanies subsets of the broader category of hierophany ought to be abandoned in favor of a categorization which makes kratophany (showings of power) the broadest category including both natural and *purportedly* non-natural dynamic appearances.

It is clear that in his establishment of a broad category of hierophany which encompasses kratophany and theophany, Eliade reifies a composite category—that of the sacred—and then assumes that both theophanies and kratophanies are species of it and not just its two exhaustive parts. This is rather like assuming that which one wants to demonstrate. Moreover, it is not clear that there is anything left of the sacred once one subtracts experiences of power and supernatural beings.

I propose, instead, that the category of kratophany be construed as the more general because what is common to hierophanies and theophanies is power described analogously. The distinction between natural and non-natural appearances of force should be an operational distinction, until such a time when it is either discovered that the non-natural can be reduced to the natural or that the non-natural appearances are irreducible.

My third recommendation is that any future taxonomy of religious showings should include their loci as both a principle of classification and a criterion for their verification. In suggesting that the locus of a manifestation must be taken in account, I am suggesting that such experiences should be indexed to whether or not the epiphany was (a) objective (or purportedly observable to any bystander, whatsoever), (b) intersubjective (or purportedly accessible to the adherents of the tradition or purportedly accessible to some subgroup meeting specific requirements) or (c) subjective (or purportedly accessible only to the subject). It is impossible to describe the origin and varieties of the powers experienced in religious appearances without describing their intensity and qualitative varieties and the theater (or loci) of their appearance. What I propose, then, is the development of a taxonomy based upon "thick" descriptions of religious appearances that would take account of the full variety of loci, purported qualities, conscious acts and dynamic intensities associated with religious manifestations. What might such a taxonomy look like?

At level one of this taxonomy, we would classify those appearances of the sacred containing experiences of power explicable in terms of ideological or social conditioning, the experience itself explained as a subjective response to objects / stimuli possessing no special (natural or supernatural) properties. Here, the purported appearance is no more than the result of social conditioning at its simplest level, the equivalent of transmitting an arbitrary but powerful emotional responses to some object, the way fear of black cats is transmitted from father to daughter. It may be further explicable, intra-traditionally, by relating the cultic object to a narrative which describes why that object is to be feared, venerated, and so on, or it may be that the best explanation for the taboo comes from some variety of cultural materialist explanation. Nevertheless, it is a feature of appearances at this level that none of the natural properties—decontextualized—would have the same effect on a person alien to the ideology and social conditioning of the group. Much, perhaps most, of what is considered taboo, charged with *sacredness* or *significance* probably falls in this category. This category's locus is characterized by a narrow intersubjectivity or a narrow psycho-pathological subjectivity; it is also the most fragile with respect to claims about the mediated realities (god's presence) or the universal religious properties of the artifact (contagion, good luck, etc.).

At the second level of this taxonomy would be those sacred appearances explicable not only on the basis of the subject's social conditioning but also upon the basis of the natural properties of the mediating artifact, process or experience itself. Thus, in the case of these appearances, one would expect an aesthetic response that might (at least in part) be intersubjective. Here, an analogy of experience across cultural boundaries might be provable, even if there were a *dynamic* residue of ideological conditioning which the outsider could not grasp. Most of those features of a religious object which have been described as sublime, uncanny, awful, wonderful, and so on, would fall into this category, if they are naturally explicable as producing analogous aesthetic (or emotional) responses across broad intercultural groups. Its locus would be considered to be broadly intersubjective or objective and its power would be naturally explicable.

Only the third taxonomic level would include the kind of appearance that may properly be called a *purported manifestation*. This consists of objects or experiences which apparently convey qualitative properties above and beyond natural properties or conscious ideological associations, and convey them with such sensorially, perceptual or psychological efficacy, such that these qualitative properties are the putative indices of some supernatural reality. Here we have (at least) two varieties: (a) a purported manifestation characterized by the subject's experience of the co-incidence of the natural qualities of a thing (or process) being wedded to a surplus of extraordinary qualities not typically attendant upon it and / or (b) a purported manifestation characterized by the irruption of an apparently veridical—but, nevertheless, extraordinary experience—into quotidian consciousness. In this category would be included experiences such as mystical union, visions (corporeal, imaginative, intellectual), locutions (auricular, imaginative, intellectual), revelations (absolute, conditioned, denunciatory), *stigmata*, bilocation, and so on. It may be that this class of purported manifestations is completely explicable according to psychopathology or neurophysiology. But before the explanation can be considered adequate, one must be able to describe sufficient conditions for the phenomenon's appearance. The subjective, intersubjective and objective loci of purported religious manifestation require especially careful empirical investigation because the *sui generis* category of the holy stands or falls on the basis of the claim that manifestations mediate experience of the transcendent. Sufficient naturalistic explanations of these phenomena would go a long way toward making this category empty.

My fourth and final recommendation for the rehabilitation of the category of manifestation is that those who study religion move away from studies done on the basis of data gleaned from texts in the direction of studies based upon field work. Most discussions of religious manifestation rely upon either anecdotal or first- or second-hand reports that come to us in written form (P. Wiebe 1997: 90–93). These are accounts that are already ideologically and theoretically loaded as well as rhetorically constructed, and, in many cases, far from being phenomenologically "thick." In their place, religionists must go back out into the "field." To construct useful descriptions they must undertake careful, rich empirical descriptions of such phenomena on the basis of living-informant reports guided by sound ethno-methodological procedures.

Suggested Readings

Alston, William P.
  1993 *Perceiving God: The Epistemology of Religious Experience.* Ithaca: Cornell University Press.
Eichrodt, Walther
  1961 *Theology of the Old Testament.* 2 vols. Translated by J. A. Baker. Philadelphia: Westminster Press.
Erricker, Clive
  1999 "Phenomenological Approaches," pp. 73–104 in Peter Connolly (ed.), *Approaches to the Study of Religion.* London: Cassell.
Eliade, Mircea
  1963b *Patterns in Comparative Religion.* Rosemary Sheed (trans.). New York: World Publishing Company.
Leeuw, Gerardus van der
  1938 *Religion in Essence and Manifestation: A Study in Phenomenology.* J. E. Turner (trans.). Princeton: Princeton University Press; original edn, 1933.
Morenz, Siegfried
  1973 *Egyptian Religion.* Translated by Ann E. Keep. Ithaca: Cornell University Press.
Muller-Ortega, Paul Eduardo
  1989 *The Triadic Heart of Siva: Kaula Tantricism of Abhinavagupta in the Non-Dual Shaivism of Kasmir.* Albany: SUNY Press.
Otto, Rudolf
  1959 *The Idea of the Holy: An Inquiry into the Non-Rational Factor in the Idea of the Divine and Its Relation to the Rational.* John Harvey (trans.). London: Oxford University Press; original German edn, 1917.
Persinger, Michael A.
  1987 *The Neuropsychological Bases of God Beliefs.* New York: Praeger.
Pyysiäinen, Ilkka
  1996 *Belief and Beyond: Religious Categorization of Reality.* Religionsveten-skapliga Skrifter, vol. 33. Åbo: Åbo Akademi.
Ryba, Thomas
  1992 *The Essence of Phenomenology and Its Meaning for the Scientific Study of Religion.* New York: Peter Lang.
Wiebe, Phillip
  1997 *Visions of Jesus: Direct Encounters from the New Testament to Today.* Oxford: Oxford University Press.

14

MYTH

Russell T. McCutcheon

Open a newspaper, a magazine or even a scholarly book and find the word "myth." The odds are that the writer uses the word to convey one of two meanings. First, "myth" commonly denotes widely shared beliefs that are simply false—as in Bruce Lawrence's *Shattering the Myth: Islam Beyond Violence* (1998), an attempt to expose and correct stereotypes of Muslims, or John Shelby Spong's question, *Resurrection: Myth or Reality?* (1994), or Naomi Wolf's best-selling *The Beauty Myth* (1992), a critique of the way women are forced to estimate their social and personal selves with reference to an impossible, ideal beauty standard. Second, "myth" is used to tag apparently fictional stories that originated in early human communities as attempts to explain commonplace but mysterious events in the natural world. Myths, in this sense, are understood to be aetiologies that explain the origins or causes of something that cannot be explained by scientific accounts. Although the first use of "myth" is harsher than the second, in both cases the word carries with it a strong judgment about ourselves and others: either we labor under falsehoods—unbelievable beliefs, stereotypes that disfigure those not like us, punishing standards of beauty, and so on—or, despite our best efforts, we do not understand the way the world actually works and so we use stories to come to the rescue where knowledge fails us.

Despite the fact that these two senses originated in dramatically different social and historical contexts, as we will see, they co-exist so comfortably in the popular imagination today because both are *modernist* in character in that they are based on the premise that one can somehow perceive and distinguish between *reality as it really is*, on the one hand, and *reality as it happens to be (mis)represented*, on the other. Without this modernist supposition, neither of these uses of the word "myth" would make much sense at all. And it is precisely the underlying premise of the two most common uses of "myth" that should occupy our attention when considering the category "myth."

Beware of Mythmakers

The term "myth" is not of our own recent invention; it comes to us from ancient Greece. Because it is with the Greeks that any commentary on myth must begin, surveys of the history of myth studies typically begin by recounting the difference between two Greek terms, *mythos* and *logos*. Although these two terms originally seem to have been synonyms, both signifying "word" or "story"—in the ancient world a *mythologos* was a storyteller—*mythos* eventually took on restricted meanings. When Greek intellectuals and critics began to question the traditional tales of gods and heroes during the period of the "sophistic enlightenment," *mythos* became an "implausible story" (Herodotus 2.23.1), mere "fabulous" tale-telling opposed to true history (Thucydides 1.22.4), or popular but false stories and even outright lies opposed to *logos*, which especially Plato defined as propositional statements open to demonstration and proof by means of logical reasoning (see Graf 1993: 1-2).

Plato's oppositional classification of *mythos* and *logos* has become a master trope in popular and scholarly discussions of myth. As for Greek thought, however, things were a little more complex than this. Richard Buxton (1994) has shown that Plato's clean, oppositional distinction between *mythos* and *logos* is not always evident in ancient Greek literature and thus may not have been as widely representative of Greek views on *mythos* as is now customarily thought. Since Plato's classification has been so axiomatic in Western myth studies, representing it as *the* Greek view, it may have more to do with the modern European "imaginary" Greece—among the most often used genealogical authorities for sanctioning everything from our own classificatory language to our culture—than with the historical Greek meaning of *mythos* and *logos*.

In addition to the possibility that Plato's classification functions as a myth of origins for modern myth scholarship, we should take into account another provocative ambiguity. In the modern era the term "mythology" usually denotes both a collection of a people's myths as well as the science of studying collections of myths. The former refers in Platonic manner to a grouping of stories spun out of the human imagination, that is, unverifiable discourses, while mythology as a scholarly activity connotes, in similarly Platonic fashion, rational, demonstrable argumentation, the trading in verifiable discourses. The scholarly *mythologos*, the teller of scientific truths, thus works both in concert and in contest with the folk *mythologos*, the teller of fabulous and fantastic tales. It would seem, getting ahead of ourselves a bit, that it is not all that clear who the mythologists really are.

We see here one instance of the messy state of the category "myth." Although it is usually used as a simple classificatory term to set off one kind of discourse from another, it turns out that the category is often *intellectually committed* to an *a priori* clean distinction between fact and fiction, truth and falsehood, fabulous delusion and scientific lucidity, us and them, just as it is *rhetorically wielded* to reinforce these oppositions by coordinating them with a scale of moral, social and political values. Hence the power to label someone's story as myth, and to classify our world-view as "scientific" over against their world-view as "mythic," is not only to classify stories, but people (are they gullible or intelligent?), societies (are they uncivilized or civilized?) and cultures (are they primitive or advanced?). The apparently straightforward distinction between false and true tales (*mythos* vs. *logos*) is therefore loaded with social significance and consequence.

For example, we would be naïve to think that Plato opposed *mythos* with the superior rationality of *logos* simply out of pure theoretical interest. Despite expressing what seems to be a sincere admiration for the talent of the poet, that is, the story-teller (*Republic* 398a; see also 568a–c), Plato thought that poets are dangerous. But why?

> The mimetic poet sets up in each individual soul a vicious constitution, by fashioning phantoms far removed from reality, and by currying favour with the senseless element that cannot distinguish the greater from the lesser, but calls the same thing now one, now the other. (*Republic* 605c)

Readers who are acquainted with the rest of the *Republic* might wonder why, if such imitation and re-presentation by means of story-telling should be disallowed, Plato is so free to tell his own story that sounds suspiciously like a *mythos* of origins to authorize his just state (*Republic* 414c–415e)? What appears, then, to be ultimately at stake in Plato's—and our?—distinction of *mythos* from *logos* is a contest for the right to define the proper constitution of the state, the right to define the proper constitution of "the good," "the true" and "the just." It was a contest in which "the myths that Plato didn't like ... were lies and the myths he liked ... were truths," as Wendy Doniger bluntly puts it (1998: 3). Plato's *mythos* was not so much an innocent classificatory term as a word that he used to censure views he did not like in the arena of public discourse and persuasion.

Turning to a more recent example, we could demonstrate how the *mythos–logos* distinction was once strategically allied to European expansionism and colonialism, an interest for which people characterized as primitive, uncivilized and gullible do come in handy as needy beneficiaries of European "civilization" (Bowler 1992; R. Williams 1980). If we throw in the once common view of European writers of the early modern era concerning the dawn of a slow but steady victory of science (*logos*) over mere superstition and religion (*mythos*), a dawn that must not only enlighten Europe but all the nations of the globe, we see once again that the classification "myth" is far from an innocuous academic label. It is instead a master signifier that authorizes and reproduces a specific world-view.

With all this in mind, there just might be something to the fact that an ancient storyteller and the modern scientific study of mythology bear the same name. When thinking about the category of myth, therefore, we must reckon with, and not evade the possibility that myth is everything and nothing at the same time. It is *the* true story or a false one, revelation or deception, sacred or vulgar, real or fictional, symbol or tool, archetype or stereotype ... Thus, instead of there being a real thing, myth, there is a thriving *industry*, manufacturing and marketing what is called "myth." "Myth" is an illusion—an appearance conjured or "construct" created by artists and intellectuals toiling away in the workshops of the myth industry. (Strenski 1987: 1–2)

To anticipate the conclusion of this essay, despite our apparent interest in talking about real things—myths that are lived, told, written down, anthologized and studied—we are continually struck by how our very judgment as to just what is and what is not a myth betrays some generally undetected logic inherent in our own social world and does not necessarily tell us about something that is self-evidently inherent in data we classify as myth.

Some Workshops in the Myth Industry

Although the use of the label "myth" to distinguish false from true stories continues to live on, the story of "myth" in the course of the past several centuries of modern scholarship fortunately is richer than that. Because there are a wealth of good resources that survey the many uses of "myth" (see for example Bolle 1968, 1983, 1987; Bolle et al. 1974; P. Cohen 1969; Doty 1986, 1999; Eliade 1973, 1991; Graf 1993: 9–56; Kirk 1973; Segal 1980; Vernant 1980: 203–260), we will only briefly sketch some of the major types here.

1. *Pre-scientific explanations of natural phenomena.* Prominent among a group of nineteenth-century anthropologists was the view that myths are attempts on the part of early human beings to explain aspects of their natural environment. This understanding of myth was articulated influentially by the German philologist Christian Gottlob Heyne (1729–1812), though he had forerunners (on Heyne and his predecessors see Graf 1993: 9–19). Heyne recovered and rehabilitated the term *mythos*, preferring it over his contemporaries' use of *fabula* (fable) which Heyne considered to be too tied up with notions of the fictive and absurd to capture what he considered the serious intent of *mythos* (Graf 1993: 10). As with so many of his contemporaries, Heyne believed that the key to understanding myths is located at their origin, which he pursued by a textual "paring knife" approach (i.e., source-critical and philological methods) on the assumption that the textualized myths available to him had accreted to themselves many additions and modifications in their oral and literary history. He concluded that

myth arose in prehistoric times, during the childhood of mankind . . .
[He] did not suppose that myth was a bizarre invention of primitive
man; instead, he thought that it came into being naturally and
inevitably at the moment when early man, overawed or frightened by
some natural phenomenon, first sought to explain it, or when,
moved by a feeling of gratitude toward some exceptional person, he
wished to recount and extol a person's deeds. (Graf 1993: 10)

This view reflects a commonplace in the scholarship of the eighteenth and
nineteenth centuries, a view that culminates in the Intellecualist tradition
associated with such figures as F. Max Müller, Herbert Spencer, Andrew
Lang, Edward B. Tylor and James G. Frazer. As suggested above, this
understanding of myth continues to dominate today's popular imagination.

2. *Tales of heroes.* For Heyne, myths were an explanation of natural phenomena
    as well as a memorialization of dramatic past events or heroic deeds, a view
    that goes back to the philosopher Euhemerus of Messene (340–260 B.C.E.),
    who suggested that tales recounting the deeds of the Olympian gods actually
    were disguised stories that glorified the exploits of real, but long dead figures.
    In the modern era, this approach—sometimes called Euhemerism—was
    reintroduced by one of the fathers of evolutionary theory, Herbert Spencer.
    Spencer argued that the historic origins of the belief in supernatural beings was
    to be found in the ancient worship of actual but long-dead ancestors. Over
    time, such ancestors came to be venerated as powerful beings (ghosts, gods,
    etc.), who were satisfied by means of ritual offerings. "Ancestor worship is the
    root of every religion," Spencer concluded, and myths were both the proof for
    and the access to the historic "roots" of religion.

3. *Expression of mythopoeic mentality.* Another line of European thought
    focused on the emotive or expressive sources and functions of myth.
    Rather than understanding myth as an attempt to explain the natural
    world, it could be taken as the spontaneous expression of what many
    label the "mythopoeic mentality." For instance, Bernard de Fontenelle
    (1657–1757) regarded myths as the evidence of a so-called "primitive
    mentality," a form of pre-logical cognition and rationality that pre-dates
    logical and scientific rationality in the evolutionary history of the human
    mind. Fontenelle then drew a direct link between ancient human beings
    and contemporary "savages" (e.g., Iroquois, Laplanders, Kaffirs), a link
    that allowed him to make inferences about ancient people by studying
    the emotional life of his "savage" contemporaries. In this tradition of
    myth scholarship we could also place the early twentieth-century
    philosopher Ernst Cassirer, a key figure in focusing attention on the
    fact that what sets humans apart from other members of the animal
    world is our ability to traffic in symbols. In the words of Percy Cohen
    (1969: 339), for Cassirer

myth-making can no more be explained or explained away than can the making of poetry or music: myth is one way of using language for expressive purposes, through the symbolic devises of metonymy [when one thing stands in for another] and synecdoche [when a part stands in for the whole] and myth-making is, in some respects, an end in itself.

For yet others, the "savage" was an appealing figure in its own right. Johann Gottfried Herder (1744–1803), for example, thought that the more "savage" a group was, the more spontaneous and alive they were. Valorizing immediate "experience" and its raw expression, Herder and other nineteenth-century Romantics evaluated myths positively as "repositories of experience far more vital and powerful than those obtainable from what was felt to be the artificial art and poetry of the aristocratic civilization of contemporary Europe" (Bolle et al. 1974: 718). Assuming that "religious" emotions are somehow different from other experiential states, myth becomes the medium by which those emotions, inspired by the numinous or the holy, are expressed and made public. A fairly coherent tradition develops around this assumption of religion as "feeling" or "experience" which is expressed by myths or other phenomena that can be studied in an attempt to gain access to religious experience. Joachim Wach's dictum that myths should be read as the "theoretical expression of religious experience" (Wach 1958: 65) is a more recent statement of a very popular tradition that continues among scholars and the general public alike. (On the problems of "experience" as an analytic category, see J. W. Scott 1991; Sharf 1998.)

4. *Social dreaming.* In some psychology-based theorizing, myths function on the social level much as dreams, nervous habits or slips of the tongue do in the life of the individual. That is, myths are thought of as the disguised expressions of anti-social but completely natural desires and wishes. Sigmund Freud (1913; see Segal 1996: vol. 1) painted a picture of the human condition as one in which individuals attempt to fulfill their private needs for pleasure (e.g., sex, food, power) while simultaneously attempting to secure their place in a larger social unit where such wish-fulfillment is rarely allowed for the sake of maintaining the social unit (e.g., to preserve family harmony few of us actually tell our family members what we really think of them). Freud theorized that to be human means one is caught in a catch-22 of the worst kind: we are stuck with completely natural wishes that we have no choice but to suppress and internalize for the relative harmony of social life. Such suppression, however, creates anxiety. Sooner or later this repression-induced anxiety builds to such a point that the repressions must be let out, but only in a disguised form (since we can never actually act on the real desire), thereby giving vent to the anti-social desires but in a more socially acceptable manner. As a cruel footnote to this state of affairs, the guilt associated with acting out

disguised desires, that is, expressing desires inauthentically, produces new anxiety and the cycle is endlessly repeated.

To be human, therefore, is to be neurotic to varying degrees, and myth is a narrative mechanism, a kind of collective therapy of neurotic desire, that allows social groups to act out their desires and fantasies while allowing them to remain a coherent social unit. For instance, what better way is there to fulfill ones love–hate relationship with authority figures (based on desires of incest and patricide) than by telling and retelling, acting and living out tales of children rising up against parents and siblings battling each other? Be it the ancient Greek myths (e.g., Hesiod's tale of the origin of the gods in the *Theogony*), biblical stories (e.g., the fratricide in the Cain and Abel story, or the sacrifice of Jesus, the supposed son of God) or modern movies, novels and soap operas, this view sees them all as narrative vehicles for projecting and momentarily resolving the inevitable and never-ending anxiety associated with social existence.

5. *Expressions of the collective unconscious.* Other psychologists see myths not as mechanisms for venting and coping with anxiety but as symbolic messages projected from ourselves and directed to ourselves. Following Carl Jung, these scholars understand myths as the means whereby aspects of our personality that are banished to our unconscious are given symbolic voice in the forms of certain archetypes (e.g., the Wise Old Man, the Earth Mother, the Innocent Virgin). We therefore ignore the messages of myths to our own peril, for they are the expressions of our full potential and true personality (Hudson 1966; Segal 1998). In our time, the late Joseph Campbell is perhaps the best known advocate of this viewpoint. Following a number of anthropological theorists before him, Campbell identifies a universal three-part *quest motif* involving departure–confrontation and change–return that comprises heroic stories told the world over throughout time. (Campbell draws attention to the exploits of Luke Skywalker in George Lucas's *Star Wars* trilogy as one of the most recent instances of this age-old narrative.) Our attraction to these stories is understood as a function of our identification with their archetypical images (e.g., the viewer becomes Luke Skywalker or maybe Darth Vadar), an identification that helps us to realize and balance the various aspects of our own personality. Campbell asserts that the proper analysis of stories as different as the adventures of Odysseus and the televised images of the Apollo astronauts splashing-down in the ocean can provide evidence of certain fundamental aspects of not just individual human psyches but also aspects of our common human need to "follow your bliss" (Joseph Campbell 1968, 1988; Noel 1990)—a recommendation that, for some, earned Campbell the title of guru to the yuppy generation (B. Gill 1989).

6. *Structuralism.* For modern scholars of myth, the challenge generally is to see these apparently illogical and fantastic narratives as very much ordered and therefore understandable. Following the anthropologist Claude Lévi-Strauss

(1972b, 1975–78), himself influenced by the structural linguistics of Ferdinand de Saussure, some scholars study myths much as one studies language: as structured public evidence of the order of human cognition itself. Myths are structured in a fashion similar to the structuredness of human language which is functional and meaningful only because of the complex inter-relationships among its basic units such as letters, phonemes, words, sentences, and so on. Structuralists thus study myths not in terms of their historical development and change (the Euhemerist approach), nor as evidence of a pre-scientific rationality (the Intellectualist approach), nor as expressions of some raw emotional or mystical mentality (mythopoeic analysis), nor by artificially isolating one of their many elements in an allegorical hunt for archetypes (Jung). Rather, structuralists think that the message of a myth results from how its elements relate to each other as part of a coherent structure (Gordon 1981; Leach 1967, 1976).

7. *Myths as truth*. The theories of myth surveyed so far obviously arise from a diverse number of disciplinary fields (anthropology, philosophy, psychology, etc.). Drawing on these and other theories, a group of scholars in the history of religions school (a designation that translates the German *Religionswissenschaft*, literally "science of religion") has developed an approach to the study of myths that is particular to much scholarship on religion. From this viewpoint, myths are stories that convey, in some veiled, encoded or symbolic form, a social group's deepest personal and social values. Although programmatically exemplified in the works of Mircea Eliade (1959b, 1960, 1963a, 1974), myths as veiled, deep truths is the operative assumption in most current scholarship on religion. Here is a representative sampling:

> Myth is above all a story that is *believed*, believed to be true, and that people continue to believe despite sometimes massive evidence that it is, in fact, a lie ... [W]hat a myth *is* is a story that is sacred to and shared by a group of people who find their most important meanings in it; it is a story believed to have been composed in the past about an event in the past, or, more rarely, in the future, an event that continues to have meaning in the present because it is remembered; it is a story that is part of a larger group of stories. (Doniger 1998: 2)

> The governing function of myth is to reveal exemplary models for all rites and all meaningful human activities. (Eliade 1991: 4)

> Myth is an expression of the sacred in words: it reports realities and events from the origin of the world that remain valid for the basis and purpose of all there is. Consequently, a myth functions as a model for human activity, society, wisdom, and knowledge. (Bolle 1987: 271)

> Myth is a narrative of origins, taking place in primordial time, a time other than that of everyday reality. (Ricoeur 1987: 273)

> Myth is a distinctive expression of a narrative that states a paradigmatic truth. (Long 1987: 94)

> *Myth* is the *first form* of intellectual explanation of religious apprehensions. (Wach 1951: 39)

Encoded in these tales (i.e. tales "dating" from when the gods walked the earth, so these authors might argue) are the abiding values that help to form and maintain a social group. For example, myths told and acted out in ritual reinforce the value that humans are at the center of an orderly, created world, or the value that despite being a unified whole society is a complex hierarchy and all of its members have their own particular duties and responsibilities. Regardless of how reality *really is*, the view of myth as veiled communication of the true constitution of the world and humanity's place in it suggests that in studying myths the modern reader can learn how past or distant societies believed reality—and their place in it—to have been.

At the heart of the "myth as truth" approach evidently is the attempt by scholars to celebrate myths as containing some sort of profound truth that "cannot be expressed in simple propositions" (Sharpe 1971: 43). "Mythology," to quote the late Italian historian of religion Raffaele Pettazzoni, "*as the science of myth*, must quit its traditional anti-mythical attitude. It must be livened by the spirit of humanism, by an attitude of sympathy towards the myth as a mark and a document of our human estate" (1954: 36, emphasis added). Studying myths thus amounts to divining our deepest human "estate" (essence), for all myths are generated by that estate and convey it, if only we apprehend the mythic narratives rightly. According to this view, the proper use of "other people's myth" means recognizing that "their myths have always been our myths, though we may not have known it; we recognize ourselves in those myths more vividly than we have ever recognized ourselves in the myths of our culture" (Doniger-O'Flaherty 1986: 224). With this sympathetic turn in myth scholarship, the distance between the liar and the truth-teller has disappeared, as has the distance between the mythmaker and the myth analyst. For, insofar as we are all parts of social groups we all have myths, myths we live by (to echo a phrase of Joseph Campbell). If the academic *study* of religion is understood as something other than the *practice* of religion, then this sympathetic turn (and it is, rightly put, *sympathetic* rather than *empathetic*) has profound implications for whether it is possible to study religion in an academic sense.

Redescribing Myth as Something Ordinary

Despite certain differences, the approaches I have outlined are unified in that all see myths either as a terribly false or as a deeply true narrative object to be read and interpreted. Common to all these approaches is the assumption that "myth" is the product, the effect or an evidentiary trace of some absent, forgotten, distant—that is, not immediately apparent—phenomenon or human intention. Thus the mission of myth scholarship has generally been construed as a reconstructive and hermeneutic labor bent on ferreting out the truth or falsity of myth, on decoding and then recovering obscured meanings. In short, common to all approaches has been the view that myths are signs of such personal or interior causes and intentions as (1) a mentality, (2) an emotional or psychological "experience," (3) a universal human "estate" such as Human Nature. Given the utter difficulties of studying such interiorized dispositions and mentalities—after all, scholarship can only examine that which is public, observable and documentable—is there another way of defining and tackling the issue of myth? Can the category "myth" be redescribed and the study of myth be rectified?

Recall the definition of myth offered by Doniger: "what a myth *is* is a story that is sacred to and shared by a group of people who find their most important meanings in it" (1998: 2). Most scholars of religion would accept this definition as straightforward and uncontroversial, but attention needs to be focused on two words: "sacred" and "important." Both words convey socially-based value judgments. After all, the word sacred comes from a Latin root that means "to set apart." It seems that deeming myths as sacred, true, essential, paradigmatic or important is somewhat circular, for what makes something sacred or true in the first place? Thinking of Eliade's understanding of myths and rituals as the apolitical containers of primordial truths—truths that are repeatedly made manifest in retellings and reenactments—we can reply that "primordiality does not emerge out of natural givenness, but is an essentially fragile social construction which—like every social construction—needs special rituals and communicative efforts [myths] in order to come into existence and be maintained" (Eisenstadt and Giesen 1995: 78). Taking this view makes yet another part of Doniger's definition stand out: she noted that "a group of people ... *find* their most important meanings *in* [myth]" (1998: 2, emphasis added). Might it not be that a group of people *fabricate* their most important meanings *by means* of myth?

Instead of perpetuating the view that myths are self-evidently meaningful things (whether true or false, oral or written or ritually performed) that can be learned, retold, recorded, interpreted and studied, I would like to suggest that we redescribe the term "myth." Let us think of it not so much as a kind narrative identifiable by its content (e.g., traditional tales of the gods or ancient heroes) as a *technique* or *strategy*. Let us suppose that myth is not so much a genre with relatively stable characteristics that allow us to distinguish myth from folk tale, saga, legend and fable (Bolle et al. 1974: 715–717; Graf 1993: 6–8) as a class of *social argumentation* found in all human cultures. Let us entertain the possibility that myths are not things akin to nouns, but *active processes* akin to verbs. Instead of saying that "a people's myths reflect, express, and explore the people's self-image" (Bolle et al. 1974: 715), or that the contents of myths act as a "pragmatic charter of primitive faith and moral wisdom" (Malinowski 1926), a shift in perspective allows us to suggest (1) that myths are not special (or "sacred") but ordinary human means of fashioning and authorizing their lived-in and believed-in "worlds," (2) that myth as an ordinary rhetorical device in social construction and maintenance makes *this* rather than *that* social identity possible in the first place and (3) that a people's use of the *label* "myth" reflects, expresses, explores and legitimizes their own self-image. To build on Malinowski, we can say that myth is the vehicle whereby any of a variety of possible social charters is rendered exemplary, authoritative, singular, unique, as something that cannot be imagined differently.

Redescribed in this manner, the study of myth becomes not just the domain of historians of religion conversant with long dead languages and cultures—their data understood by them to be "an autonomous, hermetically-sealed territory" (Buxton 1994: 14)—but the domain of a far wider collection of scholars who study the ways by which human beings the world over construct, authorize and contest their social identities (on religious studies as a domain within culture studies, see Fitzgerald 1997, 1999). No longer would myths be considered unique, symbolic, religious narratives, identified by the fact that they are "specific accounts of gods or superhuman beings involved in extraordinary events or circumstances in a time that is unspecified but which is understood as existing apart from ordinary human experience" (Bolle et al. 1974: 715). Instead, scholars would query just what it is about *these* tales—and what it is about many *other* modes of public discourse—that leads people, including scholars, to boost them into the realm of the extraordinary in the first place. After all, for the scholar in the human sciences, the data of human behavior is ordinary (which does not mean simple or simplistic) to begin with in the sense that it is *human* behavior. Myths thus are utterly mundane and assigning them an "extraordinary" status as a precondition for studying them rightly is to begin our study with a mistake that deflects us from a more interesting and productive scholarly aim: undertaking the difficult study of the mechanisms whereby societies create the extraordinary from the everyday. Pierre Bourdieu (1998: 21) puts the issue properly:

> There is nothing more difficult to convey than reality in all its ordinariness. Flaubert was fond of saying that it takes a lot of hard work to portray mediocrity. Sociologists run into this problem all the time: How can we make the ordinary extraordinary and evoke ordinariness in such a way that people will see just how extraordinary it is?

While the study of specific types of stories—stories with gods set at the beginning or the end of time, for example—is indeed fascinating and well worthwhile, would it not be far more interesting to study the mechanisms whereby just these and not other stories became important or sacred to begin with? Taking for granted the importance, the sacredness or the extraordinary character of certain stories only puts off asking what I take to be a more basic question: how is it that individual human beings accomplish, in part by dealing in myths, the all too ordinary but fascinating trick of coming together and acting collectively over great spans of time and space?

Myth as What-Goes-Without-Saying

To begin answering this question, we can appeal to Roland Barthes who examines the process of "mythification," or even "mystification," a term that might be more appropriate than "myth." For when he identifies myths he examines not stable stories but networks of actions, assumptions and representations—what other scholars might term a discourse. Like Bourdieu after him, Barthes' interest concerns the manner in which the ordinary is made to stand out, is set apart (made sacred) and made to appear extraordinary. Barthes therefore problematizes the " 'naturalness' with which newspapers, art, and common sense constantly dress up a reality which, even though it is the one we live in, is undoubtedly determined by history" (Barthes 1972: 11; see also Moriarty 1991 and Saper 1997). For Barthes, then, myth "is not defined by the object of its message, but by *the way in which it utters its message*: there are formal limits to myth, there are no 'substantial ones' " (1972: 117; emphasis added). He departs from the traditional way of defining myth with reference to its unique substance or content and opts, instead, to see myth as a particular type of human endeavor displayed in but not limited to storytelling. Breaking away from some long-held notions, Barthes answers his own rhetorical question: "Everything, then, can be a myth? Yes, I believe this" (1972: 117).

Within the field of religious studies we find a related sense of myth as human activity—this time the active process is aptly renamed "mythmaking"—in the work of the scholar of Christian origins, Burton Mack, whose most recent book is subtitled, *The Making of the Christian Myth* (1995). For Mack, the art of mythmaking "turn[s] the collective agreements of a people into truths held to be self-evident" (1995: 301). As noted by the French scholar of ancient Greece and Rome, Paul Veyne, "truth is the most variable of all measures. It is not a transhistorical invariant but a *work of the constitutive imagination* ... [N]ot only the very aim of our divergent assertions but our criteria and means of obtaining true ideas—in short our programs—vary without our realizing it" (1988: 117–118, emphasis added). According to this position, we do not find, discern or interpret truths and meanings. Rather, in every age and culture people actively *work* to selectively *make* some things true and meaningful and other things false and meaningless. If we see myth as one way of making meanings, then it is little wonder that the rhetorical mechanisms which have constructed the seemingly self-evident meaning and authority of both the Bible and the U.S. Constitution is equally interesting to scholars like Mack. Both documents are particularly powerful instances where active processes have dressed up what might otherwise be mundane and forgettable historical moments as extraordinary ones.

I can think of no better example of such practices than the familiar words used in the U.S. Declaration of Independence: "We hold these truths to be self-evident." There is a rhetoric embedded here that generally passes by unnoticed. These words *do* something, but what? The opening of the Declaration effectively removes readers from the tug-and-pull of the contingent, historical world and places them in an abstract, ahistorical realm where such things as truths are obvious, enduring and self-evident. Through this rhetoric of self-evidence, then, the long European history of philosophical, political and social debate and development which eventually led to this document—and the nation-state founded upon it—is completely obscured, as if the Declaration, and later the U.S. Constitution as well, spontaneously arose from the ground fully formed. After all, self-evidences do not have a history, they leave no trace and they are not manufactured. They simply appear and announce their existence.

Although lost on the masses of people, these so-called self-evidences were perceived by a privileged class of "Constitutional framers." Within such texts, then, there is also a rhetoric of discernment—only some of us have "eyes to see and ears to hear." Just as the pre-existent Veda was heard only by the Indian *rishis* of old, the pre-existent Qu'ran was heard only by Muhammad, the pre-existent voice of YHWH prompted a response only in some listeners, and the Christian "Word" (*logos*) which pre-existed creation itself was truly heard by only a few, so too the content of the Declaration benefits from (i.e., is authorized by) not just a rhetoric of self-evidence but by the privileged status of those wise or lucky enough to have discerned it. To push this a little further, it is wholly misleading to talk of the document being authorized, for this document cannot exist apart from the social world from which it arose and which it supports. Therefore, the all too real world of its framers and users is what ultimately gains legitimacy. Considering the manner in which many "founding fathers" of the U.S. continued their practice of owning slaves, the supposedly self-evident, timeless rights of equality, liberty and the pursuit of happiness are circumscribed in terms of the interests of a rather narrow ruling élite of land-owning white males.

Mythmaking and Social Formation

Reconceiving mythmaking as the ongoing process of constructing, authorizing and reconstructing social identities or social formations would be to create a "catalog of strategies for *maintaining* paradoxes, *fighting* over dissonances, and *surviving* [and recovering from] breakdowns" (Lease 1994: 475)—breakdowns in so much as social identity is not eternal. After all, despite the success of certain ways of producing social identities, people today do not identify themselves as Roman citizens—unless, of course, one recalls how Mussolini and the Italian fascists tried to "recover" the glorious Roman past in their attempts to forge a new Italian social identity in the mid twentieth century.

Such a catalog of strategies would amount to a map of the many social sites where tales, behaviors, institutions, clothing styles, even architectural details are used to generate and defend (and sometimes to overthrow) authority (Lincoln 1994). Acting as a sort of demythologizer reminiscent of a tradition in New Testament studies that was made famous by Rudolf Bultmann (1958), Burton Mack (1995: 11) writes:

> Social formation and mythmaking are group activities that go together, each stimulating the other in a kind of dynamic feedback system. Both speed up when new groups form in times of social disintegration and cultural change. Both are important indicators of the personal and intellectual energies invested in experimental movements ... Social formation and mythmaking fit together like hand and glove.

This reciprocal relationship between social formation and mythmaking was made clear as early as Émile Durkheim's *The Elementary Forms of Religious Life* (1995 [1912]: 425).

> A society can neither create nor recreate itself without creating some kind of ideal by the same stroke. This creation is not a sort of optional extra step by which society, being already made, merely adds finishing touches; it is the act by which society makes itself, and remakes itself, periodically.

In keeping with the Durkheimian tradition of sociological studies on religion and myth, we could say that a social formation is the activity of experimenting with, authorizing or combating, and reconstituting widely circulated ideal types, idealizations or, better put, mythifications that function to control the means of and sites where social significance is selected, symbolized and communicated. It is this tradition of scholarship on mythmaking to which Gary Lease contributes when he speaks of religions as totalized systems of meaning, or J. Z. Smith when he thinks of ritual as exercising an "economy of significance" and of myth as a "strategy for dealing with a situation" (1982c: 56; 1978a: 97). I place Roland Barthes in this tradition as well, for he speaks of the ways myths authorize contingent History by re-presenting it as necessary Nature. Because this is a tradition that sees mythmaking as an ideological activity, we also find Bruce Lincoln here. Over a decade ago (1986: 164) he noted that

> an ideology ... is not just an ideal against which social reality is measured or an end toward the fulfillment of which groups and individuals aspire. It is also, and this is much more important, a screen that strategically veils, mystifies, or distorts important aspects of real social processes.

Mythmaking is a species of ideology production, of ideal-making, where "ideal" is conceived not as an abstract, absolute value but as a contingent, localized construct that comes to represent and simultaneously reproduce certain specific social values *as if* they were inevitable and universal.

Social formation by means of mythmaking, then, is explicitly caught up in the ideological strategies of totalization, naturalization, rationalization and universalization. With Benedict Anderson we could say that social formations are based on mythic "ontological reality [that is portrayed as] apprehensible ... through a single, privileged system of re-presentation" (Anderson 1991: 14). Accordingly, Durkheim's thoughts on the creation and authorization of "some kind of ideal" find their modern equivalent in the works of the authors just named. Social formations are the ongoing results of mythmaking activity (where I see mythmaking as a discourse involving acts and institutions as well as narratives), an activity that unites into a totalized system of representation what Mack refers to as the epic past, the historical past, the historical present, the anticipated historical future and the hoped-for epic future in one narrative, behavioral and institutional system (on the production of history see Braun 1999). Where but in religions and forms of nationalism do we see this happening most effectively?

We should not forget that despite attempts to construct a past or future long removed from the present, mythmaking takes place in a specific socio-political moment and supports a specific judgment about the here and now. Myths and rituals, therefore, do not simply project consensual agreements that have been reached; they do not merely communicate some specific substance so much as give shape and authority (i.e., significance) to this or that system of judgments and messages. Myths present *one particular* and therefore contestable viewpoint as if it were an "agreement that has been reached" by "we the people" (a phrase that is part of a powerful mythic rhetoric common in the history of the U.S.). For instance, to take up Mack's use of the contemporary American situation as an example, a rhetoric that brings together references to the founding fathers (the epic past), the image of the patriarchal nuclear family of the 1950s (historical past), current crime rates, teenage pregnancy rates, abortion and divorce rates (one of many particular presents), projections for budget reductions in the next ten years (historical future), all of which contribute to the future well being or "security" of the American nation (epic future), is the consummate art of mythmaking. By means of mythmaking, the historicity and specificity of each of these elements is collated into one grand unfolding narrative. By means of a disguised or undetected ideological slippage, "is" becomes "ought," the myth of presence and self-identity is established, and value-neutral "change" is judged to be either good or bad, progressive or retrograde (Jameson 1988b: 17; Geertz 1968: 97). Mythmaking, "a particular *register* of ideology, which elevates certain meanings to numinous status" (Eagleton 1991: 188–189), has here done its work.

Evidently, this view of "myth" differs significantly from the suggestion that, because "mythlike ideologies" such as capitalism and communism have taken on greater prominence in recent time, "the word ideology might indeed be replaced, in much contemporary discussion about politics, by the term mythology" (Bolle et al. 1974: 727). The tradition of writers I have surveyed would hold just the opposite position: by means of mythmaking local, symbolic worlds of significance are authorized and naturalized by being (mis)taken for or actively portrayed as universal, literal ones. This is the role of ideology in human affairs.

Because one of the premises of all social-scientific scholarship is that all human doing is contextualized within historical (social, political, economic, gendered, etc.) pressures and influences, we must therefore understand all such doings partial and linked to specific temporally and culturally located worlds. "There is no primordium," as J. Z. Smith reminds us (1982a: xiii), "it is all history." Or, as Marx and Engels put it, "social life is essentially *practical*. All mysteries which lead theory to mysticism find their rational solution in human practice and in the comprehension of human practice" (1970: 122). Acknowledging this ensures that we do not lose sight of the fact that mythmaking allows a sleight of hand; it is the art of manufacturing, from raw materials which are by definition only part of the whole, total symbolic systems. Because social values, truths and ideals are hardly universal, because, as Durkheim noted, the "mystery that appears to surround them is entirely superficial and fades upon closer scrutiny . . ., [when one pulls] aside the veil with which the mythological imagination covered them" (1995: 431), there is an inherent contradiction embedded at the core of social formations—a point taught to us by Marx long ago. Accordingly, there is much at stake for members of a social formation to maintain the mythic status of the system of representation and signification— their very self-identity is continually at stake! As Lease comments concerning the inherent contradictions of all totalizing practices, "a society cannot live without [totalizing practices], nor can it live with them" (1994: 475). It is precisely the mythmakers (theologians, politicians, teachers, pundits and, yes, even and too often scholars of religion) who develop discourses that obscure and thereby manage these contradictions (see further McCutcheon 1998c).

"Pay No Attention to the Man Behind the Curtain"

Mythmaking, then, is the business of making "particular and contingent worldviews appear to be ubiquitous and absolute" (Arnal 1997: 317). Social formation by means of mythmaking is nothing other than the reasonable response to the inevitable social disruptions, contradictions and incongruities that characterize the ordinary human condition. Systems of social significance, encoded within narratives of the epic past and the anticipated plenary future, coordinated within behavioral and institutional systems of cognitive and social control, characterize our responses to the various incongruities and disruptions that come with historical existence: "myth both unites the group and provides an interpretive framework for coping with the exigencies of, and threats from, the natural world" (Giddens 1984: 265). Mythmaking might even be the preeminent means for creating cognitive and social continuity amidst the discontinuities of life. As Jean Baudrillard suggests, it is our way of maintaining our accumulative culture by way of "stockpiling the past in plain sight" (1994: 10). Or, as the scholar of early Christianity Ron Cameron puts it: "Religion as mythmaking reflects thoughtful, though ordinary, modes of ingenuity and labor" (1996: 39).

We should thus expect that mythmaking is a highly political affair, that "mythmaking is an everyday practice which permeates the discourse of political communicators" (Flood 1996: 275). As Flood goes on to say, when redescribed in this fashion,

> there is no need to consider myths as variant expressions of psychological archetypes. There is no need to posit a special form of consciousness or to situate the process of mythmaking within a consciousness or to situate the process of mythmaking within a psychopathology of the irrational. There is nothing strange about mythmaking There is nothing wrong with it. It is an entirely normal way of making political events intelligible in the light of ideological beliefs.

Classifying and studying so-called myths of origins, end-times, tricksters, and so on, as if these tales express some deep, abiding truths that require some kind of deep, abiding appreciation on the part of scholars, leaves this entire form of political analysis untouched—a point brought home with sharp clarity in Graeme MacQueen's critique of Alan Dundes' (1984) collection of essays by myth theorists, most of whom understand myths as essentially apolitical.

The implication of all this for scholars of religion is that if we take for granted the already established meaning and unquestioned authority of "myth"—myth's sacredness—we too may have come under its spell and, as a consequence, perpetuate a politics of which we may be unaware (Cady 1998; McCutcheon 1997c, 1998d; Murphy 1998). In so doing, we miss out on asking: What is going on when we constantly dress up our own creations in "decorative displays" to make them pass for what Barthes calls "what-goes-without-saying"? How can the descriptive "is" so smoothly become the prescriptive "ought"? If anything, I presume that Bolle's use of the phrase "expressions of the sacred in words" would attract Barthes' interest in demystification just as much as does professional wrestling, the striptease and even margarine, only to name a few cultural goodies that occupy his attention (Barthes 1972). Where historians of religion are often content to employ a purely descriptive, supposedly value-free phenomenological method simply to determine what people hold to be sacred, exemplary and paradigmatic, Barthes' and Mack's critical methods identify the strategies that construct the set-apartness of various conventions, beliefs and practices in the first place.

The gain of this redescriptive turn in myth studies is its applicability to all human efforts to construct a place beyond criticism, then to equate a particular instance of human society and culture with the "place beyond criticism." After this redescriptive turn, myths are no longer merely stories. Rather, myths are the product and the means of creating authority by removing a claim, behavior, artifact or institution from human history and hence from the realm of human doings. A rectified study of myths thus turns out to be study of mythmaking. Despite my disagreement with much scholarship on myth, I think that Bolle, Buxton and J. Z. Smith were on the right track when they suggested that "a myth has its authority not by proving itself but by presenting itself" (1974: 715). In attempting to manufacture an unassailable safe haven for the storage of social charters and "worlds," mythmakers, tellers and performers draw on a complex network of disguised assumptions, depending on their listeners not to ask certain sorts of questions, not to speak out of turn, to listen respectfully, applaud when prompted and, in those famous lines from *The Wizard of Oz*, to "pay no attention to that man behind the curtain."

Suggested Readings

Barthes, Roland
> 1972 *Mythologies*. Annette Lavers (trans.). New York: Wang and Hill.

Bolle, Kees W., Richard G. A. Buxton and Jonathan Z. Smith
> 1974 "The Nature, Functions and Types of Myths." *Encyclopaedia Britannica*. 15th edn, Vol. 24, 715–732.

Cohen, Percy
> 1969 "Theories of Myth." *Man*, September, 337–353.

Detienne, Marcel
> 1991 "The Interpretation of Myths: Nineteenth- and Twentieth-Century Theories," pp. 5–10 in Yves Bonnefoy (ed.), *Mythologies*, vol. 1. Chicago: University of Chicago Press.

Doty, William G.
> 1986 *Mythography: The Study of Myths and Rituals*. Tuscaloosa: University of Alabama Press.

Eliade, Mircea
> 1991 "Toward a Definition of Myth," pp. 3–5 in Yves Bonnefoy (ed.), *Mythologies*, vol. 1. Chicago: University of Chicago Press.

Lincoln, Bruce
    1986   *Myth, Cosmos, and Society: Indo-European Themes of Creation and Destruction.* Cambridge, MA: Harvard University Press.
    1989   *Discourse and the Construction of Society: Comparative Studies of Myth, Ritual, and Classification.* New York: Oxford University Press.
    1994   *Authority: Construction and Corrosion.* Chicago: University of Chicago Press.
MacQueen, Graeme
    1988   "Whose Sacred History? Reflections on Myth and Dominance." *Studies in Religion / Sciences religieuses* 17: 143–157.
Segal, Robert A.
    1980   "In Defense of Mythology: The History of Modern Theories of Myth." *Annals of Scholarship* 1: 3–49.
Sienkewicz, Thomas J.
    1997   *Theories of Myth: An Annotated Bibliography.* Lanham, MD: Scarecrow.

15

ORIGIN

Tomoko Masuzawa

In the beginning stands an onerous thought: nowadays, whatever else may be said about it, the term "origin" is loaded. One has the impression, indeed, that it is somehow *over*loaded. Certainly, origin can mean very many things in diverse contexts, and perhaps too many things have been already said and written about it. These meanings and opinions are abundant beyond control and, on the whole, wildly polymorphous and richly inconsistent.

On the one hand, it would seem that this is just as it should be, because origin in the strong sense—in the sense of *absolute* beginning, say, out of nothing—must mean that *everything* is already contained in it somehow. If origin is truly absolute, it eradicates any possibility of a precedent, preexisting condition or prototype—in fact, anything other than itself—that might in any way account for later developments. Absolute origin purports to account for posterity *in toto*, and as such, origin is the plenum. It stands to reason, then, that some philosophers have claimed that origin is an essentially theological idea. For, in the last analysis, the only true origin in this strong sense would be the originator of absolutely everything, and Western metaphysics has always assigned this "unique and universal" position to God. (Or at least that's what the whole world has been told lately.) Following this line of reasoning, it is often said that, to the extent that any finite thing or person purports to be the origin or originator—whether it be creative genius of the author, originality of the artist, spiritual founding of a religion or a nation—it / she / he is emulating and approximating this famous prototype, though of necessity only imperfectly. Here, insofar as the theological tenor of the idea is recognized, an important point of ramification may be mentioned: He who is the absolute origin in this prototypical, theological sense is of course also He who will be there at the end of time, and He who will preside over the last judgment or, in the event that things turn out somehow differently from what most theologians have been telling us, He will be the one Who has the last laugh. Be that as it may, this first train of thought about origin can be summarized in two brief statements. In origin is everything. Before origin, there is but nothing.

On the other hand, there is another, equally powerful train of thought, namely, that origin refers to that very nothingness—the blank, the clean slate, the virgin state, the pristine moment before anything particular and delimiting happens, hence, the absolute beginning. In this sense of the term, in order to return to or to recover origin, it is felt that one needs, precisely, to get rid of everything. This is how, for example, the origin of modern philosophy is told. Descartes is generally credited with having ushered scientific modernity into the domain of Western thought. Philosophy, it is said, after meandering in the rough seas of metaphysical nonsense for centuries, finally comes into its own with Cartesian soliloquies, *Discourse on Method* (1637) and *Meditations on the First Philosophy* (1641). As Hegel wrote: "Here we finally reach home, and like a mariner after a long voyage in a tempestuous sea, we can shout, 'Land ho!'; for with Descartes the culture and thought of modern times really begin" (Hegel 1892). In a somewhat less salutary mode, Descartes himself once likened the quest for the first principle of philosophy, or *prima philosophia*, to the method of groping in a mixed bag—or, to be precise, a basket—of good and bad apples. Instead of drawing out and inspecting the contents of the basket one at a time, he opines what is necessary at the outset is to empty the basket entirely, thus expelling both the potentially good and the bad at once, only to restore later, one at a time, those truly proven wholesome and unspoiled; only this way, he claimed, would we be assured that the basket contains no rotten apples, as our philosophical outlook would consist only of sound principles and no erroneous beliefs (Descartes 1911: II.282). As is well known, in order to achieve this unsullied first page of philosophy, Descartes began by doubting everything he possibly could, and he arrived at the famous clean slate of pure, objectless self-consciousness: *cogito*. And everything else, according to his reckoning, eventually followed from it.

It is understandable—one might say that it is structurally inevitable—that origin, *qua* that which is at once everything and nothing, should be an object of intense desire. At the same time, it follows with equal certainty and necessity that such an hyper-cathected object should be subject to strenuous prohibition. For, that which is most acutely and singularly desired is also that which must be most stringently and energetically denied. In short, the fundamental contradiction endemic to the concept (*qua* everything and nothing), as well as this logical double-bind of desire and prohibition that defines and determines its function, together make an impossible object-idea out of "origin." This constitutional difficulty, it appears, haunts every deliberation on the problem of origin, openly or surreptitiously. With this in mind, we may now look at how various attempts at getting at origins have played out, not in philosophy or theology *per se*, but in the domain more proper to the science of religion (*Religionswissenschaft*).

There is a commonly held opinion today that the quest for the origin of religion was a peculiarly and characteristically nineteenth-century preoccupation. Indeed, we find a number of intellectuals of the period who are said to have identified, correctly or not, the ultimate origin of religion or religions in general. These writers attained certain celebrity and notoriety partly because, by and large, what they thus identified turned out to be something other than the divine source, or, in any case, something other than what traditional religious authorities presumably have been claiming to be the source of religion. This is an indication that by the nineteenth century it had become permissible to look for the origin of religion not in some unknowable supernatural mystery but in human nature or in nature itself, which was assumed to be plainly in view if only we would train ourselves to see it with the rigorously empirical eye of science. Although the naturalistic accounting for the phenomenon of religion can be traced back to earlier centuries—most notably to seventeenth- and eighteenth-century Deism—it is generally felt that the naturalistic explanation of religion came into full force as it became intertwined with various theories of evolution in the middle of the nineteenth century.

It should be remembered that the so-called theory of evolution in the usual, inexact sense—the sense most pertinent to the question of the origin and development of religion—is significantly different from the strictly Darwinian theory. As we may recall, in addition to the controversy over the possible human descent from the apes, the scandal of Darwinism had to do with the notion of natural selection and the survival of the fittest. According to the latter theory, mutations of the species into new forms, and the eventual prevailing of the forms better suited for the given environment and the concomitant elimination of the forms less "fit"—that is, the processes that are tantamount to "evolution" in the properly biological sense—are essentially random and incidental occurrences. The concept of evolution in this biological sense, therefore, is not teleological or goal-oriented, and as such it is fundamentally incompatible with the notion of purposeful development, progress or providence. Indeed, this theory deprived the nineteenth-century Europeans not only of the myth of the paradisiac origin but also of the assurance or even the probability of the divinely guided course of world history, or any such narratives that posited *homo sapiens*, and Europeans in particular, at the helm. With the Darwinian theory of evolution, then, history attained for the first time a real possibility of being nothing but meandering tracks of fortuitous events, patterns of change as pointless as results of the game of chance, or a case of the proverbial tale told by an idiot ... signifying nothing.

This, to be sure, is not what is normally meant by the theory of "evolution of religion," or "origin and development of religion," as such a theory is usually attributed to various writers of the nineteenth century. As a rule, in a theory of religious evolution there is a presumption of meaningful and purposeful *development*, a presumption of the human condition generally changing and evolving for the higher and better—though the possibility of "regression" is also admitted—with something like a fulfillment, perfection, or even apotheosis projected at a certain indefinite point in the future. This is as much as to say that these so-called evolutionary theories of religion have less affinity with Darwinism or any such new varieties of natural scientific theory than with the seventeenth- and eighteenth-century Deistic idea of natural history of religion as exemplified, most notably, by the posthumously published treatise by David Hume.

Hume's *Natural History of Religion* (1957 [1757]) may be considered epoch-making in more than one sense, but the sense most relevant to our immediate concern is that this was arguably the first account that placed the origin and development of religion strictly within the domain of *human* history, that is to say, an account not directly linked to the providential, divinely guided history. Earlier Deists—such as Herbert of Cherbury (1663) and John Toland (1696)—typically presupposed that there was the original, universal, rational and ethical religion common to all humankind, and that, with a passage of time, this original pure theism became variously "corrupted," with the result that different peoples in different regions of the world came to practice divergent and idiosyncratic religions. Side-stepping these deistic presuppositions, Hume instead begins by categorically divorcing the question of the (to him) true, rational and permanent foundation of religion—the very thing that other Deists identified as the original religion—from the temporal domain of nature and history. This separation gets accomplished even before the treatise proper begins. In the author's introduction, he proclaims that, with respect to any enquiry regarding religion,

> there are two questions in particular, which challenge our attention, to wit, that concerning its foundation in reason, and that concerning its origin in human nature. Happily, the first question, which is the most important, admits of the most obvious, at least, the clearest, solution. The whole frame of nature bespeaks an intelligent author; and no rational enquirer can, after serious reflection, suspend his belief a moment with regard to the primary principles of genuine Theism and Religion. But the other question, concerning the origin of religion in human nature, is exposed to some more difficulty. (Hume 1957 [1757]: 21)

Thus first erecting the impermeable barrier between the two domains—on one side, what is ahistorical, rational and assured, and on the other side, what is historical, contingent and fraught with human frailty—Hume proceeds to explain that only the latter domain will be the subject of the book in question. No sooner than the first chapter opens he asserts, with no sign of uncertainty or scruples, that "polytheism or idolatry was, and necessarily must have been, the first and most ancient religion of mankind." Quoting the learned opinions of his day, he claims that this assertion is readily attested by the experience concerning various "barbarous nations" of the known world: "The savage tribes of AMERICA, AFRICA, and ASIA are all idolaters. Not a single exception to this rule" (Hume 1957 [1757]: 23).

In retrospect, the lasting impact of Hume's work on the future course of the study of religion has less to do with the particular scenario of historical development he had in mind, and far more to do with the fact that he effected the separation of the two domains of inquiry with such authority and finality. By declaring the rational, philosophical and theological domain to be absolutely foundational and true, he effectively liberated the domain of natural-human history from the biblical constraints and, rather ironically, rendered it invulnerable to dogmatic-theological interventions. This, of course, did not necessarily prevent those who did not share Hume's views from simply disregarding this decree of separation and meddling and interfering freely, as it were, with the affairs of the natural historians of religion. Indeed, Hume must be regarded as the first one to face this reality; the opposition forces made it necessary to suppress the publication of this very work during his lifetime. All the same, with this slim volume, he in effect issued to all posterity a license to forage the field henceforth known as (natural) history of religion(s). It is above all for the impetus Hume generated, that is, to do what one will within the contingent realm of human history, that the book is credited as something of an origin of comparative religion itself.

Following Hume's lead directly or indirectly, many nineteenth- and early twentieth-century writers proffered various accounts as to how religion began, developed, and would likely become in the future. The positivist Auguste Comte sketched world history in terms of a three-stage development: theological (fictive), metaphysical (abstract), positive (scientific). He further subdivided the theological stage into three (Comte 1830–1842), and the designations of those sub-stages are identical with the ones delineated by Charles de Brosses in the eighteenth century: fetishism (superstition), polytheism (idolatry), monotheism (ethical religion) (de Brosses 1760). The implication here is that, in Comte's own time, very many specimens of the human species known around the world were still inhabiting the earliest stages of this evolution, whereas a few Europeans at the vanguard of history, such as himself, were witnessing the dawn of the positive epoch. Similarly, J. G. Frazer's *The Golden Bough* (1924 [3 editions: 1890, 1900, 1915]) posited the developmental stages as first magical, then religious, and finally implicitly projecting the age of the scientific. The three-stage schema is also reflected in Freud's speculation on the philogenetic and ontogenetic development of humankind (1990 [1912–1913])

There are several recurrent themes in the ways in which these and other writers of their time narrated the "evolution" of religion. To begin with, and most generally, the progression is always from the lowest to the highest, from the mean, primitive and degraded to the noble, cultured and refined. This value-laden narrative trajectory also implies a transformation from the particularistic, limited conception of the divinity to the universalistic, genuine conception of the Infinite. The rising level of mental-intellectual sophistication is typically expressed in terms of the movement from materiality to spirituality, from literal, concrete language to symbolic, abstract language, and from helpless and reactive passivity to imaginative and creative activity. This complex of ideas is exemplified well in the familiar "evolutionary" scenario already mentioned: first fetishism (misguided attribution of supernatural power to merely material objects; ignorance of the spiritual), then polytheism (idolatrous worship of finite and often capricious deities in material forms; confusion of the material and the spiritual), and finally monotheism (worship of the universal, ethical deity through symbols; proper apprehension of the spiritual unencumbered by materiality).

There were, to be sure, some writers in this period whose views were more in line with the earlier Deists in the sense that they believed that there was an original, universal religion common to all humankind at the beginning of time, and that it was a monotheism. The German theologian Wilhelm Schmidt (1868–1954) was perhaps the most renowned of the advocates of the so-called primitive monotheism theory, while Andrew Lang (1844–1912), a prolific Scottish writer on diverse subjects, also came to advocate this idea late in his life and did much to popularize it. It should be noted, however, that, because these writers also believed that the primitive revelation—or at least some form of pre-knowledge of the one and the only true God—initially fell in the hands of the crudest of primitive humankind, it was assumed that this pristine knowledge or revelation could have been only very imperfectly apprehended or, more probably, promptly forgotten by those primitive recipients. For, in the estimation of these writers, the child-like mental abilities of the savage ancestors were such that they were easily swayed by all too human emotions and the material exigencies of everyday life, that is, those factors generally inimical to the rational contemplation of the purely spiritual Deity. Therefore, even if there was a time in the mythic past when the world basked in the light of true religion, much of the history of humankind that is known or knowable is tantamount to the same laborious movement from the bottom up. On the whole—as would be obvious to anyone who actually read these texts—the accounts of the history of religion presented by the primitive-monotheism-theory advocates are not appreciably different from the ones proposed by those who did not believe that any such primordial knowledge existed.

A much more fruitful way of exploring the full range of views proffered by the historians of religions of this period may be to ask how various writers situated themselves in relation to the aforementioned fundamental division first established by Hume. As we have seen, Hume made his own position clear at the outset. For him, the essential foundation of religion, or rational *grounds* of religion, was not at all the same thing as the merely contingent, temporal *beginning* of religion in human history, even though both of these notions may be taken to mean "origin" in a certain sense. Moreover, he was just as convinced of the loftiness of the rational basis of true religion as he was certain about the humbleness of the beginning of the human religious history. He was in fact interested in both these domains, and he wrote *The Natural History of Religion* to deal with the latter and a better known treatise entitled *Dialogues Concerning Natural Religion* (1750, first published 1790) to address the former.

In the nineteenth century, this division of the realms of inquiry was often expressed in terms of the distinction between "history of religion(s)" (or "comparative religion") and "philosophy of religion." Together, they were thought to constitute the general science of religion (*Religionswissenschaft*). Hence when the Dutch scholar and reputed co-founder (together with F. Max Müller) of this science, Cornelis Petrus Tiele, delivered his Gifford Lectures at the University of Edinburgh in 1896–1897, the resulting two-volume compendium was entitled *Elements of the Science of Religion*, of which the first "Morphological" volume corresponded to the historical-comparative study, whereas the second "Ontological" volume explored philosophical issues. This arrangement proved exemplary and was followed by a number of lesser known writers thereafter. In this connection we may note that, by looking at this two-ply legacy of the discipline, we can appreciate better why many scholars today continue to debate, and can never seem to agree, whether theology and philosophy of religion should have a proper place within the science of religion or, alternatively, outside the science and parallel with it.

F. Max Müller was faithful to Hume's legacy to the extent that, while he studiously pursued his immense philological research in the area of history of religions, he continued to proclaim throughout his career his conviction that all humankind without exception harbored in their hearts the intimation of the Infinite, however dimly or poorly this primordial awareness may be conceptually understood in any given society or by any given individual. In comparison to the Deists of the seventeenth and eighteenth centuries, Müller did not stress as much the rational foundation of this knowledge; yet, by his own admission, his spiritual sensibility found the greatest affinity with the rationalist philosophy of Kant. In effect, one might reasonably describe Müller's own theology as an exemplary postulate of German Idealism swaddled in the highly cultivated poetics of Romanticism.

Although no other writer may have been as articulate or insistent as Müller regarding this matter, there were indeed many others whose stance, and whose understanding of the rationale for their scholarly practice, were generally consistent with his. In fact, so long as this paragon of *Religionswissenschaft* continued to assert the inviolability and incorruptibility of the knowledge of the Infinite, others could infer that the domain of faith appropriately understood would be secure irrespective of what the science might do, and this in turn could be construed to mean that even the most thoroughly naturalistic and secularist enterprises of the history of religion would remain legitimate and safe, as it were, under the protection of the Humean edict which divided and set apart, in good Enlightenment fashion, the immutable truth of reason from the incidental facts of history. By thus disengaging the operation of the two domains, this edict appears to have served as something of a cover for the self-appointed historians of religion, since it nominally enabled them to get on with their business as soon as they finished paying due respect, à *la* Hume, to the consummate religion of universal reason. Over time, however, this sacrosanct sphere of theological conviction became less and less a matter of universality and more and more one of *privacy*. As the discursive domain of history of religions gained its academic—and public—status, the domain of theological conviction lost hold on the universal and, in turn, it became exclusively a personal affair. Henceforth this tightly circumscribed territory of the personal has come to shelter and protect, at least in principle, religious predilections of any kind whatsoever—from the most imperiously universalist to the most fanatically exclusivist—so long as they remained strictly within the sphere of scholars' private life and personal experience.

As ingenious and effective as this strategy might have been for the purpose of securing a legitimate position for the naturalistic history of religions, it is not altogether surprising that some theologians grew deeply suspicious of this convenient arrangement devised by several generations of so-called historians of religion. Thus it was that in 1881 Bishop John Wordsworth of Salisbury went on record warning against the half-truths of the natural historical approach:

> It is at present far too common a habit of mind to be satisfied with tracing out the conditions and circumstances under which a belief or a religious custom arises in the world. Some men exhaust themselves in classifying the phenomena of religion under this or that heading of myth or symbol ... But, when they have done all this useful work ... they are in danger, and leave their readers in danger, of tacitly assuming that the subject is closed, and that religion is a natural development, out of which the positive action of God, as a real existing Being, is excluded. Their mouths are full of the various ways in which other men have thought of God, but He Himself is far from their own thoughts. (Wordsworth 1893 [1881]: 78–79)

In a similar vein, in a publication dated the same year, American Sanskritist William D. Whitney—who was once remembered chiefly as a contemporary and ruthless critic of Max Müller—argued that what he termed "the so-called science of religion," unlike the science of language, could never be expected to attain the status of a true science insofar as it was ultimately nothing more than "a history of men's opinions, as inferred from modes of expression far less clear, objective, and trustworthy than are the records of speech" (Whitney 1881: 451–452).

If some theologians were wary of the separate-and-not-so-equal configuration of the two discursive fields (i.e., natural history vs. religious confession, science of religion vs. theology, the public / academic vs. the private / personal, etc.), perhaps there was a good reason for their circumspection. Nineteenth- and early twentieth-century Europe certainly saw a number of prominent writers who had no compunction about hauling a thoroughgoing naturalist theory directly into the heart of the theologico-confessional domain. For, whatever their individual intent may have been in their respective theory-building, each of these theories, if taken seriously, would have the effect of destroying the pith of "religion" as we know it. For example, Ludwig Feuerbach (1957 [1841]) famously proposed, with not much ambiguity or irony, to "translate theology into anthropology." By that he meant and wished to demonstrate that all theological propositions (such as the main precepts of Christianity) could be fully and exhaustively understood in completely naturalistic—or, in his own words, "materialistic"—terms. Such a transcription of theology into "anthropology" makes God and any other allegedly supernatural entities altogether superfluous, non-essential, and ultimately self-alienating from the human standpoint. Sigmund Freud, on the other hand, declared no such mutinous intentions, but there is little doubt that he, too, rendered the traditional, free-standing, self-validating theological discourse either redundant or half-estranged from modern sensibility, in his case, by virtue of the fact that he devised a peculiar newspeak called psychoanalysis, a brave new discourse nearly equal to Christian theology in its hyper-intelligence and its voracious explanatory power.

While neither Feuerbach's nor Freud's impact is likely to be slighted by any historian of religions endowed with sufficient hindsight, as regards the actual practices of the hitherto established mainstream *Religionswissenschaft*, each of these figures stands as something of a maverick, an intellectual nomad at once inspiring and irritating but never truly constitutive of "the discipline." The legacy of Émile Durkheim, on the other hand, is altogether differently situated. Variously crowned as a founding father of sociology, of French anthropology, or of sociology of religion, his accomplishments have been too consequential to be brushed aside as merely of historical interest, despite the fact that much of his data, and many of his theoretical propositions, have been subsequently disputed. In common accord, the significance of his role in the formation of the nomothetic-scientific study of religion is matched only by that of Max Weber. Not only did Durkheim put forward a prototype (albeit a largely speculative one) for the sociological understanding of religion, by so doing he virtually made Hume stand on his head.

In his most famous work on religion, *The Elementary Forms of Religious Life* (1995 [1912]), Durkheim offers no opinion with regard to, say, the existence and the attributes of God, the possible apperception of the Infinite, or any other like subjects of theological import. Unlike Hume, if he had a religious conviction of any kind, he did not reveal it, did not even hint that it should be of any significance whatsoever. Instead, he directly proceeds to state what he terms the "subject of our study: religious sociology and the theory of knowledge." It is here, in the introduction to the 500-page treatise, that his radical transposition of the Humean arrangement is most visible. To begin with, like Hume, Durkheim draws a distinction between the question of temporary *beginning* of religion and the question of the permanent *basis* of religion, and he also identifies the latter as the realm of rationality. What makes his endeavor radically different from that of Hume is that he purports to direct his naturalist-secularist attention not to the former but to the latter domain. Durkheim was certainly not unaware of the momentousness of this transvaluation of inquiry. There is a remarkable decisiveness and authority in his voice announcing his intentions:

> The study which I undertake is a way of taking up again the old problem of the origin of religions *but under new conditions*. Granted, if by origin one means an absolute first beginning, there is nothing scientific about the question, and it must be resolutely set aside. There is no radical instant when religion began to exist, and the point is not to find a roundabout way of conveying ourselves there in thought. Like every other human institution, religion begins nowhere. So all speculations in this genre are rightly discredited; they can consist of only subjective and arbitrary constructions without checks of any sort. The problem I propose is altogether different. I would like to find a means of discerning the ever-present causes on which the most basic forms of religious thought and practice depend. (Durkheim 1995 [1912]: 7; emphasis in the original)

As he makes amply clear in this introduction and elsewhere in the book, if he has chosen to focus on Australian totemism as the most "primitive" form of religion, this is not because he believes that totemism is historically and chronologically the *earliest* but rather because, in his estimation, it represents the most basic and structurally rudimentary form, consisting only of the minimum, that is to say, the most essential and indispensable elements.

Hence not only does Durkheim transpose the temporal and the timeless in the way he characterizes the object of his naturalistic-scientific inquiry, but by so doing he also brings into the domain of this inquiry the question of reason and rationality, such that it is now possible to speak of the origin of the faculty of reason, or, more specifically, the origin of the categories of thought. As it turns out, religion and reason have the same origin, the same basis or grounds, and that basis Durkheim claimed to be the *sui generis* reality of the collective life, that is, the ways in which members of a given societal group act, intercourse with one another and represent to themselves their sense of unity and solidarity. In effect, the origin of religion—that is to say, the "ever-present cause" of religion, as well as the ever-present cause of rationality—is *society*, that is, something natural (as opposed to supernatural), contingent and "historical" in a carefully qualified (i.e., not merely chronological) sense of the term.

As with Hume, the ground-shifting effect of Durkheim's work depended less on the validity of the specific observations he made with regard to what he construed as the most elementary (therefore essential) form of religion than on the overall transformation of the field and of the logic of inquiry. What Hume opened up almost surreptitiously in the eighteenth century as a modest, well-circumscribed area of a novel inquiry under the name of natural history of religion—that is, as an area for activities supposedly harmless to the eternal truths of religion and reason—became a foraging ground for much speculation during the nineteenth century. By the time of Freud and Durkheim, it was as though open season on big game hunting had been declared; for, as many religionists and traditionalists decried, nothing could be presumed safe and sacred any longer. According to the opinions and the complaints of these religious protesters, what the speculative "evolutionists" such as Durkheim and Freud had done was that, by claiming to have identified an origin of religion in a place entirely different from divine inspiration, they effectively *reduced* the phenomenon of religion and *violated* its essential integrity—the moralizing terms often employed by many religionists—and improperly converted it into something else, something other than "religion itself."

Fearing the imminent evaporation of "religion itself," and inferring—rather injudiciously to be sure—that the denial of the irreducible essential substance of religion would render the science of religion itself baseless and defenseless, and some even worrying that any such admission might in turn drive them out of business, many students of religion of subsequent generations protested against the methods as well as the results of the "evolutionist" search for the origin of religion. These epigonic scholars sought to shift the grounds of inquiry, above all, by shelving the issue of origin and concertedly declaring the question of the essence or foundation of religion off limits to any scientific probe.

To put this in the words of the best known proponent of this position, Mircea Eliade: "The historian of religions knows by now that he is unable to reach the "origin" of religion. What happened in the beginning, *ab origine*, is no longer a problem for the historian of religions, though conceivably it might be one for the theologian or the philosopher" (Eliade 1969: 50). His argument here is not entirely unlike that of logical positivists, in effect: what cannot be answered cannot be a problem, as far as the sound-minded, empirically responsible historians of religions are concerned. Even though this statement may leave us wondering what Eliade imagined a theologian or philosopher might do to continue tackling the seemingly impossible or, worse yet, non-existent problem, it is clear at least that this declaration of intent not to pursue origins was very much a matter of *renunciation*, a matter of "ascetic modesty" (Eliade 1969: 48) on the part of those who were resigned to a life mired in historical documents, which would never provide answers to questions such as "What is the sacred? What does a religious experience actually mean?" (Eliade 1969: 53). Without apparent irony, he likens this life of a dedicated historian, half-buried under massive data, to "a kind of *descensus ad inferos*; a descent into the deep, dark subterranean regions where he is confronted with the germinal modes of the living matter"; and in so doing, Eliade adds, the historian risks "a spiritual death; for, sadly enough, the creativity of the scholar may be sterilized" (Eliade 1969: 48–49). Cast in this language, it appears that the life of an historian is but a somewhat novel mode of carrying out a time-honored spiritual discipline, a sort of *imitatio Christi*, recommending pious labor of self-denial. For, according to Eliade (1969: 53), the historian of religion

> knows that he is condemned to work exclusively with historical documents, but at the same time he feels that these documents tell him something more than the simple fact that they reflect historical situations. He feels somehow that they reveal to him important truths about man and man's relation to the sacred. But how to grasp these truths? This is the question that obsesses many contemporary historians of religions. A few answers have been proposed already. But more important than any single answer is the fact that historians of religions asked *this* question.

A few things may be said in view of this revised mission statement for history of religions. First, it is clear that the question of origin—or what Eliade terms "obsession with origins"—is hereby suspended, rather than resolved, disabled or made to disappear. (Since Eliade himself resorts to pathological terminology here, one might add that, according to psychoanalysis, it is in the very nature of an obsession that it cannot be "renounced" because it is itself a result—a reaction formation, to be precise—of an attempt at renunciation.) It therefore stands to reason that the general work-environment of these neo-historians of religions is fraught, even more so than before, with deep ambivalence, owing to the structural tension or contradiction endemic to the very idea of origin—and the double-bind of desire and prohibition associated with the idea—to which I referred earlier in this essay. In the case of Eliade specifically, the ambivalence becomes exceptionally pronounced when his "scientific" dictum to suspend the search for origins is juxtaposed with his pet theory which holds that, baldly put, the point of religious life or quest is tantamount to a longing for origins, and that the aim of ritual acts is the reenactment of events *ab origine* (Eliade 1954). This juxtaposition results in a peculiar pair of mirroring images representing the object and the subject of *Religionswissenschaft*: on the one hand, an assembly of "religious men" indulging in the deepest human desire, jubilating among their own kind well beyond the pale of science, and on the other, an ascetic tribe of "scientists of religion" resolutely resisting this desire, feeding among the dry dust of historical documents, waiting for any intimation of "important truths" that their views from afar might yield (Masuzawa 1993: 1–6, 25–33).

Secondly, this demarcation of subject and object of the science reinscribes and reinforces the Humean edict of separation, except that, with Eliade (as well as with Rudolf Otto), rationality seems to have switched sides altogether and consequently the domain of foundational "truths" (as opposed to the domain of historical facts) could no longer be reached by rational thought but only through some self-authenticating experience unmediated by the usual cognitive faculties. In effect, Eliade would roll back all the liberties taken by the "evolutionists" and "reductionists" since the time of Hume, undo the effects of these violations, and urge the scholars to quit speculating about the dreamtime and to repair to their proper station in documentary history. Yet this newly designated seat of the neo-historian of religions is considerably more constrained and impoverished than Hume's own position. As we recall, secure in his belief in the immunity of the Deistic rationalist faith, Hume felt free to construct the "origin and development" of religion in entirely naturalistic terms, from start to finish. In contrast, Eliade's neo-historians are "condemned" to elaborate endlessly on a particularized historical narrative, which may or may not be finally meaningful, but from which both the origin and the telos are preemptively bracketed. The proper historian in Eliade's sense is thus reduced to slaving over the deluge of facts, "immersed in his documents, sometimes almost buried under their mass and weight" (Eliade 1969: 48–49), all the while straining to eavesdrop on the rumors of angels possibly echoing between the lines of hard, unyielding documentary history.

Eliade died in 1986, and there developed a small industry critiquing his legacy. Now on the eve of the twenty-first century, there may not be many scholars who would profess the Eliadean orientation as their own, compared to the number of those who would not. In fact, I suspect that the majority of historians of religions today consider themselves somehow *beyond* not only the evolutionist follies and the reductionist fallacies but also Eliade's own scruples, not to mention his unsatisfactory—still too theological, some would say—pseudo-solutions. In all their modesty, the contemporary historians seem to feel that they have overcome at least *those* stumbling blocks. Yet, having traced the seemingly intractable origin-complex constitutionally ingrained in the enterprise of history of religions from the beginning, we cannot escape the impression that the very terms in which the contemporary historians often express their sense of difference from their predecessors—"we don't speculate on the origin, the essence or the goal of religion; we just do history"—consign them exactly to the same epistemic regime that has dictated the religious-scientific inquiry, that is to say, to the infernal machine first set in motion by Hume's clever device. To be sure, given the particular configuration of institutional and ideological forces at Hume's time and place, there is no question, it seems to me, that his cunning legislation marking out a space for "natural history of religion" was enormously enabling. And since that time it has enabled the inquiry not in a monolithic way but allowed it to proceed in many unexpected directions. At the same time, it seems equally obvious that this operating system has compelled generations of scholars to tread the same origin-dominated ideological cycle over and over, the cycle that seems to be in perpetual motion thanks in part to the enduring vitality of the unresolvable contradiction within.

The question we are left with, then, is whether it is possible to write a history elsewhere, that is, in some other register than the bicameral system designed, presumably, both to "protect" and to "keep at bay" the allegedly irreducible being or basis of religion, the system which prescribes not only how history can be narrated but also, and more importantly and fundamentally, determines and dictates the supposed object (i.e., religion) in a particular, essential and ultimately unhistorical way. Can we "do history" otherwise? Is it possible, so to say, to channel history of religions in the direction of what Michel Foucault calls, after Nietzsche, *genealogy*?

Foucault describes genealogy as an alternative strategy, so to speak, for rendering and managing the past. (The past that requires rendering and managing of course is that which constitutes the present materially and ideologically.) Genealogy is above all an alternative to the prevailing historicist mode of indolent narration which is always on the side of the dominant ideology and power, as Walter Benjamin (1969) would say. Critically marshaling "relentless erudition," genealogy "rejects the metahistorical deployment of ideal significations and indefinite teleologies" and, as such, "opposes itself to the search for 'origins'" (Foucault 1977b: 140). What does this mean?

> Why does Nietzsche challenge the pursuit of the origin (*Ursprung*), at least on those occasions when he is truly a genealogist? First, because it is an attempt to capture the exact essence of things, their purest possibilities, and their carefully protected identities, because this search assumes the existence of immobile forms that precede the external world of accident and succession. This search is directed to "that which was already there," the image of a primordial truth fully adequate to its nature, and it necessitates the removal of every mask to ultimately disclose an original identity. (Foucault 1977b: 142)

At this point the neo-historians of religions might interrupt and protest: such an origin-quest is precisely what the historians do not engage in; there is no allowance for timeless essence, primordial truth, or any predetermined teleology in the historians' *modus operandi*. Yet, as we have seen, much of this disavowal comes in the form of bracketing, self-restraint, renunciation. The historians may thus resolve to *suspend* the origin-quest indefinitely, but the suspension or the renunciation of the hope of satisfaction does not automatically shift and upgrade their scholarly enterprise to a new operating system but rather it makes the same old system all the more opaque, as the latter becomes partially occluded by denial.

Meanwhile, the neo-neo-historians of the post-Eliadean epoch—would this be, roughly, *today*?—may here intervene, announcing their total disaffection with the metaphysics of origin and possibly even claiming to concur with the genealogist on this point. What, then, follows from this? As Foucault (1977b: 142) puts it,

> if the genealogist refuses to extend his faith in metaphysics, if he listens to history, he finds that there is "something altogether different" behind things: not a timeless and essential secret, but the secret that they have no essence or that their essence was fabricated in a piecemeal fashion from alien forms ... What is found at the historical beginning of things is not the inviolable identity of their origin; it is the dissension of other things. It is disparity.

Perhaps some historians are prepared to abide by this principle whole-heartedly. Of course, as it is not only a matter of principle but of practice as well, one might duly ask: What does this genealogical outlook do to something like "the history of Christianity"? Or, how does it change the nature of our business when we learn to resist the overwhelming facticity of a theoretical (yet thoroughly naturalized) object, such as "Buddhism"? How do we come to terms with the ideological construction of this facticity, which a genealogy of "Buddhism"—*not* "the history of Buddhism"—makes visible? Some answers are already in the air, and some even have made it into print, if we are to take into account such works as Philip Almond's *The British Discovery of Buddhism* (1988), Harjot Oberoi's *The Construction of Religious Boundaries* (1994), Lionel Jensen's *Manufacturing Confucianism* (1997), and—far afield but analogously and concertedly—Jonathan Z. Smith's fossorial archeology of "religion"/"religions" (1982a, 1998), or William Pietz's brilliant analysis of colonial genealogies of the discourse on fetishism (1985, 1987, 1988).

At the risk of sounding overly optimistic, I should add that any list of this sort is bound to be incomplete, partly idiosyncratic, and already out of date. It is yet to be seen, however, if and how this type of new strategic studies may engage, inflect or transform the ways in which the study of religion is generally conducted. What is even more challenging, perhaps, is whether such studies can impact and destabilize the ideology embedded in the widely prevalent, thoroughly naturalized and factualized assumptions about "religion(s)" any time soon, such that the first question our students ask will *not* be: "Tell us, what do the Hindus believe, and what's about it that they can't get along with the Muslims?" Or, in the event that any self-claimed "Hindu" or "Zen Buddhist" today proffers to give an answer to the queries of this sort—queries arising from the depth of ideological opacity and from our systematic blindness with regard to the material history that helped constitute these objects, "religion," "Buddhism," and so on—the scholars will then think of more and better options than simply to call such a person to the witness stand or to render him or her a specimen in the dubious display of the so-called world religions.

Tomoko Masuzawa

Suggested Readings

Foucault, Michel
    1977b "Nietzsche, Genealogy, History." In *Language, Counter-Memory, Practice: Selected Essays and Interviews.* Donald F. Bouchard (ed. with an Introduction), Donald F. Bouchard and Sherry Simon (trans.). Ithaca, NY: Cornell University Press.

Harrison, Peter
    1990 *"Religion" and the Religions in the English Enlightenment.* Cambridge: Cambridge University Press.

Krauss, Rosalind
    1985 *The Originality of the Avant-Garde and Other Modernist Myths.* Cambridge, MA: MIT Press.

Preus, J. Samuel
    1987 *Explaining Religion: Criticism and Theory from Bodin to Freud.* New Haven: Yale University Press.

Smith, Jonathan Z.
    1998 "Religion, Religions, Religious," pp. 269–284 in Mark C. Taylor (ed.), *Critical Terms for Religious Studies.* Chicago: University of Chicago Press.

16

PROJECTION

Stewart Elliott Guthrie

"Projection," the action of throwing out or ahead (Latin *projectio*), is a term widely used to describe or explain religion and other aspects of human thought and action by invoking supposed psychological processes. The meanings of the term, however, are diverse and may have little in common. Moreover, usages of the word projection imply varied and contested theories of perception. Since both its meaning and its perceptual basis are uncertain, projection may be regarded as a metaphor without a theory. Since the metaphor also appears misleading, I suggest that projection as a term for psychological processes and products, including religious ones, should be abandoned.

Despite its flaws, projection as a psychological term currently is well entrenched. It is common both in popular use and among academics. An anthropologist (Pandian 1997: 507), for example, thinks it is basic to anthropological theories of religion; and a scholar of religion (V. A. Harvey 1996: 67) finds it "central to an extraordinary number of widely held theories of religion" in sociology, anthropology, psychology and philosophy, and "close to the centre of some of the most influential currents of modern thought." Clearly the figure of projection strikes a chord.

A Historical Sketch

The view that religion is, in some sense, a casting of human qualities upon the nonhuman world may be old as well as popular. Thornton (1996) says that it began at least with Herodotus and continued with Lucretius and Spinoza. Others point to Xenophanes's famous remark that if lions and horses could represent their gods, these gods would look like lions and horses. Certainly Spinoza (1955) and then Hume (1957 [1757]) argued that popular religion, at least, is a product of human experience and an objectification of human needs and desires.

As a general principle of perception, something like projection has been noted at least since medieval times, as in the *Malleus Maleficarum*: "devils so stir up the inner perceptions … that they appear to be a new impression at that moment received from exterior things" (Zilboorg 1935: 54). Similarly, Thomas à Kempis wrote, "What a man is inwardly that he will see outwardly" (Murstein and Pryer 1959: 353). Nonetheless, these formulations remain sketchy. They also lack the term projection itself. Although classical and medieval Europe had (in varying degrees and combinations) the ideas that vision is a kind of touching, that perceptions somehow reflect interests, and that religion is partly a human production, they seem to have possessed neither a general psychological projectionism nor a general view of religion as projection.

The explicit application of the term projection (and of its close relative, "objectification") to perceptual processes and to religion first appears in the nineteenth century. It usually is credited to Freud (e.g., by Abeles 1993: 1885; Rieff 1979: 270; Banks 1973: 414), but in fact Freud has several predecessors. One is Ralph Waldo Emerson: "The youth, intoxicated with his admiration of a hero, fails to see that it is only a projection of his own soul which he admires." A more direct predecessor is Ludwig Feuerbach. Apparently the first explicitly to use the term (and near equivalents) to describe religion, Feuerbach wrote, "Man—this is the mystery of religion—projects his being (*vergegenständlicht sich*) into objectivity" (1854: 29, in V. A. Harvey 1995: 27). (V. A. Harvey, with Child [1967: 20], notes that Feuerbach mostly uses words other than *Projektion*, most commonly *vergegenständlichen*, "to objectify," which his translator, George Eliot, renders as "to project"; but Eliot's choice appears generally valid.)

Feuerbach is the likely source of the idea for Freud, who wrote in an 1875 letter, "I revere and admire [him] above all other philosophers" (Boehlich 1990: 76). Shafranske (1995: 201) notes that "Feuerbach's thesis that 'God is merely the projected essence of Man' … anticipated Freud's analysis," and Harvey (1995) discusses Freud's evident appropriation in some detail. A third predecessor of Freud (and a possible source for him, though Freud denied it) is Nietzsche, who seems to have suggested that paranoia is based on unconsciously projecting hostility onto other people (Chapman and Chapman-Santana 1995). Finally Marx (Marx and Engels 1964), also drawing on Feuerbach, again antedates Freud on religion as a projection, in this case a projection of social and political relations.

The metaphor of projection may have been especially accessible in the past hundred years because of the spread of films, slides, and other transparencies, beginning with nineteenth-century magic lanterns (V. A. Harvey 1996: 68). Gozzi (1995), supported by Hurry, Novick and Novick (1976: 75) who cite Freud's 1899 "Screen Memories," thinks early cinema shaped Freud's and Jung's ideas of projection. More recently Goodenough

(1965: 8, in V. A. Harvey 1995: 235) uses the metaphor specifically of religion: "Man throws curtains between himself and the [inchoate, terrifying world], and on them he projects ... pictures of divine or superhuman forces or beings."

However, an optical substrate for the idea of perception as projection appears broader and older than the projection of transparencies. Projection in cartography, in which the Earth, in part or in whole, is portrayed in two dimensions, entered the lexicon in 1557 as "map-projection," and in 1570 simply as projection. Projection as a term in drafting appeared about the same time.

Still earlier, several other kinds of optical projection were conceived (though not so named) by the ancient Greeks. Plato's cave, in which inmates take shadows on the wall for reality, is the most famous instance. A more directly relevant form is a Greek theory of vision. Shared at least by Aristotle, Euclid, Hero of Alexandria and Ptolemy, this theory makes vision consist in a touching of objects by the eye, by means of rectilinear rays emanating from it (Meyering 1989). The rays form a cone with its apex at the eye and its base at the objects constituting the visual field. This notion of vision as projection persisted in Europe as a scientific view at least until 1604, when Kepler's *Paralipomena* inverted it (Wilson 1997: 120). The concept of the evil eye and such contemporary phrases as "looking daggers" suggest that a sense of vision as projection still may be widespread.

At present, the bastions of the notion of projection are various forms of depth psychology, especially psychoanalysis; projective personality testing using techniques such as the Rorschach and Thematic Apperception tests; and certain skeptical and social-science studies of religion. Its popular currency probably stems largely from Freud (and to some degree from his daughter Anna Freud [1966]), from Feuerbach and from projective psychological testing.

Varieties of Projection

The forms and meanings of projection as a model of perception are varied, with little in common but a general connection with perception and some connotation of error. In psychology alone, for example, definitions range from the broad, unmotivated and seemingly innocuous notion of "a mental image visualized and regarded as an objective reality" to the specific, psychoanalytic "process by which we attribute our own shortcomings to others as a means of protecting ourselves from threat" (Sherwood 1979: 635). Between these two are the motivated yet sweeping "manifestation of behavior by an individual which indicates some emotional value or need" (Murstein and Pryer 1959: 370) and the apparently unmotivated but narrower "unwittingly attributing one's own traits, attitudes, or subjective processes to others" (English and English 1958: 412).

The kind of error connoted, moreover, varies with the kind of projection. For example, a subspecies of the first sort of projection above (a mental image regarded as objective) belongs to the psychology of perception and sometimes is called "eccentric" projection. This means that we locate qualities of objects in external sources, for example when we see the color of a flower as located in the flower rather than in our perceptual process. This usage claims, in an echo of eighteenth-century empiricism, that we mistakenly think we experience a world external to ourselves, whereas what we really experience are internal impacts on our sense organs. Such a mistake has little in common with the mistake of supposing that another person shares some feeling with us.

In religious studies, the meanings of projection are hardly less wide-ranging. At the most general, a contributor to Jonathan Z. Smith's *Dictionary of Religion* (1995: 861) describes projection as meaning only that "religion is based on actual experience" and sees Freud, Feuerbach, Marx, Otto and Durkheim all as sharing that view. Another writer (in Hinnells 1995: 392), somewhat more narrowly, says projectionism means "various arguments ... that 'God' is not a reality ... but a product of the human mind" and includes the views of Hobbes, Hume, Feuerbach, Marx, Nietzsche, Durkheim and Freud—again a diverse assortment. For Smart (1973b: 74) religion as projection means that the "constellations of the sacred ... are products of human activity and human signification." More specifically (in Bowker 1997: 769) projection is the "theory that God and gods are merely objectifications of human needs, ideals, or desires." This appears relatively clear. The same writer, however, finds that the notion of projection in Hindu and Buddhist doctrine has a "different significance." At most, then, one can say of projectionism in religious studies only that it implies a degree of human agency in the shaping of religion.

Although ideas of projection in religious studies derive in some measure from those in psychology, the two fields together present a broad spectrum of meanings. A number of writers have decried this diversity. In psychology, for example, Murstein and Pryer (1959: 353) write, "one would be hard pressed to find a concept so capable of multiple interpretation and so varied in meaning." Lewis, Bates and Lawrence (1994: 1295) among others note that Freud (whom they call the originator of the concept) described projection variously and vaguely. They quote Sears' (1936) opinion that it is "probably the most inadequately defined term in all psychoanalytic theory." Murray (1951: 13) says, "If 'projection' means everything it means nothing." Smythies (1954: 120), urging its abandonment, says the term is used differently and vaguely in neurophysiological theory of perception, in psychoanalysis and in neuro-anatomy. In religious studies, Harvey (1996: 67, 68) writes that it is "employed and interpreted in quite different ways" and that we should not assume that it has a single meaning.

Psychological Theory

How is it that so little consensus exists on what seems so basic and so well-known a word? Part of the answer lies in the varying views of mind, especially of perception, and in the practices of which these are part. Such views and practices, however, often are implicit rather than clearly stated. Projection in classical psychoanalysis and in projective personality testing, the strongholds of psychological projectionism, displays both diversity and uncertainty.

Theories of mind in psychoanalysis are too complex to review here, but two features stand out in Freud's writings. These are his kaleidoscopic use of the term projection and his epistemology. Freudian projection most famously is an unconscious avoidance of one's own unacceptable states of mind by attributing them to someone else. Avoidance, however, is not the only kind of projection, as Freud wrote in *Totem and Taboo* (1990 [1912–1913]: 80–81):

> Projection was not created for the purpose of defence; it also occurs where there is no conflict. The projection outwards of internal perceptions is a primitive mechanism to which, for instance, our sense perceptions are subject, and which therefore normally plays a very large part in determining the form taken by our external world.

Indeed, avoidance is only one of a panoply of forms of projection for Freud (as Hurry et al. 1976 and Lewis et al. 1994 among others show). Further, it is only one of a number of "negative" forms, abuses of a phenomenon that normally is positive.

Of the normal, positive forms, the basic one (called eccentric projection above, and noted in *Totem and Taboo*) is that we see qualities of objects such as color, texture, weight and so on as existing outside ourselves, in the objects, whereas really they are internal products of our senses. Such projection, though mistaken, produces a usable world-view. A second normal projection (which echos Feuerbach) is "endopsychic." This is based on one's dim perceptions of the workings of one's own psyche, which are projected outward because of an internal pressure and in order that we may have access to them (Freud 1901, 1919, 1950). Such projection constitutes illusions of immortality, cosmic retribution and other transcendent conditions. A third form of normal projection (reminiscent of Hume's theory of religion) is an effort to explain the natural world. It is prominent in primitive humans (Freud 1901, 1990 [1912–1913]) who, lacking knowledge of the world's events and needing explanations, project their self-knowledge for that purpose. Chief results are animism and anthropomorphism. A fourth kind of projection is infantile. It is part of the infant's differentiation of self from objects and sometimes is called the origin of projection (Freud 1920). In this, the infant assimilates (introjects) pleasurable sensations to itself and expels (projects) unpleasurable ones. Thus the infant identifies pleasure with itself and displeasure with the external world.

The other major category of Freudian projection is negative or defensive. It constitutes an abuse of normal projection, and its central purpose is to deny something objectionable about oneself. Negative projection again has a number of forms (Hurry et al. 1976). A first form is projection of cause. Whenever a noticeable internal change occurs in us (Freud 1950) we must attribute it either to an internal or to an external cause. If we cannot choose an internal one, we choose an external one. An internal cause of personal failure, for example, is emotionally unacceptable, so we attribute failure to intervention by someone else. A second form is projection of self-reproach, motivated by our ability to reject a reproach from others and our inability to reject a reproach from within. A third is projection of anxiety, by forming a phobia of some external object when one actually is threatened from within. A fourth form is the projection of "instinctual drive impulses" (Freud 1911). This disguises one's desires from oneself by shifting them to another. The unacceptable desire may be further disguised by inversion before it is projected. Illicit love, for example, first may be disguised as hatred (Freud 1911) and then projected, so that the loving person perceives the loved one as feeling hatred. Finally, Freud distinguished a negative projection in which the chief symptom is an emotional response to the feeling that has been projected: for example, a woman loves another woman, projects that condition upon her husband, and in consequence experiences jealousy of the husband (Freud 1911).

To complicate matters still further, both negative and positive projections can be internal, upon the ego: "the object has been set up in the ego itself, has been, as it were, projected on to the ego" (Freud 1916–17: 427). Two fantasies can even be projected upon each other (Freud 1899: 315, in Hurry et al. 1976: 75). Thus projection for Freud is flexible indeed.

Are all these kinds of projection really the same thing? For example, do they have the same source? Freud (1990 [1912–1913]: 115) himself is uncertain why projection occurs, concluding only that it must alleviate some strain: "I propose to avoid entering into the general problem of [its] origin. It is, however, safe to assume that [it] will be intensified when projection promises to bring . . . mental relief." This explanation proves circular. Freud explains the mental relief as escape from conflict between impulses, namely "between different impulses all of which are striving towards omnipotence—for they clearly cannot all become omnipotent." But although "striving towards omnipotence" may accurately describe the behavior of whole human beings, it does not really describe the behavior of their component parts, such as impulses. Instead, it anthropomorphizes these impulses, and in a way that is pivotal to Freud's explanation. Since in the same book Freud says anthropomorphism (which he merges with animism) is a projection, his explanation of projection as an escape from anthropomorphic impulses makes projection an escape from itself. Freud's account comes to resemble the *uroboros*, the mythical serpent that sustains its life by eating its own tail.

Freud's epistemology may be called naïvely realistic. He assumes that normal perception is passive sensory apprehension of the world as it is. The only active intervention by mind in this process is that, as noted, we experience the content of our sense impressions (color, weight, etc.) as located in the external world instead of within ourselves. This basic sensory world is the same for everyone and thus is objective. In contrast, projected perceptions that are ideational or emotional, and thus shaped by peculiar, individual needs and interests, are *ipso facto* different from normal perception: "Under conditions whose nature has not yet been sufficiently established, internal perceptions of emotional and intellective processes can be projected outwards in the same way as sense perceptions ... though they should by rights remain part of the internal world" (Freud 1990 [1912–1913]: 81). That is, perceptual projection other than that of the elementary senses constitutes a subjective view of the world, and is abnormal and misleading. Freud admits, moreover, that such projection is unexplained.

A second set of approaches to psychological projection comprises the "projective techniques," a variety of means for discovering personality traits using relatively unstructured stimuli to elicit relatively open-ended responses. The term projective technique first was used by L. K. Frank (1939), although similar methods date back at least to Galton's experiments with word association in 1879 (Symonds 1946). The best-known techniques are Hermann Rorschach's ink-blot tests, created in the 1920s, in which subjects are asked to interpret a series of ten blots, and Henry Murray's Thematic Apperception tests, developed in the 1930s, in which subjects are asked to tell stories about drawings. Other projective techniques include sentence completion, finger painting, sculpting in clay or dough, organizing toy figures and similar open-ended tasks.

Although most of these techniques include some standardized framework for interpreting responses, with Freudian theory as the most common basis, method and theory vary considerably both among and within techniques. The common assumption is only that such techniques reveal preoccupations and personality traits which subjects otherwise would be unwilling or unable to disclose. What is projected is unclear. A recent encyclopedist (in Gall 1996: 288), for instance, says simply that subjects "project their own personalities onto the stimulus." The results are widely variable, and projective tests have been criticized sharply. The encyclopedist writes that compared to "questionnaire-type personality *assessments*, projective tests are difficult to score, and [of dubious] reliability and validity." Users "have been strongly attacked for their failure to define [projection] operationally" (Murstein and Pryer 1959: 368). In personality testing as elsewhere in psychology, projection remains both protean and controversial.

Religion as Projection

Theories of religion that in some way invoke projection are equally varied. Further, what constitutes such theories is itself a matter for definition. If one means by projection only that religion is in some measure a product of human thought and action, then such theories not only are diverse but also appear as early as Xenophanes. If one means by it that religion is primarily a human product, projectionism goes back at least to Spinoza and Hume. If, however, one means specifically that religion is nothing but an objectification (or externalization) of human needs, desires and thoughts—the definition I adopt here—then the first account that is both explicit and well developed belongs to Feuerbach (1957 [1841], 1967).

Little read today, Feuerbach in the mid-nineteenth century was revolutionary, and recently both his historic influence and his current relevance have been reevaluated (Wartofsky 1977; Thornton 1996; and especially V. A. Harvey 1995). Harvey argues, for example, that Feuerbach had not one but two theories of religion, and that while the earlier and better-known one now seems obscure and difficult, the later one anticipates various current theories.

The first theory, in *The Essence of Christianity*, quickly became well known in the 1840s. Its (Hegelian) basis is that human consciousness arises in a social context and that each person becomes self-aware only through interaction with other humans. In this process, humans also become aware of themselves as different from other kinds of living beings: that is, as a species. This species-consciousness focuses on characteristic human capacities—for reason, will and feeling—that both distinguish humans as organisms and make them viable. Because these capacities are key to our survival and because we flourish to the degree that they are developed, we experience them as our species "perfections." Enchanted with them and with our distinctiveness, we reflexively picture the species as something independent of its individual members and indeed independent of time and space.

At the same time, we find that as individuals we have these perfections only imperfectly. We see ourselves as unlike the species, in that we are limited, defective and fated to die. In this predicament, our imagination, swayed by our omnipotent feelings, pictures our perfections in pure form as a transcendent being. "God," as Harvey (1995: 39) summarizes the result, "is the notion of the species transformed by the imagination into a perfect exemplar of the species, a conscious being with perfect knowledge, will, and, above all, feeling."

Feuerbach's later theory, developed in several intermediate works and set out in *Lectures on the Essence of Religion* (English trans. 1967), abandons the Hegelian themes of self- and species-consciousness and develops the naturalistic and existential themes of confrontation with dependency, anxiety and death. Here the object of religion is no longer the species and its perfections but nature, including both the nonhuman world and the involuntary, unconscious aspects of humans. Caught between a profound desire to live and to be recognized, on the one hand, and the indifference of nature, on the other, humans create a Being who can answer their deepest needs—those for immortality and for cosmic acknowledgment.

This theory, even more than the first, invokes the power of the imagination and its servitude to our feelings. It claims that our beliefs are directed by our omnipotent desires. Religion, in short, is wishful thinking. In this later work, projection in any explicit sense disappears. Whereas Feuerbach's earlier theory had both used the term projection (and several related terms) and specified a mechanism producing projection (the involuntary reification of species traits), this one does neither. Religious thought now constitutes not what people essentially *are*, but rather what they *want*. Thus the first writer on religion to treat religious thought explicitly and in detail as projection ends with something quite different.

A number of late nineteenth- and early twentieth-century writers on religion carried on Feuerbach's ideas in some form. Prominent among these are Freud, Marx, Durkheim and, in some views, Jung. Freud wrote on projection primarily as a psychoanalytic phenomenon, and when he applied the idea to religion some of the same variability appeared: religion and God represent a range of inner phenomena cast outward on the world at large. These phenomena usually are neurotic. In his most concentrated work on religion (*The Future of an Illusion*, 1927), however, projection scarcely appears. Instead, the cause of religion is wishful thinking pure and simple. Religious ideas "are illusions, fulfilment of the oldest, strongest and most urgent wishes of mankind. The secret of their strength lies in the strength of those wishes" (Freud 1989 [1927]: 38). As in the later Feuerbach, no specific mechanism of projection is offered.

Karl Marx, drawing explicitly on Feuerbach, also may be considered a projection theorist of religion (V. A. Harvey 1995: 2; McCutcheon 1997b: 112). What is projected here, however, is again different from that in Feuerbach. Though it is in part a wished-for condition (in this case retribution, in addition to general well-being) it also is an image drawn from economic and political relationships and projected as a function of cosmic order. Moreover, alienation in Marx is the cause, not the result of religion, as it is in Feuerbach; people are alienated from the means of production and hence from their labor and its product, and turn to religion for relief. "The fact that the secular foundation detaches itself from itself and establishes itself in the clouds is really only to be explained by [its] self-cleavage and self-contradictoriness" (Marx 1964: 70). Social relations, not species perfections, are at the root of religion, and Marx writes (1964: 71) that Feuerbach "did not see that the 'religious sentiment' is itself a *social product*, and [belongs] to a particular form of society." The nature of projection as such, however, has only a small place.

Émile Durkheim (1995 [1912]) also is justly called a projection theorist of religion, although he uses the term infrequently. Durkheim even uses the idea rather as does Feuerbach. In Durkheim's case, what is projected is the idealized experience of society, which its members find broadly superior to themselves. Society is more durable and more powerful than they are, requires moral behavior of them, and offers vital instruction, nurture and protection.

The consequences of these virtues of society resemble those of Feuerbach's species-perfections: just as Feuerbach's species-perfections constitute God, so Durkheim's symbolically-encoded social values and strictures constitute the sacred. The sacred, arising out of an overwhelming sense of the power and value of society, appears as more than the sum of occasional social relations. It appears independent and self-sufficient and, needing a locus, is attributed to a non-human phenomenon.

> Religious force is none other than the feeling that the collectivity inspires in its members, but projected outside the minds that experience [the feeling], and objectified. To become objectified, it fixes on a thing that thereby becomes sacred; any object can play this role ... The sacredness exhibited by the thing is not implicated in the intrinsic properties of the thing: *It is added to them.* The world of the religious is not a special aspect of empirical nature: *It is superimposed upon nature.* (Durkheim 1995 [1912]: 230; emphasis in original)

Thus yet another social scientist invokes another kind of projection, this time in a form relatively close to that of Feuerbach.

A last figure from this period, Carl Gustav Jung, sometimes also is considered a projection theorist of religion (V. A. Harvey 1995), but this designation seems doubtful. Jung evidently took the notion of projection from Freud (von Franz 1980: 1), his sometime friend and collaborator, and hence ultimately from Feuerbach. His use of the notion, however, is different from Freud's and is peripheral to his view of religion.

The mind for Jung consists of a conscious ego, an individual unconscious and a collective unconscious containing "archetypes." Projection is neither a reflex of species-feeling nor a denial of an illicit feeling, but primarily a means to a social relationship with an object, such as another person. It achieves this relationship, unknown to the ego, by attributing aspects of the individual unconscious to the object. "In order to establish this relationship, the subject detaches a content—a feeling, for instance—from himself, lodges it in the object, thereby animating it, and in this way draws the object into the sphere of the subject" (Jung 1953–76: vol. par. 784). This creates an "archaic" identity with the object, the kind of relationship predominant in children and in "primitives." The attributes one projects may actually exist in the object as well, but usually only coincidentally and minimally. Hence most projection is illusory.

Religion, however, is different from projections and independent of them. Unlike them, it is a product not of the individual but of the collective unconscious. Moreover, it is an encounter, an "immediate experience" (Jung 1938: 53, 55, 62) of the *numinosum*, something that "seizes and controls the human subject, which is always rather its victim than its creator" (Jung 1938: 4). It also appears to be one of the archetypes (which are both within and independent of the individual) and, as such, may simply be called God. Since religion is an immediate experience and since what is experienced is independent of persons, no question of projection arises.

In recent decades, views of religion as projection have continued in various disciplines, especially in the social sciences. In sociology, the best-known projectionist is Peter Berger (1969). Prominent among anthropologists are Weston La Barre (1970), Melford Spiro (1987) and A. F. C. Wallace (1966); and among psychologists, Ana-Marie Rizzuto (1979) and Fokke Sierksma (1990).

The Metaphor Turned Inside Out

Projection in psychology and religious studies, V. A. Harvey remarks (1996), looks like a metaphor in search of a theory. Its versions, as noted, have little in common. At most, it is a claim that we see "out there" what really is only inside us. But this is a claim about a location, not about a process. It is not an explanation, but a description of what is to be explained. Nonetheless, the metaphor of projection has been given the form of an explanation. People using it are attempting to answer the question, how did what is inside get out there? Their reply is, we threw it out.

Projection, however, is a metaphor that does not go very far. The image has several problems. First, it requires that we identify something that is thrown out, something else onto which it is thrown, and the manner of throwing. What or where are these? There is no clear answer. Van den Berg (1972: 19, 48) writes that "no one has ever been able to explain the way a projection takes place." Lewis, Bates and Lawrence (1994: 1296) write of projection that there is "little evidence even for its existence" and Vergote (1990: 83) calls it a "stopgap term." Smythies (1954: 129, 130, 131) wryly notes that the projection of affect assumes

> movement in space of an object. Clearly, in the process under discussion, no such movement takes place. Little pieces of affect are not projected out of my body and alighting on your body are there sensed or perceived by me ... This process of the projection of mental images is a mythical one ... [Perceptions] are processes and structures *inside* the human organism. They arise inside it and stay there.

That is, if we are throwing anything, it is only inside our own heads and from one internal concept or field to another. Once the ostensible spatial gap between subject and object is subtracted from the image, however, the remaining image of throwing is pointless.

A second problem with the metaphor is that it implies that we can tell what is thrown out from what already is there. But how do we do this? No strings lead back to the thrower. Both psychoanalysts and projective testers note the difficulty of the distinction. Von Franz (1980: 6, 4), for example, writes that a "projection cannot be unambiguously established by the judgment of an outside observer" and that "it may be that the observer's judgment is mistaken, that the projector 'was right.' " Jung (in von Franz 1980: 6) writes, "there is no scientific test that would prove the discrepancy between perception and reality." Similarly, a scholar of religion (Smart 1973b: 75–76) states that when "it is said that humans project their meanings into the universe around them, what is needed is a neutral concept of the universe to which the projected meanings can be compared. It is not, however, clear as to how we get this neutral concept."

A third difficulty is that the metaphor implies that normal, non-projecting perception is passive, unbiased and objective. This is not true. Instead, all perception starts from some particular time and place. It uses some particular organ of perception, to detect some particular kind of information, to serve some particular interest. Standing in a crowd, I do not absorb all information indifferently, but glance over the heads to find the reddish-brown curls belonging to my wife. Any head of hair that resembles it will catch my attention. There is no line, however, between perceptions shaped by these idiosyncratic needs and interests and those shaped by the total set of our needs and interests. In Nietzsche's metaphor, whatever we know about the world is what our sensory net can catch and (owing to both nature and nurture) our net is constituted by the kind of information we need to have. Fortmann, also dismantling projection, describes the situation similarly: "the perceiver does not first see an 'objective world' which he subsequently distorts through projection. He does not add subjectively to the objective, but he reads his world from the beginning" (Fortmann in Bailey 1988: 210). Applying the point to religion, Hood (1989: 337) writes, "if one's experience of God is [projected], so are other experiences."

Projection as a psychological term appears, then, to come in so many varieties because it is theoretically empty. There is nothing in it but the varying content that it putatively explains, and perhaps a tacit folk model of visual perception: that we see things by touching them with our eyes. We can do better by turning our attention to the content and to our instrumental relationship to it. When we do so, what the contents of the ostensible projections have in common is that they bear especially clearly on our interests: we see, as a commonplace has it, what we want to see.

Equally, however, we see what we do not want to see. In the crowd, I want to see a particular head. In the woods, I do not want to see a bear. In both cases, I often see the object of my interest where in fact it does not exist. Similarly in the world at large, we may or may not want to see design, purpose and other humanlike effects and presences. Whether we want to or not, we often see them where they do not exist: that is, we anthropomorphize and animate the world. The most important of these anthropomorphized forms and effects are termed religious. The question is, how does this perceptual content arise?

A different model of our perceptual situation, more or less familiar in contemporary cognitive science, answers the question better than does projection. According to this model (as I have argued elsewhere; see Guthrie 1993) our perceptual world is chronically ambiguous, since any given sensation may have any of a number of causes. A moan may be a voice or the wind, a tapping may be a signal or a wind-blown branch against the window, a tickling on our ankle a loose thread or an insect. Thus perception is interpretation; we do not just see, but always see "as."

Interpretation in turn, because it is underdetermined, is a kind of betting (Gombrich 1973). As perceptual gamblers willy-nilly, we follow the strategy of Pascal's Wager: we bet on the most important possibility. Thus we are biased, tending to choose the voice over the wind, the signal over the branch and the insect over the thread. We apparently do so on the principle, better safe than sorry. If we are right, we gain much, and if wrong, we lose little. The strategy is unconscious, a product of natural selection, and seemingly shared by other animals (Griffin 1992: 37–39).

Nothing perceptual, then, is thrown out upon the world, either in religion or elsewhere. If we must use the image of throwing at all, we should picture perceptual bias as shaping what we throw in. Beginning with the wavelengths we see and the frequencies we hear, and advancing to the most complex conceptions, our perceptual and cognitive templates determine what we admit for consideration. If perception is to be throwing, it must be introjection. If we wish to salvage anything from the metaphor, that is, we need to turn it inside out. Such an inversion would help shed more light upon our perceptual processes, not least upon those processes that help give rise to religion.

Suggested Readings

Feuerbach, Ludwig
>   1957   *The Essence of Christianity*. George Eliot (trans.), New York: Harper & Row; original German edn, 1841.

Guthrie, Stewart Elliott
>   1993   *Faces in the Clouds: A New Theory of Religion*. New York: Oxford University Press.
>   1996   "Religion: What Is It?" *Journal for the Scientific Study of Religion* 35: 412–419.

Harvey, Van Austin
    1995   *Feuerbach and the Interpretation of Religion.* Cambridge Studies in Religion and Critical Thought, vol. 1. Cambridge: Cambridge University Press.
    1996   "Projection: A Metaphor in Search of a Theory?" pp. 66–82 in D. Z. Phillips (ed.), *Can Religion Be Explained Away?* New York: St. Martin's Press.

Hurry, Anne, Jack Novick and Kerry Kelly Novick
    1976   "Freud's Concept of Projection." *Journal of Child Psychotherapy* 4(2): 75–88.

Rizzuto, Ana-Marie
    1979   *The Birth of the Living God: A Psychoanalytic Study.* Chicago: University of Chicago Press.

Sierksma, Fokke
    1990   *Projection and Religion: An Anthropological and Psychological Study of the Phenomena of Projection in the Various Religions.* Foreword by Lee W. Bailey, Jacob Faber (trans.). Ann Arbor, MI: UMI.

Smythies, J. R.
    1954   "Analysis of Projection." *British Journal for Philosophy of Science* 5: 120–133.

17

RATIONALITY

Rodney Stark

❧❧

An immense intellectual shift is taking place in the social-scientific study of religion. During the past few years many of its most venerated theoretical positions—faithfully passed down from the famous founders of the field—have been overturned. The changes have become so dramatic and far-reaching that R. Stephen Warner identified them "as a paradigm shift in progress" (1993: 1044)—an assessment that since then "has been spectacularly fulfilled," according to Andrew Greeley (1996).

As is typical in science, the emergence of a new paradigm rests both on an empirical and a theoretical basis. During the past several decades there was a resurgence in research on religious topics and a substantial number of well-established facts were accumulated. The bulk of these turned out to be inconsistent with the old paradigm. Soon, in response to the growing incompatibility between fact and traditional theory, new theories were constructed to interpret the empirical literature. These incorporate new insights, some of them imported from other branches of social science.

Since I have played an active part in empirical studies of religious phenomena and have led the way in developing these new theories, it seems appropriate for me briefly to summarize and contrast key elements of the new and old paradigms. Fuller treatment will appear in a forthcoming book (Stark and Finke).

Elements of the Old Paradigm

In the beginning, religion was a central concern of social scientists. Thomas Hobbes, Adam Smith, David Hume, Auguste Comte, Karl Marx, Friedrich Engels, Herbert Spencer, Edward Tyler, Max Weber, Ernst Troeltsch, Émile Durkheim, William James, Lucien Lévy-Bruhl, Carl Jung and Sigmund Freud each wrote extensively about religious phenomena—a corpus of "theorizing" that was for generations the received wisdom on the subject. Indeed, although these founders of social science disagreed about many things, with the exception of Adam Smith and, to a lesser extent, Max Weber, there was remarkable consensus among them on key issues concerning religion.

Religion Is False and Harmful

It is claimed that religion harms the *individual* because it impedes rational thought. As Sigmund Freud explained on *one* page of his famous book on the subject (1927: 88; cf. 1989: 54–56), religion is an "illusion," a "sweet—or bittersweet—poison," a "neurosis," an "intoxicant" and "childishness to be overcome." Moreover, Freud's views were not particularly extreme; similar claims abound in the writings of early social scientists. For example, nearly three centuries before Freud, Hobbes (1956 [1651]: I.98) dismissed all religion as "credulity," "ignorance," and "lies" in one paragraph of his enormously influential book *Leviathan*; on the next page he explained that the gods exist only in the minds of believers, being but "creatures of their own fancy," and hence humans "stand in awe of their own imaginations." A century later, David Hume attributed religious enthusiasm to "blind and terrified credulity" and to "weakness, fear, melancholy, together with ignorance" (1882 [1741]: 144), while across the channel in France, Jean Meslier (circa 1733) explained that "Our nurses are our first theologians; they talk to children about God as they talk to them of werewolves" (in Durant and Durant, 1965: 613–614). And Auguste Comte, who coined the term "sociology," dismissed religion as "hallucinations" resulting from the triumph of "the passions over reason" (1896 [1830-42]: II.548).

In similar fashion, the traditional view is that religion harms *society* because it sanctifies tyrants and justifies exploitation of the masses. According to Marx and Engels, religion "is a great retarding force, is the *vis inertiae* of history" (1955: 18) and "the parson has ever gone hand in hand with the landlord" (1955: 15). Given the general acceptance of such views, it has been a virtual article of social-scientific faith that religious movements typically are reactionary responses against enlightenment and progress. Thus, the recent growth of evangelical Protestant groups is dismissed by the contemporary heirs of the received wisdom as a "flight from modernity" (Bruce 1992; Hunter 1983)—that is, people who feel threatened by the erosion of traditional morality are flocking into religious havens. Thus did Peter Berger describe evangelical Protestant churches: "They are like besieged fortresses, and their mood tends toward a militancy that only superficially covers an underlying sense of panic" (1969: 11).

A corollary of this line of analysis is that, in addition to being harmful, religion serves as a *pain-killer* for frustration, deprivation and suffering. The influential German sociologist Georg Simmel pronounced that religion is "a sedative for the turbulence of the soul" (1959 [1906]: 32). As Kingsley Davis (1949: 352) explained,

> the ego can stand only a certain amount of frustration ... The culture that drives him to seek goals that he cannot reach also, for the sake of sanity, provides him with goals that anybody can reach. These are goals that transcend the world of actual experience, with the consequence that no evidence to attain them can be conclusive. If the individual believes he has gained them, that is sufficient. All he needs is sufficient faith, and faith feeds on subjective need. The greater his disappointment in this life, the greater his faith in the next.

Marx, of course, put it rather more succinctly, identifying religion as opium, a view that prompted his collaborator Friedrich Engels to claim that early Christianity "first appeared as a religion of slaves and emancipated slaves, of poor people deprived of all rights, of peoples subjugated and dispersed by Rome" (Marx and Engels 1955: 316). Hence, the received wisdom: *religion appeals most strongly to the lower classes.*

Religion Is Doomed

As the social sciences emerged in the wake of the "Enlightenment," the leading figures eagerly proclaimed the demise of religion. Alexis de Tocqueville wrote in his famous early nineteenth-century study, *Democracy in America*: "The philosophers of the eighteenth century explained in a very simple manner the gradual decay of religious faith. Religious zeal, said they, must necessarily fail the more generally liberty is established and knowledge diffused" (1956 [1840]: II.319). This came to be known as the *secularization thesis*: that in response to modernization, "religious institutions, actions, and consciousness, [will] lose their social significance" (B. R. Wilson 1982: 149). Toqueville, as we shall see, was virtually alone in his rejection of the secularization thesis—perhaps no other social-scientific prediction enjoyed such nearly universal acceptance for so long. Thus, the very prominent anthropologist Anthony F. C. Wallace (1966: 265) wrote in an undergraduate textbook:

> The evolutionary future of religion is extinction. Belief in supernatural beings and supernatural forces that affect nature without obeying nature's laws will erode and become only an interesting historical memory ... Belief in supernatural powers is doomed to die out, all over the world, as the result of the increasing adequacy and diffusion of scientific knowledge.

Rodney Stark

Religion Is an Epiphenomenon

A third basis of consensus among the founders is that *religion is an epiphenomenon*. Despite imputing so many harmful effects to religion, the founders clung to the claim that religion was not real—that it was but a reflection of more fundamental social phenomena. As Marx and Engels explained, "All religion ... is nothing but the fantastic reflection in men's minds of those external forces which control their daily lives" (1955: 16). In Marxist analysis, these external forces are variously the mode of production, nature, and "the forces of history." In similar fashion, in his famous study of suicide, although the topic of religion takes up a substantial portion of the book, Durkheim (1951 [1897]) did not treat religion as something in itself, but only as an elaborate reflection of the more basic reality: one's degree of social integration (Stark and Bainbridge 1997).

Over the decades, this tendency of social scientists always to seek more "fundamental"—that is, material and secular—causes of all things religious has become such a basic assumption that it is routinely invoked by the news media. Thus, for example, the reasons offered for the growth of evangelical Protestant groups and the decline of the liberal denominations are always secular and usually discreditable. Among the more common suggestions about why the evangelicals grow are repressed sexuality, urbanization, racism, sexism, status anxieties and rapid social change. Never do proponents of the old paradigm even explore possible *religious* explanations: for example, that people are drawn to the evangelical churches by a superior religious product. From their viewpoint, since all religions are false and all gods are imaginary, there can be no point in examining whether some religions are more plausible and satisfying than others. One surely need not be a believer to see the absurdity of this position—imagine applying it to science fiction novels or to horror movies.

Religion Is a Psychological Phenomenon

Fourth, proponents of the old paradigm *rarely examine religion as a social phenomenon, as a property of groups or collectivities*, but instead treat it as fundamentally *psychological*.

They often talk about religion in collective terms, but in the end they reduce it to mental states and do not use aggregate or group units of analysis. Discussions of sects, for example, typically devolve to studies of sectarian attitudes rather than comparisons of religious groups. Even when the object of study is a group (a specific sect, for example), the usual result is a case study utterly lacking in systematic comparisons with other groups. Rarely did any of the founders (nor do their heirs) examine such things as the interplay among religious groups or variations in religious social structures across societies. Even the "obvious" exceptions to this claim turn out not to be very exceptional. Thus, when Durkheim devoted a book (1912; English trans. 1995) to the thesis that religion is, in effect, society worshiping itself, his research focused on the inner life of Australian aborigines and his conclusions about such things as totemism would not have survived even rudimentary cross-cultural comparisons (Goldenweiser 1915; Runciman 1969; Evans-Pritchard 1981). Or, even when Max Weber attempted to trace the rise of capitalism to the "Protestant Ethic," for the most part he conceived of the ethic as a psychological property of the individual (Hamilton 1996)—although, quite unlike most of his peers, he did attempt to contrast several societies in terms of the presence or absence of this property. Marx's and Engels' writings on religion also are overwhelmingly psychological, despite their mandatory mentions of modes of production and social evolution. The complete version of Marx's most famous quotation on this subject is typical: "Religion is the sigh of the oppressed creature, the heart of a heartless world, just as it is the spirit of a spiritless situation. It is the *opium* of the people" (1955: 11).

This tendency continues in that the overwhelming preponderance of contemporary research is based on individuals rather than on groups. But, no amount of surveys of individual opinions will reveal answers to questions such as why some new religions succeed while most fail, or why rates of religious participation are so much higher in some societies than in others. These are not questions primarily about individuals; they can be answered adequately only by reference to attributes of *groups*—in these instances, to attributes of new religions or of societies.

The Threat of Religious Pluralism

Finally, to the extent that the founders did take any interest in religion as part of a social system (rather than of the individual consciousness), their primary concern was to condemn the *harmful effects of religious pluralism and to stress the superiority of monopoly faiths*. Only monopolies, it was asserted, can sustain the unchallenged authority on which all religions depend. In contrast, as Durkheim explained, where multiple religious groups compete, religion becomes open to question, dispute and doubt, and thereby "the less it dominates lives" (1951 [1897]: 159). Even with the contrary American example staring them in the face, those committed to the old paradigm continue to express their faith in this doctrine. Thus Steve Bruce (1992: 170):

> pluralism threatens the plausibility of religious belief systems by exposing their human origins. By forcing people to do religion as a matter of personal choice rather than as fate, pluralism universalizes "heresy." A chosen religion is weaker than a religion of fate because we are aware that we chose the gods rather than the gods choosing us.

Notice too that Bruce, like Durkheim, conforms to the practice of reducing a social phenomenon—competing religious groups—to its presumed psychological effects.

The Emergence of the New Paradigm

The immense amount of attention given to religion in the formative days of the social sciences was motivated primarily by atheism (Evans-Pritchard 1965: 15). In addition, as Jeffrey Hadden reminded us, the social sciences emerged as part of a new political "order that was at war with the old order" (1987: 590). This new order aimed to overthrow the traditional European ruling élites and repressive political and economic structures, a battle in which the churches, Protestant as well as Catholic, often gave vigorous support to the old order. In response, social scientists declared themselves against religion as well as against the state. And, although most probably were not prepared to follow Denis Diderot's proposal, "Let us strangle the last king with the guts of the last priest," most found the pairing apt and the end result desirable.

However, in the early part of the twentieth century, as the center of gravity of the social sciences shifted from Europe to America, the image of religion as a political enemy waned and anti-religious antagonisms were muted. Lacking a compelling motive to attack religion, but also tending to be personally irreligious (Leuba 1921), American social scientists mostly ignored religion altogether. Like insects embedded in amber, the views of the founders were dutifully displayed to generations of students, but the social-scientific study of religion was far more of a museum than an area of research—"It was as if the founders had said it all" (Hammond 1985: 2).

No one has summed up the period as well as Gordon W. Allport in his major psychological study of religion, published in 1950:

> Among modern intellectuals—especially in the universities—the subject of religion seems to have gone into hiding ... Whatever the reason may be, the persistence of religion in the modern world appears an embarrassment to the scholars of today. Even psychologists, to whom presumably nothing of human concern is alien, are likely to retire into themselves when the subject is broached.
>
> During the past fifty years religion and sex seemed to have reversed their positions ... Today, psychologists write with ... frankness on the sexual passions of mankind, but blush and grow silent when the religious passions come into view. Scarcely any modern textbook writers in psychology devote as much as two shamefaced pages to the subject—even though religion, like sex, is an almost universal interest of the human race. (1950: 1–2)

Following World War II, a rapidly increasing number of American social scientists—Allport among them—began to do research on religious phenomena. Their interest was stimulated by the vigor of American religion, which not only refused to conform to the secularization doctrine, but seemed to grow in popularity. Indeed, during the 1940s and the 1950s a substantial religious revival appeared to be taking place in the United States. This probably was primarily a media event sustained by the proliferation of church construction projects which were necessitated by the rapid growth of new suburbs. Nonetheless, it stimulated a great deal of research and legitimated support for such research by major granting agencies. Research on religion also was stimulated at this time by the repeated encounter with stubborn religious "effects" by those working in other areas—for example, religion has a substantial independent impact on marriage, divorce, fertility, educational attainment, infidelity, crime, drug and alcohol consumption, to name but a few (Wuthnow 1979; Stark and Bainbridge 1997; Beit-Hallahmi and Argyle 1997).

The first stirring of renewed academic interest in religion among American social scientists took the form of a regular faculty seminar on the sociology of religion which began at Harvard during the 1940s. This seminar led directly in 1949 to the organization of the Committee for the Scientific Study of Religion which in 1956 was renamed the Society for the Scientific Study of Religion (SSSR). In 1961 the SSSR first published the *Journal for the Scientific Study of Religion*. In response to the journal, membership in SSSR leaped from around 200 in 1960 to more than 800 by 1962 (Newman 1974). Meanwhile, the growth of denominational research departments prompted the organization of the Religious Research Association (RRA) in 1951, thus giving formal status to an informal "committee" that had begun to meet in 1944 (Hadden 1974). In 1959 the RRA began to publish the *Review of Religious Research*. A decade later the American Catholic Sociological Society changed its name to the Association for the Sociology of Religion and dedicated its journal, *Sociological Analysis*, entirely to social-scientific research and theorizing on religion. (In 1993 the journal was renamed *Sociology of Religion*.)

These journals were founded to provide an outlet for articles reporting social-scientific research on religion, which the existing journals too often rejected for reasons rooted in the old paradigm—that these were merely studies of a dying and objectionable phenomenon (Beckford 1985; K. Thompson 1990). The existence of these new journals stimulated a considerable increase in the number of social scientists working in the area. By 1973 the SSSR had become an international organization with 1,468 members. Consequently, a body of new, competent studies (by now numbering in the thousands) soon began to pile up—"a vast, rapidly growing literature," as Warner put it (1993: 1044). Moreover, this was not primarily a literature of polemics or of speculation. Rather, as Bryan Wilson remarked, "sociological interest in religion has found increasingly empirical expression" (1982: 11). For all that, much of it seems dull, even pedestrian, most of the new literature deals in *fact* (Argyle 1959; Argyle and Beit-Hallahmi 1975; Beit-Hallahmi and Argyle 1997). And, from the beginning, many of the facts were inconsistent with the old paradigm; indeed, researchers often expected to find the precise opposite of what they did find. For example, study after study attempted to identify religiousness as a cause or consequence of neurosis and psychopathology, but again and again the results were to the contrary (Stark and Bainbridge 1997). And any number of studies sought in vain for evidence in support of secularization (Hadden 1987; Warner 1993; Stark, in press).

In short, this has always been a literature of *discovery* and therefore quite ill-suited to a museum environment. As early as 1973 Charles Y. Glock and Phillip E. Hammond recognized that the strain between the received theoretical wisdom and the expanding corpus of research findings necessitated a new paradigm, although they were rather pessimistic that one soon would be forthcoming. However, slightly more than a decade later, in his introduction to an edited volume of essays attempting to explain the failure of the secularization thesis, Hammond (1985: 3) recognized that the first fragments of "a new paradigm" already were in view. He concluded:

> Findings may seem scattered, therefore, and theories fragmented, though this is only because the master schemes—the eventual replacements of the secularization model—have not yet come into focus. Obviously, the successor volume to this one is waiting to be born.

The new paradigm arrived as predicted, as I shall summarize below.

Elements of the New Paradigm

The new paradigm not only rejects each of the elements of the old paradigm outlined above, but it proposes the precise opposite of each. As to the claim that religion is harmful at the individual level, the new paradigm cites a huge and growing literature that finds religion to be a reliable source of better mental and even physical health. Indeed, the new paradigm directly contradicts the postulate that religion is rooted in irrationality, and the research literature is far more consistent with the new paradigm than with the old on this point. This leads to discussion of the most basic premise of the new paradigm.

On Rationality

All of the leading approaches to social theory share a common first premise or proposition. It has been stated in a great many ways, but each variant asserts the same insight: that when faced with choices, humans try to select the most rational or reasonable option. Some advocates of "rational choice theory," especially economists, limit their definition of rationality to the elegantly simple proposition: *humans attempt to maximize*—to gain the most at the least cost (Becker 1976, 1996; Iannaccone 1995). One of the greatest virtues of this version is that it lends itself so well to inclusion in mathematical models. This virtue may also be its primary shortcoming—in their daily lives humans tend to fall well short of its fulfillment.

Consequently, I prefer a formulation of the rationality axiom that softens and expands the maximization assumption. Just as those working in the area of artificial intelligence have turned to models based on what they call "fuzzy logic" (Kosko 1992), I acknowledge that human reasoning often is somewhat unsystematic and "intuitive," and that maximization is often only partial and somewhat half-hearted. Indeed, aspects of laziness probably ought to be considered in the calculation of maximization. In any event, I use the more subjective and bounded conception of rationality, the one John Ferejohn (1991) identified as the "thick" model which has sustained a substantial sociological theoretical literature going back at least as far as Max Weber (Simon 1957; March 1978; Boudon 1993; Hechter and Kanazawa 1997). It seems worthwhile to consider some of the virtues of this approach.

First, this conception of rationality recognizes that humans pursue a variety of rewards or goals and confront an array of potential costs. It is obvious that many of the things human seek tend to be somewhat mutually exclusive, and consequently "maximization" must consist of the best fit among these conflicting ends. For example, some people's best fit would be partial maximizations of the satisfactions of parenting and those of career achievement. It was mainly to deal with the complexities of the pursuit of multiple and somewhat conflicting goals that Herbert Simon (1957) coined the word "satisficing" as a substitute for "maximizing." That is, Simon combined the words "satisfy" and "suffice" to identify the tendency of humans to settle for a sufficient level of satisfaction. In addition to facing conflicting goals, humans also must function within limits, often quite severe, on their information and their available options. Consequently, I feel it excessive to use the maximizing proposition. But, being equally reluctant to resort to a neologism such as "satisficing," I adopt Simon's (1982) later formulation of *subjective rationality*. As summed up by Raymond Boudon, subjective rationality applies to all human actions that are based on what appear to the actor to be "good reasons," reasons being "good" to the extent to which they "rest upon plausible conjectures" (1993: 10). But, whatever the good reasons for making choices, the imputation of rationality always assumes *the presence of subjective efforts to weigh the anticipated rewards against the anticipated costs*, although these efforts usually are inexact and somewhat casual.

The subjective approach to rationality is entirely consistent with the axiom of symbolic interactionism that in order to understand behavior we must know how an actor defines the situation (G. H. Mead 1934; Blumer 1969), for only from "inside" can we assess the rationality—that is, the reasonableness—of a choice. As James S. Coleman put it: "much of what is ordinarily described as nonrational or irrational is merely so because observers have not discovered the point of view of the actor, from which the action *is* rational" (1990: 18).

These considerations lead me to this formulation of the principle of human rationality: *Within the limits of their information and understanding, restricted by available options, guided by their preferences and tastes, humans attempt to make rational choices.*

Let us analyze this sentence to see precisely what it does and does not mean. The first part of the sentence—*within the limits of their information*—recognizes that we cannot select choices if we do not know about them nor can we select the most beneficial choice if we have incorrect knowledge about the relative benefits of choices. The second part of the phrase—*within the limits of their ... understanding*—acknowledges that people must make choices based on the set of principles, beliefs or theories they hold about how things work. These may, of course, be false, as the history of science demonstrates, but the rational person utilizes his or her principles about the world, because these are, for the moment, the most "plausible conjectures." Finally, it is self-evident that people may only select from among *available options*, although the full range of choices actually available may not be evident to them.

However, if humans all attempt to make rational choices, why is it that they do not always act alike? Why do people reared in the same culture not all seek the same rewards? Because their choices are *guided by their preferences and tastes*. Preferences and tastes define what it is that the individual finds rewarding or unrewarding. Consequently, people may differ in what they want and how much they want it (Hechter 1994). This not only helps us understand why people do not all act alike, but why it is possible for them to engage in exchanges: to swap one reward for another.

Of course, not all preferences and tastes are variable; clearly, there are some things that virtually everyone values, regardless of their culture: food, shelter, security and affection are among them (Aberele et al. 1950). Obviously, too, culture in general, and socialization in particular, will have a substantial impact on preferences and tastes. It is neither random nor a matter of purely personal taste whether someone prays to Allah or Shiva, or indeed, whether one prays at all. Still, the fact remains that even within any culture there is substantial variation across individuals in their preferences and tastes. Some of this variation is also at least partly the result of socialization differences—for example, we probably learn as children our preferences concerning highly liturgical services. But, a great deal of variation is so idiosyncratic that people have no idea how they came to like certain things. It's as the old adage says, "There's no accounting for taste." As noted above, that people differ greatly in terms of tastes and preferences facilitates exchanges. But it also explains what often are rather remarkable differences in behavior, as will be seen.

Finally, as already mentioned, the phrase that "humans attempt to make rational choices" means that *they will attempt to follow the dictates of reason in an effort to satisfy their desired goals*. Within the limits noted, this will involve some effort to maximize the net of rewards over costs. The word "attempt" is included to note that people do not *always* act in entirely rational ways. Sometimes we act impulsively—in haste, passion, boredom or anger ("I really didn't stop to think about what I was doing"). But, most of the time normal human beings will choose what they *perceive* to be the more reasonable option, and whenever they do so, their behavior is fully rational even if they are mistaken. For example, people buy stocks hoping to profit. If their stocks decline in value that does not mean they acted irrationally, only that they were wrong about which stocks to buy.

This formulation also leaves explicit leeway for people to act in ways others would define as "unselfish" choices, but it leaves no leeway for *altruism*, if that term is defined as intentionally selecting a negative cost / benefit ratio purely for the benefit of others. Such a claim usually produces tales of heroism—a soldier who held out to the end, a parent who rushed into a burning building to save a child. Or, you may wonder, what about people like Mother Teresa who forego a comfortable life to aid the sick and the poor? How are such people acting reasonably, let alone to maximize their personal rewards and minimize their personal costs? Or, as the British sociologist Anthony Heath put it: "The people who act out of a sense of duty or friendship, it is said, cannot be accounted rational and cannot be brought within the scope of [the] rational choice [proposition]" (1976: 79). But, Heath went on:

> Of all the fallacies [about rationality], this is the least excusable. Rationality has nothing to do with the *goals* which [people] pursue but only with the *means* they use to achieve them. When we ask whether someone is behaving rationally we ... are not asking whether he [or she] is choosing the "right" goal. (1976: 79)

As Heath implies, social scientists are fully aware of people such as Mother Teresa. But, we also recognize that their behavior violates the principle of rationality *only* if we adopt a very narrow, materialistic and entirely egocentric *definition of rewards*, and if we ignore the immense variety of preferences and tastes. Human life and culture are so rich because of the incredible variety of our preferences and tastes, of things we perceive as rewarding. There is no need to suggest that a parent has acted against self-interest by rushing into a burning building. Rather, let us recognize that the ability of humans to regard the survival of a child as more rewarding than their own survival is a credit to the human spirit and to our capacity to love. To call that altruism and place it in opposition to the rationality premise is to reduce noble behavior to crazy and irrational action. In fact, the "selfish" premise of rationality is humanistic in the fullest sense. It acknowledges our capacity to find rewards in our dreams, hopes, loves and ideals.

It is all the more amazing that social scientists have refused to extend the rationality axiom to religion in light of the fact that religious teachers always have stressed maximizing behavior as the justification for faith—that belief is the most rewarding (hence most *reasonable*) option. Blaise Pascal's "wager" is a very well-known example (Durkin and Greeley 1991), but in his 148th *Pensée* he asserts the maximizing axiom with an enthusiasm that not even an economist would dare:

> All men seek happiness. There are no exceptions. However different the means they employ, they all strive towards this goal ... This is the motive of every act of every man, including those who go and hang themselves. (1966 [1670]: 45)

Indeed, most of the world's religious scriptures abound in the language of exchange. For example:

> O Indra ... may plentiful libations of the people, and singing sages' holy prayers rejoice thee ... thus may we be made partakers of the new favours that shall bring us profit. (*Rig Veda* 10:89)

> Make for Me an altar of earth and sacrifice on it your burnt offerings and your sacrifices of well-being, your sheep and your oxen; in every place where I cause My name to be mentioned I will come to you and bless you. (Exodus 21:21)

> But to those men who honour me, concentrating on me alone, who are constantly disciplined, I bring gain and security. (Bhagavad Gita 9:22)

> He that believeth and is baptised shall be saved. (Mark 16:16)

> And give glad tidings, O Muhammad, unto those who believe and do good works; that theirs are Gardens underneath which rivers flow. (Qur'ān, sûrah 2:25)

Thus, I stand with Max Weber when he wrote:

> religiously or magically motivated behavior is relatively rational behavior ... It follows rules of experience ... Thus, religious and magical behavior or thinking must not be set apart from the range of everyday purposive conduct. (1963: 1)

Recognize, too, that the rationality proposition is *only the starting assumption* of most modern social science. Thus, while of immense importance, it offers very little in the way of theory. To say, for example, that people try to be rational even when making religious choices is little more than a slogan when we confront the real explanatory tasks. Suppose we wish to explain why people select one church over another, or why they drop out of a religious movement following an initial period of enthusiasm. The rationality premise tells us to look for variations in payoffs or satisfactions, but no more than that, leaving the social scientist in the same position as a detective seeking motives in a murder case. The real work is yet to be accomplished.

The Opiate Thesis

That religion is harmful at the level of society is a political, not a scientific claim. While the old paradigm was content to identify religion as the opium of the people, the new paradigm notes that religion also often is the "amphetamines" of the people in that it was religion that animated many medieval peasant and artisan rebellions (N. R. C. Cohn 1961), generated repeated uprisings among the native peoples of Africa and North America against European encroachment (Wilson 1973), and recently served as a major centre of mobilization against the tyrants of Eastern Europe (Echikson 1990). Indeed, the whole notion that religion primarily serves to compensate the deprived and dispossessed has become untenable. The consensus among scholars rejects as "imaginary history" Engels' notion that the early Christian movement was rooted in proletarian suffering. The facts force the conclusion that Christianity's greatest early appeal was to the privileged classes (Judge 1960; Scroggs 1980; Stark 1996a). In similar fashion, since the early 1940s many researchers have attempted to connect religiousness to social class, but their findings have been weak and inconsistent. Consequently, the need for new theorizing on the role of religion in the political affairs of nations has been recognized and efforts in that direction can be found in Stark and Bainbridge (1985, 1996) and I particularly refer the reader to the recent work of Anthony J. Gill (1998).

Against the Secularization Thesis

I have devoted an entire recent essay to entombing the secularization thesis beneath a mountain of contrary fact (Stark, forthcoming). The facts are these. First, there is no consistent relationship between religious participation and modernization. Indeed, the very few significant, long-term declines in religious participation to be seen anywhere in the world are greatly outnumbered by remarkable increases. What it needed is not a simple-minded theory of inevitable religious decline, but a theory to explain variation. Second, even in nations such as those in Europe, where religious participation has *always* been quite low, the overwhelming majority express firm belief in basic religious tenets and describe themselves as religious. It is perverse to describe a nation as highly secularized (as many do) when two-thirds or more say they are "a religious person," and fewer than five percent say they are atheists. Third, the spread of science cannot result in secularization, because science and religion are unrelated: overall, scientists are as religious as anyone else and the more scientific their field, the more religious they are (Stark, Iannaccone and Finke 1996, forthcoming).

Seeking Religious Causes of Religious Phenomena

Despite their frequent claims that religion is an epiphenomenon, the founders often postulated religious effects, not all of them bad. For example, theorists as diverse as Karl Marx and Herbert Spencer took it for granted that religion reinforced the moral order, and if this placed it in league with the ruling classes, religion also was thought to sustain honesty, charity and temperance. The new paradigm is entirely compatible with the premise that religion has many effects and, indeed, a huge empirical literature finds religious people more likely to observe laws and norms and, consequently, that cities having higher rates of religious participation have lower rates of deviant and criminal behavior (Stark and Bainbridge 1997). Where the old and new paradigms part company is over the causes of religion.

The old paradigm directs social scientists to dig as deeply as necessary in order to uncover the "real" causes of religious phenomena. For example, a wave of public religious enthusiasm took place in various American cities between 1739 and 1741. In each city, "huge crowds of crying, sobbing people [gathered], thousands upon thousands of desperate souls, asking what they must do to be saved" (Wood 1993: 20). Then, at the start of the nineteenth century came widespread reports of similar activities going on in rural areas along the western frontier as again crowds gathered and people moaned and groaned for divine forgiveness. These events came to be known as the first and second "Great Awakenings" and social scientists have devoted a great deal of effort to explaining why each took place when and where it did.

Proponents of the old paradigm invariably begin their explanations by postulating a *sudden*, generalized *need* for more intense religion. Thus, William G. McLoughlin, regarded by many as the leading authority on awakenings, attributed them to sudden periods of "grave personal stress" (1978: 2). Such stress, in turn, has been traced to such "underlying causes" as floods, epidemics, crop failures, business failures, financial panics, financial booms, the incursions of a market economy, industrialization, rapid immigration and so on (Barkun 1986; Gordon-McCutchan 1983; G. M. Thomas 1989). But, a far more plausible interpretation of these "awakenings" makes no mention of any intensifications of religious needs or of the impact of social or natural crises (Jon Butler 1982, 1990; Finke and Stark 1992, T. L. Smith 1983). Instead, these scholars trace the revivals in question to organized *religious* innovations and actions. Specifically, proponents of the new paradigm note that religious organizations led by George Whitefield in the eighteenth century and Charles Finney in the nineteenth used vigorous and effective marketing techniques to sustain revival campaigns, which later historians have classified as "awakenings." In contrast to scholars who explain that because of various crises "the times" were right for huge crowds to "materialize" to hear Whitefield, for example, the new interpretation stresses that:

> Whitefield was a master of advance publicity who sent out a constant stream of press releases, extolling the successes of his revivals elsewhere, to cities he intended to visit. These advance campaigns often began two years ahead of time. In addition, Whitefield had thousands of copies of his sermons printed and distributed to stir up interest. He even ran newspaper advertisements announcing his impending arrival ... It was from these efforts that crowds "materialized." (Finke and Stark 1992: 88–89)

What Whitefield accomplished was not to exploit new religious needs, but to appeal successfully to needs going essentially unserved by the lax, state-supported churches in the American colonies at this time—something which Whitefield fully recognized, remarking during his visit to Boston in 1740, "I am persuaded, the generality of preachers [in New England] talk of an unknown and unfelt Christ. The reason why congregations have been so dead, is because they have had dead men preach to them" (Whitefield 1969 [1747]: 471).

An equally huge literature attributes the "explosive growth" of new religious movements in the United States in the late 1960s and early 1970s to profound social causes. Particular attention has been given to uncovering the secular causes of the special appeal of Eastern faiths for Americans during this period. Thus, Harvey Cox blamed the whole thing on capitalism, charging that converts to Eastern faiths had "been maddened by consumer culture" (1983: 42). Not only the sensational media, but "serious" journals abounded with equally hysterical theories. As Thomas Robbins summarized, each of these identified one or more "acute and distinctively modern dislocation which is said to be producing some mode of alienation, anomie or deprivation to which Americans are responding" (1988: 60). With her usual grasp of the essentials, Eileen Barker commented, "those who have read some of the sociological literature could well be at a loss to understand why *all* young adults are not members [of new religious movements], so all-encompassing are some of the explanations" (1986: 338).

In fact, there was *no growth*, explosive or otherwise, of new religious movements in this era (Finke and Stark 1992); the rate of new movement formation was constant from 1950 to 1990. As for the brief increase in the proportion of Eastern faiths among new American movements, capitalism had nothing to do with it. Rather, in 1965 the elimination of exclusionary rules against Asian immigration made it possible for the first time for authentic Eastern and Indian religious leaders directly to seek American followers. Consequently, there was an increase in the number of Eastern religious organizations, but the number of actual converts was minuscule. Even so, growth was the result of *religious* efforts—of face-to-face recruitment activities.

Explosive growth by new religions did in fact occur in Japan following World War II—so many new groups appeared that observers spoke of "the rush hour of the gods" (McFarland 1967). It has been assumed that the cause of this religious fervor was the devastation and suffering produced by the war. But, no similar religious activity took place in post-war Germany or in the Soviet Union, where devastation and suffering surely equaled that of Japan. On the other hand, there also was a religious "rush hour" in South Korea which was hardly touched by the war, at the end of which it was liberated from Japanese rule. The common element is religious liberty. The German state church tradition was not challenged by the occupying governments, except in the Eastern Zone where the Soviets repressed all religion. As I have demonstrated elsewhere (Stark and Iannaccone 1994; Stark 1998), state churches suppress religious competition and thus new religious groups could not prosper in either part of Germany. But, in Japan, the "MacArthur" constitution inaugurated complete religious freedom in a nation where the government previously had strictly repressed all but a few traditional religions. In South Korea, too, a policy of religious liberty replaced the prior Japanese religious repression. In both nations the emergence of new religions took place almost at once. However, the end of Japanese rule brought no similar eruption of new religions in Taiwan (Formosa) because its new Nationalist Chinese rulers did not condone religious freedom.

The notion that the war caused Japan's "rush hour" is further refuted by the fact that nearly all of what became the leading new religious movements in the post-war period originated *prior* to the war—sometimes long before. Konkō-kyō was founded in 1885, Reiyukai Kyodan in 1925, the immensely successful Sōka Gakkai movement was organized in 1930, as were PL Kyōdan and Seichō no Ie, and Risshō Kōsei-kai began in 1938 (McFarland 1967; Moroto 1976). But, government repression was sufficient to limit them to a small group of followers, often restricted to a single village or neighborhood. Thus, Neill McFarland described them as "innumerable captive and incipient religious movements" and noted that the new constitution allowed "their voice to be heard" (1967: 4). As Aiko Moroto noted, these groups originated in pre-war Japan, and what was new after the war was that "these groups came out into the open and flourished" (1976: 1). Harry Thomsen pointed out that what was new about these religions was that their new freedom allowed them to utilize "new methods of evangelism" (1963: 17). Hence, the primary "secular" cause of the proliferation of new religions in Japan and Korea was merely the legal right to function, and the rest of the story involves actions by religious organizations based on religious motives.

Therefore, while the new paradigm accepts that secular crises often do have religious consequences, it denies that secular social factors *must* underlie religious phenomena. Nor need religious causes (or secular ones for that matter) be "material" as opposed to ideas and beliefs. Proponents of the new paradigm accept that religious doctrines *per se* often have consequences. For example, the "root causes" of efforts by the early Christians to nurse the sick during the great plagues that periodically swept the Roman Empire, in contrast with their pagan neighbors who shunned and abandoned stricken family members, were doctrinal: belief that death was not final and in the obligation to be one another's keepers (Stark 1996a).

Equally obvious contemporary instances of doctrinal causation can be seen by comparing various religious movements on the basis of their capacity to sustain leaders with sufficient authority. There are many bases for legitimate authority within organizations. However, when organizations stress doctrine, as all religious movements do, these doctrines must define the basis of leadership. Who may lead and how is leadership obtained? What powers are granted to leaders? What sanctions may leaders impose? These are vital matters, brought into clear relief by the many examples of groups that failed (or are failing) for lack of doctrines defining a legitimate basis for effective leadership.

That doctrines can directly cause ineffective leadership is widely evident in contemporary New Age and "metaphysical" groups. If everyone is a "student," and everyone's ideas and insights are equally valid, then no one can say what must be done or who is to do what, when. The result is the existence of virtual non-organizations—mere affinity or discussion groups incapable of action. In similar fashion, some of the early Christian gnostic groups could not sustain effective organizations because their fundamental doctrines prevented them from ever being anything more than a loose network of individual adepts, each pursuing secret knowledge through private, personal means (Pagels 1979; M. A. Williams 1996). In contrast, from the start Christianity had doctrines appropriate for an effective structure of authority since Christ himself was believed to have selected his successors as head of the church.

Thus can one utilize religious doctrine as a causal factor vis-à-vis other religious phenomena, both individual and organizational. It is, of course, logically possible to raise the issue of from whence particular doctrines came and why these, rather than some other doctrines, were adopted. We may grant the legitimacy of such questions without promoting infinite regress or admitting that all fundamental causes are secular.

Finally, to grant causal status to doctrines forces recognition that the most fundamental aspect of any religion is its *conception of the supernatural*. Many religious doctrines and related practices presuppose supernatural beings having certain characteristics, among them consciousness and virtue. For example, it would seem unavailing to appeal to an impersonal higher power such as the Tao, and quite risky to do so to the undependable and often wicked gods of the Greek pantheon.

Social Approaches

Many of the most interesting and pressing questions facing the social-scientific study of religion require that religion be conceived of as social rather than as psychological, as a property of groups or even of whole societies. It is this emphasis on the social as against the psychological that is the most important feature of the new paradigm. To see more fully what is at issue here, consider the following questions, none of which can be reduced to psychology alone:

> Why is religious participation so low in most European nations and so high in the United States?
> Why are some Roman Catholic religious orders growing while others decline?
> Why are strict churches so much stronger than those that ask less of their members?
> Why do most sect movements fail?
> Why do cult movements thrive on the West Coasts of Canada and the United States and why are they even more successful in Europe?

I have attempted answers to these and other such questions in many recent publications which will be synthesized in a forthcoming book (Stark and Finke). In doing so I have, of course, utilized psychological assumptions and data as appropriate—I do not think psychological states are unimportant or that data on individuals (such as survey studies) are useless. Rather, my concern is to not *inappropriately* reduce group phenomena to individual traits, or to mistake attitudes for collective activity.

If stressing the social aspect of religion is a hallmark of the new paradigm, its most innovative theoretical feature is to identify religion as a subsystem within the social system: a *religious economy* (Stark 1985).

The Religious Economy

Religious organizations do not exist in a vacuum and therefore cannot be studied in isolation from their socio-cultural environments. Moreover, most of the time for most religious organizations a crucial aspect of that environment is *religious*—aspects of other religious organizations (including their doctrines), and aspects of the rules and norms governing religious activities. To facilitate analysis at this level of abstraction, my colleagues and I examine the religious life of societies within an overall conceptual and theoretical model: the *religious economy*. A religious economy is *a subsystem of all social systems* (Parsons 1951). It encompasses *all of the religious activity going on in any society*.

I use the term "economy" in order to clarify that, in terms of certain key elements, the religious subsystem of any society is entirely parallel to the subsystem involved with the secular (or commercial) economy: both involve the interplay of supply and demand for valued products. Religious economies consist of a market of current and potential followers (demand), a set of organizations (suppliers) seeking to serve that market, and the religious doctrines and practices (products) offered by the various organizations. My application of economic language to things often regarded as "sacred" is meant neither to offend nor as mere metaphor. Rather, my purpose is to facilitate immense explanatory power that can be gained by applying elementary principles of economics to religious phenomena at the group or social level—an application pioneered by Adam Smith more than two centuries ago.

As Smith recognized, and as I have demonstrated at length (Stark and Iannaccone 1994; Stark 1998), the most significant single feature of a religious economy is the degree to which it is unregulated and therefore market-driven, as opposed to being regulated by the state in favor of monopoly. Herein lies the key to explaining variations in the "religiousness" of societies, for the founders were entirely wrong about the harmful effects of pluralism and religious competition. Rather than eroding the plausibility of all faiths, competition results in eager and efficient suppliers of religion just as it does among suppliers of secular commodities, and with the same results: far higher levels of overall "consumption."

These, then, are the elements of the new paradigm. In this rapidly growing new literature, many different scholars pursue these fundamental assumptions to a great variety of conclusions, many of them not at all obvious. I am under no illusions that my colleagues and I have everything right; there undoubtedly will be many revisions and a great many extensions to come. But, there is nothing illusory about a basic paradigm shift in the social-scientific study of religion. A mountain of fact bars any return to the simple certitudes of the past.

Suggested Readings

Finke, Roger and Rodney Stark
  1992   *The Churching of America, 1776–1990: Winners and Losers in Our Religious Economy.* New Brunswick, NJ: Rutgers University Press.
Greeley, Andrew M.
  1995   *Religion as Poetry.* New Brunswick, NJ: Transaction Publishers.
Iannaccone, Laurence R.
  1992   "Sacrifice and Stigma: Reducing Free-Rising in Cults, Communes, and Other Collectives." *Journal of Political Economy* 100: 271-292.
  1994   "Why Strict Churches Are Strong." *American Journal of Sociology* 99: 1180-1211.

Stark, Rodney
   1996a *The Rise of Christianity: A Sociologist Reconsiders History.* Princeton: Princeton University Press.
   1996b "Why Religious Movements Succeed or Fail: A Revised General Model." *Journal of Contemporary Religion* 11: 133–146.
Stark, Rodney and Laurence R. Iannaccone
   1994 "A Supply-Side Reinterpretation of the 'Secularization' of Europe." *Journal for the Scientific Study of Religion* 33: 230–252.
Warner, R. Stephen
   1993 "Work in Progress Towards a New Paradigm for the Sociological Study of Religion in the United States." *American Journal of Sociology* 98: 1044–1093.
Young, Lawrence A. (Ed.)
   1997 *Rational Choice Theory and Religion: Summary and Assessment.* New York: Routledge.

18

RITUAL

Ronald L. Grimes

કે*કે

The Notion of Ritual

"Ritual" is a provocative notion, not a precisely delineated analytic category. One reason is that much of the scholarly literature fails to distinguish between the category and the thing categorized, between the idea of ritual and the enactment of rites. Another reason is that the literature has produced no coherent taxonomy of the kinds of ritual. There is no consensus whether ritual is most usefully treated as a superordinate or subordinate term. What subcategories does the category ritual include? Is festival, for instance, a kind of ritual? Alternatively, what larger category includes the smaller category ritual? Is ritual a component of religion, for example? Or of culture?

Besides the bedeviling problem of inclusion and exclusion, there is little agreement whether the terms "ritual," "rite," "ritualizing," and "ritualization" ought to be precisely defined or used as mere synonyms. There is the additional difficulty of deciding how to use related terms such as "ceremony," "magic," and "liturgy." Many scholars use the terms synonymously—except for magic, which, with few exceptions is still understood pejoratively, meaning "manipulation of supernatural powers." But is magic a kind of religion? Or a kind of ritual? Or an activity independent of both ritual and religion?

A few theorists distinguish ceremony from ritual, usually by making ceremony the less religious or less important term. For example, anthropologist Raymond Firth (1967a: 73) says:

> By *ceremony* I understand an interrelated set of actions with a social referent, and of a formal kind, that is, in which the form of the actions is regarded as being significant or important, though not valid or efficacious in itself. A *rite*, on the other hand, is also a formal set of actions, but the form in which these are carried out is regarded as having a validity or

259

efficacy in itself, through some special quality which may conveniently be termed of a mystical order, that is, not of the workaday world.

Most religious studies scholars leave the term liturgy to Christian theologians. A few writers, for example, anthropologist Roy Rappaport and I, use it as synonymous with "religious ritual." This way of using the term relieves one of the necessity of implying that all rituals are religious. Rappaport defines liturgy as "the performance of more or less invariant sequences of formal acts and utterances not encoded by the performers" (1979: 175).

Appeals to dictionaries are of little help in stabilizing usage. *The Random House College Dictionary* offers five definitions. In the first one, ritual is any "established or prescribed procedure" for "a religious or other rite." In addition to the frustrating circularity of defining ritual as a procedure for engaging in a rite, the definition hedges the question, Is ritual by definition religious? A second definition equates ritual not with a single procedure, but with a system of rites. But again, the definition is circular: ritual equals a system of rites. A third identifies ritual with a particular type of it, worship: ritual is the "observance of set forms in public worship." A fourth definition uses "ritual" to cover ritual-like procedures: "any practice or pattern ... *reminiscent* of religious ritual." The fifth treats "ritual" as a synonym for "*a book* of rites or ceremonies."

Diligent readers who try to beat the dictionary at its own game by looking up both "rite" and "ceremony" find they have not solved the conundrum so much as compounded it. "Rite" sports six definitions, most of which are synonyms for "ritual." The only exception is a usage in which "rite" refers to any historic division of Christian eucharistic liturgy, for instance, the "Eastern rite" or the "Anglican rite." The same kind of trouble plagues one who looks up "ceremony." Most uses of this term are synonymous with "ritual" and "rite." Other uses equate ceremony with formality, politeness or even meaningless observances.

If one tries to cut below the contemporary linguistic confusion by consulting an etymological dictionary hoping to arrive at the pristine simplicity of original usage, one still flounders. "Ceremony" might be based on the Latin word *caerimonia*, meaning "rites performed by Etruscan pontiffs near Rome." "Ritual," one etymological dictionary says, is derived from the Latin adjective *ritualis*, and "rite" comes from the Latin noun *ritus*. Both words simply mean "ritual," leaving us no further ahead. "Rite" is said to share the same root as "*arith*metic," and thus one might assume a vague connection between ritual and counting things or putting them in order. The most provocative claim about the etymology of the word ritual is proffered by Judy Grahn who says: "At base [that is, in Sanskrit], *rituals* and *rites* mean *public menstrual practices*" (1982: 270). *Ritu*, she believes, were practices in India meant to socialize and confirm the powers of menstruation. Although this derivation is apparently unknown or not convincing to the editors of etymological dictionaries, it is at least provocative.

Distressed in the search for a useful, ordinary-language definition of ritual, the confused may turn to scholars for help, only to find some of them, Jack Goody (1977) for instance, concluding that the word has no utility whatever. The notion of ritual not only has vague or conflicting definitions in English, it is also a Western, scholarly construct, a made-up object of study. Arguments to this effect are predicated on the observation that many languages have no word that one might translate with the English word ritual. Instead of having a general term, many people have only specific nouns—some common, some proper—that are parallels of "birthday," "Christmas," "Ramadan," "Bar and Bat Mitzvah."

But having no word for ritual does not mean there are no events in which people dance or pray, or that the word is useless. Probably any key term in scholarly discourse will expose its fictive nature after being run through the mill of cross-cultural comparison and having sustained analytical attention focused on it. So most scholars continue using the idea of ritual, along with an implicit or explicit definition of the term. Among those who offer formal ones, there is a noticeable division between broad and narrow strategies. Broadly defined, rites are, for instance, "culturally defined sets of behavior" (Leach 1968). The broader views of ritual treat it as synonymous with symbolic actions, deeds for which one can predicate not just consequences but meaning. In such definitions, ritual is a kind of communication, thus not so much one activity alongside others as an implicit dimension of all human interaction. Holding this view, one would not say, for example, that Caesarian section *is* ritual but that the symbolic dimension of Caesarian surgery is ritual. But because human actions, even ordinary ones, are fraught with meaning, most activities would become, by this definition, ritual. The broadest definitions include too much.

Many of the broad definitions are so vague as to be useless. So the majority are more tightly focused. An example of a narrow definition of ritual equates it with "traditional, prescribed communication with the sacred" (Honko 1979: 373). The more focused views often identify ritual with actions predicated on a theistic, mysterious or animistic premise, or performances by religious functionaries in sacred places. In this view, ritual is one kind of work *alongside* other kinds, for example, the deeds of midwives, dressmakers or morticians. This narrower way of defining ritual, which limits it only to religious rites, is in decline, but its advantage is that it cuts down on the confusion created by definitions with fuzzy boundaries. By using it, one can be certain what counts as ritual and what does not. The disadvantage is that it excludes emergent and non-religious ritualizing.

There is utility in both views, the narrow and the broad, because ritual is both different from and implicit in daily interactions. Ritual is both special and ordinary, so most contemporary definitions avoid the two extremes and instead specify two or three characteristics assumed to be common to all kinds of ritual. In these middle-range definitions ritual is a style of action, one that is formal, stylized, prescribed, symbolic, non-technological, repetitive, traditional and so on. Unfortunately, there is no general agreement on a single short list of qualifiers, but a typical example construes ritual as "a culturally constructed system of symbolic communication. It is constituted of patterned and ordered sequences of words and acts, often expressed in multiple media, whose content and arrangement are characterized in varying degree by formality (conventionality), stereotype (rigidity), condensation (fusion), and redundancy (repetition)" (Tambiah 1979: 119).

The Study of Ritual: A Meta-History in the Ethnographic Present

The history of the study of ritual has yet to be written. What I offer in its place is a kind of meta-history written in the timeless, ethnographic present as warning about its abstracted nature.

Rites are among the most visible aspects of a religion or culture. Ancient and contemporary travel literature is replete with tourists' accounts of public festivals and civil ceremonies. First encounters with a tradition were often mediated through visitors' encounters with ritual displays. But rites are not mere transparent windows opening into the heart of cultural values and meanings. They are also opaque; it takes enormous effort to comprehend a rite. Much early writing about ritual consisted of sketches of colorful surfaces and moving bodies. In ancient writing about ritual these exterior dimensions are bereft of cultural meaning but overlaid with the writers' own fantasies and projections. Ancient explorers, like contemporary tourists, were not in place long enough to make sustained inquiry, so their accounts transform religious enactments into aesthetic objects.

If noticing ritual begins with explorers, pilgrims and tourists, the defense of ritual begins with ritual experts. Those who lead, propagate or finance ritual activity are also obligated to interpret it—if not to the inquiring young, then to visitors; if not to visitors, then to themselves. This study of ritual from within is usually tagged with one of two clumsy labels: liturgical theology or indigenous exegesis. Rites are not merely enacted, they are also talked about. And they are talked about by those who perform them. In some societies, a class of ritual interpreters emerges as distinct from ritual performers. Although insider talk about ritual may sound like explanation, much of it is further ritualization, deeper mystification. Indigenous exegesis is, one might say, the ritualized study of ritual. More commonly, it is called the normative or theological or religious study of ritual. The purpose of studying ritual in this way is to maintain a ritual tradition's cogency, relevance and legitimacy. Insider study is not necessarily naïve. It can be quite critical, but its aims are practical and vested.

The normative study of ritual continues unabated, but it has competition. In the late nineteenth and early twentieth centuries the objectivist study of ritual begins when ethnographers enter the field to observe and document "other" people's rites, thus rendering performances as texts. Rites, taken to be enactments of religious beliefs and myths, become a privileged object of study, because they are thought to condense a society's values. In effect, ethnographers documenting rites become a second class of ritual interpreters. Unlike ritual specialists, ethnographers stand outside the sacred circle with no obvious vested interest in either the outcome or meaning of the rite. The anthropological interpretation of ritual posits hidden, tacit, unconscious or functional meanings of rites that lie beneath or behind the surfaces of the ceremonial events themselves. By virtue of their training and positions as sympathetic outsiders, social-scientific interpreters presume to have access to this hidden meaning. Thus they can explain to readers of their grant applications, articles and books what these rites mean. And asked, they sometimes even explain their discovered meanings to those who enact or lead the rites. In actuality, the social-scientific study of ritual is no less vested in its interests than the theological study of ritual; the difference lies not in *whether* it is invested but in *where* the investment is located.

In the early 1970s the study and practice of ritual in North America makes several rapid strides. Participant observers come back home announcing their initiations in far-away places; the dividing line between participation and observation is no longer sacred. In addition, ritual undergoes a drastic image change. Within a decade it becomes subversive, not conservative; creative, not traditional; exciting, not boring; processual, not structural. On the heels of this reenvisioned ritual, ritual studies emerges. It is an interdisciplinary enterprise involving performance studies, religious studies, anthropology and several other disciplines. The new constellation results in the founding of the *Journal of Ritual Studies*, along with ritual interest groups in the American Academy of Religion, the American Anthropology Association and the North American Academy of Liturgy. Ironically, shortly after the phrase "ritual studies" appears in scholarly discourse, the notions of ritual and ritual meaning are subjected to sustained critique. Dan Sperber (1975) and Frits Staal (1996) attack the assumption that rites "mean" anything. And Catherine Bell (1992) declares that ritual is not something "out there" that scholars find people doing and then describe or explain. Instead, it is a scholarly contrivance invented and defined so as to mediate classical Western dualisms such as thought and action. Bell's arguments appear to dissolve the very ground upon which she and other ritual studies scholars stand.

An Exemplary Ritual Theorist

However one names, or refuses to name, the phenomenon I persist in calling ritual, people still dance and scholars, Bell included, still write books about it.

The result is provocative but frustrating. Ritual theory is no more coherent than the history of the study of ritual. Much writing about ritual is done by people who engage in it as a sideline. As a result, contemporary students of ritual read little of each other and engage in a minimum of sustained conversation or scholarly debate. So even though there is theorizing and essaying, there is a minimum of ritual theory, by which I mean sustained, collaborative effort to agree on definitions of terms, formulate coherent classifications, conduct research that depends on previous research, and identify the co-variances, causes and consequences of rites.

For the purpose of theoretical orientation to the topic of ritual it would make little sense to summarize a dozen scholars' ideas about ritual. It is more useful to critique and build on the most promising or most fully developed scholarly writings on ritual. To that end, I will consider one key claim of Victor Turner (1920–1983), whom I take to be the most influential and prolific ritual theorist of the twentieth century.

The idea that rites conserve and consolidate social reality has its primary expression in Émile Durkheim. The notion that rites can also transform social reality has its most articulate spokesperson in Victor Turner. In the 1960s and 1970s the seed planted by Arnold van Gennep in *The Rites of Passage* (1960 [1909]) culminated in a dense grove, the prolific writings of Victor Turner. The most widely read of his works, *The Ritual Process*, was published in 1969. For Turner, the whole of ritual theory, not just rites of passage, was determined by the image of passing across a threshold or a frontier. For Turner, real ritual effects transformation, creating a major "before" and "after" difference. In Turner's hands, the *limen*, or threshold, is not just a phase in a rite but a creative "space" resulting in a temporary state known as liminality. Liminality is what enables ritual to do the work of transformation. In Turner's vision, ritual is a hotbed of cultural creativity; its work is more to evoke process than to buttress structure. Ritual that merely confirms the status quo rather than transforms it Turner preferred to call ceremony.

Turner shared the widespread assumption that rites of passage have their proper matrix in small-scale societies. Nevertheless, he was ambivalent about treating them as irrelevant to large-scale societies. Although he admitted that rites of passage achieve *maximal* expression outside of Europe and North America, Turner retained his interest in rites of passage, making them the model for understanding how ritual in general works. He treated one rite of passage, initiation, as the quintessential rite of passage, and he regarded one of its phases, liminality, as definitive of ritual. In Turner's writings liminality becomes even more autonomous than it had been for van Gennep. In fact, under Turner's influence liminality was not only an important dynamic of ritual, but a value, a virtue. The liminal had moral and religious worth. It was to become the generative, therefore primary, principle of ritual in particular and culture in general.

Especially important is Turner's identification of sacrality with liminality and secularity with social structure. The two equations were consonant with some of the values of the 1960s and 1970s inasmuch as they reversed the earlier equation of sacrality with structure and secularity with transition. When sacrality came to be identified with liminality, a new view of ritual was possible.

In Turner's view liminality is understood as "the Nay to all positive structural assertions, but as in some sense the source of them all, and, more than that, as a realm of pure possibility whence novel configurations of ideas and relations may arise" (V. Turner 1967: 97). The resulting new image of ritual was that of a generator or matrix. In Turner's theory ritual became subversive, the opposite of ceremony, the staunch conservator of culture, maintainer of the status quo and glue of society that Durkheim (1995 [1912]) had made it.

In Turner's view liminality constitutes a zone of creativity because it is a crucible capable of reducing culture to its fundamental elements, its "alphabet." This reduction allows for their playful recombination in novel or fantastic patterns. Turner refers to these elements as first principles and as building blocks. The whole set works as a template, ultimate measure or paradigm.

In a liminal state, thought Turner, a peculiarly important kind of temporary community emerges. He referred to it as *communitas* and regarded it as the "fountainhead and origin" of social structure. The generativity of liminality, then, is not limited to ritual or artistic creativity; it includes cultural and social creativity as well. Said Turner (1967: 106):

Put a man's head on a lion's body and you think about the human head in the abstract. Perhaps it becomes for you, as a member of a given culture and with appropriate guidance, an emblem of chieftainship.

There could be less encouragement to reflect on heads and headship if that same head were firmly ensconced on its familiar, its all too familiar, human body.

Liminality here breaks, as it were, the cake of custom and enfranchises speculation.

Liminality is the realm of primitive hypothesis.

As Turner turned his attention from Africa to North America and Europe, he found that the liminality-saturated model of initiation served him less and less well, so he turned his attention to other ritual types, most notably pilgrimages and festivals. Pilgrimage functioned for him as a transition type between tribal initiation and the dispersed, quirky stuff of the North American arts scene, especially experimental theater. Pilgrimage rites had some of the attributes of liminality, but pilgrimage was voluntary rather than obligatory.

Turner's tendency to treat initiation as a synonym for rites of passage in general was quite pronounced. For him, initiation is to tribal society as pilgrimage is to feudal society, but the analogy left one asking, Where does liminality appear in industrial society? Though Turner never explicitly answered the question, the implied candidate seemed to be festival, the exemplary form of ritual play. In festivity one does not have to believe but can participate "subjunctively." In festivity not only is participation optional, but so is belief. In the end, Turner dislodged liminality from its original context, traditional initiation, in order to coin a new, larger notion, the liminoid. The liminoid is constrained by no particular type of ritual—not initiation, pilgrimage or festival—so the liminoid is virtually synonymous with cultural creativity, imagination actively rendering the world a more habitable place.

Turner not only observed, interpreted and theorized about ritual; he also participated in it and created it. In fact, he was initiated by the Ndembu. Though he recognized the boundary between theory and practice, he regularly crossed it: for him the boundary was not a sacred artifact. Rather, it was a social construction, and one could—in fact, ought—to imagine it otherwise. One of the bridges between Turner's theory and his practice was pedagogy. The term he eventually used for one of his most distinctive practices was "ethno-drama," or "performing ethnography," by which he meant the imaginative re-enactment of social dramas, life crises and their corresponding rites. By the end of his life Turner himself was becoming an example of liminoid ritualizing.

Because rites of passage, liminality and *communitas* have become such generative ideas, and because they continue to be unreflectively cited and popularly venerated, we should recognize some of their limitations. For instance, is it obvious that rites transform? In some societies rites are not thought to *transform*, that is, to change things fundamentally. Instead, rites of birth, coming of age, marriage and death *protect* participants, or they may *celebrate* transformations that have already occurred by other means. The Bemba say their rites *purify* women at the moment of first menses. This is a view quite different from one which holds that the rite transforms girls into women. And it suggests that we cannot *assume* that rites transform any more than we can assume they conserve.

A brief but trenchant critique of Turner is advanced by Caroline Bynum (1996; see also Lincoln 1981). Her arguments are aimed specifically at his theory of liminality and his notion of dominant symbols. Even though her reservations are based on women's stories rather than women's rituals, they imply a rejection of basic assumptions in rites of passage theory. Bynum's argument can be summarized in four related statements:

1. Compared with men's lives, women's lives have either fewer or no turning points. Even if men's lives develop by utilizing conflict and in distinct stages, women's lives do not, or, if they do, women's dramas are often incomplete.

2. Women's symbols do not invert their lives; they enhance their lives. They emphasize continuity, not reversal.
3. Liminality is not a meaningful category for women, because either they are permanently liminal (thus the category is meaningless) or they are never truly liminal at all.
4 Liminality is a theory from the point of view of a man looking *at* women, not a theory that assumes the point of view of women looking at the world.

Thus, says Bynum, liminality is better understood as a temporary respite from obligation by élite men of power. This depiction is a far cry from the Turnerian celebration of liminality as *the* engine of ritual and culture.

The "transformationism" implicit in theories of ritual inspired by van Gennep and Turner is now in serious question. When Robbie Davis-Floyd, for instance, defines ritual as "a patterned, repetitive, and symbolic enactment of a cultural belief or value" and says "its primary purpose is transformation" (Davis-Floyd 1992: 8), she implicitly contaminates her feminist treatment of birth ritual by importing a view of ritual that is skewed by its over-reliance on the model of male initiation rites. So when claiming that rites transform, it is important not to romanticize or merely theorize. A way to avoid both errors is to specify what a rite changes and to say what degree of change transpires. In an initiation, for instance, transformation may occur in self-perception, relationships with cosmic or divine powers, access to power, knowledge or goods, kin- and other social relationships. We need to ask, What are the "before" and "after" states, and how do they compare? How significant is the change? Who is changed by a rite of passage? In some New Guinea cultures, for example, it seems that only men are ritually transformed. If so, what happens to ritual theory if we admit that liminality is a gender-specific category?

Divining the Future of Ritual

There is no end to the uses of ritual; it is a provocative notion to think, an engaging activity to enact, and sometimes difficult to know where the one activity ends and the other begins. To speculate about either the future of rites or the idea of ritual is to engage in a peculiar kind of ritual activity, divination. So divine I will, but not without inviting readers to raise a skeptical eyebrow just as one is wont to do with real diviners.

The genealogy and future of ritual practice do not depend on the fate of ritual studies or ritual theory. Those who study ritual are bit-part players. But the boundaries between practice and study are less easily separated than they once were; they are being breached coming and going. The ordained are becoming scholars of ritual, and ethnographers are participating in order to observe. Devotees of the scientific study of religion enjoy maintaining the fictive purity of religious studies against the contaminating influence of "theology" and "politics." But liturgical theologians regularly co-opt anthropological writings on ritual, and field anthropologists now embrace their informants' practices. Because of the taboo that separates theorists from practitioners, courtship across the sacred line is persistent and impassioned, and the threat is not from theologians only. People from both sides dart across the theory / practice line and then back again, sometimes within the space of a single sentence. The messiness, I predict, will continue; it is what makes ritual studies exciting as well as distressing.

The distant past of ritual theory is replete with ideas and images of ritual that deaden. They were developed in part to account for and control "primitive" societies and to account for the resistance of tribal peoples to the incursions of "civilization." Ritual, defined as guardian of social structure, was part of what made those societies at once attractive and glamorous, but also opaque and backward. This view at once exaggerated and diminished the importance of ritual. And it was incapable of making sense of the emergence of rites and the alliance of ritual with artists and revolutionaries.

The more recent past of ritual theory, the phase that culminated in Turner, flipped ritual on its ear, making of it a crowbar to be employed against closed doors and disciplinary boundaries. It was one of several conceptual and performative instruments for webbing and cobbling in the empty spaces, the corridors separating sectors of a highly differentiated society. After Turner, theologian Tom Driver (1998), for example, not only did fieldwork but also made of ritual a power capable of bringing about the "magic" of social justice. And performance theorist Richard Schechner (1993), who collaborated with Turner, made of ritual an efficacious, rather than merely entertaining, cultural activity. These activist conceptions of ritual, though open to criticism, remain an enduring legacy, and I expect to see this strand of scholarship on ritual to continue.

But the Turnerian turn is also being co-opted by New Age enthusiasts. Along with Eliade and Jung, the deceased Turner is being pressed into indentured service on the workshop circuit, where rites of passage organizations are now being legally incorporated, and where vision quests are standard fare served up on weekends, for a price. So the idea that ritual by definition transforms looks increasingly dated, an artifact of the 1960s and 1970s.

Some of the more promising directions in the study of ritual are, I believe, these (see fuller discussion in Grimes 1995: xi–xxii):

1. There are at least three major new attempts to write a theory of ritual: Caroline Humphrey and James Laidlaw's *The Archetypal Actions of Ritual* (1994), E. Thomas Lawson and Robert N. McCauley's *Rethinking Religion* (1990) and Roy Rappaport's *Holiness and Humanity: Ritual in the Making of Religious Life, Religion in the Making of Humanity* (1999). Little

progress will be made in the study of ritual until these works are thoroughly discussed and debated. Rappaport's ecological approach to ritual is especially important, because it promises to integrate cultural and biogenetic research on ritual.

2. If one follows the leads of popular culture, there needs to be continued study of ritual in its fictive, subjunctive and virtual modes. Studies of "re-behaved behavior" (Schechner 1993), the sort of action typical of theme parks and ritual tourism, continue to be fruitful. In rites performed for tourists and in re-created ceremonies trotted around the globe in road shows, there is a rich convergence of the theatrical and the religious.

   In a similar vein, several works argue for the importance and authenticity of cyber ritual (see, for instance, Brasher and O'Leary 1996). There is little doubt that the study of ritual, like the study of many other things, will have to take account of the several waves of the electronic revolution and their effects on contemporary ritual sensibilities.

3. The micro-questions, the basics of posture and gesture at the root of any ritual, and the formations of ritual sensibilities in small groups and individuals remain key topics. Although the global electronic trend, along with the cascade toward the millennium, promises ritual flair and excitement, the basic building blocks of ritual—if there are such—remain obscurely understood. If the fundamental components are not symbols, or if ritual symbols do not "mean" anything, then of what are rites constructed? And under what conditions do they emerge? Basic theoretical work at this level is still much needed.

4. There is a developing zone somewhere between ritual theory and ritual practice. For lack of a better term, I call it applied ritual studies. It resembles applied anthropology more than liturgical theology. The interest in ritual among museum curators, film makers, theater producers and other culture-brokers continues to emerge. Some of the interest is in small-scale events—birthday parties, retirement ceremonies, museum openings and the like. Some of it is large-scale—turn-of-the-millennium celebrations and gradua-tions, for instance. Some of it would put ritual to artistic use in plays, dances and film. Some of it is dangerous—rites, for instance, for those who would actively end their lives of interminable illness. One can frame these as either "job opportunities" or as "data," but if they are pursued for either motive, they may well revise how we currently theorize, define or imagine ritual.

Suggested Readings

Bell, Catherine
  1992   *Ritual Theory, Ritual Practice*. Oxford: Oxford University Press.
  1997   *Ritual: Perspectives and Dimensions*. Oxford: Oxford University Press.
Davis-Floyd, Robbie
  1992   *Birth as an American Rite of Passage: Comparative Studies of Health Systems and Medical Care*, vol. 35. Berkeley: University of California Press.
Driver, Tom F.
  1998   *Liberating Rites: Understanding the Transformative Power of Ritual*. Boulder, CO: Westview.
Grimes, Ronald L.
  1995   *Beginnings in Ritual Studies*. Revised edn. Columbia, SC: University of South Carolina Press.
Grimes, Ronald L. (Ed.)
  1996   *Readings in Ritual Studies*. Upper Saddle River, NJ: Prentice-Hall.
Humphrey, Caroline and James Laidlaw
  1994   *The Archetypal Actions of Ritual: A Theory of Ritual Illustrated by the Jain Rite of Worship*. Oxford studies in Social and Cultural Anthropology. Oxford: Oxford University Press.
Lawson, E. Thomas and Robert N. McCauley
  1990   *Rethinking Religion: Connecting Cognition and Culture*. Cambridge: Cambridge University Press.
Muir, Edward
  1997   "Introduction: What is Ritual?" pp. 1–11 in his *Ritual in Early Modern Europe*. New Approaches to European History, vol. 11. Cambridge: Cambridge University Press.
Northup, Lesley A.
  1997   *Ritualizing Women: Patterns of Spirituality*. Cleveland: Pilgrim.
Rappaport, Roy A.
  1999   *Ritual and Religion in the Making of Humanity*. Cambridge: Cambridge University Press.
Schechner, Richard
  1993   *The Future of Ritual: Writings on Culture and Performance*. London: Routledge.
Smith, Jonathan Z.
  1987b *To Take Place: Toward Theory in Ritual*. Chicago: University of Chicago Press.

19

SACRED

Veikko Anttonen

૭ન૭ન

Notwithstanding the subtleties of theological exegesis, there is no mystery or secrecy concealed in the term "sacred." It is obvious that the concept needs its own peculiar logic of understanding, according to the particular system of belief where it is used; but it also has a common-sense aspect, which is readily observable to anyone who bothers to give the concept a second thought. The religious and linguistic conventions of Western societies, which we have internalized as an inseparable part of our cognitive makeup, have given us the competence to recognize the sacred (or the holy) in our cultural environment wherever we perceive and experience the various forms whereby it is expressed. Sanctuaries and cemeteries are set apart from other buildings and spaces because they are marked as qualitatively different in the value they have for a particular religious community. The competence to decode their cultural value, however, is not restricted only to members and believers of similar faiths. Non-believers and foreign visitors too have the capacity to read their cultural significance from various information sources. The patterns and schemes of perception of their own culture make them competent to decipher the signs and symbols, architecture and behavioral rules by which the sacrality of these locations is marked. In any society anywhere, it is generally expected that the difference that the sacred makes will be respected and not violated also by people not familiar with the thought-worlds and narrative traditions of the specific ethnic or religious group.

The difference that the sacred makes is also immediately recognized when, for instance, we dress carefully for Christmas dinner and gather together as a family. We know that not only the soteriological idea of Christmas is sacred—the incarnation of God in human flesh—but the set-apartness of the whole temporal period makes us participate in its various forms of cultural representation: in the lights and other decoration of public and private spaces, in Christmas carols, gifts, foods, and in the diverse symbolism. The temporal period commemorating cosmogonic episodes in Christian mythical thinking—combined with local forms of popular traditions concerning the end of the agricultural year—are held to be qualitatively different from non-sacred times characterized by the daily routines of labor and travel. Compared to average postmodern consumerists with their secular cosmology, who may create their own "sacred" moments or whose rationality and lifestyle is safeguarded from any intervention from institutionally defined forms of transcendence, there are millions of adherents of cultural and religious traditions in the world for whom the sacrality of times and places is not only a relic from the past. Setting specific times and places apart as sacred is a fundamental structure in human cultures, without which no religion, nation-state or political ideology can insure the continuity of its power, hierarchy and authority. Such universally distributed forms of religious behavior as fasting, pilgrimage, asceticism, celibacy, religiously motivated forms of seclusion and reclusion and various forms of meditation can also be comprehended in terms of the category of the sacred. These forms of religious behavior are culturally constituted on the idea of marking one's physical and mental self as separate from the routines of everyday social life. An analytical comprehension of their sacrality cannot, however, be approached within the conceptual frames offered by religious traditions themselves. In dealing with the theory of religion, we need a special explanatory perspective in order to display the logic governing the sacred-making characteristics of these forms of activities.

Phenomenological Approaches to the Sacred

In recent scholarship, students of comparative religion have become somewhat critical in employing the sacred as an analytical category (see, e.g., Penner 1986, 1989; Lawson and McCauley 1990: 13–14, 1993: 209–210). This criticism has been due to its use as a covertly theological term in the scholarly history of comparative religion. The theological understanding of the notion of the sacred has played a more prominent role than an anthropological and what might be called a cognitive-semantic approach. Such historians and phenomenologists of religion as Nathan Söderblom, Rudolf Otto, Gerardus van der Leeuw, Joachim Wach and Mircea Eliade have held sacrality (or holiness) to be not only the hallmark of religion, but its very essence. According to these theorists, cultural systems of belief and practice cannot be given the title "religion" if there is nothing which is deemed sacred by their adherents. In their methodological approaches, the sacred has been treated as a *sui generis* ontological category, culturally schematized in human experience in the form of subjective feelings of the presence of *mysterium tremendum et fascinosum*. For the phenomenological school of thought, the sacred is comprehended as *numen*, a dynamic force that manifests itself in feelings of religious awe, in inexplicable sentiments of horror and dread, on the one hand, of overwhelming ecstasy and fascination, on the other.

The concept of the sacred has been an inseparable part of the interpretative project in hermeneutically oriented scholarship aimed at "bracketing" the transcendental element as it is experienced by a religious person. The method of bracketing (*epochē*, bracketing out and suspending judgment) has been validated by the intentional waiving of the rationalization of any psycho-dynamic or contextual condition present in such religious states. The primary goal in phenomenological research has been an urge to understand religion from within the subjective experience and to avoid issues of value-judgment and truth. The level of analysis has not been the culture, society, ideology, history, tradition or world-view, but—in Mircea Eliade's terms—the ahisto-rical religious individual, *homo religiosus* understood as a total, that is, "sacred" human being (see McCutcheon 1997b: 37–38). Although Eliade was interested in human symbolic behavior, he did not deal with methodological issues concerning gender, the human body and the contextual factors and values influencing behavior. His methodology rested on the religious conviction that beneath the historical consciousness of human beings there is a sacramental view of nature (see Morris 1987: 178–179). Eliade's scholarly work was motivated by the view that

> [w]hatever the historical context in which he is placed, homo religiosus always believes that there is an absolute reality, the sacred, which transcends this world but manifests itself in this world, thereby sanctifying it and making it real. He further believes that life has a sacred origin and that human existence realizes all of its potentialities in proportion as it is religious—that is, participates in reality. (Eliade 1959b: 202)

The essentialist arguments of the phenomenologists concerning the scholarly goal of finding the core-meaning of the sacred in human emotion or in consciousness have been heavily criticized on both philosophical and anthropological grounds. According to W. Richard Comstock, the dominance of emotion or other introspection in the discourse on the sacred in the study of religion is methodologically untenable. Comstock writes that "there is no entity called an emotion which can be examined when separated from the actor, his act, his symbolic vehicles and his goals" (Comstock 1981: 633). Rejecting the invalid distinction between external body and internal soul, he emphasizes that feeling and behavior are not distinct modalities of human expressions, but parts of the same totality. Suggesting a new behavioral approach to the sacred, Comstock advises scholars not to treat "feeling" and "behavior" as though they refer to two kinds of things on the same level of discourse. Behavior should be seen as a category that includes all kinds of activity. He says that

> much activity involves bodily movements that can be directly seen, like walking, running, kneeling, etc. Other processes also refer to bodily activities. No one will deny that thinking involves brain activity, that

perceiving involves acts of physical sensing, that feeling involves activity of the body (blushing, the dryness of the mouth, external movements like running away or embracing someone, etc.). Behaving and acting are then generic terms under which feeling is to be subsumed. (Comstock 1981: 633)

The question, "What is sacred?" should be answered, according to Comstock, in terms of a methodological shift "from the sacred as a feeling-state of the subjective mind to a distinctive kind of behavior determined by rules and open to public observation" (Comstock 1981: 636).

By emphasizing an introspective understanding of emotions and numenal structures in subjective religious experience, the phenomenologists have detached the sacred from the social matrix in which all human experience, including religious experience, takes place. By keeping the notion of the sacred detached from the cultural and cognitive processes constraining human thought and action and from socially transmitted systems of meaning, these scholars can be criticized for taking part in the very cultural process that they were supposed to study. Comstock's behavioral model, on the other hand, is a proposal to treat the sacred as "an empirical category that is as public as marriage and as observable as agriculture" (Comstock 1981: 631).

Comstock is pointing the way towards a conceptualization of the sacred as a theoretical construct, not as a category with a supernatural or transcendent referent. Employing the sacred as a methodological tool, scholars are better equipped to explicate why "humans have a capacity to behave in certain carefully prescribed ways in respect to their environment" (Comstock 1981: 630). What the concept can reveal about the human mind, and why and in what sense it should be retained in the study of religion as a technical term, are questions I shall elaborate on more closely in what follows. The criticism of phenomenological theory, however, has resulted in a cutting of the age-old bond between the categories of "sacred" and "religion." The sacred is no longer conceptualized as a dependent variable of so-called religious experience. As William E. Paden has pointed out, the sacred is not a uniquely religious category, although its religious meanings and the history of its use dominate the popular as well as scholarly discourse (Paden 1991, 1996b: 16). This is due to the so-called "prototype effect." The category of the sacred has graded membership; most persons brought up in Western societies hold that things that pertain to the category of the sacred in Judeo-Christian religious traditions are "more sacred" than things in Polynesian folk religion, for instance, which are glossed by terms denoting "sacred" in the Austronesian languages (on the theory of the prototype see Saler 1993: 202–226).

Structural-Functional Frameworks

It is within the tradition of sociology of religion, and the structural-symbolic school in anthropology, that a critical methodology based on naturalistic and explanatory theory-construction has been advanced in an attempt to unravel the constitutive factors of human cultural behavior. Such scholars as Émile Durkheim and Marcel Mauss have assessed the sacred as a category of value according to which any social, religious, ethnic or national group creates its cognitive boundaries and categorizes itself as distinct from others. For Durkheim the sacred exists only in contrast to things in the profane sphere of social life. It is the social collective that makes things sacred with regard to the symbolic representation of values which their members reaffirm and redefine in rituals in order to enhance their sense of integration as a community.

Durkheim and Mauss, in their book *Primitive Classification* (1963 [1901–1902]), were the first to suggest that the sacred should be dealt with in reference to culturally dependent classificatory systems and conceptualized in connection with the specific social constraints that generate a collective consciousness. They treated the sacred as a symbolic representation of collectivity, which unites divisions, distinctions and oppositions into a meaningful whole and gives legitimacy to the behavioral norms connected with the specific representation. Things set apart as "sacred" transcend the individual consciousness and act as a divinely legitimated source for sentiments that bind together the members of a social group. If the taxonomic status of any object which has a specific value for the local community is about to change, its category within the overall system of classification needs to be dealt with in relation to sacred things, times and places. Ritual is the only proper context for category transformations, since in ritual society creates an in-between boundary space within the social system of categories (see Leach 1976). Since ritual is the social system of behavior that makes a difference in showing the flexibility of distinctions and oppositions between social categories, it is the prime locus that in the final analysis also creates the sacred (see, e.g., J. Z. Smith 1987b; Bell 1992). The sacred and the ritual can be treated in the study of religion as analogous theoretical categories, and can be approached as symbolic vehicles whereby ethnic or other social groups maintain, secure and reorder the boundaries that generate their social edifice.

Claude Lévi-Strauss, who took structural linguistics as his point of departure, developed the Durkheimian notion of the sacred into a more general theory of the human mind. While Durkheim had a social-deterministic conception of the opposition between the sacred and the profane, Lévi-Strauss transformed the idea of oppositions into a more semiological and symbolic approach. Cultural symbolic structures and models are not grounded in specific forms of social organization, but vice versa: all social categories have a symbolic origin (Traube 1986: 2).

According to Lévi-Strauss, human beings process information on three categorical levels: the real, the symbolic and the imaginary. He treated culture as a system of communication in which thought is carried back and forth across these three structural levels by means of language (see Sullivan 1984: 152–153; Morris 1987: 266). According to Lawrence E. Sullivan,

> [the] processes of thought transform elementary structures of the mind by building symbolic bridges between contradictions. These symbolic bridges become in turn the focus of the same unceasing formal processes and are recycled as images which, in their turn, become object (or victim) of processes which reorder their relations in the attempt to give them meaning. (Sullivan 1984: 152–153)

Things, animals, persons, times and spaces set apart as sacred are in Lévi-Straussian terms symbolic bridges that carry thought back and forth on these three structural levels and become represented not only in ritual, but also in myth, epic and fiction.

In Lévi-Straussian terms, the idea of the sacred is like the numerical value zero. In itself it signifies nothing, but when joined to another number it is filled with differential significance (see J. Z. Smith 1987b: 108). In religious systems the idea of the sacred as a numerical value zero becomes evident when we think for example of the symbolism in Christian rituals. Jesus Christ can be compared to a numerical value zero: in himself he signifies nothing, but acquires meaning and acts as a source of meaning when joined to different aspects of value in Christian category systems. We need only think of Christian rites of passage. The idea of Jesus as an embodiment of sacrality is represented in liminal boundary states such as rituals of birth and baptism, confirmation, marriage and death. Jesus is used as a culturally established symbolic bridge whereby oppositions such as male / female, life / death, pure / impure, inside and outside of the sanctuary, inside and outside of the human body are brought into differential relationships. Let me here quote Jonathan Z. Smith's description of the logic of the sacred:

> Here (in the world) blood is a major source for impurity; there (in the ritual) blood removes impurity. Here (in the world) water is the central agent by which impurity is transmitted; there (in the ritual) washing with water carries away impurity. Neither the blood nor the water has changed; what has changed is their location. (J. Z. Smith 1987b: 110)

Ritual exhibits the religious system and its differences by focusing attention on one or more aspects of the systemic elements. Arnold van Gennep had a special expression for this logic: he called it the "pivoting of the sacred" (van Gennep 1960: 12–13).

In order to understand why certain values and their ritual performances receive their sacred character, it is important to conceptualize the sacred as a category-boundary which becomes actual only in social situations when the inviolability of such categories as person, gender, marriage, nation, or justice, liberty, purity, propriety, are threatened and are in danger of losing their legitimating authority as moral foundations of society and social life. By employing the sacred as an analytical category, we can, for instance, approach the heavily debated issue concerning the legalization of homosexual marriages, in particular, and the religious meanings assigned to the institution of matrimony in Judeo-Christian cultures, in general. It is not only the importance of marriage for reproduction and thus for the continuity of the human species that matter. What is primarily at issue is the fundamental significance that gender difference has as the moral foundation of society. It is not only the myth of the divine origin of matrimony which makes it sacrosanct. Likewise it is not that sexual intercourse is a sacred act and should be performed only in the context of marriage. Homosexual marriages are opposed and seen as sacrilegious and impure because an acceptance of intercourse between spouses of the same sex is seen as threatening gender difference as a fundamental category-boundary in Judeo-Christian cultures. The idea of God and the idea of the sacred can be used as arguments for either opposing or approving legalization. The absence of a gender difference in gay marriages blurs the boundary between the female and the male and is seen as threatening because— applying Lévi-Strauss's idea of the sacred—if taken out of its place, even in thought, the entire order of the universe would be destroyed. According to Lévi-Strauss "being in their place is what makes things sacred" (Lévi-Strauss 1966: 10; for an analysis of gender difference as the sacred category-boundary in public discourses on homosexual marriages see Charpentier 1996).

Connecting the Cognitive and the Cultural

It is largely agreed today that the phenomenological notion of the sacred as a dynamic force originating in another world blurs the boundaries of religious and scientific discourses. By emphasizing subjective religious experience as the primary topos of the sacred, phenomenologists have ignored the cognitive and empirical aspect, the fact that the sacred is first and foremost a cognitive category, the representations of which are culture-dependent. The scholar of religion cannot take a theological stand and address the sacred as an aspect or an agent of a presumed other-worldly reality, but must view religious categories as symbolic constructions and representations of human cognition.

Even though Durkheim tried to understand religion in connection with the operation of the human mind, he could not create a theory of the sacred separately from social organizations. Durkheim assumed that the opposition between the sacred and the profane stems from social sentiments. In Rodney Needham's words, "if the mind is taken to be a system of cognitive faculties, it

277

is absurd to say that the categories originate in social organisation ... the notion of class necessarily precedes the apprehension that social groups, in concordance with which natural phenomena are classed, are themselves classified" (Needham 1963: xxvii).

In post-structural anthropology, as in recent work in cognitive psychology, linguistics, philosophy and the study of religion, the "border area between the cognitive and the cultural" has received more serious attention (see Boyer 1993, 1994; Lawson 1993; Lawson and McCauley 1990, 1993; Lakoff 1987, 1989; M. Johnson 1987, 1991). The religious and other socially transmitted concepts and categories that constitute and organize culture-specific knowledge structures, which in turn guide and shape human behavior, do not float in the air as abstract entities, but are inseparably connected to the corporeality and the territoriality of human beings.

It is my conviction that scholars of comparative religion will have an empirically more tractable methodological tool in the notion of the sacred when it is theorized at the border between the cognitive and the cultural. The sacralities of things, objects and specific forms of behavior are to be understood as symbolic representations in which corporeality and territoriality function as constraining structures of knowledge. To behave in a sacred, culturally prescribed manner depends on the capacity to make adequate judgments about the well-formedness and relationships of cultural practices as well as the capacity to understand these as part of a larger aggregate of practices (Lawson 1993: 191). The sacred is due to the human capacity to make judgments about the ideal norms and boundaries defining and transforming the taxonomical statuses of persons, animals or objects in a specific cultural category, and to assess their cultural significance in relation to ultimate, unquestionable and unfalsifiable postulates (see Rappaport 1979: 228).

Even though there are specialists in every culture, whose competence to make the necessary judgments and whose possession of knowledge of the systemic elements in ritual practices is relied upon, any adult person has tacit knowledge of the constraints that guide and shape her or his behavior. Ethnographic evidence suggests that the human body and its locative dimensions, the notion of place, forms the cultural grammar on which sacred-making behavior is based. From this perspective the sacred can be defined as a relational category of thought and action, which becomes actualized in specific value-loaded situations when a change in the contextually interpreted boundaries of temporal, territorial or corporeal categories takes place. In traditional hunting and agricultural societies it has become operative in social situations where patterns of metaphoric and metonymic relationships between the notions of human body and territory have been linked together in order to express values that a group of people place on the strategic points of their communal life, that is, marking the qualitative difference between the inside and the outside of the human body and the territory.

George Lakoff and Mark Johnson argue that the structures of human understanding have their origin in the body. According to Johnson, patterns of conceptual significance and symbolic import are prefigured in the imaginative patternings of bodily experience. Our conceptions of reality cannot be separated from what we experience in our embodied interactions. Perceptual capacities and recurring image schemata that constrain both idiosyncratic and socially shared systems of knowledge—schemes of containment, part–whole, source–path–goal, link, cycle, scale and center–periphery—depend on the nature of human body (Lakoff 1987: 271–275, 1989: 121–123; Johnson 1987: 30–40, 1991: 6–8, 13).

The ethnographic literature shows that human life has always been a concept that is bodily confined. Just as the body is an entity with boundaries, the bodily openings are border zones (Douglas 1989: 12), through which life flows in or out, in a manner similar to people moving across international borders at entrance and exit sites. The consciousness of a living person, and the formation of conceptual categories, on which the manifestations of religion also depend, is fundamentally a corporeal consciousness. The idea of the sacred based on bodily boundaries has been developed by Mary Douglas. For her the idea of the sacred is based on the precariousness of the cultural categories guiding human thinking and behavior. The sacred is the universe in its dynamic aspect; its boundaries are inexplicable, "because the reasons for any particular way of defining the sacred are embedded in the social consensus which it protects" (Douglas 1978: xv). Sacrality does not, however, merely mean that all members belonging to a category have to conform with the prototypes defining the properties according to which membership is determined, so that the sacred order, unity, integrity or ideal norm will be maintained (see Douglas 1989; Paden 1996b; Sperber 1996b). There is also another side to the idea of sacrality, as exemplified by the French sociologists Roger Caillois (1959) and Georges Battaille (1988a, 1988b), and to which Douglas's own studies on the taxonomic status of Pangolin as an anomalous animal also bear witness (Douglas 1978). Impurity, forbiddenness and dangerousness are also characteristics of things classified as sacred. The term sacred refers here to a more general semantic concept, comprising both its positive and negative, its right-hand (religion) and left-hand (taboo) dimensions (see Burnside 1991). Menstruation, pregnancy, the post-parturition period and also the manipulation of corpses in mortuary rituals have almost universally been connected with the semantic field of the category of the sacred, in other words, with the idea of a boundary that sets socially impure members and elements apart from pure ones in the category systems of the community. The growth of things with social value (the "religious" aspect of the sacred) is to be protected against the contagious impact of substances that are not confined within the socially defined boundaries of the human body, society and territory, and which have exhausted their capacity to produce growth for the benefit of society (the "taboo" aspect of the sacred).

The categorization of social space is another major cognitive structure on which various population groups have traditionally based their symbolism of categorial boundaries. One of the most common ways of conceptualizing territorial and other spatial boundaries, as anthropologists have found, is to distinguish inhabited from uninhabited areas—and to create spiritual entities in the process. In myths and epic narratives, the supernatural world of gods and spirits is regularly located "beyond" or "beneath" the spaces and territories of human habitation (Tarkka 1994). These "other-worldly" places are situated in deserts, forests or lakes; or they are placed in some vertical relation to trees, mountains and celestial bodies. The human dwellers in the inhabited area discover evidence of this "other world" beyond in anomalous objects, times, places and phenomena which contradict and "threaten" the normal categories in terms of which the world is perceived in the flow of everyday life.

Terms denoting the "sacred" in various languages can be viewed as linguistic indices, the semantic scope of which has varied in time according to the systems of meanings whereby distinctions between persons, animals, things, objects, phenomena, topographical points in the landscape, events, experiences and so forth are made. In the Finnish language, the term *pyhä* (denoting "sacred") was originally used to designate both territorial borders and the intersections of waterways, allowing groups of settlers to separate themselves from one another and to mark the boundary between the shared inner domain of the territory claimed by them and the outer domain. In place names, *pyhä* signified the outer border of the inhabited area (Anttonen 1996). V. N. Toporov (1987) has shown how those features of the phenomenal world which contain a motive of growth have been glossed in Indo-European languages by terms denoting "sacred." The motive of growth as a condition for marking something off as sacred is manifested especially in topography and natural processes. A mountain, a hillock, or a flat treeless hilltop takes on a special meaning as "swollen," raised land; its power and substance is stronger than that of a territory which does not contain any fixed points for a dividing boundary. Likewise, sacrificing by cutting into pieces, burning or shedding of blood implies the idea of growth: a form that has cultural value (an animal, a human) is being dissolved into non-form, something that lacks fixed boundaries. The power that has supported its substance, the soul, is then regarded as a blessing for the growth and reproduction of existing or future form. The motif of growth is also connected to the symbolic value and the definition of sacrality of trees, stones, light, luster, radiance, moon and sun (Toporov 1987: 193–219).

Changing Paradigms of the Sacred

The sacred is a special quality in individual and collective systems of meaning. In religious thinking it has been used as an attribute of situations and circumstances which have some reference to the culture-specific conception of the category of God, or, in non-theological contexts, to some supreme principle of life such as love, freedom, equality or justice. Sacrality is employed as a category-boundary to set things with non-negotiable value apart from things whose value is based on continuous transactions. The difference that the sacred makes is based on culturally transmitted myths and forms of ritual representation whereby symbolic constructions of individual and collective life-values are renewed at times and in locations where contact between human beings and God or a supreme life principle becomes actual. People participate in sacred-making activities and processes of signification according to paradigms given by the belief systems to which they are committed, whether they be religious, national or ideological. Paradigms of sacralization may originate unequivocally in the mythic history of organized religions, national traditions or political ideologies, or ambiguously in conflicting and multivalent symbolic constructions of syncretic world-views and life strategies. The logic of sacralization does not necessarily have to follow the linear model from cosmogony to eschatology or from childhood to old-age, as in the mythical traditions of Judaism, Christianity and Islam. Although there have emerged both Christian and Islamic fundamentalist and anti-modern movements in the Western world, there are millions of people in Christian countries who no longer accept the whole religious tradition as a grand theory for their lives. At the same time that the number of non-affiliated people has grown in Europe in both Protestant and Catholic countries (see Dobbelaere 1993), the old religious structures have become desacralized and new or non-religious forms of sacralization are being invented.

Suggested Readings

Caillois, Roger
>   1959   *Man and the Sacred*, Meyer Barash (trans.). Glencoe, IL: Free Press.
Douglas, Mary
>   1989   *Purity and Danger: An Analysis of the Concepts of Pollution and Taboo.* London: Ark Paperbacks; original edn, London: Routledge & Kegan Paul, 1966; reprinted, London: Routledge, 1994.
Durkheim, Émile
>   1995   *The Elementary Forms of Religious Life*, Karen Fields (trans.), with an Introduction. New York: Free Press; original French ed. 1912.
Eliade, Mircea
>   1959b   *The Sacred and the Profane: The Nature of Religion*, Willard R. Trask (trans.). New York: Harcourt Brace Jovanovich.
Idinopulos, Thomas A. and Edward A. Yonan (Eds.)
>   1996   *The Sacred and Its Scholars: Comparative Methodologies for the Study of Primary Religious Data.* Studies in the History of Religions, vol. 73. Leiden: E. J. Brill.

Otto, Rudolf
    1959   *The Idea of the Holy: An Inquiry into the Non-Rational Factor in the Idea of the Divine and Its Relation to the Rational*, John W. Harvey (trans.). London: Oxford University Press; original German edn, 1917.

Parkin, David
    1991   *Sacred Void: Spatial Images of Work and Ritual Among the Giriama of Kenya*. Cambridge Studies in Social and Cultural Anthropology, vol. 80. Cambridge: Cambridge University Press.

Pyysiäinen, Ilkka
    1996   *Belief and Beyond: Religious Categorization of Reality*. Religionsvetenskapliga Skrifter, vol. 33. Åbo: Åbo Akademi.

Segal, Robert A., Carol E. Burnside, William E. Paden, Thomas Ryba and Michel Despland
    1991   "Symposium on the Sacred." *Method and Theory in the Study of Religion* 3(1): 1–46.

20

SOCIAL FORMATION

Burton L. Mack

❧ ❧

"Social formation" refers to a concept of society as a collective human construct. It differs from the less specific term, "society," by emphasizing the complex interplay of many human interests that develop systems of signs and patterns of practice, as well as institutions for their communication, maintenance and reproduction. The term social formation refers to the process by which various configurations of these systems of practice are created and relate to one another in the formation of a given society. The term is also used to refer to the resulting structure of a society formed by such a process. It is a highly abstract concept with specific connotations of importance for social theory.

The concept first emerged as a technical term in the intellectual arenas associated with the work of Louis Althusser. Earlier, in the now famous Preface to his *Contribution to the Critique of Political Economy*, and throughout, Karl Marx had used the term *Gesellschaftsformation* to refer to the shape of a society that results from a particular mode of production (Marx 1971 [1859]). For Marx, the mode of most significance was economic or material production, and the now familiar theoretical model of a basic practice (*base*) resulting in a social formation (*superstructure*) was set for testing. The subsequent history of Marxist thought and political experience did not invalidate the base / superstructure model, but found that the three variable factors in the equation (practice, production and social formation) were in need of more detailed, conceptual specification. Althusser resignified the terms of the equation by working out a complex and sophisticated concept of society as a cluster of "semiautonomous instances," whereby "instance" refers to a pattern of practice that produces socially significant effects for the structure of a society and its on-going operation.

Althusser focused upon the major triad of economic, political and ideological practices, and continued to posit economic practice as the mode of production that determined a social formation "in the last instance." But in order to account for the many practices that conjoin in the modern society, and the variety of social formations that can be observed in human history, he applied the equation of practice–production–social formation to any and all forms of social practice that reproduce themselves and function as substructures within a larger, encompassing social formation. A social formation was now conceived as a "structure of structures." In Althusser's rendering, "semiautonomy" refers to the relative independence of a pattern of practice from other practices, in the sense that each practice can develop its own rationale, principles of operation, institutions, mechanisms of maintenance and modes of production and reproduction. Since no practice can be completely independent of the others, however, bound as it is to operate within the larger "structure of structures," contradiction always attends the internal logic of a practice, and the struggle for determination of the whole defines its relations of competition and conformation to other practices. The acknowledgment of multiple practices results in a dynamic concept of society, and the notion of semiautonomy raises to the level of theoretical investigation and precision the questions of determination, power, domination and influence among the various practices.

Classical Marxist theory worked with a concept of society imagined as ranked by classes, or as layered according to the base / superstructure model in which material production was basic and other forms of practice (politics, arts, religion and ideology) were related to the basic mode of production as dependent, derived and manipulative. By introducing the notion of semiautonomy, and asking the questions of interaction, force, development and contradiction within and among the various practices of a society, Althusser made it possible to imagine every practice as a production of social effects. The result has been a quest for a comprehensive theory of social formation pursued as a humanistic, scientific and historical discipline (Resch 1992).

Postmodernist intellectuals have tended to veer away from the renewal of Marxist social theory as pursued by scholars in the tradition of Althusser, because the social and cultural histories of the twentieth century have (1) raised serious questions about universal theories, (2) focused upon the individual and the many ways in which individuals are determined by their social and cultural locations, and (3) drawn attention to cultural issues at the expense of political and economic critique. Nevertheless, the term social formation has increasingly commended itself to many critical thinkers because it connotes the dynamic processes of the human construction of social structures in ways that the older term society cannot. The importance of the term social formation has been recognized, for instance, by non-Marxist political theorists (e.g., McGowan 1991), literary critics (noted by Thurston 1993) and scholars at work on the relation between discourse and the construction of society (e.g., Lincoln 1989). And the term "practice," of fundamental importance for theories of social formation based on collective interests, activity and pursuits is now familiar as a technical term in postmodern cultural analysis. Unfortunately, neither the Marxist, Althusserian, nor postmodern contributions to the use and definition of social formation have shed much light on the quest for a social theory of religion. Althusser did discuss religious thought (theology) as an instance of ideological practice (Althusser 1971: 127–186), and Raymond Williams has often written about cultural formation from a Marxist perspective (R. Williams 1958, 1977: 115–141, 1995 [1981], 57–86). One might have hoped for a concentrated focus upon explaining religion as a semiautonomous practice on a par with other practices. That has not happened. In the Marxist tradition, religion has frequently been discounted or overlooked as a vanishing practice and thus of little theoretical interest.

In the tradition of religious studies, where one might have expected interest in exploring a social theory of religion, a Marxist approach to religion as a semiautonomous instance of human practice has not commended itself. Instead, religion has customarily been defined as an autonomous sphere of personal experience and belief determined by extra-social and superhuman attractions. There are, however, several streams of thought in the academic study of religion that have focused upon the question of religion and society. Two of the better known traditions of some theoretical interest are those stemming from the works of Max Weber and Émile Durkheim. To these should be added the large archive of knowledge about religious phenomena in social and cultural contexts documented in the fields of ethnography and cultural anthropology. American sociologists have also produced some important studies on religious institutions and groups in modern times. Of these several streams, the Weberian tradition has been the most influential among those engaged in religious studies, but this tradition has not produced a theory of religion as an integral instance of human activity in the interest of social formation.

Weber complicated the Marxist concept of economic practice, or mode of production, as basic for the constructions of a society by adding considerations of religious ideas, cultural values and political power to the factors involved in social formations. His study of *The Protestant Ethic and the Spirit of Capitalism* (Weber 1976 [1920]) is famous as an attempt to relate religious ideas to a mode of production, and a series of studies (Weber 1920) on what he called the "economic ethic" (*Wirtschaftsethik*) of the world religions was an important early attempt at cross-cultural comparison in the study of religion and culture. Weber's studies had the potential for testing the Marxist theory of economic determination and refining the concept of practice fundamental for the base / superstructure model. The Weberian tradition might have resulted in theoretical experimentation with multiple variable factors in the social formation question. Unfortunately, Weber was immersed in his own cultural mentality of the time, a dialectical Romanticism that frustrated the exercise in cross-cultural comparison, worked with a typology of "culture religions" versus "salvation religions," and gave privilege to a charismatic theory of religious innovation. This kept the question of causality or determination from being phrased in relation to social interests and the interactive relations among religious, economic and political practices. And it had the effect of shifting attention away from questions about the social origins of religion, or even from issues of religion's effect upon society, to fall instead upon analytic and historical descriptions of cultural conventions. Nevertheless, Weber's influence as a sociologist of religion, values and politics has been enormous, and major thinkers continue to find stimulus in his work. In every case, however, scholars working in the tradition of Weber have been more interested in the social logic of cultural conventions than in working toward an explanatory social theory of religion. In this tradition, religion has been taken for granted as the way in which humans respond to, think about and encounter a world of the gods, not investigated as the product of human interests in social formation and the invention of practices appropriate for those interests.

The story is quite different in the case of Émile Durkheim. He was the first social scientist to turn the observance of common practices in French, Western and "primitive" societies into data for a theory of the social origin of religion. His study of the relation between religion and society based on the totemic system in Australia in *Les formes élémentaires de la vie religieuse* (1912; English trans. 1995) theorized that religious ideas resulted from the effect of being determined by the collective in the experience of social life. But accounting for the social origin of religion is one thing; describing its practice in terms of social interests and functions another. Durkheim's recourse to the notion of the sacred as a term for the awareness of determination by the social might have resulted in a social theory of religious imagination, or at least a studied investigation of the way in which myths and rituals may relate to social forces and address issues of social import. Instead, however, a late nineteenth-century fascination with the oddity and affectivity of religious beliefs and rituals frustrated the flowering of Durkheim's promise by allowing questions of a psychological nature to slip in and sidetrack the project. Nevertheless, Durkheim's social theory of the origin of religion was a radical departure from previous scholarship, and its legacy can be traced through the work of a large number of constructive thinkers, each of whom has made substantive contributions to theory.

A recent discussion of Durkheim, Claude Lévi-Strauss, Georges Dumézil, Louis Dumont and others by Jonathan Z. Smith has created an impressive chain of intellectual labor in support of Smith's own theoretical constructions (J. Z. Smith 1987b). This tradition in the wake of Durkheim is rigorous because of its strictly social anthropology (in distinction from Romantic individualisms and psychologies of religion), its control of historical and scientific methodology, and its rational and cognitive approach to the sense and social significance of religious practices. Excellent examples of the social sense of ritual practice, for instance, can be found in Smith's book, *To Take Place: Toward Theory in Ritual* (1987b), and in his essays on "The Bare Facts of Ritual" (1982c) and "The Domestication of Sacrifice" (1987a). In these studies ritual is not an attempt to contact the gods, reenact a miraculous event of origin, dramatize the sacred, mystify participants or evoke personal transformations. Instead, ritual functions to focus attention and thoughtful reflection upon some activity recognizable to the group as common practice and important for the production, structure and maintenance of the society. In this tradition, religion is a mode of thinking about social constructs.

The relation of religious practices and social formation has also been a common theme in studies by cultural anthropologists. This tradition within the human sciences draws upon a rich reservoir of ethnographic data primarily available as descriptions of fieldwork among small, so-called "primitive" societies indigenous to specific geographical locations. Observation of these "tribal" societies has aimed at a full description of their modes of production, technologies, patterns of behavior, languages and systems of knowledge, as well as myths and rituals. During the nineteenth century the reports of primitive peoples were viewed as esoterica and the descriptions of their religious beliefs and practices were taken as evidence for the early, "prehistoric" stages of human development. Notions of "primitive" intellect and mentality resulted in theories of religion as the confused and mistaken attempt to make sense of the world. These mistaken notions would have to be corrected by the advance of "reason" and "civilization." Fortunately, the assumption of staged development in the history of human thought and civilization has now been set aside. The twentieth century has seen the emergence of a controlled fieldwork approach to the study of indigenous societies as organic units of collective activity. This approach, often associated with the influence of Franz Boas, has recognized the ethnocentric problem, provided scholarly standards for description and comparison, and resulted in an increasing appreciation of the intellectual sophistications invested in the construction of any human society.

Twentieth-century ethnography is dotted with brilliant studies of great importance for the human sciences. The list includes: the social significance of "rites of passage" (Arnold van Gennep 1960 [1909]); the discovery of the social implications of "totemism" (Durkheim 1995 [1912]); the structural relation of languages and cultures (Boas 1940); forms of intelligence required for calculation in basic technologies (Malinowski 1948); mythic systems and the logic of tripartite social structures (Dumézil 1988 [1948]); the logic of kinship systems and social structures (Lévi-Strauss 1969 [1949]); dual systems of classification in social organization, thought, mythology and knowledge (Lévi-Strauss 1966 [1962a], 1975–78 [1964–68]); the relation of ritual to social processes (Turner 1967); the social importance of the imaginary world (*habitus*) and the gap between it and actual social practice (Bourdieu 1977 [1972]); the interrelation of "primordial ties" based on attitudes toward land, language and blood kinship with cultural constructs and their manipulation by social practices (Geertz 1973); practical aspects of myths and symbols for social orientation, organization and the assignment of roles (Hultkrantz 1979); the social logic involved in responding to new social situations by recasting older mythologies and creating new (J. Z. Smith 1982b); the cognitive ingredient in myth and ritual and its significance for social structuration (J. Z. Smith 1987a, 1987b); and mythic modes of manipulating various construals of "other" peoples (J. Z. Smith 1992).

The overall result of these and other studies has been a stunning reconception of the human enterprise of social construction. It is now possible to imagine the interplay of complex systems of signs, codes and practices that make possible the formation and maintenance of a human society. Some of these systems have been analyzed in detail, their logics worked out and their significance for social organization and practice noted. The intellectual labor involved in the construction and maintenance of these systems is truly impressive. Such is the case with kinship systems, systems of classification (often of both "natural" and social phenomena and their interrelationships), social organizations and structures, the assignment of roles, technologies of production, the care of collective "memories," complex codes of behavior, rules for games and procedures for managing encounter with other peoples. It may be too early to ask for a radically social theory of human interests to account for the human enterprise of social construction. But it is already obvious that more has been involved than the customary references to (biological and psychological) "needs," "survival," "acquisition," "desire for power," "conquest," and "protection" can explain. Inordinate amounts of curiosity, delight, intellectual labor, experimentation and elaboration have been invested in the fragile craft and work required to live together in social units. It may well be that a theory of the human enterprise as a human construct will have to reduce the many practical interests involved to a profound and complex tautology. At first, the interests involved in the formation and function of the many practices and systems of signs that support social existence may appear to be disparate and unrelated, perhaps even matters best explained as forms of personal desire. One can imagine a large range of frequently acknowledged interests that come to mind when thinking about the investments humans make in their activities. But in the final analysis, it may well be that involvement in each and every practice is a form of taking interest in the conception, construction, maintenance and manipulation of a social formation itself. Thus the tautology at the highest level of theoretical abstraction: the interests humans invest in social practices, and the interests humans take in all manner of activities, are derivative modes of collective interest in the processes of social formation.

Whether that is a helpful or possible theoretical move, the implications of these studies for a theory of religion are fairly obvious. There is no reason to make an exception for religion as if it were unlike the other practices of importance for social formation. Ethnographic data do not support the notion that religion is an inexplicable persuasion or an autonomous sphere of human practice of interest only to individuals for personal pursuits. The dominant scholarly theory of religion as a personal response to manifestations of "the sacred," an experience unrelated to the constraints of the social world, is inadequate to explain the evidence in this vast, ethnographic array of social activity. The problem is that the dominant scholarly view is beholden to the modern fascination with the individual in whose interest all natural, social and religious phenomena have come to be viewed and evaluated. An adequate theory of religion will have to wrest free of any notion of religion based on modern psychologies of "personal religious experience" and embrace a thoroughly social anthropology. What might a theory of religion look like when fully integrated into the human enterprise of social construction?

Myths and rituals are modes of recording, rehearsing and manipulating a set of symbols and practices that condense collective agreements about certain features of social existence. The patterns of activity essential to the practices of a society may be thought of as rooted in agreements reached in the process of experimenting with better and less better ways to do things and think about them. They may also be thought of as the result of testing ideas, negotiating interests, pronouncing judgments, exercising power, manipulating structures of determination, inculcating conventions and so forth. Thus the modes of agreement may range from acceptance through acquiescence to submission, depending on the processes of determination in relation to particular practices. While not immutable, for challenge, contestation and change may also impinge upon the practices of a social formation, such agreements tend to settle into conventions that inform social relations. Some conventions can be taken for granted and are hardly ever noticed, others need to be rationalized by this or that ideology, and still others are anchored in codes of propriety and legitimation. An example would be the codes of honor and shame that determine proper performance and accomplishment in many societies. These codes may be articulated as folk wisdom, explored in folk tales and called upon as self-evident standards when training children, for instance, or when passing judgment on a question of behavior to call someone to task. Codes may also be changed in the course of changing practices, for the means of registry are also the mechanisms by which recoding can take place. Do myths and rituals work the same way? And if so, what specific social interests might they register and manipulate?

Two of the more obvious characteristics of myths and rituals are the ways in which they focus attention upon symbols and images in orders of time and space at a distance from the everyday world of activity, and exaggerate the descriptions of the figures and activities that inhabit and configure those imaginary worlds. We might turn these characteristics to theoretical advantage by noting that they stretch the imagination beyond the parameters of empirical observation and confirmation. On the one hand, the horizon that controls the outward limit of credibility may be as vast as all of imaginable time and space. On the other, the concentration of features in a symbol can bring thought to focus on a single point devoid of any background, and the studied movements in a ritual can unravel an action into moments so minute that time stands still. So myths and rituals trade in the manipulation of the normal senses of time, space and proportion. They are designed to exercise the imagination by placing ordinary objects in imaginary settings, creating extraordinary figures that pop into an ordinary storyline, and filling the past with marvelous moments that help account for the way things are. Can anything be said about the reasons for such extravagance, and about the objects and symbols selected for displacement and observance?

It has been customary to note that rituals are public occasions that display and confirm social structures, and that myths frequently function to confirm symbols that support a people's values, identity, structures and authorities. These observations are valid. They support the suspicion that religious practice is a human construction in the interest of social formation. But why the displacements and extravagance? And why the selection of just certain symbols? The answers may lie in the fact that the process of social formation creates and draws upon interests in and agreements about forces and features of social existence that are difficult to name and locate in the daily round of activity. Such would be the case with the sense of belonging to a people; accounting for a group's attitude toward the land; experiencing the constraints of another's views in the way in which judgments, construals and "memories" fall out; marking and honoring genealogical loyalties; finding reasons for ranking and the assignment of tasks; wondering about the workings of gifts and obligations and so on. Living together is a wondrously complex matter, after all. And it does seem that myths and rituals are ways of acknowledging that complexity by locating social determinations outside the world of the everyday while configuring them in such a way as to trigger their recognition in the everyday world. The mythic world is like an Archimedean point of advantage for looking "back" upon the real world of social practices grasped as totality. "Looking back," the social forces that function throughout the social formation as a whole can then be recognized here and there, named, thought about and accounted for. Myths and rituals affect the imagination in much the same way as any good fiction does, by making it possible to see and reflect upon features of social existence that are not readily managed in the course of other practices. In the case of myths and rituals, the selection of figures and the location of the settings tell us that interest in social forces of importance for a society as a whole have determined the imaginary constructs.

The imaginary world does not reflect the faces one actually sees in the real social world, nor is the imaginary world as lovely, sensual, detailed and inviting as the natural environment of a group and its polished artifacts. But it is much "larger" and more encompassing in that it expands the horizons of time and space beyond the limits of the perceived world within which a people actually live. And it is frequently more "fantastic" in that the agents that inhabit that world have to represent the condensed configurations of many relational and social forces. Take, for instance, the notion of ancestors "of old," or "at the beginning." If something like generational continuity is important for the process of human social formation, and if the social world is always already inhabited when any new generation comes along, it should not be surprising that the images of those who have gone before, those who first came on the scene, "established" the world as it now is, or traced out the ways to live in the world, might have to take on marvelous, extraordinary features. In this, as in every case of mythic imagination, the imagery has to collect and condense a large and complex number of powers and precedent achievements pertinent to an adequate grasp of social forces and determinations not readily accounted for by the obvious exercise of a society's practices. Thus the imaginary world created by myths, rehearsed in stories, condensed in symbols and evoked in rituals may be fantastic, but it should not be thought nonsensical. It appears to be the result of intellectual labor invested in the enterprise of social formation, the way in which the process of social formation is rationalized, registered and reproduced. It is not surprising that functionalist theorists of social formation have emphasized the way in which the mythic world corresponds to the practices and structures of determination in a society, lending legitimacy to certain configurations of power and fostering their reproduction. This function is frequently institutionalized in practices that draw upon the mythic world to support consensus, stability and the replication of the social order.

It may therefore be helpful at this point to note the ways in which the imaginary world of myth actually works in the maintenance of a social formation. The terms frequently used to designate this social phenomenon are suggestive "world-view," "symbolic world," "life-world," "habitus" and "map." In every case it is the difference between the imaginary world and the social world that is emphasized. The mythic world is not a perfect reflection of the social world. Neither is the mythic world the picture of an ideal society with which social order is constantly compared. The imaginary world of a people is frequently a motley conglomerate of disparate images that vary in intensity and clarity of profile. The gap between the social world and the mythic panoply, and the fact that the imaginary world is so richly disordered, may be thought of as creating a space for play, experimentation, thoughtful meditation, cheating, winking and / or calling one another to task. The mythic world does not inhibit the energies required to manage social relations and practices in a dynamic social formation, though it may set limits for acceptable behavioral experimentation.

Creating a backdrop for the theater of human activity is not the only way a mythic canopy functions. It may be treated like a collage in which the arrangement of its figures is susceptible to reconfiguration. It can also be thought of as a battlefield for ideological advantage when the structures of determination in a society are challenged. That is because the symbols within the mythic world can be rearranged or reconceived in the interest of calling for or rationalizing social change. Who gets to do that, by what authority and in whose interest, are very important questions of political consequence for the way in which patterns of practice and determination are given legitimacy in a society. This means that religion may be defined as a practice that produces myths and rituals of ideational consequence for the structure of a society as a whole. The institutions of religion may also be defined as a "semiautonomous instance" within a "structure of structures," in Althusser's terminology, thus accounting for the oft-noted vested interests in guaranteeing its own reproduction. It is the tension between this built-in resistance to change, and the fact that myths are arenas for ideological contestation, that describes the contradiction inherent in a religious system.

The quest for a social theory of religion is currently being pursued by scholars at work in the history of early Christianity. A seminar of the American Society of Biblical Literature is titled "Ancient Myths and Modern Theories of Christian Origins"[1] (see Mack 1996). This work may serve as a testing ground for the relation between "social formation" and "mythmaking," the terms being used to set up a series of studies for a project in the redescription of Christian origins. The discipline of early Christian studies appears to be a remarkably fertile field for such a project for four reasons. The first is that the data available, mostly texts packed with mythologies, but also some historical and archeological material, have already been subjected to layer upon layer of thorough and detailed investigation. No other chapter of human history has attracted such a concentration of scholarly attention. This means that a huge accumulation of knowledge is already available for every bit of data in need of redescription.

The second reason for the potential value of this field of study is that the hermeneutical theories traditional to the field are currently recognized as inadequate. It is now clear to many scholars in the field that the detailed descriptions of the data produced by historical, critical methods do not fit the conventional view of Christian origins. The conventional view has always followed the largely Lukan history. This acceptance of Luke's version of the gospel story has not been uncritical with regard to details, but in retrospect it can be seen that it was understandably naïve with regard to the overall pattern of the history it recounted (Cameron 1994). Naïvité was understandable because there was no other story to compete with the gospel account on the one hand, and also because there was no alternative theory of religion to question it on the other. Respectable theories of charismatic leadership, cult formation and the attraction of new religions with their offers of spiritual transformation all seemed to fit so well. But that is no longer the case. Scholars are now aware that the gospels cannot be regarded as histories, and that the histories of the gospels, as well as of all the other bits and pieces of textual and archeological evidence, do not cohere in a grand story of a unique origin for a singular religion. Instead, what we find are disparate groups and movements with different myths and rituals competing for recognition as the legitimate heirs of various social teachings and models associated with the name of Jesus as a founder-figure. The notions of a singular "ministry" and "message" of a unique Jesus, an orthodox teaching and instruction to apostles and the immediate formation of the Christian church in response to dramatic events of his death and departure, are not supported by the evidence from the first century. This Lukan "history" is actually the product of mythmaking in the interest of a particular social formation at a certain moment in the early second century.

A third reason for thinking that a redescription of Christian origins may make a contribution to the quest for a social theory of religion is that the factor of changing social circumstance is so obvious in this early history. Early Christian groups are examples of the emergence of new religious movements, and the rich history of social experimentation and mythic rationalization they document is a precious set of data. This data can complement the archive of ethnographic studies, many of which have been uninterested in or unable to account for social change and cultural encounter, concerned as they have been to detail a stable culture by synchronic description and structural analysis. Early Christian studies can add the factors of changing circumstances, mixed ethnic constituency, social experimentation and self-conscious mythmaking.

Finally, the larger social and cultural context of these investments in social and religious experimentation, the Greco-Roman age, is extremely rich in comparable phenomena, many of which have also been subjected to critical attention by scholars working in the fields of classical studies. This means that the redescription project has a ready-made resource of examples for comparison. This is an extremely important consideration, because a social theory of religion cannot be tested with examples of "religious communities" in isolation from their social and cultural worlds, nor can the work of redescribing a specific phenomenon proceed without setting up a detailed comparison with other examples in other cultures and social situations. It is true that the attempt to situate early Christian groups within the context of Greco-Roman social and cultural histories will present a challenge to New Testament scholars. That is because there is a strong tendency in this history of scholarship to make comparisons in the interest of establishing the ways in which Christianity was different from (and better than) other religions of the time. Drawing upon comparisons from farther afield, say from the archives of cultural anthropology, would therefore probably be a better approach.

Unfortunately, not many scholars of early Christianity and the Greco-Roman world are in touch with disciplines that work with ethnographic data.

One important exception to this rule is found in the work of Jonathan Z. Smith. A rather consistent approach to ethnographic data can be discerned throughout his essays. Not only has he selected phenomena for investigation that have been foundational for other theorists in the history of the history of religions. Smith has reassessed both the phenomenon and the theory derived from it by setting up a comparison with an example from another culture. Frequently the other example has been taken from the world of late antiquity, including early Christianities. Briefly, his method of analysis may be summed up in four operations: *description, comparison, redescription* and the *rectification of categories*. The approach is strictly historical and situational with respect to social and cultural impingements. The cross-cultural procedure insures that differences will be obvious, and differences are very important as indices of situational variants. However, the goal is always to isolate the similarity in respect to social, cultural and cognitive functions. Thus the categories used to designate those similarities enjoy a level of abstraction that, while still in touch with the description of empirical phenomena, are capable of contributing to the construction of a general theory.

Smith's work has provided the methodological precision and the theoretical rationale for the project in redescribing Christian origins. In application to the particular kind of data available, and the challenge of redescribing a rapidly changing history of social and ideological experimentation, the phenomena under investigation will be situated at intersections of social formation and mythmaking. The writing of texts and / or the invention of practices such as congregating, performing rituals, distributing social roles, organizing for social welfare, caring for cults of the dead and so forth, will be situated at points where the interplay of social formation and mythmaking can be analyzed. This emphasizes the dimension of change or production within the Smithian agenda of redescription, and it sets the stage for asking some serious questions about the reciprocal relationships of myth, ritual and social structuring.

If social formation is a human construct and religion is a semiautonomous practice in the interest of social construction, a study of early Christianities and their myths should complicate the dominant (Weberian and psychological) views of Christian origins sufficiently to make data available for testing alternative theories. If the gospels, for instance, can be situated at specific junctures of social history and explained as mythmaking in the interest of social formation, an attraction other than charismatic leadership or interests in personal transformation and immortality will have to be considered. This will have the result of adding the first chapters of Christian history to the ethnographic data available for the construction of a social theory of religion. The particular challenge of setting up comparisons of early Christian movements with social formations typical of ethnographic studies is that, whereas ethnography describes holistic societies, early Christian groups were experimental movements within a larger and more complex social and cultural structure. Thus the first observation one might be tempted to make about early Christian groups is that they were not holistic societies and that, as strictly religious associations, they demonstrate that religion has nothing to do with other social practices such as politics, material production, ideological competition and cultural conventions. And yet, it is not only the eventual role one form of Christianity came to play in the political structure of Western culture, but the forms of self-designation (e.g., "kingdom of God" people) and the content of the myths (e.g., Jesus as a royal figure) typical for these early Christians that suggest fundamental interests in the formation of an alternative society. If it were possible to identify and describe such an interest, early Christianities might be explained as variants of a general human interest in social formation characteristic for the times. If so, the strategies of deferral and displacement characteristic for early Christian myths would provide theorists with examples of rationalizing social formations that emerge as a minority response to, and in the context of large-scale, differentiated social configurations and multicultural challenges.

A general theory of religion will eventually have to account for the differentiated forms of religious practice and experience that have arisen in the context of the social and cultural histories of the so-called "world religions." This will have to include such things as the sense of autonomy characteristic of institutional religions, appeals to transcendent and extra-social authorities grounded in systems of "belief," and views of religion based on personal experience and the importance of individual transformation. It will not be easy to move from theories of religion formulated on the basis of ethnographic studies to analyses of interests in personal religious quests in highly complex cultures. The rub will come at the point where several questions of importance for a theory of religion converge with significant issues in the quest for a general theory of social formation itself.

Of fundamental importance for both investigations is the question of human interest, whether this question is phrased as a matter of collective "motivation," of "determination" among the several practices in the structure of a society, or of the "function" of any given instance within a spectrum of semiautonoumous practices. Debates have raged around all three terms, indicating that there is work to be done at the conceptual level of theory and testing. If it is not possible to define and demonstrate collective human interest in social formation, it may not be possible to construct a social theory of religion at all. If, on the other hand, it turns out that modern concepts of the individual and personal religious experience are beholden to social and cultural configurations within which religion as a practice may have played a suspiciously important role, it may well be that a social theory of religion will have a fundamental contribution to make to theories of social formation.

It is in any case worth noting that current quests for theoretical precision in the description of political, economic, social, cultural and religious practices converge at the point of constructing a theory of social formation. A radically social theory of religion, working with a thoroughly social anthropology, and daring the creation of concepts adequate to describe the interests and strategies basic to the collective, human invention of religious practices, would make a significant contribution to the quest for a radically social theory of social formation itself.

Note

1. The seminar's inaugural papers by Merrill Miller, Ron Cameron, Burton L. Mack, Jonathan Z. Smith and John S. Kloppenborg were published in *Method and Theory in the Study of Religion* 8 (1996).

Suggested Readings

Althusser, Louis and Étienne Balibar
    1970   *Reading Capital*, Ben Brewster (trans.). London: Verso.
Mack, Burton L.
    1995   *Who Wrote the New Testament? The Making of the Christian Myth*. San Francisco: HarperSanFrancisco.
    1996   "On Redescribing Christian Origins." *Method and Theory in the Study of Religion* 8: 247–269.
McGowan, John
    1991   *Postmodernism and Its Critics*. Ithaca, NY: Cornell University Press.
Resch, Robert Paul
    1992   *Althusser and the Renewal of Marxist Social Theory*. Berkeley: University of California Press.
Smith, Jonathan Z.
    1987   *To Take Place: Toward Theory in Ritual*. Chicago: University of Chicago Press.
    1990   *Drudgery Divine: On the Comparison of Early Christianities and the Religions of Late Antiquity*. Chicago: University of Chicago Press; London: School of Oriental and African Studies.

21

STRATIFICATION

Gustavo Benavides

❧❧

The practices and representations generally clustered under the name "religion" seem to be as concerned with erecting as with dismantling boundaries. Indeed, religious practices and representations appear to have as their function to provide the ultimate validation for the creation and the maintenance of the most tenacious differences, as well as for their radical questioning (Benavides 1989: 5). Even while not concerned with the issue of difference as such, some of the most productive definitions of religion point in that direction. For example, Rappaport's definition of sanctity as "the quality of unquestionable truthfulness imputed by the faithful to unverifiable propositions" (1971: 263) identifies the processes whereby some propositions are set apart. In so doing, this definition is concerned with the setting apart of the activities, objects or beings about which assertions are made, as well as of those uttering the propositions. More recently, and without referring to Rappaport, Burkert has written that in the ancient world religion would have been seen as necessary above all for the validation of oaths (1996: 169)—religious messages being validated through anxiety and fear (1996: 30–31). Terms such as "sacredness" or "religion," then, are used to identify the mechanisms whereby difference, distinction and rank are solidified. One would expect, therefore, that processes of social differentiation, and especially of social stratification, would be kept in place through religious means.

It would be tempting, in fact, to push further and to ask whether it was the need to render visible and keep in place inchoate social differences that led to the emergence of religion in the first place. The emergence of religion cannot be explained in purely political terms, however, for it should be remembered that before the appearance of hierarchical societies, early humans, making use of their cognitive capacities, would have needed to make other, more elementary, distinctions, paying careful attention to certain physiological processes, as well as to those components of the physical world which had to do with the satisfaction of their needs and thus with their survival. It is at this point that the connection between religion and the establishing of differences becomes visible, for paying attention to certain important activities and objects, acting in a conscientious, scrupulous manner in dealing with them, is in accordance with the most likely etymology of the Latin term *religio*, namely *relegere* or *religere*. This setting apart should remind us also of the distinction between *sacrum* (that which belongs to the gods) and *profanum* (the space in front of the temple).

Just as physical survival requires the proper functioning of basic cognitive processes, which themselves depend upon the exercise of conceptual and perceptual discrimination, in order to come into being, the symbols, myths and rituals generated by countless social groups require the existence of basic cognitive mechanisms, whose effects are amplified by ideological needs. The process of differentiation could in principle produce non-ranking, lateral divisions, but even in these cases there is the tendency not just to distinguish neutrally between right and left, but rather between a cluster of positive attributes—correct, *recht*, *Recht*, adroit, dexterity—and negative ones—sinister, *siniestro*, *gauche*, and the like. Similarly, distinctions involving front and back almost unavoidably result in equating, possibly for evolutionary reasons, the former with honor and the latter with dishonor. More frequently, such divisions involve vertical metaphors, also possibly related to our evolutionary history. When social inequality begins to emerge, it becomes reinforced by the tendency to distinguish, and then to rank, in both lateral and vertical terms, and in general by our proclivity to set objects, processes and persons apart. In turn, the beneficiaries of these processes of discrimination start making use of the cognitive mechanisms which have set them apart in the first place. Considering the recurrent nature of the gestures and metaphors employed by human groups to mark domination and subordination, it would be a mistake to act like eighteenth-century *philosophes* and regard the ritualization of difference merely as the result of a priestly conspiracy. On the other hand, despite the current unpopularity of the Enlightenment, there is much to be said for trying to discern the mutually reinforcing relationship between our cognitive proclivities and the ritualization of inequality.

What are the roots of social differentiation? Age, gender and the distinction between members and non-members of kinship-based communities appear as the most likely candidates. Even before the emergence of class-based societies, one can assume that a clear differentiation was made between one's own people and those who were perceived as potential enemies. The notion that, unless they became guests, foreigners were enemies can be seen in the tension among related terms such as Latin *hostis*, Gothic *gasts* and Old Slavic *ğosti*: the meaning of the first term being "enemy" and that of the two others, "host" (Benveniste 1973). Seeking to identify early examples of stratification based on gender and age, Bender has referred to the spatial arrangements found in upper paleolithic caves in south-west France and northern Spain. The fact that paintings are found far away from the entrance of these caves has led Bender to hypothesize that the areas of difficult access were used for male initiations (1989: 90–91). This would mean that at the very core of the emergence of social stratification we would find what Bender has described as the sharpening and sanctification of distinctions based on kin-affiliation, age-set and gender (1990: 250). Still, even though spatial–ritual separation may indicate social stratification based on gender, this explains neither the passage from differentiation to stratification, nor the workings of this stratified system.

It is beyond the scope of this essay to discuss in any detail the issue of social evolution. Suffice it to say that even though, as a reaction against nineteenth-century models, talk of evolution is still regarded with the utmost suspicion in the social sciences, and even more so in the humanities, given the connection between social evolution, stratification and the emergence of religion, it is necessary to stress the need to study religious phenomena in the context of long-term social change. In general terms, as we saw in the upper paleolithic developments studied by Bender, the dissolution of kinship-based groups in which stratification is based on gender and age gives place to one in which social differentiation begins to emerge. Döbert (1973) has proposed a process involving parallel social and religious differentiation that begins with the dissolution of kinship-based social arrangements (see also Eder 1973). At the religious level, this process entails the differentiation of gods from their domains, the availability of alternative ways of acting both for gods and for humans, and the concomitant need to keep contingency at bay through the codification of tradition (Benavides 1995b). The resulting structures are sanctified, that is, locked into place, by a variety of means. These include the use of mythical charters, ritualization of behavior and sacred kingship (Kurtz 1981: 186–191).

If we turn to social evolutionary theorizing, we can distinguish several types or models of organization. An early stage, before the dissolution of communal society, is the one represented by New Guinea's big-men. Without having coercive powers, without being sacralized, big-men encouraged and supervised lavish distribution of food in ceremonial occasions. Lacking coercive powers, however, a big-man could be abandoned by his followers if his demands were too burdensome. The instability of social arrangements in which special status was not accompanied by coercive power has led Richard Lee to remark that "big-men systems exhibit the logic of communal society pushed to the breaking-point" (1990: 240). After the breaking-point, communal societies are replaced by those intermediate societies known as chiefdoms—neither states nor egalitarian societies, these organizations have a "centralized government, hereditary hierarchical status arrangements ... but no formal, legal apparatus of forceful repression, and without the capacity to prevent fission" (Claessen and Skalník 1978: 23). It is with the emergence of chiefdoms that social authority requires religious legitimization. Chiefdoms have the tendency to be theocratic, and their political life is heavily ritualized. The mythology and ritual practices that until not too long ago surrounded—in fact, constituted—the institution of kingship were developed to set the chiefs apart from their subjects. Examining twenty-one early states, Claessen (1978: 557) found that in seventeen of them the relationship between the ruler and his subjects was based on a mythical charter; the sacral status of the ruler was found in the same number of cases, the ruler being regarded as the pivot of the state (Skalník 1978: 615). With the emergence of sacred kingship, then, we witness a further centralization of authority, with the sacred king serving as a condenser of sacredness (Kurtz 1981: 186). The parallels between the emergence of the political and religious realms becomes visible when we consider Marc Abélès' claim about sacred kingship being "synonymous with the process of autonomy of politics which places the state *in* and *above* society" (1981: 1). Translated into religious terms, the operation identified by Abélès can be understood as involving the autonomy of religion in which sacredness is found in, and placed above, society.

One of the main difficulties in discussions about social stratification involves the distinction between status and class (Weber 1980 [1922]: 177–180; Parkin 1978: 601–608). Exaggerating the differences between Weber and Marx, it is generally claimed that high status is not necessarily linked to high economic position or to the ability to exercise power. Indeed, it is the case that, in India for example, one finds economically poor ritual specialists (Brahmins) and rich untouchables; similarly, some members of the European nobilities were much poorer than subordinate and often despised groups such as merchants, groups whose display of wealth was severely restricted by sumptuary laws. Two points must be made regarding this problem. The first is that even though certain members of high-status groups may be poorer than some members of low-status groups, high-status groups *as a whole* are richer than their low-status counterparts. Even W. G. Runciman, an author who argues against ignoring the three separate dimensions of class, status and power, acknowledges "the closeness of fit between the three dimensions alike in industrial and pre-industrial societies" (1970: 132). Similarly, Bryan S. Turner, who wants "to maintain a sharper division between status and the idea of economic class," also wants "to argue that class analysis and status analysis, far from being mutually exclusive, are most productively used in combination" (1988: 12). It is symptomatic of the current attitude toward the concept of class that, while using the term "status" without further qualification, Turner feels obliged to refer to "the idea of economic class." In any case, as Ste. Croix has pointed out when referring to Greco-Roman antiquity, wealth was by far the most important marker of status. He quotes Ovid, who, not unlike the Indian texts to be mentioned later, is refreshingly candid regarding the fact that "it is property that confers rank" (*Amores* 3.8.55; Ste Croix 1975: 10, 1981: 425).

The second point has to do with the fact that high-status groups generally do everything in their power to obtain the wealth without which they could not maintain their rank for more than a couple of generations. The crucial difference between, say, medieval nobles and merchants was that, whereas the latter regarded wealth as something that could be produced through work, calculation and speculation, the former considered that either one had to be born to wealth, or one had to obtain it, booty-like, through military action. What was considered demeaning was work. It is work, therefore, and not wealth that is incompatible with high status: it is the distance established between a group and productive work that determines the group's status. Conversely, as if to mark the distance between a privileged group and work, and the closeness between it and the quest for plunder, more even than leisure, it is gratuitous, wasteful physical exertion and excess that high status groups have traditionally prized. The parallels between the gratuitous expenditure of energy and the presence of a symbolic surplus in religion—the realization, in fact, that without the presence of a symbolic surplus there is no religion is an issue that requires further exploration.

Generally, it is through military conquest that groups become subordinated. Religion does play a role in these processes, as the military activities of most societies are placed under the protection of the group's divinities. Victory, therefore, and the resulting extermination, enslavement or subordination of the conquered population are regarded as having the blessing of the conquerors' gods. Whether it is YHWH ordering the extermination of Israel's enemies, or Indra helping the *ārya* defeat the indigenous *dāsa / dasyu*, or the Christian god helping the Spaniards to defeat Aztec or Inca armies, the result is the same: a sanctified social order. Over time, the initial distance between conquerors and conquered tends to blur, although this blurring is more difficult to achieve when the physical differences between the dominant and subordinated groups are marked. But even in cases in which it is impossible to distinguish among groups by their physical characteristics, both élites and subaltern groups can validate their claims by referring to military victories or defeats. Thus, almost six centuries after the battle of Hastings, the radical Gerrard Winstanley, condemning the oppressive conditions prevalent in seventeenth-century England, could still talk of the "Norman yoke." From the opposite angle, in the early twentieth century, members of the French nobility still claimed a foreign, Frankish, ancestry that distinguished them from the ordinary French population.

In its most extreme form, the distinction between citizen and alien involves differentiating between those "well-born," free, and towards whom one feels affection from those who are not "well-born." The fact that in most languages the word for slave derives from a word that designates an alien group—the best-known being Slav / slave—points to the role that alienness plays in the generation of a radical form of subordination in which human beings are reduced to the status of property. The relationship between religion and slavery is ambiguous. As we shall see below, religious reformers such as the Buddha and Jesus did not object in principle to slavery. At the same time, certain claims made by religions such as Christianity could be used by slaves in their attempts to free themselves from their condition, a fact that led American slaveholders to regard their slaves' conversion to Christianity as endangering the social order (Raboteau 1978: 101–103). More frequently, however, that social order was sanctified—rather than challenged or inverted—by Christianity. Southern U.S. theologians, aware that the Bible does not outrightly condemn slavery, saw that institution, along with subordination based on gender and class, as the very foundation of a Christian social order (Genovese and Fox-Genovese 1986; Fox-Genovese and Genovese 1987). In Rome, 2,000 years earlier, we find religious representations on both sides of the social divide: the senatorial aristocracy considered slave rebellions as indications that the relations between Rome and the gods were strained; conversely, lower-class rebels, particularly slaves, placed their quest for social justice under religious protection.

Besides the hierarchies that result when a radical distinction is made between one's people and all the others are the cases of hierarchical differentiation within societies whose members are believed to be somehow related to each other. Mythical legitimation is generally discernible in these cases as well. An extreme example of a religiously-grounded system of hierarchy is provided by the Indian caste system, a hierarchical arrangement constituted by the interaction between the *varna* (color) and the *jati* (birth, occupation) systems. The *varna* component of the caste system can be traced back to the ideology which, according to Dumézil (1958), the ancient Indo-Aryans shared with other Indo-European groups. It is only in India, however, that a full-fledged, mythologically-grounded hierarchical system can be observed in action. Despite the parallels between the Indian and the Iranian tripartite social organizations which were based at least ideally on *varna* and *pištra* (occupation, etymologically related to color: Dumézil 1930; Benveniste 1938, 1973), it is not possible to identify in Iran a caste system similar to the one that emerged in India. Even though the priests, warriors and agriculturalists were believed to have descended from Zarathustra through his sons, or to have been established by the mythical king Yima, the Iranian tripartite system seems to have existed more as a social ideal than as a social reality (Dumézil 1930). In India, on the other hand, one finds what is perhaps the most extreme case of mythically-grounded social stratification. The *varna* system comprised *brahmán / brāhmana*, *kṣatriya / rājanya* and *vaiśya* (ritual specialists, warriors and agriculturalists), to which was added a servant class (*śūdra*).

The relation between the *varna* and the caste systems proper, comprising a large number of *jati* (Mandelbaum 1970: I.13–22), as well as the origins of the *jati* system itself, has not been satisfactorily explained. It seems to be the case that, prior to the establishment of *brāhmanas* in South India around 300 B.C.E. (Hart 1987: 481), a caste system was already in place. Morton Klass (1980: 175–178) has in fact argued that around 4,000 years ago the caste system came into existence over the entire subcontinent as a response to the spread of rice and hard-grain cultivation. He maintains that through egalitarian groups individuals sought to have access to the food surplus made possible by the new grains; stratification came about when some of the corporate groups that did not have access to land had to engage in exchanges with groups that could provide food. Klass's hypothesis about the origins of the caste system is congruent with Lee's theory about the origins of inequality: "The germs of inequality arise, not from a breakdown of the sharing ethic, but *from an effort to make it work under altered circumstances*" (1990: 238). The difference is that the altered circumstances in South Asia led not to the appearance of an "egalitarian redistributor" who would mediate among individuals, but to the emergence of an overarching ideology, locked into place by notions about purity and pollution, that would regulate the relations among the corporate groups.

Klass's reconstruction of the origins of the ancient Indian form of social stratification posits economic concerns and technological developments at the core of a caste system that mobilized practices involving purity and pollution to protect its boundaries. Economic concerns are present also at the center of the *varna* ideology that legitimizes itself mythically through the myth of *Purusha*, the primordial person, a myth of sacrifice and creation that has parallels in the mythologies of other Indo-European populations. Unlike modern apologists of the caste system, Indian texts are remarkably frank about the exploitation to which the *brāhmana* and *kṣatriya* subject members of lower castes. According to the *Aittareya Brahmana* 7, 29 (Sharma 1991: 173; B. Smith 1994: 49, 57 n. 99; see also MacQueen 1988: 148; Lincoln 1986), the *vaiśya* is "tributary to another, to be eaten by another, and one who may be dispossessed at will," while the *śūdra* is "a servant of another, to be dismissed at will, and to be murdered at will." The connection between stratification and religion becomes clear when one finds that the *Gautama Dharmasūtra* states that "when engaged in a rite enjoined by the sacred law, a person could take money by force of fraud from a *śūdra*" (Sharma 1990: 113). In general, as shown by Brian K. Smith in *Classifying the Universe* (1994), ideological persuasion is carried out through symbolic redundancy; thus a ranking fever encompasses everything: society, gods, space, time, flora, fauna.

But it is by no means self-evident that, despite the combination of brute power and ideological redundancy, the interests of élites are assimilated by members of subaltern groups. Therefore, in order to discern the effects of ideological persuasion one has to consider a society not just from the point of view of the élites, but from that of its subordinate groups as well. When that is done, one finds conflicting accounts about the pervasiveness of the élites' view.

According to Burghart (1978), Nepalese texts show the existence of not one but three competing hierarchical models, with ascetics, Brahmans and kings claiming superiority at the head of their respective hierarchies. Fuller, on the contrary, has argued that Sanskritic deities do not represent the caste hierarchy, serving rather to symbolize the upper castes' claim not to be dependent upon the lower castes; on the other hand, according to Fuller, the village deities do represent hierarchical asymmetrical relations (1988: 33–35). The most difficult issue involves the attitude of the so-called Untouchables, that is, the groups that according to the founding myth found in the *Rig Veda* and elsewhere, are not even considered to be part of the social organism. While Moffat (1979) has claimed that there is a "consensus at the bottom of caste," Mencher (1974, 1980) has shown that these subordinate groups do not accept the pretensions of the high-status castes. Relevant from the point of view of our discussion of the relationship between class and status is Mencher's demonstration of the intimate connection between low ritual status and economic misery.

Besides providing an extreme case of religiously-based stratification, the Indian caste system has been used in academic and non-academic contexts to advance culturalist explanations of ranking systems, and to make pronouncements about the universality of hierarchy, an argument associated with Dumont and his work, *Homo Hierarchicus* (1980 [1966]). Concerned with the destructive effects of the kind of consumerism so prevalent in the United States, Milner has more recently claimed that we need to achieve a "much greater insulation between economic and political power, on the one hand, and status, on the other" (1994: 16), and has explicitly proposed the culture of premodern India as a relevant model. As stated earlier, however, it is doubtful that in India, or elsewhere, wealth, power and status have been as insulated from each other as scholars such as Milner believe.

An extreme form of culturalism can be found in Clifford Geertz's fantasies about the alleged Balinese "theater state." In a much-quoted phrase, Geertz claims that, in Bali, power was "surrendered from subject to lordling, lordling to lord and lord to king," so that "power was not allocated from the top, it cumulated from the bottom" (1980: 62–63). But, as Howe has shown, besides being much poorer than their lords and owning far less land (due mostly to forced expropriations), Balinese peasants had no choice but to perform various services for rulers who did not wait for power to be "surrendered" or to "cumulate from the bottom," but who kept in place caste privileges through severe punishments (Howe 1991: 447, 449, 459). More importantly still, if one wants to consider the intimate connection between ecological conditions, social formations, and their ideological apparatus, is the fact that above the line at which wet-rice cultivation is no longer possible one does not find the hierarchical organization found in the lowlands; rather, one finds an ideology based on seniority and egalitarianism (Howe 1989: 48, 50). This means that, rather than thinking in terms of disembodied, hierarchical ideologies that happen to appear here or there, or in terms of the meaningless notion of power as the very substance of all reality, popularized by Foucault (Benavides 1997: 133), one should instead consider the constraints that ecological conditions impose on the kind of work necessary to insure the survival of populations. Wet-rice cultivation, for example, requires a degree of social differentiation—a differentiation which itself requires religious legitimation in order to be reproduced and authorized. In the case of Bali, the nature of the terrain has led to the development of a "religion of holy water" (*Agama Tirtha*), comprising a set of rituals that involve hierarchically arranged water temples by means of which irrigation is regulated (Lansing 1991). Returning to the issue of the religious legitimation of power, we could say that just as South Indian rulers invited Brahmins from the north to settle in their territories in order to provide supernatural legitimization for their social authority (Hart 1987: 481), so too Indonesian rulers seem to have welcomed Indian priests for similar reasons (Howe 1989: 64–65).

Not unlike in India, European notions of hierarchy have been based on the notion of society as an organism, whose various organs are subordinated to a central one such as the heart. As in the case of the myth of *Purusha*, European peasants were regarded as the feet of the social organism. At a higher social level, but still in a way that parallels the tense interdependence between Indian warriors and Brahmins, there was in the West a tension between complementarity and subordination, with the emperor in charge of military affairs and the protection of the social organism, and the Pope in charge of praying and legitimizing worldly authority. The European parallels with India can be pushed still further if one takes into consideration the appearance at the end of the ninth century of a tripartite ideology that divided the social world into those who prayed, those who fought, and those who worked (Duby 1978; Oexle 1979). It can be argued, in fact, that the tripartite Indo-European ideology identified by Dumézil is more visible in medieval Europe than in any other culture.

In general, whether tripartite or not, such hierarchical understanding of society was routinely legitimized through religious means, high ranking clerics being particularly vocal in their denunciation of any interpretation of the Christian myths that would have gone against their class interests. In the eighth and ninth centuries, theologians of aristocratic background such as Alcuin described Jesus as "son of the nobility" (*filius nobilium et sanctorum*, Schreiner 1974: 326–327). Hildegard of Bingen, so popular nowadays, justified accepting only women of noble birth into her convent by saying that chaos results when social unequals live together, while order reigns where the celestial hierarchy determines the distinctions in human society (Schreiner 1974: 338–339). In the tenth century, Bishop Atto of Vercelli wrote that Christ did not come to change social conditions but behavior (Oexle 1979: 427). Accordingly, the social conditions that prevailed in this world would, in fact, remain in place in the afterlife (Dinzelbacher 1979a: 22, 1979b: 29). As Dinzelbacher has shown, visions of the afterlife agree in reporting a system based on the *ordines*, in such a way that aristocratic eleventh-century visionaries report visions of heaven that resemble the assemblies of the Holy Roman Empire. Far away from this princely assembly were the slaves and the peasants, the latter being regarded by the Church as the sinners par excellence—a peasant being a slave to sin. Otherwise, peasants are barely visible. Le Goff points out that of the four peasants mentioned in the literature of the very early Middle Ages, none has a name; they are there merely in order to allow the saints to be saintly. The Church, in fact, did not canonize a peasant until the thirteenth century (Le Goff 1977 [1966]: 137).

Like the Buddhist sangha, the Church accepted since its earliest days the social order, including the practice of slavery (Ste. Croix 1975, 1985; Macmullen 1990: 143), and slaves were not allowed to become priests (Le Goff 1977: 137). Even though there were exceptions to this rule, the prohibition against the ordination of slaves lasted from the end of the fourth century until the *Codex Iuris Canonici* in 1917, which was in effect until 1983 (Landau 1991: 178, 180). According to one of its regulations (818 / 819), if an unfree person is ordained without his master's consent, the ordination is invalid (Landau 1991: 183). Augustine justified slavery, perversely explaining it as a consequence of the fall in the Garden of Eden (Ste. Croix 1975: 21, 1981: 421). Ste. Croix writes that he knows "of no general, outright condemnation of slavery inspired by a Christian outlook, before the petition of the Mennonites of Germantown in Pennsylvania in 1688" (1975: 24, 1981: 423). Despite claims by Christian apologists, it is difficult not to agree with Ste. Croix (1975: 35) and MacMullen (1990 [1986]) that little changed in the Roman empire as a result of the conversion to Christianity. Constantine decreed that slaves who had turned on their masters should be "affixed to the cross," a penalty which, as MacMullen has mischievously remarked (1990: 149), "has caused great difficulty to commentators." It should be pointed out, however, that in 922 a canon of the Synod of Koblenz determined that someone who had sold a Christian is guilty of homicide. For the Church, on the other hand, even though slavery is based on original sin, inherited from Adam and Eve, human beings could be seen as having inherited also the state that Adam and Eve enjoyed before the Fall. In that sense, the tension that seems to be present at the core of some religions makes possible the radical—but generally unsuccessful—critique of the prevailing order.

It is mainly through ritual activity that stratification is rendered visible. Ritual behavior involves managing time, delimiting and mastering space, controlling bodies (Connerton 1989). This is achieved through the control of one's demeanor, of one's gestures. From India to medieval Europe, the control of bodies was crucial in maintaining social domination. The connection between demeanor and status can be seen at work in a regulation found in Āpastamba's and Gautama's *Dharmasūtra*, according to which a *śudra* should be flogged if, in conversation, sitting, lying down or on the road, he assumed a position equal to that of a twice-born man (Sharma 1990: 120). In Vedic India, as well, rituals served as mechanisms of exclusion, so that those *śudras* who were caught listening to the recitation of Vedic chants and hymns were to be punished by having molten lead poured into their ears. In contemporary India, on the other hand, ritual continues to render visible social hierarchies, as participation in some festivities will be determined by one's caste; thus, in the Andhra village studied by Herrenschmidt (1982), members of the highest castes participate in rituals in honor of orthodox vegetarian deities, whereas Untouchables worship a carnivorous goddess.

Activities having to do with the production, procurement, and preparation of food required in pre-industrial societies an amount of time and energy, as well as an emotional investment that even poor members of industrial societies would find difficult to comprehend; consequently, food consumption, particularly involving high-protein, scarce edibles, was a central way of displaying and consolidating one's position in the social hierarchy. Readers familiar with Rappaport's studies about the connection between ritualized meat consumption and ecological regulation among the Tsembaga of New Guinea (1984 [1968]) may not be as familiar with the large number of studies about the connections between sacrificial practices, meat consumption and ranking in the ancient world. In ancient Greece, for instance, virtually all meat consumption took place in a sacrificial setting (Grottanelli 1988: 17). As the distribution of meat served as a metaphor for social differentiation and ranking, as well as for equality, this consumption took place in a way that oscillated between marking equality and rendering visible inequality (Schmitt Pantel 1985: 155–158, 1990: 15; Grottanelli 1988: 32). The same was true of Rome, where the most illustrious participants in a banquet, besides being allowed to sit, enjoyed double or triple portions, while citizens of the second rank were allowed modest portions. In Rome, as well, banquets served as a means of rendering visible the differences among the social classes. This was true even when there was the attempt, under Domitian for example, to cover those differences through lavish meals to which large numbers of people from all *ordines* were invited. But in these cases, despite the openness of the celebration, eating arrangements were such that rank differences remained in place, in Rome even more so than in Greece.

In India, when consuming cooked food one is particularly at risk of being polluted by a member of a lower caste (Mandelbaum 1970: 1.196–201). This means that commensality signals status equality; it signals also that relations of subordination will be rehearsed through metaphors involving eating. Thus when a devotee offers food to a god, and then gets back *prasada* by consuming the god's leftovers, he is placing himself in a subordinate position. More radically, Smith has shown how social relations of subordination have been presented in India through the metaphor of eating and being eaten (B. K. Smith 1990, 1994: 46–48).

Another way in which social differences have been reinforced has been through the activities that one would tend to equate with the obliteration of difference, namely games and entertainment—keeping in mind that the connection between games and cultic acts has been traditionally close. As suggested earlier, the connection between play and hierarchy is fraught with tensions, as the very possibility of leisure is inextricably connected with the expenditure of surplus energy, energy not consumed by the ever present reality of work. In any event, if we consider the Roman case, besides the structuring of time and space that took place as a result of the placement of theaters and the scheduling of games, the very structure of the seating arrangements reinforced social division. In Republican and even more so in Imperial Rome beginning with Augustus, great care was paid to the position that members of the senatorial, equestrian, and lower ranks occupied during games, as well as to the presents that these groups received from the ruler. Furthermore, as the connection between theaters and temples, and between theaters, temples and markets, became closer, the ideological function of the games as the ceremonial spaces where *unanimitas* could be choreographed grew in importance.

An issue that cannot be examined here with the attention it deserves is the role played by stratification in the genesis of the world religions—that is, the role that social differentiation, the emergence of hierarchies, and status inconsistency have played in the emergence of Buddhism, Christianity and Islam (Benavides 1998: 193–195). For example, if we approach the rise of Buddhism from the perspective of status inconsistency, we find that the early community received support from the land-based *gahapatis*, who straddled across the divide between the rural and the urban (Chakravarti 1986: 217, 1996: 65–93), and between the *varnas* (1996: 118–121). In general terms, merchant groups can be seen as constituting networks—in some cases, literally trade networks—that compensated for the disappearance of the democratic tribal political structures that were being absorbed by the large political entities then emerging in north-eastern India. Regarding the Buddha's attitude towards the prevailing social conditions, it can be said that even though it is recounted that he challenged the Brahmins' claim of ritual purity, the Buddha—like Jesus in the earliest years of Christianity—is not understood to have questioned the existence of social hierarchy. The writers of the earliest Buddhist texts, conscious of social distinctions, used an elaborate terminology to refer to social stratification: *mohabhoga kula* (wealthy family), *dalidda kula* (destitute family), *sadhana* (wealthy), *adhana* (poor), *sugata* (faring well), *duggata* (faring poorly) (Chakravarti 1986: 205). Regarding the status of the early Buddhists, based on a list of 332 monks and nuns listed in the *Thera* and *Theri Gāthā*, 41 percent belonged to *Brāhmana* castes, 30 percent to the *Gahapati*, 23 percent to the *Khattiya*, 3 percent to the *Sudda*, and 3 percent to the "degraded" castes; furthermore, if one takes into account the actual wealth and political power of this group, it turns out that almost 48 percent of them belonged to the upper strata of society (Gokhale 1965: 395; cf. Chakravarti 1996: 122).

In the Mediterranean world, triumphant Christianity was born also among interstitial groups no longer anchored by the *polis*. In a way that resembles what took place in north India at the time of the rise of Buddhism, the emergence of Christianity must be seen as inextricably related to a process that involved, on the one hand, the hardening of social hierarchies, with the concomitant loosening of social cohesion, and, on the other, the appearance of groups that, having found themselves in an interstitial position, and wanting to recreate the now lost social cohesion, ended up creating new ideologies with universal claims. The reader is referred to studies by Lane Fox (1986), Mann (1986) and Kippenberg (1991), who advance theories that could also be used to understand the emergence of Buddhism. Lane Fox has maintained that the rise of Christianity has to be seen in the context of the "loosening of the civic cohesion of the Greek city-state" (1986: 322). Mann (1986: ch. 11) has attempted to explain the emergence of Christianity in the context of the problems faced by people who sought to articulate their interstitial social and personal identity in philosophical and religious terms, and has identified the trading networks of the empire— interstitial networks that involved the transactions between autonomous, literate and highly mobile individuals—as having been crucial for the expansion of Christianity. In much greater detail, in his study of the Near Eastern salvation religions, Kippenberg (1991) has examined the rise of Christianity in terms of groups which, seeking salvation, freed themselves from the power of the local communities, creating empire-wide networks.

After its triumph, Christianity accommodated itself without difficulty to the imperial order and to the hierarchical understanding of the cosmos prevalent in the Graeco-Roman world. This accommodation applied both to the supernatural and to the ecclesiastical realms: Ješu' bar Josef, now known as the Christ, was imagined as *Christus imperator*, military language used by Tertullian to refer to the martyrs and to the Trinity (Cancik 1975), while the Roman Church recreated the Roman bureaucracy at the beginning of the fourth century (Cancik 1985: 139), eventually becoming the ultimate source of legitimation of the various political configurations that succeeded the Roman Empire.

It would be tempting to claim that "the mystical" is concerned ultimately with obliterating the distinctions posited by religion. Such a claim, however, would be only partially justified; for if it is true that in many so-called mystical systems the divisions that constitute the world are left behind, the very act of transcending creates an all too real divide between those who remain in the world of difference and those who are lifted to the rarefied realm of the mystical. Consider the case of Pseudo-Dionysius Areopagita, the mysterious sixth-century author of *The Mystical Theology*, surely one of the most influential mystical works in the history of Christianity. It is well-known that besides that book and *The Divine*

Names, Pseudo-Dionysius is the author of *The Celestial Hierarchy* and the *Ecclesiastical Hierarchy*. But this does not mean that one has to go to the latter works to find instances of hierarchy, for *The Mystical Theology* itself moves from the heights of mystical negation to the admonition to Timothy "that none of this come to the hearing of the uninformed" (1000A). The connection between Pseudo-Dionysius and the issue with which we are concerned in this essay is indeed intimate, as the word "hierarchy"—*hier-archia*, a combination of *hieros* (sacred) and *árchein* (rule, reign, govern)—was coined and defined by him: "a hierarchy is a sacred order, a state of understanding and an activity approximating as closely as possible the divine" (164D); a hierarchy "is a certain perfect arrangement, an image of the beauty of God which sacredly works out the mysteries of its own enlightenment" (165B). After Pseudo-Dionysius, the notion of hierarchy has continued to play an important role in Christian theologians' conception of the social order, and above all in the self-understanding of the Roman Church (Dolhagaray 1947).

As we have seen, not even the fact of having been saved renders hierarchies obsolete. This understanding of the afterlife is not, however, limited to the clerics of aristocratic origin; we find it also in works such as *The Mirror of Simple Souls*, a mystical treatise written towards the end of the thirteenth century by Marguerite Porete, a woman who was burned to death as a heretic in 1310. She distinguishes "peasants for whom it is sufficient only to be saved" (ch. 63), and who are saved in an "uncourtly way" (ch. 62), from the Soul that is "totally dissolved, melted and drawn, joined and united to the most high Trinity" (ch. 68). This Soul "responds to no one if she does not wish to, if he is not of her lineage. For a gentleman would not deign to respond to a peasant, even if such a one would call him or attack him in a battlefield" (85).

In India, as one would expect, renouncers are as subject to hierarchical arrangements as non-renouncers. In effect, the *Samnyāsa Upanisads* distinguish between four (*Āśrama Up.* 98) and six (*Naradaparivrajaka Up.* 174) kinds of renouncers (Olivelle 1992). Reinforcing the ambivalent relationship between the realm of renunciation and that of the world is the fact that although renouncers are supposed to have left the world behind, this world is very much present in terms of the groups from which the *samnyasin* (an ascetic or renunciant) can receive offerings, and of the kind of people who can become renouncers in the first place. Thus, according to the *Naradaparivrajaka Up.* (174), "The blind, eunuchs, outcastes, cripples, the effeminate, the deaf, the childish, the dumb, heretics, discus-bearers, phallus-bearers, Vaikhānasas, Haradvijas, mercenary teachers, bald men, and people without a sacred fire: these, although they are detached, are unfit for renunciation." The *Naradaparivrajaka* (175) states that an Avadhūta, the highest among renouncers, "is subject to no restrictions. He is given to obtaining food in the manner of a python, receiving it from all classes except the outcastes and the infamous." Furthermore, according to the *Brhat-Samnyāsa*, "ascetics shall not speak with Śudras, women, outcastes, and menstruating women" (263). But

Brahmanic renunciation is only one of the forms of mysticism found in India. From the point of view of the rejection of stratification, the medieval north Indian *Sants* are more radical than the renouncers of the *Samnyāsa Upanisads*. In the verses attributed to them one finds radical denunciations of stratification and of difference in general, whether this involves ridiculing the pretensions of Brahmins, of ascetics, of Hindus, of Muslims; in this poetry one finds an alternative to the hierarchical ideology that, according to Dumont, permeates Indian society (Lorenzen 1998: 4). Kabir scorns the classificatory frenzy found in the *Upanisads* discussed above, saying that "Monks and Yogis give up their pedigrees but still brag of their lineage" (*Sabda* 14 = Hess 1983: 48). He asks "Who's the Brahmin? Who's the Śudra?" (*Ramainī* 26 = Hess 1983: 83). For him, "The world was born from one mother. What wisdom teaches separation?" (*Ramainī* 1 = Hess 1983: 79). Kabir's *ulatbāmsī* (upside-down speech) radically questions convention, but such questioning does not remain at the purely discursive level, as the Kabir-panth can be seen as appealing to "lower caste Hindus who seek an ideology which offers them a more positive status and self image," and to tribal peoples (Lorenzen 1987: 295). In a similar vein, for Ravidas, "A family that has a true follower of the Lord is neither high caste nor low caste, lordly or poor ... Priests or merchants, labourers or warriors, half-breeds, outcastes, and those who tend cremation fires—their hearts are all the same" (Hawley and Juergensmeyer 1988: 25).

Reversals of all kinds would seem to question hierarchies, but here as well, one ought to ask whether the reversals that take place during carnivalesque situations truly question hierarchical arrangements—and, above all, manage to overthrow the social order—or whether such reversals, by rendering dominant institutional arrangements visible, actually contribute to their reinforcement (Benavides 1995c). Reversal and compensation are well known in the history of religions, and one would require at least an essay as long as this one to present even the briefest outline of the varieties of reversal found from ancient Egypt to contemporary peasant societies. It can be mentioned that according to Egyptian mythology, in the afterlife the poor man is rewarded, while the rich man is punished. In Babylon it is the goddess Sarpanītu who is in charge of reversing: she makes the rich poor and the poor rich.

After having devoted most of this essay to an examination of the ways in which hierarchies are kept in place by sacralization, it is necessary to mention other issues. One involves the parallel between social status and acceptance in principle of the reality of stratification, but not of one's place in it. The clearest example of this is the so-called process of "sanskritization" in India—that is, the relinquishing of practices considered as defiling, by groups that have accepted the normative "Brahmanic" norms, even when this entails adopting a relatively ascetic way of life. In India this generally requires changing one's diet and one's attitude towards sexuality and gender relations. The first involves giving up meat and alcohol, while the second leads to emphasizing the subordination of women and banning the remarriage of widows.

A final issue that should at least be mentioned concerns the way in which various religions, as well as varieties of a single religion, are subject to ranking. This applies not only to members of some religions classifying their own as superior to others, but even more so to the practice of drawing boundaries around official or legitimate forms of religion in order to distinguish them from those held to be illegitimate, forms which are labeled as superstition, magic, syncretism, heresy, and witchcraft (Benavides 1994, 1995a). Lest it be thought that classifications of this sort are only produced by fanatical clerics or, worse, by unenlightened scholars, it should be pointed out that the distinction between religion and superstition can be traced to Roman times, and that ordinary people do engage in this kind of discrimination, the practice of religion being precisely about making and authorizing these very distinctions. On the other hand, it should also be noted that marginal groups or individuals who are associated with so-called illegitimate forms of religion are sometimes, for that very reason, considered as endowed with supernatural powers, powers which members of dominant groups seek to utilize.

Despite the necessarily cursory manner of this examination, it should be clear that, however much some may wish to equate religion with equality, *the practices named religion are concerned above all else with the management of difference.* Although in some cases, this management means questioning or outright rejection, the fact remains that in most cases management means generation, maintenance and reinforcement.

Suggested Readings

Burkert, Walter
    1996   *Creation of the Sacred: Tracks of Biology in Early Religions.* Cambridge, MA: Harvard University Press.

Chakravarti, Uma
    1996   *The Social Dimensions of Early Buddhism.* New Delhi: Munshiran Manoharlal.

Howe, Leo
    1991   "Rice, Ideology, and the Legitimation of Hierarchy in Bali." *Man* 26: 445–467.

Lansing, J. Stephen
    1991   *Priests and Programmers: Technologies of Power in the Engineered Landscape of Bali.* Princeton: Princeton University Press.

Lenski, Gerhard E.
    1984   *Power and Privilege: A Theory of Social Stratification.* Chapel Hill: University of North Carolina Press; original edn, New York: McGraw-Hill, 1966.

Lincoln, Bruce
  1989   *Discourse and the Construction of Society. Comparative Studies of Myth, Ritual, and Classification.* New York: Oxford University Press.
Olivelle, Patrick
  1992   *Saṃnyāsa Upanisads: Hindu Scriptures on Asceticism and Renunciation.* New York: Oxford University Press.
Parkin, Frank
  1978   "Social Stratification," pp. 599–632 in Tom Bottomore and Robert Nisbet (eds.), *A History of Sociological Analysis.* New York: Basic Books.
Ste. Croix, G. E. M. de
  1981   *The Class Struggle in the Ancient Greek World from the Archaic Age to the Arab Conquests.* Ithaca, NY: Cornell University Press.
Smith, Brian K.
  1994   *Classifying the Universe: The Ancient Indian Varna System and the Origins of Caste.* New York: Oxford University Press.

22

STRUCTURE

Jeppe Sinding Jensen

"Structure" is a complex as well as a critical term in the study of religion. But that is not peculiar to the study of religion; the same holds in most other human sciences. The term structure is complex because it shares with many other terms a double reference. First, as a term, it refers to structure as a metaphysical concept in philosophical discourse, but also to an abstract theoretical concept in scientific investigations. In that sense it functions as a prerequisite of and for analysis, such as when we seek to disclose the structure of, say, this argument or of a religious system of classification. Second, the term structure also refers to concrete, empirical phenomena in the world which may be described by means of the concept, as for instance the structure of a building, of molecules or of the Paris Métro.

So, on the one hand, structure is a metaphysical[1] concept that has certain abstract, analytical and theoretical meanings depending upon the theories we relate to the concept, and, on the other hand, it is a descriptive term that refers to more or less empirical phenomena, ranging from the concrete structures of buildings and libraries (which we may identify unproblematically) to the more subtle structures of symbolic systems, such as those of religious cosmologies and mythologies, in which their structure only emerges through our analysis of the subject matter. It only adds to the complexity of the notion of structure that when we produce formal representations and draw diagrams of structures and thereby transform them into empirical matter on paper, they still remain metaphysical. They become real only in terms of our perception of things. This is because the concept of structure does not refer to an actual entity; instead, it is about the relations between entities—and "relation" is yet another metaphysical concept. Thus, the term structure refers to structure as a concept, metaphysical and theoretical and to things that have structural relations as a salient property, and these relations we may, in turn, only grasp because we possess the concept structure and understand how to use it.

Structure is a critical term because we cannot do without it. It is therefore important that we try to get our understanding and use of the term—that is, of the meanings of the concept itself and of its references—to be as intelligible and manageable as possible. The term structure can be used in so many ways and mean so many different things, abstract as well as concrete, that it must be counted among the most elusive concepts employed in the study of religion. As this exposition will demonstrate, an adequate understanding of the term is also necessary for an explanation of structuralism as a theory in the human sciences and of its application in the study of religion.

Structure is everywhere. We may reasonably presume that the physical world, as well as our mental, social and linguistic worlds are structured, but structure as an abstract notion is not the most evident matter for reflection. In the human sciences, to which the study of religion belongs, structure is mostly conceived of as a metaphysical entity, albeit no more or no less metaphysical than other abstract and cognate terms such as form, pattern or organization. Whether such concepts belong to a Platonic world of ideas or are considered as just "manners of speaking" is a truly metaphysical question not to be treated here. For our purpose it is more important to note that the concept of structure is not subjective, a something merely located in individual minds. Structure as a concept belongs to the public realm of meaning and language, it is something that we can talk about. We may of course have different opinions about it but disagreement does not entail subjectivity. Thus, the concept of structure is not a thing in the physical sense, nor is it simply a mental entity. It is, as already noted, an abstract entity and, as part of our conceptual competence and language, it is one of the prerequisites for our ability to know about physical things, to use our minds and communicate about all that through languages. Although this may sound somewhat mysterious, we shall see how structure can be made amenable to and tractable in empirical study. In fact, we would not be able to study or understand anything at all were it not for structures in our modes of cognition, in our language and in our world. Would our world make sense if it was not structured? Centuries of scientific investigation and common-sense experience have convinced us that the physical world *is* structured. It consists of many things that have properties and are the subject or objects of processes, as for instance: molecules, bacteria, snow-flakes, mammals, diamonds and galaxies. If it were not so, we could not make sense of what is going on—everything would simply be a mess. So, although structures, like properties and relations, are abstract entities they are also, in a metaphysical sense, very real; they exist and prevent the world from being a (total) mess.

The metaphysical world of thought and language is also structured, it consists of many non-physical and abstract things which also have properties and are the subjects or objects of processes, as for instance: grammar, syntax, melody, rhythm, behavior, rituals, systems of symbolic classification and religious cosmologies. If it were not so we could not make sense of what is

315

going on or even make sense of ourselves. Our making sense *of* things depends on there being structure *in* our making sense. Without structure no order, without order no rules, and without rules no meaning. Also, we would not be able to use language if it was not structured. All of this we can say because our language *is* structured, as is our cognition. Our social world is also structured or we would loose orientation and not be able to interact with each other. Our cultural and symbolic worlds are structured: What would music, literature or motion pictures be if they were not all structured?

Thus, we have epistemological, social and expressive structures—all of which only work for us as humans because of conceptualization and language. It is therefore relevant that we—in the study of religion—look primarily to the notion of structure at the level of language, because it is through language that religion is described, analyzed and interpreted. It is also, primarily, through language that religious traditions are reproduced and enacted. If language is extracted from religion, then religion becomes meaningless and untranslatable. And it ceases to be religion as we know it. On this point Terry Godlove (1989: 5–6) anticipated an oft-noted critique when he said that:

> granted that religions sometimes express their truths in language, is it not a serious distortion, perhaps even an academic fiction, to consider this aspect of religious symbolization in abstraction from its natural experiential and often ritual-bound habitat? My reply is that the question is falsely posed. In focusing on the conceptual element in religion I intend no divorce from the realm of experience and ritual, nor do I think one is possible. Indeed, I would be happy to accept the pragmatic conception of belief according to which it cannot be isolated from a disposition to act.

Simply put, the concept of structure, with all that comes with it, is of primary theoretical importance because it is a prerequisite for the rationality of religious systems of thought and action as well as for our explanations and interpretations of these systems (Jensen and Martin 1997).

Before proceeding we should have some preliminary definition of "structure." A workable definition of the concept of structure must necessarily be an abstract one, one that could run like this: *A structure is a set or network of relations which gives a phenomenon an identity as a closed system of interdependent parts.* As a point of clarification we can say that the main difference between "structure" and "system" is that a structure is a network or set of *relations*, whereas a system is a set of *elements*. It is furthermore appropriate to distinguish between "form" as the external aspects of wholes whereas structure refers to the set or network of internal relations of wholes. The most important aspect of a definition of structure is the emphasis on the priority of relations, so that structure is conceived as "a property of systems whose elements are generated out of the relations that relate them" (Caws 1995: 478). How these abstract notions concerning a metaphysical and theoretical notion of structure may "come to life" in the study of religion will be discussed below. For now, we may contrast our preliminary understanding of structure with some other uses of the term.

Etymologically, the term structure comes from the Latin term *structura*: "a building, a construction, a way of building, a layout," derived from the verb *struere* meaning "to pile up, build, arrange, order." Later it was used more specifically in science and mathematics, as well as more informally in sociology and philosophy, until the concept gained precision with the emergence of structuralism as a distinct theoretical movement in a number of academic fields in the early half of the twentieth century. On structure, dictionaries note for instance: a "way in which something is put together, organized etc.," "something arranged in a definite pattern of organization," or "organization of parts as dominated by the general character of the whole." This alone covers quite a lot and is very imprecise. Most entries in dictionaries and encyclopedias associate structure with overt and empirical arrangements of things. It is true that there are many instances of such uses of the term: we find matters as varied as "crumb structures" of farming soil, "fine structures" of microscopic biological material, "power structure" in politics, "capital structure" in the world of finance, "crystal structure" in physics, "ring structure" and "resonance structure" in chemistry, "file structure" in computing, and so forth. As most things in this world are somehow structured the list is virtually endless—and trivial as long as we operate at the level of directly observable empirical reality. In the study of human culture, for instance the study of religion, it is much more interesting to be able to investigate and disclose structures and structural relations that are not so readily observable.

In light of the assumptions already presented on the structural character of the products of the human mind and culture, it is relevant to address both the issue of structures in religion and the structures of our knowledge thereof, that is, of the study of religion itself. In the development of the sciences, including those that are concerned with human products, there has been a number of fundamental conceptual changes within the last half century. In the study of religion as well as in related academic fields, the notion of structure has played a prominent role in a turn from particularistic and historical studies towards theoretical and generalizing studies, that is, "a shift in focus, from objects to relations. It is relationships that create and define objects, not the other way around" (Culler 1986: 128). So, "for the thought of our century the world is no longer essentially a collection of independent entities, of autonomous objects, but a series of relational systems" (Culler 1986: 130). That shift of focus has profoundly affected most of the sciences, from physics and biology to linguistics and anthropology—and, in some measure, the study of religion.

To summarize: the domains and objects of the human and social sciences exist solely because they are the products of thinking minds and acting agents, they obtain their ontological status by being the products of human intentionality, that is, of human relations to the world. These relations are structured, whether they concern the physical, the social, or the mental world. The theoretical shift from particularistic or historical studies implies that we can study the systemic and structural character of such relations and we can, therefore, study religions as systematic modes of world-making.

Key Features

As already noted the term structure may refer both to an abstract concept and to a descriptive category that identifies empirical, observable forms. The latter use is less interesting here, because it retains some of the earlier empiricist and materialist ideas about the ontological primacy of observable, singular objects. We must, however, briefly review the descriptive use of the term, if only in order to be able to discern how it differs from the more abstract use of the term in later structuralist theory.

In the field of anthropology, "structural functionalism," as paradigmatically presented in the work of A. R. Radcliffe-Brown, considered structures as observable arrangements of social relationships and interactions. In the words of one prominent proponent of structuralism, Sir Edmund Leach (1987: 55):

> Social structure, in this sense, was considered to typify the morphology of the society in question, much as the bony structure of a vertebrate animal provides the principal basis for fitting a particular species into the Linnean taxonomy of all species. Indeed, Radcliffe-Brown believed that a taxonomy of all human societies could be constructed from a comparison of their social structures, societies with similar social structures being placed in the same taxonomic class.

In a similar manner, a scholar of religion may depict the layout of religious cosmologies and pantheons much in the same manner as one may depict an empirical structure of government or corporate organization by means of a box-diagram. A simple example of such a taxonomic classification would be that of monotheistic versus polytheistic religions. But in doing so we employ structure in a descriptive and empirical sense only and, if we follow the definition offered above, that means that we are actually talking about a system, that is, an arrangement of *elements*, not an arrangement of *relations*. Although disputes over terminology are often inconsequential, for the present purpose it is better that we attempt to distinguish as clearly as possible between system and structure. That is, however, not always easy and the more key features we can point out concerning structure the better for our theoretical understanding and our methodological application of the concept.

Concerning the non-empirical or abstract use of structure there are several points that should be observed. Although such structures may not be empirically verified this does not mean that they do not exist, for such structures are the precondition for order in the products of human culture, also in religion. This point has led to widespread confusion on the issue. Whereas some have maintained that studying structures in this abstract sense was simply not the business of scientific approaches, others argued that these structures may at best be considered hypothetical guesswork about the human mind and that, as such, they were a kind a psychological postulate relating to the unconscious activity of the mind. The main fallacy here is to conceive of structure by means of a posited mind/nature dualism, where it is presumed that what is not physical must by necessity be of a mental nature. A critique along these lines may argue that "the concept of the unconscious mind or structures is vague and not operational from a scientific standpoint" (Morris 1987: 268). The crucial issue here is that of the epistemological or ontological status of "unconscious structures": are they really in the world, that is, ontological, or are they only an ingredient in our knowledge of the world, that is, epistemological? As we have seen, it is necessary to conceive of structure in both senses: the world is structured and our cognition and knowledge of the world are also structured. But—and this is the most salient point in relation to the study of religion—cultural products are also structured *in themselves*, because they are the products of humans, who, following the implicit cognitive postulate of structuralism, have a propensity for creating ordered social and symbolic universes. The prime example of this, among structuralists, is human language and it is from structural linguistics that theoretical principles have been imported to such fields as literary analysis, anthropology and the study of religion.[2]

Structuralism in the human sciences is a theory about the nature and organization of cultural products, such as, in the case of religion, myths, systems of classifications, rituals; all of these are constituted by meaning. For the study of religion the main issue is that the structures of meaningful phenomena must underlie all human activity for it to be meaningful and understandable. But that can also be a matter of controversy; as Brian Morris notes:

> Then again, are the unconscious structures panhuman, substantive patterns or categories that simply provide meaning or "order" to a diversity of empirical data, as the "principle of reciprocity" is seen to explain a variety of kinship systems? Or, finally, are the structures entirely abstract, and devoid of "meaning" in the ordinary sense of the term? (1987: 268)

The answer is "Yes"; structures *are* entirely abstract and they do not have any meaning in themselves. Note again, that the whole point of the structural view is that nothing has meaning *in itself*, but only acquires meaning through its relations to other meanings, which are themselves meaningful in terms of their relations, and so on. (This will be explained below.)

The theoretical object of structuralism is the decoding of the principles by which the "human mind" operates—as it has often been stated. There is a danger of mis-translation here, because when structuralist theoreticians, who have mainly written in French, used the term *ésprit humain*, it was not as a designation for a psychological entity, as the English word "mind" suggests. Rather, it concerns the organization of thought and knowledge at an independent and public cultural level, akin to the notion of ideology, modes of thought, or, again, language—all of which are more than mere mental phenomena. Cultural and linguistic materials are not just psychological and subjective, they are also public social facts that are structured and may be explained accordingly. For instance, we may contrast a structural explanation of French grammar with a historical explanation, one that would explain French grammar and its origins as a derivation from Latin. A structural explanation, on the other hand, is not concerned with origins or causes but with how the language system *as such* is structured; how all the items and sets of items are connected in a single complex matrix. Language is structured, and the performance of it, that is, speaking French, should of course also be structured. Another illustrative analogy of the relations between systems, rules and actions is the game of chess.

Among the key notions associated with structure and structuralism are those of *code*, *transformation*, *binary opposition*, *paradigmatic* and *syntagmatic*, and *metaphors* and *metonyms*. They may be only briefly explained here.

Codes are expressive media for communication (Eco 1984: 164–188). We can communicate not only through language, but also by means of our preferred ways of dressing, our gestures, cars, musical preferences and manners of cooking.

Transformation is definable as the work of systematic difference, for instance, and more formally, when a set of relations in a mythical structure are transformed into a set of relations of social structure. Or, more informally, when "the message" I convey in one code, for example, my style of dress, is transformed, or "translated," into what I express by the kind of car I drive. Transformations are very important in that they reveal structures at work in the generative translations of cultural material. On this Claude Lévi-Strauss said (1987: 18–19):

> An arrangement is structured which meets but two conditions: that it be a system ruled by an internal cohesiveness and that this cohesiveness, inaccessible to observation in an isolated system, be revealed in the study of transformations through which similar properties are recognized in apparently different systems ... since the property of a system of signs is to be transformable, in other words *translatable*, into the language of another system with the help of substitutions.

Translations must follow rules in order to make sense; rules are thus an important aspect of the transformations. As already noted, no rules, no meaning. Moreover, transformations are more than random changes; to earn their designation, they must be logically determined and follow the principles of inversion and / or negation, in or between two modes: the *paradigmatic* and the *syntagmatic* and between two kinds of relations: the *metaphoric* and the *metonymic*.[3] The most salient feature of transformations is that they create differences in cultural meaning systems and that such differences are not capricious or haphazard, but systematic.

Binary oppositions are, for example, life–death, nature–culture, left–right and so on. A *negation* expresses a contradictory relationship, for example, man is the opposite of woman. Difference may also be conceived as an *inversion*: "upside-down" relations of the properties of men and women in terms such as brutal–tender, strong–weak. We can say that humans are not gods (negation) but that the qualities of gods are mostly inversions of human properties: they are immortal, all-powerful, all-knowing and so forth. Gods, ancestors, vampires, ghosts and zombies have some measure of human nature that has been turned "upside-down" and such differences are systematic. The "other world" of religious cosmologies is a world that is a systemic inversion of the everyday world of ordinary experience.

The *paradigmatic* mode refers to clusters of meanings conceived simultaneously, for example, the combined meanings of a myth or of an abstract concept. However, such meanings can only be expressed in a syntactical or narrative chain, that is, in a *syntagmatic* process. Edmund Leach said that "[w]e meet much the same contrast in music when *harmony*, in which different instruments make simultaneous noises which are heard in combination, is distinguished from *melody* in which one note follows another to form a tune" (1976:15). Along a complementary conception, paradigmatic relations define the possible oppositions between units which can be substituted for one another in a syntagm. For example, in the case of "the old cat," the words "young," "small," and "sick" are paradigmatically related to "old" because they can be substituted for "old" in the syntagm, just as "man" is paradigmatically related to "cat" (Penner 1989: 141). Hence, in the study of religion we can consider a cosmology of a religion as a paradigmatic total expression of a "world" and a repertoire of elements that can be combined and transformed into the actual mythical or dogmatic narratives which consist of syntagmatic sequences. In reverse transformations we (re-)construct whole and paradigmatic religious universes on the basis of their related mythical narratives, ritual performances and so on, because we work with the implicit assumption that there is some kind of system behind each particular expression.

Extensive uses of metaphors and metonyms and the mutual transformations of them are fundamental to religions. *Metaphors* are conventional symbols of similarity across domains: for example, A stands for B by association. When, for instance, God is conceived as father, healer, lord or sovereign this is an example of a metaphoric transformation, just as when groups of people, such as sports teams, named after different species of animals, are then thought to possess some of the attributes of those animals (i.e., a symbolic transfer of properties). These metaphors and transfers are often not intrinsic or self-evident; for example, only in a culture familiar with the book of Genesis is the serpent a symbol for evil. *Metonyms*, on the other hand, are symbols of similarity within the same domain: A stands for B just as parts stand for a whole, such as when crowns are metonyms for royalty. Metonymic transformations operate within the same category domain such as when a lock of hair from a person stands for that person or when a sacrificial victim is made to stand for a ritual community as a whole. Transformations between metaphoric and metonymic relations are modes of code-switching that abound in religions and in the practice of magic: Gods have human attributes. Ancestors are thought to belong to the tribe. Persons are named after patron saints. The magician works on the name or that lock of hair as if it were the person. It is a common characteristic of systems of religious classification that metonymic and metaphoric relations are blended:

> For example, consider the following argument: (1) God is a father, (2) God is a son, (3) God is a Holy Spirit. If these three assertions are regarded as separate metaphors then the words "father," "son," "Holy Spirit" are, in my terminology, alternative *symbols* for a single metaphysical concept "in the mind." But the peculiarity of religious discourse is that it denies that such formulae are metaphoric; they are said to be "true" and simultaneously "true." (Leach 1976: 70)

Structuralist theory has, in the version expounded here, primarily methodological consequences. In so far as it contains an ontology, it is one that posits the existence of cultural, symbolic and social products that are the expressions of humans who live in (more or less) ordered worlds of meaning. Religious universes are apt examples of the ways in which humans construct, organize and maintain ordered worlds. Therefore, structuralist theory is a real contribution to the study of religion. One which may, of course, be both developed and criticized (to be noted below). As in the case of religion, it is a historical product.

Historical Development

Although the history of the concept of structure in the human sciences may note scattered antecedents, the main development of theories built on notions of structure takes place in the twentieth century (Robins 1997: 222–259). Swiss linguist Ferdinand de Saussure is credited for being the originator of modern structuralist linguistics on the basis of the theoretical framework for the study of language as an independent human science set forth in his posthumous work,

Course in General Linguistics (1983 [1916]). Although Saussure did not directly labor the notion of structure, his approach had formidable consequences for the development of the modern human sciences. Basically, structuralism is "an approach to language and other systems that holds them to be autonomous, and hence to be explained by appeal to the relations between the elements in the system rather than by extra-linguistic reality" (Devitt and Sterelny 1987: 255). The question of explanation is a moot point in the assessment of structuralism, one that hinges on whether explanation is conceived of as structural or causal. On the first conception, the salient feature is the explanation of the meaning and function of elements in the system as determined in and by the system, on the other the concern is with the causes of the existence of the system (its origins) and of its practice. These views must, in the end, be complementary: language is produced by humans and it is related to extra-linguistic reality, but it must also form a system, with structures, in order to perform its task as a medium of communication.

In Saussure's theory any language (*langue*) is a system on the basis of which speech (*parole*) makes sense, so that an articulation is only understandable in relation to a system. In the study of religion this means that any ritual act, for instance, must be understood as an articulation of a cosmological system. The system is thus immanent in every expression and, because language is *the* social fact par excellence, our sociality is incorporated in all things we do or say. The idea of a "private language" is as improbable as making your own kind of money. Language and language-use are complex phenomena best understood by a principle of "ontological stratification," meaning that "the language system is a multilevel reality, and that this stratification is both social and historical in character" (Thibault 1997: 17). Saussure noted that "linguistic phenomena always present two complementary facets, each depending on the other": The ear depends on sounds from the vocal organs (and vice versa), speech depends on thought and thought on speech, language has both an individual and a social aspect; "Language at any given time involves an established system and an evolution. At any given time it is an institution in the present and a product of the past" (1983: 23–24).

With very few extensions and modifications these observations are very close to those which can be made about religion and religions. It is interesting for scholars of religion that Saussure (1983: 33, 35) considered language to be but one specific class of semiological ("of meaning") systems:

A language is a system of signs expressing ideas, and hence comparable to writing, the deaf-and-dumb alphabet, symbolic rites, forms of politeness, military signals and so on. It is simply the most important of such systems. It is therefore possible to conceive of a science *which studies the role of signs as part of social life* ... We shall call it *semiology* (from the Greek *semeîon*, "sign"). It would investigate the nature of signs and the laws governing them. Since it does not yet exist, one cannot say for certain that it will exist. But it has a right to exist ... In this way, light will be thrown not only upon the linguistic problem. By considering rites, customs, etc. as signs it will be possible, we believe, to see them in a new perspective.

This prophecy was to be fulfilled to some degree with the development of structuralism in linguistics, in anthropology and in the study of religion. Later generations have also witnessed the growth of semiology into today's theoretically advanced *semiotics*, as the field is now called.[4] The development of structuralism, in the forms relevant to the study of religion, found various courses (there were other forms of structuralism with less relevance or applicability to the study of religion). In France, around 1900, Émile Durkheim, Henri Hubert, Robert Hertz and Marcel Mauss to some extent already anticipated these developments in so far as concerns religion and the study of it. They considered religions, religious classifications, and rituals to be *social facts* that were structured around sets of oppositions, such as, for instance, the fundamental distinction between "sacred and profane," between givers and receivers of gifts, and between humans and their gods in ritual reciprocity. The exploration and investigation of such binary oppositions were later to be considered the most important feature and main program of structuralism in anthropology; an impression that somewhat trivialized the structuralist project and gave it an ill-repute for being static, simplistic, formalist and dualistic.

It was Claude Lévi-Strauss' genius and pioneering effort to transform basic linguistic notions into a theoretical framework for anthropological analysis that led to his now classic works on kinship, mythologies, totemism (1962b) and "the savage mind" (1966). His inspiration came from Durkheim, Mauss, Saussure and, from the Prague school of linguistics, Roman Jakobson and Nikolai Trubetzkoy. In 1945 Lévi-Strauss referred to the revolution in linguistics by quoting Trubetzkoy's program of four basic operations—as stated in 1933: "First, structural linguistics shifts from the study of *conscious* linguistic phenomena to the study of their *unconscious* infrastructure; second, it does not treat *terms* as independent entities, taking instead as its basis of analysis the *relations* between terms; third, it introduces the concept of *system* ...; finally, structural linguistics aims at discovering *general laws*, either by induction or ... by logical deduction" (1972a: 33). Lévi-Strauss applied these principles to the study of kinship, a primary concern of anthropologists then, and said: "Because they are symbolic systems, kinship systems offer the anthropologist a rich field, where his efforts can almost ... converge with those of the most highly developed of the social sciences, namely, linguistics" (1972a: 51). Because, "[l]ike phonemes [i.e., speech sounds], kinship terms are elements of meaning; like phonemes, they acquire meaning only if they are integrated into systems ... built by the mind on the level of unconscious thought" (1972a: 34). From there on it is only a logical step to claim that all other items of culture can be treated in a manner analogous to language systems, because culture is also built of oppositions, correlations and logical relations. All of which pertains to religion as part and parcel of culture. Lévi-Strauss primarily focused his attention on myths, or rather, mythologies, as the myths are never studied singularly but only in combinations with other myths with which they form systems, and on systems of thought and classification in tribal societies such as in his innovative studies on totemism (1962b) and so-called primitive philosophy (1966). British anthropologist Sir Edmund Leach edited an introduction to structuralist analysis (1967), produced a fine little book on Lévi-Strauss (1970) and expanded the scope of structural analysis to the field of ritual and social institutions (1976). In France, a structuralist school developed around Jean-Pierre Vernant (1980) and Marcel Detienne (1986, 1991) in the field of classical Greek mythology and culture (see also Gordon 1981).

It is fair to say that whereas only few scholars have been able to replicate the methods of Lévi-Strauss, it is the general inspiration from his approach that has been influential in a large number of areas. Formalized, strict methods and procedures of verification are understandably more difficult to achieve in the study of such complex matters as the cultural meanings of myths and religious phenomena than in more empirical linguistic areas of inquiry. Therefore, the major impact of structuralism is probably more to be found in terms of a general theoretical shift of orientation as already outlined. This is a question to which we shall return.

Outside the fields of anthropology and the study of religion there is an impressive amount of literature on developments of structuralist theory and the related areas of semiotics and narratology. The structuralist movement was especially strong in France, its home-country, during the 1960s and it spread rapidly, albeit in more specialized circles, to other European countries and North America. Leading theoreticians have also come from Eastern Europe, such as Nikolai Trubetzkoy, Roman Jakobson, Tzvetan Todorov, Yuri Lotman and Algirdas J. Greimas.

Major Variations

Lévi-Strauss' approach focused almost entirely on cultural materials from tribal societies. As the originator of structuralism in the human sciences (outside linguistics) his work did, however, spur a host of novel ways of studying aspects of the "human condition"—the fact that humans are social and cultural beings living in worlds that they have imbued with meanings. Lévi-Strauss posited a division between factual worlds as *lived in* and conceptual worlds as *thought of*. It is to the study of the latter that he devoted his efforts—without denying the primacy of the former (i.e., the material conditions of existence). On his view, the conceptual superstructures of societies and their cultural orders are systemic and they, like language, consist of constitutive units that can be elaborated into systems that synthesize ideas and facts. It may then be added that these conditions should apply, in principle, to all human societies in all ages, and to all of their cultural products. It is therefore a basic tenet of structuralist theory that it can be applied to more than the mythologies of so-called primitive societies. Structural views on cultural material have consequently been employed by theoreticians and analysts in various fields, from archeology (Tilley 1990) to sociology (Giddens 1987). The concept of structure may, as we already noted, have multiple references but here we shall only be concerned with some uses of more direct relevance to the study of religion.[5]

On the above considerations, when denoting an empirical and observable order of relations between entities in social systems, the term structure could more suitably be replaced by "organization." There are, however, modes of analysis of structures and structural composition that have affinities with the organizational view and still merit inclusion here. One concerns the internal order of narratives as presented in the studies of Vladimir Propp on the morphology of folk tales (in 1928)—a work that had a lasting influence on later structuralist analysis in narratology. Propp formally reduced the number of constituent narrative units in folk tales with an emphasis on their syntagmatic structure, that is, the sequential order of the parts of the tales. Not only sentences, but also narratives have forms of grammar and syntax constituted by the ordering of interchangeable elements. In 1909 Arnold van Gennep suggested that rituals have a three-stage pattern as their basic syntactic structure. His ideas on a common underlying structure in rituals were later elaborated by Victor W. Turner with a strong emphasis on the ritual process and its associated symbolism of structure and anti-structure (1969), and by Edmund Leach in the analysis of ritual modes of communication mediating social and symbolic categories of cosmologies (1976). Leach introduced Lévi-Strauss' principles of analysis to the study of ritual and of religious cosmologies in general—neither ritual nor religion were among Lévi-Strauss' primary fields of interest.

The structured relations between cultural cosmologies, ritual forms and social systems have been investigated by Mary Douglas who, in a number of studies on purity and pollution, sexuality, body and food taboos, applied a fundamentally structural methodology (1989). The potentials of structural analyses of religious conceptual systems and ritual actions (or, of religion generally) are far from exhausted, especially in the study of literate traditions (Penner 1989). Structural analyses may also connect with cognitive studies, because ritual actions are structured and constrained by both cultural conceptual categories and cognitive capacities as has been ingeniously demonstrated by Lawson and McCauley (1990).

Moving to the fields of more general cultural analysis, a number of scholars have shown how semantic structures consist of concepts, their grammars and their syntaxes. In the 1960s and 1970s, Roland Barthes applied the theories and methods of Saussure, Hjelmslev and Lévi-Strauss in studies of verbal, non-verbal and visual systems of signification in various domains and codes in modern society and in a formal theory of narrative (Barthes 1994). Algirdas J. Greimas, one of the most rigorous theoreticians of semiotics, was the founder and leader of the formalist Paris school. On the basis of a theory of the minimal constituent elements of meaning and their organization he developed a structural semantics and a semiotics of text and textual analysis which was later expanded to cover social and cultural norms and structures. Yuri Lotman, a leading figure of the Estonian Tartu school, developed a cultural semiotics in which culture is conceived of as a hierarchy of texts functioning as models which define their constituent culture (1990). On the less formalist side, Paul Ricoeur combined structuralism and philosophical hermeneutics in a theory of interpretation and of the constructions of other worlds of meaning, that is, the realm of symbolic cultural products through which humans come to represent and understand themselves in myths, art, music and so on. (Ricoeur 1981). Michel Foucault initially employed a structuralist perspective on the history of ideas which he viewed as a series of discontinuities where each epoch was characterized by certain forms of knowledge, governed by underlying structures, in systems of conceptual codes determining the modes of thought (1972). With Foucault and Jacques Derrida, structuralism moved into a post-structuralist or postmodern phase.[6]

In linguistics, the concept of structure has acquired a variety of usages since the time of Saussure: surface structures as representations of the phonetic forms of sentences; conversational structures; syntactic structures; phrase structures and so on. For scholars of religion, the most interesting concepts of structure relate to the works of Noam Chomsky and what was first called transformational-generative grammar and then, later, generative linguistics (Chomsky 1975; Robins 1997: 260–270). Seen as a conglomerate of more definite theoretical approaches, generative linguistics presupposes a general distinction between deep and surface structures, where basic rules assemble the elements of deep structures that are mapped onto surface structures by means of transformational rules. The *deep structures* represent the underlying level of fundamental arrangements of the elements of sentences whereas *surface structures* determine how sentences are actually pronounced or written; both levels of structure are commonly displayed in tree-diagrams. Transformative and generative grammars were introduced in order to account for the possibilities of expressing an infinite variety of sentences on the basis of a limited number of elements in any natural language (e.g., French, English, Japanese). Actual language use, termed *performance*, thus relates to a linguistic *competence* consisting in a tacit knowledge of rules and the conditions for their application.

Without delving into the complex and controversial matters concerning the relations between rules, structures and meaning, it may be discerned how some basic assumptions of this approach can be put to use in the study of religion; for instance, in the analysis of ritual or everyday religious behavior as modes of performance relating to religious conceptual systems conceived as collectively shared, and mostly subconscious, cultural competence. In Chomsky's rationalist view, humans are endowed with innate and constrained systems of possible grammars (programs for handling information) which, already at an early age, enable us to learn natural languages in all their complexity. Such conditions could apply to all instances of rule-governedness, such as the acquisition and transmission of cultural materials, including the items of religions. An important addition to the theory is an observation about the function of rules in a multi-tiered system: the elements, at each level, are combined according to the rules at the "next level up" (i.e., phonemes at the level of morphemes). For a religious conceptual system, this suggests that the overarching level of a group's cosmology is the level from which all underlying levels of representation and action are governed, or must be combined in order to "make sense." This can be seen as an instance of upward macro-reduction where parts are explained in terms of a whole. This model helps to make sense of Boyer's (1994) proposition that religions, despite their many surface variations, seem to be constructed on the basis of a finite number of general cognitive rules.

The concept of structure also plays an important role in theories in cognitive linguistics, psychology and anthropology in the form of *schema*, "a conceptual structure which makes possible the identification of objects and events" (D'Andrade 1992: 28). However diverse the theoretical assumptions governing these approaches on matters cultural and cognitive, there is a general consensus on the explanatory and interpretative importance of the concept of structure.

Critical Evaluation of Past Contributions to the Study of Religion

If, to repeat our initial hypothesis, we can only understand our physical, mental and cultural worlds because they are structured, then methodologies and theoretical frameworks emphasizing structural relations and properties should prove productive. However, structural analyses suffered a varied fate in studies of religion. When structuralism was at its height of influence in other human sciences in the 1960s and 1970s, it was scarcely noticed in the History of Religions, although biblical studies and anthropological studies on religion were somewhat more receptive to structuralist ideas. The reluctance towards an inclusion of structuralism in the methodological tool-kit can be traced to a general historical and empiricist orientation among scholars in the study of religion who distrust approaches that deal with matters non-empirical, theoretical and universal.

Skeptics have found support in the many varying claims about the nature, purpose and prospective use of structuralism. The accounts of the histories of theory and methodology in the study of religion often disagree on the features as well as on the methodological validity of structuralism. However, they seem to agree on certain recurring points of criticism. Structuralism has frequently been considered intellectually obscure, non-historical, a-methodological, non-verifiable, non-empirical, rationalist, idealist and so on (Morris 1987: 264–291). Critics have been right on some of these points, but they have also tended to disregard the productive implications. Structuralism is, almost as a rule, introduced in textbooks by way of Lévi-Strauss' 1955 article, "The Structural Study of Myth" (1972b: 206–231), in which one of his much criticized examples is that of the Greek myth on Oedipus. It is, however, erroneous to equate the entire project of structuralism, including its prospective potentials, with a single example chosen by Lévi-Strauss for its presumed familiarity to his audience. He intended to emphasize that mythologies and systems of classification are not the products of infantile speculation or cognitive disorder, nor that their empirically tractable social functions should be their most important aspect. Instead, his point was that systems of myths and their related cosmologies display their own logic, a "mythologic" as he coined it. Over the years a range of insightful and provocative (i.e., challenging conventional views) structural studies of religious and cultural systems have emerged on a variety of topics (Leach 1967, 1987; Maranda and Maranda 1971). The focus of structural analyses in the field of religion have been on the logic and coherence of mythologies and cosmologies, of ritual systems and action and, on the logic of social and cultural institutions (Penner 1989).

Concerns of the replicability and verifiability of structural analyses are a recurrent theme among its critics, and one that is justifiably problematic: "Structuralists' failure to be forthcoming about the methodological details of their approach makes it difficult either to assess the plausibility of their proposed accounts or to confirm or disconfirm their overall theoretical position" (Lawson and McCauley 1990: 42–43). Lévi-Strauss never provided an explicit and replicable methodology, only by way of example (these are, however, almost countless) did he demonstrate the plausibility of his approach. This criticism is, it seems, often somewhat beyond the point: structural analysis is, in the end, a species of interpretation and interpretation is notoriously recalcitrant to the elaboration of strict methodological rules of procedure. On this methodological problem Dan Sperber critically opines that anthropologists interpret, rather than explain, cultural representations and "[i]t is among the resulting interpretations, rather than among the observable or recordable data, that systematic resemblances and differences may be manifest. However, with a bit of interpretive ingeniousness, any two complex objects can be put in such a structural relationship" (1996a: 45). Such concerns over structuralism's lack of verifiability seem to ignore the fact that there are no data independent of theory and interpretation; the inescapability of interpretation does not mean, however, that one should view the basic Saussurean and structuralist notion of the "arbitrariness of the sign" as a license for an arbitrariness of analysis.

It is often assumed that structuralist analysis downplays the importance of historical and ethnographic detail. Contrary to widespread criticism, Lévi-Strauss is, for one, very particular about getting as much ethnographic evidence as possible to back his analyses. Nor must a structuralist, by necessity of some methodological mystique, disregard historical or philological evidence—this is amply demonstrated in the studies by the Paris school that formed around Vernant and Detienne in classical studies (Gordon 1981). Detailed ethnographic, historical and philological mastery of the material analyzed is an inevitable prerequisite for structural analysis. But it is also a structuralist's conviction that this is where the analysis begins, *not* where it ends.

Historically oriented scholars have been uneasy about the structuralist preference for analysis of synchronic systems which are treated as static entities, when, obviously, all things change and therefore should be studied diachronically. Suffice it to say that the problems of the diachronic–synchronic distinction in the form introduced by Saussure have not been sufficiently explored or solved (Culler 1986: 35–45, 84–86; Thibault 1997: 80–110). It could be argued that *diachronic* facts are facts of history, whereas *synchronic* facts are facts of theoretically guided systemic analysis; that is, they are not facts of the same order. Synchronic systems are helpful scientific constructions and they are no more static than are grammar-books or the rules of cricket. Therefore it misses the point to argue that a structural, synchronic analysis is static as opposed to a historical, dynamic analysis. For anything to remain the same or to change is still a relational property; things remain the same or change only in *relation to other things*. If it were not so, we should be unable to impose any form of order whatsoever on what we study. The simple claim of structuralism is that when we confront humanly produced cultural materials, such ordering is already present, not as fortuitous, but as a prerequisite of human language, cognition and sociality.

Prospects for Future Utility

In the study of religion it is not so much theories that are our problem—our problem is the wealth of empirical facts which we want to understand. The concept of structure and the theories associated with it are one possible solution to this problem of understanding. The concept of structure suggests that elements are organized, that they have both synchronic and diachronic aspects, that there are structures at various levels and that, finally, there are formal and causal structures. Speaking of religions, cultural systems, ideologies, world-views and the like, we may say that these are all *thought-of* worlds that exhibit certain relational and structural properties and that they are inextricably related to and fused with our *lived-in* worlds. Scholars also construct *thought-of* worlds: our explanations and our knowledge of things are also symbolic systems. For such knowledge to be scientifically valid it must be rational, but without the inherent rationalities of the systems studied that would be an impossibility. Any study of religion which disregards the rationality of the cultural systems under study, such as religions, will fail to be rational itself, because it will not be able to describe, interpret or explain the structured relations residing in its object of study. It should therefore be possible, in principle, to outline a scientific and theoretically guided systematic study of religion along the lines worked out in linguistics for the study of language. That is, however, a future prospect which requires much more serious analysis (than presently available) of the features of religious systems. However, without the conceptual apparatus made available by structural theory that would forever remain an impossibility.

There are structures in religions and these same structures warrant the interpretive accessibility of religious systems. Religious systems of beliefs, actions and institutions are meaningful, that is, they have or may be ascribed semantic content, and they may therefore in some respects be likened to languages. As with languages, they can be said to operate on three inter-dependent levels: a semantic level comprising the elements of meanings; a syntactic level concerning the ways in which these elements of meanings can be combined; and a pragmatic level of the actual religious practice, in, say, rituals or in ways of life governed by systems of purity. It must be emphasized that cultural systems of classification, including religions, operate predominantly at the subconscious levels—they are, more often than not, simply what humans do or think by routine. These systems or instances of meaning are (for the most part) not amenable to direct empirical observation, they must be produced through analysis and interpretation, but it is *only* on such conditions that conventional behavior, including that related to religion, may be construed as meaningful. Cognitive approaches rely as much upon the notion of structure operating at subconscious levels as do explicitly structuralist studies (Shore 1996). For instance, Lawson and McCauley's (1990) work on ritual complexes displays the structured nature of religious action systems, in theory and in practice. Also, Boyer's analysis (1994) of the inverted and counter-intuitive characteristics of religious representations clearly demonstrates how such representations are structured along certain schemas and consist in systematic combinations of properties and functions across ontological domains.

Some scholars (e.g., Sperber 1996a) consider causal explanation of cultural materials as more important than the interpretation of their meaning and they view structural approaches as no more than another kind of intuitively guided insight. Causal explanations, as traditionally found in the natural sciences, are reductive and explain the causes of the existence of something. However, causal explanation itself relies upon structure for there must be a presumption that the thing being explained is ordered and structured. But causal explanations are not the only mode of explanation possible. Structural explanations demonstrate the workings of systems, how elements are related and how they change under certain conditions, as for instance in biology or chemistry, without necessarily having to resort to reductive causal explanation (as found, for example, in the study of physics). Mathematics is a prime example of a system of structural explanations, whereas an investigation of the causes of mathematics is of more dubious merit. Explaining works of poetry need also not be a reductive and causal task (the poverty of most poets would suggest an economic explanation); a structural explanation situating the poetic work within a larger cultural universe seemingly makes more sense. In fact, structuralist theory and analysis have contributed to radical changes in the theory of interpretation and in hermeneutics—away from psychological notions of understanding and towards textual analysis (Ricoeur 1981). Interpretation of cultural materials consists not so much in determining what it "would mean to me" in subjective and empathetic terms, but rather what something means in specific semantic universes. Such modes of interpretation could benefit the study of religion. However, in the case of religion—being a social, cultural, psychological and cognitive phenomenon—there are indications that a combination of modes of explanation, interpretation and theoretical perspectives must be coordinated. In so far as religions encompass systems of classifications, cultural and cognitive models, human motivations, social arrangements and hierarchies of power, that are all, in some form, structured, then the potentials of structural analyses are far from exhausted.

Notes

1. The term "metaphysical" is used here not to refer to religious transcendent realms or *a priori* religious truths, but in accordance with common philosophical usage. See, e.g., Kim and Sosa 1995 and Jubien 1997.
2. There are versions of structuralism in, for example, linguistics and psychology, that need not be considered here because their impact on the study of religion is (so far) negligible.
3. For an accessible discussion of metonymy and metaphor from a linguistic perspective, see Taylor 1989; for their application in an anthropological analysis of religion and magic, see Leach 1976.
4. Semiotics in the formalist French tradition is heavily indebted to Saussure's seminal ideas and to Danish linguist Louis Hjelmslev (1899–1965). The American pragmatist philosopher C. S. Peirce (1839–1914) developed a different brand of dynamic semiotics.
5. For instance, *The Index to Britannica Online* (www.eb.co.uk) contains 107 items relevant to the query "structure"—and only a fraction of these are relevant to the study of culture and religion.
6. Contrary to widespread opinion, the term "post-structuralism" does not mean that structuralism has become obsolete, but rather that it must be subjected to radical criticism and theoretical reflexivity. A fundamental structuralist point of view still underlies the "post" positions.

Suggested Readings

Caws, Peter
  1994   *Structuralism: A Philosophy for the Human Sciences*. Atlantic Highlands: Humanities Press.

Innis, Robert E., editor
  1985   *Semiotics: An Introductory Anthology*. Bloomington: Indiana University Press.

Leach, Edmund, editor
  1967   *The Structural Study of Myth and Totemism*. A.S.A. Monographs, vol. 5. London: Tavistock.

Leach, Edmund
  1970   *Claude Lévi-Strauss*. New York: Viking.

Maranda, Pierre and Elli Köngäs Maranda (Eds.)
  1971   *Structural Analysis of Oral Tradition*. University of Pennsylvania Publications in Folklore and Folklife, vol. 3. Philadelphia: University of Pennsylvania Press.

Sturrock, John, editor
  1979   *Structuralism and Sense: From Lévi-Strauss to Derrida*. Oxford: Oxford University Press.

23

WORLD

William E. Paden

The concept of world provides a tool for understanding and analyzing the plurality, contextuality and self-positing nature of religious cultures. Thus, rather than viewing religions in terms of a given standard—whether religious or nonreligious—of what "the" world is and then seeing how they, the religions, represent "it," here the assumption is that religious systems themselves create their own versions of world. Religions are one of culture's primary systems of world definition, constructing universes of language, behavior and identity with their own particular organizing categories.

The concept world in some ways overlaps with the notions of system, belief system and world-view, but has more textured, contextualistic and behavioral reference. World encompasses all forms of habitation, action and language, and not just viewpoints, ideas or self-conscious doctrines and philosophies. Like the notion "environment," a world suggests operating life space, actively selected and negotiated. Any organism that attends to a particular environmental context has formed a version of world. In human cultures, there are multiple, alternating genres of worlds, for example, those of the military, business, arts, courtship, mathematics and sport.

World is then a systematic indicator of domain difference and specificity. The etymological meaning of the Germanic / English word "world" is "the age or life of man," (from *wer-*, "man," and *ald-*, "age"), as distinguished from the "age" or domain of the gods. In Christian cultures, where the gospels had already introduced phrases like "my kingdom is not of this world (Greek, *kosmos*)," it became conventional to distinguish "this world" of human life in contrast to "the next." As the long entry in the *Oxford English Dictionary* (1989) shows, the term world eventually invited extended uses to denote any sphere or realm, as in "the Old World and the New World," "the world of plants," "one's own world," "the world of the honeybee," "the world of the Cistercian monk." Now we have "the world of teenage romance" or "the cyberworld." What is common here is the notion of a frame of reference or domain that constitutes the horizon of certain kinds of behaviors, objects, persons or communities and thus differentiates those horizons from others so that their particular contextualities and schemas can come into focus.

Applied to human life systems, then, a world is not just a matter of conceptual representation, but also a specific form of habitation and practice—the structure of meaningful relationships in which a person exists and participates. More fully put, it is *the operating environment of linguistic and behavioral options which persons or communities presuppose, posit and inhabit at any given point in time and from which they choose courses of action.* Religious worlds, in particular, are cultural systems that organize language and behavior around engagement with postulated superhuman agencies. A person is "in" a religious world just as one can be "in" the army, "in" a game or "in" a relationship.

As an analytical concept in religious studies, "world" is most definitely not just a term for "the totality of things" in general, but rather for the particular ways totalities are constructed in any particular environment. On the one hand, the idea directs attention to the lived context, categories and realities of "insiders." In the study of religion this is critical for the goal of "understanding the other," for ideally it checks the blatant imposition of foreign classifications onto other peoples' self-representations. Yet, on the other hand, to label the insiders' systems "worlds" is not to simply validate them, admire them, or give them voice. Rather, the analytic purpose is to be able to identify the internal relationships and functions of objects and categories within a given domain, as compared with the arrangements of other life-systems. Historians of religion investigate what beliefs and actions refer to as real in the classificatory perspectives of the adherents—while also asking what they refer to within their own very different and broader horizon of explanation.

The notion of world, then, helps clarify the difference of insider and outsider points of view. Much confusion has resulted from scholars attributing their version of what religion signifies to that of the adherents themselves. What things "mean" in the world of the observer does not have to correspond to what things mean in the world of the insider. In anthropological terminology, emic categories represent terms entirely specific to a culture and its insiders. Etic categories, in contrast, represent the scholar's own concepts that have been formed by generalization and comparative analysis (for analysis and debate about these concepts in anthropology, see Headland 1990; as applied to the study of religion, see McCutcheon 1998b). The notion of world is itself an etic category—designed partly to direct attention to its emic versions.

The concept of world therefore includes not only a descriptive function, but also a redescriptive one (McCutcheon 1997c). That is, it not only is used to attend to the categories of the insider's life-world, but also to account for them within the broader conceptual resources of the outside scholar. The analyst or comparativist brings a general understanding of world formation and its shaping factors to the interpretation of any single world. In this sense, the notion of world includes and employs much of the theoretical capital of other concepts described in this *Guide*, such as culture, discourse, ideology, cognition, structure, myth, gender and classification—all of these being dimensional components or factors of world construction and lenses to analyze it. Any human world involves the variables of physical geography, language, social class, historical change, economics and even individuality; any world is an open-ended, interactive process, filled with various and complex sensory and cognitive domains, encompassing both representation and practice, both imaginal objects and bodies-in-performance. As a concept, world provides something of an integrative matrix in which the particular, faceted contributions of various disciplines can find their places.

Background of the Concept

More than a loose figure of speech, world is a concept that has undergone specialized development as a tool of the philosophic, human sciences. For example, the common-sense, descriptive move to unpack world into different domains may be accompanied by the epistemologically radical conclusion that no single one of them constitutes an absolute standard for describing the others; that the "universe" is always a product of a manner of description rather than an objectively determined referent; or that the concept of world does not assume a single, *a priori* system of knowledge in terms of which all human experience should be described.

The idea that world is not just a common, ready-made entity that humans passively receive or discover, but rather something humans also produce, has a conceptual genealogy with many branches. In each, we find concepts that "the world" is a product of the instrumentations and modes through which it is apprehended and inhabited, and that world describes versions of life-space without reducing those versions to an independent norm. These traditions include but are not limited to Kantian philosophy, phenomenology, sociology of knowledge, social anthropology and the history of religions model of Mircea Eliade.

In the first lineage, the philosopher Immanuel Kant (1724–1804) described how the mind and its categories are factors that structure reality and that without these structures there is no access to reality "in itself." From this, others developed the idea that concepts and symbol systems of all kinds become the different frames through which different kinds of "reality" take place. Ernst Cassirer (1874–1945), for example, in his "Philosophy of Symbolic Forms" (*Die Philosophie der symbolischen Formen*, 1923–29), showed how disparate forms of cultural languages like art, myth and science organize distinctive kinds of reality (Cassirer 1955). Nelson Goodman developed a radical form of relativism, summarized in his *Ways of Worldmaking* (1978), showing how the world only comes in "versions": "None of them," he writes, "tells us *the* way the world is, but each of them tells us *a* way the world is" (N. Goodman 1972: 31). A musical score, a painting or a scientific theory each compose one of these worlds, each realm with its own "schemes" (N. Goodman and Elgin 1988: 7). These are not versions of one and the same neutral, underlying world, for no version is the primordial descriptor of reality and each world version has an independence. Thus, seemingly conflicting assertions like "the sun always moves," and "the sun never moves," while at odds on the surface, need to be read within their own systems of description as statements that are true in different worlds. Truth is then a function of system genre, some truths requiring denotational, empirical criteria, and others, such as various forms of aesthetic truth, inviting "rightness" and consistency internal to the requirements of the logic of their own domain.

The second tradition is that of phenomenology, launched systematically with Edmund Husserl (1859–1938). Husserl developed the concept of a "life-world" (*Lebenswelt*), or the world as immediately experienced by subjects, as distinguished from the objectivizing conceptual world of science without human subjects in it. He focused on describing "the structures of experience" as they occur in consciousness and as they are "lived"—for example, to consciousness, time is not quantitative or homogeneous, but heterogeneous and qualitative. Martin Heidegger (1889–1976) produced an extensive, original analysis of the human situation as characterized by one's "being-in-the-world." Again, this existential focus on the structure of "habitative" existence was an alternative to philosophies that pictured consciousness, mind or subjectivity as independent of environments, and that had isolated subjects from their world fields. In the terms of existential phenomenology, what humans "are" is what they do as agents in their worlds, a world being here a mutually constitutive relation of subject and objects. Arguably in the phenomenological spirit, even the American philosopher William James (1842–1910) had analyzed seven genres of "sub-worlds"—namely, the worlds of the senses, science, abstract truths, collective prejudices, individual opinion, religion and myth, and madness (1890: 291–295), noting that "each world *whilst it is attended to* is real after its own fashion; only the reality lapses with the attention" (1890: 293).

Peter Berger's and Thomas Luckmann's *The Social Construction of Reality* (1967) and Berger's *The Sacred Canopy* (1969)—which gave particular semantic currency to the terminology of "world-construction"—encapsulated another trajectory of the category of world, the so-called "sociology of knowledge," drawing on the work of Karl Marx (1818–1883), Émile Durkheim (1858–1917), Max Weber (1864–1920) and Alfred Schütz (1899–1959). Marx and Durkheim had already developed the radical claims that the entire world of thought and knowledge, including "religion"—was a social creation. These creations are nevertheless very real in their effects. This approach went much further than just observing that thought and world views are "influenced" by social norms. Rather, it attested that knowledge is itself a *product* of human, cultural activity.

Berger and Luckmann described a basic sociological dialectic in three processes. In the first, society externalizes itself, putting its categories—like language and institutions—out onto the world; in the second, such externalization then assumes the features and "facticity" of objective reality, and this is the "objectivation" process; and in the third, that reality is then internalized as normative by society's individual members. Language, social roles and identities, which are initially our products, thus take on the aura of factuality. "[T]he fundamental coerciveness of society lies not in its machineries of social control," Berger writes, "but in its power to constitute and to impose itself as reality" (1969: 12). Society is here a world-building enterprise that must always maintain and "legitimize" its own meaningful order, or *nomos* (Greek "law") (1969: 19). Separation from the social world, in turn, constitutes *anomy*—essentially worldlessness (1969: 22). Social institutions are endowed with an ontological status "to the point where to deny them is to deny being itself—the being of the universal order of things and, consequently, one's own being in this order" (1969: 25); nomos and cosmos then become "co-extensive" (1969: 25). Religion, in Berger's view, is what "cosmizes" and sacralizes this nomos. In the face of chaos, religions ground nomic institutions in a trans-humanly legitimated realm.

A fourth trajectory is that of social anthropology *per se*, which has emphasized the culture-specific construction of world, the autonomy of "collective representations," worlds as cultural languages and mappings, and communities as systems. Representative are Robert Redfield on the notion of communities as "wholes" (1955), Mary Douglas on the boundaried character of social orders (1989 [1966]), and Clifford Geertz (1973) on the context-specific nature of cultural categories. Others, like Pierre Bourdieu (1977) and Talal Asad (1993), have drawn particular, nuanced attention to the role of "practice" in the "negotiation" of worlds. Michael Kearney's *World View* (1984) is a notable systematic analysis of cross-culturally universal categories of world-view formation, for example, the distinction of self and others, causality, classification, and notions of space and time.

Finally, and particularly influential in the vocabulary of comparative religion, has been the work of Mircea Eliade (1907–1986). Eliade made programmatic use of the concept of world, applying it as a tool of the history and phenomenology of religion. Where sociologists and anthropologists established the role of social norms in the formation of worlds, Eliade attempted to show the specific role of religious myth and ritual. Religious and nonreligious people, he posited, represent different modes of "being in the world" (1959b: 14–16), different "existential situations." Thus, for *homo religiosus* (the "religious person") the universe is constituted by "sacred histories," and sacred times and places that make the mythic realities present. What is taken as sacred becomes "the real"—it "ontologically founds the world" (Eliade 1959b: 21). To Eliade, religious world creation with its distinctive mythic style, parallels the imaginal, creative systems of novelists and artists.

In the Eliadean approach, religious worlds are those which interpret space, time, nature and human existence in terms of trans-human meanings. Thus, traditional religious cultures oriented their worlds around certain fixed, sacred points—either natural sites such as mountains or caves, or constructions such as temples or shrines, or even portable sacred objects—in the midst of otherwise homogeneous space. These "centers of the world" also function as "openings" or points of communication with the trans-human agencies which underlie existence. Where the symbolism is vertical, these points comprise an *axis mundi* (world axis), linking the world above with that below. The fundamental distinction of "our world" versus foreign, chaotic space, reflects the opposition between organized and unknown territory. Eliade calls it a traditional "system of the world" (1959b: 37) where one's own world is at the center, is believed to be founded by the gods, and involves points of communication with the gods by certain breaks in the homogeneity of space.

A second Eliadean category of religious world-making is the construction of time and history through mythic classifications. For a traditional religious world, time has a reversible quality. Religious actors orient themselves toward and define themselves in terms of the eternal "time" of the myth—the time of the great events recounted in one's sacred histories. Ritual gives access to these realities. Eliade offers the example of cultures for whom the word for world is also the word for year, indicating that the annual time of the New Year festival is also literally the time when "the world" is reborn anew through the reempowerment of the mythic forces of creation (1959b: 73).

Traditional *homo religiosus* also experiences nature as a manifestation of divine activity, so that sacrality is revealed "through the very structures of the world" (1959b: 117). This is to say that the system of nature and its features, such as the transcendence and infinity of the sky, the life-death cycle of the earth, and the dissolving but creative nature of water, all are experienced as having a trans-human, cosmic value and signification.

Finally, for Eliade, religious worlds are apt to locate all human activities, such as eating, work, art and marital life, within a cosmic or mythic framework of significance. It is the nature of the lens of mythic thinking to find its categories and archetypes manifest or divined in and through the ordinary world of objects. Transitions and events such as birth, puberty / adulthood, marriage and death, are always ritually placed within an encompassing, sacred world-view.

Besides these five approaches to world building, recent scientific models may also hold promise for religious studies, including "systems" analysis and complexity theory (Malley 1995), and biological concepts of "self-organizing systems" (Jantsch 1980). Varela, Thompson and Rosch present a cognitive science model—influenced by phenomenology and Madhyamika Buddhist dialectics—which develops the idea that mind and world arise together in an "enactive" manner (Varela et al. 1991). Some cognitivists would maintain that the human mind is engaged in a "co-evolutionary relationship" with religious systems (Malley 1995: 7). Generally, renewed interest in the application of bio-anthropology to religious behavior (Burkert 1996), in "human universals" (D. E. Brown 1991), and the cognitive basis of religious ideas (Boyer 1994; Malley 1995) may add significant conceptual resources to the notion of world-building.

Religious Worlds: Features and Dynamics

Religious systems are topographies of language and practice in which humans construe the world as a place of engagement with superhuman beings and become actors in that culturally generated system. These same religious people may also, simultaneously, live within several other organizational and behavioral systems and roles that have no trans-human reference points, for example physical, social and geographical worlds. Where a religious world version is in effect, though, one finds the language of superhuman agency, sacred, focal objects, notions of an inviolable world order, and the process of periodic, ritual world renewal.

Religion as World Script

A religious world is a particular way of seeing the world and acting in it through the matrix of languages that involve trans-human agency. Religious language names the empowering forces of the world as gods, spirits or god-like beings, evoking their presence, authority and communicative possibilities. These beings also form the ingredients of cosmologies, mythologies and sacred "histories"—which constitute a kind of semantic, categorial membrane around "one's world," explaining its origin and course, and why things are as they are. Such constructions of world and knowledge, believed to signify the realities behind appearances, create domains of experience within which human actors and religious objects evolve their interactive life. These mental mappings have been endlessly imaginative. They produce other worlds, future worlds, higher worlds, parallel spirit universes, heavens and hells, the worlds of gods and worlds produced by gods. The ordinary world, in juxtaposition with these others, accordingly may come to be seen as a place of illusion, a playground of the gods, a prison house requiring a savior, an exact mirror duplicate of "the world above" or a laborious stage in an evolutionary series.

Religious language, and thus its accompanying world version, is participatory and self-involving, unlike the language of scientific objectivity. It is itself a form of practice, involving various reciprocities of giving and receiving in relation to its postulated sacred objects; and a form of communication and performance—in some ways, a form of competency. In this sense, religious accounts of the creation and generation of the world are not just hypotheses about what happened in the past, but foundational charters and indices for how to behave in the present.

Empowered Sacred Objects

Religious worlds form around particular objects believed to be sacred. The objects come in various genres—not only as names of gods, but as the manifestations of superhuman power or authority in places and times, endowed authorities, sacraments and rites, icons and symbols, scriptures and mythic words, teachings and precepts. Sacred objects may be tangible or mental, spatial or linguistic, but they will tend to have a centripetal, centering function, serving as openings to a nonmaterial zone. They thereby become forms of bonding and reciprocal empowerment. Around them, with all their mystery, charisma, inviolateness and attention-demanding obligations, religious worlds and the logic of religious behaviors arise.

None of this indicates that a religious world is not at the same time a social world. Religious objects receive their sacrality from the collectivities they belong to. They are marks of membership or social identity. The Pope, the Ganges river, the mandalas of Soka Gakkai Buddhism, the Qur'an are holy only within their own world frames, and not in others. The absolutes, the cosmic maps, the reigning authorities, and the holy of holies of one group are irrelevant or nonexistent in other systems. Thus, thousands of "Centers of the World" sit side by side. Each group or sub-group elevates and absolutizes its own authoritative objects.

Sacred Order

Religious worlds are not just about relations with objects but also posit normative, moral orders taken to be the cosmic order itself, and these determine proper and improper behavior. Such orders draw lines forming distinctions of good and evil, right and wrong, pure and impure, and endow these boundaries with the sanctity of superhuman legitimation. Not only domains for the experience of "the other," religions are systems which monitor their own integrity by purging what is offensive, often through acts of purification. Sacred order is then not just a template for world design or a passive, aesthetic arrangement, but a process of self-maintenance in the face of wrongness and violation. The world must be kept "right," and if something is wrong with the world, it must be made right—the polarity and procedure being relative to each system. Religion is here one of the more far-reaching forms of world stability in the face of an otherwise chaotic cosmos. Religious worlds, moreover, are highly defined and developed versions of the tendency of all human worlds to seek self-preservation against threats of violation. The need to defend territory, honor, tradition, membership and collective loyalties is intimately linked with the inviolability of religious order (Paden 1996b).

Religions themselves have their own terms for world-order, such as the Hindu idea of dharma. Dharma, from a root meaning "to uphold," signifies the eternal, divinely endowed moral order, and can be synonymous with the concepts of law, duty, righteousness, religion. Chinese religions have the category of T'ien, or the "order of Heaven," reflected in all social relationships, and even Tao, the natural "way" of things; and monotheistic traditions hold conceptions of the revealed, normative Word of God manifest in scriptures such as the Qur'an, the Torah or the Bible. Religious order tends to become the guideline for all other forms of order, whether dietary, legal or political.

World Renewal

Worlds not only need to be defended but also renewed. Where the religious world is not kept up, the authority of the gods is diminished. Thus, periodic religious observances and festivals have become not only the shapers of time and calendars, but also acts that give continuing "life" to the superhuman powers. Ritual observance, then, becomes the matrix of world renewal, as Durkheim (1995 [1912]: 330–354) and later Eliade (1959b: 68–113) emphasized. Through regular acts of memorializing sacred objects and transmitting ritual behaviors, the social and mythic reality of religion are maintained as plausible and unchanging. Daily prayer for Muslims or puja for Hindus build the category of divinity into the heart of the day; Judeo-Christian Sabbath and Sunday observances return time to God on a regular weekly cycle; great annual festivals like Ramadan, the Jewish New Year or Easter, regenerate the cosmos on a pervasive, large scale. All major passages and events in life are given religious context. Thus, religious worlds are sustained and refounded periodically through commemorative and ritual practices that construct a kind of temporal geography. Without these normative, shaping intersections that mark and punctuate time, religious worlds would scarcely survive.

Varieties and Dynamics of Religious Worlds

Worlds transform, re-form, expand and extend. Buddhism completely reinterpreted what had previously been a Hindu cosmos, as Christianity did with Judaism, as Islam did with its Judeo-Christian predecessors and as Protestantism did with Catholicism. Any religion gets reshaped by new environments. Religions grow, transmute, combine, sub-divide, accommodate, migrate, die off. They are fashioned out of the stuff of endless cultural locations and genres: Where culture is territorial, so is religion; where culture is individualistic, religion reflects it; where culture is hierarchic, religion follows suit; where cultures combine, religion becomes syncretic; where culture is revolutionary, so are the gods. Likewise, religions themselves reshape cultures. They are not only reflections of social systems, but also create and recreate them, and they do this because they are themselves a form of social life.

New religious movements, numbering in the thousands when looked at globally, show how the language of spirituality constantly recreates itself to address the needs of emerging cultural identities. The enormous variety of these innovative systems shows the naturalness of religious world building, each group reconstituting a cosmology, manufacturing a revised version of history, offering a new set of ontological markers and new interactive objects of authority and communication. They do this as naturally and inevitably as any species will form a habitat.

Each purposive zone of culture, whether religious, medical, musical, commercial or political, will have its "life"—its structures, styles of productivity, goals and flow of activity. Any of them or any combination of them has a self-organizing course of its own, following the logic and strategies of its own subject matter, availability of resources, opportunities, conflict and competition, and creative leadership. Each generates its own classifications of relevant knowledge, its own lenses for construing experience. In religious terms, one who devotes his or her life "to God" comes to encounter a range of significations, processes and new experiences along the way, just as the same could be said for those who pursue other cultural genres, such as fashion designers, culinary experts or tennis players.

Religions have a tendency to spread their effects through an entire world system, and thus to totalize and universalize their influence. This drive toward extension may either take the form of so-called "world" religions which set out to win the allegiance of all cultures and thus fill the planet with their globalizing norms, or in the form of any religion that extends its influence to the entirety of educational, political and even aesthetic systems within its own cultural world. It is part of the power of "the sacred"—for example, a god—to make or authorize a world. There may also be an element of compelling, colonizing authority that attends dedication to "supreme" gods or religious founders. The public is familiar with the way fundamentalist thinking about creationism tries to take on ownership of the entirety of world-description even in the face of challenges by evolutionary science, or the way some sectarian religious groups will opt out of the secular system altogether and construct their own internally consistent and self-verifying cultures.

Comparativism and Religious Worlds

The notion of world formation supplies a basis for comparative analysis because it constitutes a common, human activity against which differences may also be discerned. The world-making model identifies both common *forms* of world-fashioning behaviors and historically different socio-cultural *contents* of world expressions.

If all religious worlds create and transmit sacred pasts, construct sacred objects, absolutize or cosmicize their moral orders and forms of authority, and periodically renew their commitments to sacred objects with calendrical and passage rites, these features are also but mythically explicit versions of themes that appear in the world making of any social group. Memory-construction, the absolutizing of values and objects, and renewal practices can be identified as comparative themes pervading the general human condition. Behaviors that otherwise might appear distant, primitive or odd, here take on a context of intelligibility as instances of common, familiar human activities.

Yet in their content, worlds are different. If all have "pasts," every past is a different genealogy than any other, even within a so-called common tradition: Pentecostalists and Catholics construct different Christian lineages, Shia and Sunni Muslims have incompatible readings of the succession of Islamic authority, Buddhist denominations affiliate with disparate genealogies of teaching authority. Indeed, every traditional village, town and city, like every family, is apt to have its own salient, chronicled memories (Braun 1999). And if all cultures have annual renewal festivals, nevertheless the content of those rites is not the same but rather a reflector of very different value orientations—such as hierarchic family relationships, moral conscientiousness, economic bonding or male prowess. If all religions draw lines distinguishing behavior that is right or pure from that which is transgressive or impure, nevertheless what it is that is pure or impure is not the same. Identifying patterns of world orientation, therefore, can actually enhance or highlight differences relative to that pattern, showing what makes a world its own and not another.

Issues and Evaluation

The notion of world is open to various forms of problematizing and debate, which may be briefly summarized:

1. It may be argued that the concept of world puts an artificial circumscription on an area that exists only in the mind of the interpreter, and thus gives a false sense of order or totality, imposing an intelligibility on things that is in fact not there. It could be said that every event is really a fluid, interdependent mixture of many networks, so complex as to be impossible to distinguish in any but an arbitrary way, and that humans essentially live in this chaos rather than in any bounded system. As anthropologist Renato Rosaldo points out, "order vs. chaos" is not the whole story of culture—there is an important, even less explored realm of behavior marked by "improvisation, muddling through, and contingent events" (Rosaldo 1989: 103).

   In response, one could show that the notion of world does not necessarily imply a fixed, boundaried system. A world can be a process of change, a form of interaction, even a momentary staging, as well as a durable institution, a long-range commitment or a changeless structure. One can be "in" a process as well as "in" a fixed order. Insofar as a world is a product of language and consciousness, it can be switched on or off in the blink of an eye. Many worlds lie both close at hand and overlapping.

2. It has been argued that "religion" is not itself a viable analytical category but only a convention, and that religious life lacks cultural autonomy (Fitzgerald 1997).

   Every analytic concept, including that of "religious worlds," has aspects of arbitrariness. But concepts may also direct attention to what otherwise would not be noticed. The notion of world points to the prospect of locating and sorting out the diversity of rule-based, purposive systems of behaviors. A religious version of world is at least potentially such an identifiable, intentional sphere or program of cultural experience.

3. Another issue, alluded to earlier, is: *Whose* religious world is being described, that of the insider or that of the interpreter? In the analogy from psychotherapy, the patient's self-description may be altogether at variance from the therapist's explanation. For the latter, the patient's world may exhibit self-deception, mental illness, social dysfunction, paranoia. No Marxist would accept a religion's description of its own world as a real account of that world.

   The two horizons of description are indeed discrepant. The study of religion is not limited to simple reiteration of the religious insider's self-description, but also involves a representation of that world, or aspects of it, within a broader repertoire of conceptual, comparative and analytical resources (Paden 1992, 1994). At the same time, if one cannot identify how objects and relationships are constituted within the experience of the insider, one lacks the basic data that is the subject matter for explanation.

4. Is the notion of world reductionistic? Does the category of world construction take away the elements of "otherness" in experience, as Paul Ricoeur worries (1980: 116)? Is world more than a construct?

Certainly the concept of world is not reducible to the metaphor of building and fabrication. Worlds are not just built, as with hammer and nails. They are environments acted upon, responded to, engaged with, practiced, performed—environments to which one "attends" (Ingold 1996: 112–117). As Ricoeur puts it, humans "render" a world, like an artist (1980: 116–120). It is the nature of religious worlds, in particular, to provide contexts in which persons may pursue various forms of engagement with "the other," with gods, with transcendence. "World" is then an open-ended affair that includes any imaginable content of experience. It gives itself through the matrices of its own designs and structures and through the receiving and configuring acts of the subject (Paden 1992: 110–135).

At the same time, the notion of world provides a referent for the analysis of religion that in some ways replaces the classical theological referents of "the Holy" or "the Divine." Thus, instead of worlds being "about" the Holy, holiness is here a feature of ways certain object-relationships drive certain kinds of behaviors in certain kinds of worlds.

5. Finally, there is the issue of whether the reference to multiple worlds ignores the reality of a *common* world. Does the world just melt down into world-versions? Is there no world in which all these other worlds subsist?

The answer must be that there is, but our understanding of it as a totality will itself still only be a world-version. The study of hundreds of religious worlds certainly leads to a larger sense of the kind of world in which these many worlds take place, and of the kinds of recurrent structures and environmental differences that condition the existence of multiple worlds. This common world then becomes the world of the interpreter, just as a physicist may form a world model that attempts to accommodate all the known data of the physical universe.

The notion of world provides an integrative matrix for linking concepts, insights and explanatory frames from the work of humanistic, social and even biological sciences. It has the versatility to distinguish large-scale or small-scale regions of kinds of activity, and it can help demarcate insiders' and outsiders' frames of reference. It differentiates domains of behavior that have an element of self-organizing purpose.

In these ways, the concept of world may be productive when applied to religion, just as religion also becomes a productive subject matter for identifying the thematics of world building as a universal human activity.

Suggested Readings

Berger, Peter
    1969   *The Sacred Canopy: Elements of a Sociological Theory of Religion.*
           Garden City, NY: Doubleday. Chs. 1 and 2.

Eliade, Mircea
    1959b *The Sacred and Profane: The Nature of Religion.* Willard R. Trask
           (trans.). New York: Harcourt, Brace Jovanovich.

Geertz, Clifford
    1983   *Local Knowledge: Further Essays in Interpretive Anthropology.* New
           York: Basic. Ch. 3.

Goodman, Nelson
    1978   *Ways of Worldmaking.* Indianapolis: Hackett. Ch. 1.

Ingold, Tim, editor
    1996   "1990 Debate: Human Worlds Are Culturally Constructed," pp. 99–146 in
           Tim Ingold (ed.), *Key Debates in Anthropology.* London: Routledge.

Kearney, Michael
    1984   *World View.* Novato, CA: Chandler & Sharp.

Paden, William E.
    1994   *Religious Worlds: The Comparative Study of Religion.* 2nd edn. Boston:
           Beacon.

Tambiah, Stanley J.
    1990   *Magic, Science, Religion, and the Scope of Rationality.* Lewis Henry
           Morgan Lectures, 1984. Cambridge: Cambridge University Press. Ch. 5.

III

LOCATION

⫷⫸

Concepts, of course, are not part of free-floating philosophical discourse, but socially, historically, and locally rooted, and must be explained in terms of these realities.

Eric Hobsbawm (1990: 9)

24

MODERNISM

Donald Wiebe

❧ ❧

"Modernism" as a term encountered in cultural history has come to be applied rather liberally to an extraordinarily broad range of cultural manifestations, including architecture, art, literature and religion. So unkempt has been its application that for some it is doubtful whether it in fact signifies a reasonably definable human phenomenon. But to restrict this term to its use in the field of religious studies, most scholars would agree that it can be appropriately applied with reference to significant developments in seventeenth- and eighteenth-century Europe, and that a proper understanding of them is essential to comprehending the role of the academic study of religion in the contemporary university. The relatively recent emergence of university programs in the academic study of religion, as John F. Wilson suggests, "may be the single most significant development associated with modernity that affects religion in new ways in our time," and students of religion, he insists, "should be the first to recognize this interface between modernity and religion [because it] is possibly the one decisively new factor in the situation we are working to understand" (J. F. Wilson 1987: 17). Wilson, unfortunately, did not elaborate on the effect of modernity on the academic study of religion, but rather chose to examine the ways in which modernity—defined simply as "a period of intense social and hence cultural change (J. F. Wilson 1987: 17)—influences religious behavior and belief. The results of that analysis, however, are rather meager, shedding no light on the "interface" of modernism and the study of religion.

In attempting to assess the influence of modernity on religion, Wilson cautions: "Our task is to understand the modern, not to either embrace or excoriate it" (J. F. Wilson 1987: 13). This is sound advice though not altogether free of paradox, being itself a product of the modern viewpoint. And it could be argued that following the advice supports the case for a "modern"—as opposed to a "traditional"—study of religion. His claim may be justified, but this does not allow the scholar to ignore the task of distinguishing descriptive historical analysis from evaluative argumentation. For without such rigorous attention the discussion of modernism would amount to little more than the expression of personal opinion. (Whether or not that effort can produce an objective account of modernism rather than mere opinion is still open to debate, but it will be attempted here.)

At least two essays in the past fifteen years have devoted explicit attention to the relation of modernism to the study of religion: Martin E. Marty's public lecture at Arizona State University, "What Is Modern about the Modern Study of Religion?" (1985) and Catherine Bell's recent review essay "Modernism and Postmodernism in the Study of Religion" (1996). Marty identifies as "modern" the fact that the study of religion today finds itself located in the university in addition to the religious setting. He recognizes that such programs of study aspire to be neutral, focused on a concern for knowledge rather than meaning, although he also insists that the consideration of what is "modern" in the study of religion today must involve acknowledging at least two "publics" in addition to the university: the "ecclesia" (religious community) and the "republic" (society at large). In so doing, however, Marty misunderstands the role of science, with its essentially detached nature, in the emergence of modern society. For Marty there is no clear line of demarcation between objectivity and engagement, thus no absolute differentiation between academy and ecclesia. "Teaching about religion instead of teaching religion," he asserts (without supporting argument, one may note) "is its own kind of quasi-creedal commitment" (Marty 1985: 8). What is peculiarly modern in the modern study of religion for Marty, then, is not its scientific character but rather the recognition that "the republic of modern religious studies" involves a multiplicity of voices—a "multiplex consciousness" (Marty 1985: 10). It is a study given over to political and religious concerns in addition to the cognitive, as can be deduced from the following warning about the evils of too narrow a view of the enterprise: "To yield all to the academics might be to obscure commitment to religion. To yield all to the religionists might be to produce a clerisy or theocracy. The interaction profits all" (Marty 1985: 9). Despite the vehemence of his claim, Marty provides the reader with an implicit critique rather than with an analytical account of modernity and its implications for the study of religion.

Although as critical of modernity as Marty, Catherine Bell has a clearer understanding of modernism and its import for the study of religion. She acknowledges that for modernists the study of religion is based on the assumption that science is a system of thought which escapes the determinations of culture. Religion, in contrast, is a system of thought "completely entangled in culture" (Bell 1996: 183)—so that modernist scholars would naturally prefer the application of scientific method in the study of religion to a study undertaken within a theological or confessional framework. By contrast, however, in a critique of J. Samuel Preus's *Explaining Religion: Criticism and Theory from Bodin to Freud* (1987) and Tom Lawson's and Robert McCauley's

Rethinking Religion: Connecting Cognition and Culture (1990), she maintains that the modern study of religion is naïve in positing a "smooth process of rational and progressively scientific thinking that yielded a 'coherent research tradition' with which to replace the reigning theological paradigm" (Bell 1996: 180); and she argues that trust in science to provide us with objective knowledge of anything is not justified. That is, according to Bell, the "moderns" too easily disregard the consequences of non-rational influences upon science. She further contends that non-rational influences even now undermine science in favor of a continued use of the theological framework for the study of religious phenomena (Bell 1996: 183). She maintains, moreover—rather ironically, as it turns out—that theology itself is a product of the Enlightenment and as such every bit as "modern" an enterprise as is science. The absolute contrast between religion and the study of religion insisted upon by modernists, she concludes, cannot be supported. Postmodernists have shown that neither religion nor science is exempt from socio-cultural influence. Insisting that "all concepts and terms are embedded in particular experiences and 'conventional perspectives'," she maintains that there is "little possibility of a shared, cross-cultural terminology that affords systematic methods of analyzing commonalities and differences in the practices we speak of as religion" (Bell 1996: 185), which for her shows that all knowing—even the so-called modern scientific knowing—is inevitably political (Bell 1996: 186).

In her conclusion Bell does not completely reject the modern notion that religion can be studied neutrally (Bell 1996: 185), for she avoids insisting that all our attempts to know "are politically, epistemologically, and morally suspect" (Bell 1996: 187). She does appear convinced, however, that the modernist debate over approaches to the study of religion—"outsider" (neutral) versus "insider" (confessional)—is now exhausted, despite "the nearly paranoid degree of anti-theology polemic of the last decade" (Bell 1996: 187), and that no resolution of that fundamental tension is possible either within a modernist or within a postmodernist framework. What is needed, she insists, is a view of science that does not simply reflect the ideology of science but instead allows for a study of religion "that is not universal or hegemonic" (Bell 1996: 188). Such a view of science, she insists rather cavalierly, can be found in Bruno Latour's analysis of the nature of modern science (1983).

That Latour's work provides a fruitful, non-confessional alternative to the scientific study of religion such as that proposed by Preus (1987) and Lawson and McCauley (1990) is doubtful. Indeed, one might even question the coherence of Latour's critique of modern science; and similarly questionable is whether it can actually provide a framework of analysis that, as Bell suggests, can transcend current theological and scientific approaches to the study of religion. I shall respond to Bell in this regard below.

As mentioned above, the term "modernism" has been used broadly to label a complex series of developments in the economic, social and political life of

Western European societies, such that they were radically transformed from simple and homogeneous to complex and highly differentiated communities. "Modernism," moreover, is intimately connected with such notions as capitalism, industrialization, urbanization and modernization. Furthermore, the transformation of the social structures of society was associated not just with material changes brought about by technology but also, and necessarily, with changes in consciousness involving the rejection of traditional religious structures of authority and the espousal of individualism. The birth of the modern revealed a new way of thinking about the human condition that involved a critique of traditional social hierarchies and a promotion of progress and emancipation. As Peter Gay points out, the moderns "called for a social and political order that would be secular, reasonable, humane, pacific, open, and free" (Gay 1977: 397). This development is elaborated by Ernest Gellner in terms of a shift from traditional martial to commercial values in which change rather than stability becomes the norm for society. As he puts it, "perpetual improvement under the name of Progress becomes the key notion of a new vision, and the basis of a new morality ... Riches are worth seeking when they are protected, and constitute the path to power, rather than the other way around" (Gellner 1997: 11).

The impact that such "modernist" changes in structures of society and consciousness have had upon religious beliefs and practices renders the issue of modernism immensely important to students of religion. And while it lends itself fruitfully to the substance of sociological theorizing as well, this will not be the focus of my essay.

Central to this transition in cultural style, as Gellner points out, is the rise of science as "an effective form of cognition" (Gellner 1997: 11). And the modernity of the intellectual developments leading to the eventual ascendancy of science will be the subject under discussion here, for these developments constitute a fundamental change of mentality from all previous traditional cultures—archaic, ancient or medieval. This development, that is, is of greater significance in our understanding of religion and the study of religion than the material changes wrought by the industrial revolution associated with this change in mentality. To present a balanced understanding of modernism as it refers to the rise of science I will make use of the analyses of Timothy Reiss (*Discourse of Modernism*, 1982) and Hans Blumenberg (*The Legitimation of the Modern Age*, 1983), whose descriptions of the phenomenon converge even though their evaluations of it diverge radically.

Modern discourse, Reiss argues, is "analytico-referential" and emerged in the West by overcoming what he calls a "theocratico-theological" discourse that predominated in the Middle Ages. "Discourse" for Reiss denotes "the visible and describable praxis of what is called 'thinking'" (Reiss 1982: 9). This parallels Foucault's notion of "episteme" in that a discourse provides the conceptual tools "that control the analysis and understanding of the majority of human practices" (Reiss 1982: 58). For Reiss (as for Foucault) there can only be one dominant discourse in effect in any period of history, although other subordinated discourses operate contemporaneously with it. Such alternative discourses, however, cannot hold effective meaning for society, he insists, because they cannot be expressed within the framework of the dominant discourse.

According to Reiss, analytico-referential discourse is most clearly represented by science (Reiss 1982: 30). To exemplify this state of affairs he points to the telescope as reflective of the new conceptual ordering of the world, wherein the linguistic sign came "to be defined as an arbitrarily selected transparent instrument placed between concept and object" (Reiss 1982: 26). This discourse, he writes,

> assumes that the world as it can be and is to be known, represents a fixed object of analysis quite separate from the forms of discourse by which men speak of it and by which they represent their thought ... Equally basic is the assumption that the proper *use* of language will not only *give* us this object in a gradual accumulation of detail (referentiality), but will also *analyze* it in the very form of its syntactic organization ... The assumption of this coincidence of universal reason and general grammar was essential. (Reiss 1982: 42)

It is a way of conceptualizing the world that "marks a total distancing of the mind from the world and the imposition of a system which belongs to the realm of discourse" (Reiss 1982: 140). This "discourse of modernism" arose out of an earlier dominant discourse which he refers to as "a discourse of patterning" (Reiss 1982: 46)—a mythic ordering of reality—dependent upon an entirely different process of conceptualizing the world, one which uses words "as though they are in some way essential and inherent in the object" (Reiss 1982: 41). Importantly, such a discourse constitutes "a system of *transformations* organizing a comprehension of society and the individual, of nature and culture, of the 'natural' and the 'supernatural'" (Reiss 1982: 49, emphasis added). Such a form of thought is mythical rather than linear; unlike the latter, it refuses to draw a distinction between the ontological and the epistemological realms and "assumes that discourse is a part of the 'world' and not distinct from it [granting privilege neither] to the enunciator of discourse [nor] to the act of enunciation" (Reiss 1982: 30). In such a system, "knowledge" subordinates the human mind "to an order of concrete events exterior to [it]" (Reiss 1982: 141). Thus knowledge is constituted by a discursive exchange "within the world" in the mythic patterning of thought, whereas in the analytico-referential discourse the expression of knowledge is "a reasoning practice upon the world" (Reiss 1982: 30). Reiss argues therefore that the patterning mode of thought is conjunctive and "totalizing" rather than disjunctive, as in the analytico-referential mode of thought. Moreover, the conjunctive mode of thought involves a form of "cognitive" union with the divine while the modern, disjunctive mode of thought accentuates human responsibility for one's being (Reiss 1982: 72, 106). Reiss concludes that in the patterning mode of thought the "concepts of *use*, *arbitrariness*, *will*, *intention*, *individual*, *person*, and *self* are all quite different [and that] they cannot but provide an utterly dissimilar practice of discourse" (Reiss 1982: 95). He consequently insists that in tracing the role of will as an aspect of self-identity—self-identity as a center of knowing—will reveal what is crucial to an understanding of the moderns (Reiss 1982: 59) and show why they were incomprehensible to their successors.

The emergence of this new disjunctive mode of discourse from within the frame of a conjunctive mode of discourse is clearly captured, Reiss suggests, in Kepler's *Somnum (Dream)*. The text of the *Somnum* does not operate in an analytical fashion, but an examination of the notes, he points out, permits "what is *contained* in the dream to become a part of an analytical knowledge," thus changing "the very structure of discourse" (Reiss 1982: 149). With this "passage from what one might call discursive *exchange within* the world to the expression of knowledge as a reasoning *practice upon* the world" (Reiss 1982: 30), Kepler's *Somnum* "manifests a moment when two different classes of discourse function with equivalent power—a moment of transition which must obviously be brief, for the one is being produced from the other" (Reiss 1982: 148).

What is seen only hesitantly in Kepler, Reiss then argues, becomes in Francis Bacon a new and dominant discourse: "*The New Organon* will view a particular class of writing and the specific organization of discourse it necessitates as the fundamental requirement of all 'right' knowing" (Reiss 1982: 198). He continues (226–227):

> Bacon's is not ... an idea of science limited to a relatively brief moment at the beginning of the seventeenth century. It remains our own. It remains indeed by and large the underlying premise behind all our discourses of truth and, therefore, behind all the forms of what we term "knowledge." For Baconian experimentalism is not *simply*, as is often claimed, the active manipulation and forcing of natural phenomena. Such manipulation is dependent, as it is for Galileo, on prior theory.

It is true that later scientific research was often affected by theological beliefs, but this does not mean that such research was not dominated by the new analytico-referential discourse. As Reiss notes, although scientific theory was not left untouched by religious belief, "[b]eing 'touched' and being organized by are two different things" (Reiss 1982: 221).

According to Hans Blumenberg, moderns adopt a rational approach to the resolution of human problems rather than a passive acceptance of the promise of salvation; in so doing, they relate to a natural, rather than a supernatural, world open to scientific understanding. And it is to this break with traditional thought to which Blumenberg devotes his attention in *The Legitimation of the Modern Age*. He sets out to refute the claims of the Romantics (and other critics of modernity) who deny that modernism constituted a rupture with the traditional mode of thought and existence in the Middle Ages, and he pays special attention to those who would refute the legitimacy of the modern age on the ground that it is little more than the secularization of Christian ideas. Thus he writes:

> The occasion for talk of the legitimacy of the modern age does not lie in the fact that this age conceives of itself as conforming to reason and as realizing this conformity in the Enlightenment but rather in the syndrome of the assertions that this epochal conformity to reason is nothing but an aggression (which fails to understand itself as such) against theology, from which in fact it has in a hidden manner derived everything that belongs to it. (Blumenberg 1983: 97)

Blumenberg's argument is that modernity constitutes a break with the dominant theme of divine omnipotence in the Middle Ages, affirming by contrast the contingency of the world—a critical commitment to rationality both in knowing the world and in living in it. Blumenberg does allow some connection with the Middle Ages in that the modern age accepted "a mortgage of prescribed [residual] questions ... as its own obligation" (1983: 65), but he nevertheless insists that the one follows from the other: "What mainly occurred in the process that is interpreted as secularization ... should be described not as the *transposition* of authentically theological questions ... into secularized alienation from their origin but rather as the *reoccupation* of answer positions that had become vacant and whose corresponding questions could not be eliminated" (1983: 65). The Enlightenment took over the explanatory functions of Christianity just as Christianity had taken over the explanatory functions of Antiquity (1983: 69). And this is characteristic of all epochal thresholds, that is, during "the phases of more or less rapid change in the basic rules for the procurement of very general explanations" (1983: 66).

According to Blumenberg, then, even though the moderns valued the legacy of Antiquity, they rejected the "fundamental Renaissance thesis of the unsurpassability of ancient literature" (1983: 125): he therefore insists "[t]hat the modern age is neither a renewal of the ancient world nor its continuation by other means" (1983: 126). Nor is it merely a continuation of Christianity, for it emerges as a response to the crises experienced by Christianity, providing a comprehensive alternative understanding of life through reason and theory (the products of a transition from naïve to self-conscious questioning of the world [1983: 237]). This last transition gave rise to an unrestricted cognitive drive, argues Blumenberg, in contrast to the Middle Ages which had linked knowledge to happiness. He continues in this vein:

From a central affect of consciousness there arises in the modern age an indissoluble link between man's historical self-understanding and the realization of scientific knowledge as the confirmation of the claim to unrestricted theoretical curiosity. The "theoretical attitude" may be a constant in European history since the awakening of the Ionian interest in nature; but this attitude could take on the explicitness of insistence on the will and right to intellectual curiosity only after it had been confronted with opposition and had to compete with other norms of attitude and fulfillment in life. (1983: 232–233)

Such "theoretical curiosity"—the search for knowledge free of all restriction in respect to other "human existential interest posited as absolute" (1983: 233)—characterizes modernity. Truth, in effect, "has become the result of a renunciation for the modern age ..., a renunciation that lies in the separation between cognitive achievement and the production of happiness" (1983: 404).

What the analyses of Reiss and Blumenberg bring into clear relief, then, is that the modern age takes shape with the ascendancy of scientific thought and that science itself, as Michael Roberts argues in *The Modern Mind* (1937: 123), is essentially due to a transformation of the notion of reason in seventeenth- and eighteenth-century thought. As Robert Hoopes puts it in *Right Reason in the English Renaissance* (1962: 161):

The intellectual history of the seventeenth century is marked by the gradual dissociation of knowledge and virtue as accepted and indivisible elements in the ideal structure of human reason, a shift from the tradition of right reason to the new tradition of scientific reasoning.

The point Hoopes makes is that "right reason" is not merely "reason" in our current sense of the term; it has a much broader meaning (1962: 4). For in earlier times the notion referred to a mode of knowing, a way of doing and a condition of being.

He explains: Right reason, may ... be thought of as a faculty which fuses in dynamic interactivity the function of knowing and being, which stands finally as something more than a proximate means of rational discovery or "a nonmoral" instrument of inquiry, and which affirms that what a man knows depends upon what, as a moral being, he chooses to make himself. (1962: 5)

Consequently, for "right reason," truth is a matter not only of the intellect but of virtue, and it involves not only the discovery of truth but the doing of good. And insofar as such a notion presupposes a belief in absolute and eternal values, it "refers not only to logical activity or discourse, but to the highest faculty and function of man" (1962: 21–22).

Hoopes goes on to show that the notion of reason distinct from "right reason" emerged in the work of seventeenth-century thinkers such as Bacon, Descartes and Hobbes, who severed cognition from virtue, so a scientific knowledge of both the natural and the social world became a distinct possibility. Science became possible by refusing to subordinate the desire to know to the achievement of non-cognitive goals (salvation and the virtuous life). "Discursive reason, as the epic repeatedly makes clear," writes Hoopes, "denotes induction or disinterested science, which discovers truths but not the Truth for Man" (1962: 198).

With this transformation of "reason," then, we witness the ascendancy of science as an objective, neutral, universalistic discourse about the world both natural and social. The precise trajectory of its rise has not been delineated here. It is important, however, to point out that essential to this development was the creation of what Toby Huff refers to as "neutral zones" in society which could politically legitimate "a disinterested agenda of naturalistic inquiry" (Huff 1993: 336) and so sustain the role of the scientist in society. Significantly, such "neutral zones" emerged, he argues, by virtue of peculiar legal developments that established the European university as an autonomous corporate entity. This breakthrough to science, according to Huff, "destroyed the received worldview and established a new and legally protected institutional location within which intellectual inquiries of the most far-reaching cultural and intellectual consequences could be carried out without hindrance" (Huff 1993: 203).

This new form of thought, as critics of modernism and postmodernists point out, has a very specific socio-historical—and perhaps geo-political—locus which makes of it yet one more "local knowledge." Although this is to some extent true of science, religious thought has a social ethos and organizational structure wholly dependent upon its social context; science is not, as Gellner shows, "*just* like the others ... [but rather] is unique and distinctive, above all in its unbelievably great cognitive and technological power which has totally transformed the world" (Gellner 1998: 184). This is a fact that postmodernists and other critics have failed to grasp. The generalization that all knowledge is really entirely "local," and the relativism this implies, is absurd. And on this matter Gellner appears incontrovertible: "It is simply not the case that all cognitive styles are equal. The technological superiority of one cognitive style has transformed the world and the rules of the social game" (Gellner 1998: 185).

In light of these intellectual developments, then, the emergence of a neutral, scientific study of religion, wholly dissociated from religion and theology in the nineteenth century, ought not to come as a surprise. The modern university had continued to develop "neutral intellectual spaces," as Huff describes them, within which anything in the natural and social worlds could be subjected to scientific analysis and explanation. Julie Reuben's *The Making of the Modern*

University (1996) leaves no room for doubt about that assessment, especially with respect to matters religious and moral. Despite Catherine Bell's concerns cited above, therefore, the modern study of religion which clearly demarcates scientific from religious modes of thought is wholly consistent with the cognitive agenda of the modern research university. The goal of disinterested knowledge as opposed to self-involving research is naïve, as Bell charges, only if the rationale of the modern university itself is naïve, and this, as I have noted, has not been established by Bell. This is not simply to reject out of hand the claim that moderns too easily dismiss the non-rational influences upon the development of science. It is rather a recognition that despite the fact that specific local conditions affect the development of science, there is a radical difference of character between scientific inquiry and other, non-universalizing, modes of thought. And contrary to Bell's suggestion, I do not believe Bruno Latour's understanding of modernity and science provides an adequate alternative framework for that task, as I shall demonstrate.

In *We Have Never Been Modern* (1993) Latour argues that science is not a peculiarly modern phenomenon that delineates a "modern" as opposed to a traditional society, be it primitive, ancient or medieval. Distinguishing the science of the modern West from the ethno-science of archaic cultures is unwarranted, he claims; we must not "create a divide between pre-logical and logical cultures" (112) and assume that knowledge of nature and society has only been achieved by moderns by virtue of their capacity "to distinguish between the laws of external nature and the conventions of society," in contrast to archaic cultures who confusedly mixed "the constraints of rationality with the needs of their societies" (130). Indeed, our culture, he maintains, must be studied in the same way archaic cultures are studied—anthropologically—because there is no fundamental difference between ancients and moderns (10). Modern Western culture, that is, has not "disenchanted" the world, and there is therefore no clear epistemological or rational asymmetry between the West and other cultures. There is consequently no need to be defend "the purity of science and rationality from the polluting influence of passions and interests; [nor to] defend ... the unique values and rights of human subjects against the domination of scientific and technical objectivity" (124), as antimodernists are wont to do.

Having argued that we are not and never have been modern, Latour admits at another juncture that we may have been modern but are no longer entirely so; and, further, he is clear that we are not premodern (127). To explain: "Moderns ... differ from pre-moderns by this single trait: they refuse to conceptualize quasi-objects [natural-social hybrids] as such" (112). More important, he is certain that not only are we not premodern but that we do not want to become premodern (in an effort to overcome what he sees as modernity's shortcomings). Significantly, it appears that becoming premodern would seriously hinder science.

Latour writes:

> The nonseparability of natures and cultures had the disadvantage of making experimentation on a large scale impossible, since every transformation of nature had to be in harmony with a social transformation, term for term, and vice versa. Now we seek to keep the moderns' major innovation: the separability of a nature that no one has constructed—transcendence—and the freedom of manoeuvre of a society that is of our making—immanence. (140)

Thus he acknowledges that "there is indeed a nature that we have not made, and a society that we are free to change; there are indeed indisputable scientific facts and free citizens" (140). He consequently admits that while the moderns' "nature–convention" distinction is not mistaken, its emergence does not require "an absolute distinction between the two terms and the continual repression of the work of mediation" (140). Finally he concedes: "We have been modern. Very well." And he cavils: "We can no longer be modern in the same way" (because the "asymmetrical rationality [of the Enlightenment] is just not broad enough for us" [142]).

The problems with Latour's analysis of modernity and modern science here are substantial. In addition to the difficulties created by his alternating rejections and affirmations of modernity, his understanding of the nature and role of scientific thought in the modern age is ambiguous at best (and appears at times simply to recapitulate the standard interpretation he is criticizing). Furthermore, Latour's talk of modernity with respect to twentieth-century developments is rather crude, for he fails to recognize that methodological doubt rather than certitude is a pervasive feature of modern science and critical reason. Thus even though modern science is "post-traditional," it does not pretend to replace ancient sureties with absolute scientific knowledge. This reflexive awareness in contemporary scientific thought, as Anthony Giddens points out, does in some sense confound Enlightenment expectations, but it is still a product of Enlightenment thought (Giddens 1991: 21). The lack of certitude in scientific knowledge, that is, does not permit the conclusion that science is indistinguishable from premodern modes of thought. Nor does the fact that Latour's hybrid natural–social realities are more difficult to treat scientifically than objects of nature justify his claim that moderns treat these realities as did the ancients. Given these difficulties with Latour's analysis of modern science, it is unclear what Bell thinks Latour provides the student of religion for the construction of an alternative framework for the study of religion that is neither modern nor postmodern. Indeed, Bell's own critique of the science of religion exhibits similar problems of consistency since the framework for the study of religion she seeks must apparently concede the political nature of all knowledge without rejecting the modern notion that religion can be studied neutrally.

To reject Latour's and Bell's arguments is not to deny, as Reiss points out (1982: 382), that since the last third of the nineteenth century scientific discourse has come under increasing attack. Reiss obviously is not alone in making such a claim. Many have criticized modernism as having fostered a purely instrumental (technological and economic) relationship of society to nature and thus of having excluded issues of moral and existential import. Indeed, we may be at the "nether end" of modernism's development, although Reiss counters that he is not sure that it will be displaced. Nevertheless, he claims that any attempt to displace modernism would be of benefit as it would make possible the recognition of the essentially "perspectival" nature of the human mind and so relativize science (which in turn would make possible the creation of new meaning [Reiss 1982: 382]). A "processive communicational network" discourse, he suggests tentatively, may provide such an alternative, "where fixity, discrete, denotated objects of knowledge, analytical knowledge itself, discursive transparency, objective grasp, [and] absence of the 'subject' would all be strangers" (382). He admits the danger that such a science-transcending discourse could simply become a new form of mysticism, although he does not consider this a risk too high to take (382 n. 44). Yet the danger cannot be ignored, for it could well entail a return to those overarching, normative structures of traditional thought and a betrayal of scientific knowledge about social life and its potential to transform society.

Neither Latour nor Reiss, it seems, have fully realized how uniquely successful has been the culture-transcending science that characterizes the modern world. As Gellner puts it, in matters of cognition, the intellectual style of modern science—whereby knowledge is made possible by freeing the thinker from social, political and cultural constraints—is sovereign, and a refusal to recognize "the universal diffusion, authority, and applicability of [this] particular cognitive style" is at least misguided if not actually fraudulent (Gellner 1998: 185). Gellner does admit that there are spheres of life in which science is inadequate for the resolution of problems—for example, for providing a sense of belonging, for fostering obligation and cooperation in society, or for consoling the afflicted. And he readily concedes that science's "defectiveness in these respects is as distinctive and conspicuous as is its superiority in the spheres of cognition and production" (184). He thus acknowledges that this new cognitive style has not been able to extend itself with much success into "the sphere of social and human phenomena" (191). And while leaving open to debate whether these social tasks are inherently impossible to accomplish, Gellner allows that the few successes of the extension of that cognitive style justify continued support for the development of an explanatory social science. This, however, does not excuse the ignoring of the defects of science (although the latter task is not one that can or need be taken up here). But neither do the defects of science to which Gellner refers provide grounds for an epistemology in which knowledge is gained by means of immersion in the "wisdom" of a cultural system which subordinates the individual. What is at stake is not wisdom, value and meaning, but rather knowledge.

It should now be clear why the modern scientific study of religion is—and should be—radically different from religious practice and articulate reflection on that practice (i.e., theology). The concern of a scientific study of religion is only with explanatory knowledge *about* religion and religions, even though such knowledge may have some relevance to issues of meaning in religion and the meaning of life. Such a study of religion is a cognitive undertaking rather than a religious quest, and it operates only within a "disenchanted" rather than an "enchanted" universe. Consequently, scholars who claim that the modernist debate over the "outsider" versus "insider" approaches to the study of religion is exhausted are simply wrong. Indeed, the critique of science and the modern academic study of religion obviously demonstrates that the debate is on-going. Unless we are to return to a premodern form of the study of religion, then, it is clear that the social sciences and the study of religion as a social science provide us with the only acceptable model for the study of religion in the modern public university.

Suggested Readings

Blumenberg, Hans
    1983   *The Legitimation of the Modern Age*. Robert M. Wallace (trans.). Cambridge MA: MIT Press.
    1987   *The Genesis of the Copernican World*. Robert M. Wallace (trans.). Cambridge MA: MIT Press.

Gay, Peter
    1966   *The Enlightenment: An Interpretation*, vol. 1: *The Rise of Modern Paganism*. New York: Norton.
    1977   *The Enlightenment: An Interpretation*, vol. 2: *The Science of Freedom*. New York: Norton; 1st edn, 1969.

Gellner, Ernest
    1992   *Postmodernism, Reason and Religion*. London: Routledge.
    1992   *Reason and Culture: The Historic Role of Rationality and Rationalism*. Oxford: Blackwell.
    1998   *Language and Solitude: Wittgenstein, Malinowski and the Habsburg Dilemma*. Cambridge: Cambridge University Press.

Preus, J. Samuel
    1987   *Explaining Religion: Criticism and Theory from Bodin to Freud*. New Haven: Yale University Press.
    1998   "The Bible and Religion in the Century of Genius." *Religion* 28: 3–27, 111–138.

Donald Wiebe

Reiss, Timothy J.

1982   *The Discourse of Modernism.* Ithaca, NY: Cornell University Press.

Reuben, Julie A.

1996   *The Making of the Modern University: Intellectual Transformation and the Marginalization of Morality.* Chicago: Chicago University Press.

Wiebe, Donald

1991   *The Irony of Theology and the Nature of Religious Thought.* Montreal: McGill-Queen's University Press.

1999   *The Politics of Religious Studies: The Continuing Conflict with Theology in the Academy.* New York: St. Martin's Press.

25

ROMANTICISM

Arthur McCalla

❦ ❦

Romanticism and the Study of Religion

Romanticism is a period in the cultural history of the West, principally Germany, Britain and France, in which mounting dissatisfaction with Enlightenment rationalism and empiricism crystalized into a set of alternatives to Enlightenment attitudes toward art, thought and life:

> In the 1790s, under the double impact of the final stage of the Enlightenment and the French Revolution, misgivings and doubts which had gradually begun to be felt in the eighteenth century suddenly acquired deeper and more perplexing significance. Old orthodoxies were shaken, old certainties were undermined. Weapons forged by the *philosophes* to assault superstition were now turned against their own most cherished beliefs about the sufficiency of human reason, the perfectibility of humanity, and the logical order of the universe. Problems which they had raised but left unsolved, because they were insoluble empirically, now seemed to be those which most urgently called for answers. From a tumult of anguished doubts, new convictions began to emerge—belief in the primacy of the imagination, the potencies of intuition, the importance of the emotions and emotional integrity, and, above all, the uniqueness and value of every human being in a constantly changing cosmos. (Honour 1991: 21)

The study of religion was an important part of the Romantic quest for alternatives to Enlightenment rationalism and empiricism. The Romantics rarely considered themselves "scientists of religions"; most placed themselves somewhere along a continuum from scholar to poet to prophet (several moved back and forth along the continuum). As a result, Romantic approaches to the study of religion are embedded within symbolic visions, lyric and epic poems, philosophies of history, Orientalisms, Traditionalisms and even theologies, as well as in works explicitly conceived as investigation of religion or religions.

In this essay, the Romantic study of religion is discussed under the rubrics of philosophy of religion, histories of religions, disenchanted Romanticism and the Romantic contribution to the study of religion. It treats German idealism as the philosophical wing of Romanticism, and discusses Romantic religious thought and literature only where and to the extent that they bear on the study of religion.

Philosophy of Religion

Romantic philosophy of religion may be understood as a set of responses to Immanuel Kant's critique of metaphysics and natural theology. Kant's (1724–1804) *Critique of Pure Reason* (1781) made the noumenal realm of ultimate truth inaccessible to rational knowledge. The exercise of reason is legitimate only within the bounds of experience; since metaphysics and natural theology deal with matters beyond experience, reason can say nothing about them. This does not mean that Kant had no place for religion. In his *Critique of Practical Reason* (1788) Kant argued that the legitimate locus of religion is the moral life. *Religion within the Limits of Reason Alone* 1960 [1793] extended Kant's attempt to situate religious concepts, beliefs and practices within the moral life.

Friedrich Schleiermacher (1768–1834) accepted Kant's critique of metaphysics and natural theology, but rejected his assimilation of religion to morality. In *On Religion: Speeches to Its Cultured Despisers* [*Über die Religion: Reden an die Gebildeten unter ihren Verächtern*] (1988 [1799]), Schleiermacher defined religion as an intuition or feeling of total dependence on the Infinite. This intuition or feeling of dependence is an autonomous, irreducible and universal moment in human experience that lies beneath and is the source of the positive forms of the various religions of the world. Though his analysis implies that the various religions, beneath their specific dogmas, rituals, and so on, have a common source in the natural human experience of the Infinite, Schleiermacher was a Christian theologian who, in *The Christian Faith* [*Der christliche Glaube*] (1928 [1821–1822]) and elsewhere, argues that Christianity is the highest expression of the universal experience. (On Schleiermacher, see Gerrish 1984; Welch 1972 1:59–85).

The philosophical career of F. W. J. von Schelling (1770–1854) may be divided into four major periods: transcendentalist idealism, under the influence of J. G. Fichte (to 1796); systems synthesizing the history of consciousness and nature (to 1806); the investigation, under the influence of Boehmist theosophy, of freedom, consciousness and the will, leading to a logical analysis of the dynamic ontological relations that constitute the eternal process that is God (to 1820); and the system of positive philosophy wherein he sought empirical verification for the ontological categories deduced in his logical analysis of the divine nature. The epistemological basis for all these systems is an attempt to elude Kantian epistemological pessimism by reconceptualizing reason as an intuition that permits direct apprehension of the ontological Absolute. (In the terminology of German idealism, "the Absolute" and "Spirit" are synonyms for God.)

Myth and religion play increasingly important roles in Schelling's philosophy. In the second period, in which he identified nature and the history of human consciousness as manifestations in matter and time of the self-unfolding of Spirit, myth is an expression of the creative movement of Spirit but as such is subordinate to art. In the third period, myth and religion replace art as the key diagnostic tool in analyzing the unfolding of the self-manifestation and self-actualization of God. In the fourth period, Schelling undertook a massive, uncompleted systematic history of religions as positive proof for the truth of his analysis of the divine nature. The philosophy of religion is fundamental to Schelling's third and fourth periods. Mythologies and religions are the expressions in human consciousness (including the subconscious) of the self-actualization of God. A science of religions is possible precisely because myths and religions unfold according to this essential dynamic and therefore possess a systematic character capable of discovery. Such a science of religion—irreducible to any other science because myths and religions take their structure directly from the ontological Absolute itself—requires symbolic, psychological and historical approaches that allow the investigator to discern the manifestation of the ontological Absolute in human consciousness. (On Schelling, see Tilliette 1970; Reardon 1985: 88–116; Beach 1994: 17–67.)

G. W. F. Hegel (1770–1831) agrees with Schelling that mythologies and religions are progressive expressions of the self-actualization and self-realization of Spirit within the historical process. Unlike Schelling, however, Hegel insists that religion, like art, permits only an imperfect union with Spirit because it is symbolic or representational in form whereas Spirit, or Mind, is ultimately rational. Humanity and Spirit may be truly reconciled only at the level of speculative knowledge, that is, by means of concepts rather than symbols, or through philosophy rather than religion. Religion and philosophy share the same subject matter, but philosophy treats it at a higher level. While Hegel's continuation of Enlightenment intellectualism in his valorization of concepts over symbols has led some to classify him as a theorist of Romanticism rather than a Romantic, his historicism, organicism and reconceptualization of reason as grasping the ontological Absolute are fundamental characteristics of philosophical Romanticism. (On Hegel, see Jaeschke 1990; Kolb 1992; Merklinger 1993.)

In Britain, Samuel Taylor Coleridge (1772–1834) responded to Kant's challenge to religious knowledge by distinguishing between understanding and reason. His distinction, a variation of Schelling's reconceptualization of reason, concedes that Enlightenment rationalism, or the understanding, cannot attain ontological truth but insists that another human faculty can. This faculty, the "organ of the supersensuous" that directly apprehends ontological truth, is reason or imagination. This epistemology, while consistent with literary Romanticism, including the great poetry of Coleridge's early collaboration with William Wordsworth, underlies his approach to religious knowledge in later theological works such as *Aids to Reflection* (1825). Reason or the imagination produces subjective knowledge of the interpenetration of the finite and the Infinite. (On Coleridge, see MacNiece 1992; Perkins 1994; Reardon 1985: 29–58.)

Schleiermacher, Schelling, Hegel and Coleridge treat religion as a distinctive part of culture, a body of symbols and experiences that are set off from other symbols and experiences by their relative capacity to manifest the Infinite in the finite. By approaching the study of religion through an analysis of human consciousness and experience and the symbolic products expressive of that consciousness and experience, the Romantics transformed Enlightenment discourse on natural religion and shifted the focus of the philosophy of religion away from rational defenses of the content of revelation and to the identification of the distinctive character of religious experience, religious language, or religious practice vis-à-vis other cultural phenomena. In so doing they founded an important strand of modern philosophy of religion (see Proudfoot 1987: 309–310; Despland 1979: 488–507).

Histories of Religions

In terms of pages written, the preponderant genre of Romantic study of religion is the history of religions. German philosophical idealism, whether Hegelian or Schellingian, points to the data of the history of religions as the empirically demonstrable exemplification of the unfolding of the self-actualization of Spirit.

Hegel's Berlin lectures on the history of religions (1821–1831) identified the mythological and religious traditions of humanity as unique moments in the dialectical evolution of Spirit, and classified them from magic to Christianity according to their increasing perfection (see Hegel 1984–1987). Hegel's conceptual approach to the history of religions was taken up, with epochal effect, by David Friedrich Strauss in *The Life of Jesus* (1835) and Ludwig Feuerbach in *The Essence of Christianity* (1857 [1841]), both of whom read Christianity itself as a mythology. But with these works, which equate mythology with illusion and error, we have broken with Romanticism. So Hegel's posterity does not belong in this essay; it is rather Schelling, for whom mythology embodies spiritual truth, who both wrote and inspired the most influential Romantic histories of religions.

Schelling, in the second period of his philosophical career, considered art to be the principal expression of the creative movement of Spirit and, accordingly, he showed little interest in the history of religions. Other scholars, however, attempted to fill out the transcendental metaphysics of his philosophy of nature with the positive content of the history of religions. The most notable attempts were made by Joseph von Görres (1776–1848) and Friedrich Creutzer (1771–1858). Görres' *History of Asiatic Mythologies* [*Mythengeschichte der asiatischen Welt*] (1810) presents the history of religions as a record of the progressive separation of humanity from Spirit. Görres identifies the primitive religion of humanity—the original self-revelation of Spirit—as a pure monotheism and locates it in ancient India. Over time this primitive monotheism progressively degraded into the diverse beliefs, practices and doctrines of the world's religions. Though degenerate, the mythologies and religions of all peoples preserve remnants of the primitive revelation of Spirit. These remnants, and something of the original self-revelation of Spirit, are recoverable for modern humanity through a hermeneutic of myth. (On Görres, see Bürke 1958; Feldman and Richardson 1972: 381–383.)

Creutzer took his friend Görres' diffusionist account of a pure Indian monotheism successively corrupted into polytheistic mythologies as the historical framework for his widely-read *Symbolism and Mythology of Ancient Peoples* [*Symbolik und Mythologie der alten Völker*] (1810–1812). Creutzer, however, modified Görres' history of religions on the philosophical level by declaring that the original self-revelation of Spirit took symbolic form. Symbols preserve the primal union of Spirit and matter (Nature) by holding the Infinite and finite in indivisible unity; myth provides commentary on symbols. On the historical level, Creutzer's volumes describe how wandering Indian priests transmitted the pure primitive monotheism to all other ancient peoples. Because, however, these ignorant peoples proved incapable of grasping the purely symbolic religion, the priests provided illustrative stories—myths, rites, mystery cults—that at once convey and distort the content of the symbols. The various polytheisms therefore possess a core of truth, albeit now severely distorted. Christianity, in turn, refocused the divine truths diffused among the various paganisms. Modern mythography, according to Creutzer, similarly reconstructs the primitive monotheism by retrieving the traces of truth preserved in the various mythologies. (On Creutzer, see Feldman and Richardson 1972: 387–389.)

The privileging of India in Görres' and Creutzer's histories of religions reminds us that Romanticism drew on and contributed materially to what has been called the Oriental Renaissance. Though the Oriental Renaissance, a creation of philologists, linguists, archeologists and explorers as well as poets and philosophers, is neither identical to nor co-terminous with Romanticism, its attempt to renew the intellectual life of the West by broadening its cultural resources beyond the classical and Hebrew sources recognized by the

Enlightenment was seized on and exploited by Romantics from the early works of Novalis and Friedrich Schlegel (who declared "it is in the Orient that we must seek the highest Romanticism") to the late works of Victor Hugo and Jules Michelet. When, however, these writers discuss Indian religions, they tend to interpret them in light of their own beliefs. The translations of excerpts from the *Ramayana* and the *Bhagavad Gita* included in Schlegel's *On the Language and Wisdom of India* [*Über die Sprache und Weisheit der Indier*] (1808), for example, give them a strongly monotheistic tone. (On Oriental Renaissance and Romanticism, see Schwab 1984; Gérard 1963.)

Schelling's opinion of the history of religions had changed dramatically by the time he began to work on his positive philosophy. He had long since come to agree with Creutzer (Schelling largely ignored Görres) that the history of religions possesses philosophical value. Beginning with the treatise, *On the Deities of Samothrace* [*Über die Gottheiten von Samothrace*] (1815), and continuing through his "historico-critical" studies of mythology and religion comprising the *Philosophy of Mythology* [*Philosophie der Mythologie*] (1842) and *Philosophy of Revelation* [*Philosophie der Offenbarung*] (1841, both published posthumously in 1854), Schelling now attempted a comprehensive analysis of the history of religions as at once a narrative of the life of God revealed in and through the world process and empirical verification for the dynamic structure of God's eternal nature previously deduced through his logical analysis.

Philosophy of Mythology arranges the mythologies and religions of the ancient world into a history of religions according to the degree to which each manifests the progressive actualization of the divine nature. The entire mythological process is fulfilled and completed in the attainment of a three-in-one Supreme God in the Eleusinian Mysteries (Zagreus, Bacchus and Iakchos are recognized as three different manifestations of Dionysus). The attainment in the Mysteries of a three-in-one Supreme God brought the Greeks to the threshold of an explicit formulation of absolute monotheism and prepared the classical world for the reception of the Christian revelation. Revelation is necessary because myth, while it intuits divine unity and ultimate spiritual harmony, is incapable of fully expressing human freedom. Schelling identifies Judaism as the transitional phase from mythology to revelation. The disclosure of the person of the Father is the first fulfillment of mythological anticipation; yet, while Judaism signals the end of myth, it is incomplete revelation because the Son must still appear as man to actualize the truth. *Philosophy of Revelation* presents Christianity as the fulfillment of the history of mythology. In his Munich lectures on the positive philosophy (1827–1841), Schelling sketched a third epochal transformation in the theogonic process: from revelation to the philosophical religion of Spirit. Just as revelation presumed mythology, philosophical religion presumes the Christian revelation because it is Christ who opens the possibility of the final era of full freedom. The age of the Spirit, as the fulfillment of the actualization of God's life in history, will bring history to a close and restore fallen human consciousness. (On Schelling's history of religions, see Beach 1994; O'Meara 1982; R. Brown 1977.)

In France, the idea of primitive revelation gave rise to a set of histories of religions analogous to those worked out in Germany. As in Germany, it served to combat the doctrines of the Enlightenment, but in France, especially in its initial use in the works of the Catholic Traditionalists, the content of the primitive revelation was explicitly identified with the doctrines of the Catholic Church.

Louis de Bonald, Joseph de Maistre and the early Félicité de Lamennais, linking the Protestant Reformation, the Enlightenment and the French Revolution in an unholy trinity of cause and effect, identified rationalism and individualism as the enemies of religious truth and socio-political stability and proclaimed the authority of the Catholic Church as the sole bulwark against both intellectual and social anarchy. Though Catholic Traditionalist epistemology substitutes the authority of revealed tradition for the Romantic faculties of speculative reason, intuition or imagination, Traditionalism is intimately linked to contemporaneous Romanticism not only by its opposition to the Enlightenment but by its historicism and organicism. Catholic Traditionalist histories of religions accordingly are structurally similar to German idealist histories of religions.

Louis de Bonald's (1754–1840) history of religions, which must be pieced together from *Theory of Political and Religious Power* [*Théorie du pouvoir politique et religieux*] (1796) and *Primitive Legislation* [*Législation primitive*] (1802), is built on the Traditionalist principles of a universal primitive revelation and its transmission through language to all humanity. Bonald claims to rectify Enlightenment ideas of natural religion—whether Charles de Brosses and Nicolas-Antoine Boulanger's immoral and cruel affront to human reason or Jean-Jacques Rousseau's interior faith arising from the innate goodness of uncorrupted human beings—by showing that natural religion, properly understood, is the knowledge of God and of the immortality of the soul revealed to earliest humanity through language. While all peoples of the world received through primitive revelation and language the same natural religion, the corrupting power of the imagination has produced the diverse beliefs and practices encountered by missionaries and travelers. For the proper development of natural religion Bonald points to Judaism and Christianity. The Judaic religion, he says, is only natural religion developed in a manner appropriate to the needs of a particular society and the character of a certain people. Christianity is the Judaic religion fully developed, perfected and fulfilled so that it is appropriate for all societies, for all peoples, for all times. Bonald understands natural religion, Judaism and Christianity as the three sequential ages of monotheism, or the religion of the unity of God. There has therefore been only one true religion in the world since earliest times (paganisms are corruptions of true religion, not independent religions). And since Christianity is the fulfillment of the one true religion, the Christian truths must have been present in natural religion as the plant is present in the seed; conversely, Christianity must be both as old as the world and the universal religion of humanity.

Bonald's history of religions rests almost entirely on logical reasoning and is rarely supported with historical evidence. Félicité de Lamennais (1782–1854), who buttressed Traditionalism with his philosophy of "general reason" or "*sensus communis*," devoted the third and fourth volumes of his *Essay on Indifference to Religion* [*Essai sur l'indifférence en matière de religion*] (4 vols, 1818–1823) to compiling historical evidence for the existence of a universal primitive revelation and its transmission though the ages. After Lamennais abandoned Traditionalism in the late 1820s Augustin Bonnetty's journal, *Annales de philosophie chrétienne* (founded 1830) served as the primary voice of Traditionalist history of religions. (On Catholic Traditionalist histories of religion, see Derré 1962; McCalla 1998.)

The affinity of Traditionalism with Romanticism is confirmed by the fusion of Catholic Traditionalist and German idealist histories of religions by Ferdinand d'Eckstein ("baron Sanskrit"). Eckstein (1790–1861) published in Paris his own journal, *Le Catholique* (1826–1829), to which he gave the subtitle: "a periodical devoted to the universality of knowledge through the unity of doctrine." The linguistic, philological and mythographic studies published in *Le Catholique* bear witness to the existence of a universal primitive revelation, or natural religion, that carries within itself the eternal religious truths, that is corrupted into idolatry, and that develops through Judaism to its fulfillment in Christianity. For Eckstein, as for the Catholic Traditionalists, the principle of unity implies that Christianity is the universal religion. But whereas the Traditionalists used this logic to laud Catholicism, Eckstein used it to defend the spiritual value of Oriental religions. Not only do all religions retrain traces of the primitive revelation but the farther back one goes in a given tradition the purer—because closer to the original revelation—these traces will be. Hence, the religions of India, widely considered in the Romantic period the most ancient religions, are our best guide to the primitive revelation. Moreover, since Christianity participates in primitive wisdom as its highest expression, the religions of India are compatible with, and indeed essentially identical to, Christianity. Eckstein pointedly refers to the religions of the ancient world as "anterior Christianity." (On Eckstein, see Burtin 1931.)

A final example of a French Romantic history of religions grounded on the idea of primitive revelation is that of Pierre-Simon Ballanche (1776–1847). Ballanche's philosophy of history, worked out in a series of works collected under the overarching title of *Essays on Social Palingenesis* [*Essais de Palingénésie sociale*] (1827–1831), contains a history of religions in which the sequence of religions marks the intellectual, social and spiritual development of the human race. What is notable about Ballanche's history of religions is that the divine truth that is contained in the primitive revelation and that unfolds over the course of the positive religions of the world to its fulfillment in Christianity is the doctrine that humanity successively overcomes the effects of the Fall through social progress and by means of suffering endured within the historical process. Ballanche accordingly identifies the history of religions with specific phases of social progress; the Saturn–Jupiter–Bacchus sequence of divinities in Greek mythology, for example, is a symbolic expression of the three social orders through which all peoples of the ancient world passed in the course of their development. (On Ballanche, see McCalla 1998.)

Ballanche is a transitional figure between two phases of French Romanticism. Beginning in the late 1820s and increasingly after the July Revolution of 1830 some French Romantics disengaged their intellectual and aesthetic project from the political royalism and Catholic orthodoxy with which it originally had been allied. The politically liberal and often anticlerical French Romanticism of 1830 incorporated the Enlightenment ideals of liberty and social progress into the Romantic program of historicism, organicism and transcendence; its motto was "progress under the guidance of providence." This shift in the nature of Romanticism is as evident in histories of religions as in other intellectual or literary forms. An exemplar of this new sort of Romantic history of religions already existed in the form of Benjamin Constant's *On Religion, Considered in its Origin, its Forms, and its Developments* [*De la Religion, considérée dans sa source, ses formes et ses développements*] (5 vols, 1824–1831).

Constant (1767–1830) first approached the study of religions from the critical perspective of the Scottish Enlightenment, intending a work along the lines of David Hume's *Natural History of Religion* 1957 [1757]. Subsequent encounters with German philosophers and Swiss pietists having modified his critical attitude toward religion, Constant increasingly emphasized individual feeling and conscience as the essence of religion. *De la Religion* correspondingly evolved into an account of the emergence out of external religious forms of religious *sentiment*, understood as the universal and overwhelming need of human beings to communicate with superior spiritual forces. Depicting the various religions of the world, with their rituals, doctrines and institutions, as transient, superficial and authoritarian shells for the enduring, innate and liberating religious *sentiment*, Constant's history of religions traces a progressive development from sacerdotal, authoritarian religions, in which religious *sentiment* is largely suppressed, to non-sacerdotal, open, progressive religions in which it is given free rein. The modern phase of this development marks the decline of traditional religions as shells for religious *sentiment* and the emergence in their place of a public morality embodied in social and political institutions. Constant argues that continued religious evolution in post-Revolutionary France requires the abandonment of Roman Catholic orthodoxy, with its dogmas, priests and coercive support from the restored

Bourbon monarchy, in favor of an undogmatic, tolerant faith based on the religious *sentiment* of individuals. In short, the political liberalism that was emerging in early nineteenth-century France manifests the current stage in the evolution of religious *sentiment* that is the history of religions. (On Constant, see Fontana 1991; P. Thompson 1978; Hogue 1964.)

Constant was familiar with the mythographies of both Creutzer and Schelling, but whereas the German Romantics considered symbol and / or myth as permitting the grasp of spiritual truths inaccessible to discursive reason, Constant's history of religions traces the decline of symbol and myth in favor of morality and interior feeling. Constant's history of religions was picked up and further rationalized in the literary work of the 1830s of Alphonse de Lamartine (1790–1869). In *Travels in the Orient* [*Voyage en Orient*] (1835), *An Angel's Fall* [*La chute d'un ange*] (1836) and *Jocelyn* (1838), Lamartine combined the Enlightenment values of reason and liberty with Constant's notion that in the course of intellectual progress doctrines and religions become obsolete. Religions, Christianity included, are way-stations along the path of humanity's intellectual progress. (On Lamartine, see Bénichou 1988: 21–109; Hunt 1941.)

That humanity, in the course of its intellectual, social and spiritual development, supersedes outworn religions is also the basis of Edgar Quinet's (1803–1875) history of religions. He dramatized this view in his 1833 prose epic, *Ahasvérus*, before publishing his lectures on the history of religions as *The Genius of Religions* [*Le génie des religions*] (1841). Quinet's version of human progress is the story of a ceaseless struggle for liberty, first of human tribes against the necessity of Nature, then of reason against dogma and sacerdotal systems and finally, in modern times, of individuals against despotisms that seek to restrain their moral self-determination. The shift from history of religions to social and political history merely marks, as for Constant, a new phase in a single, providentially-directed process of perfectibility. Quinet's conviction that civil society arises out of religion and political and social revolutions extend humanity's understanding of the divine purpose allow him to present his study of contemporary political history, *Christianity and the French Revolution* [*Christianisme et la révolution française*] (1845), as the continuation of his history of religions. (On Quinet, see Aeschimann 1986; Hunt 1941.)

The histories of religion discussed in this section, despite their differences, have certain fundamental elements in common—and it is these elements that make them *Romantic* histories of religions. (1) Teleological developmentalism: Romantic histories of religions subordinate their empirical data to a teleological organic developmentalism according to which the preexistent essence of humanity unfolds according an *a priori* pattern. (2) Reductionism: by interpreting their empirical data in light of a teleological developmentalism, Romantic histories of religions reduce the multiplicity of religious phenomena empirically encountered in the world to a single, unified transcendent order.

They then claim this data as empirical corroboration for the reality of that transcendent order. (3) Historicization of figurism: Romantic histories of religion historicize the venerable Christian exegetical mode of figurism. Non-Christian religions, instead of being read as inferior parallels of the Christian revelation, become stages in the unfolding of religious truth. In this way the Romantics vastly expanded the category of sacred history to include both non-Christian religions as "anterior Christianity" and the works of the Romantics themselves as the expression of religious truth in the modern period.

Disenchanted Romanticism

The Romantic approaches to the study of religion outlined so far are, like the poetry and other cultural products of high Romanticism, expressions of an epistemological optimism, or the conviction that human beings possess extra-rational faculties that permit direct apprehension of the metaphysical order or the divine will for humanity. This optimism was maintained by some Romantics (Victor Hugo, above all), but in France from the 1830s and increasingly in the 1840s a new wave of Romantics began to doubt both that their imaginative or intuitive insights truly correspond to metaphysical reality and that human history is a providentially-guided ascension. Writers like Charles Nodier (1780–1844) and Gérard de Nerval (1808–1855)—whom Honoré de Balzac dubbed the "School of Disenchantment"—perceived an abyss between the promises of high Romanticism and their own experiences. It is this abyss that separates the faith of Creutzer or Schelling or Ballanche or Quinet that the study of mythologies discloses spiritual truth from Nerval's decision to entitle his collection of sonnets on mythological themes *Chimaera* [*Les Chimères*] (1844–1854). Imagination and intuition retain their privileged status for these disenchanted writers, as do the favored Romantic devices of metaphor, symbol and myth. But whereas they formerly revealed metaphysical reality by expressing the Infinite in the finite, these devices are now used to explore the nature of human creativity, knowledge and religiosity. The disenchanted view draws out something inherent in high Romanticism. In reflecting on their own historicity, the high Romantics linked world-views to historical eras and thereby prepared for the loss of their cherished ideals in the movement of history. (On disenchanted Romanticism, see Bénichou 1992.)

Disenchantment in no way reduced the Romantic interest in religion. Nodier and Nerval investigated, both as scholars and as seekers, a wide range of religious traditions, including esotericism and popular superstitions. Nerval, when accused of having no religion, famously replied that he had at least seventeen. Nevertheless, for the disenchanted Romantics the study of religion is no longer the logical analysis of the eternal divine nature, the substitution of religious experience for rational theology, or the tracing of the unfolding of

Spirit or of God's plan for humanity through the history of positive religions. In place of these high Romantic approaches to the study of religion the disenchanted Romantics treat religions as sets of narratives and images, produced by the innate human impulsion to create forms, purporting to mediate between humanity and the transcendent or metaphysical realm. But because the correspondence between these religious forms and metaphysical reality is at best uncertain and at worst illusory, the sacred, rather than signifying an ontological presence, points to an ontological absence and an epistemological crisis. Disenchanted Romantic study of religion directs attention away from the assertion of metaphysical truth and toward the forms—narratives, symbols, images, codes—in which such assertions are expressed (see Despland 1994: 144, 149). The result is what we may identify as a second Romantic philosophy of religion. Disenchanted Romantic philosophy of religion retains the high Romantic emphasis on cultural forms and religious experience, but shifts the focus from their metaphysical referent to analysis of the forms and the experience themselves.

The Romantic Contribution to the Study of Religion

Mainline Enlightenment thought about religion attributed its origin to the domination of wonder, fear and imagination over reason in the first human beings. The continued existence of such manifest absurdity was attributed to the ignorance of the masses and its usefulness in maintaining the despotisms of church and state. Enlightenment theorists of religion explained religion by reducing it to fantasies about the natural world (naturalism) and/or history (euhemerism). The high Romantics retained these loci for the study of religion, but countered Enlightenment rationalist reductionism by re-attaching them to ontology: nature and history become the realms in which Divinity expresses or reveals itself. From the present-day perspective of the study of religion as the naturalistic description and explanation of a certain set of human practices and representations, the Romantics in some respects represent a step back from Enlightenment study of religion inasmuch as they renounced naturalistic explanation and subsumed the study of religion within religious thought itself. In other respects, however, the high Romantics contributed importantly to the development of this perspective. Romantic philosophy of religion integrated religion into the cultural expressions of humanity and established the philosophical concept of religion within the autonomous effort of humanity to understand itself. Romantic histories of religions, expressions of the fundamental Romantic values of historicism and organicism, similarly add a historical and, especially in France, social dimension to the study of religion absent from Enlightenment approaches. Further, they integrated Eastern and aboriginal religions, including newly recovered languages and texts, into the study of religion, directed attention to symbol and myth and established comparison based on developmental pattern.

In the early nineteenth century a flood of philological, epigraphic, linguistic and archeological discoveries transformed the study of religion. As examples, rather than an exhaustive list, we cite the translations from Avestan by A. H. Anquetil-Duperron and from Sanskrit by William Jones, the decipherment of Egyptian hieroglyphics by J. F. Champollion, the textual criticism of Buddhist scriptures by Eugène Burnouf and the comparative grammar of Franz Bopp (see Pinard de la Boullaye 1922: 228–238). While these works of erudition were carried out primarily outside Romanticism, the Romantic interest in religions as the cultural expressions of spiritual truth contributed greatly to the establishment of an intellectual climate that supported and encouraged them.

If, however, Romantic interest in myth and religion encouraged these studies, their ultimate effect on Romantic approaches to the study of religion was devastating. Until about 1840 the work of Creutzer, Schelling and other high Romantics continued to be widely praised, imitated and translated. While Creutzer, for example, had been attacked in the 1820s and 1830s by J. G. J. Hermann, J. H. Voss and C. A. Lobeck for what they called his mysticism, and by Otfried Müller for exaggerating the influence of the India on Greece, his influence on a younger generation of mythographers was maintained and strengthened outside Germany by a French translation of his principal work. J. D. Guigniaut's translation of *Symbolism and Mythology of Ancient Peoples* [*Religions de l'antiquité, considérée principalement dans leurs formes symboliques et mythologiques*] (1825–1851), in which Guigniaut amended and supplemented Creutzer's work in light of contemporary scholarship, was a notable event in French mythography. Jules Michelet credited Guigniaut with thereby founding the study of religion in France, while Ernst Renan hailed him as the renewer of mythological studies in France. It was only from the 1840s, in the work of scholars such as Alfred Maury, Ernst Renan and F. Max Müller, that the sun finally set on Creutzer's system. Applying the work of the philologists, linguists, archeologists, and so on, these and other scholars demonstrated that high Romantic histories of religions were based on fanciful etymologies and symbolisms in the service of preconceived metaphysical frameworks. It is precisely in opposition to such approaches to the study of religion that Müller proclaimed his approach as the Science of Religion.

Romantic histories of religions unquestionably subordinated their empirical data to *a priori* teleological metaphysics. Nevertheless, the denunciations of the *soi-disant* scientists of religion must not be permitted to obscure either their own indebtedness to the Romantics (Schelling played a crucial role in Müller's intellectual formation) or the real advances contained in Romantic histories of religions.

While Romantic histories of religions did not survive mid and late nineteenth-century attacks, the philosophies of religion of which they were the empirical exemplification underlie several highly influential twentieth-century approaches to the study of religion. The characteristic Romantic assertions of religious experience as an autonomous, irreducible and universal intuition or feeling of the Infinite, of human cultural expressions as the medium through which divine revelation is mediated, and of the various religions of the world as the positive forms in which the essence of religion manifests itself, are fundamental to the work of Nathan Söderblom, Rudolf Otto, Friedrich Heiler, Gerardus van der Leeuw, William Brede Kristensen, Paul Tillich and Joachim Wach, among others. The neo-Romanticism of these scholars of religion, salient differences among them notwithstanding, is principally attributable to the influence of Schleiermacher and Schelling.

Creutzer has similarly enjoyed an afterlife as the inspiration for later approaches to the study of religion. The most notable example of the continuing influence of Creutzer in the later nineteenth century is Johann Jakob Bachofen (1815–1887). Bachofen explicitly declared, in *An Essay on Ancient Mortuary Symbolism* [*Versuch über die Gräbersymbolik der Alten*] (1859), that "myth is the exegesis of the symbol" (1967:48). The twentieth-century philosophies of symbolism of Aby Warburg, Ernst Cassirer, Paul Ricoeur and Karl Kerényi pick up this tradition. In the twentieth century, the principal advocate of Creutzer's approach to the study of religion has been Jan de Vries. Contrasting the dominion of *ratio* over emotion and imagination in the objective approach of later nineteenth-century positivists and evolutionists with the visionary, intuitive approach to religion of the Romantics, and Creutzer in particular, Vries decries the spiritual impoverishment of a rational approach to the study of religion and advocates a study of religion in the Romantic mode, only purged of its factual errors (Vries 1967: ix, 61, 220).

Twentieth-century neo-Romantic study of religion reacts against critical approaches that treat religions as human phenomena that are to be explained naturalistically. This essay has argued that the Romantics, their metaphysical presuppositions notwithstanding, contributed importantly to the development of post-Enlightenment critical study of religion. It is difficult to make the same argument for the neo-Romantics. While they have unquestionably encouraged interest in the field, their resubordination of the study of religion to high Romantic ontology and epistemology has undermined the status of the study of religion within the modern university.

And yet the influence of Romanticism on contemporary study of religion need not be detrimental. The work of a Nodier or a Nerval, in which the sacred points to an ontological absence and attention is drawn away from the assertions of doctrines and beliefs and toward the forms in which they are expressed, brings us to the heart of postmodern reflection on absence and narrativity. Julia Kristeva, for example, devotes a chapter of *Black Sun: Depression and Melancholy* to Nerval's "El Desdichado," the first poem in the *Chimaera* collection. The poem's images of a black sun, a dispossessed prince, a ruined tower symbolize a past that is lost, and recoverable, if at all, only in poetry. Religious doctrines and beliefs, like the rest of humanity's symbolic resources, offer modern men and women the melancholy experience of the absence of an absolute authority. In the absence of a transcendent referent, meaning must be sought in a constantly negotiated relationship of texts to individuals (Kristeva 1987: 152–182). Contemporary studies of religion that focus on absence and narrativity (see Despland 1994) apply, often to the Romantics themselves, an approach to the study of religion pioneered by the disenchanted Romantics.

Suggested Readings

Abrams, M. H.
  1971   *Natural Supernaturalism: Tradition and Revolution in Romantic Literature*. New York: Norton.
Beach, Edward Allen
  1994   *The Potencies of God(s): Schelling's Philosophy of Mythology*. Albany: State University of New York Press.
Charlton, D. G. (Ed.)
  1984   *The French Romantics*, 2 vols. Cambridge: Cambridge University Press.
Despland, Michel
  1994   *Reading an Erased Code: Romantic Religion and Literary Aesthetics in France*. Toronto: University of Toronto Press.
Feldman, Burton and Robert D. Richardson
  1972   *The Rise of Modern Mythology, 1680–1860*. Bloomington: Indiana University Press.
Hunt, Herbert J.
  1941   *The Epic in Nineteenth-Century France*. Oxford: Blackwell.
O'Meara, Thomas
  1982   *Romantic Idealism and Roman Catholicism: Schelling and the Theologians*. Notre Dame, IN: University of Notre Dame Press.
Reardon, Bernard M. G.
  1985   *Religion in the Age of Romanticism*. Cambridge: Cambridge University Press.
Schwab, Raymond
  1984   *The Oriental Renaissance: Europe's Rediscovery of India and the East, 1680–1880*, Gene Patterson-Black and Victor Reinking (trans.). New York: Columbia University Press.
Smart, Ninian, John Clayton, Patrick Sherry and Steven T. Katz, (eds)
  1985   *Nineteenth-Century Religious Thought in the West*, 3 vols. Cambridge: Cambridge University Press.

26

POSTMODERNISM

Johannes C. Wolfart

It seems that even commonplace concepts in the study of religion defy the delimitation, identification and classification which are themselves the defining feature of any "Guide to the Study of Religion." Probably, this has something to do with the incongruity of religious traditions and that tradition of encyclopedic enterprises in which such a guide stands. Generally religious knowledge and the knowledge contained in modern handbooks are considered two entirely distinct species. Certainly the modern university—for all intents and purposes a living, breathing encyclopedia—traditionally did not make place for the study of religion. In more recent decades that has changed and many universities and colleges have established religion departments, as distinct from theological faculties, on the basis that a modern knowledge about religion, as distinct from religious knowledge, is possible and even desirable. This has not been uncontroversial, even within the academic field thus constituted, and many departments have experienced rifts over the appropriateness of a variety of non-theological approaches to religion. Nonetheless, the present *Guide* is conceived wholly in accordance with that "modern" attitude to the study of religion.

Moreover, the editors have ordered this essay on "postmodernism" under the sub-heading "location," in recognition of the extreme difficulty of a strictly modern approach to this particular topic. In fact, in certain modernist quarters the decision to locate rather than "define" would be taken as an unwarranted accession to postmodernist criticism. And yet the *Guide* remains essentially modern in its purpose as a classificatory analysis of the study of religion. Indeed, in certain postmodernist quarters the declaration of a purpose itself would be taken as a fatal concession to the constraints of modernism. And so one might identify a second nexus of confutation in our modernist approach to "postmodernism" within the field of the Study of Religion: the ambivalence of postmodernism to modernism.

The difficult relations of the modern study of religion to both theology and the category of religion as traditionally constituted are relatively well rehearsed (for extensive recent discussions also McCutcheon 1997; D. Wiebe 1999). Likewise, the debates between modernists and postmodernists which still raged in the academy less than a decade ago, are now largely fossilized and widely anthologized (see, for example, Bové 1995; for an overview of implications for the study of religion see Bell 1996). What remains virtually unexplored, however, is the symbiotic agency of traditional theological and postmodern conceptions of religion. This symbiosis, moreover, amounts to much more than a politically expedient alliance of two groups bent on attacking the modern academic study of religion. Rather, from a historian's point of view, all three knowledge systems—traditional religious, modern and postmodern—interact within the confines of a modernity which is much more expansive than is generally recognized. Thus there is a very real historical affinity of traditional (almost exclusively Christian and predominantly Protestant) theology and postmodern epistemology. The rest of this essay explores the historical and historiographical conditions of that affinity.

Postmodernism and "Modernism"

So what is postmodernism? Scholarly opinions vary widely and range from the banal correctness of Alister McGrath's: "A general cultural development, especially in North America, which resulted from the general collapse in confidence of the universal rational principles of the Enlightenment" (McGrath 1995: 404) to the quite unscholarly illumination of Ernest Gellner's assessment: "metatwaddle" (Gellner 1992: 41).

In fact, one might consider, in the manner of a postmodernist, that there are as many postmodernisms, or "readings" of postmodernism, as there are observers. Yet what all postmodernists appear to share is a self-conscious rhetoric of epistemic rupture or intellectual revolution. In this, at least, proponents of postmodernism are very much like the humanists of the Renaissance or the rationalists of the Enlightenment. That is, much like their Renaissance or Enlightenment predecessors, postmodernists appear to validate their intellectual positions with reference to an exterior reality marked by the passage of the world from one age to another. In this manner all postmodernisms are the function of a particular historiographical operation. Three things should be noted in this regard.

1. The success of this operation demands the meticulous establishment of a previous age as distinct from one's own. Just as the champions of the Renaissance created the image of the medieval "dark ages" or Enlightenment men of reason claimed to be leaving behind ignorance and superstition, so postmodernists differentiate their own age, the postmodern, from the modern age on the basis of very particular constructions of the latter.

2. The imagined mode of progression from one age to another is just as significant as the invention of discrete ages. The Renaissance humanists subscribed to a classical Greek model, usually associated with the works of Thucydides and Polybius, which described a cyclical chronological progression of the ages. Thus they considered their age, which they dubbed "re-birth," not so much a new age as an old age reborn. By contrast, postmodernists do posit the progression of the ages in linear, teleological or even eschatological terms. Granted, many postmodernists would fiercely resist being labeled "new agers." Yet few would deny that various so-called new-age conceits are part and parcel of the "postmodern condition" (see below). Moreover, the widespread adherence to linear models of chronological progression, marked by the near universal application of the "post-" prefix (as in post-industrial, post-capitalist, post-structural, post-modern), reflects the influence of Judeo-Christian sacral chronologies. Here it is worth noting, for example, that the recent *HarperCollins Dictionary of Religion* (J. Z. Smith 1995), while it contains no entry for either "poststructural" or "postmodern," does cover "postdiluvial."

3. The rhetoric or conceit of epistemic rupture or intellectual revolution is just that: a construct. Thus it is now widely accepted that many Renaissance humanists had as much in common with the medieval schoolmen as they did with the academics of antiquity (Kristeller 1974; see also Bietenholz 1985–1987). Luther's theological breakthrough, which traditionally marked the beginning of the Reformation, has also been contextualized in terms of both late medieval scholasticism and popular religion (Oberman 1963, 1989; Ozment 1971, 1980). Likewise, the heroes of the eighteenth-century Enlightenment were engaged primarily in thoroughly unenlightened battles along lines drawn in accordance with confessional or religious allegiances. For example, John Locke was bluntly dismissive of the critical remarks on his *Essay Concerning Human Understanding* (1690) published by the Cambridge neo-Platonist theologian John Burnet. Nevertheless, Burnet was not alone in his mistrust of Locke's empiricism, being joined apparently by significant portions of the English public, as well as foreign luminaries such as Leibniz. The impression of a Lockean rupture was nonetheless established over the course of the following centuries. One suspects that this has as much as anything to do with the suppression of his critics' work: Leibniz's criticisms were not published in English before 1981 and Burnet's attack remained unpublished until 1989 (Watson 1989: 9–19). It should come as no surprise then, that postmodernists engage rather than simply reject or supersede the modern age in a number of important ways.

For at least three reasons, therefore, any discussion of postmodernism must take into account the modern as it is viewed by postmodernists. There is some considerable scope for confusion here, since the term "modern" is put to two very different uses in contemporary scholarship. In the first instance it is used by literary critics, art historians, architectural theorists, musicologists and the like to describe formal cultural and stylistic developments in the early part of the twentieth century. Broadly these developments were marked by a reaction against the imperial-age aestheticism of the Edwardians or Wilhelmians. This rejection is widely considered a consequence of the traumatic disillusionment experienced by the "lost generation" of World War I. The works of James Joyce, Wassilij Kandinsky, Le Corbusier and Arnold Schönberg are all considered seminal in this regard. Since their work was marked by a rigorous, often austere, attention to fundamental form at the expense of ornament, the postmodern reaction has been marked by stylistic promiscuity and exuberant ornamentation. Inasmuch as the modern style was a function of World War I, the postmodern style might be related to the trivialization of that experience by the excesses of World War II and the Nuclear Age. This postmodern tendency was first remarked in architecture, especially in North America, and it is in this form that it remains publicly most visible.

Enlightenment-Centered Modernity and the Historicist Critique

A quite different sense of the term "modern," however, is that understood by historians, historians of science, philosophers and the like. Their critical use of the modern—and the postmodern reaction—profoundly affects the study of religion. Generally historians agree that some time around 1500 C.E. the outlook of Europeans ceased to be medieval and began to be increasingly ... well ... "modern." Economic historians point to the development of commerce and the accumulation of capital, social historians to increasingly urban social formations, political historians to the bureaucratization and centralization of the state, church historians to various forms of reformation, historians of science and technology to geographic discoveries, the spread of printing and the publication of Copernicus' theory. The list goes on. Obviously, one great attraction of a "modern age" concept which encompasses the last five hundred years is its ability to absorb the widest range of existing historiographical schemes. Yet this concept of the modern is more than simply a convenient name for a variety of historiographies forced to cooperate institutionally. These historiographies are already linked by the same implicit assumptions, especially the idea of a "progression of the ages" itself, established by the joint influence of schemes of world history first developed both in the Renaissance and the Reformation. These schemes, whose influence continues through the agency of canonical courses in "Western Civilization," "History of Religions" and the like, all locate a predominance of change over continuity sometime in and around 1500 C.E. In this sense there is an historical reality to the historiographical concept of the modern: the *idea* of progression from one age to another has certainly had its historical effects. Yet, in their eagerness to target the Enlightenment many observers—including extremely influential ones such as Hans Blumenberg, Michel Foucault, Thomas Kuhn and Perry Anderson—have reduced a complex of historiographical imaginations, past and present, to a simple historical reality. That is, they have proceeded in many instances as if the "modern age" itself was an extended historical event.

In his *Legitimation of the Modern Age* (1983) Blumenberg argued that a superior modern epistemology, fundamentally more legitimate than its predecessors, emerged sometime around the middle of the second millennium. Blumenberg's work is largely an engagement with Karl Löwith's "secularization" thesis, which posited the endurance of largely Christian theological modes in the acquisition and expression of historical knowledge (Löwith 1949). Blumenberg's interest appears to be less a critique of Löwith's thesis than a refinement and extension of his central idea to include the canons of scientific knowledge. He expressed this orientation in *The Genesis of the Copernican World* (1987), which more or less overtly theologized the acceptance of heliocentrism, long considered a harbinger of secular science, and for Blumenberg the marker of the beginning of the modern age.

Michel Foucault's work, especially his *Archeology of Knowledge* (1972), is much more widely read, especially in the North American academy, than that of Blumenberg. Foucault argued, chiefly on the basis of examples from classificatory literature, that some time around 1500 C.E. European epistemology shifted its focus from similarity to difference. This change ultimately resulted in the preeminence of mental operations grounded in the production of rigid and uniform identities, on the one hand, and intolerance and exclusion, on the other. Of course terms such as *"identity," "intolerance," "exclusion,"* and so on, are today habitually associated with social dynamics. And indeed, Foucault did seek to disclose what he regarded as the fundamental connection between social and epistemic formation. Perhaps his most celebrated work remains that on social definition, for example *The Birth of the Clinic* (1973b) or *Discipline and Punish* (1977a).

At first glance Hans Blumenberg and Michel Foucault appear to have very little in common, especially ideologically. Furthermore, where Blumenberg was interested chiefly in the epistemology of the natural sciences, Foucault interrogated the somewhat more diverse knowledge of what we might term "human sciences" or "social sciences." Yet both of them were interested in establishing a longer history of modern, scientific knowledge than that which had dominated the Western academy since the eighteenth century. Moreover, Blumenberg and Foucault both took aim at a model of scientific knowledge which was ontological and fixated on a somewhat mysterious critical juncture known as the "Enlightenment." Instead of an eighteenth-century revolution in Western thought, Foucault and Blumenberg both posited much earlier—and perhaps even more fundamental—changes in European modes of knowing. But where Blumenberg tried to locate the scientific Enlightenment within the confines of a much broader modern age of theological design, Foucault's relocation was based on an explicitly un-theologically and determinedly anthropological model. For him the impulse to knowledge of the dominating kind was to be understood in terms of a basic human impulse to dominate. Thus Foucault coined the term "power-knowledge," in adaptive allusion to Nietzsche's infamous "will-to-power," to describe the driving force behind the tandem emergence of *both* modern epistemology *and* modern social relations.

While Blumenberg and Foucault thus approached modernity with entirely different agendas, they shared a basic premise: a simple relocation of the revolutionary juncture in Western thought to an earlier time, a move which nonetheless entailed the conservation of the concept of intellectual revolution or even breakthrough. In a particular and important way, therefore, they shared an approach, one which I call "historical idealism."

A very different critical approach is exemplified by the efforts of Thomas Kuhn and Perry Anderson. Once again, these two represent very different ideological inclinations. Compared with Blumenberg and Foucault, however, they share a destructive attitude to the very concept of Enlightenment, at least insofar as this is conceived as a unique revolution in thought or modes of knowing.

Kuhn's *Structure of Scientific Revolutions*, first published in 1962 (Kuhn 1970), is now widely considered one of the foundational texts of the History of Science. Kuhn posited that scientific knowledge is subject to some of the same forces (cultural, institutional, political, etc.) which determine social relations. Since these forces are largely inertial, there are no radical ruptures or revolutionary scientific "discoveries" in the common sense. Instead knowledge and society together progress by incremental adjustment; enough adjustments might in the long run add up to a significant shift which could, ultimately, warrant or necessitate the adoption of what Kuhn called a new "paradigm," or general theoretical model. Grossly simplified, then, Kuhn recast scientific revolutions as effects—as opposed to causes—of historical change. Consequently, while in Kuhnian terms the eighteenth century may well be the site of a paradigm shift of revolutionary significance, that shift is to be properly located historically somewhere within an "extended" modern age (Kuhn 1970: 7). Likewise Perry Anderson's *Lineages of the Absolutist State* (1974) recast political absolutism, long understood as a theoretical determinant of state formation in the seventeenth and eighteenth centuries, as a logical consequence of long-range political and economic developments. Like many of his generation of British historians, Anderson was influenced by the work of Karl Marx. Thus the concentration of political authority, often seen as an act of will, intellectual or otherwise, on the part of monarchs such as Louis XIV ("l'état, c'est moi"), was explained by Anderson in broader, conjunctural terms. Logically, the reaction to absolutism, normally claimed as the province of the Enlightenment, would have to be understood in much the same terms. According to Anderson the last several centuries of the so-called *ancien régime* were marked by a dialectical relationship of aristocracy and bourgeoisie. In these terms the intellectual values we now associate with the Enlightenment are simply the synthetic ideological outcome of this class competition.

Thus Blumenberg, Foucault, Kuhn and Anderson, each in his own way, undertook to historicize the knowledge revolution called the Enlightenment, the central feature of a genesis myth which legitimizes the modern academy and its product. Yet where Blumenberg and Foucault simply relocated the beginnings of modern thinking, Kuhn and Anderson criticized the conception of knowledge as a causative force in historical change or even as an autonomous historical entity. As a result of both of these broadening approaches to the modern age, the legitimacy of three propositions associated with the Enlightenment in particular have come under fire: the definitive knowability of things (i.e., *the truth*); the knowability of things by the application of the five senses (i.e., *empiricism*); and the higher knowledge attained by the application to sensory knowledge of innate human cognitive abilities (i.e., *reason*). It is worth noting the unlikelihood that any of the four authors discussed above sought to attack any of the above propositions *per se*. In fact all four of them managed highly successful academic careers, suggesting aptitude for a game whose rules remain largely defined by the above propositions. In other words, they were all thoroughly "modern" in their outlook, even as they all reformed the meaning of that word. This assessment is potentially controversial only in the case of Foucault, who has become a hero of the postmodernists, some of whom wish to claim him as one of their own. Yet even in the opinion of Hayden White, his most significant English interpreter, Foucault remains not only but also a representative of the thoroughly modern French Structuralist movement (White 1978: 230). Moreover, in their success these modernist critics of modernism have attracted many academic admirers and imitators of lesser finesse and agility, many of whom have taken to distinguishing themselves as "postmodernists."

Hermeneutic Critiques of the Enlightenment

These critics are joined by followers of a very different and more direct critical assault on modernist epistemology. Once again, the work of four individuals— Ferdinand de Saussure, Ludwig Wittgenstein, Jacques Derrida and Richard Rorty—illustrates a general theme underlying a range of positions here. As suggested above, historicists potentially undermined the legitimacy of modernism by fiddling with the parameters of its own Enlightenment myth, especially the timing and nature of the all-important transformation in modes of thought (mythic legitimacies are notoriously susceptible to apparently minor changes). By contrast, certain philosophical trends, especially in the philosophy of language, directly challenge the particular content of modern epistemology in terms of the three propositions already outlined. Because of their predominant interest in interpretative meanings, proponents of this direction have been identified generally as "hermeneuticists." They have also been called, with some justification, "textualists." The common critical claim that they are "cognitive relativists" or "anti-realists" is perhaps too simplistic since, as has been widely observed, most of them have learned to tie their own shoelaces. That is not to say that certain aspects of the textualist argument have not been taken to absurd extremes. Yet while the moral responsibility (*à la* Socrates) of the master for the exuberant excesses of his pupils remains an open question largely as a matter of canonical convention, the direct causal connection between expression and reception cannot be established. Hence even the harshest critics of postmodernism, such as Christopher Norris, are careful to distinguish between the position of Jacques Derrida and his postmodernist disciples, first and foremost among them Jean Baudrillard (Norris 1992: 20).

In fact, Norris points out that Derrida has a very strong relationship to modernism, especially in his epistemology, which does not question the validity of truth claims *per se*, but rather the wisdom (one suspects from the point of view of the maintenance of any credible truth concept whatsoever) of claims to absolute certainty (Norris 1992: 46). This affords Derrida a basis for his famous critical technique of "deconstruction," which, Norris is at pains to point out, bears no resemblance to the sensational anti-realism or relativism / nihilism peddled by garden variety postmodernists like Baudrillard (Norris 1992: 35–38).

Indeed, it seems that what Saussure, Wittgenstein and Rorty all share with Derrida—a point not widely appreciated by their postmodernist admirers, nor by their detractors—is that they are all linguistic determinists, either by default or by virtue of their skepticism, depending on how you look at it. "Linguistic determinism" is used here in a sense other than that normally understood by linguists and often associated with the work of Benjamin Lee Whorf (Whorf 1956; Lucy 1992). Instead, for textualists the realities of language are neither necessarily nor predictably related to the realities of extra-linguistic worlds. As a matter of practical choice as much as anything else, therefore, textualists treat reality, insofar as they treat it at all, only as linguistic reality. Meanings are real, if anything is; and in some instances only meanings are real. Critics apparently take this to mean that reality is simply always linguistically *mediated* and so rendered philosophically irrelevant. What is the point, they say, of second-hand knowledge of the axiomatic referent? But textualists are not so foolish as to insist on a foundational condition which is not really foundational at all. What they do say, however, is that if language ultimately determines our reality, it does so indeterminately. That is, regardless of whether language is foundational or not, it cannot be objective or stable. This is the basic point of the semiotic theory attributed to Saussure, in which meaning never inhered in either the signifier or the signified, but in an arbitrary union of the two as sign (Saussure 1983 [1916]). Likewise, for Wittgenstein the authority of the referent object receded entirely in the practice of his famous "language games" (Brand 1979).

In recent years linguistic determinism has been applied most flamboyantly by Jacques Derrida and Richard Rorty. On the surface these two have much in common. Derrida conjures with a practical textualism in which entire worlds are constructed, deconstructed and reconstructed as "mere" texts. Rorty conceives the import of all linguistic operations not in terms of their reference or relevance to objects, but rather in terms of their rhetorical character. Together Derrida and Rorty have probably received the lion's share of credit and blame for the philosophical development of postmodernism. Yet in their respective ideological and institutional contexts they are actually very different. Rorty has been widely identified as a neo-pragmatist, a label which he shares with other American intellectuals who claim the ability to transcend the ideological polarizations of the Cold War era. Of course the adoption of a trans-ideological position is by no means neutral, ideologically speaking. Nor was it when the first school of American pragmatists had its heyday, in the greatest age of American economic imperial expansion. Likewise there is quite a good fit between Rorty's neo-pragmatism and the interests of neo-conservative Global Marketeers (Rorty 1968, 1982; Saatkamp 1995). The interaction of Derrida with his political surroundings is quite different. While he appears to have left behind the terms of critical debate established in the successes of intellectual Marxism in France in the 1960s and 1970s, he has definitely not abandoned criticism (Derrida 1976, 1992, 1997). Certainly his textualist practices allow for characteristically sharp observation and commentary. More importantly, however, his insistence on the fundamental indeterminacy of language and the radical plurality of meanings is a direct challenge to enduring French cultural and political elites who still exercise unique authority through the agency of the Académie Française and the integrated national education system. The marked contrast to the American situation—where post-revolutionary attempts to harness linguistic identity to the interest of the state faded rapidly after the pioneering efforts of Daniel Webster—does not fully explain the difference between Derrida and Rorty. It should be noted that there is a living tradition of American Marxist ideological criticism, which includes the work of Kenneth Burke, Fredric Jameson and Frank Lentricchia. It is not difficult to imagine why this has received scant attention compared to Rorty's neo-pragmatism.

Lineages of the Relativistic State

Since the late 1970s various attempts at fusing historicist and hermeneutic approaches have exerted their influence in the humanities and social sciences.

Works such as Hayden White's *Tropics of Discourse* (1978) raised considerable interest in the narrative dimensions of knowledge. What has become known as the "linguistic turn" practically swept through those disciplines which had also witnessed the greatest excesses of structuralism and quantitative methods. For example, Marshall Sahlins' anthropology made fundamental use of what he perceived as the diachronic or narrative character of cultural structures. For Sahlins epistemology itself was first and foremost a serial effect (Sahlins 1981, 1985). In history, too, the linguistic turn and the promise of a *return* to narrative was immediately embraced as a relief from the increasingly abstract "cliometrics" of the 1960s and 1970s (Stone 1979).

But none of this tells us very much about "postmodernism" *per se*, nor how it has affected the study of religion. Both depend largely on the three major critical streams in modern scholarship discussed above and how their constructions or destructions of the old myth of Enlightenment are received in various quarters. Taking Fredric Jameson's formulation of Jean François Lyotard's famous working definition of postmodernism as "incredulity toward metanarratives" (Lyotard 1984: xxiv), one might expect religion and postmodernism to relate antipathetically. But as Talal Asad's work highlights, not all metanarratives are created equal. It is moreover in a zone defined by competing metanarratives—basically competing ideologies of church and state—that proponents of religious positions and postmodernists find themselves in close sympathy.

Certain political cultures which we might call "modern revolutionary," in particular the political ideologies of the United States and the Soviet Union, have exercised inestimable influence on the academy in this regard. In the latter case the official atheism of the Communist Party was enforced more or less effectively from shortly after the Russian Revolution until the terminal crisis of Party government in the early 1990s. This policy was generally reflected, one assumes, in the shape of the academy. Significantly, in the post-revolutionary politics of the United States the anti-confessional arguments of the Enlightenment were also absolutized. The salient consequence for American political culture is the infamous liberal exclusion from the public sphere, in the name of toleration, of those ideologies and institutions deemed "religious." It should be noted that while this did not entail any official state atheism, it did have profound implications for the place of religion within the academy. Judging by the venerable criterion of numismatic evidence, Americans never officially relinquished their trust in God. In practice, however, the professional associations representing academic disciplines—for example the American Historical Association—have excluded anything smacking of religion since they were established in the nineteenth century (Rothberg 1998).

Yet this coincidence of the interests of the modern state with Enlightenment secularism is not nearly as axiomatic as Asad (1993) implies. Certainly U.S. and Soviet models of the academy have dominated the world since 1945, but as regards matters of religion their influence has been neither total nor straightforward. In Canada, for example, the political culture generally values the toleration credited to the privatization of religion in the Enlightenment. Yet public education with overt confessional orientation continues to thrive at the same time. In the Federal Republic of Germany the situation is stranger still. After World War II the allied powers established an American-style constitutional state. Yet the allies also encouraged, again influenced by the Americans, a public role for religious ideologies and institutions. These were to serve both as an expurgative of fascism and as a bulwark against communism, both of which were notoriously godless (i.e. "modern"). Thus the new German state maintained, at least in some jurisdictions, confessional public education supported by an opt-out system of tithing fully integrated with the mechanism for income taxation. The party which dominated national government from 1949 to 1990 and beyond, moreover, identified itself as "Christian Democratic." In the eighteenth century this might have appeared somewhat contradictory; in the late twentieth century it is merely "postmodern." In any case, critics of public life in the Federal Republic of Germany—first and foremost among them Jürgen Habermas—reacted to what they see as a reactionary compromise with vigorous reformulations of modernism. Not surprisingly Habermas has also produced one of the most effective and persistent critiques of postmodernism (Habermas 1981).

The situation in the North American academy is quite different. Here a reaction to the *status quo* has taken the form of an attack on every exposed flank of the Enlightenment academy (and there are many). In recent years many observers have, like Alister McGrath, conflated these critical approaches to a single "postmodernism." In reality, however, they emerged in the 1970s as a variety of distinct critical discourses, most notably feminism and what was then called Black Studies. Since that time postcolonialism, a plethora of ethnic studies, diverse approaches in gender studies, and so forth have joined the list of fields which take as their mandate a study of the "Other" from a "subjective" point of view. The overall advantage, institutionally speaking, of the postmodernists is that in their interpretation of these critical perspectives one need not be "Other" to study the same. Thus postmodernists have been able to domesticate more overtly confrontational discourses, thereby establishing both themselves and these discourses in a notoriously inertial academy. Certainly the peculiar political dynamics of the academy have played a crucial role in this process, a point made by E. Gellner in his wicked formulation of a postmodernist academic motto: "Sturm und Drang und Tenure" (Gellner 1992: 41).

The reactionary potential of postmodernism has long been a mainstay of modernist critiques, especially in Britain, where a shared language and a spate of hiring to offset a "braindrain" granted North American postmodernism an easy entry (Callinicos 1990; Norris 1992). Yet the realization of that potential to date has gone largely unremarked in the academy in general. Not so in religion departments across North America. Here postmodernism has been a hot topic for some time, for reasons which only appear relatively straightforward. From its inception as an academic discipline, the study of religion has been split, one might say, between the spiritually illuminated and the intellectually enlightened. That is, the discipline has been the shared province of both traditional subjectivists (including theologians) and modern objectivists. Because the academy as a whole existed on an intellectual basis and within a political context both of which were firmly objectivist, the subjectivists were once genuinely beleaguered. All that has changed. In 1984 Mark C. Taylor published *Erring: A Postmodern A / Theology* and the response was terrific. In 1985 the *Journal of the American Academy of Religion* (*JAAR*) contained not a single article or review relative to postmodernism. By 1986 an entire issue revolved around a symposium held to discuss Taylor's work. Since that time *JAAR*, the *Journal of Religion* and similar organs have published a steady stream of discussion, not of postmodernism and *religion*, but of postmodernism and *theology*. Mark C. Taylor remains the undisputed master of the "field" and his own output remains steady. In addition he also edits a series *Postmodernism and Religion* for the University of Chicago Press (interested readers can get a hypertextual taste-test at http://www.press.uchicago.edu). The impression one gets from this work is one of simple hope that postmodernism will permit miraculous transcendence of those debates concerning modernism and religion in which many departments have become hopelessly mired (Grassie 1997). Yet there has also been dissent. One of the first critical responses came from Huston Smith. He added to his well-known critique of modernism the charge that postmodernism simply could not grasp the ontological transcendence which Smith, following William James, considers constitutive of religion (H. Smith 1990). More recently other criticism has come from the side of modernists who have restated the objectivist position with great conviction and have attempted to mount a "cognitive re-turn" to surpass the "linguistic" one (Benavides 1997; Segal 1997).

In general, however, the increasing incidence of the buzzword "pluralism" in the titles of articles and books under review bespeaks an enamorment of the field with the disappearance of critical judgment. The political significance of this tendency, moreover, appears not to have gone entirely unnoticed (Kamitsuka 1996). While some religionists embrace this development—as per Gellner's scathing commentary—simply to advance their own careers, others are obviously in pursuit of less personal agendas. They are nonetheless equally opportunistic: under the cover of postmodern pluralism (or, at least, relativism) they are seeking to reestablish theological judgments as intellectually creditable and otherwise legitimate determinants of public life. George Marsden is perhaps the best-known, but by no means the only, advocate of this position. According to Marsden's *The Outrageous Idea of Christian Scholarship*, current pluralistic principles dictate that "faith-informed scholarship" must be recognized by public universities, especially since these have already accorded standing to women's studies and gay studies (Marsden 1997: 10–13). The argument departs from an initial sleight of hand: Marsden conflates the specific critical perspectives (which, it has already been suggested, are thoroughly modernist in any case) of, say, feminism with perspectivalism in general. From this Marsden then reextracts the legitimacy of other uncritical or "faith-informed" perspectives. Anyone acquainted with Marsden's work over the last decades will hardly be surprised, either by his agenda or by his rhetorical abilities. His equation of Christians with other persecuted minorities charging systemic injustice and seeking "empowerment" will also fail to startle even casual observers of the cultural politics of Middle America. What is somewhat astonishing, however, is the warm welcome Marsden has received in the North American academy in general. For example, shortly after the appearance of *The Outrageous Idea* the *Chronicle of Higher Education* carried an extensive positive review article entitled "A Welcome Revival of Religion in the Academy" (Wolfe 1997).

This susceptibility to Marsden's particular brand of special pleading can be related to more general intellectual—as opposed to recent American political—history. It is my concluding argument that the history of modern thought, conceived in the broadest terms, has both shaped postmodern arguments and has conditioned a postmodernist predisposition, albeit in many cases an unwitting predisposition, to theological rhetoric. My explanation therefore goes well beyond Marsden's expectation that postmodernism has rendered a whole generation psychically impotent (for a brilliant spoof of postmodernist intellectual paralysis see Leyner 1997). Instead, it suggests the historical formation of a distinct postmodernist vocabulary and, more importantly, a postmodernist mode of self-legitimation which draw heavily on early modern Protestant traditions.

This is not to obscure that approach, adopted primarily by writers of residual materialist inclination, which appears to draw legitimacy for postmodern discourse from the observation of corresponding external social, cultural, economic and political realities: "the postmodern condition" (Lyotard 1984; D. Harvey 1989; Jameson 1991). By far the most common strategy of late, however, has been simply to establish legitimacy for postmodernism by identifying intellectual lineages or academic histories as alternatives to the myth of an Enlightenment-centered modernity. As a general rule these alternative histories emphasize a time formerly treated conjointly by historians as Renaissance-Reformation. In the last twenty years or so the term "early modern" has come into use as a more neutral label. For our purposes the salient point about the period is that it preceded the Enlightenment. Moreover, the Enlightenment can be seen as a dual reaction, both positive and negative, to the early modern world. For example, in Renaissance humanism champions of the Enlightenment located the roots of their religious toleration; the phase of confessional warfare immediately following the Reformation they cast as a reason for turning away from religion. So it is not without complication that postmodernists today tout their sympathy with the early moderns as a thoroughgoing disavowal of the Enlightenment. Certainly most North American postmodernist scholars, at least those outside of the study of religion *per se*, appear keen to maintain an appearance of enlightened secularity. Thus the early modern interest in rhetoric, various—including purely ludic—textual practices, stylistic and other historical allusions, and so on, which many postmodernists claim as their heritage, are located strictly in the Renaissance and apparently not in the Reformation (for an exception to the rule, see Wojciehowski 1995). Yet inasmuch as the Enlightenment was a response to the most unfortunate consequences of the Reformation, one would expect a retrograde rejection of the Enlightenment to entail certain engagements with the Reformation as well as the Renaissance. In any case, the distinction between the two halves of the early modern age today seems rather less clear to historians than it did only a few decades ago.

What this emphasis on Renaissance and neglect of Reformation does, in effect, is belie the considerable contribution to postmodernism of explicitly theological or even "religious" concepts and expressions. This particular early modern heritage remains largely unexplored and can here only be adumbrated. According to E. Gellner the one unifying substantive characteristic of postmodernism is an obsession with something called "meaning" (Gellner 1992a: 22–26). For this reason postmodern practice in general has been called, among other things, hermeneutical. Yet hermeneutics, as it was practiced by, say, the Greeks or the Fathers of the Church, was primarily cultic and explicitly privileged. The unrestricted access to meaning, proliferation of interpretative perspectives and its consequences (i.e., "polysemia") did, however, figure largely in the Reformation. Yet Luther and others who were ultimately credited with establishing Protestant confessions did so chiefly by attempting to control the democratic hermeneutic tendencies of the so-called Radical Reformation (Williams 1962). Thus Luther's highly successful *Small Catechism* of 1529 was an attempt to put the genie of scriptural interpretation back in the bottle. Nearly all articles were followed by the odd didactic interrogative—"Was *ist* das?" ("What *is* that?"; possibly related to the Latin commonplace *id est*)—which severely limited interpretative perspective. Yet in certain instances even Luther could not avoid altogether the risk of hermeneutic reflection on the "meanings" of particular words or rituals, hence: "Was *heißt* Amen?" ("What does Amen *mean*?") and "Was *bedeutet* denn solch Wassertaufen?" ("What does such water baptism *signify*?") (Luther 1958 [1529]: 3–13, emphasis mine; Kohls 1980).

Of course most postmodernists would be quick to point out that they consider the linguistic theory of Saussure to be more significant, despite its apparent post-Enlightenment modernism, than the rhetorical genius of Luther or the rebel peasants' *Twelve Articles of the Upper Swabian Peasants* (Baylor 1991: 231–238). Yet it seems that the gulf separating them may be rather smaller than one would expect—it may not even amount to a very small enlightenment. What attracts postmodernists to Saussure is his theory's ability to suspend, or even to transcend, the otherwise apparently intractable mutual opposition of idealism and realism. Yet the exact same problem was tackled by every theologian of the Reformation, in the quest for the meanings of the eucharist. Notoriously, the question of the balance of the real and the ideal in the eucharist emerged as the only stumbling block to agreement between Luther and Zwingli at the Colloquy of Marburg. (Incidentally, Alister McGrath's summary of the dispute is the site of one of the more significant typographical errors or polysemic incidents in the history of publishing. According to McGrath, Luther and Zwingli failed to agree at Marburg: they "were unable to agree on the meaning of such phrases 'this is my tody' [sic] (which Luther interpreted literally, Zwingli metaphorically)" [McGrath 1988]). In any case, eucharistic theories proliferated throughout the sixteenth century, but by the 1630s it was possible for an anonymous commentator to classify eucharistic theories in accordance with a scheme which cast as *Zeichen* (sign) the eucharistic tension between bread and wine (signifier) and the divinity (signified). Moreover, production of meaning or signification—*Bedeutung*— was determined by no fixed relationship of sign to signifier, with opinions ranging along a whole spectrum of possibilities. The shared Swiss provenance of the most radical theory of theological signs and Saussure's theory of linguistic ones should be considered purely coincidental, yet their similarity is remarkable. To this day, moreover, the work of avowedly secular post-modernists is loaded with theological concepts which have served as equivocations of real experience and transcendent expectation in the long and varied history of Christianity. Thus, for example, James Dicenso's meticulous Derridaean critique of Mark C. Taylor's theology must rely, for better or for worse, on concepts with considerable theological pasts, such as "hypostasis" (Dicenso 1992: 39–40).

So what does this tell us about "religion and postmodernism"? That they are perhaps inextricably linked historically, via the traditions of Protestant Christianity. Moreover, that they are certainly linked historiographically, insofar as postmodernists legitimize their repudiation of the Enlightenment with reference to an early modernity. That George Marsden's attempt to harness the postmodernist repudiation of Enlightenment secular hegemony to a Protestant Christian agenda, while it may be an expedient, is no accident. Moreover, in its intrinsic dependence on modes of extracting "meaning" which are religious (if only because they cannot be of the Enlightenment), postmodernism can be considered no less hegemonic than modernism. Thus it has become possible to make pretensions to "authentic" postmodernism (Raschke 1990). On a more than incidental note: the simultaneous distinction and confusion of the *authentic* and the *authoritative* (homophony notwith-standing, these terms have entirely distinct Greek and Latin etymologies) is an early modern conceit which allowed people to claim precisely what they claim they were not claiming.

Finally, we must be mindful of the pharmacologists' commonplace that all medicines have two effects: those we know about and those we don't know about. In the case of the postmodernist remedy for the Enlightenment, it turns out that the revaluation of theological judgments is a real, if unintended, consequence. Now that we know about the serious side-effects, perhaps postmodernism should come with a warning: "May impair your ability to operate intellectual machinery safely. If you are postpositively pregnant consult your metaphysician. Do not mix with alcohol."

Suggested Readings

Appleby, Joyce et al. (Eds.)
1996 *Knowledge and Postmodernism in Historical Perspective*. New York: Routledge.
Bell, Catherine
1996 "Modernism and Postmodernism in the Study of Religion." *Religious Studies Review* 22: 179–190.
Gellner, Ernest
1992a *Postmodernism, Reason and Religion*. London: Routledge.
Grassie, William
1997 "Postmodernism: What One Needs to Know." *Zygon* 23: 83–94.
Habermas, Jürgen
1981 "Modernity Versus Postmodernity." *New German Critique* 22: 3–14.
Jarvis, Darryl S. L.
1998 "Postmodernism: A Critical Typology." *Politics and Society* 26: 95–142.
Lyotard, Jean François
1984 *The Postmodern Condition: A Report on Knowledge*. Geoff Bennington and Brian Massumi (trans.). Minneapolis: University of Minnesota Press.
Norris, Christopher
1992 *Uncritical Theory: Postmodernism, Intellectuals and the Gulf War*. London: Lawrence & Wishart.

27

DISCOURSE

Tim Murphy

"Discourse" is a unique theoretical construct in that it throws both the object of scientific analysis and that analytical activity itself into question in one and the same gesture. For to look at discourse means to look at both the object of analysis, the text, culture, speech under study, as well as the way in which the scholarly analysis itself is put into discourse. Discourse theory, then, opens the question of the very foundations of its own enterprise.

Three intellectual currents merge in the historical formation of discourse theory. First, the New Rhetoric school, exemplified in the work of such theorists as I. A. Richards and Kenneth Burke, extended the traditional domain of rhetoric to encompass the very manner in which acts, motives, scenes, and so forth, were put into discourse. They argued that rhetoric was not merely a passive instrument to express a writer's content, but was itself an active force in structuring the form of discourse. Second, Russian formalism, especially in the work of Mikhail Bahktin, brought literary discourse to the foreground as an independent object of study in itself. Formalism sought to show that discourse functioned autonomously, and could not be reduced to social, psychological or autobiographical factors. Third, the structuralist revolution was the largest single catalyst in the formation of a science of discourse. The initial insight of structuralist linguistics of the autonomy of language as a system (*langue*) from concrete instances of speech acts (*parole*; see Saussure 1983) and the subjects who perform them was quickly applied to the study of literary texts. Together, these three trends colluded in going against Romantic theories of writing as coming from "within" the author, or historicist textual interpretation, which saw the text as a product of its context. Discourse emerged as a distinct theoretical entity.

All of this history converged in the 1960s in the intellectual scene in France. Here we find the major figures in the propulsion of discourse theory from a school of literary analysis to being a contender for a major methodological school in the human sciences. Michel Foucault, Jacques Lacan and Roland Barthes, along with Julia Kristeva, must be counted among the founders of discourse theory. Together, they launched a program of applying the insights of discourse theory to a wide variety of the human sciences, for example, psychoanalysis, film, photography, literature, culture, philosophy, biology, linguistics and economics. Although many theoretical and philosophical questions emerged unanswered by this labor, its net effect was to change the way many scholars understood their own research.

This group of thinkers spawned a second generation of scholars. The main achievement of this group of scholars was to apply the methods developed earlier to specific disciplines. Thus, for example, Hayden White (1978, 1987) applies insights from Barthes and Burke to the discourse of the historical text, showing how tropology lies at the very structure of narrative, and James Clifford (1986, 1988) applies discourse theory to the ethnographic text, showing how the form of the text itself determines what it can and cannot represent. Thus, in ethnographers' writings on "other" people we do not see the native other, as if through a window, but we see the ethnographer and the science of ethnography itself, as if in a mirror.

Tzvetan Todorov (1981: 3–6) has explained the distinctness of discourse theory by contrasting it with two other approaches to texts (or signifying practices generally). Discourse theory is not hermeneutics. The latter attempts to rename the meanings of the text, that is, to condense the text to a second set of meanings, meanings which nevertheless are "faithful" to the text. Neither is discourse theory to be mistaken for "the science of literature." This science attempts to explain the coming-to-be of the text on the basis of some domain of reality outside of the text. Thus, psychoanalysis will explain the text in terms of the author's psyche; Marxist criticism will explain the text as an effect of class struggle, and so forth. Whereas hermeneutics tries valiantly to stay within the text's own reference, the science of literature begins and ends outside the text to tell the story of its causation.

Discourse theory may be understood as a midpoint between these two approaches. Like hermeneutics, discourse theory deals with the text as a relatively autonomous object. Like the science of literature, however, it understands the text to be a product of something which cannot be said strictly to reside within the text, but rather within which the text itself resides. This other, which is both within the text and without it, is *discourse*. As such, discourse theory "is therefore an approach to literature at once 'abstract' and 'internal'" (Todorov 1981: 6). That is, discourse as ensembles of language, constitute the text (i.e., are inside it), but the text itself is made up of braids of discourse which both precede the text and lead out of it.

The term "discourse" in discourse theory is used in two different ways, never fully distinct, yet conceptually and analytically they can be differentiated. On the one hand, discourse may simply refer to language ("discourse" in the more common sense of the term); on the other hand, the meaning of the term may be extended to designate not just language systems but any unified, coded or systematic practice of signification. So, discourse as a distinct theoretical object may either be generically defined as "groups of words greater than the sentence" or, when defined more theoretically, as

> a perspective of quotations, a mirage of structures; we know only its departures and returns; the units which have resulted from it (those we inventory) are themselves, always, ventures out of the text, the mark, the sign of a virtual digression toward the remainder of a catalog ... they are so many fragments of something that has always been *already* read, seen, done, experienced; the code is the wake of that *already*. (Barthes 1974: 20)

The text cannot be seen as a self-contained system of signifiers and signifieds, for its system of meanings draws upon a series of preexistent meanings, meanings of formulae, tropes, clichés, conventions, genres, taxonomies, myths, characters, histories, ideologems and other historical-cultural-semantic items. A particular text comes into being as an ensemble of discourses, as "a multi-dimensional space in which a variety of writings, none of them original, blend and clash. The text is a tissue of quotations drawn from the innumerable centers of culture" (Barthes 1977a: 146). The specific text, then, is *parole* to the *langue* of discourse.

The effect of discourse on the theoretical apprehension of the text is absolutely basic: "in their interweaving, these voices (whose origin is 'lost' in the vast perspective of the *already-written*) de-originate the utterance" (Barthes 1974: 21). The meanings of the text are diffused out of the author's pen and the physical bounds of the book and into the cultural codes of the "already." This is not to say that discourse makes texts indeterminate. Rather, discourse makes texts irreducibly plural. They can be seen as indeterminate only if plurality itself is seen as a principle of indetermination while unity or convergence is seen as the sole criterion for meaningfulness. Discourses, although they cannot be reconstituted fully, are *known* because they are specific, though difficult to isolate because they tend to blend into, draw upon, and entail other discourses.

Take, for instance, debates over the sources of the New Testament. Scholars argue that we can find historical influences from Platonism, Stoicism, Gnosticism, mystery religions, Jewish apocalypticism, and even early rabbinic Judaism. Typically, a scholar will argue for the more or less exclusive influence of one of these factors on a particular section of the text. Discourse theory would see all of these as the "already" of the text, that is, those fragments of discourse which precede the text, and of which the text is itself composed. Consequently, the text is plural: it is an ensemble of all of these discourses, each sometimes more and sometimes less foregrounded. Discourse theory would refuse to reduce the text to its social context, for that too is plural, nor would it reduce the text to the author's intentions. Finally, mere etymology of terms, as in traditional biblical exegesis, would not suffice, because the terms derive their meaning by their place within a specific, historical discourse.

As noted, discourse need not refer to language or verbal texts. Many theorists have extended the idea of discourse to include any system of interrelated meanings, regardless of the specific form these take. Thus, one can analyze types of behavior, clothing, furniture, architecture, painting and so forth, and find discrete sets of meanings which manifest themselves in these objects, which pass between them, and which make them significant. Bruce Lincoln has done this with ritual:

> Like myth, ritual is best understood as an authoritative mode of symbolic discourse and a powerful instrument for the evocation of those sentiments (affinity and estrangement) out of which society is constructed. The differences between the two, although hardly negligible, are in large measure a matter of genre, ritual discourse being primarily gestural and dramatic; mythic discourse, verbal and narrative. (Lincoln 1989: 53)

Ritual performs its characteristic effects by means of transmitting a distinct set of coded meanings. Those who participate in the discourse of the ritual understand its meanings and therefore "get" its message. These messages are conveyed not by language, but by symbolic, coded behavior in combination with symbols. The ritual embodies and acts out a discourse (or discourses). For example, Lincoln shows how the ceremonial features of the Feast of Tara in medieval Ireland symbolically replicates the structure of society. Rituals express social relations and norms in indirect ways, and these help foster social cohesion.

Roland Barthes has given a similar analysis of fashion. Fashion, he says, "appears essentially—and this is the final definition of its economy—as a system of signifiers, a classificatory activity, much more a semiological than a semantic order" (Barthes 1990: 208). Although clothing clearly has a non-linguistic function, it also signifies. The fashion system is that system of relations in which the meaning of signifiers of clothing lives. Ultimately, Barthes says, the signified of fashion is Fashion itself. Although developed out of ordinary material, a "real garment," as Barthes calls it—its *being*—is this signification. In other words, within the signifying system of Fashion, the *purpose* of the garment is not to clothe someone but to signify Fashion itself, and along with it, those values and that social status that attend those who are judged to be "fashionable." The garment is not merely "natural," or utilitarian; it is semiotic.

Discourse theory, however, moves beyond a method of analysis of signification in that it argues that discourse is the means by which the world is socially constructed. Discourse theory developed at the same time and, indeed, was a principal means for the critique of traditional theories of representation. Neither language nor the mind is seen as a mirror which reflects the essential content of reality. Instead, both are seen as productive activities which construct the objects that they apprehend. Discourse theory has argued that this happens at two levels: at the level of verbal discourse, the text constructs its object; and at the sociological level, society is constructed in and by discourse.

Michel Foucault was one of the first theorists to argue that discourses, including scientific discourses, do not mimetically re-present their objects. Rather, the objects of scientific analysis and inquiry are products of discourse and discursive displacements. Using the example of the science of biology, Foucault argues:

> Historians want to write histories of biology in the eighteenth century; but they do not realize that biology did not exist then, and that the pattern of knowledge that has been familiar to us for a hundred and fifty years is not valid for a previous period. And that, if biology was unknown, there was a very simple reason for it: that life itself did not exist. All that existed was living beings, which were viewed through a grid of knowledge constituted by natural history. (Foucault 1970: 127–128)

This is to say that the distinct taxonomic category "life" did not exist prior to the taxonomy in which it is a category. Such taxonomies Foucault describes as products of the underlying "order" or set of implicit rules for the formation of discourse. To put life, or sex, or labor or language into discourse, there must be some implicit set of rules that allows such objects to arise within discourse, that provides the linguistic and conceptual space within which they are intelligible. It would be both naïve and unhistorical to say that such objects themselves naturally make sense to human beings in the immediacy of perception. The history of science itself refutes this.

For discourse theory, the construction of reality is not merely something given to intellectual objects; it is one of the basic facts of mundane, social life. Exactly what is meant by the "construction of reality" has been the subject of much confusion. Fortunately, Ernesto Laclau and Chantal Mouffe have given one of the better explications of this meaning of "discourse":

> We use it to emphasize the fact that every social configuration is meaningful. If I kick a spherical object in the street or if I kick a ball in a football match, the physical fact is the same, but its meaning is different. The object is a football only to the extent that it establishes a system of relations, and these relations are not given by the mere referential materiality of the objects, but are rather, socially constructed. This systematic set of relations is what we call discourse. (Laclau and Mouffe 1987: 104)

Their argument, then, is that like the "football," which materially is nothing more than a spherical object made of leather, becomes a football, with all of its signifying capacities, only within the system of relations we know as the rules of soccer, so all other objects become particularly significant only within specific social configurations. This is not to say that discourse brings the material object into existence, or that the material object is dependent for its existence on discourse. Discourse theory is not a form of idealism. It is only to say that the raw materiality of mind-independent objects has little to do with their life in society. They become objects for human beings by virtue of the place within a system of relations, relations which have an undeniable signifying element.

Laclau and Mouffe extend this analysis to the whole of society:

> Every social practice is ... articulatory [or discursive]. As it is not the internal moment of a self-defined totality, it cannot simply be the expression of something already acquired, ... it always consists in the construction of new differences. The social *is* articulation insofar as 'society' is impossible. (Laclau and Mouffe 1985: 113–114)

This strange object we call "society" (and the same can be said about "culture," "religion," etc.) is nothing more than an ensemble of discourses, or discursive articulations. "Society," in other words, is not a substance which subsists under or behind particular manifestations; it is simply the ongoing practice of its various and multiple articulations.

This idea allows discourse theory to solve a very important theoretical problem which has plagued the idea of the social construction of reality ever since Peter Berger and Thomas Luckmann announced the idea several decades ago (Berger and Luckmann 1967). The problem is, who or what is the constructing subject of this totality, or society as a whole? In their analysis, Berger and Luckmann, as well as other theorists, fall back on the model of individual human consciousness with such concepts as "projection" or "objectification." This merely begs the question, however, because the answer they give is that "society" is the constructing agent (subject) of society. But what *is* society? Can we really speak of collective phenomena on the model of individual consciousness? Discourse theory holds that a "society" is an always shifting ensemble of discourses. Therefore, translating the constructive activity out of subjectivity and into discourse (understood as a structured set of relations) eliminates this problem.

This brings us to the question of the subject's relation to discourse, and here again we see one of the unique aspects of discourse theory. Unlike much criticism and unlike some versions of the science of literature, discourse theory is unconcerned with the agent of writing or the "author": "Linguistically, the author is never more than the instance of writing, just as *I* is nothing other than the instance of saying I: language knows a 'subject,' not a 'person,' and this subject, empty outside of the very enunciation which defines it, suffices to make language 'hold together'" (Barthes 1977a: 145). Not only is the author not the god-like originator of the text, discourse itself, by its own structural power, stands over and against, even endures, its activators:

> What is a strong system [of discourse]? It is a system of language which can function in all situations, and whose energy subsists, whatever the mediocrity of the subjects using it: the stupidity of certain Marxists, of certain psychoanalysts, or of certain Christians in no way jeopardizes the force of the corresponding systems, of the corresponding discourses). (Barthes 1989: 108)

Just as Saussure had argued that the system of relations which constitutes language exists independently of specific users of language, so the structure and internal logic of discourses also exists independently of its users. Discourse structures the act of speech, not vice versa.

It has not proved sufficient, however, merely to discard the subject. The fact remains that people experience themselves as thinking, acting, feeling, willing and the like, and this fact must somehow be explained in light of discourse theory's strong claim to disposing of the subject. This has been done by arguing not that the subject does not exist, but by insisting that the subject is constituted by and in discourse. None have done this more thoroughly or radically than Émile Benveniste and Jacques Lacan.

How is the subject defined in discourse? How is it present in discourse? As Benveniste has argued, the subject *is* its articulation: "What then is the reality to which this *I* or *you* refers? It is solely the 'reality of discourse,' and this is a very strange thing. *I* cannot be defined except in terms of 'locution,' not in terms of objects as a nominal sign is. *I* signifies 'the person who is uttering the present discourse containing *I*'" (Benveniste 1971: 218). That is, the subject is defined by its other, by the difference, by the play of difference in its on-going articulations. We must, however, be clear that the subject, like the Saussurean sign, is not a positive term in this articulation. As the Barthean code referred to an "already," to something that was prepared in advance by the structures of cultural systems of signification, so it is also with the subject. Its very possibility is determined by forms of articulation which, paradoxically, are not "it." Benveniste's conclusion, then, is: "Language is the possibility of subjectivity because it always contains the linguistic forms appropriate to the expression of subjectivity, and discourse provokes the emergence of subjectivity because it consists of discrete instances" (Benveniste 1971: 227). Unlike Cartesianism, discourse sees the subject as located in language, not in consciousness, and so the structure of language determines the nature of subjectivity. Whereas classical theories of language held that the mind exists prior to language and "uses" language to express thought, discourse theory holds that language, as a concrete, social structure, exists prior to individuals and, therefore, that it is only because of language that subjectivity is possible.

And it is not only the *I*, the conscious ego, which is constituted by discourse, but the unconscious also. Summarizing Lacan, Kaja Silverman points out:

> With the subject's entry into the symbolic order it is reduced to the status of a signifier within the field of the Other. It is defined by a linguistic structure which ... determines its entire cultural identity. Lacan insists that the subject is linguistically coerced not only at the level of the preconscious, as Freud would argue, but at that of the unconscious as well. Within his scheme "the unconscious is the discourse of the Other"; its desires are those of an already constituted social order. (Silverman 1983: 166)

No facet, then, of subjectivity can be seen as "natural" in the specific sense of being outside of cultural, discursive construction. Even the desires of the subject are constructed from a field of relationships which is always before it and beyond it, and so eludes it. Since there is no "subject in itself," the subject is only this ensemble of articulations. Or, to paraphrase Nietzsche, there are no "facts" about the subject, only its various interpretations or articulations. Discourses produce subjects (or what Laclau and Mouffe call "subject positions," the basic repertoire of types in a culture), subjects do not produce discourse (though they "activate" particular instances of it, often in very eccentric combinations, which may be ideologically coded as "creativity" or "uniqueness").

The past uses of discourse theory in religious studies do not present us with much material for analysis; when it comes to discourse theory and religion, we find ourselves in mostly uncharted territory. We may have begun to assume something similar about the category "religion" as Foucault did about language, life and labor, but no one has yet done for "religion" what Foucault has done for the human sciences generally, that is, try to explicate, both structurally and historically, the rules which make "religion" a possible object of discourse and, therefore, of analysis.

There are two works, however, which have taken up the method of discourse theory, Bruce Lincoln's *Discourse and the Construction of Society* (1989), and Tomoko Masuzawa's *In Search of Dreamtime: The Quest for the Origin of Religion* (1993). Although both can be fairly counted as examples of discourse theory in the study of religion, the two works could not be more different in objective, approach and tone. Lincoln works exclusively at the object language level, and produces a virtual theory of religion as a legitimating or contesting discourse. Masuzawa works exclusively at the meta-language level, taking classical texts in the study of religion as her *data*. A brief look at both will illustrate some possibilities for the application of discourse theory to the field of religious studies.

Bruce Lincoln sets out to examine

> how certain specific modes of discourse—myth, ritual, and classifica-
> tions—can be, and have been, employed as effective instruments not only

for the replication of established social forms ..., but more broadly for the construction, deconstruction, and reconstruction of society itself ... Together, discourse and force are the chief means whereby social borders, hierarchies, institutional formations, habituated patterns of behavior are both maintained and modified. (Lincoln 1989: 3)

The "specific modes of discourse" which Lincoln analyzes are those social, historical discourses—myth, ritual and taxonomy—which are used in concrete social situations by specific social actions either to construct social relations or to contest given constructions in order to construct new forms of social relations. According to Lincoln, the characteristic effect of these discourses is, in an example of imperial expansion, "the transformation of these [colonized] peoples' consciousness so that they come to consider themselves members of an imperial society rather than the vanquished subjects of a foreign nation" (Lincoln 1989: 4). As we noted above, discourse produces subjectivity. Lincoln argues that the subjective effect of discourse lies in its "sentiment evocation"— social subjects either grow to identify with a discursively defined group or they come to feel estranged from it.

Lincoln's analysis of the medieval Irish royal banquet at Tara provides an example. What he finds is that every aspect of the banquet, especially seating arrangements and portions of meat served, signify social relations. Seating is hierarchical relative to the king's position; portions are graded from the most to the least desirable cuts of meat. Thus a noble would sit near the king and eat from the hind flank, while a non-noble would sit at the far end and eat from the front shoulder. In each case, society is signified, that is, replicated, as a meaningful order by means of the performance of a ritual act.

Tomoko Masuzawa's work, on the other hand, takes direct aim at the meta-language of "religion" and the narratorial subject who has been employed in the academic study of religion. She states her goal as follows:

What is sought here is a critique that departs fundamentally from the kind of vaguely narcissistic self-criticism within the confines of an "ethics of science"—"Are we *fair* in our representations of the 'primitives'?"— which ultimately refuses to question the positional structure of the knowing and the known, and thus remains insistently blind to the question of power. What is called for instead is a critical inquiry about the practice of knowledge and power, about the politics of writing, as it pertains to the study of religion. (Masuzawa 1993: 6)

Here we find something like the antithesis of Lincoln's approach. Masuzawa looks at the *writing*, not of "religion," but of the academic study of religions itself. She analyzes religious studies' structural relations to its presumed object of study ("the religions"), religious studies' implicit assumptions of hierarchies, its repressions, ploys and evasions. All of this is done by way of a *textual analysis* of some of the major works of Mircea Eliade, Émile Durkheim, F. Max Müller and Sigmund Freud. Her point is not that their arguments are logically or scientifically invalid, nor is it that they are not true in the sense of failing to correspond to the "real" data. Rather, she wants to demonstrate those specific textual strategies by which the object "religion" is constructed, not so that we may do the science of religion better, but so that we may better understand what it is that the science of religion *does*. In this, her project much resembles that of Foucault's *The Order of Things*, whereas Lincoln's is more like Barthes' *Mythologies*.

One could, at this point, describe the past exercise of discourse theory in religious studies as having been brought to an impasse. This, however, would assume some teleological norm of "scientific results" which would be quite difficult to derive from discourse theory itself, fully granting, however, that such normative discourse is common enough in relation to the goals of science. Again, such normative teleological discourse would seem to be data for, not the result of, discourse theory. As such, the question may be left aside, except to use it to segue to a final question: What might be discourse theory's future in the study of religion?

Futurology is perhaps one of the more futile human occupations. Given that limitation, however, we may make the following remarks about the future prospects of discourse theory in the study of religion. As can be discerned from the above discussion, the central challenge presented to discourse theory is to find some way to retain a critical stance towards the object level of discourse (the data of religion) while remaining reflexively self-critical about the meta-level of discourse (the study of the data of religion). At the object level, on the one hand, no one has yet attempted to describe religion *as* discourse—in a manner in which discourse is not seen merely as the "instrument" of some non-discursive reality—and to work out the implications of such a theoretical definition. On the other hand, Masuzawa's *In Search of Dreamtime* stands virtually alone as an example of a discourse analysis working at the meta-level. This indicates that there is *more* to be done, but also that there is more to be done than *this*.

A rich suggestion—as yet not taken up by anyone—for the future of discourse theory in the study of religion comes from Jonathan Z. Smith. Although neither an advocate nor a practitioner of discourse theory in *stricto sensu*, he makes the following suggestion for the *program* of religious studies. In an article entitled "Sacred Persistence: Toward a Redescription of Canon," Smith argues for the idea of canon as the basis for understanding the construction of continuity which makes up a tradition. That is, canon, a fixed set of "texts" along with methods for the interpretation of these texts, can indicate the perimeters of a tradition without resort to the classical substantialist and essentialist notions of historical continuity. Smith frames the problem thus:

> I should like to reflect further on the notion of canon as a way of exploring the proposition that sacrality persists insofar as there are communities which are persistent in applying their limited body of tradition; that sacred persistence . . . is primarily exegesis; that, if there is anything distinctive about religion as a human activity, it is a matter of degree rather than kind, what might be described as the extremity of its enterprise for exegetical totalization. (J. Z. Smith 1982d: 44)

How do canon and interpretation achieve this continuity? They achieve this apparent perdurance and permanence by a simple yet tensely paradoxical and precarious combination of fixed and mutable elements. Canon, as Smith describes it, is a sub-genre of the genre "list" (J. Z. Smith 1982d: 44). The distinction between the two, however, is the degree of closure: "The only formal element that is lacking to transform a catalog [a kind of list] into a *canon* is the element of closure: that the list be held to be complete" (J. Z. Smith 1982d: 48). Once a list is closed, it becomes a canon not just because it is closed, but because such closure creates a new and dramatic possibility:

> This formal requirement generates a corollary. Where there is a canon, it is possible to predict the necessary occurrence of a hermeneute, of an interpreter whose task it is continually to extend the domain of the closed canon over everything that is known or everything that exists without altering the canon in the process. It is with the canon and its hermeneute that we encounter the necessary obsession with exegetical totalization. (J. Z. Smith 1982d: 48)

The perpetuity of the canon, or at least the appearance of such perpetuity, forms one pole of the dynamic of continuity. Adaptation *via* interpretation forms the other pole: "It is the genius of the diviner [for Smith, a key instance of the canon / hermeneute relationship] in his role as hermeneute to match a public set of meanings with a commonly known set of facts" (J. Z. Smith 1982d: 51).

Although this is not a call for discourse theory proper, it certainly opens a window for a rapprochement between discourse theory, a typically "fringe" methodology, and the more central concerns of the study of religion as a disciplinary field. There are many possible ways to construct the synthesis between understanding religion as an interpretive practice and as a discursive practice, but allow me to venture the following. If we return to the discussion of Todorov above, we may say that "interpretation" is the production of a second discourse out of and upon a definite discursive domain. What a discourse theorist would study, then, include the following: historically, the configurations of domains which "count" and those which do not for a given religious tradition; the diachronic activity of appropriating traditional bodies of discourse into and for the present; the analytic operation of exactly *how* an interpretation is "applied" to an object being interpreted—or fails to be applied; the social situation of the parties positioned within and by the discourse, that is, its mode and object of address, and so forth. Insofar as the "semiotic turn" in social, cultural and literary theory remains viable, these modes of analysis hold promise for future areas of research.

A return to Roland Barthes may allow us another way to describe the future situation of discourse theory in religious studies. On the one hand, it is characteristic that the more objectively minded theorists who draw upon Barthes invariably use his very early work, *Mythologies*—the only work by Barthes cited by Lincoln, for example. In the most *avant-garde* (an entirely relative term) literary theory, on the other hand, it is the "later Barthes" of works such as *S/Z* or *The Pleasure of the Text*—works rarely cited by those who rely heavily on *Mythologies*—who is used to develop theory and analysis. Perhaps one way to think about the future of discourse theory in religious studies is to rethink these two Barthes and the critical impulses they represent. In this vein, Barthes himself noted: "Is it not the characteristic of reality to be *unmasterable*? And is it not the characteristic of any system to *master* it? What then, confronting reality, can one do who rejects mastery? Get rid of the system as apparatus, accept *systematics* as writing" (Barthes 1977b: 172). Like discourse, reality is over-determined and therefore unmasterable. So we must reject the notion that science mirrors the world, and ever bear in mind that scholarly products are of the same substance as the cultural phenomena we study: they are both, finally, discourse.

Suggested Readings

Barthes, Roland
    1973   *Elements of Semiology*, Annette Lavers and Colin Smith (trans.). New York: Hill and Wang.
    1977a "From Work to Text," pp. 153–164 in *Image–Music–Text*, Essays selected and trans. by Stephen Heath. New York: Hill and Wang.
    1989   "From Science to Literature," pp. 3–10 in *The Rustle of Language*, Richard Howard (trans.). Berkeley: University of California Press.
Clifford, James
    1986   "On Ethnographic Allegory," pp. 98–121 in James Clifford and George E. Marcus (eds.), *Writing Culture: The Poetics and Politics of Ethnography*. Berkeley: University of California Press.
Culler, Jonathan D.
    1981   *The Pursuit of Signs: Semiotics, Literature, Deconstruction*. Ithaca: Cornell University Press.

Foucault, Michel
    1972   *The Archeology of Knowledge and the Discourse on Language*, A. M.
            Sheridan Smith (trans.). New York: Harper & Row; original French edn,
            1966; reprint, London: Routledge, 1995.
Laclau, Ernesto and Chantal Mouffe
    1987   "Post-Marxism Without Apologies." *New Left Review* 166: 79–106.
Todorov, Tzvetan
    1990   *Genres in Discourse*, Catherine Porter (trans.). Cambridge: Cambridge
            University Press.
White, Hayden
    1987   *The Content of the Form: Narrative Discourse and Historical Representation.*
            Baltimore: Johns Hopkins University Press.

28

CULTURE

Bruce Lincoln

☙ ☙ ☙

Let me begin by observing that although the term "culture" is a seemingly indispensable part of my professional and everyday vocabulary, whenever I have tried to think through just what it means or how and why we all use it, the exercise has proved both bewildering and frustrating. As a result, I am always on the lookout for serviceable alternatives and my list now includes such items as discourse, practice, ethos, *habitus*, ideology, hegemony, master narrative, canon, tradition, knowledge/power system, pattern of consumption and distinction, society, community, ethnicity, nation and race, all of which manage to specify some part of what is encompassed within the broader, but infinitely fuzzier category of "culture." In some measure, that breadth—which is the strength as well as the weakness of this enormously supple and elusive concept—involves a set of complexities and ambiguities I would like to explore in the following pages.

Group and Collective Identity

The first of these ambiguities arises within anthropological and sociological models (see Barth 1969; Bernstein 1975; Geertz 1973; Goody 1982; Lamont and Fournier 1992; Leach 1954), where the term "culture" often refers both to a group of people and to some X the group shares, which defines them in the same moment they define it. I want to come back and give more serious attention to the question of what this X is, but for the moment let me provisionally suggest it includes a people's communications, artifacts and standard behaviors, but is more importantly associated with the preferences encoded in and transmitted through these items, which are more its vehicles than its essence.[1] Regardless of how we understand the X that is culture's content, however, we will still need to theorize the relation between the group and its shared-and-defining X, recognizing that neither of these is immanent, autochthonous or simply given by nature.

Rather, both group and culture are products of human activity and, what is more, each one is simultaneously product and (re-)producer of the other, in much the fashion of chickens-and-eggs. Thus, people with a specific collective identity make distinctive items of culture which are transmitted to successive generations, imbue more people with the same identity, and they in turn make more items of a similar sort, which they transmit to still further generations, in a cycle of symbiotic co-production that has neither clear beginning nor foreseeable end.

Japanese, African-American or Trobriand culture, for instance, is constituted out of that which these various peoples make, do, say, think, feel and judge to be good, while people constitute themselves as "Japanese," "African-American" or "Trobriand" by participating in things that they constitute as the distinguishing aspects and marks of their group. These may include such seemingly superficial—but emotionally evocative and highly consequential—signs as wearing certain clothes, holding or moving one's body in a certain manner, or eating certain foods, either as part of regular practice or on ceremonial and public occasions. Speaking a certain language (including dialect, sub-dialect and local accent) is also important, particularly if we understand this to include sharing not just language *per se*, but a repertoire of stories, proverbs, jokes and formulaic expressions. One might extend the sense of "language" further still to include nonverbal systems of signification like art, architecture, dance and music or one might treat them separately, but the extent to which one engages with local idioms of each also conditions one's participation in culture. Also crucial is participating in certain rituals and ceremonies, observing certain rules of etiquette, and—most broadly—manifesting behavior and showing a sensibility that those who constitute themselves as members of the group (1) recognize as their own; (2) recognize in themselves; (3) recognize in those people with whom—*as a result*—they feel bound by sentiments of affinity; and (4) recognize as lacking in those from whom—once more, *as a result*—they feel themselves estranged.

Cultural identity and belonging are not simply ascribed or inherited by birth; they also—and more importantly—emerge from processes in which people are slowly educated by those around them to make judgments the group considers appropriate about a great host of things, and to make meta-judgments about the relative value of their own and others' judgment. Judgments are made in widely disparate domains, and to the extent that the standards in these domains cohere and are shared by members of the group, we may speak of cultural integration.

Perfect integration, of course, is never accomplished, and there are always disagreements that separate fractions of the group from one another. These cultural divides indicate lines of actual or potential conflict, and they often correlate to differences that are social, economic, generational and / or geographic in nature. Such differences notwithstanding, a viable degree of integration remains possible even within a diverse population, so long as the group's defining principles are not overly narrow, rigid or monolithic. Ideally they identify a range of possibility in which difference and discussion are permitted, even encouraged, with the result that actors can interact in situations of lively interest and debate specific judgments of specific items. In the process, they can gradually renegotiate their values, while also reaching finely tuned meta-judgments about themselves and each other.

Those whose behavior and judgments consistently fall outside the range the group construes as normative (people whose clothes, food or music seem weird and off-putting, for instance) thereby prompt meta-judgments that identify them as outsiders: foreigners, tourists, occupying troops, country cousins, recent immigrants, oreos, wannabees and other species of aliens and barbarians. Similarly, those whose judgments play at the edges of the culturally permissible are subject to meta-judgments that relegate them to a correspondingly marginal social status. Marginality is the ordinary situation of children, for instance, whose failures of acculturation are tolerated and indulged precisely because they are understood to be temporary and corrigible. More painful is the devalued status accorded those whose enduring deficiencies lead them to be branded philistines, bumpkins, louts and the like.[2] Worse still is the fate of those who once enjoyed full membership in the group, but broke sharply with its values and—as a result—are judged to be deviants, criminals, heretics and traitors. Here, we can recognize some very basic—if not always pretty— social and political processes, for "culture" is the prime instrument through which groups mobilize themselves, construct their collective identity and effect their solidarity by excluding those whom they identify as outsiders, while simultaneously establishing their own internal hierarchy, based on varying degrees of adherence to the values that define the group and its members (regarding such processes, see Goffman 1963; Hasenfratz 1982; and Elias and Scotson 1994).

Hegemony and Stratification

This line of analysis—which grows out of works by social scientists such as Pierre Bourdieu, Norbert Elias, Edmund Leach, Fredrik Barth, Stuart Hall, Basil Bernstein, Dick Hebdige and others—can also be applied to models of culture more concerned with the arts than with matters ethnographic (see Bourdieu 1984; Hartman 1997; Jameson 1981; Williams 1995). To this end, we might observe that every work of art creates an aesthetic and moral universe that resembles and interacts with those created by other works in the same tradition or canon. Individually and collectively, they invite would-be readers, viewers and listeners into the spaces of the imagination they create. Those audiences who accept such invitations and experience the moral and aesthetic universe of these works as meaningful, comfortable and familiar are not just influenced or transformed by the content of the works at the level of their individual personhood, but they also join in a community. Not a national or ethnic community, to be sure, but a different sort of cultural community that constitutes itself in similar fashion, by excluding those who choose not to participate, and by ranking insiders on the refinement and quality of the judgments they have internalized and learned to reproduce for themselves. Among such groups one might note classicists, traditionalists, the avant garde, the cool, the hip, the retro and countless other subcultures defined by taste and style (Hebdige 1979). Similarly, one can note different subcultures among sports fans (golfers as opposed to aficionados of professional wrestling, for instance), music lovers (by preferred style and radio station), shoppers (by preferred merchandise, brand or stores), moviegoers, TV viewers, pulp fiction readers (all subcategorized by genre) and virtually infinite others.

This last set of examples bring us to a second area of ambiguity in theorizing culture, for within the humanities that term can be used for an entity rather different from the ones we have been discussing thus far: something that often gets called "high" culture or Culture with a capital "C," as opposed to popular and mass culture or culture with a lower-case "c." Acknowledging that all these usages are legitimate in their own way, the problem becomes identifying what this capital-C Culture is, specifying how it differs from its lower-case homophone, and understanding how the two are related. Given the preceding discussion, I understand lower-case-c culture as the sum of all communications circulating within a group that the group recognizes as its own, and through which it constitutes itself and distinguishes itself from others. Capital-C Culture is a highly significant subset of this totality.

More precisely, capital-C Culture consists of the "choice" works and the "select" genres that enjoy greatest aesthetic privilege, social cachet and official support. It is the subset of culture that is valorized, often to the point of fetishization, by the fraction of society that is itself most valorized, and which represents itself—with considerable, but never total success—as the custodian and arbiter of the group's core values. Different fractions can (and do) play this role in different societies and different historic moments. Sometimes it is elders, particularly male elders, who are able to decide what is really good and what really counts. Then again, this may be the prerogative of aristocrats, priests, intellectuals, critics, the wealthy or those who are able to convert their material and other assets—above all, the respect they enjoy—into a controlling interest in the institutions and processes that form and evaluate taste.

Within the operant logic of such systems, it is claimed that the things-judged-best by the people-judged-best hold this status because they embody and reveal the ideals toward which everyone ought aspire, but which only truly "cultured" souls can fully appreciate and internalize. If one steps outside that logic, however, and asks where these values come from and whom they benefit (a move far easier to make when considering a culture other than one's own), the self-serving aspects of the process become evident. Regularly one finds that a well-situated fraction claims as one of its privileges (and one that is key to preserving all of the others) the right to speak for the group as a whole. In this capacity, they misrepresent—occasionally in cynical fashion, but more often with sincere conviction—preferences that redound to their own benefit as if these were eternal and transcendent values. To use Gramscian terms, capital-C Culture is nothing other than hegemony, and the remainder of lower-case-c culture is that which hegemony seeks to suppress, contain and devalue.

Language, Culture, Hegemony

With regard to Antonio Gramsci, whom I consider one of the most astute theorists of culture, it is worth digressing to note the way his concept of hegemony grew out of his interest in language. A contrast with Marx is instructive. Marx took religion as the paradigm for his theory of ideology, and thus viewed ideology as something invariably mystificatory, but potentially dispensable, that can (and must!) be vanquished by an antithetical style of thought and discourse: that which he called "science." In contrast, Gramsci understood culture as similar to language: something that is neither inevitably misleading, nor ultimately dispensable, nor possessed of a neat antithesis that can serve as a weapon against it. Instead of seeking alternatives to language or culture, he thus sought alternatives within them.

Many factors contributed to the development of Gramsci's views, including his Sardinian origins, his knowledge of European history, his engagement in politics, his attitudes to the Catholic Church, his reading of Marx, Lenin and the idealist philosophy of Benedetto Croce. But the template on which he organized these, as Franco Lo Piparo has shown (1979), came from his work in linguistics at the University of Turin from 1911 to 1918. There, Gramsci studied under Matteo Bartoli, founder of the "Neo-linguist" school of thought. Bartoli was particularly interested in processes of language change and diffusion, and was particularly impressed by the way Latin replaced the ancient languages of Iberia, Gaul and Dalmatia, while leaving Greek—a language attached to a more prestigious culture—virtually intact.[3]

Bartoli envisioned Gramsci as his successor and as a thinker who would rout the rival "Neo-grammarians." Under his tutelage, Gramsci developed two areas of expertise.[4] The first was the Church's use of Latin throughout the Middle Ages as an élite medium of communication for clerics and cosmopolitan intellectuals, while popular classes adopted the many vernaculars that developed after the fall of Rome: Venetian, Ligurian, Piedmontese, Neapolitan,

Sardinian and many others. Second, Gramsci gave critical study to the nineteenth-century proposals designed to create a common language for the newly unified Italian state. Most of these involved the use of schools and other state apparatuses to promote one privileged vernacular (most often Tuscan) as the language of the nation as a whole—more precisely, as its sole language, which educated, progressive citizens were expected to use by preference. Since the state was unable to stamp out the other vernaculars swiftly and completely, however, it was prepared to tolerate them, so long as they accepted the subordinate status of "dialects," that is, instruments fit for use in domestic and local settings, especially by women, children and illiterates.

Neo-grammarian theory treated language as a natural system, subject to evolutionary processes such as sound shifts, that were governed by the physiology of speech. In contrast, Bartoli and his circle used the case of Latin, neo-Latin, Italian and the vernaculars to argue that language is not a natural phenomenon, but something acutely social and historic; further, that change results not from competition among languages themselves, but rather from competition among the people who speak them. Languages that receive the support of powerful institutions like the state or the church enjoy a distinct advantage in this competition, but even so, they cannot be imposed by brute force. Rather, populations must also be educated and led to adopt as their own what was previously an alien tongue, associated with an alien group and culture.

Invariably, there are limits on the ability of a dominant (or hegemonic) language to supplant or obliterate those with which it struggles. Dialects, argots and other embattled tongues continue to be used by certain speakers for certain purposes, and each usage carries within it elements of an alternative value system, sense of identity and view of existence. Although these languages change under the hegemon's pressure (sometimes slowly, sometimes fast), the hegemon is also transformed—conceivably, even overthrown—by the strength of their resistance. Gramsci took this dynamic, eminently political model of language from Bartoli and expanded it into a theory of culture in all its diverse aspects: art, literature, philosophy, folklore, ethics, religion, common sense and so on.

Notwithstanding the strong appeal and broad applicability of Gramsci's ideas, when one tries them out on the contemporary cultural landscape, they raise a third set of complexities and problems. At the most concrete level, it can be surprisingly difficult to tell which aspects of culture are actually hegemonic. Shakespeare or Disney? Aristotle or Oprah? More abstractly, when culture becomes a commodity, does hegemony correlate to small audiences, élite status and the backing of prestigious non-profit institutions or to mass audiences, corporate sponsorship and mega-profits? This question has still other dimensions, but before I can address them, it seems advisable to revisit the question I earlier deferred: how can we define that X which is the content of culture?

Ethics, Aesthetics, Religion

Although culture involves and depends on a great many things—for example, a language, economy, relations of production and communication—its core content, I believe, consists of two elements, to which a third is often added. I want to return to this third element shortly, and to explore its logical and historic relation to the other two. But for the moment, let me begin with the two invariant elements, which I would identify as aesthetics and ethics. By these terms I mean to signal the two areas in which groups articulate their characteristic and defining preferences or what some are inclined to call "values." Under the heading of aesthetics, I would thus include all practice and discourse concerned with "taste," that is, the evaluation of sensory experience and all matters of form and style. In similar fashion, I take ethics to include abstract discussion of moral tenets, concrete practice and casuistic evaluations regarding specific behaviors performed by (and upon) specific categories of person: How does a gentleman treat a lady? What can a beggar expect from a lord? Must one answer a psychopath truthfully? Can one kill in self-defense?

Along these lines, every item of culture offers ideas and examples of what is good and what is pleasing, not just for their audiences' edification, but also for their evaluation: How good is this image of the good? How pleasant this experience of the pleasing? To reach such meta-judgments, audiences call into play everything they have learned about the good and the pleasing from all the other items of culture they have encountered and all the judgments they have heard offered. And as they do this, other members of the group make meta-judgments about them: How good is this person's notion of the good? How pleasing her appreciation of the pleasing? How fully does she share and appreciate the values our group takes as its own and seeks to foster? Do her judgments conform sufficiently to those judgments we share that we may safely consider her one of our own? Or do they show her to be marginal in ways that make us hold her at a distance and treat her with suspicion or even disdain?

Although they might be derived from other sources, I have adapted these categories of the aesthetic and the ethical from Søren Kierkegaard. Where I have treated them as separate and equally necessary spheres of culture, however, Kierkegaard took them to be successive stages of individual developments.[5] In his view, the ethical represents a position of greater maturity than the aesthetic, a sense of what is morally good being more responsible than a taste for what is sensually pleasing. Moreover, Kierkegaard acknowledged a third category, which for him was most important of all: that of the religious. And just as a move from the aesthetic to the ethical implied advancement from a self-gratifying exploitation of inanimate objects (or people treated as objects) to a more mature concern for other human subjects, so he took the religious to imply something higher still: a concern with that which transcends the human.

I have chosen to omit this last Kierkegaardian category from my model of culture, albeit with a certain ambivalence. In part, I do so because my understanding of religion differs strongly from Kierkegaard's, and I would prefer to minimize the possibility for confusing our positions. For him, religion involves an individual leap of faith and an embrace of paradoxes, culminating in the conviction that the eternal would (and did) enter into the temporal. In contrast, I work with a polythetic model that focuses on aspects of religion that are manifest in intersubjective social relations, rather than those that are intensely personal and interior. Briefly, I take religion to include four different components, which can relate to one another in various ways, including disjuncture and contradiction. These components are:

1. A discourse that claims its concerns transcend the human, temporal and contingent, while claiming for itself a similarly transcendent status.
2. A set of practices informed and structured by that discourse.
3. A community, whose members construct their identity with reference to the discourse and its attendant practices.
4. An institution that regulates discourse, practices and community, reproducing and modifying them over time, while asserting their eternal validity and transcendent value.

While I recognize the importance of religion (and make my living studying it), I still hesitate to make it a core component of culture, and base this view on a fairly simple historic observation. Thus, whereas ethics and aesthetics are salient concerns for all human cultures, the role of religion varies over time, space and social stratum. In particular, it has been much attenuated since the eighteenth century, particularly in Europe, North America and many of their former colonies. I thus theorize culture as necessarily and invariably involving two central domains (ethics and aesthetics), alongside a third domain (religion), which often plays a role of prime importance, but from which, in certain historical instances, it has been displaced and relegated to a subordinate, even marginal position. It is of some interest, then, to specify what role religion plays when it does remain a central part of culture and to inquire when, where, why and how it came to lose that role. Of particular interest, I think, is the way religion connects to the other domains of culture: specifically, the capacity of religious discourse to articulate ethical and aesthetic positions in a uniquely stabilizing fashion. What religion does—and this, I submit, is its defining characteristic—is to invest specific human preferences with transcendent status by misrepresenting them as revealed truths, primordial traditions, divine commandments and so forth. In this way, it insulates them against most forms of debate and critique, assisting their transmission from one generation to another as part of a sacred canon.

Even so, critique can never be silenced. When religious assertions secure the hegemony of specific aesthetic and ethical preferences, particularly those that benefit society's dominant fractions, insurgency is likely to take the form of religious contestation. Heresies, heterodoxies, folk beliefs and practices, calls for reform, claims of miracles and revelations, theological disputes, liturgical squabbles, inventive hermeneutics, anti-clerical jokes and gossip are all such moments of struggle. Within European history the most dramatic examples are furnished by the Protestant Reformation and Catholic Counter Reformation of the sixteenth and seventeenth centuries. So terrible was the violence and so bitter the hatreds stirred up by religious difference in those centuries that episodes like the Peasants' War (1524–1525), the campaigns of the Duke of Alba and his "Council of Blood" in the Spanish Netherlands (1567–1576), the St. Bartholomew's Day Massacre (1572), the Thirty Years' War (1618–1648) and the English Revolution (1642–1653) threatened the nations of Europe with social, political and cultural disintegration of unprecedented dimensions.

Voltaire spoke of these Wars of Religion as having unleashed "a type of barbarism that the Herulii, the Vandals, and the Huns never knew" (*Essai sur les moeurs* [1745], chap. 121; see also chaps. 129, 187). The critique of religion he advanced, along with other Enlightenment *philosophes* from Bayle, Locke and Hobbes through Hume, Diderot, Helvétius, d'Holbach, Lessing, Kant and others, is not incidental to or detachable from the bulk of their thought. As I see it, their celebration of "reason" is best understood as an attempt to constitute an alternative to that which they characterized as "superstition," that is, the religious discourse, practices and institutions their rivals took to be normative (see, for example, Gay 1966 and Manuel 1967). Here, it is worth recalling that publication of the *Encyclopédie* was (temporarily) suppressed by decree of Louis XV for its "irreparable damage to morality and religion," while Pope Clement XIII threatened those who read or owned it with excommunication.[6] Nor was the Pope wrong to feel threatened, for the project of the Enlightenment *philosophes* was a radical revision of the nature of culture that would displace religion from its dominant position, thereby freeing up ethical and aesthetic debate and reflection. This audacious endeavor was undertaken, moreover, in the wake of bloody religious conflicts, with the determination that such horrors would not be repeated.

Here, it is worth considering briefly Kant's much-discussed essay, "Was ist Aufklärung?" As is well-known, Kant begins by defining Enlightenment (*Aufklärung*) as "mankind's exit from its self-incurred immaturity," an immaturity he understood as "the inability to make use of one's own understanding without the guidance of another." As becomes clear in the course of the essay, the other who most obstructs the exercise of independent reason is an authority simultaneously religious and political, and the path to enlightenment is cleared of this obstacle when the prince ceases to cloak himself in religious aura and to prescribe religious orthodoxy (Kant 1996 [1784]). Speaking further about the space for religious liberty and pluralism that enlightened despots like Frederick the Great opened up, Kant went on to say "it is an illuminating example to such a government that public peace and unity have little to fear from this freedom. Men work their way by themselves bit by bit out of barbarity if one does not intentionally contrive to hold them in it."

The subtext in this passage is clear and firm: it is not religious difference that leads to conflict and barbarism, but the attempt of state and church to enforce religious unanimity and to use religion as a central instrument for the consolidation of their power that does so. Toward the end of his essay Kant went on to assert, "I have placed the main point of enlightenment—mankind's exit from its self-imposed immaturity—primarily on religious matters" (1996 [1784]: 62–63).

As a result of the *philosophes* efforts, theoretical and polemic, the role of religion was severely curtailed throughout western Europe. Among the prime beneficiaries of this was the secular nation-state, which learned to derive its legitimacy from the people it governed rather than God, and which built up its power by taking over many functions previously controlled by religious institutions: law, education, moral discipline and surveillance, social relief, record keeping and others. The vast expansion and intrusiveness of state power is, of course, one of the chief problems that follow from the Enlightenment's reorganization of culture, as countless critics have made clear.[7] That power is only partially checked by the institutions and media of civil society: philosophy, literature, the arts, sciences, journalism and popular culture which also gained at religion's expense and became the prime venues in which ethical and aesthetic issues are seriously engaged. At the same time, however, and for the same reason, these media have become the chief battlegrounds in the cultural conflicts of modernity.

Institutions and Industry

Space does not permit me to explore the skirmishes that break out within the ethical and aesthetic arenas of "culture" when religion is no longer able to protect hegemonic preferences by cloaking them in a fictive transcendence. Within the aesthetic, one might point to the all-too-familiar quarrels about music, clothes, coiffures and food that are also quarrels about race, class and ethnicity. Or within the ethical, the equally common arguments about etiquette, sensitivity and commitment that are also arguments about gender and age. Blurring of the border between ethics and aesthetics is also possible, as in the assertive politics of style summed up in the slogan "Black is beautiful."

Unmediated conflict between the aesthetic and the ethical is also apparent in aspects of the "culture wars" within contemporary American society, and this brings me back to a question I left suspended. Who and what holds hegemony in American culture today? Shakespeare or Disney? Aristotle or Oprah? Such examples point to a longstanding struggle over cultural preferences and national identity that is waged by two very different apparatuses, each of which represents the interests of different social fractions.

Painting with broad and rapid strokes, we can identify one side of that struggle with cultural *institutions*—for example, museums, libraries, symphony halls, opera and ballet companies, colleges and universities—that are structured in non-profit fashion, patronized by old moneyed families and the upwardly mobile, who seek to restructure their identity through an immersion in Culture, with hope of thus "bettering" themselves. These institutions consider it their mission to display and celebrate, for the edification of society at large, those classic items of high culture that present images of the good in a manner that is pleasing, such that the ethical thereby encompasses the aesthetic. Not coincidentally, these items are identified as "treasures" and "masterpieces," which is to say rare, expensive and difficult to understand or appreciate.

On the other side stands the culture *industry*: movie studios, TV networks, record companies, mass market publishers, fashion designers, advertising agencies and others who manufacture and traffic in images and signs. Like that of most entrepreneurs, their interest lies in maximizing their clientele, market share and profit. Toward that end, they develop product lines and promotional campaigns that deliver sensuous pleasure and excitement, while making occasional concessionary gestures in the direction of "the good." Their products are readily affordable, their audiences large, young and desiring immediate rather than delayed gratifications. In the items of mass culture they market, the aesthetic regularly overpowers the ethical.

Although it would be simplistic to depict this as a showdown between Boston Brahmins and Hollywood Hucksters, that caricature manages to capture the components of class, generation, race and region at play in the over-determined conflict of élite and mass culture. Their differences notwithstanding, both apparatuses are manipulative and dangerous. The one seeks to stabilize values as a means of protecting class privilege and prestige; the other seeks to destabilize them, as a means to open new markets and make a quick dollar.

Freudian critics have described the conflict of élite and mass culture as a battle between the superego and id, which seems reasonable enough, as does Plato's idea of competition between the "spirited" and "appetitive" fractions of society, which he also treats as aspects of the soul (*Timaeus* 69d–70a; see also *Republic* 439d–441a and 442b). What I find attractive in these models is that in each case, conflict between the two elements they identify is made more likely by debilitation of a third, which in other, more stable circumstances enjoys the paramount position. For Freud, this third, ruling element was the ego; for Plato, it was the rational part of soul and society, which he identified with philosophy. In the Kierkegaardian model, the same role falls to religion.

While all of these systems have their attractions, ultimately I prefer the Kierkegaardian model, and this for several reasons. First, its categories of ethics and aesthetics focus attention on culture as the domain of preferences, judgments and meta-judgments. Second, it permits one to understand the historic transformation of culture that was effected by the Enlightenment through its critique of religion. Third, as an ancillary benefit, it helps make sense of some contemporary debates about popular culture. Large fractions of American society seem to believe that a sea of "garbage" and "filth" threatens to overwhelm "everything that is decent," in nothing short of apocalyptic fashion.[8] To reverse this anticipated triumph of the aesthetic over the ethical, they advance three overlapping kinds of proposal that fall in classically Kierkegaardian categories. One calls for intervention in the aesthetic through censorship, V-chips, increased support for high culture and a return to the canonical classics. A second focuses on the ethical, urging more support for "values" in schools, public rhetoric and policy, as well as more jails, police and harsher enforcement of more punitive laws.

Although I have little sympathy for either of these positions, I am willing to listen and respond respectfully, so long as it remains clear that their favored buzzwords ("decency," "values," "law and order," etc.) are not categorical imperatives, as they would like to believe, but highly rhetorical signifiers that encode the speaker's preferences. As such, they remain open to question, debate and revision. This, however, is not enough for many, who wish to construe their preferences as something absolute and unchanging. Toward that end, they deploy the term "values" in conjunction with a number of weighty modifiers: "family values," "traditional values," "time-honored" or "eternal values," "Judeo-Christian," "Christian" or "sacred values" even. Here, we can perceive—and need to resist—attempts to silence alternatives and foreclose the possibility of contestation by misrepresenting contingent human preferences as if they were transcendent verities.

This is the task accomplished by religion in all human societies prior to the Enlightenment and in those societies left relatively untouched by the Enlightenment's revision of culture. This is also why the third kind of proposal—which calls for prayer in the schools, evangelical revival, Bible-based morality and fundamentalist interpretation of Scripture—seeks to reverse the Enlightenment's restructuring of culture. Their goal is to restore religion to its paramount position, from which it can stabilize embattled hegemonies, and put an end to conflict by establishing—once and for all—in the ethical domain, what is good and what is not; in the aesthetic, which pleasures ought be permitted and which ones ought be suppressed and sanctioned. Others are making similar attempts in other parts of the globe (governing parties in Iran, Afghanistan, Israel, Serbia and the Sudan; powerful movements in Algeria, Egypt, India, Turkey, parts of eastern Europe and Latin America). Sometimes they gain their immediate objectives, and sometimes they do not, but whatever success they have comes wrapped in cruel irony. Restoring religion to a dominant position within culture hardly puts an end to conflict; it simply insures that a culture's most bruising conflicts will assume religious, rather than ethical or aesthetic character, and in that form they can be more destructive than ever. When one rejects the Enlightenment's values *en masse* and dispenses with its model of culture, one risks not just a return of the repressed, but novel Wars of Religion.[9]

Notes

1. My views here are informed by, but contrast somewhat with those in Clifford Geertz's influential essay, "Religion as a Cultural System" (1966). Where Geertz theorizes culture as a system of symbols that organize life and confer meaning on it, I am more inclined to see it as a system of preferences through which people constitute their collective identity.
2. Or, as Miss Manners recently put it, when counseling a gentleman disposed to employ a spoon where others more commonly use forks: "People who defy the simple customs of their own people arouse an amount of scorn that even Miss Manners finds surprising" (*Minneapolis Star Tribune* [11 September, 1996]: E4).
3. A bibliography of Bartoli's writings appears in his *Saggi di linguistica spaziale* (1945: xxi–xxxii). Among the most important are his translation of Meyer-Luebke, *Grammatica storica della lingua Italiana e dei dialetti Toscani* (1926), his *Introduzione alla neo-linguistica: principi – scopi – metodi* (1925) and the volume he co-authored with Bertoni, *Breviario di neolinguistica* (1925). In the first letter he wrote from prison, Gramsci asked his landlady to send him the copy of this last volume, which he had left behind when arrested by Mussolini's police. When this request proved unsuccessful, he made two subsequent attempts to obtain a copy (Gramsci 1994, vol. 1: 35, 145, 160).
4. On Gramsci's relation to Bartoli, see Gramsci 1994, vol. 1: 84; on his own linguistic studies, see Gramsci 1994, vol. 1: 247, 296–297, 360–361. The sections of Gramsci's *Notebooks* that deal with language have also been collected and translated (Gramsci 1984; see also Mansfield's introduction [1984]).
5. One can also derive these categories from Kant, who grouped them together with logic. For reasons outlined below, I find Kierkegaard's system of greater utility and interest. In treating them as aspects of collective culture, rather than stages of individual development, I have sought to redress some of the problems identified by Adorno (1989).
6. Publication of the *Encyclopédie* began in 1751 and was suspended in 1759, after the first seven volumes had appeared. The final ten volumes came out in 1765, after Diderot had obtained the king's tacit permission (see Wood 1987: 111).
7. Horkheimer and Adorno 1972 is of prime importance, as are numerous writings of Foucault (for example, 1977a, 1973a). See also Burchell, Gordon and Miller 1991.
8. If examples are really necessary, see Green et al. 1996; Romanowski 1996; Carter 1993; Medved 1992; Bennett 1992; and Bloom 1987.
9. Earlier versions of this chapter were presented at Bates College, Dartmouth College and Reed College. I am grateful to my colleagues at all three institutions for helpful discussion and criticism and to Martin Riesebrodt, who read and commented on my original manuscript.

Suggested Readings

Asad, Talal
  1993   *Genealogies of Religion: Discipline and Reasons of Power in Christianity and Islam.* Baltimore: Johns Hopkins University Press.
Barthes, Roland
  1972   *Mythologies*, Annette Lavers (trans.). New York: Hill and Wang.
Bloch, Maurice
  1989   *Ritual, History, and Power: Selected Papers in Anthropology.* Monographs on Social Anthropology, vol. 58. London: Athlone.
Bourdieu, Pierre
  1993   *The Field of Cultural Production: Essays on Art and Literature*, Randal Johnson (ed. and Introduction). Cambridge: Polity.
Certeau, Michel de
  1997a *Culture in the Plural*, Luce Giard (ed. and Introduction), Tom Conley (trans. and Afterword). Minneapolis: University of Minnesota Press.
  1997b *The Capture of Speech and Other Political Writings*, Luce Giard (ed. and Introduction), Tom Conley (trans. and Afterword). Minneapolis: University of Minnesota Press.
Clifford, James
  1988   *The Predicament of Culture: Twentieth-Century Ethnography, Literature, and Art.* Cambridge, MA: Harvard University Press.
Dirks, Nicholas, Geoff Eley and Sherry Ortner (Eds.)
  1994   *Culture / Power / History: A Reader in Contemporary Social Theory.* Princeton: Princeton University Press.
Elias, Norbert
  1983   *The Civilizing Process*, 3 vols., Edmund Jephcott (trans.). New York: Pantheon.
Gramsci, Antonio
  1985   *Selections from Cultural Writings*, David Forgacs and Geoffrey Nowell-Smith (eds.), William Boelhower (trans.). Cambridge, MA: Harvard University Press.
Hall, Stuart, editor
  1996   *Modernity: An Introduction to Modern Societies.* Cambridge, MA: Blackwell.
Lawson, E. Thomas and Robert McCauley
  1990   *Rethinking Religion: Connecting Cognition and Culture.* Cambridge: Cambridge University Press.
Lincoln, Bruce
  1989   *Discourse and the Construction of Society: Comparative Studies of Myth, Ritual, and Classification.* Oxford: Oxford University Press.
Nelson, Cary and Lawrence Grossberg, editors
  1988   *Marxism and the Interpretation of Culture.* Urbana: University of Illinois Press.
Sahlins, Marshall D.
  1976   *Culture and Practical Reason.* Chicago: University of Chicago Press.

29

COLONIALISM

David Chidester

৵৵

Why study religion and religions? In a series of lectures on *The Religions of the World* published in 1847, British theologian Frederick Denison Maurice proposed that the study of religions provided knowledge that was useful for a nation that was currently "engaged in trading with other countries, or in conquering them, or in keeping possession of them" (Maurice 1847: 255; see Chidester 1996: 131–132). Over a century later, in the first edition of his popular survey of world religions published in 1958, *The Religions of Man*, American scholar of religion Huston Smith reported that his series of lectures to officers of the U.S. Air Force provided useful knowledge because "someday they were likely to be dealing with the peoples they were studying as allies, antagonists, or subjects of military occupation" (H. Smith 1958: 7–8; see McCutcheon 1997b: 180–181). Certainly, these recommendations for the study of religion suggest a remarkable continuity from British imperialism to American neo-imperialism in justifying the study of religion as an intellectual instrument of international trade, military conquest and political administration. In an era that is widely regarded as postcolonial, how should we understand the historical relationships of power and knowledge that have linked the study of religion with colonialism?

In recent years, scholars in a variety of academic disciplines have worked to relocate the production of knowledge within the power relations of colonial situations. Beginning with the critical essays collected in *Anthropology and the Colonial Encounter* (Asad 1973), social and cultural anthropologists have taken the lead in developing colonial and postcolonial analysis. In the field of literary studies, the groundbreaking work of Edward Said, *Orientalism* (1978; see Said 1986, 1989, 1993; Parry et al. 1998), has redirected the study of European literature during the colonial and imperial era towards a critique of the power relations involved in European representations of "others" at the center and boundaries of empire. For historians, efforts to recover the histories of

423

colonized "people without history" (Wolf 1982) has required new methods for analyzing consciousness, subjectivity, agency, meaning and power in colonial situations. As an interdisciplinary enterprise, gender studies has made a particularly strong contribution to the analysis of meaning and power under colonialism. Although the academic study of religion has generally lagged behind these developments in colonial and postcolonial research, recent efforts to locate the history of the study of Buddhism (Lopez 1995) and indigenous African religion (Chidester 1996) in specific colonial situations suggest the potential for revising our understanding of both religion and the study of religion in the modern world.[1]

Although European colonialism has been a global phenomenon, it has produced specific local effects in different times and places. Accordingly, the best entry into colonial studies is provided by historical ethnographies of specific colonial situations. Important regional studies of colonial situations have provided resources for reinterpreting the ways in which religion has operated in contexts of intercultural contact, encounter and exchange in the Americas, Africa, the Middle East, South Asia, East Asia and the Pacific Islands.[2] While recognizing the theoretical diversity and historical specificity of colonial studies, it is nevertheless possible to make some general observations about religion and the study of religion under colonial conditions before considering postcolonial prospects for the academic study of religion.

Colonial Situations

In simple definition, colonialism is the use of military and political power to create and maintain a situation in which colonizers gain economic benefits from the raw materials and cheap labor of the colonized. More than merely a matter of military coercion and political economy, however, colonialism represents a complex intercultural encounter between alien intruders and indigenous people in what Mary Louise Pratt (1992) has called "contact zones." In analyzing those colonial encounters, we need to consider both their material and cultural terms and conditions. In the political economy of colonialism, cultural forms of knowledge and power, discourse and practice, techniques and strategies, played an integral role in the formation of colonial situations.

European explorers, traders, conquerors and colonial administrators operated with an ideology of territorial expansion and intercultural negation that became thoroughly integrated into European modes of thinking about and engaging with the larger world. According to the early nineteenth-century German philosopher G. W. F. Hegel, for example, all great nations "press onward to the sea" because "the sea affords the means for the colonizing activity—sporadic or systematic—to which the mature civil society is driven"

(1974: 282–283). By taking to the sea, Hegel argued, colonizers solved certain internal problems (such as poverty, overpopulation and limited markets) that blocked the development of a mature civil society. But they also encountered "barbarians" in strange lands who were allegedly incapable of developing the maturity of civilization. In relation to such permanent children, Hegel insisted, "The civilized nation is conscious that the rights of the barbarians are unequal to its own and treats their autonomy as only a formality" (1967: 219). In this formulation, with its thematics of distance and difference, denial and domination, the philosopher only recapitulated the basic ingredients of a European culture of colonialism.

On colonized peripheries, however, indigenous people deployed a range of strategies for engaging these European territorial claims and cultural representations. On the one hand, reversing the alien terms of European religious signification was an option. During the era of sixteenth-century Spanish conquests in the Americas, for example, the conquistadors were armed with a theological formula, the *Requirement*, that was designed to be read before a gathering of natives to enact what historian Patricia Seed (1995) has called a "ceremony of possession" that certified Spanish claims on new land. In a carefully constructed chain of references, the *Requirement* announced to Native Americans that the Spanish conqueror who stood before them represented the authority of the King of Spain in Castile, who represented the authority of the Pope in Rome, who represented the authority of the Apostle Peter in Jerusalem, who represented the ultimate authority of the supreme God who had created heaven and earth. Although the *Requirement* invited the natives to freely convert to Christianity, the text concluded that those who refused would experience the force of total warfare and that the deaths and damages that resulted would be their fault (Seed 1995: 69).

In response to this colonial ultimatum, indigenous people could submit or resist. But people also found ways to reappropriate and reverse the chain of references that spanned the Atlantic Ocean to link the New World with the Old. For example, the Andean nobleman Guaman Poma, who had lived through the Spanish conquest of the Inca empire, the subjugation of the Andean people and the dispossession of native lands, published a book in 1621 that reversed the terms of the *Requirement*. Drawing upon the new Christian resources, Guaman Poma argued that under colonial conditions "the world is upside-down." To restore the proper order of the world, he proposed, the chain of references established by Spanish colonization had to be reversed. According to Guaman Poma, the restoration of Inca political sovereignty would reveal the order of a world in which the mineral wealth of Peru supported the Spanish King in Castile, who supported the Catholic Pope in Rome, who supported the religion of the God of heaven and earth. In reversing these alien religious terms, therefore, Guaman Poma tried to intervene in a world that had been turned upside down by Spanish colonization (Adorno 1985; MacCormack 1988).

On the other hand, reworking the familiar terms of indigenous religious signification was also an option. In Africa, for example, indigenous myths of sea and land were recast to make sense out of the strange encounters and violent oppositions of colonial contact. "It is well-documented from missionary reports," as historian Wyatt MacGaffey has observed, "that in the seventeenth century white people were believed to live under the ocean." Drawing on earlier mythic themes, this identification of Europeans with the sea, as MacGaffey has concluded, "is not derived from experience but is a fundamental postulate in terms of which experience is interpreted" (1994: 257). Using this symbolic template for interpreting the experience of colonialism, Africans could reconfigure the encounter in terms of the mythic opposition between sea and land.

Under the impact of British colonization in nineteenth-century southern Africa, myths of the sea were reworked to make sense of the military incursions, dispossession of land and new relations of power. As the Xhosa chief Ngqika observed, since the Europeans were people of the sea—the "natives of the water"—they had no business on the land and should have stayed in the sea (Campbell 1815: 526). The Xhosa religious visionary and war-leader Nxele developed this political observation about sea and land into an indigenous theology that identified two gods: Thixo, the god of the white people, who had punished white people for killing his son by casting them into the sea, and Mdalidiphu, the god of the deeps, who dwelled under the ground but had ultimate dominion over the sea (Peires 1979). Similarly, during the first half of the nineteenth century, a Zulu emergence myth was reworked in terms of this colonial opposition between land and sea. In the beginning, uNkulunkulu created human beings, male and female, but also black and white. While black human beings were created to be naked, carry spears and live on the land, white human beings were created to wear clothing, carry guns and live in the sea (Bleek 1952: 3–4). For these African religious thinkers, therefore, the mythic origin—the *primordium*—was clearly located in the new era that opened with the colonial opposition between people of the sea and people of the land. By appropriating foreign religious resources and recasting local religious resources, indigenous people all over the world struggled to make sense out of colonial situations.

An important facet of the European colonial project, however, was the assertion of control not only over material, but also over symbolic, cultural and religious resources. In nineteenth-century southern India, for example, British colonial interventions in religion on the Malabar coast succeeded in reifying religious differences and separating religious communities of Hindus and Christians that had lived in harmony for centuries. Tracing their traditional origin to the first-century apostle of Jesus, and their spiritual power to ongoing connections with Christian holy men of West Asia, the St. Thomas Christians of the Malabar coast had maintained close relations with the Hindu rulers of the region. Sharing the same military disciplines and upper-class status with the Hindu *rajas*, the St. Thomas Christians received patronage, financial support and royal protection for their churches, shrines and festivals. In exchange, the Christians supported the shrines and participated in the festivals of the Hindu ruling class.

This interreligious cooperation changed dramatically, however, after the British East India Company established its domination of the region in 1795. Under the authority of the British Resident, Colonel John Monro, between 1810 and 1819, the network of economic, social and religious exchange between Christians and Hindus was broken. Directing state funds for the construction and repair of their churches, Monro exempted St. Thomas Christians from paying taxes and tributes to Hindu officials. Since these funds were also used to support Hindu temples, shrines and festivals, St. Thomas Christians were thereby removed from the system of mutual exchange by which high-caste Hindus and Christians had cooperated in supporting religion. Increasingly, St. Thomas Christians became targets for the animosity of high-caste Hindus. By the 1880s, while riots frequently broke out between them, annual religious festivals, which had been events of interreligious celebration, became occasions for interreligious provocation when Hindus and St. Thomas Christians marched past each other's shrines, as one observer reported, "howling, screaming, and crying out obscene words" (Bayly 1989: 294).

British colonial interventions, therefore, had succeeded in reifying the boundaries between two religions—Hindu and Christian—that had been part of the same network of social class, martial culture and religious worship in southern India. As many analysts have observed, the British colonial reification of religious boundaries not only reinforced a certain kind of European Christianity in India, but also produced the modern religious classification, "Hinduism" (Frykenberg 1993; see Inden 1990; Pandey 1990). Under colonial conditions, the primary categories of the study of religion—"religion" and "religions"—emerged as potent signs of identity and difference.

Colonial Comparative Religion

As a sustained reflection on religious difference, the study of religion has its historical roots not only in the European Enlightenment, but also in this long history of colonialism. On the frontiers of colonial encounter, European explorers, travelers, missionaries, settlers and colonial administrators recorded their findings on indigenous religions all over the world. With remarkable consistency over a period of five hundred years, these European observers reported that they had found people in the Americas, Africa and the Pacific Islands who lacked any trace of religion. At the beginning of the sixteenth century, the explorer Amerigo Vespucci observed that the indigenous people of the Caribbean had "no religion" (Berkhofer 1978: 6–8). In the seventeenth century, the traveler Jacques le Maire insisted that among the inhabitants of the Pacific Islands there was "not the least spark of religion" (Callender 1766–1768: 2.308). In the context of expanding trading relations in eighteenth-century West Africa, the trader William Smith reported that Africans "trouble themselves about no religion at all" (1744: 26). Well into the nineteenth century, European observers persisted in claiming that the aboriginal people of Australia had "nothing whatever of the character of religion, or of religious observance, to distinguish them from the beasts that perish" (D. Collins 1804: 354; Lang 1861: 374). These examples could be almost endlessly multiplied. As this global litany of denial accumulated, it developed multiple layers of strategic significance in European colonial encounters with indigenous people. Because they supposedly lacked such a defining human characteristic as religion, indigenous people had no human rights to life, land, livestock or control over their own labor that had to be respected by European colonizers. In this respect, the denial of the existence of any indigenous religion—this discovery of an absence—reinforced colonial projects of conquest, domination and dispossession.

Obviously, the discovery of an absence of religion implied that European commentators in colonial situations were operating with an implicit definition of religion, a definition that was certainly informed by Christian assumptions about what counted as religion. More significantly, however, these denials indicated that the term "religion" was used as an oppositional term on colonial frontiers. In its ancient genealogy, of course, *religio* was always a term that derived is meaning in relation to its opposite, *superstitio*. As the linguist Émile Benveniste observed, the "notion of 'religion' requires, so to speak, by opposition, that of 'superstition'" (1973: 522). On contested colonial frontiers, however, the conceptual opposition between religion and superstition was often deployed as a strategic denial of indigenous rights to land, livestock or labor. In the eastern Cape of southern Africa, for example, the beliefs and practices of indigenous Xhosa people were explicitly denied the designation "religion" during the first half of the nineteenth century by European travelers, missionaries, settlers and colonial magistrates who were trying to establish British military control over the region. Supposedly lacking any trace of religion, the Xhosa allegedly were immersed in superstition. Invoking the defining opposite of religion in this particular colonial situation, the traveler Henry Lichtenstein, for example, reported that the Xhosa's "superstition, their belief in magic or enchantment, and in omens and prognostics, is in proportion to their want of religious feelings" (1928: 301, 311–313). As a recurring motif in European reflections on religious difference in open frontier zones, this opposition between religion and superstition served the colonial project by representing indigenous people as living in a different world.

How did European observers move from the denial to the discovery of indigenous religions in colonial situations? Although that question has to be investigated through detailed attention to historical conditions in specific regions, a general answer can be suggested by the experience of the Xhosa in the eastern Cape of southern Africa. According to the reports of every European commentator, the Xhosa lacked any trace of religion until 1858 when they were placed under a colonial administrative system—the magisterial system—that had been designed by the Cape Governor, Sir George Grey, for the military containment, surveillance and taxation of indigenous people in the eastern Cape. Following his researches on indigenous traditions in Australia and New Zealand, Sir George Grey was both a professional colonial administrator and an amateur scholar of religion. It was the new context of colonial containment, however, that inspired the magistrate J. C. Warner (1858) to be the first to use the term, "religion," for Xhosa beliefs and practices. Insisting that the Xhosa had a religious system, Warner worked out a kind of proto-functionalist analysis by determining that Xhosa religion was a religion because it fulfilled the functional "purposes" of providing psychological security and social stability. Although Warner hoped that the Xhosa religion would ultimately be destroyed by military conquest and Christian conversion, he concluded that in the meantime their indigenous religious system could function to keep them in their place just like the colonial magisterial system.

Throughout southern Africa, the European "discovery" of indigenous religions can be correlated with the colonial containment of indigenous people. While the discovery of a Zulu religious system followed the imposition of the colonial location system in Natal in the 1840s, the recognition of a Sotho-Tswana religious system was delayed until the colonial reserve system was imposed after the destruction of their last independent African polity in the 1890s. By that point, however, when colonial administrators assumed that every African in the region was contained within the urban location system or the rural reserve system, European commentators found that every African in southern Africa had been born into the same "Bantu" religion (Chidester 1996). The southern African evidence suggests, therefore, that the "discovery" of indigenous religions under colonial conditions was not necessarily a break-through in human recognition. As a corollary of the imposition of a colonial administrative system, the discovery of an indigenous religious system was entangled in the colonial containment of indigenous populations.

Ironically, the colonial project of containment that sought to keep people in place at the same time generated theoretical terms for the displacement of indigenous people. Throughout the colonized world, European observers developed theories of history, genealogy and descent that traced indigenous people back to cultural centers in the ancient Near East. In the Americas, for example, European travelers, missionaries and colonizers during the seventeenth century argued that Native Americans were descended from ancient Israel, a claim that was stated succinctly in 1650 in the title of Thomas Thorowgood's book, *Jews in America, or Probabilities that the Americans are of that Race*. By implication, if they were actually Jews from ancient Israel, then Native Americans did not really belong in America (Eilberg-Schwartz 1990: 32–37; Huddleston 1967: 70–71).

In southern Africa, European commentators also traced the genealogy of indigenous people back to the ancient Near East. Anticipated by the early eighteenth-century findings of the German visitor Peter Kolb, who traced the Khoikhoi or "Hottentot" religious system of the subjugated indigenous people of the Cape back to the Judaism of ancient Israel, nineteenth-century European commentators argued that all Africans in southern Africa came from the north. The Xhosa had been ancient Arabs, the Zulu had been ancient Jews, and the Sotho-Tswana had been ancient Egyptians (Chidester 1996). Besides transposing the religious differences of the ancient Near East onto the southern African landscape, thereby reifying the ethnic, cultural and religious differences that had been shaped by colonialism, this fanciful genealogy also implied that indigenous Africans were not actually indigenous to southern Africa because they originally belonged in the Near East. Similarly, a British colonial comparative religion that traced Hinduism back to ancient Indo-European migrations that originated in Siberia or Persia could work not merely as a historical reconstruction, but also as a strategy of displacement. Pursuing this contradictory dual mandate of structural containment and historical displacement, colonial comparative religion operated throughout the world to deny, discover, locate and displace the beliefs and practices of the colonized.

Imperial Comparative Religion

In his inaugural lectures on the science of religion in 1870, F. Max Müller, who has often been regarded as the "founder" of the modern study of religion (Sharpe 1985: 35), demonstrated that the culture of British colonialism and imperialism permeated his understanding of the academic study of religion. First, the study of religion was a science of distance and difference. The distance between the metropolitan center and the colonized periphery was conflated with the difference between the civilized and the barbarian, the savage or the primitive. In developing a comparative method for the study of religion, Max Müller and other metropolitan theorists played on this theme of distance and difference in order to infer characteristics of the "primitive" ancestors of humanity from reports about contemporary "savages" living on the colonized periphery of empire. "Though the belief of African and Melanesian savages is more recent in point of time," as Max Müller observed in his 1870 lectures, "it represents an earlier and far more primitive phase in point of growth" (1873: 25). In similar terms, E. B. Tylor, the "father of anthropology," asserted that the "hypothetical primitive condition corresponds in a considerable degree to modern savage tribes, who, in spite of their difference and distance ... seem remains of an early state of the human race at large" (1903: 1.16). Whatever their differences, nineteenth-century metropolitan theorists of religion, such as Max Müller, Tylor, John Lubbock, Herbert Spencer, Andrew Lang, W. Robertson Smith and James Frazer, employed a comparative method, which came to be known as *the* comparative method, that used reports about the different, the exotic and the savage from distant colonized peripheries to draw conclusions about the evolutionary origins of religion (see Ackerknecht 1969; Bock 1966; Dundes 1986; Eggan 1965; Hammel 1980; Hoenigswald 1963).

Second, the study of religion was a science of denial and domination. "Let us take the old saying, *Divide et impera*," Müller proposed, "and translate it somewhat freely by 'Classify and conquer'" (1873: 122–123). More than merely a rhetorical flourish, this "old saying" provided legitimation for an imperial comparative religion that aspired to global knowledge over the empire of religion. Classification according to language gave Müller a measure of conceptual control over the library of the sacred texts of the world. But imperial conquest enabled him to develop theories of religion that were anchored in British India and British South Africa. In his last work to be published before his death, a pamphlet, *The Question of Right between England and the Transvaal*, which was printed and widely distributed by the Imperial South African Association, Müller asserted that the British Empire "can retire from South Africa as little as from India" (1900: 11). These two imperial possessions, he suggested, were essential for maintaining the global power and authority of the British Empire. But they were also essential for Müller's imperial comparative religion that mediated between "civilized" Great Britain and the "exotic" and "savage" peripheries of empire. While his edition of the *Rig Veda* and his expertise on the religious heritage of India were made possible by the financial support of the East India Company, Müller's imperial comparative religion rested on comparative observations that depended heavily on the British possession of South Africa. Although he observed that in the empire of religion there was "no lack of materials for the student of the Science of Religion" (1873: 101), Müller knew that those raw materials had to be extracted from the colonies, transported to the metropolitan centers of theory production, and transformed into the manufactured goods of theory that could be used by an imperial comparative religion.

In his relations with South Africa, for example, Müller was engaged in a complex process of intercultural mediation in order to transform raw religious materials into theory. First, Africans on the colonized periphery were drawn into this process as informants—often as collaborators, sometimes as authors—as they reported on religious innovations, arguments and contra-dictions in colonial contexts. The Zulu informant Mpengula Mbande, for example, reported arguments about uNkulunkulu, tracking African disagree-ments about whether he was the first ancestor of a particular political grouping, the first ancestor of all people, or the supreme god who created all human beings. Second, local European "experts" on the colonized periphery

431

synthesized these religious conflicts and contradictions into a "religious system." Relying heavily on Mbande's local fieldwork, the Anglican missionary Henry Callaway became the leading authority in the world on Zulu religion and, by extension, on "savage" religion in general, by publishing his classic text, *The Religious System of the Amazulu* (1868–1870). Like other "men on the spot" in colonized peripheries, Callaway corresponded with the metropolitan theorists in London (Benham 1896: 215, 239, 341; Callaway 1874). However, his exposition of the Zulu "religious system" was dissected by those metropolitan theorists in the service of a third mediation, the mediation between the "primitive" ancestors of humanity, who could supposedly be viewed in the mirror of the Zulu and other "savages," and the "civilized" European. What was construed as a religious system in the colony, therefore, was taken apart and reassembled in London as religious data that could be used in support of an evolutionary progression from the primitive to the civilized.

As Jean Paul Sartre observed, "the colonial situation manufactures colonizers as it manufactures colonies" (1965: xxv–xxvi). On colonial peripheries and at imperial centers, nineteenth-century comparative religion played a role in manufacturing European colonial discourse, especially through its representations of "others" in colonized regions such as "exotic" India and "savage" South Africa. As Nicholas Dirks has proposed, these efforts contributed to manufacturing colonizers as "agents of Western reason" (1992: 6). At the end of the twentieth century, we must still wonder about the colonial and imperial legacies that have been inherited by the academic study of religion. In our attention to structure and history, morphology and genealogy, psychological and social functions, and other analytical concerns, do we reproduce the containments and displacements of "others" that were so important to European colonial and imperial projects? Do we still produce knowledge about "allies, antagonists, or subjects of military occupation?" However these questions might be answered, it is clear that a critical academic study of religion must be self-reflexive and self-critical of the political implications of its theory and practice.

Postcolonial Prospects

As we find in postcolonial studies generally, postcolonial prospects for the academic study of religion are largely a matter of location. In *Orientalism* (1978), Edward Said used the analytical term "strategic location" to capture the subject position of European authors in relation to the broad discursive formations of European colonialism and imperialism. In more recent developments within postcolonial theory, however, attention has shifted away from the critique of European colonial representations of "others" to a recovery of the subjectivity and agency of the colonized. At the risk of oversimplifying the complex theoretical controversies that have raged in this emergent field, we can identify two extreme positions in postcolonial studies—*indigeneity* and *hybridity*—that are relevant to the future of the academic study of religion.

First, *indigeneity*, or "indigenism" (Dirlik 1997), represents a range of analytical strategies based on a "cultural differentialism" (Ahmad 1995) that links the recovery of place, the authenticity of tradition and the assertion of self-determination in a project to forge postcolonial meaning and power on indigenous terms. Privileging the self-representation of indigenous people who have passed through the experience of colonization, indigeneity generates analytical terms for recovering the purity of local traditions from the defiling effects of global imperialism. Drawing inspiration from political struggles against colonialism, indigeneity engages the precolonial not merely through a romantic politics of nostalgia but also through the liberation movements of the colonized world. In this respect, the work of the radical psychiatrist Frantz Fanon, who actively identified with the liberation struggles of colonial Africa, has informed an understanding of indigenous tradition that is both postcolonial and post-romantic. "Colonization is not satisfied merely with holding a people in its grip and emptying the native's brain of all form and content," Fanon observed. "By a kind of perverted logic, it turns to the past of oppressed people, and distorts, disfigures and destroys it" (Fanon 1963: 170). While the recovery of a "pure" tradition from colonial distortions and disfigurements was therefore part of his postcolonial project, Fanon linked that recovery of the past with a present of struggle—armed, violent struggle—against colonialism. Although Fanon's position has been characterized as a type of "nativism," it was an indigeneity that sought to forge a new humanity in the modern world by means of a militant anti-colonialism (see Parry 1987).

Certainly, recent examples could be multiplied of postcolonial religious indigeneity in which religious "traditionalists" have deployed "modern" means to assert their power, place, purity and authenticity. Insisting that the only indigenous religion of India is Hinduism, the Rashtriya Svayamsevak Sangh has actively engaged in electoral politics on the platform of "Hindu-ness" (*Hindutva*) in ways that have not just recovered but have actually redefined what it means to be a Hindu in contemporary Indian society (Lochtefeld 1996). Rejecting colonial constructions of African mentality, a variety of African movements have nevertheless promoted visions of African humanity and personality, communalism and socialism, in the interests of a postcolonial African renaissance (Appiah 1988; 1991; Eze 1997a; Mudimbe 1988). Arguing that indigenous land should be regarded as sacred and communal rather than alienable property, Native Americans continue to press cases for the recovery of traditional sacred land in the modern courts of law in the United States (Michaelsen 1995). The failure of almost all of these land claims has suggested to many scholars of Native American religion that the long history of colonial occupation, with its denial, containment and displacement of indigenous religion, has not ended in America (see J. Martin 1997).

While some scholars of religion have embraced indigeneity as their own strategic location, they have had to contend with trends in postmodern, poststructural and other postcolonial analysis that have generally undermined any confidence in the continuity or uniformity of tradition. With respect to historical continuity, influential research on the "invention of tradition" has shown how supposedly timeless traditions—even the primitive, the archaic or the exotic traditions that fascinated colonial and imperial comparative religion—can turn out to have been recent productions (Hobsbawm and Ranger 1985). For example, the Indian caste system, which has supposedly been a perennial feature of Hinduism from time immemorial, has been investigated in recent research as a complex product of indigenous interests and colonial order. In defense of indigeneity, however, as Rosalind O'Hanlon has argued, it is possible to reject the British colonial "notion of an ageless caste-bound social order" while not attributing the entire historical process to a "colonial conjuring" that produces a picture of Indians "who are helpless to do anything but reproduce the structures of their own subordination" (1989: 98, 104, 100). In this respect, indigeneity has made an important contribution by stressing the agency of the colonized as historical actors in the formation of religious, social and political structures (see Trotter 1990).

The "invention of structures," however, has also been called into question, most effectively in the work of Benedict Anderson (1991) on "imagined communities," which analyzed colonial instruments—the census, the archive, the administrative system and so on—for the production of an imaginary sense of social uniformity, but also in the general distrust of any "essentialism" that has been the result of postmodern theory. However, even an anti-essentialist critical theorist such as Gayatri Spivak can propose that in some situations a "strategic essentialism" might be necessary to intervene on behalf of the marginal, oppressed or "subaltern" in struggles over representation in colonial relations (1987: 202). For advocates of indigeneity in the academic study of religion, some form of "strategic essentialism" seems to be necessary in order to pursue an authentic recovery of traditions that however much they might be "invented" or "imagined" nevertheless produce real effects in the real world (see Parry 1994).

Second, *hybridity*, or "hybridization" (Bhabha 1994), captures a range of analytical strategies that follows a logic not of place but of displacement. As a strategic location, hybridity is dislocated in migration and diaspora, contact and contingency, margins and mixtures. As a theoretical intervention in both colonial situations and the postcolonial horizon, attention to hybridity rejects the binary distinction between the colonist and the colonized (Parry 1987: 28–29). According to the most vigorous proponent of colonial hybridity, the cultural theorist Homi Bhabha, the analysis of colonialist situations should focus on neither "the noisy command of colonial authority" nor "the silent repression of native traditions" (Bhabha 1994: 112). Rather, analysis should be directed towards the cultural space in between, the intercultural space of contacts, relations and exchanges. According to Bhabha, intercultural relations in colonial situations are based, "not on the exoticism of multiculturalism or the *diversity* of cultures, but on the inscription and articulation of culture's *hybridity*." In the colonial contact zone of intercultural relations, Bhabha insists, "it is the 'inter'— the cutting edge of translation and negotiation, the *in-between* space—that carries the burden of the meaning of culture" (1994: 38–39).

As Homi Bhabha and other postcolonial theorists have developed this analysis of cultural hybridity, emphasis has shifted from the self-representation of indigenous people in their traditional places to the translations, negotiations and improvisations of the displaced. Migrants, exiles and diaspora communities have received special attention. For example, cultural theorist Stuart Hall has adapted the notion of hybridity as a strategic location for analyzing a dispersed Afro-Caribbean identity that was formed out of the New World that was "the beginning of diaspora, of diversity, of hybridity and difference." In clarifying the New World origin of this diaspora identity, Hall has insisted that it does not entail a politics of nostalgia that evokes myths of "scattered tribes whose identity can only be secured in relation to some sacred homeland to which they must at all costs return, even if it means pushing other people into the sea. This is the old, the imperializing, the hegemonizing, form of 'ethnicity.'" By contrast to such an ethnic, dominating, imperializing, or even indigenous sense of place, purity and essence, which Hall identifies with the hegemonic constructions of colonialism and imperialism, the diaspora identity that he is interested in exploring "is defined, not by essence or purity, but by the recognition of a necessary heterogeneity and diversity; by a conception of 'identity' which lives with and through, not despite, difference; by hybridity" (Hall 1990: 235).

In the study of religion, this postcolonial notion of hybridity has been anticipated by the term, "syncretism" (Stewart and Shaw 1994). Although the term has borne the burden of suggesting impure or illicit mixtures of religion, it has more recently been recovered as a medium of religious innovation. For religious studies, as Ella Shohat has noted in postcolonial studies, " 'Hybridity' and 'syncretism' allow negotiation of the multiplicity of identities and subject positionings which result from displacements, immigrations and exiles without policing the borders of identity along essentialist and originary lines" (1992: 108). Liberated from the "policing of borders" inherent in colonial constructions of genealogical origins and systemic essences, a postcolonial study of religion can engage the complex and contested negotiations over person, place and power that inevitably arise in intercultural relations. Classifications of persons, orientations in time and space, and the power animating these classifications and orientations have all been negotiated, contested and renegotiated in colonial relations. On the postcolonial horizon, religion might be redefined as an open and fluid set of discursive, practical and social strategies for negotiating person and place in an intercultural world (Chidester 1991: 4–5).

As the academic study of religion reorients itself in a world that is simultaneously global and local, as it engages in what Fredric Jameson (1988a) has called a new "cognitive mapping," it might find that the most significant religious negotiations have been conducted over vast bodies of water. In the emergence of modernity, the religious negotiations over the meaning and power of the "fetish" in the Atlantic world and the "cargo" in the Pacific world have raised all the questions of spirituality and materiality, agency and subjectivity, encounter and exchange, that have been both the legacy of colonialism and the challenge of postcolonialism. While the "fetish" that emerged out of mercantile capitalist trading relations in West Africa has been so thoroughly theorized—Marx's objectification of desire, Freud's desired object—that it has even provided a postcolonial definition of modern political power as "state fetishism" (Taussig 1992; see Apter and Pietz 1993; Pietz 1985, 1987, 1988), the "cargo" that captured the imagination of a colonized Pacific world awaits further theoretical reflection. As many adherents of cargo movements in the Pacific realized, the truth of the cargo remains hidden: Since you cannot get it by working for it in wage labor or praying for it in Christian churches, you must have to steal it (see Trompf 1994). The truth of the cargo, therefore, is submerged in the intercultural process of stealing back and forth sacred symbols, including the symbols of wealth, that has been an integral part of all the hybrid or syncretistic negotiations that have been conducted in colonial situations.

Of course, not all negotiating positions are equal. In the culture of late capitalism, global capitalism or neo-imperial capitalism at the end of the twentieth century (Jameson 1984), indigeneity can look like nostalgia for the premodern, hybridity like alienation in the postmodern (Ahmad 1992, 1995). As the academic study of religion comes to terms with its colonial legacy, it might also develop its postcolonial potential to deploy its resources of critique and analysis, interpretation and explanation, empathy and engagement, in a changing world order. As a science of identity and difference, the academic study of religion might actually be well positioned to rise to the challenge of the postcolonial through sustained attention to the strategic locations and dislocations of the human in new contact zones.

Notes

1. Innovations in colonial and postcolonial analysis in the field of anthropology appear, for example, in Cooper and Stoler (1997), Fabian (1983), Stocking (1987, 1991) and N. Thomas (1994). In the field of literary studies, a profile of analytical trends can be suggested by consulting Adam and Tiffin (1991), Brantlinger (1988), Darby (1998), Gikandi (1996), Low (1996), Mignolo (1995), Moore-Gilbert (1997) and Spurr (1993). Significant discussions of historical theory and method in colonial and postcolonial studies can be found in B. S. Cohn (1997), Dirks (1992), Prakash

(1995) and R. Young (1990). Recent developments in colonial and postcolonial gender analysis appear in Jolly (1994), McClintock (1995), McClintock et al. (1997), Ram and Jolly (1998) and Stoler (1995).

2. Among the historical ethnographies of intercultural contact, encounter and exchange under colonial conditions, the following are particularly useful for analyzing colonialism: in the Americas (Gilroy 1993; Greenblatt 1991; Hulme 1986; MacCormack 1991; Seed 1991; Taussig 1980; 1987; Todorov 1984); in Africa (Comaroff and Comaroff 1991, 1997; Werbner and Ranger 1996); in the Middle East (Mitchell 1991); in South Asia (Breckenridge and Van der Veer 1993; Deepika and Vasudeva 1996; Guha 1997; Inden 1990; Nandy 1983; Schwarz 1997; Singh 1996); in East Asia (Barrow 1997; Wiener 1995); and in the Pacific Islands (Sahlins 1985; Thomas 1991, 1997).

Suggested Readings

Bhabha, Homi K.
  1994   *The Location of Culture.* London: Routledge.
Breckenridge, Carol A. and Peter van der Veer
  1993   *Orientalism and the Postcolonial Predicament: Perspectives on South Asia.* South Asia Seminar Series, vol. 44. Philadelphia: University of Pennsylvania Press.
Chidester, David
  1996   *Savage Systems: Colonialism and Comparative Religion in Southern Africa.* Studies in Religion and Culture. Charlottesville: University Press of Virginia.
Comaroff, Jean and John L. Comaroff
  1997   *Of Revelation and Revolution,* vol. 2: *The Dialectics of Modernity on a South African Frontier.* Chicago: University of Chicago Press.
Long, Charles H.
  1986   *Significations: Signs, Symbols, and Images in the Interpretation of Religion.* Philadelphia: Fortress.
Lopez, Donald S., Jr., editor
  1995   *Curators of the Buddha: The Study of Buddhism under Colonialism.* Chicago: University of Chicago Press.
Prakash, Gyan, editor
  1995   *After Colonialism: Imperial Histories and Postcolonial Displacements.* Princeton Studies in Culture / Power / History. Princeton: Princeton University Press.
Pratt, Mary Louise
  1992   *Imperial Eyes: Travel Writing and Transculturation.* London: Routledge.
Said, Edward W.
  1978   *Orientalism.* New York: Pantheon.
Taussig, Michael
  1987   *Shamanism, Colonialism, and the Wild Man: A Study in Terror and Healing.* Chicago: University of Chicago Press.

30

IDEOLOGY

Gary Lease

"Ideology" marks the twentieth century as no other term. Since the social and political upheavals in the United States and France at the end of the eighteenth century, revolution, of course, has laid claim to first rank among modern-era concepts. And since Freud, the notion of "the unconscious" has gained strong currency as the chief marker of our age. But neither term has the breadth and extension of ideology; neither concept has exercised such inclusiveness as ideology; and neither word has replaced so many others as has ideology. It is not to be wondered, then, that the study of religion, that many-headed Hydra of modernity, is inextricably, even intimately, linked to the notion of ideology.

Ideology as Category

Ideology does not take its origins in Western culture's antiquity or even in the Middle Ages, as do so many other political and social concepts. Rather, it is in the overthrow of these older, traditional categorical systems during the French Revolution (1789) that the word first was formed. In the beginning, the so-called French Ideologists sought only to name their new science, but due to Napoleon's later use of the term, and the resulting political / public relations campaigns, the word lost its original philosophical and quite a-political meaning, to be transformed into a polemical slogan during the first half of the nineteenth century. As a result, the notion assumed its status as a battle cry, a function it has not lost to this day. It is also in this guise that Marx and Engels appropriated the term and provided it with the specific meaning that still attaches to this label in many disparate areas of dispute. The end result is that the very term ideology has been ideologized.

Initially, ideology refers to a pattern of thought, a way of life, and a political course of action—in other words, a more or less coherent system of ideas—that are bound to sets of ideas with little or no connection to reality, indeed are opposed to experiential reality. Ideology thus presupposes a gap between theory and practice, between idea and reality. It is only when the belief in the primacy of thought is attacked as the reverse of what the actual state of human consciousness is, that ideology also assumes the secondary meanings of illusion and self-deception. In this form, then, ideological criticism becomes the process by which unrecognized impediments in the process of establishing truth are revealed.

For the purpose of the study of religions, however, it is important to note that the current primary reference of the concept ideology is to a special form of illusion, namely the belief that ideas are the chief elements in human politics and history. Despite logical consistency, the presence of scientific rationality, and even practical evidences, what characterizes ideology in its usual applications is the hidden, even repressed role of the key historical, social and economic interests, motives and determinations that produced the seemingly disembodied system of ideas to begin with.

The History of Ideology

It was the French Ideologist, Antoine Destutt de Tracy (1754–1836), who first coined the term "ideology" (1801–1807). As the founder of a *science of ideas*, Destutt hoped to study the origin of human conceptualization, not as norms but as products. Such a science would, in his view, serve as a foundation for the rest of human knowledge. Following the English philosopher John Locke, Destutt sought merely to observe and describe the actions of the human mind, emphasizing that ideology, properly conceived, would be nothing other than a part of zoology. This is so, according to Destutt, because all ideas take their origin in the senses and achieve expression in language. By investigating the relationship between ideas and the (linguistic) signs that matched them, he hoped to achieve for his science of ideas the same strict precision that rules in such other fields as mathematics and the natural sciences. As such, ideology would be the scientific basis of human society: politics, law, morality and education would flow from it.

The influence exercised by the Ideologists, however, throughout revolutionary and post-revolutionary France, especially in the form of a-religious and empirical teachings in the schools, led to a clash with Napoleon. Initially he had been friendly toward the Ideologists, even inviting Destutt to accompany him on his military campaign in Egypt. But after assuming sole power in France in 1799 (the coup of the 18th Brumaire), Napoleon saw the need to consolidate his position by restoring, in a controllable form, both church and state (Concordat with the Roman Church, 1801). This move led inexorably to a break with the anti-theological and liberal teachings of the Ideologists. There was little doubt in Napoleon's mind that the Ideologists, now disqualified by him as merely "metaphysicians and fanatics," were working counter to his notions of supreme power. Indeed, their concepts of state and society were, for the Emperor, but abstract theories that had nothing to do with political reality. By giving the term ideology a new meaning, Napoleon attempted to make the Ideologists ridiculous: an idea is for him no longer a sensually grasped content projected by the human imagination, but rather merely a theory disconnected from reality. As such, any discourse about ideas was disqualified as substanceless theorizing. With one blow Napoleon had turned ideology into a pejorative characterization of all philosophical theories, particularly those that may have laid claim to some practical political legitimacy. As a consequence, ideology was seen throughout Europe as the hallmark of dreamers, theoreticians, doctrinaire professors, people of principle, writers of fiction, insane projections, and so on. This was especially true for the followers of natural law theory and the supporters of a restoration of the monarchical political order that had been swept away in the tide of the French Revolution. True, and particularly in Germany, there was also a positive conception of ideology: Goethe, and later Heine, saw the power of ideas realized in the wars of liberation fought precisely against Napoleon, and they viewed their victory for freedom as the reverse of his version of ideology. But in the main, ideology remained at the mid-nineteenth century a term of derision and a polemical slogan—a sense of the term that we still find in use to this day.

Of long-lasting importance for the development of the term ideology is, of course, the role played by Karl Marx. Tracing the history of ideology in Marx's writings is extremely complicated. For one thing, the key text authored by Marx and Engels dealing with ideology, *The German Ideology* (1970 [1845–46]), was not published in any form until early in the twentieth century (1903–1904), and in its entirety only in 1932. Apparently, both Marx and Engels thought that the notion of ideology was so transparent that a precise delineation of its meaning was unnecessary. The result was a myriad of different nuanced uses of the term in their writings, which in turn led to a wide number of Marxian-based conceptions of ideology that could simply not be undone by such late revelations of what Marx and Engels may have thought ideology was at the beginning of their careers. What is clear, however, is that Marx found the notion of ideology associated with Napoleon to be the proper one: ideology for him was, at least to begin with, an act of theorizing that was distant from reality, and above all foreign to political practice. From this point of departure it was not long before Marx spoke of his now famous "alienated consciousness," a consciousness permeated by abstract projections and mental spider webs. Only later was one able to see that already in *The German Ideology* Marx and Engels had made this interpretation of ideology even more precise. Here they took on the so-called Young Hegelians, those critics of Hegel who, in the judgment of Marx and Engels, had stood reality (and also Hegel) on its head: ideas, concepts, thoughts, projections do not determine human life and history; to maintain that position is to turn the true relationship between being and consciousness *ideologically* upside down. Of course Marx and Engels did know what that relationship should be: it is only individuals, their actions and the material conditions of their lives that determine their history; the entire mental production of human beings is conditioned by the development of the products of their labor and the exchange of those products. According to Marx and Engels, ideologies, unfortunately, see this process in reverse: rather than viewing the progression of consciousness from material production, ideologies maintain the independence of thought and spirit.

One consequence of this legendary position—consciousness does not determine life, but rather life determines consciousness—was that, in the Marxian view, morality, religion, metaphysics, and other ideologies lose any claim to social and historical autonomy. Since Marx and Engels argued that the genuine relationship between humans and reality lies in the material preconditions of life, it was easy for them to proceed to the analysis of the products of human action as the source of an empirical confirmation. Reality was expanded to include, however, not only the material conditions but also the social conditions of human life, namely the class interests that were hidden by ideologies. In fact, in later Marxian thought, this becomes one of the chief tasks of ideology: to hide the true interests that lie behind the goals and acts of the power-wielding classes (e.g., the nobility, the bourgeoisie). This forgetting of the genuine, material motivations for thought and action is the product of self-delusion rather than conscious intention: ideology is therefore a process of self-alienation. Consciously or not, such self-alienation as found in religion, morality, and so on, is therefore revealed as a lie. Ideology results from the attempt to make the *super-structure* of ideas autonomous and independent of the true relationship between consciousness and reality. Indeed, for Marx religion is one of those areas of human activity that, by its very nature, must understand its norms and beliefs as eternal, holy and, above all else, as unchanging; as such, religion strives to break the connection between itself and the class interests that lie at its foundation. Religion, in other words, is ideology *per se*.

The post-Marxian development of socialism and social democracy, however, led to often quite different results. Georg Lukacs (1955), for example, considered a reified or independent consciousness as the product of capitalism's terrible effect on the worker. Such an autonomous consciousness must achieve *ideological* maturity, must gain accurate knowledge about its true class situation—must, in other words, reach a state of authentic class consciousness. At that point, for Lukacs, ideology is no longer a theory independent of practice, but instead is the location of unity between theory and practice. This is, however, a position that neither Marx nor Engels would have represented. Nor would Theodor Adorno's (1964) understanding of ideology have been happily accepted by Marx and Engels. Ideology in his sense is precisely society itself, but society in its essential appearance. For Adorno there is no false consciousness that is independent of society, making ideologies somehow stand apart from history. Rather, the consciousness that is ideology is the duplication of the society from which it springs. Although Herbert Marcuse viewed ideology as restricted to the one-dimensional reality of technological development, Jürgen Habermas went even further, finding ideology in the identification of possessions and humanity. One of the most recent attempts to reconceptualize the notion of ideology is found in the work of the sociologist Niklas Luhmann (1977) who sees ideology as the value system by which members of a society determine which consequences of their actions are acceptable and which are not. For Luhmann ideology is primarily, if not completely, comprehensible as a function of human society, not as separate and autonomous thought.

Critique and Evaluation

Religion, observed the sociologist Peter Berger (1969), is the "audacious attempt to conceive of the entire universe as being humanly significant." Or put another way, religions are systems of meaning, and as such they are ideologies. For if the history of the term has taught us anything, it is that, whether considered to be false or authentic, ideologies are precisely systems of ideas that are organized to produce meaning for human actions. And religions are exactly such constructions, claiming to be models for all other theorizing. Religion is therefore not simply one ideological creation among others—though it is certainly that—but also a key node for the distribution of power or control over the texts and limits of consciousness. Luhmann is therefore correct when he maintains that the key to understanding ideology is its function: a religion represents just such a function as the self-evident pattern of human experience, and thus of reality.

But religion and ideology are not the only constructs to share the function of providing meaning: world-views, mythologies and cosmologies also strive to systematize human meaning. Are they therefore all the same as ideology? Hardly! Despite Ninian Smart's (1981, 1983) tendency to mix and match these categories, the lines of distinction are important to observe. A world-view, for example, deals with the difficulty of comprehending the relationship between humans and the world in which they are located, and imposing a meaning upon that connection. A cosmology, on the other hand, strives to present as complete a picture as possible of the relationship between the world and the nature that inhabits that world, humanity included; such a presentation may or may not lead to the establishment of meaning, or a pattern of relationships between all the players.

Mythology is perhaps the most difficult of these categories to determine, and at the same time the most relevant to understanding both ideology and religion. For mythologies deal directly with constituting data as self-evident; analyzing mythology seeks to understand not only how this process works, but also to what purpose it is undertaken. It is only within such a framework that we can ask about religion, ideology, world-view and cosmology.

One can perhaps most easily grasp the function of mythologies as the meta-codes which govern the choice (selection) of the actual interpretive codes used to decipher experience and the expression of experience. Myths, in other words, both govern the choice of a code (world-view, cosmology, ideology, religion) and judge its application. Precisely as meta-code, mythologies establish what gets to count, or what is considered self-evident in a culture, be that in the realm of the so-called sacred or the general cultural code.

Religions, as specific forms of ideology, are culture-wide interpretations or code applications, dedicated to making manifest the latent meaning behind the text of the culture at large; myths, particularly in their manifestation within a religion, are the governing tools or codes by which this production is performed. These basic tools or codes are always about relationships: origins to world to humans. A major consequence therefore of understanding religions as ideologies is that they only make sense when viewed as human productions rather than as external impositions. Finally, religions also allow the accessing of world-views and cosmologies by establishing an absolute claim to do so: the meaning of the world, or a world-view, and the representation of that world, or a cosmology, can only, according to religion, be interrelated by means of that religion and its mythology. Precisely, however, because religions are ideologies, and therefore changeable, every person has a world-view, and every person has a cosmology, but not every person has a religion.

Traditional religions, however, particularly those in Western culture and those claiming universal legitimacy, reject any identification with ideology as inauthentic and destructive. For them religion cannot be ideology for the simple fact that religions (or their religion) are true and thus certainly are not in any sense manifestations of an alienated consciousness. In contrast, the view represented here, following Louis Althusser's (1971) lead, holds that ideologies are the inevitable result of human consciousness. Among the key functions of consciousness is to process the myriad stages of identification with which human beings construct the world around them. As the chief tool for doing so, consciousness makes use of definition, or the establishment of relationships as *objects* which are consequently subject to use and control. To identify both self and world and have them remain stable and separable, consciousness stamps them as independent and external, rather than seeing them as the products of cultural and representational imagination. As a result, humans are constantly bringing forth new identifications and linking them up with previous identifications in a feverish attempt to provide definitions capable of covering all possible experiences. Such a plurality of definitions, in turn, demands a catalog or ranking of their relationships of one to another; tests are produced which allow one to locate new definitions within the catalog. These catalogs are ideologies.

The presence of such catalogs in human lives, and more particularly in commonly shared human lives, leads inevitably to a struggle over the power to control their formation and their application. Who, for example, defines the ranking with a particular catalog? How, and with what force, is that primary definitional act exercised? The answers to these questions form the stuff of ideologies, or the dynamic process by which such catalogs cease to be ever changing, contestable systems of judgment and, instead, come to be understood as self-evident and fundamental to human existence. Such self-evident systems of definition and classification must constantly be legitimated in order to head off the collapse of the intricate patterns of relationship which make up the supportive ideologies. Any society, I would argue, is forever and inextricably bound up with the process of sustaining its basically shared catalogs of definitions and classifications for human experience of the world. Any society, in other words, is always producing and legitimating sets of ideologies.

In order to sustain such sets, or systems of ideologies, authority is needed to impose them on those segments of a society which may have constructed quite different, or variant catalogs of definitions. Force may be employed, and the role of law codes to regulate the function of such force in maintaining broad-based ideologies is well known. *Constitutions*, for example, have as their reason for being the provision of such a self-evidently understood and accepted framework for ideologies and their attendant rules of enforcement (law), that the very basis of the societies for which they were created cannot be called into question. *Religion*, on the other hand, frequently serves as the label for those systems of legitimation which attempt to anchor their foundation outside of, or external to, the ideologies being legitimated. In either case, stability is the desired product. And stability promises a constant, unvarying pattern of relationship between inside and outside, or more prosaically, between self and others. In overcoming separation and distinction, stability of ideology becomes both inclusive and exclusive, that is, it assumes all experiences available to the society in question and rejects all those experiences which might be used to question the accepted set.

But what happens if such questioning does occur? What happens if the stability, no matter how powerfully enforced, breaks down and the catalog of definitions which makes up a society's ideologies no longer is understood to be self-evident? Inevitably, chaos and the competition of ideologies results. It is precisely religion, however, always the preeminent discourse of definition, that is opposed to such chaos. Together with law, religion works tirelessly against the dismantling of ideological systems, trying to stem any encroaching chaos by shoring up the once-self-evident catalogs of definitions which are the substance of a society's ideologies. Religion, in other words, is always the enemy of revolution, since revolution can only mean the subversion and destabilizing of ideological systems. As such, revolution is also the ever-present shadow of religion. Where you find history and religion, ideology and revolution both lie at their roots and are not far behind. For both history and religion are not true in the sense that their stories are full, complete and forever unchanging, though each would have you believe that is indeed the case. Rather, history and religion are only interpretations, or better, ideological narratives: how one views, represents and comprehends a subject, event or experience is very much dependent upon the ideology underlying the interpretive effort; that is why history and religion are so full of mysteries, not clarity. There are no real artifacts to go on: you have to reconstruct it all. Due to the interspacing of ideology between us and reality, the past, present and future are not self-revealing: we have to *make it up*. Not every ideology is a religion, but every religion is ideology.

Ideology and the Study of Religion

There is widespread agreement that doing religion is not the same as studying religion. If we were to take the notion of religion as ideology as our point of departure, then three directions offer contemporary and future scholarship the most fruitful sources for the study of religion: tracing the natural history of religions; the interaction between religion and the law; and the anchoring of a theory of religion in the biological sphere.

A so-called natural history seeks to trace the emergence, or primal identity; development, or mature identity; and dissolution, or death of identity. Understanding religion as ideology grants us the flexibility to apply such analytic categories to religions. This is so because tracking the development or patterns of change in a particular religion over time allows us to understand it as ideologically determined, that is, as contingent. Without a coherent account of the process of change that lies between the narrated emergence and the present point of observation, establishing the identity of a religion becomes difficult if not impossible. And without an identity, there is not intelligibility. One need only witness the current chaos reigning in the world of Christian origins: soon tracing this area of study will have mainly ethnographic interest.

The result of such an approach would mean that one never comes to closure on what constitutes the object of such a history. The target, or particular religion under review, would always be shifting, would always be contingent, would never be final, just as with our other rational objects of knowledge. Indeed, the evidences that one might adduce for such a history would also always be in movement. The ethical, moral, ritual and intellectual choices that adherents of a specific religion consider to be demanded by their beliefs, or demanded by *religion* in general, would constantly be changing, would never be absolute. A

445

natural history of a religion could never, therefore, posit the *reality* or, better, the validity of any religion's claims or persuasions (beliefs) as the object and intelligibility, but rather only the origins, the history and the death of such claims and their resulting functions. In other words, desire and need are not identical: a genuine science of religion would acknowledge that a choice of reality does not constitute hegemony over all of reality or over others. Study of religion, precisely as ideology, is not the giving or bearing of testimony to the truth of a particular religion, or of religion in the abstract: it is not an act of belief.

The question of what place religion occupies in our larger social life is an almost classic case of the intimate relationship between religion and the law, as well as to the broader political setting in which law is found. A colleague of mine observed some years ago that the parallel to the slogan of that well-known Jewish teacher of antiquity, Jesus of Nazareth, who said that *the meek shall inherit the earth*, was none other than the observation of that contemporary social critic and baseball manager of the 1950s, Leo Durocher, who noted that *nice guys finish last*. There are very real tensions between these two stances, tensions that come from competitive ideologies. In our own time we have seen National Socialist Germany co-opt the major Christian churches in its spasm of totalitarian control and self-destruction, using particularly Roman Catholicism to organize public ritual and the celebration of fascist political domination. Again, in Yugoslavia, or more specifically Croatia, we have seen the church co-opted by a national movement hardly distinguishable from its German masters; now Archbishop Stepinac, who welcomed his fascist allies with such enthusiasm, is being praised by the Roman Catholic Pope as a martyr and has been beatified. In the United States there continues sharp controversy over whether the Congress and the states should amend the Constitution to permit prayer in school classrooms; the struggle is, of course, over the questions of *"which* prayer?" and *"whose* composition?" Religion and law, in other words, is one of the most thorny but also most potentially fruitful areas for the study of religion today precisely because it is in the law, and in a religion's relationship to the law, that the struggle between competing ideologies becomes most clear.

As biologists probe ever deeper into the structure of the human brain, as the final mapping of the human genome becomes ready for us in the next few years, more and more students of religion are questioning the possibility that religion is *hard-wired* into the human genetic structure. Or at the very least, that evolutionary hangovers (experiential adaptations), rather than specific genes, lie at the heart of the human creation we call religion. What if, for example, we were to view religion as a set of artifacts, artifices and strategies by which the human species moved from being a prey species to a predator species? In other words, what if the ideological understanding of religion took as its point of departure a notion of religion as a complex strategy designed as a system of values, reinforced by ritual, to locate our origin and our fate outside of ourselves, with the goal of this strategy being the effort to cope with an initial prey experience and eventual shift to outright predation, ultimately ending in preying upon ourselves? What if the human species is chased by the ghosts of predators past, and still displays its strategic adaptations for surviving those predators? Other constructions are, of course, not only possible but likely if one were to take seriously the ideological character of religion.

Understanding religions as ideologies will liberate the study of religions and their traditions in ways we can only dimly anticipate, leading to more profound, and more accurate ways of determining both the role religions play in wider society, and the definitions of what gets to count as religion in that society.

Suggested Readings

Althusser, Louis
> 1971   "Ideology and the State." In *Lenin and Philosophy, and Other Essays*. Ben Brewster (trans.). New York: Monthly Review Press.

Berger, Peter
> 1969   *The Sacred Canopy: Elements of a Sociological Theory of Religion.* Garden City, NY: Doubleday.

Bocock, Robert and Kenneth Thompson, editors
> 1985   *Religion and Ideology: A Reader*. Manchester: Manchester University Press.

De Man, Paul
> 1996   *Aesthetic Ideology*. Andrzej Warminski (ed.). Minneapolis: University of Minnesota Press.

Eagleton, Terry
> 1991   *Ideology: An Introduction*. London: Verso.

Henry, Michael
> 1979   *The Intoxication of Power: An Analysis of Civil Religion in Relation to Ideology*. Dordrecht, Holland: D. Reidel.

Lease, Gary
> 1995b   'Odd Fellows' in the Politics of Religion: Modernism, National Socialism, and German Judaism*. Berlin: Mouton de Gruyter.

Smart, Ninian
> 1981   *Beyond Ideology: Religion and the Future of Western Civilization*. San Francisco: Harper & Row.

Tal, Uriel
> 1975   *Christians and Jews in Germany: Religion, Politics, and Ideology in the Second Reich, 1870–1914*. Ithaca, NY: Cornell University Press.

Thompson, Kenneth
> 1986   *Beliefs and Ideology*. London: Tavistock.

Van Dijk, Teun A.
> 1998   *Ideology: A Multidisciplinary Approach*. London: Sage.

Žižek, Slavoj, editor
> 1994   *Mapping Ideology*. London: Verso.

EPILOGUE

Critical inquiry need assume neither cynicism nor dissimulation to justify probing beneath the surface, and ought to probe scholarly discourse and practice as much as any other.

Bruce Lincoln (1996: 226)

31

PLAY

Sam D. Gill

అలా అలా

Play, among its many and varied meanings, may denote a type of structural dynamics, a being at once of two minds or a holding at once of mutually exclusive positions. Play as this sort of structurality, to use Jacques Derrida's term, offers insight and promise for creatively engaging the challenges of the modern academic study of religion.

Religion is a generic category imagined and developed to address issues distinctive to a Western heritage. That the study of religion be academic requires it to be descriptive, its scope to be world-wide and spanning history, its methods to be comparative, and its goal to be comprehension and appreciation rather than conversion. That the study of religion be modern demands it to embrace cultural and religious diversity without the principal intent to collapse difference. That the study of religion be postmodern demands it to forgo (or at least to persistently acknowledge the impact of) objectivist and essentialist premises and to embrace the responsibility for creating and constructing its subjects as well as discovering and observing them. Thus the academic study of religion finds itself repudiating aspects of both its religious and intellectual heritages (inseparable from Western religious ideas) and, even more seriously, challenging its own most fundamental understanding of its subject, religion (based heavily on the prototype of Christianity). The acknowledgment that there is no being-presence, no essential ground, it would seem, contradicts most religious views of the world, the views of our subjects. The acceptance of diverse world-views—some exclusive, most claiming ultimate truth—does the same.

Frankly, I find this conundrum one of the most interesting issues facing the academic study of religion. It is what can make this field of study important to the academy and to the world beyond. Our challenge is to find a meaningful way to hold together at once two or more irreconcilable positions and to do so without smoke and mirrors and without forced or too easy difference-denying solutions. Our ability to do this is among the crowning human capabilities. That this ability, which may be called "play," is a common one at the root of so much human pleasure and so many aspects of human culture—symbol, metaphor, language, humor, art and religion—is all the more satisfying.

Play emerges early in human development. Jean Piaget described the dynamics of human development in terms of two strategies: accommodation and assimilation. Accommodation is when the child holds the experience of the world as the base on which to develop and adjust concepts and ideas, that is, knowledge and awareness of the *real* world. Assimilation (the term "projection" may communicate the idea more directly) is a complementary strategy in which the developing child builds a sense of self (*ego*) by projecting her or his ideas on the world. The first is necessary to accommodate the facticity and independent existence of the world in which we live (*reality*) while the second is necessary to relate meaningfully as individual human beings through such operations as imagination and interpretation and it is required for all forms of human expression from language to art (*ego*). Piaget, and later Erik Erikson, saw these strategies as interdependent rather than separable. While they structurally oppose one another, they are necessarily held in common in developing human beings through a structurality Piaget referred to as play which he understood as "distinguished by a modification, varying in degree, of the conditions of equilibrium between reality and ego … Play is to be conceived as being both related to adapted thought by a continuous sequence of intermediaries, and bound up with thought as a whole, of which it is only one pole, more or less differentiated" (Piaget 1962: 150).

This understanding of play as a kind of structural dynamic was presented as early as the late eighteenth century by Friedrich Schiller in *On the Aesthetic Education of Man* (1967 [1793]). He described play as a human drive (*Spieltrieb*). Schiller investigated the distinctions of being human in terms of a series of opposing pairs of drives or forces (*Trieb*). For example, he recognized two contrary "challenges to man," which he called the sensuous and formal drives. The sensuous drive insists on attention to the present and the wholly subjective. All potentialities are fully manifest. The formal drive, on the other hand, strives toward universality, generality and law. Seen as the product of these drives, human beings externalize all that is within them and give form to all that is outside them (Schiller 1967: XIV.1). While these forces oppose one another,[1] Schiller found neither impulse to be dispensable. It is not a matter of choosing between them, because when either acts exclusive of the other the result is the loss of the human being: the sensuous drive acting alone leaves the person as a moment of sensation while one becomes an idea, a species, when only the formal drive is active. Further, both drives require restriction and moderation. "Perfection," in Schiller's scheme, is attained only through "a reciprocal action between the two drives, reciprocal action of such a kind that the activity of the one both gives rise to, and sets limits to, the activity of the

452

other, and in which each in itself achieves its highest manifestation precisely by reason of the other being active" (Schiller 1967: XIV.1). When both drives work "in concert," the reciprocal action amounts to the emergence of a third drive, the play drive (*Spieltrieb*). According to Schiller this play drive is "directed towards annulling time within time [the contribution of the sensuous drive], reconciling becoming with absolute being and change with identity [the contribution of the formal drive] ... The play-drive, in consequence, as the one in which both the others act in concert, will exert upon the psyche at once a moral and physical constraint; it will, therefore, since it annuls all contingency, annul all constraint too, and set man free both physically and morally" (Schiller 1967: XIV.3 and 5).[2] The interaction and movement among the two opposed mutually exclusive forces—that is, in the interplay of the drives—achieve a kind of transcendence (play) of the opposing drives that Schiller identified with freedom, with perfection and with beauty.[3] Though two centuries old, Schiller's view of play in some ways anticipates postmodernity where play is an important concept.

Near the end of his essay, "Structure, Sign, and Play in the Discourse of the Human Sciences," Jacques Derrida places his readers in the jaws of the alternative approaches to interpretation. He writes in typical Derridian style:

> There are two interpretations of interpretation, of structure, of sign, of freeplay [*jeu*]. The one seeks to decipher, dreams of deciphering, a truth or an origin which is free from freeplay and from the order of the sign, and lives like an exile the necessity of interpretation. The other, which is no longer turned toward the origin, affirms freeplay and tries to pass beyond man and humanism, the name man being who, throughout the history of metaphysics or of ontotheology—in other words, through the history of all his history—has dreamed of full presence, of reassuring foundation, the origin and the end of the game. (Derrida 1970: 264)

Derrida holds the choice to be trivial, writing that we must "first try to conceive of the common ground, and the *différence* of this irreducible difference" (Derrida 1970: 265). That is, we must play both irreconcilable options at once and in doing so transcend to a new level of awareness of structural dynamics. In Derrida's terms play is of structurality rather than of structure (that limits freeplay). Play emerges from the rupture he identified with Nietzsche's critique of metaphysics, with Freud's critique of self-presence, and with Heidegger's destruction of the determination of being as presence. Play is born of the loss of center, of fixedness, of the awareness of "a field of infinite substitutions in the closure of a finite ensemble" (Derrida 1970: 249). This is, of course, the domain of the sign.

In "A Theory of Play and Fantasy," the essay that has in recent years replaced Johan Huizinga's *Homo Ludens*[4] as the standard defining work on play, Gregory Bateson focuses his attention on the meta-communicative aspects of play, recognizing that play is possible only if the participating organisms are capable of some degree of meta-communication. Play, in his analysis, always contains the message "this is play" rather than that which without this meta-communication would be considered something else. Observing monkeys playing, Bateson realized that their playful nips denoted bites, but still they did not denote what would be denoted by bites. Thus he saw that play could be described as a meta-message: "These actions, in which we now engage, do not denote what would be denoted by those actions which these actions denote." In other words, the actions must be framed by the meta-message "this is play." The statement "this is play," as Bateson analyzes it, establishes "a paradoxical frame comparable to Epimenides' paradox" (Bateson 1972: 184). Epimenides, the Cretan, stated that all Cretans are liars. This is a self-referential paradox. If his statement is true, then it is false; if false, then it falsifies itself. "This is play" allows the holding at once of the statements "this action denotes something" and "this action does not denote what these actions denote."

Bateson's work focused attention on the interplay between play and the boundary that distinguished play from not-play. Choices made within play, unlike those in not-play, necessarily invoke the interrelationship of the content of play with the boundary condition "this is play." Play is moebiatic in this sense: the inside and outside are so seamlessly connected as to be self-problematizing. To play is also in some sense to say, "this is play" which is also in some sense to ask, "what is play?" Play is a boundary that presents alternatives governed by self-contradiction such that each leads to and negates the other in an apparent endless cycle. Play demands choice among equally valued alternatives. Choice depends upon a hierarchy of values. Choice involves movement. But when any choice is made (thus seemingly to pass beyond play) the immediate attractiveness of the not chosen alternative invokes self-doubt and self-reflection on and problematization of the hierarchy of values which led to the now-questioned choice. And on and on. The result is an oscillatory movement in at least two planes—the movement back and forth among alternatives within the frame of play seeking resolution through choice and the movement back and forth between the domain in which choice is demanded and the boundary conditions that frame the choices (see Handelman 1992). I believe play is often experienced as enjoyable because it celebrates the distinctive human capacity to simultaneously do one thing and its opposite and to be aware of the process by which it is possible to do the impossible. Yet, seen in this way, we can also appreciate why play is often opposed to work (where choices are experienced as satisfying terminations) and that play may be experienced as frustrating or dangerous.

The experience of play is autotelic—what Csikszentmihalyi (1990) calls "flow"—because its self-referential and paradoxical character challenges one to do all of the following at once: to make choices, to reflect on the process of making choices, and to question our understanding of how choices are made. It is autotelic because it challenges us to end that which turns endlessly upon itself. To attempt to end play by making a choice only initiates a new cycle of play and often at a new level.

Interestingly, Jean Baudrillard's understanding of the way our brains work is similar:

> There is no better model of the way in which the computer screen and the mental screen of our own brain are interwoven than Moebius's topology, with its peculiar contiguity of near and far, inside and outside, subject and object within the same spiral. It is in accordance with this same model that the information and communication are constantly turning round themselves in an incestuous circumvolution, a superficial conflation of subject and object, within and without, question and answer, event and image and so on. The form is inevitably that of a twisted ring reminiscent of the mathematical symbol for infinity. (Baudrillard 1993: 56)

The academic study of religion may be clarified by rethinking it *sub specie ludi*.[5] In my view, Jonathan Z. Smith offers the best foundation for this development. Fundamental to understanding this aspect of his work is to discern the playful character of the academic method by which Smith conducts his work. *Juxtaposition* is his initiating operation. He places side by side interpretations, quotations and their sources, approaches or ideas in such a way that they demand *comparison*. An engaging juxtaposition motivates an interplay, rather than a resolution, among the elements. That interplay is fueled by *difference*, because it is in difference that the operation is interesting and creative. If the elements can be happily reduced to sameness, the process abruptly ends. Play stops. Difference gives rise to thought, to hypothesis and theory, to explanation. Smith's is a comparative method framed by juxtaposition and fueled by difference directed less toward final resolution than toward raising questions and revealing insights. Smith's method is akin to play as described above.

The structurality we are calling play is evident in Smith's understanding of the categories he, and many others, hold most fundamentally religious: place, myth and ritual. Place, for Smith, is accounted for most powerfully in the dynamics of map and territory. He recognizes religion as well as the study of religion as a mapping process and to account for the history of the study of religions he articulates two mapping strategies—locative and utopian.[6] A locative vision of the world emphasizes place, while a utopian vision emphasizes the value of being in no place (J. Z. Smith 1978a: 101). But Smith warns against using this distinction as a pair of categories into which to sort religions. The structurality of play is engaged here by Smith in a powerful construction that builds upon the acknowledgment of the interdependence of these two mapping strategies as well as the classical terms of sacred and profane (chaos in Smith's revision). In acknowledging the power of the incongruity and difference that forces the elements of these pairs to be held together despite their opposition, Smith articulates a third, yet unnamed, mapping strategy found in some traditions that "are more closely akin to the joke in that they neither deny nor flee from disjunction, but allow the incongruous elements to stand. They suggest that symbolism, myth, ritual, repetition, transcendence are all incapable of overcoming disjunction. They seek, rather, to play between the incongruities and to provide an occasion for thought" (J. Z. Smith 1978: 309). Here again is a "third thing" arising from the dynamic interplay among two juxtaposed and opposed elements. Though Smith here identifies this strategy as a third category of religious traditions, it is clear from the study of his work that it may be understood as more pervasive and fundamental than a minor category. It can be shown that this third strategy corresponds with his understanding of both religion and the academic study of religion as species of play (see S. D. Gill 1998a).

Smith shows us that religion arises in and exists because of the play of difference which he repeatedly demonstrates in his studies of myth and ritual. For Smith, myth is a story concocted and told to deal with a situation. Myth is always applied and its distinctive character is the dynamic process of relating the story to an existential situation. Smith writes:

> There is delight and there is play in both the "fit" and the incongruity of the "fit," between an element in the myth and this or that segment of the world that one has encountered. Myth, properly understood, must take into account the complex processes of application and inapplicability, of congruity and incongruity. Myth shares with other genres such as the joke, the riddle and the "gospel" a perception of a possible relation between two different "things" and it delights in the play in-between. (J. Z. Smith 1978a: 206)

For Smith the power of myth is located in the play that arises in the process of application, in the oscillation between "fit" and "no fit," rather than the resolution of "fit" (see also J. Z. Smith 1978a: 300). For Smith, myth is best understood as a species of play.

Smith's understanding of ritual is not a simple translation from story to action. In Smith's presentation, which itself creates and plays among incongruities, ritual is a controlled environment that resolves incongruities that commonly exist in the course of life and thus contrasts with myth:

> *Ritual represents the creation of a controlled environment* where the variables (i.e., the accidents) of ordinary life may be displaced *precisely* because they are felt to be so overwhelmingly present and powerful. *Ritual is a means of performing the way things ought to be in conscious tension to the way things are in such a way that this ritualized perfection is recollected in the ordinary, uncontrolled, course of things.* (J. Z. Smith 1982c: 63; emphasis in original)

Like his view of myth, Smith sees ritual as serving practical purposes, as existing only in application, only in meeting the needs of historical and cultural situations. Whereas myth offers a perspective on an existential situation creating a gap that cannot be overcome, thus initiating a play that gives rise to meaning, ritual is itself motivated by existing incongruities that, in the course of life, can never be overcome. Ritual thus appears to lean towards a locative strategy. But, particularly in his study of ritual in *To Take Place*, Smith makes it clear that ritual also has its creativity and power in its ability to provide occasion for reflection. In his discussion of Indic sacrificial ritual Smith writes:

> Ritual is a relationship of differences between "nows"—the now of everyday life and the now of ritual place; the simultaneity, but not the coexistence, of "here" and "there." ... The absolute discrepancy invites thought, but cannot be thought away. One is invited to think of the potentialities of the one "now" in terms of the other; but the one cannot become the other. Ritual precises ambiguities; it neither overcomes nor relaxes them. (J. Z. Smith 1987b: 110)

And a clearer description of play structurality would be difficult to find.

Though elsewhere (S. D. Gill 1998a) I have discussed more fully J. Z. Smith's study of religion in terms of play, there is one other aspect of his work that must be considered here and that is his widely known statement "map is not territory" which titles his perhaps best known essay as well as a collection of his essays. Smith concludes his essay "Map is Not Territory" (J. Z. Smith 1978a: 289–309) with the rather problematic statement, "We [academics] need to reflect on and play with the necessary incongruity of our maps before we set out on a voyage of discovery to chart the worlds of other men. For the dictum of Alfred Korzybski is inescapable: 'Map is not territory'—but maps are all we possess" (J. Z. Smith 1978a: 309). It is important to try to understand what Smith means here. Smith's statement seems motivated by the scholarly voyage that takes us to the world occupied by "other" people, a real world presumably and one independent of us. While Smith reminds us that our maps are not equivalent to the worlds of others, reminding us that they are (I presume) interpretations, he concludes with the conundrum "but maps are all we possess." I believe that Smith is reminding us here that we do not have, in any significant way, access to the actual worlds or realities of others, except as they are presented in texts. He sees religion as primarily confined to the analysis and interpretation of texts. The conundrum is not resolved in that Smith still acknowledges this real world of the other as ultimately our subject. And in another place he writes that "it is both wonderful and unaccountable, perhaps even comic or crazy, that sometimes our playful imagination, our arguments about and mental construals of the world, turn out to have real consequences" (J. Z. Smith 1978b: 18). We find here, as in his view of ritual, a multi-level complex of playful juxtapositions.

I think this conundrum might now be further enriched. Scholarship is at once a construct, an interpretation, to meet the interests of the academy and it has "real consequences." There is an interplay between reality and our study of it. This playful act of imagination is clearly in line with the moebiatic thought articulated by Jean Baudrillard in *Simulacra and Simulation* (1994). We must recognize that our construals may be but preceding simulacra of our subject reality, that is, projections made without adequate constraint, amounting to the construction (fabrication) of our subject.[7] When scholarship shapes the world to correspond with our academic mappings of it, Korzybski's statement is shifted to "map is *now* territory." Though we have but the most tenuous access to the reality we study, our studies often significantly shape these actual realities. These issues raised with respect to the academic study of religion make us unsure of where we stand to perform our tasks and Smith boldly proclaims that there is no place on which we might stand firmly and without reservation. To take a stance in this complex world without recognizing that it is problematic is either religious, narrow-minded or naïve. Yet to refuse to take any stand at all puts us out of business, it renders us silent. But this issue takes us back to where I began this essay. Now we might recognize that what I have described, based on the analysis of a variety of scholars, as play, a particular kind of structurality, is central to Jonathan Smith's understanding of religion, the academic study of religion, and it characterizes his academic methods. One hope for the future of the academic study of religion, one which acknowledges and works with the complex contemporary world, is to practice it *sub specie ludi*.

What remains is to consider what a study of religion might look like if conducted in the terms of play. Though J. Z. Smith has yet to systematically present his studies explicitly in the terms of play, his scholarship offers both a model and the foundation for development of a study of religion in terms of play.

As a constructed generic category religion is itself of a meta-language that makes possible some general comprehension and discourse about an aspect of being human and about human cultures. The academic study of religion has a play structurality in that doing it always also involves the meta-message "this is academic not religious"—to be "religious" would be to identify with one of the alternative positions that engage the academic study of religion and would therefore negate any possibility of being engaged by the play structurality—signaling a passage through a boundary of paradox very like that of play. The study of religion as play juxtaposes alternatives that demand comparison but defy resolution. This oscillatory activity gives rise to another dimension of concern, the juxtaposition of the items compared and the constructed academic categories invoked. In other words, the interpretive study of any particular cultural practice cannot be done without also raising issues of the categories and theories in which it is framed, and this cannot be grasped without comparison with the practices of other religions. The experience of this play structurality engages movement between the content (alternative religions, etc.) and the boundary (the academic study and all of its constructs) raising questions such as "what is religion?" (see also S. D. Gill 1998b: esp. chs. 2 and 3).

This does not mean that specific religions or our understanding of religion need exclude play. J. Z. Smith has convincingly shown that the meaning and vitality of place, myth and ritual (all of these are academically constructed analytic categories) is a result of the play of fit. Religion and its constituents, as Smith imagines them, involve the oscillatory and iterative negotiation of fit without final resolution. But the academic study of religion, while framing different concerns than do religions, gains its meaning and vitality through the same process.

Many of the frequently-considered problems related to how our subjects understand what we are doing are clarified by a play approach to the academic study of religion. This academic study arises out of a Western intellectual and cultural heritage and is meaningful primarily in these terms. The proposition is that academic studies of the whole world—a task demanding the concoction and development of abstract generic comparative categories, categories not necessarily present to our subjects—effectively addresses the concerns that have arisen in our own tradition. To expect our subjects either to agree with, be interested in, or to even comprehend our business is, it seems to me, an undesirable recent phase of our own colonization and missionization. Though this view does not deny our responsibility to them, indeed, quite the opposite. It is in the juxtaposition and comparison (of the type that acknowledges both sameness and unresolvable difference) of others that our subjects are brought into juxtaposition with our constructed categories, ideas and theories. The academic study of religion is moebiatic and Janus-like in structure. As it attempts to understand others in their own terms, it cannot help but recognize that our results are powerfully determined by our expectations. To avoid madness (and bad scholarship) we must see this process in terms of play.

This play approach to the study of religion encourages an interactive model of interpretation requiring the interplay of ego and reality, the interplay between interpreter and the independent subject that is interpreted. In the academic study of religion I think far too little attention has been given to the technical aspects of interpretation. We have not really known how to interpret or to evaluate a legitimate and satisfying interpretation. An interactive interpretation is completely free to re-ontologize reality in terms of the perspectives of the interpreter, but it must also be constrained by the real and independent subject (see S. D. Gill 1998b: esp. ch. 2).

The academic study of religion is then in some important sense like the creation of engaging narratives in which we tell the tales of the religions of "other" people. Our writings are fictive in the sense both of being about those we are not (they are beyond our full comprehension) and are motivated to address issues of our own making. We make and tell our tales in the attempt to live morally and meaningfully as modern (should I say postmodern?) citizens of a complex and diverse world. It is a peculiar necessity, a defining principle, that our tales lay aside the role of discovering Truth, of reporting objective reality. While we tell tales of how "other" people come to Truth and to understand how it shapes their lives, we must acknowledge that doing so (and doing so seriously) forces us to set aside or qualify any claim to the truth of what we are doing. But we are constrained in an important way not experienced by other storytellers—novelists, for example—whose genres are distinguished as hyper-realities. We tell the tales of real people and we must not shirk the responsibility of being constrained by the facticity of their existence. We cannot go about our task assuming that what we do does not affect the real worlds of the actual people that give inspiration to our tales. The greatest absurdity in what we do is that, because our knowledge is always in some respects a product of our theories, we can never objectively know those whom we choose as our subjects, but we are nonetheless always in interaction with them, as partners in a dance. Our stories cannot exist without our real subjects. We must acknowledge that our writings are fictive, in that they are the products of our theoretical perspectives, and we must constrain these fictions by the real and independent presence of others. The academic study of religion *sub specie ludi* embraces this paradox oscillating playfully among the irreconcilable alternatives, knowing that doing so also gives rise to the play between the studies of our subjects and the paradox-creating frame in which we work. What we write then is hyper-real, but it must also be real. Hyper-real, on the one hand, in that it is distinguished by imaginative academics creating stories, arguing hypotheses and concocting theories. All these are fictions to be judged only in terms of the history of similar writings. Yet, on the other hand, writings of the academic study of religion must also be demonstrably grounded in the reality of the subject. Without this grounding, what we do is finally not academic at all.

Notes

1. In the contemporary popular domain there are a variety of correlations with these drives, interestingly suggesting that they can and do exist independent of one another. Gender stereotypes correlate male with the formal (reason) and female with the sensuous (intuition). Personality type stereotypes identify artists with the sensuous and scientists with the formal. In journalistic terms inspired by split brain research these types are often naïvely distinguished by hemispherical brain designations: left and right brained. To me it is fascinating that, though this has been persistently recognized since at least Schiller, we have failed (in large measure) to see the inseparability of these opposing forces, that it is the interactivity that is key to human creativity and vitality.

2. There are the many memorable passages from Schiller attesting to his understanding of play. For example, "With beauty man shall only play, and it is with beauty only that he shall play ... Man only plays when he is in the full sense of the word a human being, and he is only a human being when he plays" (1967: XV.8 and 9). And, "it is precisely play and play alone, which of all men's states and conditions is the one which makes him whole and unfolds both sides of his nature at once" (1967: XV.7). Finally,

> the utmost that experience can achieve will consist of an oscillation between the two principles, in which now reality, now form, will predominate. Beauty as Idea, therefore, can never be other than one and indivisible, since there can never be more than one point of equilibrium; whereas beauty in experience will be eternally twofold, because oscillation can disturb the equilibrium in twofold fashion, including it now to the one side, now to the other. (1967: XVI.1)

3. More recently Charles Sanders Peirce wrote of play in a fashion similar to and dependent upon Schiller. He made explicit his connection with Schiller's understanding of play and, interestingly, the first book of philosophy he studied intensely as a teen was Schiller's *On the Aesthetic Education of Man*. Near the end of his life Peirce discussed play in his essay "A Neglected Argument for the Reality of God" (1908). A full understanding of Peirce's views on play requires an extensive study well beyond the scope of this essay, but I believe that he identified "Pure Play" with abduction (hypothetic inference), which both precedes and encompasses the creative interplay of induction and deduction, a play that affirms yet transcends the opposition. Peirce, I believe, saw play as the creative force of discovery. See Peirce, especially 1931–58: 6.452–493.

4. Johan Huizinga's work (1970 [1939]) is of little importance to the study of play as it designates some sort of structurality, some dynamic of certain types of structures. Huizinga sees play largely as *agon* (contest) which might have led him to understand play as structurality, but he was more bent on using play as an excuse to demonstrate his extensive knowledge of cultural history and to criticize modernity. For further critique of Huizinga see also Ehrmann (1968).

5. I realize how cursory is this discussion of play. While it may appear to some to be a light or trivial topic, play has a firm place in philosophy and anthropology. There is not yet the much needed comprehensive history of the study of play which would most certainly include contributions by Gadamer (1989), Bakhtin (1981) and others, as well as much fuller consideration of those I have so summarily presented.

6. The term "strategy" is mine. J. Z. Smith simply presents them as maps, that is, map types or categories of maps. I feel it is much more consistent with the dynamic playful character of his broader study of religion to call them strategies and it reminds others of Smith's warning that these should not be used as categories by which to label religions. For a fuller discussion on this point see S. D. Gill 1998a.

7. This issue is considered in depth in S. D. Gill 1998b, especially chs. 1, 2, 7 and 8.

Suggested Readings

Bateson, Gregory
    1972   "A Theory of Play and Fantasy," pp. 177–193 in *Steps to an Ecology of Mind*. New York: Ballantine.

Baudrillard, Jean
    1994   *Simulacra and Simulation*. Sheila Faria Glaser (trans.). Ann Arbor: University of Michigan Press.

Derrida, Jacques
    1970   "Structure, Sign and Play in the Discourse of the Human Sciences," pp. 247–265 in Richard Macksey and Eugenio Donato (eds.), *The Languages of Criticism and the Sciences of Man*. Baltimore: Johns Hopkins University Press.

Gill, Sam D.
    1998a "No Place to Stand: Jonathan Z. Smith as *Homo Ludens*, the Academic Study of Religion as *Sub Specie Ludi*." *Journal of the American Academy of Religion* 66: 283–312.

Handelman, Don
    1992   "Passage to Play: Paradox and Process." *Play and Culture* 5:1–19.

Schiller, Friedrich
    1967   *Friedrich Schiller: On the Aesthetic Education of Man in a Series of Letters*. E. M. Wilkinson and L. A. Willoughby (eds.). Oxford: Clarendon; original German edn, 1793.

Smith, Jonathan Z.
    1978a "Map Is Not Territory," pp. 289–309 in *Map Is Not Territory: Studies in the History of Religions*. Chicago: University of Chicago Press.
    1978b "Playful Acts of Imagination." *Liberal Education* 73, 5:14–20.

REFERENCES

REFERENCES

Aarne, Antii and Stith Thompson
  1961   *The Types of the Folktale: A Classification and Bibliography.* Helsinki: Academia Scientiarum Fennica.
Abbott, L. A., F. A. Bisby and D. J. Rogers
  1985   *Taxonomic Analyses in Biology: Computers, Models and Databases.* New York: Columbia University Press.
Abélès, Marc
  1981   " 'Sacred Kingship' and the Formation of the State," pp. 1–13 in Henri J. M. Claessen and Peter Skalník (eds.), *The Study of the State.* The Hague: Mouton.
Abeles, Norman
  1993   "Projective Personality Traits," pp. 1885–1890 in Frank N. McGill (ed.), *Survey of Social Science: Psychology Series*, vol. 4. Pasadena, CA: Salem.
Aberele, David F., Albert K. Cohen, Arthur K. Davis et al.
  1950   "The Functional Prerequisites of a Society." *Ethics* 60:100–111.
Abrams, M. H.
  1971   *Natural Supernaturalism: Tradition and Revolution in Romantic Literature.* New York: Norton.
Achinstein, Peter
  1968   *Concepts of Science: A Philosophical Analysis.* Baltimore: Johns Hopkins University Press.
Ackerknecht, Edwin
  1969   "On the Comparative Method in Anthropology." pp. 117–125 in Robert F. Spencer (ed.), *Method and Perspective in Anthropology.* Gloucester, MA: Peter Smith.
Ackerman, Robert
  1987   *J. G. Frazer: His Life and Work.* Cambridge: Cambridge University Press.
  1991   *The Myth and Ritual School: J. G. Frazer and the Cambridge Ritualists.* New York: Garland.
Adam, Ian and Helen Tiffin (Eds.)
  1991   *Past the Last Post: Theorizing Post-Colonialism and Post-Modernism.* New York: Harvester Wheatsheaf.
Adams, Charles J.
  1974   "Religions, Classification of." *Encyclopaedia Britannica* 15th edn, Vol. 15: 628–634.

Adkins, Lisa and Diana Leonard
  1996   "Reconstructing French Feminism: Commodification, Materialism and Sex," pp. 1–23 in Diana Leonard and Lisa Adkins (eds.), *Sex in Question: French Materialist Feminism*. London: Taylor and Francis.

Adorno, Rolena
  1985   "The Rhetoric of Resistance: The 'Talking' Book of Felipe Guaman Poma." *History of European Ideas* 6:447–464.

Adorno, Theodor W.
  1964   *Jargon der Eigentlichkeit. Zur deutschen Ideologie*. Frankfurt: Suhrkamp.
  1989   *Kierkegaard: Construction of the Aesthetic*, Robert Hullot-Kentor (ed. and trans.). Theory and History of Literature, vol. 61. Minneapolis: University of Minnesota Press.

Aeschimann, Willy
  1986   *La pensée d'Edgar Quinet. Étude sur la formation de ses idées*. Paris: Anthropos.

Ahmad, Aijaz
  1992   *In Theory: Classes, Nations, Literatures*. London: Verso.
  1995   "The Politics of Literary Postcoloniality." *Race and Class* 36, 3:1–20.

Ainsworth, G. C. and P. H. A. Sneath (Eds.)
  1962   *Microbial Classification: The Twelfth Symposium of the Society for General Microbiology*. Cambridge: Cambridge University Press.

Akoun, A. A., F. Morin and J. Mousseau
  1972   "A Conversation with Claude Lévi-Strauss." *Psychology Today* 5.

Allport, Gordon W.
  1950   *The Individual and His Religion: A Psychological Interpretation*. New York: Macmillan.
  1963   "Behavioral Science, Religion, and Mental Health." *Journal of Religion and Health* 2:187–197.

Almond, Philip C.
  1988   *The British Discovery of Buddhism*. Cambridge: Cambridge University Press.

Alston, William P.
  1967   "Religion." In P. Edwards (ed.), *The Encyclopedia of Philosophy*. New York: Macmillan.
  1993   *Perceiving God: The Epistemology of Religious Experience*. Ithaca, NY: Cornell University Press.

Althusser, Louis
  1969   *For Marx*, Ben Brewster (trans.). London: Allen Lane.
  1971   *Lenin and Philosophy, and Other Essays*, Ben Brewster (trans.). New York: Monthly Review Press.

Althusser, Louis and Étienne Balibar
  1970   *Reading Capital*, Ben Brewster (trans.). London: Verso.

Amit-Talai, Vered and Caroline Knowles
  1996   *Re-Situating Identities: The Politics of Race, Ethnicity, and Culture*. Peterborough, ON: Broadview.

Ammerman, Nancy T.
  1994   "Telling Congregational Stories." *Review of Religious Research* 35:289–299.

References

Anderson, Benedict

    1991   *Imagined Communities: Reflections on the Origin and Spread of Nationalism*. 2nd edn. London: Verso.

Anderson, Perry

    1974   *Lineages of the Absolutist State*. London: New Left Books.

Anttonen, Veikko

    1996   "Rethinking the Sacred: The Notions of 'Human Body' and 'Territory' in Conceptualizing Religion," pp. 36–64 in Thomas A. Idinopulos and Edward A. Yonan (eds.), *The Sacred and Its Scholars: Comparative Methodologies for the Study of Primary Religious Data*. Studies in the History of Religions, vol. 73. Leiden: E. J. Brill.

Appadurai, Arjun

    1986   Ed. *The Social Life of Things: Commodities in Cultural Perspective*. Cambridge: Cambridge University Press.

    1996   "Number in the Colonial Imagination." In Arjun Appadurai (ed.), *Modernity at Large: Cultural Dimensions of Globalization*. Minneapolis: University of Minnesota Press.

Appiah, K. A.

    1988   "Out of Africa: Topologies of Nativism." *Yale Journal of Criticism* 1, 2.

    1991   "Tolerable Falsehoods: Agency and the Interests in Theory," pp. 63–90 in Jonathan Arqac and Barbara Johnson (eds.), *Some Consequences of Theory*. Baltimore: Johns Hopkins Unversity Press.

Appleby, Joyce O. et al. (Eds.)

    1996   *Knowledge and Postmodernism in Historical Perspective*. New York: Routledge.

Apter, Emily and William Pietz (Eds.)

    1993   *Fetishism as Cultural Discourse*. Ithaca, NY: Cornell University Press.

Argyle, Michael

    1959   *Religious Behavior*. Glencoe, IL: Free Press.

Argyle, Michael and Benjamin Beit-Hallahmi

    1975   *The Social Psychology of Religion*. London: Routledge & Kegan Paul.

Arnal, William E.

    1994   Review: Jonathan Z. Smith, *Drudgery Divine: On the Comparison of Early Christianities and the Religions of Late Antiquity*. *Method and Theory in the Study of Religion* 6:190–199.

    1997   "Making and Re-Making the Jesus Sign: Contemporary Markings on the Body of Christ," pp. 308–319 in William E. Arnal and Michel Desjardins (eds.), *Whose Historical Jesus?* Studies in Christianity and Judaism / Études sur le christianisme et le judaïsme, vol. 7. Waterloo, ON: Wilfrid Laurier University Press.

Aron, Raymond

    1970   *Main Currents in Sociological Thought II: Durkheim, Pareto, Weber*, Richard Howard and Helen Weaver (trans.). Garden City, NY: Doubleday.

Asad, Talal

    1973   Ed. *Anthropology and the Colonial Encounter*. London: Ithaca.

    1993   *Genealogies of Religion: Discipline and Reasons of Power in Christianity and Islam*. Baltimore: Johns Hopkins University Press.

Atran, Scott
    1990   *Cognitive Foundations of Natural History: Towards an Anthropology of Science*. Cambridge: Cambridge University Press; Paris: Éditions de la Maison des sciences de l'homme.
    1994   "Core Domains Versus Scientific Theories: Evidence from Systematics and Itza-Maya Folkbiology." In Lawrence A. Hirschfeld and Susan A. Gelman (eds.), *Mapping the Mind: Domain Specificity in Cognition and Culture*. Cambridge: Cambridge University Press.
    1996a   "From Folk Biology to Scientific Biology." In D. R. Olson and N. Torrance (eds.), *Handbook of Education and Human Development*. Oxford: Blackwell.
    1996b   "Modes of Thinking About Living Kinds: Science, Symbolism and Common Sense." In D. R. Olson and N. Torrance (eds.), *Modes of Thought: Explorations in Culture and Cognition*. Cambridge: Cambridge University Press.

Atran, Scott and Dan Sperber
    1991   "Learning Without Teaching: Its Place in Culture," pp. 39–55 in Liliana Tolchinsky Landsmann (ed.), *Culture, Schooling, and Psychological Development*. Norwood, NJ: Ablex.

Auffarth, Christoph
    1995   "Gaben für die Götter—für die Katz? Wirtschaftliche Aspekte des griechischen Götterkults am Beispiel Argos." In Hans G. Kippenberg and Brigitte Luchesi (eds.), *Lokale Religionsgeschichte*. Marburg: Diagonal-Verlag.

Austin, John L.
    1961   *Philosophical Papers*. Oxford: Clarendon.

Bachofen, Johann Jakob
    1967   *Myth, Religion, and Mother Right: Selected Writings of J. J. Bachofen*, Ralph Manheim (trans.). Princeton: Princeton University Press.

Bahri, Deepika and Mary Vasudeva (Eds.)
    1996   *Between the Lines: South Asians and Postcoloniality*. Asian American History and Culture Series. Philadelphia: Temple University Press.

Bailey, Lee W.
    1988   "Religious Projection: A European Tour." *Religious Studies Review* 14:207–211.

Bakhtin, Mikhail M.
    1981   *The Dialogic Imagination: Four Essays by M. M. Bakhtin*, Michael Holquist (ed.), Caryl Emerson and Michael Holquist (trans.). Austin: University of Texas Press.

Baldwin, David A.
    1989   *Paradoxes of Power*. Oxford: Blackwell.

Banks, Robert
    1973   "Religion as Projection: A Re-Appraisal of Freud's Theory." *Religious Studies* 9:401–426.

Barbosa, Alice P.
    1969   *Teoria e prática dos sistemas de classificação*. Rio de Janeiro: Instituto Brasileiro de Bibliografia e Documentação.

Barker, Eileen
 1986 "Religious Movements: Cult and Anti-Cult Since Jonestown." *Annual Review of Sociology* 12:329–346.
Barkun, Michael
 1986 *Crucible of the Millennium: The Burned-Over District of New York in the 1840s*. Syracuse, NY: Syracuse University Press.
Barlow, Tani E. (Ed.)
 1997 *Formations of Colonial Modernity in East Asia*. Durham, NC: Duke University Press.
Barnhart, Robert K.
 1988 *The Barnhart Dictionary of Etymology*. New York: H. W. Wilson.
Barsalou, Lawrence W.
 1987 "The Instability of Graded Structure: Implications for the Nature of Concepts." In Ulric Neissner (ed.), *Concepts and Conceptual Development: Ecological and Intellectual Factors in Categorization*. Cambridge: Cambridge University Press.
 1992 *Cognitive Psychology: An Overview for Cognitive Scientists*. Hillsdale, NJ: Lawrence Erlbaum.
Barth, Fredrik (Ed.)
 1969 *Ethnic Groups and Boundaries: The Social Organization of Culture Difference*. Boston: Little, Brown.
Barthes, Roland
 1972 *Mythologies*, Annette Lavers (trans.). New York: Hill and Wang.
 1973 *Elements of Semiology*, Annette Lavers and Colin Smith (trans.). New York: Hill and Wang.
 1974 *S/Z*, Richard Miller (trans.). New York: Hill and Wang.
 1975 *The Pleasure of the Text*, Richard Miller (trans.). New York: Hill and Wang.
 1977a *Image–Music–Text*, Stephen Heath (trans.). New York: Hill and Wang.
 1977b *Roland Barthes by Roland Barthes*, Richard Howard (trans.). New York: Hill and Wang.
 1989 *The Rustle of Language*, Richard Howard (trans.). Berkeley: University of California Press.
 1990 *The Fashion System*, Matthew Ward and Richard Howard (trans.). Berkeley: University of California Press.
 1994 *The Semiotic Challenge*, Richard Howard (trans.). Berkeley: University of California Press; first trans. edn, New York: Hill and Wang, 1988.
Bartoli, Matteo
 1945 *Saggi di linguistica spaziale*. Turin: Università di Torino.
Bataille, Georges
 1988a "Attraction and Repulsion I: Tropisms, Sexuality, Laughter and Tears," pp. 103–112 in Denis Hollier (ed.), *The College of Sociology (1937–39)*. Betsy Wing (trans.). Theory and History of Literature, vol. 41. Minneapolis: University of Minnesota Press; original French edn, 1979.
 1988b "Attraction and Repulsion II: Social Structure," pp. 113–124 in Denis Hollier (ed.), *The College of Sociology (1937–39)*. Besty Wing (trans.). Theory and History of Literature, vol. 41. Minneapolis: University of Minnesota Press; original French edn, 1979.

Bateson, Gregory
    1972   "A Theory of Play and Fantasy," pp. 177–193 in *Steps to an Ecology of Mind*. New York: Ballantine.

Baudrillard, Jean
    1993   *The Transparency of Evil: Essays on Extreme Phenomena*, James Benedict (trans.). London: Verso.
    1994   *Simulacra and Simulation*, Sheila Faria Glaser (trans.). Ann Arbor: University of Michigan Press.

Baylor, Michael, G. (Ed.)
    1991   *The Radical Reformation*. Cambridge: Cambridge University Press.

Bayly, Susan
    1989   *Saints, Goddesses, and Kings: Muslims and Christians in South Indian Society, 1700–1900*. Cambridge South Asian Studies, vol. 43. Cambridge: Cambridge University Press.

Beach, Edward Allen
    1994   *The Potencies of God(s): Schelling's Philosophy of Mythology*. Albany: State University of New York Press.

Beattie, John H. M.
    1964   *Other Cultures: Aims, Methods and Achievements in Social Anthropology*. London: Cohen & West.
    1966   "Ritual and Social Change." *Man* 1:60–74.

Beauvoir, Simone de
    1949   *The Second Sex*, H. M. Parshley (trans.). New York: Knopf.

Bechtel, William and Adele A. Abrahamsen
    1991   *Connectionism and the Mind: An Introduction to Parallel Processing in Networks*. Oxford: Blackwell.

Beck, Brenda
    1969   "Color and Heat in South Indian Ritual." *Man*, N. S. 4.

Becker, Gary S.
    1976   *The Economic Approach to Human Behavior*. Chicago: University of Chicago Press.
    1996   *Accounting for Tastes*. Cambridge, MA: Harvard University Press.

Beckford, James A.
    1985   "The Insulation and Isolation of the Sociology of Religion." *Social Analysis* 46:347–354.

Beckner, Morton
    1959   *The Biological Way of Thought*. Berkeley: University of California Press.

Beit-Hallahmi, Benjamin and Michael Argyle
    1997   *The Psychology of Religious Behaviour, Belief and Experience*. London: Routledge.

Bell, Catherine
    1992   *Ritual Theory, Ritual Practice*. Oxford: Oxford University Press.
    1996   "Modernism and Postmodernism in the Study of Religion." *Religious Studies Review* 22:179–190.
    1997   *Ritual: Perspectives and Dimensions*. Oxford: Oxford University Press.

Bellah, Robert N.
    1970   "Civil Religion in Modern America," pp. 229–252 in *Beyond Belief: Essays*

on Religion in a Post-Traditional World. Berkeley: University of California Press.

Ben-Rafael, Eliezer
1982   *The Emergence of Ethnicity: Cultural Groups and Social Conflict in Israel.* Contributions in Ethnic Studies, vol. 7. Westport, CT: Greenwood.

Benavides, Gustavo
1989   "Religious Articulations of Power," pp. 1–12, 197–202 in Gustavo Benavides and M. W. Daly (eds.), *Religion and Political Power.* Albany: State University of New York Press.
1994   "Resistance and Accommodation in Latin American Popular Religiosity," pp. 37–67 in Anthony Stevens-Arroyo and Ana María Díaz-Stevens (eds.), *An Enduring Flame: Studies on Latino Popular Religiosity.* New York: City University of New York.
1995a   "Syncretism and Legitimacy in Latin American Religion," pp. 19–46 in Anthony Stevens-Arroyo and Andrés Pérez y Mena (eds.), *Enigmatic Powers: Syncretism with African and Indigenous Peoples' Religions Among Latinos.* New York: City University of New York.
1995b   "Cognitive and Ideological Aspects of Divine Anthropomorphism." *Religion* 25:9–22.
1995c   "On Ranters, Fools and Antinomians; or When Does Transgression Transgress?" Unpublished paper, American Academy of Religion. Philadelphia, 20 November.
1997   "Postmodern Disseminations and Cognitive Constraints." *Religion* 27:129–138.
1998   "Modernity," pp. 186–204 in Mark C. Taylor (ed.), *Critical Terms for Religious Studies.* Chicago: University of Chicago Press.

Bender, Barbara
1989   "The Roots of Inequality," pp. 83–95 in Daniel Miller, Michael Rowlands and Christopher Tilley (eds.), *Domination and Resistance.* London: Unwin Hyman.

Bendroth, Margaret Lamberts
1993   *Fundamentalism and Gender, 1875 to the Present.* New Haven: Yale University Press.

Benham, Marian S.
1896   *Henry Callaway M.D., D.D., First Bishop of Kaffraria, His Life History and Works: A Memoir.* London: Macmillan.

Bénichou, Paul
1988   *Les Mages romantiques.* Paris: Gallimard.
1992   *L'École du désenchantement.* Paris: Gallimard.

Benjamin, Walter
1969   "Theses on the Philosophy of History." In *Illuminations: Essays and Reflections,* Hannah Arendt (ed.), Harry Zohn (trans.). New York: Schocken.

Bennett, William J.
1992   *The De-Valuing of America: The Fight for Our Culture and Our Children.* New York: Summit.

Benveniste, Émile
    1938   "Traditions indo-iraniennes sur les classes sociales." *Journal asiatique* 230:529–549.1971
          Problems in General Linguistics, Mary Elizabeth Meek (trans.). Coral Gables, FL: University of Miami Press.
    1973   *Indo-European Language and Society*, Elizabeth Palmer (trans.). Studies in General Linguistics. London: Faber & Faber.

Berger, Peter L.
    1969   *The Sacred Canopy: Elements of a Sociological Theory of Religion*. Garden City, NY: Doubleday.

Berger, Peter L. and Thomas Luckmann
    1967   *The Social Construction of Reality: A Treatise in the Sociology of Knowledge*. Garden City, NY: Doubleday.

Berkhofer, Robert F., Jr.
    1978   *The White Man's Indian: Images of the American Indian from Columbus to the Present*. New York: Knopf.

Berlin, Brent O.
    1992   *Ethnobiological Classification: Principles of Categorization of Plants and Animals in Traditional Societies*. Princeton: Princeton University Press.

Berlin, Brent O., Dennis Breedlove and Peter Raven
    1973   "General Principles of Classification and Nomenclature in Folk Biology." *American Anthropologist* 74.

Berlin, Brent O. and Paul D. Kay
    1969   *Basic Color Terms: Their Universality and Evolution*. Berkeley: University of California Press.

Bernstein, Basil B.
    1975   *Class, Codes, and Control: Theoretical Studies Towards a Sociology of Language*. New York: Schocken.

Bhabha, Homi K.
    1994   *The Location of Culture*. London: Routledge.

Bietenholz, Peter G. (Ed.)
    1985–   *Contemporaries of Erasmus: A Biographical Register of the*
       87   *Renaissance and Reformation*, 3 vols. Toronto: University of Toronto Press.

Blake, William
    1997   [1804] "Jerusalem." In D. V. Erdman (ed.), *The Poetry and Prose of William Blake*. Garden City, NY: Doubleday.

Blatavsky, Helena Petrovna
    1889   *The Key to Theosophy*. New York: Theosophical Publishing Company.

Blau, Peter Michael
    1964   *Exchange and Power in Social Life*. New York: Wiley.
    1986   "Microprocess and Macrostructure," pp. 83–100 in Karen S. Cook (ed.), *Social Exchange Theory*. Beverly Hills, CA: Sage.

Bleek, W. H. I.
    1952   *Zulu Legends*, J. A. Engelbrecht (ed.). Pretoria: Van Schaik; original edn, 1857.

References

Bloch, Maurice

  1989 *Ritual, History, and Power: Selected Papers in Anthropology.* Monographs on Social Anthropology, vol. 58. London: Athlone.

  1992 *Prey Into Hunter: The Politics of Religious Experience.* Cambridge: Cambridge University Press.

Bloom, Allan

  1987 *The Closing of the American Mind: How Higher Education Has Failed Democracy and Impoverished the Souls of Today's Students.* New York: Simon & Schuster.

Blumenberg, Hans

  1983 *The Legitimation of the Modern Age,* Robert M. Wallace (trans.). Cambridge, MA: MIT Press.

  1987 *The Genesis of the Copernican World,* Robert M. Wallace (trans.). Cambridge, MA: MIT Press.

Blumer, Herbert

  1969 *Symbolic Interactionism: Perspective and Method.* Englewood Cliffs, NJ: Prentice-Hall.

Blunt, Alison and Gillian Rose (Eds.)

  1994 *Writing Women and Space: Colonial and Postcolonial Geographies.* New York: Guilford.

Bly, Robert

  1990 *Iron John: A Book About Men.* Reading, MA: Addison-Wesley.

Boas, Franz

  1940 *Race, Language, and Culture.* New York: Macmillan; Free Press, 1966.

  1966 *Kwakiutl Ethnography,* Helen Codere (ed.). Chicago: University of Chicago Press.

Bock, Kenneth E.

  1966 "The Comparative Method of Anthropology." *Comparative Studies in Society and History* 8:269–280.

Bocock, Robert and Kenneth Thompson (Eds.)

  1985 *Religion and Ideology: A Reader.* Manchester: Manchester University Press.

Boehlich, W. (Ed.)

  1990 *The Letters of Sigmund Freud to Edward Silberstein 1871–1881,* A. Pomerans (trans.). Cambridge, MA: Belknap Press of Harvard University Press.

Bolle, Kees W.

  1968 *The Freedom of Man in Myth.* Nashville, TN: Vanderbilt University Press.

  1983 "Myths and Other Religious Texts," pp. 297–363 in Frank Whaling (ed.), *Contemporary Approaches to the Study of Religion.* Berlin: Mouton.

  1987 "Myth: An Overview," pp. 261–273 in Mircea Eliade (ed.), *Encyclopedia of Religion,* vol. 10. New York: Macmillan.

Bolle, Kees W., Richard G. A. Buxton and Jonathan Z. Smith

  1974 "The Nature, Functions, and Types of Myth." *Encyclopaedia Britannica* 15th edn, Vol. 24: 715–732.

Bossy, John

  1982 "Some Elementary Forms of Durkheim." *Past and Present* 95:3–18.

Bottomore, Tom
    1991   "Social Formation." In Tom Bottomore (ed.), *A Dictionary of Marxist Thought*. 2nd revised edn. Oxford: Blackwell.

Bouchard, Constance Brittain
    1991   *Holy Entrepreneurs: Cistercians, Knights, and Economic Exchange in Twelfth-Century Burgundy*. Ithaca, NY: Cornell University Press.

Boudon, Raymond
    1993   "Toward a Synthetic Theory of Rationality." *International Studies in the Philosophy of Science* 7:5–19.

Bourdieu, Pierre
    1972   *Esquisse d'une théorie de la pratique*. Geneva: Droz.
    1977   *Outline of a Theory of Practice*, Richard Nice (trans.). Cambridge Studies in Social Anthropology, vol. 16. Cambridge: Cambridge University Press; original French edn, 1972.
    1984   *Distinction: A Social Critique of the Judgment of Taste*, Richard Nice (trans.). Cambridge, MA: Harvard University Press.
    1990   *The Logic of Practice*, Richard Nice (trans.). Stanford, CA: Stanford University Press; London: Polity.
    1993   *The Field of Cultural Production: Essays on Art and Literature*, Randal Johnson (ed.). Cambridge: Polity; New York: Columbia University Press.
    1998   *On Television*, Priscilla Parkhurst Ferguson (trans.). New York: New Press.

Bové, Paul A.
    1995   (ed.) *Early Postmodernism: Foundational Essays*. Durham, NC: Duke University Press.

Bowker, John
    1997   (ed.) *The Oxford Dictionary of World Religions*. Oxford: Oxford University Press.

Bowler, Peter
    1992   "From 'Savage' to 'Primitive': Victorian Evolutionism and the Interpretation of Marginalized Peoples." *Antiquity* 66:721–729.

Boyarin, Daniel
    1993   *Carnal Israel: Reading Sex in Talmudic Culture*. Berkeley: University of California Press.
    1997   *Unheroic Conduct: The Rise of Heterosexuality and the Invention of the Jewish Man*. Berkeley: University of California Press.

Boyer, Pascal
    1990   *Tradition as Truth and Communication: A Cognitive Description of Traditional Discourse*. Cambridge: Cambridge University Press.
    1993   "Pseudo-Natural Kinds," In Pascal Boyer (ed.), *Cognitive Aspects of Religious Symbolism*. Cambridge: Cambridge University Press.
    1994   *The Naturalness of Religious Ideas: A Cognitive Theory of Religion*. Berkeley: University of California Press.

Braithwaite, R. B.
    1964   "An Empiricist's View on the Nature of Religious Belief," pp. 229–252 in John Hick (ed.), *The Existence of God*. New York: Macmillan; original edn, Cambridge: Cambridge University Press, 1955.

References

Brand, Gerd (Ed.)

1979   *The Central Texts of Ludwig Wittgenstein*, Robert E. Innis (trans.). Oxford: Blackwell.

Brantlinger, Patrick

1988   *Rule of Darkness: British Literature and Imperialism, 1830–1914*. Ithaca, NY: Cornell University Press.

Brasher, Brenda and Stephen O'Leary

1996   "The Unknown God of the Internet: Religious Communication from Ancient Agora to the 'Virtual Forum'." In Charles Ess (ed.), *Philosophical Perspectives on Computer-Mediated Communications*. Albany: State University of New York Press.

Braude, Ann

1997   "Women's History is American Religious History," pp. 87–107 in *Retelling U.S. Religious History*. Berkeley: University of California Press.

Braun, Willi

1999   "Amnesia in the Production of (Christian) History." *Bulletin of the Council of Societies for the Study of Religion* 28 (1):3–8.

Breckenridge, Carol A. and Peter van der Veer

1993   *Orientalism and the Postcolonial Predicament: Perspectives on South Asia*. South Asia Seminar Series, vol. 44. Philadelphia: University of Pennsylvania Press.

Brittan, Arthur

1989   *Masculinity and Power*. Oxford: Blackwell.

Brod, Harry

1987   *The Making of Masculinities: The New Men's Studies*. Boston: Allen & Unwin; reprinted, New York: Routledge, 1992.

Brody, Baruch A.

1967   "Logical Terms, Glossary of," pp. 57–77 in Paul Edwards (ed.), *The Encyclopedia of Philosophy*, vol. 5. New York: Macmillan.

Brosses, Charles de

1760   *Du culte des dieux fétiches, ou parallèle l'ancienne religion de l'Egypte avec la religion actuelle de Nigritie*. Paris: n.p.; reprinted, Paris: Fayard, 1988.

Brown, Cecil H.

1977   "Folk Botanical Life Forms: Their Universality and Growth." *American Anthropologist* 79.

1979   "Folk Zoological Life Forms: Their Universality and Growth." *American Anthropologist* 81.

1984   *Language and Living Things: Uniformities in Folk Classification and Naming*. New Brunswick, NJ: Rutgers University Press.

Brown, Donald E.

1991   *Human Universals*. Philadelphia: Temple University Press.

Brown, Robert F.

1977   *The Later Philosophy of Schelling: The Influence of Boehme on the Works of 1809–1815*. Lewisburg: Bucknell University Press.

Bruce, Steve (Ed.)

1992   *Religion and Modernization: Sociologists and Historians Debate the Secularization Thesis*. Oxford: Clarendon.

Bruce, Steve
    1993   "Religion and Rational Choice: A Critique of Economic Explanations of Religious Behavior." *Sociology of Religion* 54:193–205.
    1995   "The Truth About Religion in Britain." *Journal for the Scientific Study of Religion* 34:417–430.
Buchignani, Norman
    1982   *Anthropological Approaches to the Study of Ethnicity*. Occasional Papers in Ethnic and Immigration Studies. Toronto: The Multicultural History Society of Ontario.
Bultmann, Rudolf K.
    1958   *Jesus Christ and Mythology*. New York: Scribner.
Burchell, Graham, Colin Gordon and Peter Miller (Eds.)
    1991   *The Foucault Effect: Studies in Governmentality*. Chicago: University of Chicago Press.
Burghart, Richard
    1978   "Hierarchical Models of the Hindu Social System." *Man* 13:519–536.
Bürke, Georg
    1958   *Vom Mythos zur Mystik. Joseph von Görres' mystische Lehre und die romantische Naturphilosophie*. Ensiedeln, n.p.
Burkert, Walter
    1985   *Greek Religion*, John Raffan (trans.). Cambridge, MA: Harvard University Press.
    1996   *Creation of the Sacred: Tracks of Biology in Early Religions*. Cambridge, MA: Harvard University Press.
Burnside, Carol E.
    1991   "The Left Hand of the Sacred." *Method and Theory in the Study of Religion* 3:3–9.
Burrow, J. W.
    1966   *Evolution and Society: A Study in Victorian Social Theory*. Cambridge: Cambridge University Press.
Burtin, Nicolas
    1931   *Un Semeur des idées au temps de la restauration: Le Baron d'Eckstein*. Paris: Boccard.
Butler, Jon
    1982   "Enthusiasm Described and Decried: The Great Awakenings as Interpretive Fiction." *Journal of American History* 69:305–325.
    1990   *Awash in a Sea of Faith: Christianizing the American People*. Studies in Cultural History. Cambridge, MA: Harvard University Press.
Butler, Judith
    1990   *Gender Trouble: Feminism and the Subversion of Identity*. New York: Routledge.
Buxton, Richard G. A.
    1994   *Imaginary Greece: The Contexts of Mythology*. Cambridge: Cambridge University Press.
Bynum, Caroline Walker
    1996   "Women's Stories, Women's Symbols: A Critique of Victor Turner's

Theory of Liminality," pp. 71–86 in Ronald L. Grimes (ed.), *Readings in Ritual Studies*. Upper Saddle River, NJ: Prentice-Hall.

Cady, Linell
  1998   "The Public Intellectual and Effective Critique." *Bulletin of the Council of Societies for the Study of Religion* 27, 2:36–38.

Caillois, Roger
  1959   *Man and the Sacred*, Meyer Barash (trans.). Glencoe, IL: Free Press.

Callaway, Henry
  1868– *The Religious System of the Amazulu*. Springvale, SA: Springvale Mission;
  70   reprinted, Cape Town: Struik, 1970.
  1874   *A Fragment on Comparative Religion*. Natal: Callaway.

Callender, John
  1766– *Terra Australis Cognita; or Voyages to the Terra Australis*, 3 vols.
  68   Amsterdam: Israel.

Callinicos, Alex
  1990   *Against Postmodernism: A Marxist Critique*. New York: St. Martin's Press.

Cameron, Ron
  1994   "Alternate Beginnings—Different Ends: Eusebius, Thomas, and the Construction of Christian Origins," pp. 501–525 in Lukas Bormann, Kelly Del Tredici and Angela Standhartinger (eds.), *Religious Propaganda and Missionary Competition in the New Testament World: Essays Honoring Dieter Georgi*. Supplements to Novum Testamentum, vol. 74. Leiden: E. J. Brill.
  1996   "Mythmaking and Intertextuality in Early Christianity," pp. 37–50 in Elizabeth A. Castelli and Hal Taussig (eds.), *Reimagining Christian Origins: A Colloquium Honoring Burton L. Mack*. Valley Forge, PA: Trinity Press International.

Campbell, John
  1815   *Travels in South Africa*. London: Black, Parry.

Campbell, Joseph
  1968   *The Hero with a Thousand Faces*, 2d edn. Princeton: Princeton University Press.
  1988   *The Power of Myth*, Betty Sue Flowers (ed.). New York: Doubleday.

Cancik, Hubert
  1975   "*Christus Imperator*. Zum Gebrauch militärischer Titulaturen im römischen Herrscherkult und im Christentum," pp. 112–130 in Heinrich von Stietencron (ed.), *Der Name Gottes*. Düsseldorf: Patmos.
  1985   "Augustin als konstantinischer Theologe," pp. 136–152 in Jacob Taubes (ed.), *Der Fürst dieser Welt: Carl Schmitt und die Folgen*. Religionstheorie und politische Theologie, vol. 1. Munich: Fink-Schöningh.

Canfield, Robert L.
  1978   "Religious Myth as Ethnic Boundary," pp. 35–42 in Jon W. Anderson and Richard F. Strand (eds.), *Ethnic Processes and Intergroup Relations in Contemporary Afghanistan*. Occasional Paper of the Afghanistan Council of the Asia Society, no. 15. New York: Afghanistan Council of the Asia Society.

Capps, Walter H.
   1995   *Religious Studies: The Making of a Discipline*. Minneapolis: Fortress.
Carey, John
   1998   Review: Peter Ackroyd, *The Life of Thomas More. The Sunday Times Books*, 22 February.
Carey, Susan
   1996   "Cognitive Domains as Modes of Thought," In D. R. Olson and N. Torrance (eds.), *Modes of Thought: Explorations in Culture and Cognition*. Cambridge: Cambridge University Press.
Carrasco, David
   1990   *Religions of Mesoamerica: Cosmovision and Ceremonial Centers*. Religious Traditions of the World. San Francisco: Harper & Row.
Carroll, John B. (Ed.)
   1956   *Language, Thought, and Reality: Selected Writings of Benjamin Lee Whorf*, Foreword by Stuart Chase. Cambridge, MA: MIT Press.
Carter, Stephen
   1993   *The Culture of Disbelief: How American Law and Politics Trivialize Religious Devotion*. New York: Basic.
Cartledge, Paul
   1997   "Historiography and Ancient Greek Self-Definition," pp. 23–42 in Michael Bentley (ed.), *Companion to Historiography*. London: Routledge.
Cassirer, Ernst
   1925   *The Philosophy of Symbolic Forms*, vol. 2: *Mythical Thought*, Ralph Manheim (trans.). New Haven: Yale University Press.
   1955   *The Philosophy of Symbolic Forms*, 3 vols., Ralph Manheim (trans.). New Haven: Yale University Press.
Caws, Peter
   1994   *Structuralism: A Philosophy for the Human Sciences*. Atlantic Highlands: Humanities Press.
   1995   "Structure," pp. 477–479 in Jaegwon Kim and Ernest Sosa (eds.), *A Companion to Metaphysics*. Oxford: Blackwell.
Certeau, Michel de
   1984   *The Practice of the Everyday Life*, Steven Redall (trans.). Berkeley: University of California Press.
   1997a *Culture in the Plural*, Luce Giard (ed. and Introduction), Tom Conley (trans. and Afterword). Minneapolis: University of Minnesota Press.
   1997b *The Capture of Speech and Other Political Writings*, Luce Giard (ed. and Introduction), Tom Conley (trans. and Afterword). Minneapolis: University of Minnesota Press.
Chadwick-Jones, J. K.
   1976   *Social Exchange Theory: Its Structure and Influence in Social Psychology*. London: Academic Press.
Chakravarti, Uma
   1986   "The Social Philosophy of Early Buddhism and the Problem of Inequality." *Social Compass* 33:199–221.
   1996   *The Social Dimensions of Early Buddhism*. New Delhi: Munshiran Manoharlal.

Chambers, Iain and Lidia Curti
  1996   (eds.) *The Post-Colonial Question: Common Skies, Divided Horizons.* London: Routledge.
Chapman, A. H. and Miriam Chapman-Santana
  1995   "The Influence of Nietzsche on Freud's Ideas." *British Journal of Psychiatry* 166:251–253.
Chapman, Malcolm, Maryon McDonald and Elizabeth Tonkin
  1989   "Introduction: History and Social Anthropology," pp. 1–21 in Malcolm Chapman, Maryon McDonald and Elizabeth Tonkin (eds.), *History and Ethnicity.* Association of Social Anthropologists of Britain and the Commonwealth Monographs, vol. 27. London: Routledge.
Charlton, D. G. (Ed.)
  1984   *The French Romantics*, 2 vols. Cambridge: Cambridge University Press.
Charpentier, Sari
  1996   "Exploring Gender Difference in the Study of Religion: Gender Difference as 'Sacred' in the Debate of Gay Marriage in Finland." Unpublished paper.
Cheal, David J.
  1988   *The Gift Economy.* London: Routledge.
Chen, Hsinchih
  1995   "The Development of Taiwanese Folk Religion, 1683–1945." Unpublished dissertation, University of Washington, Seattle.
Chidester, David
  1991   *Shots in the Street: Violence and Religion in South Africa.* Boston: Beacon; Cape Town: Oxford University Press.
  1996   *Savage Systems: Colonialism and Comparative Religion in Southern Africa.* Studies in Religion and Culture. Charlottesville: University Press of Virginia.
Child, Arthur
  1967   "Projection." *Philosophy: The Journal of the Royal Institute of Philosophy* 42:20–36.
Chomsky, Noam
  1975   *Reflections on Language.* New York: Pantheon.
  1993   *Language and Thought.* Anshen Transdisciplinary Lectureships in Art, Science, and the Philosophy of Culture, vol. 3. Wakefield, RI: Moyer Bell.
Christ, Carol P.
  1987   *Laughter of Aphrodite: Reflections on a Journey to the Goddess.* San Francisco: Harper & Row.
  1992   "Feminists—Sojourners in the Field of Religious Studies," pp. 82–87 in Cheris Kramarae and Dale Spender (eds.), *The Knowledge Explosion: Generations of Feminist Scholarship.* New York: Teachers College Press.
Claessen, Henri J. M.
  1978   "The Early State: A Structural Approach," pp. 533–596 in Henri J. M. Claessen and Peter Skalník (eds.), *The Early State.* The Hague: Mouton.
Claessen, Henri J. M. and Peter Skalník
  1978   "The Early State: Theses and Hypotheses," pp. 3–29 in Henri J. M. Claessen and Peter Skalník (eds.), *The Early State.* The Hague: Mouton.
  1981   (Eds.) *The Study of the State.* The Hague: Mouton.

Clark, Elizabeth and Herbert W. Richardson (Eds.)
1996 *Women and Religion: A Feminist Sourcebook of Christian Thought*, Revised and expanded edn. San Francisco: HarperCollins; original edn, 1977.

Clarke, David L.
1968 *Analytical Archeology*. London: Methuen.

Clarke, Peter B. and Peter Byrne
1993 *Religion Defined and Explained*. London: Macmillan; New York: St. Martin's Press.

Clifford, James
1986 "On Ethnographic Allegory," pp. 98–121 in James Clifford and George E. Marcus (eds.), *Writing Culture: The Poetics and Politics of Ethnography*. Berkeley: University of California Press.

1988 *The Predicament of Culture: Twentieth-Century Ethnography, Literature, and Art*. Cambridge, MA: Harvard University Press.

Cohen, Abner
1969 *Custom and Politics in Urban Africa: A Study of Hausa Migrants in Yoruba Towns*. Berkeley: University of California Press.

Cohen, Percy
1969 "Theories of Myth." *Man*, September, 337–353.

Cohen, Ronald
1978 "Ethnicity: Problem and Focus in Anthropology." *Annual Review of Anthropology* 7:379–403.

Cohn, Bernard S.
1987 "The Census, Social Structure and Objectification in South Asia." In Bernard S. Cohn (ed.), *An Anthropologist Among the Historians and Other Essays*. Delhi: Oxford University Press.

1997 *Colonialism and Its Forms of Knowledge: The British in India*. Princeton: Princeton University Press.

Cohn, Norman R. C.
1961 *The Pursuit of the Millennium*. New York: Harper & Row.

Coleman, James S.
1973 *The Mathematics of Collective Action*. Methodological Perspectives. Chicago: Aldine.

1990 *Foundations of Social Theory*. Cambridge, MA: Harvard University Press.

Collins, David
1804 *Account of the English Colony of New South Wales, 1798–1804*. London: T. Cadell and W. Davies.

Collins, Randall
1981 "The Microfoundations of Macrosociology." *American Journal of Sociology* 86:984–1014.

Comaroff, Jean and John L. Comaroff
1991 *Of Revelation and Revolution*, vol. 1: *Christianity, Colonialism, and Consciousness in South Africa*. Chicago: University of Chicago Press.

1997 *Of Revelation and Revolution*, vol. 2: *The Dialectics of Modernity on a South African Frontier*. Chicago: University of Chicago Press.

Comstock, Gary David and Susan E. Henking (Eds.)
1997   *Que(e)rying Religion: A Critical Anthology*. New York: Continuum.
Comstock, W. Richard
1981   "A Behavioral Approach to the Sacred: Category Formation in Religious Studies." *Journal of the American Academy of Religion* 49:625–643.
Comte, Auguste
1830–   *Cours de philosophie positive*. Paris: Bachelier, 1896; *The Positive*
42   *Philosophy*, Harriet Martineau (trans. and ed.). New York: C. Blanchard, 1955.
1851–   *Système de politique positive, ou traité de sociologie, instituant la religion*
54   *de l'humanité*, 4 vols. Paris: Carilian-Goeury, V. Dalmont; English trans., *System of Positive Polity, or, Treatise on Sociology: Instituting the Religion of Humanity*. London: Longmans, Green & Co., 1875.
Conklin, Harold C.
1972   *Folk Classification: A Topically Arranged Bibliography of Contemporary and Background References Through 1971*. New Haven: Department of Anthropology, Yale University.
Connerton, Paul
1989   *How Societies Remember*. Themes in the Social Sciences. Cambridge: Cambridge University Press.
Connolly, Peter (Ed.)
1999   *Approaches to the Study of Religion*. London: Cassell.
Cooey, Paula M., William R. Eakin and Jay B. McDaniel (Eds.)
1992   *After Patriarchy: Feminist Transformations of the World Religions*. Maryknoll, NY: Orbis.
Cook, Karen S. (Ed.)
1986   *Social Exchange Theory*. Beverly Hills, CA: Sage.
Cooper, Frederick and Ann Laura Stoler (Eds.)
1997   *Tensions of Empire: Colonial Cultures in a Bourgeois World*. Berkeley: University of California Press.
Cornell, Stephen
1996   "The Variable Ties That Bind: Content and Circumstance in Ethnic Processes." *Ethnic and Racial Studies* 19:265–289.
Cox, Harvey
1983   "Interview." In Steven J. Gelberg (ed.), *Hare Krishna, Hare Krishna*. New York: Grove.
Csikszentmihalyi, Mihaly
1977   *Beyond Boredom and Anxiety*. San Francisco: Jossey-Bass.
1990   *Flow: The Psychology of Optimal Experience*. New York: Harper & Row.
Culler, Jonathan D.
1981   *The Pursuit of Signs: Semiotics, Literature, Deconstruction*. Ithaca, NY: Cornell University Press.
1986   *Saussure*, 2d edn. London: Fontana.
Daly, Mary
1978   *Gyn / Ecology: The Metaethics of Radical Feminism*. Boston: Beacon.

References

Darby, Phillip
    1998   *The Fiction of Imperialism: Reading Between International Relations and Postcolonialism*. London: Cassell.

Daudin, Henri
    1926a   *De Linné à Jussieu. Méthodes de la classification et idée de série en botanique et zoologie 1740–1790*. Paris: Alcan.
    1926b   *Cuvier et Lamarck. Les classes zoologique et idée de série animale 1790–1830*. Paris: Alcan.

Davidson, Donald
    1980   *The John Locke Lectures*, unpublished; cited with permission of the author.
    1984   *Inquiries Into Truth and Interpretation*. Oxford: Clarendon.
    1989   "The Myth of the Subjective," pp. 159–172 in Michael Krausz (ed.), *Relativism: Interpretation and Confrontation*. Notre Dame: University of Notre Dame Press.

Davis, John
    1992   *Exchange*. Concepts in Social Thought Series. Minneapolis: University of Minnesota Press.

Davis, Kingsley
    1949   *Human Society*. New York: Macmillan.

Davis-Floyd, Robbie
    1992   *Birth as an American Rite of Passage*. Comparative Studies of Health Systems and Medical Care, vol. 35. Berkeley: University of California Press.

Delphy, Christine
    1996   "Rethinking Sex and Gender," pp. 30–41 in Diana Leonard and Lisa Adkins (eds.), *Sex in Question: French Materialist Feminism*. London: Taylor and Francis.

De Man, Paul
    1996   *Aesthetic Ideology*. Andrzej Warminski (ed.). Minneapolis: University of Minnesota Press.

Derré, Jean-René
    1962   *Lamennais, ses amis, et le mouvement des idées à l'époque romantique, 1824–1834*. Paris: Klincksieck.

Derrida, Jacques
    1970   "Structure, Sign and Play in the Discourse of the Human Sciences," pp. 247–265 in Richard Macksey and Eugenio Donato (eds.), *The Languages of Criticism and the Sciences of Man*. Baltimore: Johns Hopkins University Press.
    1976   *Of Grammatology*, Gayatri Spivak (trans.). Baltimore: Johns Hopkins University Press.
    1992   *Acts of Literature*, Derek Attridge (ed.). New York: Routledge.
    1994   *Specters of Marx: The State of the Debt, the Work of Mourning and the New International*, Peggy Kamuf (trans.). New York: Routledge.
    1997   *Deconstruction in a Nutshell: A Conversation with Jacques Derrida*, John D. Caputo (ed.). New York: Fordham University Press.

References

Descartes, René
    1911   *The Philosophical Works of Descartes*, 2 vols., Elizabeth S. Haldane and G. R. T. Ross (trans.). Cambridge: Cambridge University Press.

Despland, Michel
    1979   *La Religion en occident. Evolution des idées et du vécu*. Montreal: Fides.
    1994   *Reading an Erased Code: Romantic Religion and Literary Aesthetics in France*. Toronto: University of Toronto Press.

Detienne, Marcel
    1986   *The Creation of Mythology*, Margaret Cook (trans.). Chicago: University of Chicago Press.
    1991   "The Interpretation of Myths: Nineteenth- and Twentieth-Century Theories," pp. 5–10 in Yves Bonnefoy (ed.), *Mythologies*, vol. 1. Chicago: University of Chicago Press.

Devitt, Michael and Kim Sterelny
    1987   *Language and Reality: An Introduction to the Philosophy of Language*. Oxford: Blackwell.

Dicenso, James J.
    1992   "Deconstruction and the Philosophy of Religion: World Affirmation and Critique." *Philosophy of Religion* 31:29–43.

Dilthey, Wilhelm
    1976   *Selected Writings*, Hans Peter Rickman (ed. and trans.). Cambridge: Cambridge University Press.

Dinzelbacher, Peter
    1979a   "Reflexionen irdischer Sozialstrukturen in mittelalterischen Jenseitsschilderungen." *Archiv für Kulturgeschichte* 61:16–34.
    1979b   "Klassen und Hierarchien im Jenseits," pp. 20–39 in Albert Zimmermann (Ed.), *Soziale Ordnungen im Selbstverständnis des Mittelalters*. Miscellanea Mediaevalia, vol. 12. Berlin: Walter de Gruyter.

Dirks, Nicholas B. (Ed.)
    1992   *Colonialism and Culture*. Comparative Studies in Society and History Book Series. Ann Arbor: University of Michigan Press.

Dirks, Nicholas, Geoff Eley and Sherry Ortner (Eds.)
    1994   *Culture / Power / History: A Reader in Contemporary Social Theory*. Princeton: Princeton University Press.

Dirlik, Arif
    1997   *The Postcolonial Aura: Third World Criticism in the Age of Global Capitalism*. Boulder, CO: Westview.

Dobbelaere, Karel
    1993   "Church Involvement and Secularization: Making Sense of the European Case." In Eileen Barker, James A. Beckford and Karel Dobbelaere (eds.), *Secularization, Rationalism, and Sectarianism: Essays in Honour of Bryan R. Wilson*. Oxford: Clarendon.

Dolhagaray, B.
    1947   "Hiérarchie," pp. 2362–2382 in *Dictionnaire de théologie catholique*, vol. 6.II. Paris: Librairie Latouzey et Ané.

Doniger, Wendy
1998   *The Implied Spider: Politics and Theology in Myth.* New York: Columbia
        University Press.

Doniger-O'Flaherty, Wendy
1986   "The Uses and Misuses of Other People's Myths." *Journal of the
        American Academy of Religion* 54:219–239.

Dorson, Richard M.
1968   *The British Folklorists: A History.* Chicago: University of Chicago Press.

Doty, William G.
1986   *Mythography: The Study of Myths and Rituals.* Tuscaloosa: University of
        Alabama Press.
1996   "Joseph Campbell's Myth and / versus Religion." *Soundings* 79:421–445.
1999   "Exploring Politico-Historical Communications of Mythologies." *Bulletin
        of the Council of Societies for the Study of Religion* 28, 1.

Douglas, Mary
1978   *Implicit Meanings: Essays in Anthropology.* London: Routledge & Kegan
        Paul.
1989   *Purity and Danger: An Analysis of the Concepts of Pollution and Taboo.*
        London: Ark Paperbacks; original edn, London: Routledge & Kegan Paul,
        1966; reprinted, London: Routledge, 1994.

Doutté, Edmund
1898–   "Mahomet Cardinal." In *Mémoires de la société d'agriculture, commerce,*
99   *sciences et les arts de la Marne,* series 2, vol. 1, part 2. Châlons-sur-Marne:
        Musée de Châlons-en-Champagne.

Downs, Laura Lee
1993   "If 'Woman' is Such an Empty Category Then Why Am I Afraid to Walk
        Alone at Night?: Identity Politics Meets the Postmodern Subject."
        Comparative Studies in Society and History 35:414–437.

Döbert, Rainer
1973   "Zur Logik des Übergangs von archaischen zu hochkulturellen Religion-
        systemen," pp. 330–363 in Klaus Eder (ed.), *Die Enstehung der
        Klassengesellschaften.* Frankfurt am Main: Suhrkamp.

Driver, Tom F.
1998   *Liberating Rites: Understanding the Transformative Power of Ritual.*
        Boulder, CO: Westview.

Du Cange, Charles Du Fresne
1733–   *Glossarium ad scriptores mediae et infimae aetatis,* Revised edn., 6 vols.
36   Paris: Caroli Osmont.

Duberman, Martin B., Martha Vicinus and George Chauncey, Jr. (Eds.)
1989   *Hidden from History: Reclaiming the Gay and Lesbian Past.* New York:
        Meridian.

Dubetsky, Alan
1976   "Kinship, Primordial Ties, and Factory Organization in Turkey: An
        Anthropological View." *International Journal of Middle East Studies*
        7:433–451.

Dumézil, Georges
1930 "La préhistoire indo-iranienne des castes." *Journal asiatique* 216:109–130.
1958 *L'Idéologie tripartie des Indo-Européens*. Brussels: Latomus.
1988 *Mitra-Varuna: An Essay on Two Indo-European Representations of Sovereignty*, Derek Coltman (trans.). New York: Zone Books; original French edn, 1948.

Dumont, Louis
1980 *Homo Hierarchicus: The Caste System and Its Implications*, 2d edn, Mark Sainsbury, Louis Dumont and Basia Gulati (trans.). Chicago: University of Chicago Press; original publication, 1966.

Dundes, Alan
1984 (Ed.) *Sacred Narrative: Readings in Theory of Myth*. Berkeley: University of California Press.
1986 "The Anthropologist and the Comparative Method in Folklore." *Journal of Folklore Research* 23:125–146.

Dunn, Oliver and James E. Kelly, Jr.
1989 *The Diário of Christopher Columbus's First Voyage to America 1492– 1493, Abstracted by Fray Bartolomé de las Casas*. Norman: University of Oklahoma Press.

Dunnell, Robert C.
1971 *Systematics in Prehistory*. New York: Free Press.

Durant, Will and Ariel Durant
1965 *The Age of Voltaire*. New York: Simon & Schuster.

Durkheim, Émile
1912 *Les Formes élémentaires de la vie religieuse*. Paris: F. Alcan.
1951 *Suicide: A Study in Sociology*, John A. Spaulding and George Simpson (trans.), George Simpson (ed.). Glencoe, IL: Free Press; original French edn, 1897.
1995 *The Elementary Forms of Religious Life*, Karen E. Fields (trans.) with an Introduction. New York: Free Press; original French edn, 1912.

Durkheim, Émile and Marcel Mauss
1963 *Primitive Classification*, Rodney Needham (ed. and trans.). London: Cohen & West; Chicago: University of Chicago Press; orginal French edn, 1901–1902.

Durkin, John, Jr. and Andrew M. Greeley
1991 "A Model of Religious Choice Under Uncertainty: On Responding Rationally to the Nonrational." *Rationality and Society* 3:178–196.

Dworkin, Andrea
1981 *Pornography: Men Possessing Women*. London: Women's Press.
1987 *Intercourse*. New York: Free Press.

D'Andrade, Roy G.
1992 "Schemas and Motivation," pp. 23–44 in Roy G. D'Andrade and Claudia Strauss (eds.), *Human Motives and Cultural Models*. Publications of the Society for Psychological Anthropology. Cambridge: Cambridge University Press.
1995 *The Development of Cognitive Anthropology*. Cambridge: Cambridge University Press.

D'Arms, John
 1990   "The Roman *Convivium* and the Idea of Equality," pp. 308–320 in Oswyn Murray (ed.), *Sympotica: A Symposium on the Symposion*. Oxford: Clarendon.

Destutt de Tracy, Antoine Louis Claude
 1801– *Éléments d'idéologie*. Paris: Lévi.
 07

Eagleton, Terry
 1991   *Ideology: An Introduction*. London: Verso.

Echikson, William
 1990   *Lighting the Night: Revolution in Eastern Europe*. London: Sidgwick & Jackson; New York: William Morrow.

Eco, Umberto
 1984   *Semiotics and the Philosophy of Language*. London: Macmillan; Bloomington: Indiana University Press.

Eder, Klaus
 1973   "Die Reorganisation der Legitimationsformen in Klassengesellschaften," pp. 288–299 in Klaus Eder (ed.), *Die Entstehung von Klassengesellschaften*. Frankfurt am Main: Suhrkamp.

Edgeworth, Francis Y.
 1961   *Mathematical Psychics: An Essay on the Application of Mathematics to the Moral Sciences*. New York: A. M. Kelly; original edn, London: C. K. Paul, 1881.

Edwards, Rem Blanchard
 1972   *Reason and Religion: An Introduction to the Philosophy of Religion*. New York: Harcourt Brace Jovanovich.

Eggan, Fred
 1965   "Some Reflections on Comparative Method in Anthropology," pp. 357–372 in Melford E. Spiro (ed.), *Context and Meaning in Cultural Anthropology*. New York: Free Press.

Ehrmann, Jacques
 1968   "*Homo Ludens* Revisited," pp. 31–51 in Jacques Ehrmann (ed.), *Game, Play, Literature*. Boston: Beacon.

Eichrodt, Walther
 1961   *Theology of the Old Testament*. 2 vols. Translated by J. A. Baker Philadelphia: Westminster Press.

Eilberg-Schwartz, Howard
 1990   *The Savage in Judaism: An Anthropology of Israelite Religion and Ancient Judaism*. Bloomington: Indiana University Press.

Eisenstadt, Shmuel and Bernhard Giesen
 1995   "The Construction of Collective Identity." *Archives européennes de sociologie* 36:72–102.

Eisler, Riane
 1987   *The Chalice and the Blade: Our History, Our Future*. Cambridge, MA: Harper & Row.

Ekeh, Peter P.
 1974   *Social Exchange Theory: The Two Traditions*. London: Heinemann.

Eliade, Mircea
  1954   *The Myth of the Eternal Return*, Willard E. Trask (trans.). Bollingen Series, vol. 46. New York: Pantheon; original French edn, 1949.
  1959a "Methodological Remarks on the Study of Religious Symbolism," pp. 86–107 in Mircea Eliade and Joseph M. Kitagawa (eds.), *The History of Religions: Essays in Methodology*, With preface by Jerald C Brauer. Chicago: University of Chicago Press.
  1959b *The Sacred and the Profane: The Nature of Religion*, Willard R. Trask (trans.). New York: Harcourt Brace Jovanovich.
  1960   *Myths, Dreams and Mysteries: The Encounter Between Contemporary Faiths and Archaic Realities*. London: Harvill.
  1963a *Myth and Reality*, Willard R. Trask (trans.). New York: Harper & Row.
  1963b *Patterns in Comparative Religion*. New York: World Publishing Company.
  1964   *Shamanism: Archaic Techniques of Ecstasy*. Princeton: Princeton University Press.
  1969   *The Quest: History and Meaning in Religion*. Chicago: University of Chicago Press.
  1973   "Myth in the Nineteenth and Twentieth Centuries," pp. 307–318 in Philip P. Weiner (ed.), *Dictionary of the History of Ideas*, vol. 3. New York: Scribner.
  1974   *The Myth of the Eternal Return*, Willard R. Trask (trans.). Princeton: Princeton University Press.
  1991   "Toward a Definition of Myth," pp. 3–5 in Yves Bonnefoy (ed.), *Mythologies*, vol. 1. Chicago: University of Chicago Press.
Elias, Norbert
  1983   *The Civilizing Process*, 3 vols., Edmund Jephcott (trans.). New York: Pantheon.
Elias, Norbert and John L. Scotson
  1994   *The Established and the Outsiders: A Sociological Enquiry Into Community Problems*. London: Sage.
Ellmann, Mary
  1968   *Thinking About Women*. New York: Harcourt, Brace & World.
Ellwood, Robert S.
  1980   *Mysticism and Religion*. Englewood Cliffs, NJ: Prentice-Hall.
Elman, Jeffrey L. et al.
  1996   *Rethinking Innateness: A Connectionist Perspective on Development*. Neural Network Modeling and Connectionism. Cambridge, MA: MIT Press.
Elster, Jon
  1989a *The Cement of Society: A Study of Social Order*. Studies in Rationality and Social Change. Cambridge: Cambridge University Press.
  1989b *Solomonic Judgments: Studies in the Limitations of Rationality*. Cambridge: Cambridge University Press.
Emerson, Richard M.
  1962   "Power-Dependence Relations." *American Sociological Review* 27:31–41.
  1964   "Power-Dependence Relations: Two Experiments." *Sociometry* 27:282–298.

1972a "Exchange Theory, Part I: A Psychological Basis for Social Exchange," pp. 38–57 in Joseph Berger, Morris Zelditch and Bo Anderson (eds.), *Sociological Theories in Progress*. Boston: Houghton-Mifflin.

1972b "Exchange Theory, Part I: Exchange Relations and Networks," pp. 58–87 in Joseph Berger, Morris Zelditch and Bo Anderson (eds.), *Sociological Theories in Progress*. Boston: Houghton-Mifflin.

Engels, Friedrich
1972 *The Origin of the Family, Private Property, and the State, in the Light of the Researches of Lewis H. Morgan*, With an introd. and notes by Eleanor Burke Leacock. New York: International Publishers; original German edn, 1884.

English, Horace B. and Ava Champney English
1958 "Projection," p. 412 in Horace B. English and Ava Champney English (eds.), *A Comprehensive Dictionary of Psychological and Psychoanalytical Terms*. New York: Longmans, Green & Co.

Erikson, Erik H.
1950 *Childhood and Society*. New York: Norton.
1962 *Young Man Luther: A Study in Psychoanalysis and History*. New York: Norton.
1972 "Play and Actuality," pp. 127–167 in Maria W. Piers (ed.), *Play and Development*. New York: Norton.

Ermarth, Michael
1978 *Wilhelm Dilthey: The Critique of Historical Reason*. Chicago: University of Chicago Press.

Erricker, Clive
1999 "Phenomenological Approaches, pp. 73–104 in Peter Connolly (ed.), *Approaches to the Study of Religion*. London: Cassell.

Evans-Pritchard, E. E.
1937 *Witchcraft, Oracles, and Magic among the Azande*. Oxford: Clarendon.
1965 *Theories of Primitive Religion*. Oxford: Clarendon.
1981 *A History of Anthropological Thought*. New York: Basic.

Eze, Emmanuel Chukwudi
1997a (Ed.) *Postcolonial African Philosophy: A Critical Reader*. Oxford: Blackwell.
1997b *Race and the Enlightenment: A Reader*. Oxford: Blackwell.

Fabian, Johannes
1983 *Time and the Other: How Anthropology Makes Its Object*. New York: Columbia University Press.

Faivre, Antoine
1998 "Renaissance Hermeticism and the Concept of Western Esotericism," pp. 109–123 in Roelof van den Broek and Wouter J. Hanegraaff (eds.), *Gnosis and Hermeticism from Antiquity to Modern Times*. Albany: State University of New York Press.

Fanon, Frantz
1963 *The Wretched of the Earth*, Constance Farrington (trans.). New York: Grove.

References

Feinberg, Leslie
  1996   *Transgender Warriors: Making History from Joan of Arc to Dennis Rodman*. Boston: Beacon.
Feldman, Burton and Robert D. Richardson
  1972   *The Rise of Modern Mythology, 1680–1860*. Bloomington: Indiana University Press.
Ferejohn, John A.
  1991   "Rationality and Interpretation: Parliamentary Elections in Early Stuart England," pp. 279–305 in Kristen Renwick Monroe (ed.), *The Economic Approach to Politics: A Critical Reassessment of the Theory of Rational Action*. New York: HarperCollins.
Ferro-Luzzi, Gabriella E.
  1986   "The Polythetic-Prototype Concept of Caste." *Anthropos* 81.
Feuerbach, Ludwig
  1957   *The Essence of Christianity*, George Eliot (trans.). New York: Harper & Row; English trans. 1854, original German edn, 1841.
  1967   *Lectures on the Essence of Religion*, Ralph Mannheim (trans.). New York: Harper & Row.
  1972   *The Fiery Brook: Selected Writings of Ludwig Feuerbach*, Zawar Hanfi (trans. and Introduction). Garden City, NY: Anchor.
Finke, Roger and Rodney Stark
  1992   *The Churching of America, 1776–1990: Winners and Losers in Our Religious Economy*. New Brunswick, NJ: Rutgers University Press.
Firth, Raymond
  1967a *Tikopia Ritual and Belief*. Boston: Beacon.
  1967b (Ed.) *Themes in Economic Anthropology*. A.S.A. Monographs, vol. 6. London: Tavistock.
  1973   *Symbols: Public and Private*. London: Allen & Unwin.
  1996   *Religion: A Humanist Perspective*. London: Routledge.
Fitzgerald, Timothy
  1991   "Krishnamurti and the Myth of God Incarnate." *Asian Philosophy* 1, 2:109–126.
  1997   "A Critique of 'Religion' as a Cross-Cultural Category." *Method and Theory in the Study of Religion* 9:91–110.
  1999   *The Ideology of Religious Studies*. New York: Oxford University Press.
Flood, Gavin
  1996   *Political Myth: A Theoretical Introduction*. New York: Garland.
Fodor, Jerry A.
  1983   *The Modularity of Mind: An Essay on Faculty Psychology*. Cambridge, MA: MIT Press.
Fontana, Biancamaria
  1991   *Benjamin Constant and the Post-Revolutionary Mind*. New Haven: Yale University Press.
Fortmann, Han M. M.
  1964– *Als Ziende de Onzienlijke. Een cultuurpsychologische Studie over de
  68   religieuze Waarneming en de zogenaande religieuze Projectie*, 4 vols. Hilversum: Gooi en Sticht.

Foucault, Michel
 1970 *The Order of Things: An Archeology of the Human Sciences.* New York: Pantheon; original French edn, Paris: Gallimard, 1966.
 1972 *The Archeology of Knowledge and the Discourse on Language,* A. M. Sheridan Smith (trans.). New York: Harper & Row; original French edn, 1966; reprint, London: Routledge, 1995.
 1973a *Madness and Civilization: A History of Insanity in the Age of Reason,* Richard Howard (trans.). New York: Vintage.
 1973b *The Birth of the Clinic: An Archeology of Medical Perception,* Alan M. Sheridan (trans.). London: Tavistock.
 1977a *Discipline and Punish: The Birth of the Prison,* Alan Sheridan (trans.). New York: Pantheon.
 1977b "Nietzsche, Genealogy, History." In *Language, Counter-Memory, Practice: Selected Essays and Interviews,* Donald F. Bouchard (ed. with an Introduction), Donald F. Bouchard and Sherry Simon (trans.). Ithaca, NY: Cornell University Press.
 1978 *The History of Sexuality,* vol. 1, Robert Hurley (trans.). New York: Pantheon.
 1980 "Nietzsche, Genealogy, History." In *Language, Counter-Memory, Practice: Selected Essays and Interviews,* Donald F. Bouchard (ed.), Donald F. Bouchard and Sherry Simon (trans.). Ithaca, NY: Cornell University Press.

Fowler, James W.
 1981 *Stages of Faith: The Psychology of Human Development and the Quest for Meaning.* San Francisco: Harper & Row.

Fowler, W. Warde
 1978 "The Latin History of the Word *Religio*," pp. 330–336 in Whitfield Foy (ed.), *Man's Religious Quest: A Reader.* London: Croom Helm.

Fox-Genovese, Elizabeth and Eugene D. Genovese
 1987 "The Divine Sanction of Social Order: Religious Foundations of the Southern Slaveholders' World View." *Journal of the American Academy of Religion* 55: 211–233.

Frank, K. L.
 1939 "Projective Methods for the Study of Personality." *Journal of Psychology* 8: 389–413.

Fraser, Robert
 1990 *The Making of the Golden Bough: The Origins and Growth of an Argument.* New York: St. Martin's Press.

Frazer, James George
 1924 *The Golden Bough: A Study in Magic and Religion.* Abridged edn. New York: Macmillan.

Frege, Gottlob
 1960 *Translations from the Philosophical Writings of Gottlob Frege.* 2d edn, Peter Geach and Max Black (eds.). Oxford: Blackwell.

Freud, Anna
 1966 *The Ego and the Mechanisms of Defense.* New York: International Universities Press.

Freud, Sigmund
 1899 "Screen Memories." In *The Standard Edition of the Complete Psychological Works of Sigmund Freud*, vol. 3, James Strachy (ed. and trans.). New York: Norton.

 1901 *The Psychopathology of Everyday Life*. In *The Standard Edition of the Complete Psychological Works of Sigmund Freud*, James Strachy (ed. and trans.), vol. 3. New York: Norton.

 1907 "Obsessive Actions and Religious Practices." In *The Standard Edition of the Complete Psychological Works of Sigmund Freud*, vol. 9, James Strachy (ed. and trans.). London: Hogarth.

 1911 *Psycho-Analytic Notes on an Autobiographical Account of a Case of Paranoia (Dementia Paranoides)*. In *The Standard Edition of the Complete Psychological Works of Sigmund Freud*, James Strachy (ed. and trans.), vol. 12. New York: Norton.

 1913 *The Interpretation of Dreams*, A. A. Brill (trans.). London: Allen.

 1916–17 *Introductory Lectures on Psycho-Analysis*. In *The Standard Edition of the Complete Psychological Works of Sigmund Freud*, James Strachy (ed. and trans.), vols. 15, 16. New York: Norton.

 1919 "The Uncanny." In *The Standard Edition of the Complete Psychological Works of Sigmund Freud*, vol. 17, James Strachy (ed. and trans.). New York: Norton.

 1920 *Beyond the Pleasure Principle*. In *The Standard Edition of the Complete Psychological Works of Sigmund Freud*, James Strachy (ed. and trans.), vol. 18. New York: Norton.

 1927 *Die Zukunft einer Illusion*. Leipzig: Internationaler psychoanalytischer Verlag.

 1930 *Civilization and Its Discontents*, J. Riviere (trans.). London: Hogarth.

 1935 *A General Introduction to Psychoanalysis*, J. Riviere (trans.). New York: Washington Square.

 1950 "Extracts from the Fliess Files." In *The Standard Edition of the Complete Psychological Works of Sigmund Freud*, vol. 1, James Strachy (ed. and trans.). New York: Norton.

 1963 *Studies in Parapsychology: The Uncanny, Dreams and Telepathy, Neurosis of Demonical Possession*, Philip Rieff (trans.). New York: Crowell-Collier.

 1967 *Moses and Monotheism*, Katherine Jones (trans.). New York: Vintage; original German edn, 1937.

 1989 *The Future of an Illusion*, With a biographical Introduction by Peter Gay, James Strachey (ed. and trans.). New York: Norton; original German edn, 1927.

 1990 *Totem and Taboo*, James Strachey (ed. and trans.). New York: Norton; original edn, 1912–13.

Fromm, Erich
 1950 *Psychoanalysis and Religion*. New Haven: Yale University Press.

Frykenberg, Robert Eric
 1993 "Constructions of Hinduism at the Nexus of History and Religion." *Journal of Interdisciplinary History* 23: 523–550.

Fuller, C. J.
  1988   "The Hindu Pantheon and the Legitimation of Hierarchy." *Man* 23: 19–39.
Gadamer, Hans-Georg
  1989   *Truth and Method*, Garrett Barden and John Cumming (trans.). New York: Crossroad; original German edn, 1960.
Gage, Matilda Joslyn
  1985   *Woman, Church, and State: A Historical Account of the Status of Women Through the Christian Ages, with Reminiscences of the Matriarchate.* Salem, NH: Ayer; original edn, New York: Truth Seeker, 1893.
Gall, Susan (Ed.)
  1996   *The Gale Encyclopedia of Psychology*, s.v, "Projective techniques." Detroit: Gale.
Gati, I. and Amos Tversky
  1984   "Weighting Common and Distinctive Features in Perceptual and Conceptual Judgments." *Cognitive Psychology* 16.
Gay, Peter
  1966   *The Enlightenment: An Interpretation*, vol. 1: *The Rise of Modern Paganism*. New York: Norton.
  1977   *The Enlightenment: An Interpretation*, vol. 2: *The Science of Freedom*. New York: Norton; 1st edn, 1969.
Geertz, Clifford
  1960   *The Religion of Java*. Chicago: University of Chicago Press.
  1966   "Religion as a Cultural System," pp. 1–46 in Michael Banton (ed.), *Anthropological Approaches to the Study of Religion*. A.S.A. Monographs, vol. 3. London: Tavistock; reprinted in Clifford Geertz, *The Interpretation of Cultures*. New York: Basic, 1973.
  1968   *Islam Observed: Religious Development in Morocco and Indonesia*. New Haven: Yale University Press.
  1973   *The Interpretation of Cultures: Selected Essays*. New York: Basic.
  1980   *Negara: The Theater State in Nineteenth-Century Bali*. Princeton: Princeton University Press.
  1983   *Local Knowledge: Further Essays in Interpretive Anthropology*. New York: Basic.
Gellner, Ernest
  1992a   *Postmodernism, Reason and Religion*. London: Routledge.
  1992b   *Reason and Culture: The Historic Role of Rationality and Rationalism*. Oxford: Blackwell.
  1997   "Knowledge of Nature and Society," pp. 9–17 in Mikulas Teich, Roy Porter and Bo Gustafsson (eds.), *Nature and Society in Historical Context*. Cambridge: Cambridge University Press.
  1998   *Language and Solitude: Wittgenstein, Malinowski, and the Habsburg Dilemma*. Cambridge: Cambridge University Press.
Gennep, Arnold van
  1909   *Les Rites de passage*. New York: Johnson Reprint, 1969.
  1960   *The Rites of Passage*, Monika B. Vizedom and Gabrielle Cafee (trans.). Chicago: University of Chicago Press.

Genovese, Eugene D. and Elizabeth Fox-Genovese
  1986   "The Religious Ideals of Southern Slave Society." *Georgia Historical Society* 70:1–16.
Gerrish, B. A.
  1984   *A Prince of the Church: Schleiermacher and the Beginnings of Modern Theology*. Philadelphia: Fortress.
Gerth, H. H. and C. Wright Mills (Eds. and trans.)
  1946   *From Max Weber: Essays in Sociology*. New York: Oxford University Press.
Gérard, René
  1963   *L'Orient et la pensée romantique allemande*. Paris: Didier.
Giddens, Anthony
  1984   *The Constitution of Society: Outline of the Theory of Structuration*. Berkeley: University of California Press.
  1987   "Structuralism, Post-Structuralism and the Production of Culture," pp. 195–223 in Anthony Giddens and Jonathan H. Turner (eds.), *Social Theory Today*. Stanford, CA: Stanford University Press.
  1991   *Modernity and Self-Identity: Self and Society in the Late Modern Age*. Stanford, CA: Stanford University Press.
Gikandi, Simon
  1996   *Maps of Englishness: Writing Identity in the Culture of Colonialism*. New York: Columbia University Press.
Gilder, George F.
  1973   *Sexual Suicide*. New York: Quadrangle.
Gill, Anthony J.
  1998   *Rendering Unto Caesar: The Roman Catholic Church and the State in Latin America*. Chicago: University of Chicago Press.
Gill, Brendan
  1989   "The Faces of Campbell." *New York Review of Books*, 28 September, 16–19.
Gill, Sam D.
  1998a "No Place to Stand: Jonathan Z. Smith as *Homo Ludens*, the Academic Study of Religion as *Sub Specie Ludi*." *Journal of the American Academy of Religion* 66:238–312.
  1998b *Storytracking: Texts, Stories, and Histories in Central Australia*. New York: Oxford University Press.
Gillmore, Mary Rogers
  1986   "Implications of Generalized Versus Restricted Exchange," pp. 170–189 in Karen S. Cook (ed.), *Social Exchange Theory*. Beverly Hills, CA: Sage.
Gilman, Charlotte Perkins
  1903   *The Home: Its Work and Influence*. New York: McClure, Phillips & Co.
  1911   *The Man-Made World; or, Our Androcentric Culture*. New York: Charleton.
  1966   *Women and Economics: A Study of the Economic Relation Between Men and Women as a Factor in Social Evolution*, Carl N. Degler (ed.). New York: Harper & Row; original edn., 1898.

Gilroy, Paul
    1993   *The Black Atlantic: Modernity and Double Consciousness.* London: Verso.

Gleason, Maud W.
    1990   "The Semiotics of Gender: Physiognomy and Self-Fashioning in the Second Century C.E." pp. 389–415 in David M. Halpern, John J. Winkler and Froma I. Zeitlin (eds.), *Before Sexuality: The Construction of Erotic Experience in the Ancient Greek World.* Princeton: Princeton University Press.
    1995   *Making Men: Sophists and Self-Presentation in Ancient Rome.* Princeton: Princeton University Press.

Glock, Charles Y. and Phillip E. Hammond (Eds.)
    1973   *Beyond the Classics? Essays in the Scientific Study of Religion.* New York: Harper & Row.

Godlove, Terry F.
    1989   *Religion, Interpretation, and Diversity of Belief: The Framework Model from Kant to Durkheim to Davidson.* Cambridge: Cambridge University Press.

Goetz, Hans-Werner
    1992   "Der 'rechte' Sitz. Die Symbolik von Rang und Herrschaft im hohen Mittelalter im Spiegel der Sitzordnung," pp. 11–47 in Gertrude Blaschitz et al. (eds.), *Symbole des Alltags-Alltag der Symbole. Festschrift für Harry Kühnel zum 65. Geburtstag.* Graz: Akademische Druck und Verlagsanstalt.

Goffman, Erving
    1963   *Stigma: Notes on the Management of Spoiled Identity.* Englewood Cliffs, NJ: Prentice-Hall.

Gokhale, B. G.
    1965   "The Early Buddhist Elite." *Journal of Indian History* 43:391–402.

Goldenweiser, Alexander A.
    1915   "A Review of *Les Formes*." *American Anthropologist.*

Goldstone, R.
    1994   "The Role of Similarity in Cognition." *Cognition* 52.

Gombrich, Ernst H.
    1973   "Illusion and Art," pp. 193–244 in R. L. Gregory and Ernst H. Gombrich (eds.), *Illusion in Nature and Art.* London: Duckworth.

Goodenough, Erwin R.
    1965   *The Encyclopedia of Religious Experience.* New York: Basic.

Goodman, Jordan
    1997   "History and Anthropology," pp. 783–804 in Michael Bentley (ed.), *Companion to Historiography.* London: Routledge.

Goodman, Nelson
    1972   *Problems and Objects.* Indianapolis: Bobbs-Merrill.
    1978   *Ways of Worldmaking.* Indianapolis: Hackett.

Goodman, Nelson and Catherine Z. Elgin
    1988   *Reconceptions in Philosophy and Other Arts and Sciences.* Indianapolis: Hackett.

Goody, Jack
  1961   "Religion and Ritual: The Definitional Problem." *British Journal of Sociology* 12.
  1977   "Against 'Ritual': Loosely Structured Thoughts on a Loosely Defined Topic," pp. 25–35 in Sally F. Moore and Barbara G. Myerhoff (eds.), *Secular Ritual*. Assen: Van Gorcum.
  1982   *Cooking, Cuisine and Class: A Study in Comparative Sociology*. Themes in the Social Sciences. Cambridge: Cambridge University Press.
Gopnik, Alison and Henry M. Wellman
  1994   "The Theory Theory," pp. 257–293 in Lawrence A. Hirschfeld and Susan Gelman (eds.), *Mapping the Mind: Domain Specificity in Cognition and Culture*. Cambridge: Cambridge University Press.
Gordon, Raymond L. (Ed.)
  1981   *Myth, Religion, and Society: Structuralist Essays by M. Detienne, L. Gernet, J.-P. Vernant, and P. Vidal-Naquet*, With an Introduction by R. G. A. Buxton. Cambridge: Cambridge University Press.
Gordon-McCutchan, R. C.
  1983   "Great Awakenings." *Social Analysis* 44:83–95.
Gotthelf, Allan and James G. Lennox (Ed.)
  1987   *Philosophical Issues in Aristotle's Biology*. Cambridge and New York: Cambridge University Press.
Gottschalk, Louis R. (Ed.)
  1963   *Generalization in the Writing of History*. Report, Social Science Research Council (U.S.), Committee on Historical Analysis. Chicago: University of Chicago Press.
Gozzi, Raymond, Jr.
  1995   "The Projection Metaphor in Psychology." *Et Cetera* 52:197–201.
Graf, Fritz
  1993   *Greek Mythology: An Introduction*, Thomas Marier (trans.). Baltimore: Johns Hopkins University Press.
Grahn, Judy
  1982   "From Sacred Blood to the Curse and Beyond," pp. 265–279 in Charlene Spretnak (ed.), *The Politics of Women's Spirituality: Essays on the Rise of Spiritual Power Within the Feminist Movement*. New York: Anchor.
Gramsci, Antonio
  1984   "Notes on Language." *Telos* 59:127–150, with an Introduction by Steven Mansfield.
  1985   *Selections from Cultural Writings*, David Forgacs and Geoffrey Nowell-Smith (eds.), William Boelhower (trans.). Cambridge, MA: Harvard University Press.
  1994   *Letters from Prison*, Frank Rosengarten (ed.), Raymond Rosenthal (trans.). New York: Columbia University Press.
Grassie, William
  1997   "Postmodernism: What One Needs to Know." *Zygon* 23:83–94.
Greeley, Andrew M.
  1995   *Religion as Poetry*. New Brunswick, NJ: Transaction Publishers.

1996   "The New American Paradigm: A Modest Critique." Paper, German Sociological Association Annual Meetings. Cologne, Germany.

Green, John C. et al. (Eds.)

1996   *Religion and the Culture Wars: Dispatches from the Front.* Religious Forces in the Modern Political World. Lanham, MD: Rowman & Littlefield.

Greenblatt, Stephen

1980   *Renaissance Self-Fashioning from More to Shakespeare.* Chicago: University of Chicago Press.

1991   *Marvelous Possessions: The Wonder of the New World.* Chicago: University of Chicago Press.

Griffin, Donald

1992   *Animal Minds.* Chicago: University of Chicago Press.

Griffin, Susan

1978   *Woman and Nature: The Roaring Inside Her.* New York: Harper & Row.

Grimes, Ronald L.

1985   *Research in Ritual Studies: A Programmatic Essay and Bibliography.* Metuchen, NJ: Scarecrow.

1995   *Beginnings in Ritual Studies.* Revised edn. Columbia, SC: University of South Carolina Press.

1996   (ed.) *Readings in Ritual Studies.* Upper Saddle River, NJ: Prentice-Hall.

Grosby, Steven

1994   "The Verdict of History: The Inexpungable Tie of Primordiality—A Response to Eller and Coughlan." *Ethnic and Racial Studies* 17:164–171.

Gross, Rita M.

1977   (ed.) *Beyond Androcentrism: New Essays on Women and Religion.* Missoula, MT: Scholars Press.

1993   *Buddhism After Patriarchy: A Feminist History, Analysis, and Reconstruction of Buddhism.* Albany: State University of New York Press.

1996   *Feminism and Religion: An Introduction.* Boston: Beacon.

Grottanelli, Cristiano

1988   "Uccidere, donare, mangiare. Problematiche attuali sul sacrificio antico," pp. 3–53 in Cristiano Grottanelli and N. F. Parise (eds.), *Sacrificio e società nel mondo antico.* Bari: Laterza.

Grünschloss, Andreas

1994   *Religionswissenschaft als Welt-Theologie: Wilfred Cantwell Smiths interreligiöse Hermeneutik.* Forschungen zur systematischen und ökumenischen Theologie, vol. 71. Göttingen: Vandenhoeck & Ruprecht.

Guha, Ranajit

1997   *Dominance Without Hegemony: History and Power in Colonial India.* Cambridge, MA: Harvard University Press.

Guillaumin, Colette

1982   "The Question of Difference." *Feminist Issues* 2:33–52.

Gumperz, John J. and Stephen C. Levinson (Eds.)

1996   *Rethinking Linguistic Relativity.* Studies in the Social and Cultural Foundations of Language, vol. 17. Cambridge: Cambridge University Press.

Guthrie, Stewart Elliott

 1993　*Faces in the Clouds: A New Theory of Religion.* New York: Oxford University Press.

 1996　"Religion: What is It?" *Journal for the Scientific Study of Religion* 35:412–419.

Habermas, Jürgen

 1981　"Modernity Versus Postmodernity." *New German Critique* 22:3–14.

Haddad, Yvonne Yazbeck and John L. Esposito (Eds.)

 1998　*Islam, Gender, and Social Change.* New York: Oxford University Press.

Hadden, Jeffrey K.

 1974　"A Brief Social History of the Religious Research Association." *Review of Religious Research* 15:128–136.

 1987　"Toward Desacralizing Secularization Theory." *Social Forces* 65:587–611.

Hahn, Ulrike and Nick Chater

 1997　"Concepts and Similarity." In Koen Lamberts and David R. Shanks (eds.), *Knowledge, Concepts, and Categories.* Cambridge, MA: MIT Press.

Hall, Stuart

 1990　"Cultural Identity and Diaspora," pp. 222–237 in Jonathan Rutherford (ed.), *Identity, Community, Culture, Difference.* London: Lawrence & Wishart.

 1996　(Ed.) *Modernity: An Introduction to Modern Societies.* Cambridge, MA: Blackwell.

Hamilton, Richard F.

 1996　*The Social Misconstruction of Reality: Validity and Verification in the Scholarly Community.* New Haven: Yale University Press.

Hammel, E. A.

 1980　"The Comparative Method in Anthropological Perspective." *Comparative Studies in Society and History* 22:145–155.

Hammond, Phillip E. (Ed.)

 1985　*The Sacred in a Secular Age: Toward Revision in the Scientific Study of Religion.* Berkeley: University of California Press.

Hancock, Roger

 1967　"Metaphysics, History of," pp. 289–300 in Paul Edwards (ed.), *The Encyclopedia of Philosophy,* vol. 5. New York: Macmillan.

Handelman, Don

 1992　"Passage to Play: Paradox and Process." *Play and Culture* 5:1–19.

Hanson, Norwood Russell

 1958　*Patterns of Discovery: An Inquiry Into the Conceptual Foundations of Science.* Cambridge: Cambridge University Press.

Harris, Marvin

 1968　*The Rise of Anthropological Theory: A History of Theories of Culture.* New York: Thomas Y. Crowell.

 1979　*Cultural Materialism: The Struggle for a Science of Culture.* New York: Random House.

Harrison, Peter

 1990　*"Religion" and the Religions in the English Enlightenment.* Cambridge: Cambridge University Press.

Hart, George L.
1987 "Early Evidence for Caste in South India," pp. 467–491 in Paul Hockings (ed.), *Dimensions of Social Life: Essays in Honor of David G. Mandelbaum*. Berlin: Mouton de Gruyter.

Hartman, Geoffrey H.
1997 *The Fateful Question of Culture*. Wellek Library Lecture Series at the University of California, Irvine. New York: Columbia University Press.

Hartsock, Nancy C. M.
1983 *Money, Sex, and Power: Toward a Feminist Historical Materialism*. Longman Series in Feminist Theory. New York: Longman; Boston: Northeastern University Press, 1985.

Harvey, David
1989 *The Condition of Postmodernity: An Enquiry Into the Origins of Cultural Change*. Oxford: Blackwell.

Harvey, Van Austin
1987 "Hermeneutics," pp. 279–287 in Mircea Eliade (ed.), *The Encyclopedia of Religion*, vol. 6. New York: Macmillan.
1995 *Feuerbach and the Interpretation of Religion*. Cambridge Studies in Religion and Critical Thought, vol. 1. Cambridge: Cambridge University Press.
1996 "Projection: A Metaphor in Search of a Theory?" pp. 66–82 in D. Z. Phillips (ed.), *Can Religion Be Explained Away?* New York: St. Martin's Press.

Hasenfratz, Hans-Peter
1982 *Die toten Lebenden: Eine religionsphänomenologische Studie zum sozialen Tod in archaischen Gesellschaften, zugleich ein kritischer Beitrag zur sogenannten Strafopfertheorie*. Beihefte der Zeitschrift für Religions- und Geistesgeschichte, vol. 24. Leiden: E. J. Brill.

Hawley, John Stratton
1994 (ed.) *Fundamentalism and Gender*. New York: Oxford University Press.

Hawley, John Stratton and Mark Juergensmeyer
1988 *Songs of the Saints of India*. New York: Oxford University Press.

Headland, Thomas N., Kenneth L. Pike and Marvin Harris (Eds.)
1990 *Emics and Etics: The Insider / Outsider Debate*. Newbury Park, CA: Sage.

Heath, Anthony F.
1976 *Rational Choice and Social Exchange: A Critique of Exchange Theory*. Themes in the Social Sciences. Cambridge: Cambridge University Press.

Hebdige, Dick
1979 *Subculture: The Meaning of Style*. London: Methuen; reprinted, London: Routledge, 1991.

Hechter, Michael
1994 "The Role of Values in Rational Choice Theory." *Rationality and Society* 6:318–333.

Hechter, Michael and Satoshi Kanazawa
1997 "Sociological Rational Choice Theory." *Annual Review of Sociology* 23:191–214.

Hegel, Georg Wilhelm Friedrich

1892   *Lectures on the History of Philosophy*, 3 vols., Elizabeth S. Haldane and Frances H. Simson (trans.). London: Kegan Paul.

1967   *Philosophy of Right*, T. M. Knox (trans.). Oxford: Oxford University Press.

1974   *The Essential Writings*, F. Weiss (ed.). New York: Harper.

1984–   *Lectures on the Philosophy of Religion*, 3 vols. Peter C. Hodgson (ed.), R.
87   F. Brown, Peter C. Hodgson and J. M. Stewart (trans.). Berkeley: University of California Press.

Heilbrun, Carolyn G.

1973   *Toward a Recognition of Androgyny*. New York: Knopf.

Hennig, Willi

1950   *Grundzüge einer Theorie der phylogenetischen Systematik*. Berlin: Deutscher Zentralverlag.

1966   *Phylogenetic Systematics*, D. Dwight Davis and Rainer Zangerl (trans.). Urbana: University of Illinois Press.

Henry, Michael

1979   *The Intoxication of Power: An Analysis of Civil Religion in Relation to Ideology*. Dordrecht, Holland: D. Reidel.

Herbert of Cherbury

1663   *De religione gentilium. Errorumque apud eos causis*. Amsterdam: no publisher; English trans., *Pagan Religion*, John Anthony Butler (trans.). Ottawa: Dovehouse, 1996.

Herrenschmidt, Olivier

1982   "Quelles fêtes pour quelles castes?" *L'Homme* 22, 3:31–55.

Hess, Eva

1983   *The Bījak of Kabir*. San Francisco: North Point.

Hewitt, Marsha A.

1996   "How New is the 'New Comparativism'? Difference, Dialectics, and World-Making." *Method and Theory in the Study of Religion* 8:15–20.

Hick, John

1964   (Ed.) *The Existence of God*. New York: Macmillan; original edn, Cambridge: Cambridge University Press, 1955.

1987   "Religious Pluralism," pp. 331–333 in Mircea Eliade (ed.), *The Encyclopedia of Religion*, vol. 12. New York: Macmillan.

Hinnels, John R. (Ed.)

1995   *A New Dictionary of Religions*. Oxford: Blackwell.

Hirsch, E. D.

1967   *Validity in Interpretation*. New Haven: Yale University Press.

Hirschfeld, Lawrence A.

1994   "Is the Acquisition of Social Categories Based on Domain-Specific Competence or on Knowledge Transfer?" pp. 201–233 in Lawrence A. Hirschfeld and Susan Gelman (eds.), *Mapping the Mind: Domain Specificity in Cognition and Culture*. Cambridge: Cambridge University Press.

Hobbes, Thomas

1839   *The English Works of Thomas Hobbes of Malmesbury; Now First Collected and Edited by Sir William Molesworth, Bart*, vol. 1. London: John Bohn.

1956   *Leviathan*, I. Chicago: Henry Regnery; original edn, 1651.

1968   *Thomas Hobbes: Leviathan*, C. B. MacPherson (ed.). Harmondsworth: Penguin.

Hobsbawm, Eric J.

    1990   *Nations and Nationalism Since 1780: Program, Myth, Reality*. Wiles Lectures. Cambridge: Cambridge University Press.

    1997   *On History*. New York: New Press.

Hobsbawm, Eric J. and Terence Ranger (Eds.)

    1983   *The Invention of Tradition*. Past and Present Publications. Cambridge: Cambridge University Press.

Hodgart, Matthew

    1955   "In the Shade of *The Golden Bough*." *Twentieth Century* 157:111–119.

Hoenigswald, Henry M.

    1963   "On the History of the Comparative Method." *Anthropological Linguistics* 5:1–11.

Hoenigswald, Henry M. and Linda F. Wiener (Eds.)

    1987   *Biological Metaphor and Cladistic Classification: An Interdisciplinary Perspective*. Philadelphia: University of Pennsylvania Press.

Hoffman, Lawrence

    1996   *Covenant of Blood: Circumcision and Gender in Rabbinic Judaism*. Chicago: University of Chicago Press.

Hogden, Margaret T.

    1936   *The Doctrine of Survivals: A Chapter in the History of the Scientific Method in the Study of Man*. London: Allenson.

Hogue, Helen H. S.

    1964   *Of Changes in Benjamin Constant's Books on Religions*. Geneva: Droz.

Holm, Jean and John Bowker (Eds.)

    1994   *Women in Religion*. Themes in Religious Studies Series. London: Pinter.

Holmberg, David H.

    1989   *Order in Paradox: Myth, Ritual, and Exchange Among Nepal's Tamang*. Ithaca, NY: Cornell University Press.

Homans, George C.

    1974   *Social Behavior: Its Elementary Forms*. 2d edn. New York: Harcourt Brace Jovanovich.

Honko, Lauri

    1979   "Theories Concerning the Ritual Process," pp. 369–390 in Lauri Honko (ed.), *Science of Religion: Studies in Methodology*. The Hague: Mouton.

Honor, Hugh

    1991   *Romanticism*. Harmondsworth: Penguin.

Hood, Ralph

    1989   "The Relevance of Theologies for Religious Experiencing." *Journal of Psychology and Theology* 17:336–342.

Hoopes, Robert

    1962   *Right Reason in the English Renaissance*. Cambridge, MA: Harvard University Press.

Horkheimer, Max and Theodor W. Adorno

    1972   *Dialectic of Enlightenment*, John Cumming (trans.). New York: Seabury.

Horton, Robin
1993   *Patterns of Thought in Africa and the West: Essays on Magic, Religion and Science*. Cambridge: Cambridge University Press.

Howe, Leo
1989   "Hierarchy and Equality: Variations in Balinese Social Organization." *Bijdragen tot de taal-, land- en volkenkunde* 145:47–71.
1991   "Rice, Ideology, and the Legitimation of Hierarchy in Bali." *Man* 26:445–467.

Huddleston, Lee Eldridge
1967   *Origins of the American Indians: European Concepts, 1492–1729*. Latin American Monographs, vol. 11. Austin: University of Texas Press.

Hudson, Wilson M.
1966   "Jung on Myth and the Mythic," pp. 181–191 in Wilson M. Hudson (ed.), *The Sunny Slopes of Long Ago*. Dallas, TX: Southern Methodist University Press.

Huff, Toby E.
1993   *The Rise of Early Modern Science: Islam, China and the West*. Cambridge: Cambridge University Press.

Huizinga, Johan
1970   *Homo Ludens: A Study of the Play Element in Culture*. New York: Harper & Row; original edn., 1939.

Hull, David L.
1988   *Science as a Process: An Evolutionary Account of the Social and Conceptual Development of Science*. Science and Its Conceptual Foundations. Chicago: University of Chicago Press.

Hultkrantz, Åke
1979   *The Religions of the American Indians*, Monica Setterwall (trans.). Berkeley, CA: University of California Press.

Hume, David
1882   *Essays: Moral, Political and Literary*. London: Longmans, Green & Co.; original edn, 1741.
1957   *The Natural History of Religion*, H. E. Root (ed.). Stanford: Stanford University Press; original edn., 1757.

Humphrey, Caroline and James Laidlaw
1994   *The Archtypal Actions of Ritual: A Theory of Ritual Illustrated by the Jain Rite of Worship*. Oxford Studies in Social and Cultural Anthropology. Oxford: Oxford University Press.

Hunt, Herbert J.
1941   *The Epic in Nineteenth-Century France*. Oxford: Blackwell.

Hunter, James Davison
1983   *American Evangelicalism: Conservative Religion and the Quandary of Modernity*. New Brunswick, NJ: Rutgers University Press.
1987   *Evangelicalism: The Coming Generation*. Chicago: University of Chicago Press.

Hurry, Anne, Jack Novick and Kerry Kelly Novick
1976   "Freud's Concept of Projection." *Journal of Child Psychotherapy* 4, 2:75–88.

Iannaccone, Laurence R.
    1992   "Sacrifice and Stigma: Reducing Free-Rising in Cults, Communes, and Other Collectives." *Journal of Political Economy* 100:271–292.

    1994   "Why Strict Churches Are Strong." *American Journal of Sociology* 99:1180–1211.

    1995   "Voodoo Economics? Reviewing the Rational Choice Approach to Religion." *Journal for the Scientific Study of Religion* 34:76–89.

Idinopulos, Thomas A. and Brian C. Wilson (Eds.)
    1998   *What is Religion? Origins, Definitions, and Explanations.* Leiden: E. J. Brill.

Idinopulos, Thomas A. and Edward A. Yonan (Eds.)
    1996   *The Sacred and Its Scholars: Comparative Methodologies for the Study of Primary Religious Data.* Studies in the History of Religions, vol. 73. Leiden: E. J. Brill.

Inden, Ronald B.
    1990   *Imagining India.* Oxford: Blackwell.

Ingold, Tim (Ed.)
    1996   *Key Debates in Anthropology.* London: Routledge.

Innis, Robert E. (Ed.)
    1985   *Semiotics: An Introductory Anthology.* Bloomington: Indiana University Press.

Inwood, Michael
    1995   *A Hegel Dictionary.* Oxford: Blackwell.

Irigaray, Luce
    1985   *This Sex Which Is not One*, Catherine Porter and Carolyn Burke (trans.). Ithaca, NY: Cornell University Press.

Jacobson, Jessica, Ichijo Atsuko and Anthony D. Smith (Eds.)
    1997   *Ethnicity and Religion.* Special Issue: *Ethnic and Racial Studies* 20, 2.

Jaeschke, Walter
    1990   *Reason in Religion: The Foundations of Hegel's Philosophy of Religion*, J. Michael Stewart and Peter C. Hodgson (trans.). Berkeley: University of California Press.

James, Edwin Oliver
    1961   *Comparative Religion: An Introductory and Historical Study.* New York: Barnes and Noble.

James, William
    1890   *The Principles of Psychology.* New York: Henry Holt.

    1902   *The Varieties of Religious Experience: A Study in Human Nature.* London: Longmans, Green & Co.

Jameson, Fredric
    1981   *The Political Unconscious: Narrative as a Socially Symbolic Act.* Ithaca, NY: Cornell University Press.

    1984   "Postmodernism, or the Cultural Logic of Late Capitalism." *New Left Review* 146:53–92.

    1988a "Cognitive Mapping," pp. 347–357 in Cary Nelson and Lawrence Grossberg (eds.), *Marxism and the Interpretation of Culture.* Urbana: University of Illinois Press.

1988b   *The Ideologies of Theory: Essays 1971–1986*, 2 vols. Minneapolis: University of Minnesota Press.

1991   *Postmodernism, or, The Cultural Logic of Late Capitalism*. Durham, NC: Duke University Press.

Jantsch, Erich

1980   *The Self-Organizing Universe: Scientific and Human Implications of the Emerging Paradigm of Evolution*. Pergamon International Library of Science, Technology, Engineering and Social Studies. Oxford: Pergamon.

Jarvie, Ian C.

1964   *The Revolution in Anthropology*. New York: Humanities Press.

Jarvis, Darryl S. L.

1998   "Postmodernism: A Critical Typology." *Politics and Society* 26:95–142.

Jastrow, Morris, Jr.

1902   *The Study of Religion*. New York: Charles Scribner's Sons.

1981   *The Study of Religion*, Introduction by William A. Clebsch and Charles H. Long. Chico, CA: Scholars Press; original edn, London: Scott, 1901.

Jensen, Jeppe S. and Luther H. Martin (Eds.)

1997   *Rationality and the Study of Religion*. Acta Jutlandica, Teologisk Serie, vol. 19. Aarhus, Denmark: Aarhus University Press.

Jensen, Lionel M.

1997   *Manufacturing Confucianism: Chinese Traditions and Universal Civilization*. Durham, NC: Duke University Press.

Johnson, L. A. S.

1970   "Rainbow's End: The Quest for an Optimal Taxonomy." *Systematic Zoology* 19.

Johnson, Mark

1987   *The Body in the Mind: The Bodily Basis of Meaning, Imagination, and Reason*. Chicago: University of Chicago Press.

1991   "Knowing Through the Body." *Philosophical Psychology* 4:3–18.

Jolly, Margaret

1994   *Women of the Place: Kastum, Colonialism, and Gender in Vanuatu*. London and Philadelphia: Harwood.

Jones, C. and E. Heit

1993   "An Evaluation of the Total Similarity Principle." *Journal of Experimental Psychology: Learning, Memory and Cognition* 19.

Jones, Robert Alun

1984   "Robertson Smith and James Frazer on Religion," pp. 31–58 in George W. Stocking, Jr. (ed.), *Functionalism Historicized: Essays on British Social Anthropology*. History of Anthropology, vol. 2. Madison: University of Wisconsin Press.

Jordan, Louis

1905   *Comparative Religion: Its Genesis and Growth*. Edinburgh: T. & T. Clark.

Joy, Morny and Eva K. Neumaier-Dargyay (Eds.)

1995   *Gender, Genre and Religion: Feminist Reflections*. Waterloo, ON: Wilfrid Laurier University Press.

Jubien, Michael
    1997   *Contemporary Metaphysics*. Oxford: Blackwell.

Judge, E. A.
    1960   *The Social Patterns of Christian Groups in the First Century*. London: Tyndale.

Jung, Carl G. and C. Kerényi
    1963   *Essays on a Science of Mythology*, R. F. C. Hull (ed.). New York: Harper & Row.

Jung, Carl Gustav
    1938   *Psychology and Religion*. New Haven: Yale University Press.
    1953– *The Collected Works of C. G. Jung*, H. Read, M. Fordham, G. Adler and
    76   W. McGuire (eds.), R. F. C. Hull (trans.). Princeton: Princeton University Press.

Juschka, Darlene
    1997   "Religious Studies and Identity Politics: Mythology in the Making." *Bulletin of the Council of Societies for the Study of Religion* 26, 1:8–11.

Just, Roger
    1989   "Triumph of the Ethnos," pp. 71–88 in Malcolm Chapman, Maryon McDonald and Elizabeth Tonkin (eds.), *History and Ethnicity*. Association of Social Anthropologists of Britain and the Commonwealth Monographs, vol. 27. London: Routledge.

Kamitsuka, David G.
    1996   "The Justification of Religious Belief in the Pluralistic Public Realm: Another Look at Postliberal Apologetics." *Journal of Religion* 76:588–606.

Kant, Immanuel
    1960a *Philosophy of Material Nature: The Complete Texts to Prolegomena to any Future Metaphysics and Metaphysical Foundations of Natural Science*, James W. Ellington (trans.). Indianapolis, IN: Hackett.
    1960b *Religion Within the Limits of Reason Alone*, Theodore M. Greene and John R. Silber (trans.). New York: Harper & Row.
    1996   "An Answer to the Question: 'What is Enlightenment'," pp. 58–64 in James Schmidt (ed.), *What is Enlightenment? Eighteenth-Century Answers and Twentieth-Century Questions*. Berkeley: University of California Press.

Kaufman, Michael (Ed.)
    1987   *Beyond Patriarchy: Essays by Men on Pleasure, Power, and Change*. New York: Oxford University Press.

Kearney, Michael
    1984   *World View*. Novato, CA: Chandler & Sharp.

Keen, Sam
    1990   *Fire in the Belly: On Being a Man*. New York: Bantam.

Kehrer, Günter
    1983   *"Vor Gott sind all gleich". Soziale Gleichheit, soziale Ungleichheit und die Religionen*. Düsseldorf: Patmos.

Kenrick, Paul and Peter C. Crane
    1997   *The Origin and Early Diversification of Land Plants: A Cladistic Study*. Washington, DC: Smithsonian.

Kim, Jaegwon and Ernest Sosa (Eds.)
  1995   *Companion to Metaphysics.* Oxford: Blackwell.

King, Ursula
  1987   (Ed.) *Women in the World's Religions, Past and Present.* New York:
         Paragon.
  1990   "Religion and Gender," pp. 275–286 in Ursula King (ed.), *Turning Points
         in Religious Studies: Essays in Honour of Geoffrey Parrinder.* Edinburgh:
         T. & T. Clark.
  1995   "Introduction: Gender and the Study of Religion," pp. 1–38 in Ursula King
         (ed.), *Religion and Gender.* Oxford: Blackwell.

Kippenberg, Hans G.
  1991   *Die vorderasiatischen Erlösungsreligionen in ihrem Zusammenhang mit
         der antiken Stadtherrschaft: Heidelberger Max-Weber-Vorlesungen 1988.*
         Frankfurt am Main: Suhrkamp.

Kirk, G. S.
  1973   *Myth: Its Meaning and Functions in Ancient and Other Cultures.* Berkeley:
         University of California Press.

Kitagawa, Joseph M.
  1983   "Humanistic and Theological History of Religions with Special Reference
         to the North American Scene." In Peter Slater and Donald N. Wiebe (eds.),
         *Traditions in Contact and Change: Selected Proceedings of the XIVth
         Congress of the International Association for the History of Religions.*
         Waterloo, ON: Wilfrid Laurier University Press.

Kittel, Gerhard and Gerhard Friedrich (Eds.)
  1964– *Theological Dictionary of the New Testament,* 10 vols., Geoffrey W.
  76   Bromiley (trans.). Grand Rapids, MI: Eerdmans.

Klass, Morton
  1980   *Caste: The Emergence of the South Asian Social System.* Philadelphia:
         Institute for the Study of Human Issues.

Kohls, Ernst-Wilhelm (Ed.)
  1980   *Evangelische Katechismen der Reformationszeit vor und neben Martin
         Luthers kleinem Katechismus.* Gütersloh: Gerd Mohn.

Kolb, David (Ed.)
  1992   *New Perspectives on Hegel's Philosophy of Religion.* Albany: State
         University of New York Press.

Komarovsky, M.
  1950   "Functional Analysis of Sex Roles." *American Sociological Review* 15.

Komter, Aafke E. (Ed.)
  1996   *The Gift: An Interdisciplinary Perspective.* Amsterdam: Amsterdam
         University Press.

Kosko, Bart
  1992   *Neural Networks and Fuzzy Systems: A Dynamical Systems Approach to
         Machine Intelligence.* Englewood Cliffs, NJ: Prentice-Hall.

Kramarae, Cheris and Dale Spender (Eds.)
  1992   *The Knowledge Explosion: Generations of Feminist Scholarship.* New
         York: Teachers College Press.

Krauss, Rosalind
    1985   *The Originality of the Avant-Garde and Other Modernist Myths.* Cambridge, MA: MIT Press.

Krishnamurti, J.
    1969   *Freedom from the Known.* London: Victor Gollancz.
    1985   *Truth and Actuality.* London: Victor Gollancz.

Kristeller, Paul O.
    1974   *Medieval Aspects of Renaissance Learning: Three Essays,* Edward P. Mahoney (ed. and trans.). Durham, NC: Duke University Press.

Kristeva, Julia
    1987   *Soleil noir. Dépression et mélancholie.* Paris: Gallimard.

Krymkowski, Daniel H. and Luther H. Martin
    1998   "Religion as an Independent Variable: An Exploration of Theoretical Issues." *Method and Theory in the Study of Religion* 10:187–198.

Kuenen, Abraham
    1882   *National Religions and Universal Religions.* London: Williams & Norgate.

Kuhn, Thomas S.
    1970   *The Structure of Scientific Revolutions.* 2d edn. Chicago: University of Chicago Press; original edn., 1962.

Kurtz, Donald V.
    1981   "Legitimation of Early Inchoate States," pp. 177–200 in Henri J. M. Claessen and Peter Skalník (eds.), *The Study of the State.* The Hague: Mouton.

La Barre, Weston
    1970   *The Ghost Dance: The Origins of Religion.* New York: Dell.

Lachmann, Ludwig M.
    1986   *The Market as an Economic Process.* Oxford: Blackwell.

Laclau, Ernesto
    1997   "The Death and Resurrection of the Theory of Ideology." *Modern Language Notes* 112:297–321.

Laclau, Ernesto and Chantal Mouffe
    1985   *Hegemony and Socialist Strategy: Towards a Radical Democratic Politics.* London: Verso.
    1987   "Post-Marxism Without Apologies." *New Left Review* 166:79–106.

Lakoff, George
    1987   *Women, Fire, and Dangerous Things: What Categories Reveal About the Mind.* Chicago: University of Chicago Press.
    1989   "Cognitive Semantics," pp. 119–154 in Umberto Eco, Marco Santambrogio and Patrizia Violi (eds.), *Meaning and Mental Representations.* Advances in Semiotics. Indianapolis: Indiana University Press.

Lambert, Malcolm D.
    1992   *Medieval Heresy: Popular Movements from the Gregorian Reform to the Reformation.* Oxford: Blackwell.

Lamont, Michelle and Marcel Fournier (Eds.)
    1992   *Cultivating Differences: Symbolic Boundaries and the Making of Inequality.* Chicago: University of Chicago Press.

References

Landau, Peter
    1991   "Frei und unfrei in der Kanonistik des 12. und 13. Jahrhunderts am Beispiel der Ordination der Unfreien," pp. 177–196 in Johannes Fried (ed.), *Die abendländische Freiheit vom 10. zum 14. Jahrhundert. Der Wirkungszusammenhang von Idee und Wirklichkeit im europäischen Vergleich.* Sigmaringen: Jan Thorbecke.

Lane Fox, Robin
    1989   *Pagans and Christians.* New York: Knopf.

Lang, John Dunmore
    1861   *Queensland, Australia: A Highly Eligible Field for Emigration, and the Future Cotton-Field of Great Britain, with a Disquisition on the Origin, Manners, and Customs of the Aborigines.* London: E. Stanford.

Lansing, J. Stephen
    1991   *Priests and Programmers: Technologies of Power in the Engineered Landscape of Bali.* Princeton: Princeton University Press.

Laqueur, Thomas
    1990   *Making Sex: Body and Gender from the Greeks to Freud.* Cambridge, MA: Harvard University Press.

Latour, Bruno
    1993   *We Have Never Been Modern*, Catherine Porter (trans.). Cambridge, MA: Harvard University Press.

Lawrence, Bruce
    1998   *Shattering the Myth: Islam Beyond Violence.* Princeton: Princeton University Press.

Lawson, E. Thomas
    1993   "Cognitive Categories, Cultural Forms and Ritual Structures," pp. 188–206 in Pascal Boyer (ed.), *Cognitive Aspects of Religious Symbolism.* Cambridge: Cambridge University Press.
    1996   "Theory and the New Comparativism, Old and New." *Method and Theory in the Study of Religion* 8:31–35.

Lawson, E. Thomas and Robert N. McCauley
    1990   *Rethinking Religion: Connecting Cognition and Culture.* Cambridge: Cambridge University Press.
    1993   "Crisis of Conscience, Riddle of Identity: Making Space for a Cognitive Approach to Religious Phenomena." *Journal of the American Academy of Religion* 61:201–223.

Le Goff, Jacques
    1977   "Les paysans et le monde rural dans la littérature du haut Moyen Age (Ve–VIe siècle)," pp. 131–144 in *Pour un autre Moyen Age. Temps, travail et culture en Occident.* Paris: Gallimard; original edn, 1966.

Leach, Edmund
    1954   *Political Systems of Highland Burma: A Study of Kachin Social Structure.* London: London School of Economics and Political Science.
    1961a   "Golden Bough or Gilded Twig." *Daedalus* 90:371–399.
    1961b   *Rethinking Anthropology.* London: Athlone.
    1964   "Anthropological Aspects of Language: Animal Categories and Verbal

Abuse." In Eric H. Lenneberg (ed.), *New Directions in the Study of Language*. Cambridge, MA: MIT Press.

1965   "On the 'Founding Fathers': Frazer and Malinowski." *Encounter* 25:24–36.

1966   "Virgin Birth." *Proceedings of the Royal Anthropological Institute* 67:39–49.

1967   (Ed.) *The Structural Study of Myth and Totemism*. A.S.A. Monographs, vol. 5. London: Tavistock.

1968   "Ritual." In David L. Sills (ed.), *International Encyclopedia of the Social Sciences*, vol. 13. New York: Macmillan.

1970   *Claude Lévi-Strauss*. New York: Viking.

1976   *Culture and Communication: The Logic by Which Symbols Are Connected: An Introduction to the Use of Structuralist Analysis in Social Anthropology*. Themes in the Social Sciences. Cambridge: Cambridge University Press.

1987   "Structuralism," pp. 54–64 in Mircea Eliade (ed.), *The Encyclopedia of Religion*, vol. 14. New York: Macmillan.

Leach, Edmund and Jerry W. Leach (Eds.)

1983   *The Kula: New Perspectives on Massim Exchange*. Cambridge: Cambridge University Press.

Lease, Gary

1994   "The History of 'Religious' Consciousness and the Diffusion of Culture." *Historical Reflections/Réflexions historiques* 20:453–479.

1995a   (Ed.) *Pathologies in the Academic Study of Religion: North American Institutional Case Studies*. Special Issue: *Method and Theory in the Study of Religion*, vol. 7, 4. Berlin: Mouton de Gruyter.

1995b   *'Odd Fellows' in the Politics of Religion: Modernism, National Socialism, and German Judaism*. Berlin: Mouton de Gruyter.

1998a   "Religion gleich Weltbild? Zur Problematik einer Begriffsbestimmung." In Dieter Zeller (ed.), *Religion im Wandel der Kosmologien*. Frankfurt: Peter Lang.

1998b   "What are the Humanities and Why Do They Matter? The Case of Religion and Public Life." *Bulletin of the Council of Societies for the Study of Religion* 27:91–95.

Lechner, Frank J.

1991   "The Case Against Secularization: A Rebuttal." *Social Forces* 69:1103–1119.

1996   "Secularization in the Netherlands?" *Journal for the Scientific Study of Religion* 35:252–264.

Lee, Richard B.

1979   *The !Kung San: Men, Women, and Work in a Foraging Society*. Cambridge: Cambridge University Press.

1990   "Primitive Communism and the Origin of Social Inequality." In Steadman Upham (ed.), *The Evolution of Political Systems: Sociopolitics in Small-Scale Sedentary Societies*. Cambridge: Cambridge University Press.

1993   *The Dobe Ju/'Hoansi*. Case Studies in Cultural Anthropology. Fort Worth, TX: Harcourt Brace College Publishers; original edn, *The Dobe !Kung*. New York: Holt, Rinehart and Winston, 1984.

Leeuw, Gerardus van der

1938   *Religion in Essence and Manifestation: A Study in Phenomenology*, J. E. Turner (trans.). Princeton: Princeton University Press; original edn, 1933.

Lenin, Vladimir I.

1976   *Philosophical Notebooks*, vol. 38 of *The Collected Works*, Stewart Smith (ed.), Clemence Dutt (trans.). Moscow: Progress Publishers.

Lenski, Gerhard E.

1984   *Power and Privilege: A Theory of Social Stratification*. Chapel Hill: University of North Carolina Press; original edn, New York : McGraw-Hill, 1966.

Lentricchia, Frank

1983   *Criticism and Social Change*. Chicago: University of Chicago Press.

Lepowsky, Maria

1993   *Fruit of the Motherland: Gender in an Egalitarian Society*. New York: Columbia University Press.

Lerner, Gerda

1979   *The Majority Finds Its Past: Placing Women in History*. New York: Oxford University Press.

Leuba, James H.

1912   *A Psychological Study of Religion*. New York: Macmillan.

1921   *The Belief in God and Immortality: A Psychological, Anthropological and Statistical Study*. Chicago: Open Court; original edn, 1916.

Lewis, I. M.

1971   *Ecstatic Religion: An Anthropological Study of Shamanism and Spirit Possession*. Harmondsworth: Penguin.

1976   "Misfortune and the Consolation of Witchcraft," pp. 68–91 in *Social Anthropology in Perspective: The Relevance of Social Anthropology*. Harmondsworth: Penguin.

1986   *Religion in Context: Cults and Charisma*. Cambridge: Cambridge University Press.

Lewis, J. Rees, B. C. Bates and S. Lawrence

1994   "Empirical Studies of Projection: A Critical Review." *Human Relations* 47:1295–1319.

Leyner, Mark

1997   "Geraldo, Eat Your Avant-Pop Heart Out." *New York Times*, 21 December, Sect. 4, 11.

Lévi-Strauss, Claude

1949   *Les Structures élémentaires de la parenté*. Paris: Presses Universitaires de France.

1962a   *La Pensée sauvage*. Paris: Plon.

1962b   *Totemism*, Rodney Needham (trans.). Harmondsworth: Penguin.

1964–   *Mythologiques*, 3 vols. Paris: Plon.
68

1966   *The Savage Mind*. Chicago: University of Chicago Press; London: Weidenfeld & Nicholson; original French edn, 1949.

1969   *The Elementary Structures of Kinship*, John Harle Bell, Richard von

Sturmer and Rodney Needham (trans.). Boston: Beacon; original French edn, 1949.

1972a "Structural Analysis in Linguistics and in Anthropology," pp. 31–54 in *Structural Anthropology*, vol. 1, Claire Jacobson and Brooke Grundfest Schoepf (trans.). Harmondsworth: Penguin; original French edn, 1945.

1972b "The Structural Study of Myth," pp. 206–231 in *Structural Anthropology*, vol. 1, Claire Jacobson and Brooke Grundfest Schoepf (trans.). Harmondsworth: Penguin; original French edn, 1955.

1975– *Introduction to a Science of Mythology*, 3 vols, John and Doreen
78   Weightman (trans.). New York: Harper & Row; original French edn, 1964–68.

1978 " 'Preface' to Roman Jakobson." In Claude Lévi-Strauss (ed.), *Six Lectures on Sound and Meaning*. Cambridge, MA: MIT Press.

1987 "The Scope of Anthropology," pp. 3–32 in *Structural Anthropology*, vol. 2, Claire Jacobson and Brooke Grundfest Schoepf (trans.). Harmondsworth: Penguin.

Lichtenstein, Martin Karl Heinrich
1928 *Travels in Southern Africa in the Years 1803, 1804, 1805*, 2 vols, Ann Plumbtre (trans.). Cape Town: Van Riebeeck Society; original edn 1811–1812.

Liddell, Henry George, Robert Scott and Henry Stuart Jones (Eds.)
1968 *A Greek-English Lexicon*. Oxford: Clarendon.

Lienhardt, R. G.
1961 *Divinity and Experience: The Religion of the Dinka*. Oxford: Clarendon.

Lincoln, Bruce
1981 *Emerging from the Chrysalis: Studies in Rituals of Women's Initiations*. Cambridge, MA: Harvard University Press.

1986 *Myth, Cosmos, and Society: Indo-European Themes of Creation and Destruction*. Cambridge, MA: Harvard University Press.

1989 *Discourse and the Construction of Society: Comparative Studies of Myth, Ritual, and Classification*. New York: Oxford University Press.

1994 *Authority: Construction and Corrosion*. Chicago: University of Chicago Press.

1996a "Mythic Narrative and Cultural Diversity in American Society," pp. 163–176 in Laurie Patton and Wendy Doniger (eds.), *Myth and Method*. Charlottesville: University Press of Virginia.

1996b "Theses on Method." *Method and Theory in the Study of Religion* 8: 225–277; reprinted in Russell T. McCutcheon (ed.), *The Insider / Outsider Problem in the Study of Religion: A Reader*. Cassell: 1999.

Lo Piparo, Franco
1979 *Lingua, intellettuali, egemonia in Gramsci*. Bari: Laterza.

Lochtefeld, James G.
1996 "New Wine, Old Skins: The Sangh Parivar and the Transformation of Hinduism." *Religion* 26:101–118.

Long, Charles H.
1963 *Alpha: The Myths of Creation*. New York: George Braziller.

1986   *Significations: Signs, Symbols, and Images in the Interpretation of Religion*. Philadelphia: Fortress.

1987   "Cosmogony," pp. 94–100 in Mircea Eliade (ed.), *Encyclopedia of Religion*, vol. 4. New York: Macmillan.

Lopez, Donald S., Jr. (Ed.)

1995   *Curators of the Buddha: The Study of Buddhism Under Colonialism*. Chicago: University of Chicago Press.

Lorenzen, David

1987   "The Kabir-Panth and Social Protest," pp. 281–303 in Karine Schomer and W. H. McLeod (eds.), *The Sants: Studies in a Devotional Tradition of India*. Delhi: Motilal Banaridass; Berkeley, CA: Berkeley Religious Studies Series.

1998   *Praises to a Formless God: Nirgūni Texts from North India*. Albany: State University of New York Press.

Lotman, Juri M.

1990   *Universe of the Mind: A Semiotic Theory of Culture*, Ann Shukman (trans.). London: Tauris.

Low, Gail Ching-Liang

1996   *White Skin, Black Masks: Representation and Colonialism*. London: Routledge.

Löwith, Karl

1949   *Meaning in History: The Theological Implications of the Philosophy of History*. Chicago: University of Chicago Press.

Luckmann, Thomas

1967   *The Invisible Religion: The Problem of Religion in Modern Society*. New York: Macmillan.

Lucy, John Arthur

1992   *Language Diversity and Thought: A Reformulation of the Linguistic Relativity Hypothesis*. Studies in the Social and Cultural Foundations of Language, vol. 12. Cambridge: Cambridge University Press.

Luhmann, Niklas

1977   *Funktion der Religion*. Frankfurt am Main: Suhrkamp.

Lukacs, Georg

1955   *Schicksalswende: Beiträge zu einer neuen deutschen Ideologie*. Berlin: Aufbau Verlag.

Luther, Martin

1958   *Der Kleine Katechismus Doktor Martin Luthers*, Arbeitsgemeinschaft für gemeinsame liturgische Texte in deutscher Sprache (ed.). Gütersloh: Rufer-Verlag; original edn, 1529.

Lutyens, Mary

1988   *Krishnamurti: The Open Door*. London: John Murray.

Lydgate, John

1967   *Lydgate's Fall of Princes*, Henry Bergen (ed.). London: Published for the Early English Text Society by Oxford University Press; original edn, 1430(?).

Lyotard, Jean François

1984   *The Postmodern Condition: A Report on Knowledge*, Geoff Bennington and Brian Massumi (trans.). Minneapolis: University of Minnesota Press.

MacAloon, John J. (Ed.)

    1984   *Rite, Drama, Festival, Spectacle: Rehearsals Toward a Theory of Cultural Performance.* Philadelphia: Institute for the Study of Human Issues.

MacCormack, Sabine

    1988   "*Pachacuti*: Miracles, Punishments, and Last Judgment: Visionary Past and Prophetic Future in Early Colonial Peru." *American Historical Review* 93:960–1006.

    1991   *Religion in the Andes: Vision and Imagination in Early Colonial Peru.* Princeton: Princeton University Press.

MacGaffey, Wyatt

    1994   "Dialogues of the Deaf: Europeans on the Atlantic Coast of Africa," pp. 249–267 in Stuart B. Schwartz (ed.), *Implicit Understandings: Observing, Reporting, and Reflecting on the Encounters Between Europeans and Other Peoples in the Early Modern Era.* Studies in Comparative Early Modern History. Cambridge: Cambridge University Press.

Mack, Burton L.

    1995   *Who Wrote the New Testament? The Making of the Christian Myth.* San Francisco: HarperSanFrancisco.

    1996   "On Redescribing Christian Origins." *Method and Theory in the Study of Religion* 8:247–269.

MacMullen, Ramsay

    1990   "What Difference Did Christianity Make?" pp. 142–155, 327–335 in *Changes in the Roman Empire: Essays in the Ordinary.* Princeton: Princeton University Press.

MacNiece, Gerald

    1992   *The Knowledge That Endures: Coleridge, German Idealism, and the Logic of Romantic Thought.* New York: St. Martin's Press.

MacQueen, Graeme

    1988   "Whose Sacred History? Reflections on Myth and Dominance." *Studies in Religion / Sciences religieuses* 17:143–157.

Mair, Douglas and Anne G. Miller

    1991   (eds.) *A Modern Guide to Economic Thought: An Introduction to Comparative Schools of Thought in Economics.* Brookfield, VT: Edward Elgar.

Malinowski, Bronislaw

    1922   *Argonauts of the Western Pacific: An Account of Native Enterprise and Adventure in the Archipelagoes of Melanesian New Guinea*, Preface by James G. Frazer. London: G. Routledge.

    1926   *Myth in Primitive Psychology.* London: Routledge & Kegan Paul.

    1948   *Magic, Science and Religion, And Other Essays.* Boston: Beacon; Garden City, NY: Doubleday, 1955.

Malley, Brian E.

    1995   "Explaining Order in Religious Systems." *Method and Theory in the Study of Religion* 7:5–22.

    1997   "Causal Holism in the Evolution of Religious Ideas: A Reply to Pascal Boyer." *Method and Theory in the Study of Religion* 9:389–399.

Mandelbaum, David Goodman
  1970   *Society in India*, 2 vols. Berkeley: University of California Press.
Mann, Michael
  1986   *The Sources of Social Power*, 2 vols. Cambridge: Cambridge University Press.
Mansfield, Steven
  1984   "Introduction: Antonio Gramsci, 'Notes on Language'." *Telos* 59:119–126.
Manuel, Frank Edward
  1967   *The Eighteenth Century Confronts the Gods*. New York: Atheneum; original edn, Cambridge, MA: Harvard University Press, 1959.
Maranda, Pierre and Elli Köngäs Maranda (Eds.)
  1971   *Structural Analysis of Oral Tradition*. University of Pennsylvania Publications in Folklore and Folklife, vol. 3. Philadelphia: University of Pennsylvania Press.
March, James G.
  1978   "Bounded Rationality, Ambiguity, and the Engineering of Choice." *Bell Journal of Economics* 9:587–607.
Marett, R. R.
  1932   *Faith, Hope, and Charity in Primitive Religion*. Lowell Institute Lectures, 1930. New York: Macmillan.
  1936   *Tylor*. London: Chapman and Hall.
Margolis, Howard
  1982   *Selfishness, Altruism, and Rationality: A Theory of Social Choice*. Cambridge: Cambridge University Press; Chicago: University of Chicago Press, 1984.
Marsden, George
  1997   *The Outrageous Idea of Christian Scholarship*. New York: Oxford University Press.
Martin, James Alfred
  1987   "Religious Experience," pp. 323–330 in Mircea Eliade (ed.), *The Encyclopedia of Religion*, vol. 12. New York: Macmillan.
Martin, Joel
  1997   "Indians, Contact, and Colonialism in the Deep South: Themes for a Postcolonial History of American Religion," pp. 149–180 in Thomas A. Tweed (ed.), *Retelling U.S. Religious History*. Berkeley: University of California Press.
Martin, Luther H.
  1993   "The Academic Study of Religion in the United States: Historical and Theoretical Considerations." *Religio. Revue Pro Religionistiku* 1:73–80.
  1994   "The Anti-Individualistic Ideology of Hellenistic Culture." *Numen* 41:117–140.
  1996   "Introduction: The Post-Eliadean Study of Religion and the New Comparativism." The New Comparativism in the Study of Religion: A Symposium. *Method and Theory in the Study of Religion* 8:1–3.
  1997a "Akin to the Gods or Simply One to Another? Comparison with Respect to Religions in Antiquity." In Hans-Joachim Klimkeit (ed.), *Vergleichen und Verstehen in der Religionswissenschaft*. Wiesbaden: Harrassowitz.

1997b   "Biology, Sociology and the Study of Religion: Two Lectures." *Religio. Revue Pro Religionistiku* 5:21–35.

1999   "Religious Syncretism, Comparative Religion and Spiritual Quests." *Method and Theory in the Study of Religion* 11.

Forth-coming   "Secular Theory and the Academic Study of Religion." In Tim Jensen and Mikael Rothstein (eds.), *Secular Theories of Religion: A Selection of Recent Academic Perspectives*. Copenhagen: The Museum Tusculanum Press.

Martineau, Harriet

1840   *Woman's Rights and Duties Considered with Relation to Their Influence on Society and Her Own Condition*. London: J. W. Parker.

1985   *Harriet Martineau on Women*, Gayle Graham (ed.). New Brunswick, NJ: Rutgers University Press.

Marty, Martin

1985   *What is Modern about the Modern Study of Religion?* The University Lecture in Religion at Arizona State University. Tempe: Department of Religious Studies, Arizona State University.

Marx, Karl

1844   "A Contribution to the Critique of Hegel's *Philosophy of Right*: Introduction." In Robert C. Tucker (ed.), *The Marx-Engels Reader*. New York: Norton, 1972.

1964   "Theses on Feuerbach," pp. 69–72 in Reinhold Niebuhr (ed. and Introduction), *On Religion: Karl Marx and Friedrich Engels*. New York: Schocken.

1971   *A Contribution to the Critique of Political Economy*, Maurice Dobb (ed.), S. W. Ryazanskaya (trans.). London: Lawrence & Wishart; original German edn, 1859.

1987   *Economic and Philosophic Manuscripts of 1844*, Martin Milligan (trans.). Buffalo, NY: Prometheus.

Marx, Karl and Friedrich Engels

1955   *On Religion*. Moscow: Foreign Language Publishing House.

1964   *On Religion: Karl Marx and Friedrich Engels*, Reinhold Niebuhr (ed.). New York: Schocken.

1970   *The German Ideology, Part One*, C. J. Arthurs (trans.). New York: International Publishers.

Masuzawa, Tomoko

1993   *In Search of Dreamtime: The Quest for the Origin of Religion*. Religion and Postmodernism. Chicago: University of Chicago Press.

Mathieu, Nicole-Claude

1980   "Masculinity / Feminity." *Feminist Issues* 1:51–69.

1996   "Sexual, Sexed and Sex-Class Identities: Three Ways of Conceptualizing the Relationship Between Sex and Gender," pp. 42–71 in Diana Leonard and Lisa Adkins (eds.), *Sex in Question: French Materialist Feminism*. London: Taylor and Francis.

Maurice, Frederick D.

1847   *The Religions of the World and Their Relations to Christianity*. London: John W. Parker.

Mauss, Marcel

    1990   *The Gift: The Form and Reason for Exchange in Archaic Societies*, W. D. Halls (trans.). Foreword by Mary Douglas. New York: Routledge; original French edn, 1925.

Maybury-Lewis, David and Uri Almagor (Eds.)

    1989   *The Attraction of Opposites: Thought and Society in the Dualist Mode.* Ann Arbor: University of Michigan Press.

Mayr, Ernst

    1969   *Principles of Systematic Zoology.* New York: McGraw-Hill.

    1982   *The Growth of Biological Thought.* Cambridge, MA: Harvard University Press.

    1988   *Toward a New Philosophy of Biology.* Cambridge, MA: Harvard University Press.

McCalla, Arthur

    1998   *A Romantic Historiosophy: The Philosophy of History of Pierre-Simon Ballanche.* Leiden: E. J. Brill.

McClintock, Anne

    1995   *Imperial Leather: Race, Gender, and Sexuality in the Colonial Contest.* London: Routledge.

McClintock, Anne, Aamir Mufti and Ella Shohat (Eds.)

    1997   *Dangerous Liaisons: Gender, Nation, and Postcolonial Perspectives.* Cultural Politics, vol. 11. Minneapolis: University of Minnesota Press.

McClung, Nellie L.

    1972   *In Times Like These.* Toronto: University of Toronto Press; original edn, 1915.

McCutcheon, Russell T.

    1997a   "Classification and the Shapeless Beast: A Critical Look at the AAR Research Interest Survey." *Religious Studies News* 12, 3:7–9.

    1997b   *Manufacturing Religion: The Discourse on Sui Generis Religion and the Politics of Nostalgia.* New York: Oxford University Press.

    1997c   "A Default of Critical Intelligence? The Scholar of Religion as Public Intellectual." *Journal of the American Academy of Religion* 65:443–468.

    1998a   "The Economics of Spiritual Luxury: The Glittering Lobby and the Parliament of Religions." *Journal of Contemporary Religion* 13:51–64.

    1998b   "Redescribing 'Religion' as Social Formation: Toward a Social Theory of Religion," pp. 51–71 in Thomas A. Idinopulos and Brian C. Wilson (eds.), *What is Religion? Origins, Definitions, and Explanations.* Studies in the History of Religions, vol. 81. Leiden: E. J. Brill.

    1998c   "Talking Past Each Other: Public Intellectuals Revisited." *Journal of the American Academy of Religion* 67:911–917.

    1999   (Ed.) *The Insider / Outsider Problem in the Study of Religion: A Reader.* Controversies in the Study of Religion. London: Cassell.

McFarland, H. Neill

    1967   *Rush Hour of the Gods: A Study of New Religious Movements in Japan.* New York: Macmillan.

McGowan, John

    1991   *Postmodernism and Its Critics.* Ithaca, NY: Cornell University Press.

McGrath, Alister E.
    1988   *Reformation Thought: An Introduction*. Oxford: Blackwell.
McKay, James
    1982   "An Exploratory Synthesis of Primordial and Mobilizationist Approaches to Ethnic Phenomena." *Ethnic and Racial Studies* 5:395–420.
McLoughlin, William G.
    1978   *Revivals, Awakenings, and Reform: An Essay on Religion and Social Change in America, 1607–1977*. Chicago: University of Chicago Press.
Mead, George Herbert
    1934   *Mind, Self, and Society: From the Standpoint of a Social Behaviorist*. Chicago: University of Chicago Press.
Mead, Margaret
    1935   *Sex and Temperament in Three Primitive Societies*. New York: William Mary.
Medin, D., R. Goldstone and D. Gentner
    1993   "Respects for Similarity." *Psychological Review* 100.
Medved, Michael
    1992   *Hollywood vs. America: Popular Culture and the War on Traditional Values*. New York: HarperCollins.
Mencher, Joan P.
    1974   "The Caste System Upside-Down, or the Not-So Mysterious East." *Current Anthropology* 15:469–479.
    1980   "On Being an Untouchable in India: A Materialist Perspective," pp. 261–294 in Eric B. Ross (ed.), *Beyond the Myths of Culture*. New York: Academic Press.
Mensching, Gustav
    1959   *Die Religionen: Erscheinungsformen, Strukturtypen und Lebensgesetze*. Stuttgart: W. Kohlhammer.
    1976   *Structures and Patterns of Religion*. Delhi: Motilal Banarsidass.
Merklinger, Philip
    1993   *Philosophy, Theology, and Hegel's Berlin Philosophy of Religion, 1821–1827*. Albany: State University of New York Press.
Merton, Robert K.
    1968   *Social Theory and Social Structure: Toward the Codification of Theory and Research*. New York: Free Press; original edn, 1949.
Mervis, Carolyn and Eleanor Rosch
    1981   "Categorization of Natural Objects." *Annual Review of Psychology* 21.
Messer-Davidow, Ellen, David R. Shumway and David J. Sylvan (Eds.)
    1993   *Knowledges: Historical and Critical Studies in Disciplinarity*. Knowledge, Disciplinarity and Beyond. Charlottesville: University Press of Virginia.
Meyering, Theo C.
    1989   *Historical Roots of Cognitive Science: The Rise of a Cognitive Theory of Perception from Antiquity to the Nineteenth Century*. Dordrecht: Kluwer.
Michaelsen, Robert S.
    1995   "Dirt in the Court Room: Indian Land Claims and American Property Rights," pp. 43–96 in David Chidester and Edward T. Linenthal (eds.), *American Sacred Space*. Bloomington: Indiana University Press.

Michel, A.
1959   *Famille, industrialisation, logement.* Paris: Centre nationale de recherche scientifique.
1960   "La Femme dans la famille française." *Cahiers internationaux de sociologie.*

Mignolo, Walter D.
1995   *The Darker Side of the Renaissance: Literacy, Territoriality, and Colonization.* Ann Arbor: University of Michigan Press.

Mill, John Stuart
1988   *The Subjection of Women,* Susan Muller Okin (ed.). Indianapolis: Hackett; original edn, London: Longmans, Green, Reader & Dyer, 1869.

Mills, Sara
1994   "Knowledge, Gender, and Empire," pp. 29–50 in Alison Blunt and Gillian Rose (eds.), *Writing Women and Space: Colonial and Postcolonial Geographies.* New York: Guilford.

Milner, Murray
1994   *Status and Sacredness: A General Theory of Status Relations and an Analysis of Indian Culture.* New York: Oxford University Press.

Milner, Vincent L.
1872   *Religious Denominations of the World, Comprising a General View of the Origin, History and Condition of the Various Sects of Christians, the Jews, the Mahometans, as Well as the Pagan Forms of Religion Existing in the Different Countries of the Earth.* Philadelphia: J. W. Bradley.

Minnich, Elizabeth Kamarck
1990   *Transforming Knowledge.* Philadelphia: Temple University Press.

Mitchell, Timothy
1991   *Colonising Egypt.* Berkeley: University of California Press; original edn, Cambridge: Cambridge University Press, 1988.

Moffat, Michael
1979   "Harijan Religion: Consensus at the Bottom of the Caste." *American Ethnologist* 6:244–260.

Mohanty, Chandra Talpade
1991a   "Cartographies of Struggle: Third World Women and the Politics of Feminism," pp. 1–50 in Chandra Talpade Mohanty, Ann Russo and Lourdes Torres (eds.), *Third World Women and the Politics of Feminism.* Bloomington: Indiana University Press.
1991b   "Under Western Eyes: Feminist Scholarship and Colonial Discourses," pp. 51–80 in Chandra Talpade Mohanty, Ann Russo and Lourdes Torres (eds.), *Third World Women and the Politics of Feminism.* Bloomington: Indiana University Press.

Molm, Linda
1986   "Linking Power Structure and Power Use," pp. 101–129 in Karen S. Cook (ed.), *Social Exchange Theory.* Beverly Hills, CA: Sage.

Moore-Gilbert, Bart
1997   *Postcolonial Theory: Context, Practice, Politics.* London: Verso.

Moran, Gabriel
1992   *Uniqueness: Problem or Paradox in Jewish and Christian Traditions.* Maryknoll, NY: Orbis.

Morenz, Siegfried
    1973   *Egyptian Religion.* Translated by Ann E. Keep. Ithaca: Cornell University Press.

Moriarty, Michael
    1991   *Roland Barthes.* Stanford, CA: Stanford University Press.

Moroto, Aiko
    1976   "Conditions for Accepting a New Religious Belief: A Case Study of Myochikai Members in Japan." Unpublished MA thesis, University of Washington, Seattle.

Morris, Brian
    1987   *Anthropological Studies of Religion: An Introductory Text.* Cambridge: Cambridge University Press.

Mudimbe, V. Y.
    1988   *The Invention of Africa: Gnosis, Philosophy and the Order of Knowledge.* Bloomington: Indiana University Press.

Muir, Edward
    1997   *Ritual in Early Modern Europe.* New Approaches to European History, vol. 11. Cambridge: Cambridge University Press.

Müller, F. Max
    1871   *Lectures on the Science of Language: Delivered at the Royal Institution of Great Britain, 1861 and 1863.* 6th edn. London: Longmans, Green & Co.

    1873   *Introduction to the Science of Religion: Four Lectures Delivered at the Royal Institution with Two Essays of False Analogies, and the Philosophy of Mythology.* London: Longmans, Green & Co.

    1878   *Lectures on the Origin and Growth of Religion: As Illustrated by the Religions of India.* London: Longmans, Green & Co.; reprinted in Bryan S. Turner (ed.), *The Early Sociology of Religion,* vol. 2. London: Routledge / Thoemmes Press, 1997.

    1884   *Biographical Essays.* New York: Scribners.

    1900   *The Question of Right between England and the Transvaal: Letters by the Right Hon. F. Max Müller with Rejoinders by Professor Theodore Mommsen.* London: Imperial South African Association.

Muller-Ortega, Paul Eduardo
    1989   *The Triadic Heart of Siva: Kaula Tantricism of Abhinavagupta in the Non-Dual Shaivism of Kasmir.* Albany: SUNY Press.

Murphy, Tim
    1994   "*Wesen und Erscheinung* in the History of the Study of Religion: A Poststructuralist Perspective." *Method & Theory in the Study of Religion* 6:119–146.

    1998   "The 'One' Behind the 'Many'." *Bulletin of the Council of Societies for the Study of Religion* 27, 2:39–40.

Murray, H. A.
    1951   "Foreword." In H. H. Anderson and Gladys L. Anderson (eds.), *An Introduction to Projective Techniques.* New York: Prentice-Hall.

Murstein, Bernard and Ronald S. Pryer
    1959   "The Concept of Projection: A Review." *Psychological Bulletin* 56:353–374.

Myrdal, A. and V. Klein
  1956 *Women's Two Roles: Home and Work*. London: Routledge & Kegan Paul.
Nagata, Judith A.
  1979 *Malaysian Mosaic: Perspectives from a Poly-Ethnic Society*. Vancouver: University of British Columbia Press.
Nandy, Ashis
  1983 *The Intimate Enemy: Loss and Recovery of Self Under Colonialism*. Delhi: Oxford University Press.
Narotzky, Susana
  1997 *New Directions in Economic Anthropology*. Anthropology, Culture, and Society. London: Pluto.
Nattier, Jan
  1995 "Visible and Invisible: Jan Nattier on the Politics of Representation in Buddhist America." *Tricycle* 5, 1:42–49.
Needham, Rodney
  1963 "Introduction." In Émile Durkheim and Marcel Mauss, *Primitive Classification*. London: Cohen & West; Chicago: University of Chicago Press.
  1972 *Belief, Language, and Experience*. Chicago: University of Chicago Press.
  1973 (Ed.) *Right and Left: Essays on Dual Symbolic Classification*, Foreword by E. E. Evans-Pritchard. Chicago: University of Chicago Press.
  1975 "Polythetic Classification: Convergence and Consequences." *Man* N. S. 10.
  1980 *Reconnaissances*. Toronto: University of Toronto Press.
Nelson, Cary and Lawrence Grossberg (Eds.)
  1988 *Marxism and the Interpretation of Culture*. Urbana: University of Illinois Press.
Neusner, Jacob
  1973 *The Idea of Purity in Ancient Judaism*, With a critique and commentary by Mary Douglas. Studies in Judaism in Late Antiquity, vol. 1. Leiden: E. J. Brill.
  1974– *A History of the Mishnaic Laws of Purity*, 22 vols. Leiden: E. J. Brill.
  77
Newman, Peter
  1965 *The Theory of Exchange*. Englewood Cliffs, NJ: Prentice-Hall.
Newman, William M.
  1974 "The Society for the Scientific Study of Religion: The Development of an Academic Society." *Review of Religious Research* 15:137–151.
Niebuhr, Reinhold (Ed.)
  1964 *Karl Marx and Friedrich Engels on Religion*. New York: Schocken.
Nisbet, Robert A.
  1974 *The Sociology of Emile Durkheim*. Oxford and New York: Oxford University Press.
Noel, Daniel C. (Ed.)
  1990 *Paths to the Power of Myth: Joseph Campbell and the Study of Religion*. New York: Crossroad.

Norris, Christopher
  1992   *Uncritical Theory: Postmodernism, Intellectuals and the Gulf War.*
          London: Lawrence & Wishart.

Northup, Lesley A.
  1997   *Ritualizing Women: Patterns of Spirituality.* Cleveland: Pilgrim.

Nosofsky, R.
  1988   "Choice, Similarity and the Context Theory of Classification." *Journal of
          Experimental Psychology: Learning, Memory and Cognition* 10.

Oakley, Ann
  1972   *Sex, Gender and Society.* London: Temple Smith.

Oberman, Heiko
  1963   *The Harvest of Medieval Theology: Gabriel Biel and Late Medieval
          Nominalism.* Cambridge, MA: Harvard University Press.

  1989   *Luther: Man Between God and Devil*, Eileen Walliser-Schwarzbart
          (trans.). New Haven: Yale University Press.

Oberoi, Harjot
  1994   *The Construction of Religious Boundaries: Culture, Identity, and Diversity
          in the Sikh Tradition.* Chicago: University of Chicago Press.

Oexle, Otto Gerhard
  1979   "Die funktionale Dreiteilung der Gesellschaft nach Adalbero von Laon.
          Deutungsschemata der sozialen Wirklichkeit in früheren Mittelalter," pp.
          421–474 in Max Lerner (ed.), *Ideologie und Herrschaft im Mittelalter.*
          Darmstadt: Wissenschaftliche Buchgesellschaft.

O'Hanlon, Rosalind
  1988   "Recovering the Subject: *Subaltern Studies* and Histories of Resistance in
          Colonial South Asia." *Modern Asian Studies* 22:184–224.

  1989   "Cultures of Rule, Communities of Resistance: Gender, Discourse, and
          Tradition in Recent South Asian Historiography." *Social Analysis* 25.

Olivelle, Patrick
  1992 *Samnyāsa Upanisads: Hindu Scriptures on Asceticism and Renunciation.*
          New York: Oxford University Press.

Olivelle, Patrick
  1993   *The Asrama System: The History and Hermeneutics of a Religious
          Institution.* New York: Oxford University Press.

Olson, Carl (Ed.)
  1987   *The Book of the Goddess, Past and Present: An Introduction to Her
          Religion.* New York: Crossroad.

Olzak, Susan and Joane Nagel
  1986   (eds.) *Competitive Ethnic Relations.* Orlando, FL: Academic Press.

O'Meara, Thomas
  1982   *Romantic Idealism and Roman Catholicism: Schelling and the Theolo-
          gians.* Notre Dame, IN: University of Notre Dame Press.

Onions, C. T.
  1966   *Oxford Dictionary of English Etymology.* Oxford: Oxford University
          Press.

Ortner, Sherry
  1974   "Is Female to Male as Nature is to Culture?" pp. 67–87 in Michelle

Zimbalist Rosaldo and Louise Lamphere (eds.), *Woman, Culture and Society*. Stanford, CA: Stanford University Press.

1996 *Making Gender: The Politics and Erotics of Culture*. Boston: Beacon.

Otto, Rudolf

1932 *Mysticism East and West: A Comparative Analysis of the Nature of Mysticism*, Bertha L. Bracey and Richenda C. Payne (trans.). London: Macmillan.

1969 *The Idea of the Holy: An Inquiry Into the Non-Rational Factor in the Idea of the Divine and Its Relation to the Rational*, John W. Harvey (trans.). London: Oxford University Press; original German edn, 1917.

Ozment, Steven

1971 (Ed.) *The Reformation in Medieval Perspective*. Chicago: Quadrangle.

1980 *The Age of Reform, 1250–1550: An Intellectual and Religious History of Late Medieval and Reformation Europe*. New Haven: Yale University

Paden, William E.

1991 "Before 'the Sacred' Became Theological: Rereading the Durkheimian Legacy." *Method and Theory in the Study of Religion* 3:10–23.

1992 *Interpreting the Sacred: Ways of Viewing Religion*. Boston: Beacon.

1994 *Religious Worlds: The Comparative Study of Religion*. 2d edn. Boston: Beacon.

1996a "Elements of a New Comparativism." *Method and Theory in the Study of Religion* 8:5–14.

1996b "Sacrality as Integrity: 'Sacred Order' as a Model for Describing Religious Worlds." pp. 3–18 in Thomas A. Idinopulos and Edward A. Yonan (eds.), *The Sacred and Its Scholars: Comparative Methodologies for the Study of Primary Religious Data*. Studies in the History of Religions, vol. 73. Leiden: E. J. Brill.

1998a "Elements of a New Comparativism." In Kimberley C. Patton and Benjamin C. Ray (eds.), *A Magic Still Dwells: Comparative Religion in a Postmodern Age*. Berkeley: University of California Press.

1998b "Sacrality and Worldmaking: New Categorial Perspectives." In Tore Ahlbäck (ed.), *Methodology of the Study of Religions*. Scripta Instituti Donneriani Aboensis, vol. 17, 1. Åbo: Donner Institute.

Pagels, Elaine

1979 *The Gnostic Gospels*. New York: Random House.

Pagitt, Ephraim

1635 *Christianographie, or, The Description of the Multitude and Sundry Sorts of Christians in the World not Subject to the Pope*. London: T. P. & W. for M. Costerden.

Pailin, David A.

1984 *Attitudes to Other Religions: Comparative Religion in Seventeenth and Eighteenth Century Britain*. Manchester: Manchester University Press.

Pals, Daniel L.

1996 *Seven Theories of Religion*. New York: Oxford University Press.

Pandey, Gyanendra

1990 *The Construction of Communalism in Colonial North India*. Delhi: Oxford University Press.

Pandian, Jacob
    1997   "The Sacred Integration of the Cultural Self," pp. 505–516 in Stephen D. Glazier (ed.), *Anthropology of Religion: A Handbook*. Westport, CT: Greenwood.

Parkin, David
    1991   *Sacred Void: Spatial Images of Work and Ritual Among the Giriama of Kenya*. Cambridge Studies in Social and Cultural Anthropology, vol. 80. Cambridge: Cambridge University Press.

Parkin, Frank
    1978   "Social Stratification," pp. 599–632 in Tom Bottomore and Robert Nisbet (eds.), *A History of Sociological Analysis*. New York: Basic.

Parrish, Fred L.
    1941   *The Classification of Religions: Its Relation to the History of Religions*. Scottdale, PA: Herald Press.

Parry, Benita
    1987   "Problems in Current Theories of Colonial Discourse." *Oxford Literary Review* 9, 1–2:27–58.
    1994   "Resistance Theory/Theorising Resistance or Two Cheers for Nativism," pp. 172–193 in Francis Barker, Peter Hulme and Margaret Iverson (eds.), *Colonial Discourse/Postcolonial Theory*. Essex Symposia, Literature, Politics, Theory. Manchester: Manchester University Press.

Parry, Benita, Keith Ansell-Pearson and Judith Squires (Eds.)
    1998   *Cultural Readings of Imperialism: Edward Said and the Gravity of History*. New York: St. Martin's Press.

Parry, Jonathan P.
    1982   "The Sarcophagous Ascetics of Benares." In Maurice Bloch and Jonathan P. Parry (eds.), *Death and the Regeneration of Life*. Cambridge: Cambridge University Press.

Parry, Jonathan P. and Maurice Bloch (Eds.)
    1989   *Money and the Morality of Exchange*. Cambridge: Cambridge University Press.

Parsons, Talcott
    1951   *The Social System*. Glencoe, IL: Free Press.

Partin, Harry B.
    1987   "Classification of Religions." In Mircea Eliade (ed.), *The Encyclopedia of Religion*, vol. 3. New York: Macmillan.

Pascal, Blaise
    1966   *Pensées*, A. J. Krailsheimer (trans.). Harmondsworth: Penguin Classics; original French edn, 1670.

Patton, Laurie L.
    1996   "Myth and Money: The Exchange of Words and Wealth in Vedic Commentary," pp. 208–244 in Laurie L. Patton and Wendy Doniger (eds.), *Myth and Method*. Charlottesville: University Press of Virginia.

Paulus, Paul B. (Ed.)
    1983   *Basic Group Processes*. Springer Series in Social Psychology. New York: Springer-Verlag.

Peel, J. D. Y.

References

1969   "Understanding Alien Thought Systems." *British Journal of Sociology* 20:69–84.

Peirce, Charles Sanders
1931– *Collected Papers*, Hartshorne C. and P. Weiss (eds.). Cambridge, MA:
58   Harvard University Press.

Peires, J. B.
1979   "Nxele, Ntsikana and the Origins of the Xhosa Religious Reaction." *Journal of African History* 20:51–62.

Penner, Hans H.
1986   "Structure and Religion." *History of Religions* 25:236–254.
1989   *Impasse and Resolution: A Critique of the Study of Religion*. Toronto Studies in Religion, vol. 8. New York: Peter Lang.
1994   "Holistic Analysis: Conjectures and Refutations." *Journal of the American Academy of Religion* 62:977–996.
1995   "Why Does Semantics Matter to the Study of Religion?" *Method and Theory in the Study of Religion* 7:221–249.

Perkins, Mary Anne
1994   *Coleridge's Philosophy: The Logos as Unifying Principle*. Oxford: Clarendon.

Persinger, Michael A.
1987   *The Neuropsychological Bases of God Beliefs*. New York: Praeger.

Petras, John W.
1975   *Sex: Male, Gender: Masculine: Readings in Male Sexuality*. Port Washington, NY: Alfred.

Pettazzoni, Raffaele
1954   *Essays on the History of Religions*, H. J. Rose (trans.). Studies in the History of Religions; Supplements to Numen, vol. 1. Leiden: E. J. Brill.

Piaget, Jacques
1962   *Play, Dreams and Imitation in Childhood*, G. Gattegno and F. M. Hodgson (trans.). New York: Norton.

Pietz, William
1985   "The Problem of the Fetish, I." *RES: Anthropology and Aesthetics* 9:23–45.
1987   "The Problem of the Fetish, II." *RES: Anthropology and Aesthetics* 13.
1988   "The Problem of the Fetish, IIIa." *RES: Anthropology and Aesthetics* 16:105–123.

Pinard de la Boullaye, Henri
1922   *L'Étude comparée des religions*, 2 vols. Paris: G. Beauchesne.

Pingaud, Bernard
1965   "Comment en devient structuraliste." *L'Arc* 26.

Pinker, Steven
1994   *The Language Instinct: How the Mind Creates Language*. New York: William Morrow.
1997   *How the Mind Works*. New York: Norton.

Plaskow, Judith and Joan Arnold Romero (Eds.)
1974   *Women and Religion: Papers of the Working Group on Women and Religion, 1972–73*, Rev. edn. Missoula, MT: Scholars Press.

Pocock, J. G. A.
    1962   "The Origins of Study of the Past: A Comparative Approach." *Comparative Studies in Society and History* 4:209–246.

Polanyi, Karl
    1968   *Primitive, Archaic, and Modern Economies: Essays of Karl Polanyi,* George Dalton (ed.). Garden City, NY: Anchor; Boston: Beacon, 1971.

Poole, Fitz John Porter
    1986   "Metaphors and Maps: Towards Comparison in the Anthropology of Religion." *Journal of the American Academy of Religion* 54:411–457.

Porete, Marguerite
    1993   *The Mirror of Simple Souls,* Ellen L. Babinsky (trans.). New York: Paulist Press.

Prakash, Gyan (Ed.)
    1995   *After Colonialism: Imperial Histories and Postcolonial Displacements.* Princeton Studies in Culture / Power / History. Princeton: Princeton University Press.

Pratt, Mary Louise
    1992   *Imperial Eyes: Travel Writing and Transculturation.* London: Routledge.

Preus, J. Samuel
    1987   *Explaining Religion: Criticism and Theory from Bodin to Freud.* New Haven: Yale University Press.
    1998   "The Bible and Religion in the Century of Genius." *Religion* 28:3–27, 111–138.

Proudfoot, Wayne
    1985   *Religious Experience.* Berkeley: University of California Press.
    1987   "Philosophy of Religion," pp. 305–311 in Mircea Eliade (ed.), *The Encyclopedia of Religion,* vol. 11. New York: Macmillan.

Purdue, A. W.
    1998   "Review: Peter Gay, *The Naked Heart: The Bourgeois Experience, Victoria to Freud.*" *Times Higher Education Supplement,* 20 February.

Pye, Michael (Ed.)
    1994   *The Continuum Dictionary of Religion.* New York: Continuum.

Pyysiäinen, Ilkka
    1996   *Belief and Beyond: Religious Categorizaton of Reality.* Religionsvetenskapliga Skrifter, vol. 33. Åbo: Åbo Akademi.

Raboteau, Albert J.
    1978   *Slave Religion: The "Invisible Institution" in the Antebellum South.* Oxford: Oxford University Press.

Radcliffe-Brown, A. R.
    1952   *Structure and Function in Primitive Society: Essays and Addresses.* London: Cohen & West.

Ram, Kalpana and Margaret Jolly (Eds.)
    1998   *Maternities and Modernities: Colonial and Postcolonial Experiences in Asia and the Pacific.* Cambridge: Cambridge University Press.

Rappaport, Roy A.
    1971   "Ritual, Sanctity, and Cybernetics." *American Anthropologist* 73:59–76.
    1979   *Ecology, Meaning, and Religion.* Richmond, CA: North Atlantic Books.

1984   *Pigs for the Ancestors: Ritual in the Ecology of a New Guinea People.* New Haven: Yale University Press; original edn, 1968.

1999   *Ritual and Religion in the Making of Humanity.* Cambridge: Cambridge University Press.

Raschke, Carl A.

1990   "Fire and Roses: Toward an Authentic Post-Modern Religious Thinking." *Journal of the American Academy of Religion* 57:671–689.

Rawls, John

1971   *A Theory of Justice.* Cambridge, MA: Belknap Press of Harvard University Press.

Reardon, Bernard M. G.

1966   *Religious Thought in the Nineteenth Century: Illustrated from Writers of the Period.* Cambridge: Cambridge University Press.

1985   *Religion in the Age of Romanticism.* Cambridge: Cambridge University Press.

Reat, N. Ross and Edmund F. Perry

1991   *A World Theology: The Central Spiritual Reality of Humankind.* Cambridge: Cambridge University Press.

Redfield, Robert

1955   *The Little Community: Viewpoints for the Study of a Human Whole.* Chicago: University of Chicago Press.

Reiss, Timothy J.

1982   *The Discourse of Modernism.* Ithaca, NY: Cornell University Press.

Resch, Robert Paul

1992   *Althusser and the Renewal of Marxist Social Theory.* Berkeley: University of California Press.

Reuben, Julie A.

1996   *The Making of the Modern University: Intellectual Transformation and the Marginalization of Morality.* Chicago: University of Chicago Press.

Ricoeur, Paul

1970   *Freud and Philosophy: An Essay on Interpretation,* Denis Savage (trans.). New Haven: Yale University Press.

1976   *Interpretation Theory: Discourse and the Surplus of Meaning.* Forth Worth, TX: Texas Christian University Press.

1980   "Review of Goodman's *Ways of Worldmaking.*" *Philosophy and Literature* 4:107–120.

1981   *Hermeneutics and the Human Sciences: Essays on Language, Action, and Interpretation,* John B. Thompson (ed. and trans.). Cambridge: Cambridge University Press; Paris: Éditions de la Maison des sciences de l'homme.

1987   "Myth and History," pp. 273–282 in Mircea Eliade (ed.), *Encyclopedia of Religion,* vol. 10. New York: Macmillan.

Ridley, Mark

1986   *Evolution and Classification: The Reformation of Cladistics.* London: Longman.

Rieff, Philip

1979   *Freud: The Mind of the Moralist.* Chicago: University of Chicago Press.

Rips, Lance J.
    1995   "The Current Status of Research on Concept Combination." *Mind and Language* 10.

Rizzuto, Ana-Marie
    1979   *The Birth of the Living God: A Psychoanalytic Study*. Chicago: University of Chicago Press.

Robbins, Thomas
    1988   *Cults, Converts, and Charisma: The Sociology of New Religious Movements*. London: Sage.

Roberts, Michael
    1937   *The Modern Mind*. London: Faber & Faber.

Robins, R. H.
    1997   *A Short History of Linguistics*. 4th revised edn. London: Longman.

Romanowski, William D.
    1996   *Pop Culture Wars: Religion and the Role of Entertainment in American Life*. Downers Grove, IL: InterVarsity.

Rorty, Richard
    1968   *The Linguistic Turn: Recent Essays in Philosophical Method*. Chicago: University of Chicago Press.
    1982   *Consequences of Pragmatism: Essays, 1972–1980*. Minneapolis: University of Minnesota Press.

Rosaldo, Renato
    1989   *Culture and Truth: The Remaking of Social Analysis*. Boston: Beacon.

Rosch, Eleanor
    1978   "Principles of Categorization." In Eleanor Rosch and Barbara B. Lloyd (eds.), *Cognition and Categorization*. Hillsdale, NJ: Lawrence Erlbaum.
    1981   "Prototype Classification and Logical Classification: The Two Systems," In E. Scholnick (ed.), *New Trends in Cognitive Representation: Challenges to Piaget's Theory*. Hillsdale, NJ: Lawrence Erlbaum.

Rosch, Eleanor and Barbara B. Lloyd (Eds.)
    1978   *Cognition and Categorization*. Hillsdale: Lawrence Erlbaum.

Rosch, Eleanor and Carolyn Mervis
    1975   "Family Resemblances: Studies in the Internal Structure of Natural Categories." *Cognitive Psychology* 7.

Rosch, Eleanor, Carolyn Mervis, Wayne Gray, et al.
    1976   "Basic Objects in Natural Categories." *Cognitive Psychology* 8.

Rosen, Lawrence
    1984   *Bargaining for Reality: The Construction of Social Relations in a Muslim Community*. Chicago: University of Chicago Press.

Rosman, Abraham and Paula G. Rubel
    1971   *Feasting with Mine Enemy: Rank and Exchange Among Northwest Coast Societies*. New York: Columbia University Press.

Ross, Gillian
    1971   "Neo-Tylorianism: A Reassessment." *Man* N. S. 6:105–116.

Rossi, Alice S.
    1988   (ed.) *The Feminist Papers: From Adams to de Beauvoir*. Boston: Northeastern University Press.

Rothberg, Morey
1998 "History in the Public Arena: The AHA and the Smithsonian."
      Perspectives 36, 1: 24–26.
Rubin, Gayle
1975 "The Traffic in Women: Notes on the 'Political Economy' of Sex," pp.
      157–210 in R. R. Reiter (ed.), *Toward an Anthropology of Women*.
      London: Monthly Review Press.
Rudolph, Kurt
1985 "Development as a Problem for the History of Religions," pp. 81–98, 111–
      114 in *Historical Fundamentals and the Study of Religion: Haskell
      Lectures Delivered at the University of Chicago*. New York: Macmillan.
Ruhlen, Merritt
1991 *A Guide to the World's Languages*, vol. 1: *Classification, With a Postscript
      on Recent Developments*. Stanford: Stanford University Press.
Runciman, W. G.
1969 "The Sociological Explanation of 'Religious' Beliefs." *Archives euro-
      péennes de sociologie* 10:149–191.
1970 "Class, Status and Power?" pp. 102–140 in *Sociology in Its Place and
      Other Essays*. Cambridge: Cambridge University Press.
Ryba, Thomas
1991 "The Philosophical Loadings of Rudolf Otto's Idea of the Sacred."
      Method and Theory in the Study of Religion 3: 21–40.
1992 *The Essence of Phenomenology and Its Meaning for the Scientific Study of
      Religion*. New York: Peter Lang.
1994a "The Idea of the Sacred in Twentieth-Century Thought: Four Views."
      Analecta Husserliana 43:21–42.
1994b "The Magister Internus: An Augustinian Proto-Phenomenology of Faith as
      Desire and Teacher." *Analecta Husserliana* 43:307–329.
Saatkamp, Herman J., Jr.
1995 (ed.) *Rorty and Pragmatism: The Philosopher Responds to His Critics*.
      Nashville, TN: Vanderbilt University Press.
Sahlins, Marshall D.
1972 *Stone Age Economics*. Chicago: Aldine-Atherton.
1976 *Culture and Practical Reason*. Chicago: University of Chicago Press.
1981 *Historical Metaphors and Mythical Realities: Structure in the Early
      History of the Sandwich Islands Kingdom*. Association for Social
      Anthropology in Oceania Special Publications, no. 1. Ann Arbor:
      University of Michigan Press.
1985 *Islands of History*. Chicago: University of Chicago Press.
Said, Edward W.
1978 *Orientalism*. New York: Pantheon.
1986 "Orientalism Reconsidered," pp. 210–229 in Francis Barker (ed.),
      *Literature, Politics, and Theory: Papers from the Essex Conference,
      1976–84*. London: Methuen.
1989 "Representing the Colonized: Anthropology's Interlocutors." *Critical
      Inquiry* 15:205–225.

1993   Culture and Imperialism. New York: Knopf.

Saiving, Valerie
   1960   "The Human Situation: A Feminine View," pp. 25–42 in Carol P. Christ
and Judith Plaskow (eds.), Womanspirit Rising: A Feminist Reader in
Religion. San Francisco: Harper & Row.

Saler, Benson
   1993   Conceptualizing Religion: Immanent Anthropologists, Transcendent
Natives, and Unbounded Categories. Leiden: E. J. Brill.

Saper, Craig J.
   1997   Artificial Mythologies: A Guide to Cultural Invention. Minneapolis:
University of Minnesota Press.

Sartre, Jean-Paul
   1965   "Introduction." In Albert Memmi, The Colonizer and the Colonized,
Howard Greenfeld (trans.). New York: Orion.

Saussaye, P. D. Chantepie de la
   1891   Manual of the Science of Religion. London: Longmans, Green & Co.

Saussure, Ferdinand de
   1983   Course in General Linguistics, W. Barkin (trans.). New York: Duckworth;
original French edn, 1916.

Schacter, Daniel L.
   1996   Searching for Memory: The Brain, the Mind, and the Past. New York:
Basic.

Schechner, Richard
   1993   The Future of Ritual: Writings on Culture and Performance. London:
Routledge.

Schedler, Norbert O.
   1974   Philosophy of Religion: Contemporary Perspectives. New York: Macmillan.

Schiller, Friedrich
   1967   Friedrich Schiller: On the Aesthetic Education of Man in a Series of
Letters, E. M. Wilkinson and L. A. Willoughby (eds.). Oxford: Clarendon;
original German edn, 1793.

Schilling, Robert
   1987   "Numen," pp. 21–22 in Mircea Eliade (ed.), The Encyclopedia of Religion,
vol. 11. New York: Macmillan.

Schimmel, Annemarie
   1960   "Summary of the Discussion." Numen 7:235–239.

Schleiermacher, Friedrich
   1928   The Christian Faith, H. R. Macintosh and J. S. Stewart (eds.). Edinburgh:
T. & T. Clark; Philadelphia: Fortress, 1976; original German edn, 1821–
1822.

   1977   Hermeneutics: The Handwritten Manuscripts, Heinz Kimmerle (ed.),
James Duke and Jack Forstman (trans.). Missoula, MT: Scholars Press.

   1988   On Religion: Speeches to Its Cultured Despisers, Richard Crouter (trans.).
Texts in German Philosophy. Cambridge: Cambridge University Press;
original German edn, 1799.

Schmitt Pantel, Pauline

    1985   "Banquet et cité grecque." *Mélanges de l'école française de Rome et d'Athènes* 97:135–158.

    1990   "Sacrificial Meal and *Symposion*: Two Models of Civic Institutions in the Archaic City?" pp. 14–33 in Oswyn Murray (ed.), *Sympotica: A Symposium on the Symposion*. Oxford: Clarendon.

Schreiner, Klaus

    1974   "Zur biblischen Legitimation des Adels. Auslegungsgeschichtliche Studien zu 1. Kor. 1,26–29." *Zeitschrift für Kirchengeschichte* 85:317–357.

Schreiner, Olive

    1914   *Woman and Labour*. Toronto: S. B. Gundy.

Schwab, Raymond

    1984   *The Oriental Renaissance: Europe's Rediscovery of India and the East, 1680–1880*, Gene Patterson-Black and Victor Reinking (trans.). New York: Columbia University Press.

Schwartz, Barry

    1967   "The Social Psychology of the Gift." *American Journal of Sociology* 73:1–11.

Schwarz, Henry

    1997   *Writing Cultural History in Colonial and Postcolonial India*. Critical Histories. Philadelphia: University of Pennsylvania Press.

Scott, George M., Jr.

    1990   "A Resynthesis of the Primordial and Circumstantial Approaches to Ethnic Group Solidarity: Towards an Explanatory Model." *Ethnic and Racial Studies* 13:147–171.

Scott, Joan Wallach

    1991   "The Evidence of Experience." *Critical Inquiry* 17:773–797.

    1993   "The Tip of the Volcano: A Reply to Laura Lee Downs." *Comparative Studies in Society and History* 35:438–443.

Scroggs, Robin

    1980   "The Sociological Interpretation of the New Testament: The Present State of Research." *New Testament Studies* 26:164–179.

Searle, John B.

    1967   "Proper Names and Descriptions." In P. Edwards (ed.), *The Encyclopedia of Philosophy*. New York: Macmillan.

Sears, R. R.

    1936   "Experimental Studies of Projection." *Journal of Social Psychology* 7:151–163.

Seed, Patricia

    1991   "Colonial and Postcolonial Discourse." *Latin American Research Review* 26:181–200.

    1995   *Ceremonies of Possession in Europe's Conquest of the New World, 1492–1640*. Cambridge: Cambridge University Press.

Segal, Robert A.

    1980   "In Defense of Mythology: The History of Modern Theories of Myth." *Annals of Scholarship* 1:3–49.

    1996   (ed.) *Theories of Myth: From Ancient Israel and Greece to Freud, Jung, Campbell, and Lévi-Strauss*, 6 vols. New York: Garland.

1997   "Postmodernism and the Social Scientific Study of Religion." *Religion* 27:139–149.

1998   (ed.) *Encountering Jung on Mythology*. Princeton: Princeton University Press.

Sellars, Wilfrid
1997   *Empiricism and the Philosophy of Mind*, With an Introduction by Richard Rorty and a Study Guide by Robert Brandom. Cambridge, MA: Harvard University Press.

Sen, Amartya
1979   "Rational Fools: A Critique of the Behavioral Foundations of Economic Theory," pp. 1–15 in Henry Harris (ed.), *Scientific Models and Man*. Herbert Spencer Lectures, 1976. New York: Oxford University Press.

Sered, Susan Starr
1998   *Women of the Sacred Groves: Divine Priestesses of Okinawa*. New York: Oxford University Press.

1998a "De-Gendering Religious Leadership: Sociological Discourse in an Okinawan Village." *Journal of the American Academy of Religion* 66:589–611.

1999   "Religiously Doing Gender: The Good Woman and the Bad Woman in Israeli Ritual Discourse." In Randi R. Warne (ed.), *Feminist Contributions to Method and Theory in the Study of Religion*, Special Issue: *Method & Theory in the Study of Religion*, vol. 11. Leiden: E. J. Brill.

Shafranske, Edward P.
1995   "Freudian Theory and Religious Experience," pp. 200–230 in Ralph W. Hood (ed.), *Handbook of Religious Experience*. Birmingham, Alabama: Religious Education Press.

Sharf, Robert
1998   "Experience," pp. 94–116 in Mark C. Taylor (ed.), *Critical Terms for Religious Studies*. Chicago: University of Chicago Press.

Sharma, Arvind
1987   (ed.) *Women in World Religions*. Albany: State University of New York Press.

1994a *Religion and Women*. Albany: State University of New York Press.

1994b *Today's Woman in World Religions*. Albany: State University of New York Press.

Sharma, R. S.
1990   *Śūdras in Ancient India: A Social History of the Lower Order Down to Circa A.D. 600*. Delhi: Motilal Banarsidass.

1991   *Aspects of Political Ideas and Institutions in Ancient India*. Delhi: Motilal Banarsidass.

Sharpe, Eric J.
1971   *Fifty Key Words: Comparative Religion*. Richmond, VA: John Knox.

1986   *Comparative Religion: A History*. 2d edn. La Salle, IL: Open Court; original edn, London: Duckworth, 1975.

1987   "Comparative Religion," pp. 578–580 in Mircea Eliade (ed.), *The Encyclopedia of Religion*, vol. 3. New York: Macmillan.

Shera, Jesse H.
  1965   *Libraries and the Organization of Knowledge*, D. J. Forkett (ed.). London: Crosby, Lockwood & Sons.
  1966   *Documentation and the Organization of Knowledge*, D. J. Foskett (ed.). London: Crosby, Lockwood & Sons.
Sherwood, G. G.
  1979   "Classical and Attributive Projection." *Journal of Abnormal Psychology* 88: 635–640.
Shils, Edward
  1957   "Primordial, Personal, Sacred and Civil Ties: Some Particular Observations on the Relationships of Sociological Research and Theory." *British Journal of Sociology* 8:130–145.
Shipley, Joseph T.
  1963   *Dictionary of Early English*. Paterson: Littlefield, Adams & Co.
Shohat, Ella
  1992   "Notes on the Post-Colonial." *Social Text* 31–32:99–113.
Shore, Bradd
  1996   *Culture in Mind: Cognition, Culture, and the Problem of Meaning*. Foreword by Jerome Bruner. New York: Oxford University Press.
Sienkewicz, Thomas J.
  1997   *Theories of Myth: An Annotated Bibliography*. Lanham, MD: Scarecrow.
Sierksma, Fokke
  1990   *Projection and Religion: An Anthropological and Psychological Study of the Phenomena of Projection in the Various Religions*, Foreword by Lee W. Bailey, Jacob Faber (trans.). Ann Arbor: University of Michigan Press.
Silk, Mark
  1987   "The Hot History Department." *New York Times Magazine*, 19 April.
Silverman, Kaja
  1983   *The Subject of Semiotics*. Oxford: Oxford University Press.
Simmel, Georg
  1959   *Sociology of Religion*, Curt Rosenthal (trans.). New York: Philosophical Library; original German edn, 1906.
  1990   *The Philosophy of Money*, 2d edn, Frisby, David (ed.), David Frisby and Tom Bottomore (trans.). London: Routledge.
Simon, Herbert A.
  1957   *Models of Man: Social and Rational*. New York: John Wiley & Sons.
  1982   *Models of Bounded Rationality*. Cambridge, MA: MIT Press.
Simpson, George G.
  1961   *Principles of Animal Taxonomy*. New York: Columbia University Press.
Singh, Jyotsna G.
  1996   *Colonial Narratives / Cultural Dialogues: "Discoveries" of India in the Language of Colonialism*. London: Routledge.
Smart, Ninian
  1969   *The Religious Experience of Mankind*. New York: Scribners.
  1973a   *The Phenomenon of Religion*. London: Macmillan.
  1973b   *The Science of Religion and the Sociology of Knowledge*. Princeton: Princeton University Press.

1981   *Beyond Ideology: Religion and the Future of Western Civilization*. San Francisco: Harper & Row.

1983   *Worldviews: Crosscultural Explorations of Human Beliefs*. New York: Scribner's & Sons.

1996   *The Dimensions of the Sacred: An Anatomy of the World's Beliefs*. California: University of California Press.

Smart, Ninian, John Clayton, Patrick Sherry and Steven T. Katz (Eds.)

1985   *Nineteenth-Century Religious Thought in the West*, 3 vols. Cambridge: Cambridge University Press.

Smith, Brian K.

1987   "Exorcizing the Transcendent: Strategies for Defining Hinduism and Religion." *History of Religions* 27:33–54.

1989   *Reflections on Resemblance, Ritual, and Religion*. New York: Oxford University Press.

1990   "Eaters, Food, and Social Hierarchy in Ancient India: A Dietary Guide to a Revolution in Values." *Journal of the American Academy of Religion* 58:201–229.

1994   *Classifying the Universe: The Ancient Indian Varna System and the Origins of Caste*. New York: Oxford University Press.

Smith, Edward E.

1988   "Concepts and Thought." In Edward E. Smith and Robert J. Sternberg (eds.), *The Psychology of Human Thought*. Cambridge: Cambridge University Press.

Smith, Edward E. and Douglas L Medin

1981   *Categories and Concepts*. Cognitive Science Series, vol. 4. Cambridge, MA: Harvard University Press.

Smith, Edward E. and S. Sloman

1994   "Similarity- Versus Rule-Based Categorization." *Memory and Cognition* 22.

Smith, Huston

1958   *The Religions of Man*. New York: Harper & Row; revised and updated edn, *The World's Religions*. San Francisco: HarperSanFrancisco, 1991.

1990   "Postmodernism's Impact on the Study of Religion." *Journal of the American Academy of Religion* 58:653–670.

Smith, John E.

1994   *Quasi-Religions: Humanism, Marxism, and Nationalism*. New York: St. Martin's Press.

Smith, Jonathan Z.

1974   "Animals and Plants in Myth and Legend." *Encyclopaedia Britannica* 15th edn, Vol. 1: 911–918.

1978a   *Map Is Not Territory: Studies in the History of Religions*. Leiden: E. J. Brill; University of Chicago Press, 1993.

1978b   "Playful Acts of Imagination." *Liberal Education* 73, 5:14–20.

1982a   *Imagining Religion: From Babylon to Jonestown*. Chicago: University of Chicago Press.

1982b   "A Pearl of Great Price and a Cargo of Yams," pp. 90–101 in *Imagining Religion: From Babylon to Jonestown*. Chicago: University of Chicago Press.

1982c "The Bare Facts of Ritual," pp. 53–65 in *Imagining Religion: From Babylon to Jonestown*. Chicago: University of Chicago Press.

1982d "Sacred Persistence: Toward a Redescription of Canon," pp. 36–52 in *Imagining Religion: From Babylon to Jonestown*. Chicago: University of Chicago Press.

1987a "The Domestication of Sacrifice," pp. 191–235 in Robert Hamerton-Kelly (ed.), *Violent Origins: Walter Burkert, René Girard, and Jonathan Z. Smith on Ritual Killing and Cultural Formation*. Stanford, CA: Stanford University Press.

1987b *To Take Place: Toward Theory in Ritual*. Chicago: University of Chicago Press.

1990 *Drudgery Divine: On the Comparison of Early Christianities and the Religions of Late Antiquity*. Chicago: University of Chicago Press; London: School of Oriental and African Studies.

1992 *Differential Equations: On Constructing the 'Other'*. The University Lecture in Religion at Arizona State University. Tempe: Department of Religious Studies, Arizona State University.

1995 (ed.) *The Dictionary of Religion*. San Francisco: HarperCollins.

1996a "A Matter of Class: Taxonomies of Religion." *Harvard Theological Review* 89: 387–403.

1996b "Social Formation of Early Christianities: A Response to Ron Cameron and Burton Mack." *Method and Theory in the Study of Religion* 8:271–278.

1998 "Religion, Religions, Religious," pp. 269–284 in Mark C. Taylor (ed.), *Critical Terms in Religious Studies*. Chicago: University of Chicago Press.

1999a "Afterword," In Kimberley C. Patton and Benjamin C. Ray (eds.), *A Magic Still Dwells: The Case for Comparative Religion in the Postmodern Age*. Berkeley: University of California Press.

1999b "Close Encounters of a Diverse Kind." In Susan Mizruchi (ed.), *Religion in an Era of Cultural Studies*. Princeton: Princeton University Press.

Smith, Timothy L.

1983 "My Rejection of the Cyclical View of 'Great Awakenings' in American Religious History." *Social Analysis* 44:97–101.

Smith, W. Robertson

1972 *Lectures on the Religion of the Semites: First Series, the Fundamental Institutions*. New York: Schocken; original edn, 1889.

Smith, Wilfred Cantwell

1964 *The Meaning and End of Religion: A New Approach to the Religious Traditions of Mankind*. New York: New American Library.

1981 *Towards a World Theology: Faith and the Comparative History of Religion*. Philadelphia: Westminster; London: Macmillan; Maryknoll, NY: Orbis, 1989.

Smith, William

1744 *A New Voyage to Guinea*. London: Nourse.

Smith-Rosenberg, Carroll

1985 *Disorderly Conduct: Visions of Gender in Victorian America*. New York: Oxford University Press.

Smythies, J. R.
  1954   "Analysis of Projection." *British Journal for Philosophy of Science* 5:120–133.
Sokal, Robert R. and P. H. A. Sneath
  1963   *Principles of Numerical Taxonomy.* San Francisco: W. H. Freeman.
  1973   *Principles of Numerical Taxonomy,* 2d edn. San Francisco: W. H. Freeman.
Southwold, Martin
  1978   "Buddhism and the Definition of Religion." *Man* N. S. 13.
Spelman, Elizabeth V.
  1988   *Inessential Woman: Problems of Exclusion in Feminist Thought.* Boston: Beacon.
Spender, Dale (Ed.)
  1983   *Feminist Theorists: Three Centuries of Women's Intellectual Traditions.* London: Women's Press.
Sperber, Dan
  1975   *Rethinking Symbolism,* Alice L. Morton (trans.). Cambridge Studies in Social Anthropology. Cambridge: Cambridge University Press.
  1996a   *Explaining Culture: A Naturalistic Approach.* Oxford: Blackwell.
  1996b   "Why Are Perfect Animals, Hybrids, and Monsters Food for Symbolic Thought?" *Method and Theory in the Study of Religion* 8:143–169; original French edn, "Pourquoi les animaux parfaits, les hybrides et les monstres, sont-ils bon à penser symboliquement?" *L'Homme* 15 (1975).
Spicer, Edward
  1971   "Persistent Cultural Systems." *Science* 174:795–800.
Spinoza, Benedict de
  1955   *The Chief Works of Benedict de Spinoza: On the Improvement of the Understanding; The Ethics; Correspondence,* R. H. M. Elwes (trans.), with an Introduction. New York: Dover.
Spiro, Melford E.
  1966   "Religion: Problems of Definition and Explanation," pp. 85–126 in Michael Banton (ed.), *Anthropological Approaches to the Study of Religion.* A.S.A. Monographs, vol. 3. London: Tavistock.
  1968   "Virgin Birth, Parthenogenesis and Physiological Paternity." *Man* N. S. 3:242–261.
  1982   *Buddhism and Society : A Great Tradition and Its Burmese Vicissitudes.* 2d expanded edn. Berkeley: University of California Press; original edn, New York: Harper & Row, 1970.
  1987   *Culture and Human Nature: Theoretical Papers.* Benjamin Kilborne and L. L. Langness (eds.). Chicago: University of Chicago Press.
Spivak, Gayatri Chakravorty
  1987   *In Other Worlds: Essays in Cultural Politics.* London: Methuen.
Spong, John S.
  1994   *Resurrection: Myth or Reality?* San Francisco: HarperSanFrancisco.
Spurr, David
  1993   *The Rhetoric of Empire: Colonial Discourse in Journalism, Travel Writing, and Imperial Administration.* Post-Contemporary Interventions. Durham, NC: Duke University Press.

534

Staal, Frits
    1996   "The Meaninglessness of Ritual," pp. 483–494 in Ronald L. Grimes (ed.), *Readings in Ritual Studies*. Upper Saddle River, NJ: Prentice-Hall.

Stace, W. T.
    1955   *The Philosophy of Hegel*. New York: Dover.

Stanner, W. E. H.
    1967   "Reflections on Durkheim and Aboriginal Religion." In M. Freedman (ed.), *Social Organization: Essays Presented to Raymond Firth*. London: Frank Cass.

Stanton, Elizabeth Cady
    1974   *The Woman's Bible*. Seattle: Coalition Task Force on Women and Religion; original edn, 1895.

Stark, Rodney
    1985   "From Church-Sect to Religious Economies," pp. 139–149 in Phillip E. Hammond (ed.), *The Sacred in a Secular Age: Toward Revision in the Scientific Study of Religion*. Berkeley: University of California Press.
    1996a *The Rise of Christianity: A Sociologist Reconsiders History*. Princeton: Princeton University Press.
    1996b "Why Religious Movements Succeed or Fail: A Revised General Model." *Journal of Contemporary Religion* 11:133–146.
    1998   "Explaining International Variations in Religiousness: The Market Model." *Polis*, Special Issue: *Ricerche e studi su società e politica in Italia*.
    Forth- "Secularization, R.I.P." *Sociology of Religion* 59.
    coming

Stark, Rodney and William Sims Bainbridge
    1980   "Towards a Theory of Religion: Religious Commitment." *Journal for the Scientific Study of Religion* 19:114–128.
    1985   *The Future of Religion: Secularization, Revival, and Cult Formation*. Berkeley: University of California Press.
    1996   *A Theory of Religion*. New Brunswick, NJ: Rutgers University Press; original edn, New York: Peter Lang, 1987.
    1997   *Religion, Deviance, and Social Control*. New York: Routledge.

Stark, Rodney and Roger Finke
    Forth- *Understanding Religion: The New Social Science Paradigm*.
    coming

Stark, Rodney and Laurence R. Iannaccone
    1994   "A Supply-Side Reinterpretation of the 'Secularization' of Europe." *Journal for the Scientific Study of Religion* 33:230–252.

Stark, Rodney, Laurence R. Iannaccone and Roger Finke
    1996   "Religion, Science and Rationality." *American Economic Review* 86:443–437.
    Forth- "Rationality and the Religious Mind." *Economic Inquiry*.
    coming

Ste. Croix, G. E. M. de
    1975   "Early Christian Attitudes to Property and Slavery," pp. 1–38 in Derek Baker (ed.), *Church, Society and Politics*. Studies in Church History, vol. 12. Oxford: Blackwell.

1981   *The Class Struggle in the Ancient Greek World: From the Archaic Age to the Arab Conquests.* Ithaca, NY: Cornell University Press.

Steinen, Karl von den
1894   *Unter den Naturvölkern Zentral-Brasiliens.* Berlin: Dietrich Reimer.

Stewart, Charles and Rosalind Shaw (Eds.)
1994   *Syncretism / Anti-Syncretism: The Politics of Religious Synthesis.* London: Routledge.

Stocking, George W., Jr.
1987   *Victorian Anthropology.* New York: Free Press.
1991   *Colonial Situations: Essays in the Contextualization of Ethnographic Knowledge.* History of Anthropology, vol. 7. Madison: University of Wisconsin Press.

Stoler, Ann Laura
1995   *Race and the Education of Desire: Foucault's History of Sexuality and the Colonial Order of Things.* Durham, NC: Duke University Press.

Stoltenberg, John
1989   *Refusing to Be a Man: Essays on Sex and Justice.* New York: Meridian.
1993   *The End of Manhood: A Book for Men of Conscience.* New York: Dutton.

Stone, Lawrence
1979   "The Revival of Narrative: Reflections on a New Old History." *Past and Present* 95:3–24.

Strathern, Marilyn
1988   *The Gender of the Gift: Problems with Women and Problems with Society in Melanesia.* Studies in Melanesian Anthropology, vol. 6. Berkeley: University of California Press.

Strenski, Ivan
1987   *Four Theories of Myth in Twentieth-Century History: Cassirer, Eliade, Lévi-Strauss, and Malinowski.* Iowa City: University of Iowa Press.

Sturrock, John (Ed.)
1979   *Structuralism and Sense: From Lévi-Strauss to Derrida.* Oxford: Oxford University Press.

Sullivan, Lawrence E.
1984   "Lévi-Strauss, Mythologic and South American Religions," pp. 147–176 in Robert L. Moore and Frank E. Reynolds (eds.), *Anthropology and the Study of Religion.* Studies in Religion and Society Series. Chicago: Center for the Scientific Study of Religion.

Symonds, Percival
1946   *Encyclopedia of Psychology*, Philip Lawrence Harriman (ed.). New York: Philosophical Library.

Tal, Uriel
1975   *Christians and Jews in Germany: Religion, Politics, and Ideology in the Second Reich, 1870–1914.* Ithaca, NY: Cornell University Press.

Tambiah, Stanley J.
1969   "Animals Are Good to Think and Good to Prohibit." *Ethnology* 8.
1979   "A Performative Approach to Ritual." *Proceedings of the British Academy* 65:119.
1989   "Ethnic Conflict in the World Today." *American Ethnologist* 16:335–349.

1990   *Magic, Science, Religion, and the Scope of Rationality.* Lewis Henry Morgan Lectures, 1984. Cambridge: Cambridge University Press.

Tarkka, Lotte

1994   "Other Worlds – Symbolism, Dialogue and Gender in Karelian Oral Poetry," pp. 250–298 in Anna-Leena Siikala and Sinikka Vakimo (eds.), *Songs Beyond the Kalevala: Transformations of Oral Poetry.* Studia Fennica. Folkloristica, vol. 2. Helsinki: Finnish Literature Society.

Tart, Charles T.

1975   (ed.) *Transpersonal Psychologies.* New York: Harper & Row.

Taussig, Michael

1980   *The Devil and Commodity Fetishism in South America.* Chapel Hill: University of North Carolina Press.

1987   *Shamanism, Colonialism, and the Wild Man: A Study in Terror and Healing.* Chicago: University of Chicago Press.

1992   *The Nervous System.* London: Routledge.

Tavard, George H.

1973   *Woman in Christian Tradition.* Notre Dame, IN: Notre Dame University Press.

Taylor, A. E.

1964   "The Argument from Religious Experience," pp. 153–164 in John Hick (ed.), *The Existence of God.* New York: Macmillan; original edn, Cambridge: Cambridge University Press, 1955.

Taylor, John R.

1989   *Linguistic Categorization: Prototypes in Linguistic Theory.* Oxford: Clarendon; New York: Oxford University Press.

Taylor, Mark C.

1984   *Erring: A Postmodern A / Theology.* Chicago: University of Chicago Press.

Thagard, Paul

1996   *Mind: An Introduction to Cognitive Science.* Cambridge, MA: MIT Press.

1998   *Mind Readings: Introductory Selections in Cognitive Science.* Cambridge, MA: MIT Press.

Thibault, Paul J.

1997   *Re-Reading Saussure: The Dynamics of Signs in Social Life.* London: Routledge.

Thomas, George M.

1989   *Revivalism and Cultural Change: Christianity, Nation Building, and the Market in the Nineteenth-Century United States.* Chicago: University of Chicago Press.

Thomas, Nicholas

1991   *Entangled Objects: Exchange, Material Culture, and Colonialism in the Pacific.* Cambridge, MA: Harvard University Press.

1994   *Colonialism's Culture: Anthropology, Travel and Government.* Cambridge: Polity.

1997   *In Oceana: Visions, Artifacts, Histories.* Durham, NC: Duke University Press.

Thompson, Kenneth

1986   *Beliefs and Ideology.* London: Tavistock.

1990   "Religion: The British Contribution." *British Journal of Sociology* 41:531–535.

Thompson, Patrice
    1978   *La religion de Benjamin Constant. Le pouvoir de l'image*. Pisa: Paccini.

Thompson, Stith
    1946   *The Folktale*. New York: Holt, Rinehart & Winston.
    1955–   *Motif-Index of Folk Literature: A Classification of Narrative Elements*
    58   *in Folktales, Ballads, Myths, Fables, Medieval Romances, Exempla, Fabliaux, Jest-Books, and Local Legends*, vols. 1–6. 2d edn. Bloomington: Indiana Unversity Press.

Thomsen, Harry
    1963   *The New Religions of Japan*. Rutland, VT: Charles E. Tuttle.

Thornton, Stephen P.
    1996   "Facing up to Feuerbach." *International Journal for Philosophy of Religion* 39:103–120.

Thorowgood, Thomas
    1650   *Jews in America, or Probabilities that the Americans Are of That Race*. London: n.p.

Thurston, John
    1993   "Social Formation." In Irena R. Makaryk (ed.), *Encyclopedia of Contemporary Literary Theory*. Toronto: University of Toronto Press.

Tiele, Cornelius Petrus
    1877   *Outlines of the History of Religion, to the Spread of the Universal Religions*. London: Trubner & Co.
    1884   "Religions," *Encyclopaedia Britannica* 9th edn, Vol. 20.

Tilley, Christopher Y.
    1990   (ed.) *Reading Material Culture: Structuralism, Hermeneutics, and Post-Structuralism*. Oxford: Blackwell.

Tilley, Virginia
    1997   "The Terms of the Debate: Untangling Language About Ethnicity and Ethnic Movements." *Ethnic and Racial Studies* 20:497–522.

Tilliette, Xavier
    1970   *Schelling. Une philosophie en devenir*, 2 vols. Paris: J. Vrin.

Tobler, Adolf and Erhard Lommatzsch
    1962   *Altfranzösisches Wörterbuch*. Fascicle 46. Berlin: Weidmann.

Tocqueville, Alexis de
    1956   *Democracy in America*, 2 vols., Henry Reeve (trans.). New York: Vintage; original French edn, 1835–40.

Todorov, Tzvetan
    1981   *Introduction to Poetics*, Richard Howard (trans.). Minneapolis: University of Minnesota Press.
    1984   *The Conquest of America: The Question of the Other*, Richard Howard (trans.). New York: Harper & Row.
    1990   *Genres in Discourse*, Catherine Porter (trans.). Cambridge: Cambridge University Press.

Toland, John
    1696   *Christianity not Mysterious: Or, a Treatise Shewing, That There is Nothing*

in the Gospel Contrary to Reason, not Above It: And That No Christian Doctrine Can Be Properly Call'd a Mystery. London: S. Manship.

Tong, Rosemarie
   1989   *Feminist Thought: A Comprehensive Introduction.* Boulder, CO: Westview.

   1998   *Feminist Thought: A More Comprehensive Introduction.* Boulder, CO: Westview.

Topitsch, Ernst
   1961   "Begriff und Funktion der Ideologie." In Ernst Topitsch, *Sozialphilosophie zwischen Ideologie und Wissenschaft.* Neuwied am Rhein: H. Luchterhand.

Toporov, V. N.
   1987   "Ob Odnom Archaichnom Indoeuropeiskom Elemente v Drevnerusskoi Duhovnoi Kul'ture *Sv t-," pp. 184–252 in *Jaziky Kul'tury i Problemy Perevodimosti.* Moscow: Nauka.

Tosh, John (Ed.)
   1991   *Manful Assertions: Masculinities in Britain Since 1800.* London: Routledge.

Traube, Elizabeth G.
   1986   *Cosmology and Social Life: Ritual Exchange Among the Mambai of East Timor.* Chicago: University of Chicago Press.

Tréguier, Michel
   1970   "Entrevue radiodiffusé." In Catherine Backès-Clément (ed.), *Claude Lévi-Strauss ou la structure et le malheur.* Paris: Seghers.

Troeltsch, Ernst
   1913   "The Dogmatics of the *religionsgeschichtliche Schule*," pp. 87–108 in James Luther Adams and Walter E. Bense (eds.), *Ernst Troeltsch: Religion in History.* Minneapolis: Fortress, 1991.

Trompf, G. W.
   1994   *Payback: The Logic of Retribution in Melanesian Religions.* Cambridge: Cambridge University Press.

Trotter, David
   1990   "Colonial Subjects." *Critical Quarterly* 32, 3:3–20.

Tuana, Nancy
   1993   *The Less Noble Sex: Scientific, Religious, and Philosophical Conceptions of Woman's Nature.* Bloomington: Indiana University Press.

Tuana, Nancy and Rosemarie Tong (Eds.)
   1995   *Feminism and Philosophy: Essential Readings in Theory, Interpretation, and Application.* Boulder, CO: Westview.

Turner, Bryan S.
   1988   *Status.* Minneapolis: University of Minnesota Press.

Turner, Jonathan
   1986   "Social Exchange Theory: Future Directions," pp. 223–238 in Karen S. Cook (ed.), *Social Exchange Theory.* Beverly Hills, CA: Sage.

Turner, Victor
   1967   *The Forest of Symbols: Aspects of Ndembu Ritual.* Ithaca, NY: Cornell University Press.

1968   *The Drums of Affliction: A Study of Ritual Processes Among the Ndembu of Zambia*. Oxford: Clarendon.

1969   *The Ritual Process: Structure and Anti-Structure*. Chicago: Aldine; Ithaca, NY: Cornell University Press, 1991.

Tversky, Amos

1977   "Features of Similarity." *Psychological Review* 84.

Tversky, Amos and I. Gati

1978   "Studies of Similarity." In Eleanor Rosch and B. Lloyd (eds.), *Cognition and Categorization*. Hillsdale, NJ: Lawrence Erlbaum.

Tylor, Edward Burnett

1903   *Primitive Culture: Researches into the Development of Mythology, Philosophy, Religion, Language, Art and Custom*, 2 vols. 4th revised edn. London: John Murray; original edn, 1871.

Underhill, Evelyn

1911   *Mysticism*. London: Methuen.

Ursin, Johann Heinrich

1563   *Historisch-theologischer Bericht vom Unterschied der Religionen die heute zu Tage auf Erden sind*. Nuremburg.

Van den Berg, J. H.

1972   *A Different Existence: Principles of Phenomenological Psychopathology*. Pittsburgh, PA: Duquesne University Press.

Van Dijk, Teun A.

1998   *Ideology: A Multidisciplinary Approach*. London: Sage.

Varela, Francisco J., Evan Thompson and Eleanor Rosch

1991   *The Embodied Mind: Cognitive Science and Human Experience*. Cambridge, MA: MIT Press.

Vergote, Antoine

1990   "Confrontation with Neutrality in Theory and Praxis," pp. 74–94 in Joseph H. Smith and Susan A. Handelman (eds.), *Psychoanalysis and Religion*. Baltimore: Johns Hopkins University Press.

Vernant, Jean Pierre

1980   *Myth and Society in Ancient Greece*, Janet Lloyd (trans.). London: Methuen.

Veyne, Paul

1988   *Did the Greeks Believe in Their Myths? An Essay on the Constitutive Imagination*, Paula Wissing (trans.). Chicago: University of Chicago Press.

Vico, Giambattista

1948   *The New Science of Giambattista Vico*, Thomas Goddard Bergin and Max Harold Fisch (trans.). Ithaca, NY: Cornell University Press.

Vincent, Joan

1974   "The Structuring of Ethnicity." *Human Organization* 33:375–379.

von Franz, Marie-Louise

1980   *Projection and Re-Collection in Jungian Psychology*. London and La Salle, IL: Open Court.

Vries, Jan de

1967   *The Study of Religion: A Historical Approach*, Kees W. Bolle (trans.). New York: Harcourt, Brace & World.

Waal, Frans B. M. de
  1982   *Chimpanzee Politics: Power and Sex Among Apes.* London: Cape; New York: Harper & Row.
Waardenburg, Jacques
  1973   *Classical Approaches to the Study of Religion*, 2 vols. The Hague: Mouton.
  1978   "Gerardus Van der Leeuw as a Theologian and Phenomenologist," pp. 187–220 in *Reflections on the Study of Religion.* The Hague: Mouton.
Wach, Joachim
  1944   *Sociology of Religion.* Chicago: University of Chicago Press.
  1951   *Types of Religious Experience: Christian and Non-Christian.* Chicago: University of Chicago Press.
  1958   *The Comparative Study of Religions*, Joseph M. Kitagawa (ed.). New York: Columbia University Press.
Wallace, Anthony F. C.
  1966   *Religion: An Anthropological View.* New York: Random House.
Ward, Duren J. H.
  1909   *The Classification of Religions: Different Methods, Their Advantages and Disadvantages.* Chicago: Open Court.
Warne, Randi R.
  1998   "(En)Gendering Religious Studies." *Studies in Religion/Sciences religieuses* 27:427–436.
  Forth-   "Making the Gender-Critical Turn." In Tim Jensen and Mikael Rothstein
  coming.a (eds.), *Secular Theories on Religions: A Selection of Recent Academic Perspectives.* Copenhagen: Museum Tusculanum.
  Forth-   "Feminist Theology." In Lorraine Code (ed.), *Encyclopedia of Feminist*
  coming.b *Theories.* London: Routledge.
Warner, J. C.
  1858   "Mr. Warner's Notes," pp. 57–109 in John MacLean (ed.), *A Compendium of Kafir Laws and Customs.* Mount Coke: Wesleyan Mission Press.
Warner, Marina
  1976   *Alone of All Her Sex: The Myth and the Cult of the Virgin Mary.* New York: Simon & Schuster.
Warner, R. Stephen
  1993   "Work in Progress Towards a New Paradigm for the Sociological Study of Religion in the United States." *American Journal of Sociology* 98:1044–1093.
Wartofsky, Max
  1977   *Feuerbach.* Cambridge: Cambridge University Press.
Watson, George
  1989   (ed.) *Remarks on John Locke by Thomas Burnet with Locke's Replies.* Doncaster: Brynmill.
Watson, L. and M. J. Dallwitz
  1985   *Australian Grass Genera: Anatomy, Morphology, Keys and Classification.* 2d edn. Canberra: Australian National University Press.
Watson, L., M. J. Dallwitz and C. R. Johnston
  1986   "Grass Genera of the World: 728 Detailed Descriptions from an Automated Database." *Australian Journal of Botany* 33.

References

Weber, Max
1920 *Gesammelte Aufsätze zur Religionssoziologie*, Band 1. Tübingen: J. C. B. Mohr.
1946 "Religious Rejections of the World and Their Directions," pp. 323–329 in H. H. Gerth and C. Wright Mills (eds. and trans.), *From Max Weber: Essays in Sociology*. New York: Oxford University Press; original German edn, 1915.
1963 *The Sociology of Religion*, Introduction by Talcott Parsons, Ephraim Fischoff (trans.). Boston: Beacon; original German edn, 1922.
1976 *The Protestant Ethic and the Spirit of Capitalism*, Introduction by Anthony Giddens, Talcott Parsons (trans.). London: Allen & Unwin; original English trans. 1930; original German edn, 1904–1905 / 1920.
1980 *Wirtschaft und Gesellschaft. Grundriss der Verstehenden Soziologie*. Tübingen: J. C. B. Mohr (Paul Siebeck); original edn, 1922.
Welch, Claude
1972 *Protestant Thought in the Nineteenth Century*, vol. 1: *1799–1870*. New Haven: Yale University Press.
Welter, Barbara
1966 "The Cult of True Womanhood." *American Quarterly* 18:151–174.
Werbner, Richard P. and Terence Ranger (Eds.)
1996 *Postcolonial Identities in Africa*. London: Zed Books.
Whaling, Frank (Ed.)
1995 *Theory and Methods in Religious Studies: Contemporary Approaches to the Study of Religion*. Berlin: Mouton de Gruyter.
1999 "Theological Approaches," pp. 226–274 in Peter Connolly (ed.), *Approaches to the Study of Religion*. London: Cassell.
White, Hayden
1978 *Tropics of Discourse: Essays in Cultural Criticism*. Baltimore: Johns Hopkins University Press.
1987 *The Content of the Form: Narrative Discourse and Historical Representation*. Baltimore: Johns Hopkins University Press.
Whitefield, George
1969 *George Whitefield's Journals*. Gainsville, FL: Scholars' Facsimiles and Reprints; original edn., 1747.
Whitney, William D.
1881 "On the So-Called Science of Religion." *Princeton Review*, May.
Whorf, Benjamin Lee
1956 *Language, Thought and Reality: Selected Writings of Benjamin Lee Whorf*, John B. Carroll (ed.). Cambridge, MA: MIT Press.
Wiebe, Donald
1991 *The Irony of Theology and the Nature of Religious Thought*. Montreal: McGill-Queen's University Press.
1992 "On the Transformation of 'Belief' and the Domestication of 'Faith' in the Academic Study of Religion." *Method and Theory in the Study of Religion* 4:47–67.
1996 "Is the New Comparativism Really New?" *Method and Theory in the Study of Religion* 8:21–29.

References

1999   *The Politics of Religious Studies: The Continuing Conflict with Theology in the Academy.* New York: St. Martin's Press.

Wiebe, Phillip

1997   *Visions of Jesus: Direct Encounters from the New Testament to Today.* Oxford: Oxford University Press.

Wiener, Margaret J.

1995   *Visible and Invisible Realms: Power, Magic, and Colonial Conquest in Bali.* Chicago: University of Chicago Press.

Wilk, Richard R.

1996   *Economies and Cultures: Foundations of Economic Anthropology.* Boulder, CO: Westview.

Wilken, Robert L.

1972   *The Myth of Christian Beginnings.* Garden City, NY: Doubleday.

Williams, George H.

1962   *The Radical Reformation.* Philadelphia: Westminster.

Williams, Michael Allen

1996   *Rethinking "Gnosticism": An Argument for Dismantling a Dubious Category.* Princeton: Princeton University Press.

Williams, Raymond

1958   *Culture and Society, 1780–1950.* New York: Columbia University Press; New York: Doubleday, 1959.

1976   *Keywords: A Vocabulary of Culture and Society.* London: Fontana.

1977   *Marxism and Literature.* Oxford: Oxford University Press.

1980   "Social Darwinism," pp. 86–102 in *Problems in Materialism and Culture: Selected Essays.* London: Verso.

1995   *The Sociology of Culture.* Chicago: University of Chicago Press; original edn, *Culture.* London: Fontana, 1981.

Wilson, Bryan R.

1973   *Magic and the Millennium: A Sociological Study of Religious Movements of Protest Among Tribal and Third-World Peoples.* London: Heinemann.

1982   *Religion in Sociological Perspective.* Oxford: Oxford University Press.

Wilson, Catherine

1997   "Discourses of Vision in Seventeenth-Century Metaphysics," pp. 117–138 in David Michael Levin (ed.), *Sites of Vision: The Construction of Sight in the History of Philosophy.* Cambridge, MA: MIT Press.

Wilson, John F.

1987   "Modernity and Religion: A Problem of Perspective," pp. 9–18 in William Nicholls (ed.), *Modernity and Religion.* Supplements to *Studies in Religion / Sciences Religieuses,* vol. 19. Waterloo, ON: Wilfrid Laurier University Press.

Winch, Peter

1970   "Understanding a Primitive Society," pp. 78–111 in Bryan R. Wilson (ed.), *Rationality.* Key Concepts in the Social Sciences. Oxford: Blackwell.

Wittgenstein, Ludwig

1953   *Philosophical Investigations,* G. E. M. Anscombe (trans.). London: Blackwell; New York: Macmillan.

References

Wittig, Monique
    1992   *The Straight Mind and Other Essays*. Boston: Beacon.

Wojciehowsky, Dolora A.
    1995   *Old Masters, New Subjects: Early Modern and Poststructuralist Theories of Will*. Stanford, CA: Stanford University Press.

Wolf, Eric
    1982   *Europe and the People Without History*. Berkeley: University of California Press.

Wolf, Naomi
    1992   *The Beauty Myth: How Images of Beauty Are Used Against Women*. New York: Doubleday.

Wolfe, Alan
    1997   "A Welcome Revival of Religion in the Academy." *Chronicle of Higher Education*, 19 September.

Wood, Allen W.
    1987   "The Enlightenment," pp. 109–113 in Mircea Eliade (ed.), *The Encyclopedia of Religion*, vol. 5. New York: Macmillan.

Wood, Gordon S.
    1993   "Founding a Nation, 986–1787." In Arthur M. Schlesinger, Jr. (ed.), *The Almanac of American History*. New York: Barnes and Noble.

Wordsworth, John
    1893   *The One Religion: Truth, Holiness, and Peace Desired by the Nations, and Revealed by Jesus Christ. Eight Lectures*. Oxford: Parker; 1st edn, 1881.

Wright, Almroth
    1913   *The Unexpurgated Case Against Woman Suffrage*. New York: Paul B. Hoeber.

Wright, Erik Olin
    1985   *Classes*. London: Verso.

Wuthnow, Robert (Ed.)
    1979   *The Religious Dimension: New Directions in Quantitative Research*. New York: Academic Press.

Wyschogrod, Edith
    1990   *Saints and Postmodernism: Revisioning Moral Philosophy*. Religion and Postmodernism. Chicago: University of Chicago Press.

Yandell, Keith E.
    1993   *The Epistemology of Religious Experience*. Cambridge: Cambridge University Press.

Yengoyan, Aram A.
    1989   "Language and Conceptual Dualism: Sacred and Secular Concepts in Australian Aboriginal Cosmology and Myth." In David Maybury-Lewis and Uri Almagor (eds.), *The Attraction of Opposites: Thought and Society in the Dualist Mode*. Ann Arbor: University of Michigan Press.

Young, D. J. and L. Watson
    1970   "The Classification of the Dicotyledons: A Study of the Upper Levels of the Hierarchy." *Australian Journal of Botany* 18.

Young, Lawrence A. (Ed.)

    1997   *Rational Choice Theory and Religion: Summary and Assessment.* New York: Routledge.

Young, Robert

    1990   *White Mythologies: Writing History and the West.* London: Routledge.

Young, Serenity (Ed.)

    1993   *An Anthology of Sacred Texts By and About Women.* New York: Crossroad.

Zaehner, R. C.

    1957   *Mysticism, Sacred and Profane: An Inquiry into Some Varieties of Praeternatural Experience.* Oxford: Clarendon.

Zilboorg, G.

    1935   *The Medical Man and the Witch During the Renaissance.* Baltimore: Johns Hopkins University Press.

Žižek, Slavoj (Ed.)

    1994   *Mapping Ideology.* London: Verso.

Zuesse, Evan M.

    1987   "Ritual," pp. 405–422 in Mircea Eliade (ed.), *The Encyclopedia of Religion*, vol. 12. New York: Macmillan.

INDEX